MASS ORATORY AND POLITICAL POWER IN THE LATE ROMAN REPUBLIC

This book highlights the role played by public political discourse in shaping the distribution of power between Senate and People in the late Roman Republic. Against the background of the current debate between "oligarchical" and "democratic" interpretations of Republican politics, Robert Morstein-Marx emphasizes the perpetual negotiation and reproduction of political power through mass communication. It is the first work to offer an extensive analysis of the ideology of Republican mass oratory and to situate its rhetoric fully within the institutional and historical context of the public meetings (*contiones*) in which these speeches were heard. Examples of contional orations, drawn chiefly from Cicero and Sallust, are subjected to an analysis that is influenced by contemporary political theory and empirical studies of public opinion and the media, rooted in a detailed examination of key events and institutional structures, and illuminated by a vivid sense of the urban space in which the *contio* was set.

ROBERT MORSTEIN-MARX is Professor of Classics at the University of California, Santa Barbara. He is the author of *Hegemony to Empire: the Development of the Roman* Imperium *in the Greek East, 149–62 BC* (Berkeley and Los Angeles, 1995).

MASS ORATORY AND POLITICAL POWER IN THE LATE ROMAN REPUBLIC

ROBERT MORSTEIN-MARX

CAMBRIDGE
UNIVERSITY PRESS

PUBLISHED BY THE PRESS SYNDICATE OF THE UNIVERSITY OF CAMBRIDGE
The Pitt Building, Trumpington Street, Cambridge, United Kingdom

CAMBRIDGE UNIVERSITY PRESS
The Edinburgh Building, Cambridge, CB2 2RU, UK
40 West 20th Street, New York, NY 10011–4211, USA
477 Williamstown Road, Port Melbourne, VIC 3207, Australia
Ruiz de Alarcón 13, 28014 Madrid, Spain
Dock House, The Waterfront, Cape Town 8001, South Africa

http://www.cambridge.org

First published 2004

Printed in the United Kingdom at the University Press, Cambridge

Typeface Adobe Garamond 11/12.5 pt.   *System* LATEX 2ε   [TB]

A catalogue record for this book is available from the British Library

Library of Congress cataloguing in publication data
Morstein-Marx, Robert.
Mass oratory and political power in the late Roman Republic / Robert Morstein-Marx.
p.   cm.
Includes bibliographical references and index.
ISBN 0 521 82327 7 (hardback)
1. Speeches, addresses, etc., Latin – History and criticism.   2. Rome – Politics and
government – 265–30 BC.   3. Communication – Political aspects – Rome.   4. Rome – History –
Republic, 265–30 BC.   5. Power (Social sciences) – Rome.   6. Public meetings – Rome.
7. Rhetoric, Ancient.   8. Oratory, Ancient.   I. Title.
PA6083.M67   2003
875′.0109358 – dc21   2003053220 CIP

ISBN 0 521 82327 7 hardback

To Sara, Eric, and Matthew

Contents

Figures and maps

Acknowledgments

This project began more than a decade ago with a paper delivered to the annual meeting of the American Philological Association in December 1992, which contained in fifteen minutes' compass the kernel of the argument of this book. Many interruptions, professional and private, have slowed its progress, and it has at times been nerve-wracking to monitor the constant stream of new publications emerging from the very debates that gave rise to this book. In retrospect, I find that while some of my points have now been anticipated, at least in part, many others have been greatly enriched by work that has come out since 1992, and that there still seems to be room for my own synthesis of the material. I know well that this will be far from the last word on the *contio* and Republican mass oratory. My greatest hope for the book is that it might stimulate, rather than foreclose, further debate on some central, though relatively neglected, phenomena of Roman political life.

It is a real pleasure to recall how many colleagues and friends have assisted me in this project over the years. Constraints of space prevent me from expressing my gratitude to all as fully as I would like, yet the signal services of some must be publicly acknowledged. Andrew Dyck, Erich Gruen, Alexander Yakobson, and two anonymous readers for the Press took up the burden of reading the penultimate draft of the manuscript; their comments, corrections, and objections contributed immeasurably to the value of this work. (Of course, any slips and errors that remain are my own responsibility alone.) Nathan Rosenstein read and commented on an earlier draft and cheerfully answered many a query that I would have been too embarrassed to ask others. Fergus Millar generously allowed me to see a draft of *The Crowd in Rome* in advance of its publication, and over the whole course of this project has been most kind and supportive despite our numerous points of disagreement – which on my part, at least, seem to be rather fewer now than when I began. My thinking has been repeatedly stimulated by conversations with Anthony Corbeill, who also kindly showed me some of his work in advance of publication, as did Michael Alexander. Malcolm Bell, then Mellon Professor at the American Academy in Rome, obtained for me the necessary permit to study the remains of the Republican Rostra under the pavement of the Forum, and the Soprintendenza archeologica di Roma (Area archeologica Foro Romano-Palatino) efficiently and courteously afforded access to that monument on the appointed day. Most references were checked by my successive research assistants, Debra Nousek and Greg Smay, who corrected a number of slips and offered useful suggestions. To all I wish to convey my warmest thanks, as I do also, for other suggestions, assistance, and other kindnesses, to Christer Bruun, Harriet Flower, Jerise Fogel, Nicholas Horsfall, Matthew Roller, Richard Saller, Jeffrey Tatum, William Turpin and Ellen Magenheim. For their helpful and friendly responses I also thank the audiences on which earlier versions of parts of the argument were tested, at Berkeley, the University of Pennsylvania, Smith College, Toronto, the University of Southern California, meetings of the American Philological Association, the Classical Association of the Canadian West, and the University of California at San Diego Working Seminar on Ancient Politics and Contemporary Political Science.

Two important books that were published in 2002 and came into my hands too late to be integrated into the present argument are Peter Holliday's *Origins of Roman Historical Commemoration in the Visual Arts* (Cambridge: Cambridge University Press) and Fergus Millar's *Roman Republic in Political Thought* (Hanover, NH and London: University Press of New England); I urge readers to consult the first especially in connection with my third chapter and the second with my introduction and conclusion. I have tried to give due attention to all relevant works published through 2001. It would be unrealistic to assume that I have done so with fully equal success in all the fields and sub-disciplines represented in this book, ranging from Republican political history to Ciceronian oratory to Roman topography, monuments and coins, and I apologize in advance to any whose work has been unjustly overlooked. In this connection, I would like to thank especially Karl-Joachim Hölkeskamp, who very kindly shared some of his remarkable bibliographical knowledge and in particular offered guidance with recent German scholarship. Here at the University of California, Santa Barbara, my colleagues in the Political Science Department, Peter Digeser and Eric Smith, offered valuable and stimulating bibliographical suggestions in their field. I would also like to thank Michael Sharp, Commissioning Editor for Classics at Cambridge University Press, for the interest he took in this project and the efficiency with which he has seen it through. Readers, as well as I, owe thanks too to Jan Chapman, my indefatigable copy-editor, who removed countless blemishes from the final typescript and never balked at the extra labor that my corrections and reconsiderations entailed.

The fundamental work of this book was done during a year's leave from teaching in 1994–95, supported by a fellowship from the American Council of Learned Societies that was supplemented by the Regents of the University of California. A UC Regents' Junior Faculty Fellowship and a UC Regents' Humanities Faculty Fellowship funded much-needed research assistants. Two sabbatical quarters granted by the University of California, Santa Barbara, and the Department of Classics were crucial for producing interim and final drafts. I am most grateful to all of the entities and individuals involved in these decisions for their touching faith in the outcome.

But the greatest debt of gratitude is owed to my wife, Sara Lindheim, whose patience I relied on at a time when she had her own book to write. This book is lovingly dedicated to her, and to Eric and Matthew, the two luminous boys she somehow also found time to bring into the world.

Note on translations

The quotation on p. 63 from *The Aeneid of Virgil*, translated by Allen Mandelbaum (© copyright 1971), is reproduced courtesy of Bantam Books.

Translations on pp. 122 and 188 are reproduced from *Cicero's Letters to Atticus*, translated and edited by D. R. Shackleton Bailey, vol. 1, Cambridge University Press, 1965, pp. 159 and 145 respectively.

Translations on pp. 142–43, 220, and 261 are reproduced from CICERO: "PHILIPPICS," translated and edited by D. R. Shackleton Bailey. Copyright © 1986 by the University of North Carolina Press. Used by permission of the publisher.

All other translations are by the author.

Abbreviations

C	A. C. Clark, ed., *Q. Asconii Pediani orationum Ciceronis quinque enarratio* (OCT), Oxford, 1907
CIL	*Corpus Inscriptionum Latinarum*
Cr	J. W. Crawford, ed., *M. Tullius Cicero: the Fragmentary Speeches*, 2nd edn., Atlanta, 1994
FGrH	F. Jacoby, *Fragmenta der griechischen Historiker*, Berlin and Leiden, 1923–
Gordon	A. E. Gordon, *Illustrated Introduction to Latin Epigraphy*, Berkeley, 1983
Greenidge–Clay	A. H. J. Greenidge and A. M. Clay, *Sources for Roman History, 133–70 BC*, rev. by E. W. Gray, Oxford, 1960
IIt	*Inscriptiones Italiae*
ILLRP	A. Degrassi, *Inscriptiones latinae liberae rei publicae*, 2 vols., Florence, 1965
ILS	H. Dessau, *Inscriptiones latinae selectae*, 5 vols., Berlin, 1892–1916
L	W. M. Lindsay, ed., *Sextus Pompeius Festus: De verborum significatu quae supersunt cum Pauli epitome* (Teubner), Leipzig, 1913
LTUR	*Lexicon Topographicum Urbis Romae*, 6 vols., Rome, 1993–2000
M	B. Maurenbrecher, ed., *C. Sallusti Crispi Historiarum reliquiae*, 2 vols., Leipzig, 1891–93
MRR	T. R. S. Broughton, *Magistrates of the Roman Republic*, 3 vols., New York, 1951–86
OLD	P. W. Glare, ed., *Oxford Latin Dictionary*, Oxford, 1982
ORF	E. Malcovati, *Oratorum Romanorum Fragmenta*, 4th edn., Torino, 1976

Peter	H. Peter, *Historicorum Romanorum Reliquiae*, 2nd edn., 2 vols., Leipzig, 1906–14
RE	A. Pauly, G. Wissowa, and W. Kroll, *Real-Encyclopädie der classischen Altertumswissenschaft*, Stuttgart and Munich, 1893–
Roman Statutes	M. H. Crawford, ed., *Roman Statutes* (Bull. of the Institute of Classical Studies 64), 2 vols., London, 1996
RRC	M. H. Crawford, *Roman Republican Coinage*, 2 vols., Cambridge, 1974
St	T. Stangl, ed., *Ciceronis Orationum Scholiastae*, Vienna, 1912
TLL	*Thesaurus Linguae Latinae*, Leipzig, 1900–

CHAPTER I

Introduction

MASS ORATORY AND POLITICAL ACTION

At around sundown on January 18, 52 BC, the battered corpse of the popular hero P. Clodius Pulcher, murdered earlier that day on the Appian Way on the orders of T. Annius Milo, was carried through the Porta Capena into Rome, borne on the litter of a senator who had passed by the scene of the crime and, after giving instructions for the conveyance of the body, prudently retraced his steps.[1] A huge crowd of the poorest inhabitants of the metropolis and slaves flocked in mourning and indignation to the impromptu cortège as it made its way to Clodius' house on the upper Sacred Way, on the lower slope of the northern Palatine (see maps 1 and 2, pp. 43–44);[2] there his widow set the body on display in the great atrium of the house, poured forth bitter lamentations, pointed out his wounds to the angry multitude. The crowd kept vigil through the night in the Forum,[3] and next morning reassembled at Clodius' house in vengeful mood, joined now by two tribunes of the plebs, T. Munatius Plancus and Q. Pompeius Rufus. The tribunes called upon the gathering multitude to carry the corpse on its bier down to the Forum and onto the Rostra, the speakers' platform, where the wounds inflicted by Milo's cutthroats and gladiators could be seen by all. At that very spot, on the morning of the previous day, Pompeius Rufus and a third tribune, the future historian C. Sallustius Crispus, had harangued the People,[4] no doubt inveighing against Milo's candidacy, against which they had been fighting a determined struggle for weeks in favor of protégés of the great Pompey. Now, a day later, the tribunes had better material: they unleashed a fiery discourse in place of a funeral eulogy, whipping up

---

[1] My narrative is largely a paraphrase of Asconius' introduction to Cicero's *Pro Milone* (32–33 C).

[2] For a plausible identification of the location and remains of the house (formerly that of M. Aemilius Scaurus at the corner of the Sacra Via and Clivus Palatinus, bought by Clodius in 53), see Carandini 1988: 359–73, esp. 369, n. 35; cf. E. Papi, *LTUR* ii.85–86, 202–204.

[3] App. *B Civ.* 2.21.

[4] Asc. 49 C (cf. Cic. *Mil.* 27, 45, where a date of January 17 is intentionally and misleadingly suggested).

indignation against Milo over the corpse of his enemy. Afterwards, their audience, passionately stirred, needed little prompting from an old Clodian partisan, a civil servant ("scribe") named Sex. Cloelius, to make a suitable pyre for their hero: carrying his corpse into the adjacent Senate-house, they heaped up benches, tables, and other unconventional fuel such as state documents, and set the whole building aflame. The Curia, a monument of the much-hated Sulla and the oligarchic régime he had installed, was consumed by the flames, which spread to the Basilica Porcia next door and damaged hallowed monuments in the Comitium in front, the focal point of the city. Flushed with consciousness of impunity, the roving mob turned to more pragmatic ends, attacking and ransacking the house of the *interrex* in an attempt to force an immediate election of consuls (thus to ensure Milo's defeat), then Milo's house, where it at last met some determined resistance. Deflected thence, this "Clodian mob" seized funerary replicas of the rods (*fasces*) that were the emblem of executive power (*imperium*) and offered them first to Milo's consular competitors in what may have amounted to a symbolic popular election, then to Pompey in his suburban villa, calling on him variously as consul and as dictator.[5]

The burning of the Senate-house caused some revulsion of feeling among the urban populace. This encouraged Milo to return to the city that very night (January 19) and resume his candidacy. He distributed "gifts" to the tribes with extravagant generosity, and a few days afterwards a friendly tribune, M. Caelius Rufus, held a public meeting, probably at the Rostra itself, where he could make good rhetorical use of the burnt-out shell of the Curia at his back, and, no doubt, of a well-compensated audience, which he hoped (one source plausibly claims) could be induced to simulate a public acquittal.[6] Caelius, together with his mentor, Cicero, and Milo himself, spoke in his defense, blending what was true – that Milo had not planned to ambush Clodius – with what was, in fact, false – that Clodius had lain in

---

[5] The funerary riot has now been interestingly analyzed by Sumi 1997. On the *scriba* Cloelius, see Benner 1987: 156–58; Damon 1992. "Hallowed monuments" refers to the statue of Attus Navius (Plin. *HN* 34.21; see below, p. 96). Lambinus' persuasive emendation of Cic. *Mil.* 91, printed in Clark's OCT and defended by him at Clark 1895: 81–82, shows that the crowd brought the *fasces* to a *contio* before the Temple of Castor, perhaps as if assembling for a legislative vote of the *concilium plebis*. Of Milo's two known houses, the one on the Clivus Capitolinus, which seems to have enjoyed a reputation as a kind of fortress (Cic. *Mil.* 64), seems a more obvious and immediate target for a mob in the Forum than his other house on the Cermalus (*pace* Sumi, pp. 85–86; on the houses, see Maslowski 1976; E. Papi, *LTUR* II.32). Sumi, p. 86, believes the attack on Lepidus' house followed two days afterwards (cf. Asc. 43 C); contra, Ruebel 1979: 234–36, and B. A. Marshall 1985: 169.

[6] For this particular claim, see App. *B Civ.* 2.22; note the similar charge made by Q. Metellus Scipio in the Senate (Asc. 35 C: *ad defendendos de se rumores*). Ruebel's date of *c.* Jan. 27 (Ruebel 1979: 237, n. 14) is only approximate.

wait for Milo on the Appian Way. The speeches were interrupted, however, by the attack of an armed mob led by the other tribunes.[7] At about the same time, on January 23, one of these tribunes, Q. Pompeius Rufus, sought to stoke public indignation against Milo further by accusing him in another public meeting of trying, in addition, to assassinate Pompey.[8]

A chaotic struggle in the Forum and the streets of Rome now ensued, leading ultimately to Pompey's appointment as sole consul and (sometime in March, after an additional, intercalary month) the passage of legislation to deal with the violence of mid-January. It now becomes impossible to follow the events in sequence and full detail; but it is clear that the flurry of public meetings continued, and that the *contio* – the "informal," that is, non-voting, form of popular assembly where public speeches were heard – remained a central stage of political action. Successfully turning the tables of public opinion after the débacle of the burning of the Senate-house, Munatius Plancus, Pompeius Rufus, and Sallust assiduously kindled and tended the flame of popular indignation against Milo with their "daily speeches" (or "meetings"):[9] by turns they came before the People to assail senatorial schemes to fix the outcome of any trial by procedural maneuvers, to present (alleged) witnesses of Milo's suspicious actions after the event,[10] to pour scorn on Milo's excuse for not turning over his slaves (who were acknowledged to have been the actual perpetrators) to give evidence under torture,[11] to arouse suspicion that he was making attempts on Pompey's life,[12] to incite popular anger against Milo's most prominent defenders, Cicero, Cato, and no doubt Caelius,[13] and finally, on the day before the verdict was due, to urge the People "not to allow Milo to slip from their hands," that is, to show up in force at the trial and display their anger to the jurors as they went to cast their vote.[14] Certainly they won the battle for the hearts and minds of the People. According to our valuable source, Cicero's commentator Asconius, by the eve of the trial the urban populace generally,

[7] Compare App. *B Civ.* 2.22 with Cic. *Mil.* 91.   [8] Asc. 50–51 C.

[9] *Cotidianae contiones*: see Asc. 51 C; cf. 37 C, Cic. *Mil.* 12. *Contio* can describe the meeting, the audience, or the speech delivered there: Gell. *NA* 18.7.5–8.

[10] Asc. 37 C.

[11] This would be the occasion for the *turbulenta contio* calmed by Cato: Cic. *Mil.* 58 (see Pina Polo 1989: no. 330). For the practice of exposing opponents to popular anger, see below, pp. 161–72; for the controversy, see Asc. 34–35 C.

[12] Asc. 51–52 C; cf. 36, 38 C.

[13] Asc. 37–38 C; Cic. *Mil.* 47, 58. For Caelius, see Asc. 36 C: his denunciation of Pompey's laws, and Pompey's response, almost certainly belong in *contiones* preceding the popular votes, since the senatorial decree had already been passed.

[14] Asc. 40, 42, 52 C; cf. Cic. *Mil.* 3, 71. For the individual *contiones* of the first half of 52, see the catalog of Pina Polo 1989: 304–6, nos. 326–36.

not merely the *Clodiani*, was bitterly hostile to Milo and indeed to Cicero because of his unpopular defense of the man.[15] Whether or not popular indignation actually was a leading factor in the outcome of the trial,[16] it is tolerably clear that the tribunes' effective use of the contional stage to mobilize public opinion produced the circumstances in which Pompey's sole consulship became thinkable, ensured passage of the Pompeian laws which closed Milo's most promising escape route, and (along with Pompey as sole consul, of course) forced the Senate to acquiesce in endorsing that legislation as the basis for Milo's trial.[17]

Asconius' account of these events, which I have followed closely above, is exceptionally detailed by the standards of Roman Republican history – comparable in its density to some of the most vivid narratives in the letters of Cicero, but wider in perspective and far less partisan. Through it we see, with unusual clarity, the importance of the public sphere[18] of Roman politics, which has until recently tended (at least in Anglophone scholarship) to be downplayed in favor of a substratum of personal and private connections of "friendship" and patronage, ostensibly the "real" field of power, cloaked by the clouds of political rhetoric. Following the lead of Ronald Syme's *Roman Revolution*, with its brilliant penetration of the "screen and sham" of the Roman constitution and masterly puncturing of rhetorical hypocrisy, we have tended to dismiss, and finally to overlook, public, political speech altogether.[19] For Syme, famously, "as in its beginning, so in its last generation, the Roman Commonwealth, 'res publica populi Romani,' was a name; a feudal order of society still survived in a city-state and governed an empire"; moreover, "in all ages, whatever the form and name of government, be it monarchy, republic, or democracy, an oligarchy lurks behind the façade; and Roman history, Republican or Imperial, is the history of the governing class."[20] It followed that the Roman historian's true business was to penetrate the façade, to get behind the speechifying and legislating that

---

[15] Asc. 37–38 C. To his credit, Asconius implicitly distinguishes between the *infensa/inimica multitudo* discussed here and the *Clodiani* whose shouts ruined Cicero's performance (41–42 C). For the employment of prepared claqueurs and hecklers, see below, pp. 131–36.

[16] See n. 15; Asconius, for what it is worth, believed, or assumed, that the verdict was determined by the key facts established in the case (53 C): cf. chap. 7, n. 66.

[17] The tribunes foiled, or distorted, the will of the Senate by vetoing half of a divided motion: Cic. *Mil.* 12–14, with Asc. 43–45 C. On the nature of the division, see chap. 3, n. 219.

[18] A phrase I am not using in the quasi-technical sense given it by Jürgen Habermas, but merely to denote the open, communal realm of speech and action.

[19] For "Screen and a sham," see Syme 1939: 15; "rhetorical hypocrisy," ibid., chap. 11, "Political Catchwords."

[20] Syme 1939: 11–12; 7.

garishly but superficially flashed across it, in order to lay bare the abiding reality of factional maneuver.

There is truth here, of course. Yet it has become increasingly clear that this model of Roman politics, whose core Syme adopted from his German predecessors, Matthias Gelzer and Friedrich Münzer, and brilliantly wedded to a compellingly dark vision and historiographical style drawn from Tacitus, simply leaves too much out of the picture. In 1986 Fergus Millar complained that "we have ceased to listen sufficiently to the actual content of oratory addressed to the people."[21] He was right. Just look at Syme's own version – admittedly very brief, highly selective, but all the more telling for that – of the narrative of the prelude to Milo's trial reviewed above:

When Milo killed Clodius, the populace in Rome, in grief for their patron and champion, displayed his body in the Forum, burned it on a pyre in the Curia, and destroyed that building in the conflagration. Then they streamed out of the city to the villa of Pompeius, clamouring for him to be consul or dictator.

The Senate was compelled to act. It declared a state of emergency and instructed Pompeius to hold military levies throughout Italy. The demands for a dictatorship went on: to counter and anticipate which, the *Optimates* were compelled to offer Pompeius the consulate, without colleague. The proposal came from Bibulus, the decision was Cato's.

The pretext was a special mandate to heal and repair the Commonwealth. With armed men at his back Pompeius established order again and secured the conviction of notorious disturbers of the public peace, especially Milo, to the dismay and grief of the *Optimates*, who strove in vain to save him.[22]

To be sure, the outraged populace is there: explicitly, in reference to its mourning for "their patron and champion," and perhaps implicitly in the description of subsequent developments. (Or does Syme imply that it was in fact the invisible hand of Pompey which "compelled" the Senate to act, which orchestrated "demands" for a dictatorship and ultimately "compelled" the *optimates* to make him sole consul?) The remarkable feature, however, is the amazing disappearing act of the tribunes, "daily *contiones*" and all.[23] In this account there is no mediation, through political speech, between the levels of senatorial and popular action, and the *populus Romanus* (or at least the urban plebs), is reduced to a kind of arbitrary and mysterious automaton that on exceptional occasions such as this one trespasses upon the proper aristocratic business of politics. That is no accident, since it is presupposed by Syme's model of Republican politics. Here, where a remarkably

---

[21] Millar 1986: 1.   [22] Syme 1939: 39. Compare Millar 1998: 181–85.

[23] Note, too, how it is Pompey – no mention of tribunes, *Clodiani*, the urban plebs or even the jurors – who "secured the conviction" of Milo and others.

informative source allows us an extraordinarily complete picture of a Republican crisis, the insidious occlusion of political speech becomes quite conspicuous. I say "insidious" because an appropriate skepticism toward the truth-value of political speech has here grown out of all proportion, to the point where it comes dangerously close to an *a priori* assumption, not susceptible of verification or refutation, applicable to any polity and thus hardly revelatory of anything peculiar to Rome. Hypocrisy is not uniquely Roman; but to the extent that it was indeed a salient characteristic of the political life of the Republic, it after all demonstrates fairly decisively the power of ideological speech. When Sallust writes that Republican politicians exploited "specious pretexts" such as "defending the rights of the People" or "upholding the authority of the Senate" in order to amass personal power under the pretext of the public good,[24] he evidently presumes that such ideas possessed real potency among his contemporaries.

On the other hand, to the extent that some historians' bias against speech and symbol does not simply arise from, say, the attractions of a persona of skeptical cynicism or a personal inclination toward philosophical materialism, but seems to be founded on empirical judgments about the Romans themselves, this has been until recently manifestly the result of the unique prestige enjoyed by the "patron–client" model of Roman politics, especially in the English-speaking world, no doubt in good part because of the great influence of Syme's work.[25] But recent studies have demonstrated that the increasingly exclusive (and sterile) emphasis on the patron–client model is misplaced and misleading.[26] Perhaps the jury is still out on the question of the precise explanatory force we are to give to patronage in Republican politics – a very real factor, surely, though not the fundamental one.[27] Yet what John North has harshly but aptly labelled the "frozen waste theory" of Republican politics, implying "that voting behaviour in the assemblies could be regarded as totally divorced from the opinions, interests and prejudices of the voters themselves," is really no longer viable.[28]

The king is dead, then, but we still linger in a conceptual and methodological interregnum. Alternative models of Republican politics have been

---

[24] Sall. *Cat.* 38.3.

[25] Note that Matthias Gelzer, whose youthful masterpiece of 1912, *Die römische Nobilität*, serves as a "foundation document" for the patron–client model, never took the possible implications of that brilliant study so far as did his intellectual descendants in the Anglophone "prosopographical school."

[26] Especially Brunt 1988: 382–502; Morstein-Marx 1998; Yakobson 1999; Mouritsen 2001: esp. 67–79, 96–100.

[27] See Pani 1997: 132–40; Morstein-Marx 2000b; or Jehne's observation (Jehne 1995a: 55–56) that patronage will often have been politically neutralized precisely because it was so all-pervasive.

[28] North 1990a: 6–7 (= North 1990b: 280).

adumbrated but have not yet been fully articulated, much less won generalized assent, although renewed interest in the ways in which the Roman
People participated in what was after all called the *res publica* is strongly
manifested in a rising torrent of recent studies.[29] Nearly two decades after
the publication of Millar's seminal article calling upon us to "place in the
centre of our conception the picture of an orator addressing a crowd in the
Forum,"[30] we have learned much about the ubiquity and importance of
the *contio* as a political institution but have only just begun to explore the
nature, dynamics, and implications for the distribution of power of this
vital point of contact between the two political entities of the Republic –
Senatus Populusque Romanus.[31] And Millar's increasingly provocative claims
for the "democratic" status of the Roman Republic have sparked significant
resistance, generally conceding his point about the importance of public
speech in the *contio* but challenging his "optimistic" reading of its consequences.[32] On the other hand, a new study of popular participation in the
Republic now goes so far in the opposite direction as to conclude that "Late
republican Rome emerges . . . as a place with little contact or communication between elite and populace, where the world of politics remained
largely separate from the one inhabited by the urban masses."[33] Clearly
there is work to be done.

I start with the premise that Millar was right to make the *contio*, with
its crucial scenario of the orator "using the arts of rhetoric to persuade
an anonymous crowd," the proper focus of investigation for those seeking
to illuminate the nature of popular participation in the *res publica* and

---

[29] Besides works already listed in nn. 26–28, and others focused on the *contio* noted below (n. 31), see
especially Millar 1984 and 1989; Yakobson 1992; Flaig 1995a; and Hölkeskamp 2000. Note too, the
recent surveys of Pani 1997: esp. 140–69; and Lintott 1999: esp. 191–213.

[30] Millar 1986: 1.

[31] Hölkeskamp 1995 and 2000 offers a stimulating challenge to Millar's views on the political effects
of the *contio* (further elaborated in Millar 1995 and 1998), even while corroborating his claim for
the central importance of this venue of élite-mass interaction. See also Bell 1997; Laser 1997: esp.
138–82; Mouritsen 2001: 38–62 (somewhat polemical); and, more generally, Fantham 1997. The most
comprehensive recent studies of the *contio* specifically are Pina Polo 1989 and 1996; a convenient
English summary of some of his findings appears in Pina Polo 1995.

[32] In particular, Hölkeskamp 1995 and 2000, who emphasizes instead the importance of the *contio*
for élite image-building, both individual and collective. Cf. Bell 1997; also Jehne 1995b. For the
evolution of Millar's claims, note that in his earlier work on the subject he does not call the Republic
a "democracy" *tout court*, but, borrowing explicitly from Polybius, speaks of a "democratic element"
or "features" (Millar 1984: 14–19 is particularly illustrative), occasionally writing as if the Republic
had a "proper place in the history of democratic values" (Millar 1986: 9). In Millar 1995, however,
it became "undeniable that the constitution of the Roman republic was that of a direct democracy"
(p. 94), and in Millar 1998 the assertion appears stronger, for example, "the constitution of the
Roman *res publica* made it a variety of democracy" (p. 208; cf. p. 11). On all of this, see now Millar
2002.

[33] Mouritsen 2001: 132–33.

the ideological structure of the communal, civic world rather than Syme's "feudal order of society."[34] The unique importance of the *contio* lies in the fact that orators' attempts to win decisive public support in such meetings were the chief feature of the run-up to any vote on legislation, that most direct assertion of the Popular Will which, as Millar well shows, more or less covered the gamut of major political issues, foreign or "imperial" as well as domestic. (In the Republic, *all* legislation was passed by popular vote: in this sense, at least, Rome might be called a "direct democracy" in form.[35]) Magistrates promulgated bills orally in a *contio*, at the same time posting up written copies of their proposals on whitened boards, and after 98 BC the passage of three successive market-days (thus a minimum of seventeen to twenty-five days), when the influx of people from outside the city would ensure maximum publicity, was required before the vote could be taken.[36] During this period a flurry of *contiones* will have taken place, mostly called by the proposer of the legislation, seeking to rally public enthusiasm for his bill.[37] Since successful legislation was at the same time one of the most important means by which the politician advanced his own "career," nursing the popular support necessary for continued success in the repeated electoral competitions that shaped a senator's life, or for pursuit of his own projects and interests, it will be obvious that the *contio* was a place where important convergences of interest were continually negotiated between the "élite" who supplied the speakers and the "mass" who made up the audience.[38]

But the significance of the *contio* is hardly to be strictly limited to the legislative field, as crucial as that was in the actual practice of Roman politics.

---

[34] So too Hölkeskamp 1995: esp. 25–35, despite his divergent thesis. Quotation from Millar 1986: 1.

[35] Millar 1998: 209. Institutional peculiarities such as the system of group voting (rather like the American electoral-college system) and the bias toward wealth in the Centuriate Assembly (little used, however, for legislation by the late Republic), as well as the lack of any process of legislative initiative "from the floor," make the phrase somewhat misleading.

[36] On the length of the so-called *trinundinum*, I accept the conclusion of Lintott 1965 and 1968a, *pace* Mommsen 1887: III.376, n. 1, and Michels 1967: 191–206, who argue for a full three Roman weeks. The aim, obviously, was maximal publicity, for which the three market-days, not a set number of days, was what was important (see *ILLRP* 511 = *ILS* 18, lines 23–24; cf. Lintott 1965: 284; Pina Polo 1989: 96–99; and for *contiones* on market-days, see pp. 82–84); presumably the text was expected to be presented in three successive nundinal *contiones* at the time of promulgation (Plut. *Pomp.* 25.3: ἀναγνωσθέντων δὲ τούτων) and it was also publicly posted on *tabulae* or an *album* (πινάκια or σανίδες): see Cass. Dio 42.22.4–23.1, 32.3; Cic. *Leg. agr.* 2.13, *Sest.* 72 (*tabulae*); Mommsen's claim that texts of promulgated bills were also filed in the *aerarium* before being voted into law is refuted by von Schwind 1940: 29–33. On promulgation generally, see Mommsen 1887: III.370–78, or more briefly, M. H. Crawford 1996: 9–11; Crawford 1988 argues that the reading of proposed laws in *contiones* was a highly effective means of publicizing the content of a law among the populace generally.

[37] See chap. 5.

[38] Millar frequently criticizes the use of the term "élite" to refer to those who "played a political role" in Rome (e.g. Millar 1998: 4–5), but his complaint that it is "circular" to do so seems to me to

Millar rightly stressed how much political activity took place directly under the gaze of the "Roman People in the Republic" according to what he calls an "ideology of publicity."[39] The legislative, electoral, and somewhat vestigial judicial powers of the People presupposed continuous direct observation by the citizenry of their present and potential leaders and, on the part of the politicians, constant cultivation of a public image in speeches on a variety of occasions, including religious ritual, spectacles, and the various forms of public or private pageantry such as funerals, public banquets, or triumphs. Of all these venues, the ubiquitous *contiones* were perhaps the most important for the purposes of self-advertisement, communication, and ritualized communal action. No wonder, then, that in turbulent times magistrates virtually "lived on the Rostra" and held "daily *contiones*"; sometimes the same day saw more than one meeting, held by different officials.[40]

The *contio* was, quite simply, center stage for the performance and observation of public, political acts in the Roman Republic. Even when legislation was not being explicitly mooted, an enormous variety of public meetings took place in the Forum in any given year. Most important for present purposes, it appears to have been standard practice for decrees of the Senate to be read out to the People in a *contio* called immediately afterwards, usually by the same magistrate who had presided over the senatorial meeting; he might then offer his own narrative and commentary (as does

have force only if it is used to *define* them. I see no tautology in using the word as fairly accurate descriptor to denote, quite literally, the "elect" – which anyone "worthy" (*dignus*) of the distinction of political office (*honor*) in Rome obviously was – without any necessary connotation of inherited status. (See now Millar 2002: 170–71.) The term has the advantage over "aristocracy" of leaving open the question of the advantages of birth: even if four out of five consuls had consular ancestors (Badian 1990a: 409–12), it is of course true that the Roman Senate, far from being closed to new blood, positively depended on it for its perpetuation (see, e.g., Hopkins and Burton, in Hopkins 1983: 107–16). Still, the élitist character of the criteria of *dignitas* ("worthiness") for office-holding, the social and political aura surrounding *nobilitas*, and the practical requirement of wealth for election, also made the present and past magistrates who constituted the Senate an élite in the evaluative sense of the term: see, recently, Hölkeskamp 2000: 211–23 (cf. Morstein-Marx 1998: 260–88, and from a somewhat different perspective Yakobson 1999: 184–225). As for relative sizes of this "élite" and the "mass," we may note that the Senate comprised roughly 600 men in the Ciceronian period (300 before Sulla), while the number of adult male citizens in Rome must have been roughly comparable to that of grain recipients in 46 BC, i.e. 320,000 (Suet. *Iul.* 41.3), out of a total urban population estimated as between 700,000 and 1,000,000 (Brunt 1971a: 376–83; Morley 1996: 33–39; Lo Cascio 1997: 24) and a total adult male citizenry numbering perhaps a few million (below, n. 51). For actual numbers in the *contio*, see below, chap. 2, n. 36.

[39] Millar 1984 and 1986: esp. 8. For the phrase, Millar 1998: 45. On publicity, and the dynamics of face-to-face interaction between mass and élite in the central spaces of Rome, see now Döbler 1999, who, however, gives surprisingly short shrift to the *contio* (pp. 136–41, 199–210).

[40] Cic. *Brut.* 305: *et hi quidem habitabant in rostris*; Tac. *Dial.* 36.3: *hinc contiones magistratuum paene pernoctantium in rostris*. For the phrase *contiones cotidianae*, see Cic. *Brut.* 305–6; *Clu.* 93, 103; *Mil.* 12; *Sest.* 39, 42; Asc. 51 C; cf. Tac. *Dial.* 40.1 (*contiones adsiduae*). Pina Polo 1989: 86. Two *contiones*, see Asc. 49 C; note also that the informer Vettius was brought before two *contiones* in succession in 59, first by Caesar, then by Vatinius: Cic. *Att.* 2.24.3; *Vat.* 24, 26.

Cicero in the *Third Catilinarian*), or perhaps invite a leading ally to speak in addition (so Cicero in the *Fourth* and *Sixth Philippics*). It is clear that a crowd hungry for information often lurked about the Curia on these occasions.[41] All other news and important announcements, from dispatches of generals from the battlefield to magisterial edicts, were delivered to the People *in contione*: Cicero's *Second Catilinarian* comes readily to mind, informing the People of Catiline's flight from the city while they watched the Senate being summoned.[42] The *contio* was also the essential setting for major, public, illocutionary speech acts: Sulla abdicated the dictatorship in a *contio*;[43] in 63 Cicero declined a consular province in a *contio*;[44] Caesar's and Pompey's final offers of peace on the eve of civil war in 49 were read out in *contiones*;[45] in the run-up to another civil war, young Octavian promised to pay Caesar's legacy to the People in a *contio*.[46] At their first *contio* upon assuming office magistrates not only thanked the People for their election and praised their ancestors but indicated how they would administer their magistracy; praetors in particular would describe the principles by which they would dispense justice.[47] Then there were the *contiones* called in order for the People to witness an important legal act, and implicitly to enforce its execution: magistrates, senators, or even candidates for office were required by certain laws to swear obedience to them publicly, *in contione*;[48] immediately upon election, magistrates-designate swore in a *contio* that they would uphold the laws, and at the end of their term, consuls (perhaps all magistrates) swore in another *contio* that they had administered their office in accordance with the laws, perhaps often adding a justificatory account of their tenure of the office, as Cicero attempted to do.[49] To complete the picture we might add the *contiones* of victorious generals at the end of their triumphal procession; those of censors in connection with the

---

[41] See pp. 246–48.

[42] Pina Polo 1989: 139–46; Achard 1991: 207. Assembling: Cic. *Cat.* 2.26: *quem* [sc. *senatum*] *vocari videtis*.

[43] App. *B Civ.* 1.104; Quint. *Inst.* 3.8.53.   [44] Cic. *Pis.* 5; *Fam.* 5.2.3.

[45] Plut. *Pomp.* 59.2; *Caes.* 30.2; Cic. *Att.* 7.17.2, 18.1, 19; 8.9.2. Cf. other examples of letters from absent *principes* read out in the *contio*: Cic. *Dom.* 22; Cass. Dio 39.16.2, 63.5.

[46] Octavian: Cass. Dio 45.6.3. Decimus Brutus' edict barring Antony from his province was posted up on the day the *Fourth Philippic* was delivered (Cic. *Fam.* 11.6a.1; *Phil.* 4.7), December 20, 44; it was surely read out in the same or an earlier *contio*.

[47] Cic. *Fin.* 2.74; Suet. *Tib.* 32.1. Cf. Cic. *Leg. agr.* 2.5–10, esp. 6–7; Plut. *Aem.* 11. Sallust's speech of Marius (*Iug.* 85) is to be set against this background.

[48] *In contione*: Cic. *Att.* 2.18.2; App. *B Civ.* 1.29–31; Plut. *Mar.* 29.4–6 (note the pressure exerted by the crowd); *CIL* I² 582 = *Roman Statutes* 7, Lives 16–24. Millar 1986: 8; Pina Polo 1989: 160–61.

[49] Oath upon election: Livy 31.50.7, with Mommsen 1887: 1.619–22. Cicero's "swearing-out": Cic. *Fam.* 5.2.7; *Pis.* 6–7; *Sull.* 33–34; *Rep.* 1.7; Cass. Dio 37.38. Similarly, Bibulus in 59 was prevented by Clodius from delivering a speech in addition to his oath: Cass. Dio 38.12.3. Mommsen 1887: 1.625; Pina Polo 1989: 157–59.

quinquennial revision of the citizen rolls and *lustrum*; the nomination of replacements to the augural college *in contione* (from 104); and the lottery in a *contio* among candidates for a place among the Vestals. Even noble funerals held at the Rostra took the form of a *contio*.[50] Even more than the more noteworthy sort of meeting that fuelled a legislative campaign or heated political controversy, the routine nature of some of these *contiones* demonstrates how central the institution was to the (urban) citizen's political experience, for they convey a strong sense that publicity and the flow of information to the citizenry were taken very seriously.

In a provocative recent study, however, Henrik Mouritsen rejects this view, chiefly on the grounds that the crowds that attended these meetings – perhaps numbering several thousand people at most – in fact constituted only a tiny proportion of the mass of eligible voters scattered the length of the Italian peninsula, or even just in Rome; further, they can often be shown to have been particular, highly variable, and sharply partisan in their makeup.[51] For Mouritsen, the Roman People were largely sidelined – or apathetically stood apart – from a political process which actually had very little connection with their interests.[52] The attack on the democratic credentials of such a system is well directed. Yet he clearly goes much too far in his zeal to counter Millar's emphasis on the *contio*. While on the whole he is eager to interpret public meetings as little more than political rallies,[53] there is unresolved tension, even conflict, between this view and other aspects of his argument, so that in the end a coherent picture of the function of the *contio* in the Republic fails to emerge. For example, if these meetings possessed great symbolic importance as a kind of ritual enactment of popular freedom, or the "effective symbolic manifestation of the sovereignty of the people over the senate,"[54] then it remains mysterious how such weighty significance could have accrued to smallish partisan demonstrations divorced from the real concerns of the populace. And as it happens, Mouritsen is indeed prepared at times to grant the *contio* what sounds like a fairly large role: for example, public meetings gave the "popular" leaders of the late Republic "an opportunity to demonstrate the *popular support*

---

[50] For the immense variety of such "minor *contiones*," see Pina Polo 1989: 147–70. For augurs and Vestals, see *Rhet. Her.* 1.20; Gell. *NA* 1.12.11.
[51] Mouritsen 2001: esp. 38–62. On the numbers and makeup of contional crowds, see chap. 2, n. 36 and chap. 4, pp. 128–36. The total male citizen population in the Ciceronian period may be variously estimated at 1–2 million (Brunt 1971a: 91–120), or, as seems increasingly plausible, something closer to 3 million (Lo Cascio 1994a, 1994b, 2001). See now Morley 2001.
[52] Mouritsen 2001: e.g. 91–92: "Few political issues . . . had implications which reached much beyond the elite"; p. 144: "the people of Rome never became fully integrated into the political process."
[53] Mouritsen 2001: 52: "essentially 'party'-meetings." [54] Mouritsen 2001: 13–14, 49.

on which they based their policies and claim to influence."[55] The great innovation of these "popular" leaders, as he persuasively maintains, was to mobilize the voting power of much wider sectors of the citizen population, especially from the lower class;[56] but if they got these people into the voting-pens, why not also to the Rostra? After all, "even Clodius had to present his case to his constituency on every single occasion" and "each bill . . . had to be communicated persuasively to the *plebs.*"[57] If public meetings in fact served the important function in late-Republican politics of binding "popular" politicians to a notably broadened base of support, then the connection between *populus* and contional audiences cannot be so remote as Mouritsen insists in his direct comments on the question.[58] When we add that the *contio* was *the* authorized locus of face-to-face communication between the Senate and the populace (as was first emphasized by Millar and will be demonstrated at length in this study), then its significance is clear for all those inquiring into how the dyadic system of the Republic – "the Senate and People of Rome" (*SPQR*) – actually worked, even though it is quite true that the *actual* audiences of *actual* public meetings in late-Republican Rome cannot remotely be equated with the *actual* collectivity of Roman citizens, and thus that such meetings do not remotely meet a modern standard of democratic legitimacy.

The importance of the *contio* is sufficiently established by the fact that it was the venue where political leaders sought to influence, in both the short and long term, that portion of the citizenry who actually exercised the sovereign right of the *populus Romanus* to decide by vote most of the fundamental matters of the Commonwealth: the fate of all laws, the results of all elections, and thus (indirectly, and subject to relatively limited censorial supervision) even the conscription of the august council of the Senate itself. The central act of Republican politics is, as Millar claimed, the "orator addressing a crowd in the Forum." But this may not take us very far in the direction of democracy.

---

[55] Mouritsen 2001: 49 (my emphasis). Note also pp. 45–46: "formal consultation of the people for whom politics mattered – and who mattered for the politicians"; the people "who mattered" for Clodius were, however, admittedly "working-class" (p. 59).

[56] Mouritsen 2001: 79.

[57] Mouritsen 2001: 86. Note how here "local networks" of the *vici* and *collegia* are emphasized over public meetings as lines of communication. But earlier Mouritsen allows that the rhetorical influence of speeches in the *contio*, if only in the form of "soundbites and slogans," extended beyond their immediate audience into "broader sections of the population" (pp. 55–56).

[58] Indeed, that there *was* felt to be a strong connection (see below, pp. 120–28) seems incomprehensible on this view. To my mind, any persuasive account of the *contio* will need to elucidate this connection.

DEMOCRATIC PERSUASION

The debate on the possible democratic effects of the *contio* has thus far been conducted without much explicit reflection on key concepts or the underlying theoretical framework. Millar himself eschewed explicit discussion of the meaning of such potentially problematic ideas as "persuasion" or "popular demands," and others have not remedied the omission.[59] In my view, however, the distribution of power between speaker and audience is not an eternal "given" but a product of specific material and ideological circumstances. Only a more probing analysis of the communication-situation in the *contio* will yield progress in the debate about the democratic effects of public speech in Republican Rome. It is necessary, therefore, to preface this study with some theoretical considerations that complicate any attempt, such as Millar's, to adopt a "democratic" interpretation of contional persuasion and communication. They will also usefully adumbrate the major themes of the argument of this book. The reflections that follow are non-dogmatic and highly eclectic, though I hope not arbitrarily so. On the whole, theoretical eclecticism in an empirical study may be a virtue rather than a vice, since for the examination of actual human society nothing seems more dubious than a single, totalizing perspective.

The association of persuasion with democracy is a very old and quite natural one. But that does not mean that it is unproblematic.[60] It is therefore unfortunate that Millar did not offer an explicit analysis of how, in his view, persuasion in the *contio* worked to produce the democratic effects he saw. In the absence of any such overt treatment of the communication-situation, we are left to infer an implicit model from the development of his arguments. To judge from Millar's emphasis on speakers' need, for success, to satisfy popular "demands" in an environment of "genuine," open debate,[61] his argument seems to presuppose what I would call a "common-sense" model of the contional speech situation, according to which, in order to be persuasive to his audience, a speaker is obliged to make his

---

[59] Mouritsen, for example, seems to distinguish between proper "persuasion" and "rabble-rousing" (and interestingly takes the latter as inconsistent with democracy), but declines to clarify and defend the distinction (Mouritsen 2001: 74; cf. 54, 55–56).

[60] For the Athenian debate, see especially Yunis 1996; for modern theorists' efforts to articulate a deliberative conception of democracy, see Bohman and Rehg 1997.

[61] This is sketched out most fully in Millar 1986, and applied to the period after the Social War in Millar 1995, and 1998: 217–26. For "genuine debate," see Millar 1998: 84 (cf. pp. 46–47). The chief elements of Millar's developed view are perhaps most crisply expressed in Millar 1995 (for the driving force of popular demands, see pp. 103–8). See Millar 1998: 225, for an explicit assertion of the democratic nature of the Republic's "modes of persuasion" (viz., "by the delivery of speeches to those who turned up"). Cf. also Achard 1991: 89; Laser 1997: 142.

arguments conform closely to their values, beliefs, fundamental conceptions and wishes of the short or long term. Consequently, given the competitive rivalry among politicians seeking to tap the sources of popular power, the speaker is, to some undefined extent, influenced or even controlled by his *audience*, who oblige him to enunciate and satisfy their desires. Since Millar sees the Republic as "a political system based on popular power and directed to popular gratification,"[62] it would seem that he presumes a relation between Roman orator and audience rather like the one Josiah Ober more explicitly employs in his important study of the function of rhetoric in Athenian democracy: "at the practical level of discourse in the courtroom and the Assembly, the orator had to conform to his audience's ideology or face the consequences: losing votes or being ignored."[63]

On deeper consideration, however, this sort of model begins to look too simple to do the work required of it. Most striking to me are its deficiencies in three crucial areas:

(1) *The ideological effects of discourse. Contiones* were a persistent point of contact and face-to-face exchange between senators, who did the talking, and the (symbolically present) Roman People, who listened but might also reply, as we shall see. Inevitably, in such meetings the fundamental political conceptions of the audience, repeatedly invoked in the service of the immediate purpose, must have been defined, shaped, and revised in a complex and constantly reiterated interaction between listener, speaker, and the larger social and political contexts. Even when ostensibly *informing* the populace of current events, contional speech should not be assumed to have simply described relatively objective realities and contemporary circumstances, but should rather be seen as playing an important role in creating and perpetuating the perceived "truths" and "natural" parameters of action that conditioned citizens' responses to political questions. So, for example, when in Cicero's *Third Catilinarian Oration*, the orator-consul, even while describing the penetration of the urban conspiracy of 63 to the worried and news-hungry populace, casts himself as the near-omniscient agent of Jupiter, tirelessly defending the People, in their ignorance, from the inhuman plots of depraved aristocrats, and calls upon them to repay this debt by protecting him in the future, we can readily see how he is

---

[62] Millar 1995: 100.
[63] Ober 1989: 43–44. From this fundamental premise eventually emerges Ober's notion of "mass control of political ideology," which alone permits the potential of a formally democratic constitution to be realized (p. 337). Ober cites Aristotelian paternity for the view that "an orator who wishes to persuade a mass audience must accommodate himself to the ethos – the ideology – of his audience" (p. 43), but the passages he cites (p. 43, n. 101: among the more significant, *Rh.* 2.13.16 [1390a25–27], 2.21.15 [1395b1–11], and 2.22.3 [1395b27–1396a3]) seem much more circumscribed.

seeking to shape *both* the audience's understanding of the situation *and* their consideration of appropriate responses, with reference to a wide shared background of moral and civic assumptions as well as beliefs about the natural order.

We should therefore view the oratory of the *contio* as a uniquely important political "discourse" (or "genre of discourse") – that is, an interrelated series of utterances and practices embedded in a specific political context and linked to a certain type of social action – with a heavy ideological content.[64] (Following most contemporary work on ideology, I reject the traditional Marxist sense of the word ["false consciousness"], which is always pejorative and bound to distinctly Marxist notions of "class" and "society," but find the word invaluable as a convenient designation for the collection of beliefs, values, and core concepts that contribute to the distribution of power in a society, typically implicitly or covertly.[65]) Now, whatever one thinks of Louis Althusser's dark musings about "Ideological State Apparatuses," there can be little doubt that he hit upon something important when he observed that ideology "summons" or "interpellates" individuals to take up a position already defined through existing discourses, and thus constitutes them as ideological subjects.[66] Just so, I would say, the member of a contional crowd was again and again "hailed" to locate himself without critical reflection within the discourse and the ideology it perpetuated. To take a simple but pointed example, we may note how speakers in the assembly typically addressed whatever crowd stood in front of them as the actual embodiment of the *populus Romanus*, with all that the august title entailed – sometimes with paradoxical consequences, as when Cicero calls upon his audience for the *Pro lege Manilia* (*In Support of the Manilian Law*),

[64] I am using "discourse," therefore, not in the special Habermasian sense, but in the sense commonly employed in contemporary social and political criticism. For a lucid introduction to "discourse theory," particularly in the version promoted by the work of E. Laclau and C. Mouffe, see Howarth and Stavrakis 2000. See also Wodak et al. 1999 (esp. 7–48), an interesting, recent case study, in the "Critical Discourse Analysis" school, of the creation of modern Austrian national identity through speeches, media reporting, interviews, and so on.

[65] Eagleton 1991 provides an excellent critical history of the concept. Some object to the vagueness of the term, but as Teun van Dijk remarks (1998: 1), "ideology" is no "fuzzier" than other indispensable words of social analysis such as "society," "group," "action," "power," "discourse," "mind," and "knowledge." Indeed, I have doubts about an attempt such as van Dijk's to define "ideology" both more sharply and globally, since its usefulness seems to depend on specific contexts. With Eagleton (pp. 7–8), I do not share Michel Foucault's well-known aversion to the concept (Foucault 1980: 118).

[66] See the famous essay, "Ideology and Ideological State Apparatuses," in Althusser 1971: 121–73, esp. 162–63: "I shall then suggest that ideology 'acts' or 'functions' in such a way that it 'recruits' subjects among the individuals (it recruits them all), or 'transforms' the individuals into subjects (it transforms them all) by that very precise operation which I have called *interpellation* or hailing, and which can be imagined along the lines of the most commonplace everyday police (or other) hailing: 'Hey, you there!' "

probably a heterogeneous crowd of largely foreign, partly even Hellenic, descent, not to abandon the Imperial traditions of "*our* ancestors" who had destroyed the city of Corinth, defeated the great Hellenistic kings, and crushed Carthage.[67] Given the *contio*'s centrality in the political experience of the Roman community, it might be seen as a – perhaps *the* – major instrument of ideological production in the Republic.

If, then, we think of oratory in the *contio* as ideological discourse, and acknowledge the force of Althusser's observation that individual subjects are produced by discourse and located thereby within ideology, then it follows that the *contio*-goer was by no means the autonomous agent implied by what I have called the "common-sense" model of persuasion: one, in short, capable and disposed to take up an independent, critical stance from which to assess a speaker's arguments according to an independent perception of his interests and the public good. On the contrary, the conceptual framework through which he would interpret what he heard was itself the product of contional discourse. In the absence of alternative, powerful sources of communication, he could hardly be expected to "stand outside of" that discourse and its ideological content; indeed, if the discourse be relatively univocal, he might even be its prisoner.

Add to this the fact that, in the *contio*, the distinction between speaker and listener was also characterized by socio-political differentiation and a hierarchical relationship – with negligible exceptions, those who spoke were members of the political élite drawn from the higher echelons of society – and the potential for an élite hegemony over contional discourse rather than the opposite would appear, in principle, to be very great indeed.[68] Objections in a Foucauldian mode, such as that the speaker too cannot "stand outside" a perpetual discourse in which he too is located, or, more fundamentally, that power suffuses society like an electrical current and is not simply exerted from the top downward, have, of course, some weight. But, since it was an educated and trained élite that actually articulated contional discourse, while the audience was restricted to listening and vocally conferring or withholding approval of what that élite had brought before it, it would seem quite implausible to deny to the political élite of Republican Rome a high degree of agency in, and control over, the generation

---

[67] Cic. *Leg. Man.* 11–12, 14, 54–55. A few years later Cicero complains that *contiones* were now dominated by disruptive Phrygians, Mysians, and similarly decadent "Greeks" (*Flac.* 17), not to mention Jews (66–67).

[68] This evokes Antonio Gramsci's concept of "cultural hegemony," whose usefulness and problems for the historian are well examined by Lears 1985.

of contional discourse, within the limits imposed by its own ideological perspective and the exigencies of the moment.

All of this might seem to be a rather abstract kind of objection to the "common-sense" model whereby speakers had to accommodate themselves to their audiences' beliefs and wishes in order to succeed. A circumscribed illustration of the nature of the problem might be helpful. An angry Roman crowd, desperate at the soaring price of grain in the city, must have been about as demanding an audience as one could imagine. One would have been foolish indeed to address it in terms that were not in some real sense appropriate to its circumstances and beliefs. Yet, to judge from some surviving samples of contional oratory, it is evident that, by exploiting certain dispositions (deference to authority and respect for élite traditions of public service, say) to counter others (hunger and social resentment, for example), a speaker might *suppress* what would seem to be the true Voice of the People rather than being driven by the requirements of the speech situation to express it. In a speech that Sallust (who, as we shall see, should be considered a good source for the nature of contional rhetoric) puts in the mouth of a consul during a dangerous scarcity of grain in 75, Gaius Cotta assuages popular anger by directly evoking the semi-mythical tradition of self-immolation for the public good, rhetorically carrying out such a *devotio* himself and thereby in effect "proving" his total dedication to the interests of the Roman People at a time when that link between mass and élite had become dangerously frayed.[69] Two generations earlier, P. Scipio Nasica was supposedly blunter: his response – effective, we are told – to an audience's outcry under similar circumstances was, "Silence, please, Citizens; for I know better than you what is good for the Republic."[70] Setting aside for the present the question of the historical authenticity of either of these utterances,[71] we may note that in both instances the speaker indeed appeals to certain elements of the pre-existing disposition of his audience, but in neither case would we say that he has become the people's mouthpiece, or in any profound sense accommodated himself to popular demands and aspirations. In both cases, the speaker's strategy is entirely predicated on the power of ideology; such appeals, I assume, would have been hopelessly counterproductive before audiences with a very different ideological makeup – say, one of modern European or North American voters. It doubtless remains true that a speaker could not (cannot) succeed

---

[69] Sall. *Hist.* 2.47.10–13. See chap. 7, n. 77, and p. 262 for further remarks on this example.

[70] Val. Max. 3.7.3 = *ORF* 38.3, pp. 157–58 (text at chap. 6, n. 111).

[71] Note that the authors of the texts in which these speeches are embedded considered them plausible ways of addressing a *contio*.

in gaining his end without, to a great extent, making use of the considerations, values, and beliefs held by his audience. That, clearly, rather than "ideological control" (in Ober's phrase) is what Aristotle was talking about; and in that very limited sense, indeed, one might say that the disposition of the audience calls forth his voice (although this disposition should then also be seen as to some significant degree the *product* of *previous* élite discourse). Yet, if that were all that there was to it, then all rhetoric would be inherently democratic, which a moment's reflection induces us to doubt.

(2) *The problem of public opinion.* Nothing would seem more obvious than that, at least at times, the People want something. For example, in the illustrations that I have just drawn upon, it would be perversely skeptical to deny that the urban populace really wanted bread. However, for concrete political action to follow (legislation, for example), such manifest and powerful but as yet inarticulated needs or desires must be translated into specific proposals; and it is only in this form that they may be voted on – the standard test of the popular will. Yet the unspecific, pre-existing "want" and the popular mandate that is the ultimate outcome do not necessarily have a direct and uncomplicated relationship with each other. Gabinius' proposal that Gnaeus Pompey (for example) be given supreme command over the entire Mediterranean and its coasts for three years to pursue a war against the pirates is not a simple, transparent reflection of the generalized urban panic at the prospect of continuing food shortages that formed its context.[72] Nor does the overwhelming popular vote in favor of the proposal suggest that *this* is what was being demanded by the citizenry before Gabinius promulgated his plan. The point is that the formal procedures for ascertaining and authoritatively measuring the popular will also simultaneously fashion it, *at a minimum* by reducing it to the level of specificity necessary for concrete adjudication. Consequently, the nature of pre-existing public opinion, before anyone has sought in some way to articulate and then to measure it, can only be a guess (though there may be better or worse guesses).

The highly problematic nature of the deceptively simple phrase "public opinion" is well demonstrated by the political scientist John Zaller, with the help of the whole social-scientific panoply of questionnaires and quantitative analysis unavailable to ancient historians. The question, "If the public had an opinion and there was no pollster around to measure it, would public opinion exist?"[73] turns out to pose quite a conundrum. More precisely, Zaller makes a compelling case that what emerges as "public opinion" is

---

[72] The *lex Gabinia* of 67, the debate on which is examined below, chap. 5.   [73] Zaller 1992: 265.

the product of interaction with, if not outright prompting by, whoever is defining and measuring it – frequently, of course, with the ulterior motive of exploiting it. This produces something like a pollster's uncertainty principle.

None of this is to deny that the public has hopes, fears, values, and concerns that are, to a large extent, independent of élite discourse . . . The claim, rather, is that the public's feelings are, in their unobserved state, unfocused and frequently contradictory. Which of these feelings becomes activated for expression as public opinion depends on a complex process in which pollsters, among others, are key players.[74]

Political leaders, on this view, are neither "passive instruments of majority opinion" nor "attempt[ing] openly to challenge it"; rather, they "attempt to play on the contradictory ideas that are always present in people's minds, elevating the salience of some and harnessing them to new initiatives while downplaying or ignoring other ideas."[75] As for the origin of these ideas and their structural interrelationship, they are themselves heavily influenced by élite discourse, with (somewhat embarrassingly) the most politically aware and involved portion of the population being most susceptible; in particular, ideological divergence among the public is closely dependent on the emergence of such a division in élite media sources, with those most closely attuned to politics falling into step the soonest.[76]

    V. O. Key, Jr., an early and (for his time) a relatively "optimistic" analyst of American voting behavior, once offered a striking metaphor to explain why electoral results cannot necessarily be interpreted as a transparent popular verdict or mandate: "the voice of the people is but an echo," namely, of what candidates and parties have put in at the other end of the echo chamber. He meant at least two things by this. In part he was simply enunciating the famous principle rather saltily, but effectively, enunciated as "garbage in, garbage out." But also he meant that "As candidates and parties clamor for attention and vie for popular support, the people's verdict can be no more than a selective reflection from among the alternatives and outlooks presented to them."[77] The metaphor nicely highlights the problem we are faced with. Just how can an "echo" influence what it echoes? If, and to the extent that, the citizen-auditor does not autonomously bring *his own* conceptions of his needs and interests to the contional speech situation, then the "common-sense" model's assumption of indirect audience *control* over the speaker's words becomes correspondingly implausible.

[74] Zaller 1992: 95. [75] Zaller 1992: 95–96.
[76] Zaller 1992: 185–215, esp. 208–11, building on Converse 1964: 206–61. [77] Key 1966: 1–8.

A closely related problem is that of the intellectual autonomy of citizens who receive their political knowledge and information through the mediation of élites (e.g. newspaper and television reporting). Some recent work on the effects of the modern mass media upon democratic deliberation is indeed fairly optimistic about the capacity of the general public to sort, evaluate, and make use of the information they receive through mediating élite sources.[78] Yet even "optimists" about the rationality of the modern voting public agree that however active citizens may be in the construction of their political realities and ultimately of their desires, the success of their attempts to determine their own destiny is dependent on a series of variables of which the "competition and diversity" of opinion in their sources of information are paramount.[79] This must give us pause, since in fact there was no serious alternative source of political information to the Roman citizen *other* than what he heard in the *contio*. Describing his own penetration of the urban conspiracy of 63 as consul and the proceedings within the Senate under his own presidency that convinced the council of the conspirators' guilt, Cicero delivering the *Third Catilinarian Oration* combined functions that we tend to think of as separate, rather as if a modern President or Prime Minister delivered the prime-time news. The question of the range of "competition and diversity" of opinion *across contiones* held by different persons, often adversaries, I leave to the study proper. At this point I wish only to mark out a problem.

All of this, then, complicates the "common-sense model" of persuasion, which presumes that speakers are obliged to meet fairly specific demands on the part of their audiences, since those demands, when they first come to be articulated, are the result of interaction with the speakers themselves, who are, indeed, the ones articulating them and have supplied much of the information on which calculations of interest could be based. As we also found above at the ideological level of social beliefs, values, and concepts, here too at the concrete level of their immediate fears, needs, and desires, the autonomy of members of the audience as agents and judges of their own (and the public's) interest, which alone produces their leverage over speakers, is potentially deeply eroded.

---

[78] See esp. Neuman, Just, and Crigler 1992; Page 1996.

[79] Esp. Page 1996: 123, 126, 128. Also, Page and Shapiro 1992: chap. 9, whose list of crucial factors for avoiding public dependence on élite discourse includes: "(1) predispositional differences among experts that parallel those among the public; (2) institutional incentives for experts to develop effective solutions; (3) a press that covers all expert viewpoints; (4) politicians and activists that keep within the parameters of public opinion; (5) citizenry capable of aligning itself with the élite faction that shares its predispositions."

(3) *The "less-than-ideal" speech situation.* Jürgen Habermas's career-long effort to anchor the critique of modern society, and thus to vindicate philosophically the Enlightenment project of Reason against the Nietzschean vacuum of postmodernism, is based on the claim that all cooperative social action is premised upon a fundamental presupposition of rationality: that is, that implicit in every attempt to coordinate action with others through *communication* rather than force or intimidation is a promise to justify that action, if necessary, by giving reasons that would be found acceptable to the others involved. For Habermas, every speech act – say, for example, "we must increase defense spending" – contains four "validity claims" as to its *intelligibility, truth, truthfulness* or *sincerity,* and *normative rightness* (in this case, that the proposal makes sense linguistically, is in fact true, is an honest representation of the speaker's opinion, and is consistent with social norms), each of which the speaker implicitly "warrants" and undertakes to "redeem" with good reasons if challenged. "Communicative action" in Habermas's sense characterizes social action only if and when this kind of communicative rationality, with its potential for an exchange of good reasons leading to consensus, underlies it (even if only implicitly). The alternative, when agents pursue their own interest without regard for persuasion of other rational subjects, is called by Habermas "strategic action"; and when strategic action is surreptitiously pursued under the *guise* of communicative action – as when, say, a legislator publicly advocates spending for a plausible reason to which he does not, in fact, adhere while covertly pursuing another end, such as satisfying a contributor to his campaign, thus violating the "sincerity" validity claim – then the result is "systematically distorted communication," a vicious perversion of social rationality.[80]

The circumstances for proper communicative action, on the other hand, are encapsulated in the Habermasian term, "ideal speech situation": essentially, as Thomas McCarthy puts it, "absence of constraint – both external (such as force or the threat of force) and internal (such as neurotic or ideological distortions) . . . [T]he structure is free from constraint only when for all participants there is a symmetrical distribution of chances to select and employ speech acts, when there is an effective equality of opportunity for the assumption of dialogue roles."[81] Only such conditions would ensure

---

[80] The central works for present purposes are Habermas 1984–87 and 1996. Useful orientation may be found in McCarthy 1982 and S. K. White 1995; a lucid explication of the theory prefaces the otherwise rather technical critique of Habermas by Heath 2001: 1–48. On "systematically distorted communication," see Habermas 2001: 131–70.

[81] McCarthy 1982: 306. On the "ideal-speech situation," see ibid., pp. 291–310, and for the chief source-text, Habermas 1973: 211–65, esp. 252–60.

that the rational consensus that emerges has been driven by "the unforced force of the better argument," to use Habermas's most famous phrase. Now, he is perfectly aware that this ideal has arguably never been realized and perhaps never will. However, it is a uniquely important sort of *ideal*, since if Habermas is right, then unlike many other ideals this is one we cannot live without, or more accurately, society cannot function without. More to the point for us, only the standard of the "ideal speech situation" enables us to distinguish a rational consensus from a false one;[82] thus in historical or sociological studies it "allows for a systematic understanding of the different *sorts* of failure and provides the norms or standards for *criticizing* them."[83]

Habermas, then, helps us to see just how rigorous – indeed, generally speaking, counterfactual – are the requirements of open and transparent persuasion that are so quietly presupposed in the "common-sense model." Above all, there must be complete reciprocity among the participants in discussion, and an equal opportunity for all to engage in and influence the course of public debate, including the right to contribute to the agenda or to challenge justifications.[84] The current "deliberative-democracy" school of political theorists, for whom Habermas has been a major philosophical source, has sought to work out these criteria more fully in real-world terms.[85] For instance, as Jack Knight and James Johnson elaborate the demands of discursive equality, there must be "procedural guarantees that afford equal access to relevant deliberative arenas at both agenda-setting and decision-making stages," and also rather heavy substantive requirements, such as the neutralization of inequalities in the "social distribution of power and resources," and even in the capacity to influence others (including capacity "to formulate authentic preferences," to use "cultural resources" such as the dominant language and concepts, not to mention skills, knowledge, and especially simple access to good information).[86] For good measure, Knight and Johnson add "mechanisms to foster equality of opportunity of political influence" such as governmental expenditure to improve education, diet, and environment of the disadvantaged.[87] For deliberation to be democratic in fact rather than merely in form, James Bohman points out, all participants must be above a "floor" of "political poverty," that is, the minimal threshold of capabilities below which participants are systematically excluded from influence upon ostensibly deliberative decisions, and below a "ceiling" of

---

[82] Habermas 1973: 257.   [83] B. Fultner, in Habermas 2001: xxi.   [84] Habermas 1973: 255–56.

[85] See Bohman and Rehg 1997, and especially Jon Elstner's introductory essay (pp. 3–33).

[86] Knight and Johnson 1997, quoted at 281, 294, and 298. On access to information, see 1997: 299, and n. 88 below.

[87] Knight and Johnson 1997: 304–9.

such great social power that those above it can determine in advance the results of any apparently deliberative process.[88]

We may safely conclude, even without further investigation, that Republican Rome was not a "deliberative democracy." However, not even Millar has said that it was. The point of lingering so long over what is manifestly an ideal of democratic deliberation is not speciously to refute the "democratic" thesis by defining democracy in such a way that it is placed well out of reach, but to highlight the limitations and potentially distorting simplifications of the "common-sense" model of persuasion, which alone would give strong content to Millar's application of the word "democracy" to the Roman Republic. Of course, every model is a simplification of reality. That is not in itself the problem with the "common-sense model"; the problem is rather that there are grounds to doubt that its omissions are justifiable in the present area of investigation. But such doubts can only gain substance through empirical study of the ways in which the *contio* and its rhetoric worked in the late Roman Republic. The distribution of power between speaker and audience in any actual situation is not given *a priori* but can only be discerned through an investigation of a whole variety of circumstantial factors that determine the degree of intellectual independence possessed by an audience. Of particular interest in this study will be the economy of knowledge/information in late Republican Rome: that is, how, and by whom, it was distributed and controlled.

RHETORICAL EVIDENCE

A central concern of this book is to explore how political speech negotiates the distribution of power between speaker and audience. That raises the question of evidence for a phenomenon as transitory as speech. While I shall make much use of ancient *descriptions* of public meetings (in narrative histories, for example, or speeches or letters) and also draw much from our growing knowledge of the physical space in which they were held, the most important class of evidence for the present purpose consists of the surviving published examples of contional oratory. Only the speeches themselves (set, of course, in the context provided by other evidence, and "tested" against it for consistency) can provide the material we need to answer

[88] Bohman 1997. Admittedly, Bohman (like Knight and Johnson 1997), influenced by Amartya Sen's "capabilities" approach to equality, goes well beyond Habermas here, who seems quite prepared to countenance great asymmetries between participants in deliberation, among them that of access and control over information (p. 342). On this point, however, Bohman's criticism of Habermas strikes me as quite valid.

the questions of interest here – questions rather like those posed about US presidential inauguration speeches by the political scientist Richard A. Joslyn:

What expectations or norms about popular participation are revealed and encouraged in political discourse? Is the public's role a circumscribed one of observation, obedience, quiescence, and occasional indications of consent? Or is the public encouraged to take a more active role in public affairs? Is the public encouraged to be skeptical or reassured? Is the public encouraged to be participant or quiescent? . . . Does discourse politicize or narcotize the public?[89]

These are not the kinds of questions that have traditionally concerned the Roman historian, and it will therefore be necessary to borrow much from the toolbox of the students of Roman oratory and political rhetoric. But in place of the extended analysis of rhetorical strategies that is characteristic of current work on Cicero, for example, the questions in this study will work mostly at a different level, where lurk the usually latent presuppositions about the relationship between orator and mass audience and the distribution of power between them.

As it happens, the quantity of material in this class of evidence is not small, at least by the standards of ancient history. Of more-or-less complete contional speeches, we possess the published versions of no fewer than nine by Cicero, the oral originals of which were delivered over a span of more than twenty years from his debut on the Rostra to his final, ill-fated crusade against Mark Antony. They are: the *Pro lege Manilia* (*In Support of the Manilian Law*, also known as *De imperio Cn. Pompei*, *On the Command for Pompey*), a speech in support of the law conferring the Mithridatic command on Pompey the Great delivered in Cicero's praetorship in 66; the second and third speeches *De lege agraria* (*On the Agrarian Law*) of January, 63, when upon assuming his consular duties Cicero fought the agrarian proposal of the tribune P. Servilius Rullus; the *Pro Rabirio perduellionis reo* (*In Defence of Rabirius on a Charge of Treason*) of the same year, delivered at the final *contio* of the trial before the People of a man accused of murdering the tribune L. Saturninus in 100, almost four decades before;[90] the *Second* and *Third Catilinarians* (*In Catilinam*),

---

[89] Joslyn 1986: 315.

[90] The background and precise nature of Rabirius' trial are highly controversial. I follow in essentials the judicious analysis of Tyrrell 1978 (esp. pp. 37–50, 60–61, 70–75, 84–89, 131; cf. also Tyrrell 1973), who establishes to my satisfaction that the speech was indeed delivered in a capital trial (rather than a mere pecuniary case involving a fine, as has often been supposed from §8) on a charge of *perduellio* brought by the tribune, T. Labienus, in the first instance (rather than on appeal [*provocatio*] from the prior decision of the *duumviri perduellionis*), to be concluded with a vote by the Centuriate

based on speeches Cicero made on November 9[91] and December 3, 63, both conveying important political news to the citizenry and rallying public support behind the consul; the *Post reditum ad Quirites* (*Speech of Thanks to the Citizens*), an address of September 5, 57 (probably[92]) thanking the People for the law that had restored Cicero from exile; and the *Fourth* and *Sixth Philippics*, delivered on December 20, 44, and January 4, 43, mobilizing popular enthusiasm for Cicero's last great crusade, the civil war against Mark Antony.

A potential problem that cannot be shirked, however, is the fact that the speech as originally, orally delivered and its published, written version were by no means the same thing. Cicero's speech in defense of Milo in 52 BC is at best an idealized version of what Cicero would have said had the Clodian crowd not ruined the speech with its interruptions; the five books of the *actio secunda* against Verres (like the *Second Philippic*) were never even delivered, since the defense forfeited the case after Cicero's opening statement, yet they were still fully "written up" as if they had been, complete with imaginative dramatizations of the reactions of the defense to the author's overpowering oratory. These are, of course, special cases whose "counter-factual" status was known to ancient critics and whose idealized fictionalization took in no one. But even the normal sort of published version of a speech actually delivered in roughly the same form, length, and circumstances, cannot be taken to be a verbatim record of a rhetorical event. Orators typically wrote down speeches *after* the event, drawing on very recent – but highly trained – memory as well as written-out portions (especially openings) and

Assembly (rather than the tribes, as has been supposed from reference to the *rostra* at §25: see below, chap. 2, n. 93). Work published since Tyrrell's study does not, it seems to me, overturn these points: Liou-Gille 1994 presumes, without new argument, the validity of the generally discredited notion that the speech belongs to an appeal; Alexander 1990: no. 221 follows the reconstruction of the case as one involving only a fine, but with hesitation; while the elaborate hypothesis of Primmer 1985: 9–14, 25–49 contradicts *perduellionis reo* in Cic. *Pis.* 4 (chap. 6, n. 100), and the supposed inconsistency between Cicero's pride in his performance (attested by his publication of the speech, as well as the just-cited passage) and Dio's version of the conclusion of the matter (by Metellus' dissolution of the centuriate assembly: 37.27.3) may simply be a choice of emphasis (Dio's well-known anti-Ciceronianism is invoked by Primmer himself: p. 28). Final day: *Rab. perd.* 5. See too Gruen 1974: 279, n. 69; on the procedure of *iudicia populi*, see Santalucia 1998: 84–88; Lintott 1999: 152–53.

[91] Accepting the "traditional" dating of *Cat.* 1 (Nov. 8): see, however, now Berry 1996: 236–37, in favor of the alternative date one day earlier.

[92] Cic. *Att.* 4.1.5. The date, strictly, is only that of the preceding *Post reditum in senatu*; but it is almost certain that this speech was delivered immediately upon adjournment of the senatorial meeting at which its "twin" was given (Nicholson 1992: 126–28). Cf. *Phil.* 3–4 and 5–6, with chap. 7, nn. 23, 24. The alternative possibility, which Nicholson advances hesitantly, is that it was delivered on the actual day of Cicero's arrival, *before* the senatorial speech, in keeping with the primacy of the debt to the People (*Red. pop.* 1–5); it is certainly unthinkable that Cicero failed to thank the People in a *contio* (the final possibility Nicholson raises).

more-or-less complete notes (*commentarii*) for important sections. There is no sign that the necessary means – fully prepared texts, shorthand – for verbatim reproduction were generally exploited, although the practices existed; nor was this extreme degree of exactitude considered an objective of publication.[93]

Even so, at present the debate seems to be favoring proponents of the view that the published speeches are, in substance and form, fair, if not by our standards exact, reflections of the oral original: the "commemoration of a speech delivered," as Quintilian puts it.[94] The speeches for Milo and Verres (as well as the *Second Philippic*) were special cases, whose exceptional nature cannot be taken to be indicative of Cicero's normal practice of publication except in so far as they prove that an orator *could* publish what was well known to be a substantially or wholly fictionalized speech. (At the same time, the effort taken by Cicero to make these speeches fit the actual or implied circumstances of delivery should equally be noted: even these "fictions" are not wholly divorced from historical reality.) On the other hand, in the usual instance – the subsequent publication of an actually delivered speech that was, and was known to have been, delivered in full – there is no good evidence that the published versions distort the content or form of the original.[95] On the contrary, the (admittedly exiguous) evidence we have for Cicero's editing of written versions implies that while stylistic improvements, for example, were made as a matter of course, accuracy in representing the arguments actually employed and the circumstances of the speech was valued and expected.[96] Furthermore, Cicero, who should know, as a rule treats published speeches as good evidence of an orator's actual, orally realized, speeches in his magisterial survey of the history of Roman

---

[93] See now Alexander 2003: 16–24, for a good discussion of the process of reconstruction. For writing after oral delivery, see Cic. *Tusc.* 4.55 and *Brut.* 91; for verbatim, written preparation of only selected, important portions of the speech, see Quint. *Inst.* 10.7.30.

[94] Quint. *Inst.* 12.10.51: *monumentum actionis habitae.* Riggsby 1999: 178–84 and now Alexander 2003: 15–26 make many good points while reviewing the contours of this old debate (esp. the contributions of Humbert, Laurand, and Stroh). For the opposing view, see now Ledentu 2000 and Achard (below, n. 110).

[95] The *locus classicus* is Pliny's claim at *Ep.* 1.20.8, as interpreted especially by Humbert. On this crux, see now Riggsby 1999: 180, and Alexander 2003: 24–25. It might be added that Pliny has a personal stake in this argument, which may have led him to a hopeful interpretation of the Ciceronian evidence (note *puto*, 1.20.7): he wants to mobilize Cicero in favor of *magnitudo* against a critic who subordinates everything to *brevitas* (1.20.1–5). See also, in general, Quint. *Inst.* 12.10.49–57.

[96] Note especially *Att.* 1.13.5; 13.44.3; 15.1a.2, and the *tituli* summarizing the content of omitted argumentation at *Mur.* 57; *Font.* 20; and perhaps *Cael.* 19 – a convention that evidently presumes an expectation of fidelity to the delivered version (cf. Riggsby 1999: 180). Alexander 2003: 19 rightly emphasizes the attention to factual accuracy implied by Cicero's known corrections.

oratory in the *Brutus*.[97] Elsewhere, he unhesitatingly takes a striking passage from the published version of one *contio* as something actually said.[98]

Thus, to take Cicero's *contiones* as a fair reflection of what was actually said, without pressing details too strongly, is in fact justifiable. But in any case, my objective in this work is not so much to assess the effectiveness of any particular Ciceronian rhetorical "move" in its original, oral performance (although some such judgments of this sort will be inevitable), but above all to delineate the larger patterns and contours of popular political speech, making use not of isolated particulars but of ideas, themes, and underlying structures of thought that repeat themselves and forge complementary connections with other speeches in the sample. Consequently, for my main purpose, I do not need to assume that congruence between oral and written versions was extremely close, but – a less demanding requirement – that the *nature and style of rhetoric* did not undergo a substantial change in the transition between these two states. What matters most for us, for example, is not whether the published text of Cicero's *Second Catilinarian* reflects very closely the speech he actually delivered to the populace on the morning of November 9, 63, but whether we can accept it as a good example of the sort of speech Cicero, at the time of writing, thought appropriate to that specific occasion and *its implied audience*. Whatever we make of the former question (and, as we have seen, extreme skepticism here may be misplaced), we can be fairly confident about the latter.

The reason is the exemplarity of published orations. Wilfried Stroh, rejecting the formerly common view that speeches were fundamentally reworked in order to appeal to the different "audience" of a written text, forcefully drove home the point that published speeches were intended above all to serve as rhetorical models and memorials of oratorical brilliance: "the

---

[97] E.g. *Brut.* 65, 68–69, 77, 82–83, 114–16, 117, 122, 131, 153, 163, 177. The exceptions Cicero allows are explained by reference to special circumstances and seem to prove the rule. For example, the oral tradition might attest to greater merit than seemed warranted on the evidence of published speeches, so that one was led to conjecture that a famed speaker did not give equal attention to writing (thus, Ser. Sulpicius Galba, cos. 144: §§91–94, cf. 82, 295; for the distinction to be drawn between these two talents, see also §§95, 205, and for a published product that fell short of oratorical repute, §104 [Ti. Gracchus and C. Carbo]; cf. §298 [L. Crassus]). Or, indeed, the quality of a published oration might surpass the assessment of an orator by the tradition, as in the case of C. Fannius (cos. 122), leading some to doubt whether the speech was the product of his pen at all, although Cicero himself accepts instead the evidence of the published speech (§99–100). Also, in one case Cicero claims to know that another man produced the written versions of speeches originally composed and delivered by a noted orator (P. Sulpicius, tr. pl. 88: §205). Finally, the published version of a speech might itself betray abbreviation of certain parts: §164 (L. Crassus' *suasio* on the *lex Servilia Caepionis*; see below). Cf. the use of *tituli*, above, n. 96.

[98] Cic. *De or.* 1.225–27: L. Crassus on the *lex Servilia Caepionis* (see below).

very *oratio scripta* itself can only achieve its new purpose – the purpose of instruction by example – when its nature remains that of an oral speech in a historical setting, that is, when it shows the student how one should speak under specific circumstances, before a specific audience, on a specific occasion."[99] The written version of a speech will therefore have been expected to reflect closely the actual circumstances of delivery, including the assumptions of the orator-author as to the distinct nature, disposition, and what we would call the ideological perspective of the kind of audience to which the original was delivered. As it happens, Quintilian enunciates the principle fairly explicitly.[100] So, for example, Cicero recalls studying in his youth Lucius Crassus' speech to the citizens in favor of a judicial law, delivered and probably published in 106, the year of Cicero's birth: it was like a teacher to him.[101] The remarkable nature of this speech, as Cicero recalls, was that while it defended the interests of the Senate and extolled its authority, it made use of the populist style of invidious attack to arouse indignation against the supposed collusion of equestrian judges and prosecutors (the result of a judiciary law of the popular hero Gaius Gracchus).[102] It is evident that what this speech taught the young Cicero was largely predicated on fidelity to the rhetorical and political circumstances Crassus faced, including the type and disposition of the original audience.

Evidence for the conclusion that published contional speeches, if somewhat improved, remained true in the presumptions of their rhetoric to their original (type of) audience, may be drawn from a comparison of Cicero's (published) contional speeches with other kinds of oration (senatorial and forensic). Of particular interest here are Cicero's "paired" speeches on identical themes delivered successively before senatorial and popular venues: *On the Agrarian Law* 1 and 2, the *Post reditum* speeches of 57, and *Philippics* 3–4 and 5–6.[103] The mere fact, indeed, that Cicero published these juxtaposed "twins" suggests in itself that he wished to demonstrate to future senators how the same theme should be treated before the two distinct

---

99 Stroh 1975: 52–53 (my translation); see pp. 21, 51–54. For "exemplarity" as the chief purpose of publication, Stroh calls Cicero's *Brutus* to witness (122, 127, 164); also Cic. *Att.* 2.1.3, 4.2.2; *Q Fr.* 3.1.11. See also Classen 1985: 5–8, 367; Fuhrmann 1990: 56–57; Vasaly 1993: 9–10. Stroh was not, of course, the first to make the point: cf. Mack 1937: 11–12.

100 Quint. *Inst.* 12.10.53: *omnia quae ad obtinendum quod intendimus prodesse credemus adhibenda sunt, eaque et cum dicimus promenda et cum scribimus ostendenda sunt, si modo ideo scribimus ut doceamus quo modo dici oporteat.*

101 Cic. *Brut.* 164: *Mihi quidem a pueritia quasi magistra fuit.*

102 Cic. *Brut.* 164: *in qua et auctoritas ornatur senatus, quo pro ordine illa dicuntur, et invidia concitatur in iudicum et in accusatorum factionem, contra quorum potentiam populariter tum dicendum fuit.*

103 *Cat.* 1 and 2, 3 and 4, are of course comparable, but do not fall in quite the same category, since circumstances are substantially different before each of the two audiences.

deliberative bodies.[104] Close rhetorical and linguistic examination of the "paired" speeches has shown how elements as diverse as style, emotional and intellectual register, historical perspective, and contemporary political outlook all vary with remarkable consistency, in ways that are convincingly interpreted as corresponding to the change of implied (original) audience and circumstances of delivery.[105] This is not just a simple matter of alternatively praising or denigrating the Gracchi, or the different ways in which the names of Sulla and Marius are invoked;[106] much less obvious features prove to be distinctive to each audience. For example, in the major speech on the agrarian law directed to the People, Cicero makes much more frequent use of questions and exclamations than in the surviving portion of the senatorial speech, employs far more historical and geographical allusions, and quotes extensively from the text of the law, a tactic he eschews almost entirely in the substantial surviving portion of the speech delivered in the Senate.[107] In the *Philippics* and the *Post reditum* speeches, on the other hand, Cicero places extraordinary emphasis on his own person and his personal bond to his listeners when speaking in the *contio*, relegating other leading men and the Senate as an institution largely to the background. Further, the popular *Post reditum* and *Philippics* speeches are distinguished by heightened emotionalism and religiosity; their senatorial "twins," by their indulgence in invective and interest in legality.[108] One scholar has recently drawn attention to Cicero's relatively prodigious exploitation of the device of apostrophe ("*Quirites!*") in addresses to the People compared with in the senatorial speeches, and plausibly explained the sharp contrast by referring to the special demands of mass oratory.[109] In short, the many rhetorical differences – both striking and subtle – between Cicero's published popular and senatorial orations, leave little doubt that he took considerable pains *in the written versions* of his speeches to keep his arguments, emphases, and style precisely adapted to the nature of the audience that had heard the original, as was called for in a rhetorical model. The contrary notion, still current in some quarters, that what one might call the "intellectual register" as well as the political ideology of Cicero's published *contiones* were raised *ex post facto* to appeal above all to the interests

---

[104] Mack 1937: 11.
[105] Mack 1937; Classen 1985: 304–67. See also Thompson 1978: esp. iii–vi, 133–38.
[106] On contional invocation of these figures, see pp. 110–13 and p. 216.
[107] Classen 1985: 310–13, 319, 326, 334, 342, and esp. 361–66. Cf. Thompson 1978: 28–46, 86–99; Sklenář 1992; for Leonhardt 1998/99, however, see chap. 2, n. 95.
[108] Mack 1937: e.g. 20, 27, 32–33, 43, 51–52, 61–62, and esp. 73–79, 113–14. His conclusions are somewhat qualified by Thompson (above, n. 105). On the *Post reditum* speeches, see also Nicholson 1992: 102–6.
[109] Leovant-Cirefice 2000.

of his educated senatorial and equestrian readership not only lacks positive evidence but clashes head-on with this fact.[110]

In sum, the published speeches available to us are not verbatim transcriptions but (in one scholar's piquant reformulation of Quintilian) "representations of genuine speeches."[111] But "genuine" deserves as much emphasis as does "representation." While a published contional oration cannot be treated as an exact copy of the words spoken on the occasion of delivery, it can be taken to reflect well the type of rhetoric that was thought suitable to that occasion and such audiences. That is what is most important for us. It is regrettable that we cannot be sure we have the exact words of any speaker in an assembly – not to mention our comparable lack of direct evidence for delivery, gesture, and setting – but perhaps this is no graver than is the evidentiary basis for most other aspects of ancient history.

Further evidence for the rhetoric of the *contio* can be found in the extant historical narratives of the Republican period, most notably, those of Sallust, Livy, Cassius Dio, and, to stretch traditional generic boundaries somewhat, Plutarch; these all contain numerous descriptions of public meetings and, not infrequently, parts or the whole of addresses supposedly delivered in them. As sources of facts about these specific meetings and their speeches, these must be subjected to the usual historians' tests of authority, which means of course that complete orations contained in these narratives must be assessed according to the conventions of ancient historiographical writing. Individual historians followed differing methodological principles in the dramatic recreation of direct speech, but none, we may be certain, was pretending to offer a verbatim record of what was actually said on the occasion. As a rule, then, I take a *contio* given in direct (i.e. "quoted") speech only as evidence of what the author thought suitable to the circumstances he was aware of and describing in his narrative. On this premise, most such "embedded" speeches are of little use to us. Livy's direct knowledge of the realities of late-Republican political life in the city is suspect, and in any case the *contiones* in the extant portion of his text belong so far in the distant past that the relationship between his recreation and his own

---

[110] Achard 1981: esp. 25–30. Achard supposes as well that Cicero's contional rhetoric was directed to uncharacteristically well-off crowds after 63, after his pretence of being a "Friend of the People" was unmasked in the Catilinarian crisis. Yet this is only a hypothesis invoked to make sense of what Achard perceives to be elements of non-populist rhetoric. We should not presume to know *a priori* what kind of rhetorical moves would work before the *plebs contionalis*, but accept that the published *contiones* are themselves the best evidence of that, unless there is some clear and compelling reason not to do so; I do not believe that Achard ever offers such a reason (see chap. 6, n. 19). See also now Achard 2000, and Ledentu 2000.

[111] Zetzel 1993: 450.

present is highly problematic. Dio is much further removed from the late Republic, and is particularly free in his invention of speeches; Plutarch, on the other hand, as a biographer does not so freely take the historian's license of relating, or creating direct speech. In my view, only those five *contiones* embedded in the surviving portions of the works of Sallust can be taken as reliable evidence of the nature of contional rhetoric.[112] "When a senator writes history," wrote Syme, "he knows how to render the speech of a politician";[113] as stated in my opening narrative, Sallust had been a demogogic tribune himself, and unlike these other writers had first-hand experience of speaking in a late-Republican public meeting. The Sallustian *contiones* are particularly valuable as a kind of control with which to limit the otherwise Ciceronian bias of our evidence for contional rhetoric: in particular, Sallust offers us two such speeches delivered by tribunes of the plebs whose "popular" critique of the oligarchy provides an invaluable shift in perspective from the typically Ciceronian effort to exploit popular speech to buttress senatorial leadership. For this reason, too, "fragments" (that is, surviving quotations) of popular speeches delivered or published by other men sometimes have a value out of all proportion to their small size.[114] It is a great shame that we lack even a single substantial fragment of the popular oratory of Publius Clodius, the leading if hardly paradigmatic popular politician of the last decade of the Roman Republic; yet with the help of Sallust and the fragments, that lacuna is unfortunate, but hardly crippling, for this investigation.

PLAN OF THE WORK

Starting from a core assumption that political power must be perpetually negotiated and reproduced through public discourse, I seek in this book to examine how mass communication shaped the distribution of power between the Roman People and their political élite in the late Republic. I shall argue that, while an emphasis on the centrality of public speech and deliberation to the political culture of the Roman Republic is fully justified (and can be further corroborated), this did not, in fact, make the political system more than minimally responsive to popular needs; indeed overall,

---

[112] Specifically, those of Memmius and Marius in the *Jugurtha* (30.4–32.1; 84.5–85.50) and those of Lepidus, Cotta, and Macer in the *Histories* (1.55; 2.47, 3.48 M).

[113] Syme 1964: 198. On Sallust's speeches in general, see Büchner 1982: 238–43; and La Penna 1968: 325–32, who well stresses his interest in using speeches not so much for dramatic or psychological purposes but for representing the verbal dimension of historical action.

[114] For example, the fragment of Gaius Gracchus' speech on the *lex Aufeia* (*ORF* 48.XII, pp. 187–88); L. Crassus on the *lex Servilia iudiciaria* (*ORF* 66.V, pp. 243–45).

despite the ways in which the existence of this alternative, popular source of power encouraged persistent division within a competitive governing élite, the discourse of the *contio* strongly reinforced its hegemony and buttressed the traditional order.[115] To maintain these two propositions simultaneously may appear paradoxical, but the work is written in the conviction that the tension between them is only apparent and that a persuasive account of the role of public political speech in the Roman Republic will need to do full justice to both. Whatever the fate of my larger argument in the "marketplace of ideas," it is my hope that the following chapters will help to construct a richer picture of the relationship between public speech and political power in the Roman Republic, and to raise some productive questions about public deliberation, communication, and the flow of knowledge in all political systems that involve a mass public.

The plan of the book is readily sketched. It is a necessary preliminary to the argument to set the Republican *contio* precisely in its institutional and physical context: public meetings of this type had a specific place in political culture *and* in the physical setting of the city of Rome which will need to be firmly grasped at the outset (chapter 2, "Setting the stage"). At the conclusion of the chapter, a review of Cicero's explicit observations on the character of contional oratory will give a sense of how élite speakers themselves were apt to view this rhetorical venue and its peculiar demands. In chapter 3 ("Civic knowledge"), I enter upon one of the central issues for my argument, using the best extant samples of contional oratory to assess the level of civic knowledge possessed by the crowds who gathered to listen to it. Elite sources regularly referred to the audiences of public meetings as "ignorant men" (*imperiti*). How ignorant actually *was* the Roman plebs? The evidence of political and historical references on contemporary coins as well as an appreciation of the "collective memory" embedded in the monuments that surrounded the scene of interaction between orator and citizen will help to set the allusions in the *contio* into a wider cognitive and ideological context and offer some degree of control over my hypotheses. It will also become apparent how effectively contional oratory (in interaction with other communicative media, such as monuments) drew citizens into the political life of the *res publica*.

---

[115] In very broad terms it may be said that I join Millar against Mouritsen on the first proposition, and Hölkeskamp against Millar on the second (above, nn. 31–33). To my mind, however, Hölkeskamp offers an exaggerated, one-sided picture of élite domination, partly by collapsing distinctions that should be drawn between the middle and late Republic, partly by a tendency to view the citizen audience as relatively passive consumers of élite ideology rather than active, but disadvantaged, co-constructors of contional discourse.

With a better idea of the kind of audience to which public oratory had to be "pitched" I can turn in chapter 4 to the rich variety of methods politicians used – claqueurs, "claptraps," and other forms of audience manipulation – to make their words appear to be nothing less than the Voice of the People, a central strategy of Republican politics which, somewhat paradoxically, proves how important popular legitimation was held to be. Such observations bring us, of course, to the realm of political theater, and the next chapter (chapter 5: "Debate") seeks to demonstrate further, with reference to several important legislative controversies, that precisely this, rather than the kind of reasoned and "empowering" debate on important policy issues desiderated by democratic idealists, was, by and large, characteristic of the Roman public assembly. These two chapters together seek to develop a nuanced model of the *contio* as political instrument (drawing its force both from an ideology of popular primacy and from the sheer weight of urban collective action) rather than as a setting for authentic public deliberation.

As is shown by the repetition of the opening rubric in their titles (6: "Contional ideology: the invisible 'Optimate'"; 7: "Contional ideology: the political drama"), the final two chapters present a single argument divided only by a conveniently timed shift of focus. This pair is meant to be read in close succession; only a preliminary conclusion closes the first, and a comprehensive summary of the argument is postponed until the end of the second. Here I seek to show how public oratory, the sole authoritative medium of political information and interpretation, produced and perpetuated an ideological structure for the citizenry that reinforced the cultural hegemony of the political élite and quietly foreclosed the development of a more active, assertive form of deliberative participation on the part of the Roman People.

CHAPTER 2

Setting the stage

The first chapter introduced the central problems and themes of this book. It remains, however, to bring into sharper focus the phenomenon to be investigated. The Republican *contio* or public meeting had a well-defined place within a great complex of traditional political practices (Rome had no written constitution) and further *took* place in specific central locations in the city of Rome which, with their familiar monuments and historical associations, drew it into a symbolic context as well as a distinctive urban milieu. The chief purpose of this chapter is to sketch out these two contexts – one institutional and pragmatic, the other physical and symbolic – not merely to provide the necessary background for what is to come but also to invite reflection on the relationship between public deliberation, its material setting, and political practice. In the final part of this chapter I turn to a third kind of context, that of rhetorical theory, looking briefly at Cicero's explicit characterization of the nature of contional rhetoric, drawn partly from his essays on oratory, partly from incidental comments scattered elsewhere through his works. The main focus of attention in this book will be on actual practice and actual rhetoric as they are revealed by specimens of contional oratory and narratives of actual events; but the more theoretical descriptions collected at the end of this chapter will show what a contemporary master thought public speech was like – or, alternatively, should be like.

THE *CONTIO*

The urban *contio* may be briefly and simply defined as that form of popular assembly which was summoned to listen to a speech (or speeches) rather than to vote.[1] The feature that fundamentally distinguishes the *contio*, or

---

[1] Military assemblies, also called *contiones*, which of course would normally take place in the field (*militiae*), do not pertain directly to this study. I also leave aside as special cases funerary *contiones*, for

"public meeting," from other popular assemblies in Republican Rome is that it had no *formal* power, and indeed produced no *formal* expression of its will. As Aulus Gellius puts it, "to hold a *contio* is to speak to the People without taking a vote."[2] Thus *contiones* are sometimes dubbed "informal assemblies" by moderns, and consequently they have been relatively little studied in comparison to the "formal" voting assemblies, curiate, tribal, and centuriate. That is a mistake, because they had a clear and essential place in the traditional legislative machinery, as we saw in the last chapter (original promulgation *in contione*, followed by more meetings over the weeks up to the vote). As we shall see in later chapters (4–5), these meetings, and the responses to them of the citizenry, other magistrates such as tribunes and consuls, or the Senate, tended to seal the fate of bills, so that by the time they came up for a vote the results rarely occasioned any surprise.[3] Clearly, then, as Millar insisted, *contiones* were the life of the Roman legislative process – not to mention their crucial function as the chief conduit of authoritative information to the citizenry.

This separation of public deliberation from voting was, according to Cicero in his defense of L. Valerius Flaccus in 59, a master-stroke of Rome's eminently wise founding fathers; they thus emphatically rejected the Greek precedent whereby (again according to Cicero) ignorant mobs, encouraged to loiter by their dangerous practice of sitting in assembly, both deliberated and voted without a pause for reflection and instruction by their betters. (It is not irrelevant that some of the weightiest testimony against Cicero's client, on trial for extortion as governor of Asia, came in the form of public decrees of the Greek cities.) But the passage is worth quoting in full, for it offers a useful introductory characterization of the *contio* while at the same time betraying a series of élite anxieties about popular participation in political decision-making:

Our ancestors, those extremely wise and scrupulous men, decided that public meetings (*contiones*) should have no legal force; they decided that whatever the *plebs* desired to decree or the *populus* to enact should be approved or rejected after the public meeting was adjourned, after the people had been allotted to their divisions and distinguished by tribes and centuries according to their order, wealth-class, and age, after the supporters [of the law] had been heard, and its content had been promulgated and made known for many days. But the city-states of Greece are entirely managed by unrestrained, seated assemblies. Thus, to say nothing of

---

the pronouncement of eulogies from the Rostra, and triumphal *contiones*, held by victorious generals after the procession to the Capitol (on these, see Pina Polo 1989: 147–50, 165–68; for funerary orations, see Flower 1996: 128–58).
[2] Gell. *NA* 13.16.3.   [3] On the rarity of a negative vote, see below, pp. 124–26.

the Greece of today, which was cast down and ruined long ago through its own decisions, that Greece of antiquity, which once flourished in strength, imperial power, and fame, was laid low by this one evil, the unrestrained freedom and license of its assemblies. When men inexperienced in all affairs, ignorant novices, had taken their seats in a theater, then they would undertake useless wars, set subversive men in charge of the state, and expel their most patriotic citizens from the city.[4]

This fascinating passage tends to provoke a smile from the modern reader – not entirely justly, given the checks placed by modern representative democracies upon the kind of rule-by-assembly Cicero has in mind – but I suspect that among its original audience there were many more grave nods of approval than smirks. For Cicero, the clear separation of voting from listening to speeches in a traditional Roman *contio*, the necessity of standing through all deliberations, and not least the ponderous mechanism by which the chaotic human mass was sorted and rationalized into its constituent voting categories before a binding decision could be reached, all had a salutary restraining effect upon the impulsiveness of the naturally anarchic multitude. We would do well to pay some attention to these notions, however strange they appear to us.

More will be said below on the question of the composition of contional audiences; for the present, however, the important thing is that access to public meetings was totally unrestricted, and limited only by the brevity of advance notice: it will have been impractical even to exclude non-citizens and slaves.[5] In this connection we should also note that Cicero claims that in his own day the traditional standards of contional restraint were slipping; implicitly he suggests that in contemporary practice public meetings had begun to enjoy a measure of "force," in this context evidently "decision-making capacity," contrary to the excellent prescriptions of the ancestors.[6] It is evident that the complaint is based on the fact that "popular" magistrates had begun to overemphasize, or distort, the significance of the *contio* as an

---

[4] Cic. *Flac.* 15–16.

[5] Pina Polo 1989: 70–73, and 1996: 127–34; Botsford 1909: 146–47; Liebenam, *RE* IV (1901) 1151. Thus the only effective way to bar non-citizens from participation in *contiones* (as distinct from the voting assemblies) was to ban them from the city, which must have given some impetus to the exclusionary measures of 126 and 122 (Noè 1988: 57–58; Gabba, 1994: 106). Cf. Fannius' invidious appeal in 122: *ORF* 32.3, p. 144, no. 3. One should be duly skeptical of Cicero's assertions regarding the servile status of Clodius' mobs (see chap. 3, n. 9); but App. *B Civ* 2.120 claims that slaves, who dressed like free men, had long been available to be hired for *contiones* by 44 (cf. also 2.22: θεράποντές τε ὄντες οἵ πλείους).

[6] Cic. *Flac.* 15: *O morem praeclarum disciplinamque quam a maioribus accepimus, si quidem teneremus! sed nescio quo pacto iam de manibus elabitur* [note the present tense]. *Nullam enim illi nostri sapientissimi et sanctissimi viri vim contionis esse voluerunt . . .*

expression of the popular will: elsewhere Cicero decries as untraditional, and a "practice of Greeklings," the way in which a leading opponent of the attempts to recall him from exile in 57 used to ask of his audiences at public meetings (in what Cicero represents as a parody of the formal phraseology of legislation) "whether or not they desired me to return (*velletne me redire*)", and then to claim that the "half-dead shouts of hirelings" in response showed that the Roman People rejected the proposal.[7] By making a pretence of expressing the Will of the People (not to mention by the audience's expressing itself at all, in the form, necessarily, of shouts[8]) *contiones*, in Cicero's view, were becoming rather too much like Greek assemblies. But it is also true that this development made the problem of the uncontrolled makeup of the contional crowd potentially serious; we begin to understand better why Cicero makes so much of sorting the audience out before it is allowed to bind the community by means of a vote.[9]

Cicero's stress on the standing attitude of the Roman audience vis-à-vis the seated position of the Greeks, which produces "rashness" (*sedentis contionis temeritate*) and contributes to the "unrestrained freedom and license of [their] meetings,"[10] is also worth a few moments' reflection, despite its apparent silliness. It does, in fact, seem intuitively obvious that a standing audience is not likely to linger for too many hours of speechifying, particularly if initiatives are not taken from the floor and the meeting is not going to conclude by taking some formal measure of its will. As Cicero suggests, then, the peculiar nature of the traditional Roman *contio* imposed some discipline of time, and thus constraints of behavior, both on speakers and their audience. To judge from the length of Cicero's published contional speeches, most must have lasted perhaps twenty minutes to an hour at most; only the major speeches for and against legislation (*suasiones* and

---

[7] Cic. *Sest.* 126. Of course, Cicero's example is part of a larger polemic in which he seeks to downgrade the importance of the *contio* as an index of public sentiment, or hedge it about with conditions: for example, it must be the right *kind* of *contio*, not one packed with paid partisans, in particular (§§106–8; cf. 114: *quod illum esse populum Romanum qui in contione erat arbitrabatur*, and §127: *videtisne igitur quantum <intersit> inter populum Romanum et contionem?*). The consequence of the argument, in fact, is the highly tendentious and self-interested claim that the contemporary *contio* was in general the least useful indicator of popular sentiment at this time of general satisfaction.

[8] Note the references to shouting in Cicero's caricature of Greek assemblies at *Flac.* 15: *porrigenda manu profundendoque clamore multitudinis concitatae*; 19: *audire strepitum imperitorum*.

[9] The separation of voting from deliberation, then, was not quite "pure technicality," as Millar asserts (1995: 113), even if on the (proportionally rare) occasions when a *contio* was immediately followed by a legislative vote, the interval of time and alteration in the makeup of the multitude will presumably have been small.

[10] Cic. *Flac.* 16; note also *Cum in theatro imperiti homines . . . consederant . . .* For the Circus Flaminius, see below, n. 89.

dissuasiones) will have been substantially longer.[11] It might also be noted that nothing, other than the audience's interest, kept them in attendance. This too must have had an effect on speakers, for one who suffered the grave humiliation of being deserted by his *contio*, as did C. Scribonius Curio as tribune in 90, was not likely to show his face again: Curio "fell silent," as Cicero puts it, evidently for the rest of his year in office.[12]

Contiones were regulated by a series of clearly articulated constitutional rules and customs, which further belies the conception of them as "informal assemblies."[13] Most important, they could be summoned only by a magistrate of quaestorian rank or higher during his term of office (i.e., no pro-magistrates); in practice, the great majority of significant public meetings were held by tribunes of the plebs, with the consuls and finally praetors well behind.[14] Unlike voting assemblies, public meetings could be summoned on market-days, *dies nefasti*, and other days on which voting

---

[11] The two examples of legislative *contiones*, Cicero's *Pro lege Manilia* (which fills 30 pp. in the Oxford edition), and *De lege agraria* 2 (at 48 pp.), are far longer than the non-legislative public speeches in Cicero's corpus (*Cat.* 2 and 3: 13 pp., 27 pp.; *Red. pop.*: 12 pp.; *Phil.* 4 and 6: 6 pp., 8 pp.; the legislative *Leg. agr.* 3, at only 6 pp., is a brief reply to his opponents at a length typical of non-legislative public speeches), with the special exception of the judicial *contio* in defense of Rabirius (16 pp., plus a lacuna of unknown length – delivered, apparently, within half a Roman hour [§6]). Within these two broad categories, there is also a clear distinction between the major speeches that Cicero delivered while consul in his "own" *contio* (*Leg. agr.* 2, *Cat.* 2–3) and those he gave before an assembly presided over by someone else as a less senior magistrate (*Leg. Man.*) or *privatus* (*Red. pop.; Phil.* 4, 6), while the remarkable length of the Catilinarian *contiones* also makes sense in view of the state of crisis and the extraordinary hunger for authoritative information to which those speeches respond. The variation in length of these published speeches, therefore, evidently accords well with the differing circumstances of their implied setting and need not be attributed to arbitrary and inconsistent expansion for publication (see pp. 25–31). Without pretending to specious precision, then, I assume that the length of Cicero's published *contiones* approximates roughly that of the oral originals. The temporal ranges I suggest in the text are based on a rate of some three or four minutes per page (see Wellesley 1971: 31; for possibly greater speed, however, consider the *Pro Rabirio* [above]). Incidentally, the extant Sallustian *contiones* cluster around four pages in length (Marius' speech of thanks for the consulship is the longest at 6 pp., balanced by Cotta's brief oration at 2 pp.; the rest are about 4 pp. long); they appear therefore to be moderately compressed (say, by about half to a third) relative to the norm for orally delivered *contiones*.

[12] Cic. *Brut.* 305; cf. 192.

[13] For the constitutional details, the fullest modern account is Pina Polo 1989: 41–91. Taylor 1966: 15–33 remains the standard introduction in English; Botsford's old account (1909: 139–51) is still useful. See also Mommsen 1887: esp. 1.197–202, 389–96; Liebenam, *RE* IV (1901) 1149–53.

[14] Pina Polo calculates that roughly 50 percent of late-Republican *contiones* mentioned in our sources were held by tribunes, and that of the roughly ninety known speakers more than fifty were tribunes, barely thirty were consuls, and fewer than ten were praetors (Pina Polo 1996: 52). For magistrates with the right to hold *contiones*, see Pina Polo 1989: 43–51; Mommsen withdrew his original view that the power was restricted to major magistrates and censors (1887: 1.200, with p. xix, n. 1). According to Festus (34 L), priests too could hold *contiones*, but presumably only on religious business within their special area of competence: Pina Polo 1989: 54–64.

was banned,[15] but clear rules governed interference by one magistrate with another's *contio*: consuls and praetors could pre-empt meetings of all magistrates beneath them in rank, while tribunes' *contiones*, it seems, could not be interrupted (*avocari*) by any magistrate.[16] Indeed, the formal grounds of the summons to the Senate on Gaius Gracchus' fatal day, according to the only source that offers explicit information on the point, was his interference with a *contio* held by a tribune, Minucius.[17]

There is no good evidence that *contiones* were scheduled in advance, excepting those, of course, that formed part of the proceedings of a legislative vote (or popular trial).[18] One might suppose that especially important meetings might be announced on the previous day in order to insure maximal attendance, but it must be emphasized that there is no direct evidence for this; this may be because the power to call a "snap" meeting conferred on the magistrate some control over the composition of his audience.[19] An immediate summons indeed appears to have been the norm: the magistrate simply had his herald first make the announcement from the Rostra (or another *templum*), then sent him to do the same throughout the city,

---

[15] Pina Polo 1989: 81–86; Lintott 1999: 44. Market-days: in view of Cic. *Att.* 1.14.1, Botsford 1909: 139–40 is surely correct against Mommsen 1887: 1.199.

[16] Pina Polo 1989: 65–68. Tribunes could also presumably resort to their right of veto (*intercessio*) to stop the (non-tribunician) *contiones* of other officials.

[17] *De vir. ill.* 65.5, who suggests that Gracchus summoned a competing *contio*, despite his lack at this point of magisterial power: *in forum descendit, et imprudens contionem a tribuno plebis avocavit; qua re arcessitus* . . . Cf. Oros. 5.12.5; Plut. *C. Gracch.* 13–14.

[18] The only evidence known to me for scheduling in advance is Madvig's emendation, accepted by Clark in his 1909 OCT but not by Marek in the 1983 Teubner edn., of the unanimous consensus of our manuscripts at Cic. *Leg. agr.* 2.13: *contionem in primis [in pridie Idus,* Madvig] *advocari iubet.* Madvig's complaint was based on the supposed absence of any idea of seriality (1873: 204). But in fact Cicero does wish to stress that, rather than formally promulgating the law immediately in his first *contio* (cf. *legem hominis contionemque exspectabam*), Rullus refused to go public right away with the text of the law (*lex initio nulla proponitur*), which had been worked up in secret, and instead first (*in primis*: cf. *OLD*, s.v. *imprimis*, 2) gave an incomprehensible speech that continued to leave the situation in suspense, only a good bit later (*aliquando tandem me designato*, §13 *fin.*) following up with the formal promulgation of the law (*lex in publicum proponitur*). Thus, "in the beginning no law was posted [or promulgated]; first [here, almost "instead"] he ordered an assembly to be summoned." The MS reading is thus perfectly consistent with the picture we have otherwise of immediate gathering in response to a summons (*summa cum exspectatione concurritur*); and I would add that it is dubious method to introduce by emendation something unique in our evidence: a *contio* summoned according to a calendar date, hence presumably not just for the next day (*in posterum [diem]*). Finally, nothing is gained here rhetorically by supplying this exact date: a *contio* on December 12 would have been only Rullus' third day in office – hardly a suspicious delay!

[19] Mouritsen 2001: 42, thinks of a day's advance notice, but gives no evidence. T. Munatius Plancus' plea to the People in a *contio* to show up in force on the last day of Milo's trial, combined with the closure of *tabernae* throughout the city (Asc. 40–41 C; cf. below, n. 29, and on the practice, p. 129), shows what was possible, if broad attendance were indeed desired.

perhaps following the line of the old city walls (see map 1, p. 43).[20] Then, after the herald had obtained "as much silence throughout the Forum as was possible in any central square,"[21] the presiding magistrate opened the meeting with a prayer that the outcome be fortunate to the Roman People; no formal auspication seems to have been necessary, in keeping with the absence of formal and binding decision-making.[22] He then spoke himself, or brought forward onto the speaker's platform other speakers at his sole discretion (*contionem dare, in contionem producere*), who addressed the People while he took his seat on his tribunician bench or, if a consul or other high magistrate, curule chair.[23] The speakers thus presented might be other magistrates or, more often, private citizens, typically authoritative senators but on occasion men of modest station, even women, if their purpose was to attest publicly to some allegation;[24] the magistrate might also "bring forth" notable adversaries, ostensibly perhaps in accordance with the principle that the other side ought at some point at least to be represented in discussion, but usually, in fact, to bring the pressure of public opinion

[20] Livy 4.32.1; App. *B Civ.* 2.127; Varro, *Ling.* 6.86–95; Festus 34, 100, 101 L. Varro alone mentions the traversing of the walls; the commentaries he cites were at least in part anachronistic for his own time (§95). For the initial announcement *in templo*, see Varro, *Ling.* 6.87; for the Rostra as *templum*, see n. 22. Festus' comment on *inlicium* appears to confirm that the procedure for summoning *contiones* was identical to the one that Varro describes for censorial *lustra*, meetings of the *comitia centuriata*, and judicial *contiones*. The difficult passage of Varro still demands full legal-constitutional exegesis: for the present, see Taylor 1966: 100–101 and 156–57, n. 41; Vaahtera 1993: 112–15; and the notes of P. Flobert's 1985 Budé text and of E. Riganti's 1978 Pàtron edition. On summoning *contiones*, see Pina Polo 1989: 87–89; the *praeco* seems sometimes to have been called by the more general term *accensus* (Varro, *Ling.* 6.88–89, 95). To summon individuals, at least by the late Republic, consuls sent a lictor, tribunes a *viator* (Varro, ap. Gell. 13.12.6; Cic. *Font.* 39; *Vat.* 22; cf. Livy. 6.15.1); on the powers of *vocatio* and *prensio*, see below, chap. 5, n. 53. On these various assistants, see Mommsen 1887: 1.355–66.

[21] The phrase is Asconius' (41 C), from his account of the trial of Milo.

[22] Variants of the phrasing of the *solemne carmen precationis* (Livy 39.15.1) in Cic. *Div.* 1.102; Varro, *Ling.* 6.86; Livy 1.17.10; 3.34.2, 54.8. The fact that the Rostra was an inaugurated *templum* (Cic. *Vat.* 24; Livy 8.14.12; other evidence listed in Vaahtera 1993: 108, n. 65) was relevant to its use for voting, since this was required for auspication and probably for the actual act of casting the ballots (hence the *pontes*; Livy 2.56.10 and 3.17.1 suggest that voting-platforms had formally to be a *templum*). On all this, see Vaahtera, pp. 107–12. Carafa 1998: 117 and Pina Polo 1989: 189–91 rightly return to Mommsen's view, against Coarelli's popular reconstruction, that the inaugurated *templum* included the Rostra but not the Comitium (see below, pp. 42ff.) as a whole, which is never described as such. Vaahtera seems to concur for the late Republic, though not in "the earliest times" when voting was by acclamation (p. 115; cf. p. 108, n. 65).

[23] Pina Polo 1989: 74–80. Thommen 1989: 176–79, lists those known to have been brought before a *contio* by tribunes. Seated position: Cic. *Brut.* 161, 217; Livy 38.51.6; Plut. *Cat. Min.* 27.4. Antony's alleged threat while seated on the podium of the Temple of Castor "with the whole Roman People listening" (Cic. *Phil.* 3.27; 5.21) is puzzling, since it would otherwise appear that the presiding magistrate and those he "produced" in his *contio* sat only while another was speaking. Since this is clearly a highly invidious comment it may be unwise to take it entirely at face value.

[24] See, e.g., Asc. 37 C (a freedman); Cic. *Att.* 2.24.3 (L. Vettius, the habitual informer); Val. Max. 3.8.6 (Sempronia, sister of Ti. Gracchus). For the (supposed) norm, see Cic. *Vat.* 24 (below, n. 112).

to bear.[25] Finally, the meeting was dismissed by the magistrate's herald or attendants. If this happened to be a *contio* immediately preceding a vote (legislative or judicial), the meeting could then be directly – though surely not quickly, in view of the ponderous process of discrimination and sorting that had to precede any vote – converted into a voting assembly.[26]

The question who actually attended meetings of this kind is as complicated as it is important. Full consideration of this vexed problem will have to be left to a later chapter,[27] but a few preliminary observations may suffice for the present. Clearly, meetings that were always in the center of the city of Rome and were regularly summoned on the same day with little or no advance notice, must normally have drawn an overwhelmingly urban audience except when their import was such as to draw a significant influx from the country, or they happened to coincide with major festivals or weekly market-days (as must frequently have been the case of those meetings called to discuss legislation).[28] While the mechanism of summoning *contiones* appears to have been meant to make the whole city aware of the event, it seems unlikely, given the rapidity with which they were called, that those who spent their day far from the Forum would have been able to make their way there for a meeting except under exceptional circumstances.[29] A famous passage of Plautus reminds us that the Forum was daily frequented by people who were far from representative of the Roman citizenry as a whole, a fact noted more prosaically by other sources as well.[30] The Forum was, after all, not merely a focal point of public life but also the business center of Rome: shops and meeting-places for all kinds of moneymaking ringed the Forum and the arteries leading out of the central square.[31] The men who spent their days in this setting had immediate and convenient

---

[25] See below, pp. 161–72.

[26] The term for simple dismissal is *contionem dimittere*; for adjournment before reorganization as *comitia*, *contionem summovere* (Pina Polo 1989: 91, with references; cf. Vaathera 1993: 113, n. 95).

[27] See pp. 128–36.

[28] Pina Polo 1996: 131. Festivals: Achard 1981: 28; cf. the *contiones* preceding the vote on Cicero's recall (pp. 148–49).

[29] According to Asc. 41 C, the *tabernae* were closed *throughout the city* on the last day of Milo's trial, after the tribune T. Munatius Plancus had called upon the populace to show up in full force that day. This seems to imply the expectation that inhabitants of all parts of the city might come to the Forum for the closing of the trial; with a day's advance warning it is conceivable that the same may have been done for a particularly important *contio*. On the closing of the *tabernae*, see p. 129.

[30] Plaut. *Curc.* 466–84, with Vanderbroeck 1987: 87–90. Key texts are Q. Cicero (?), *Comment pet.* 29: *multi homines urbani, industrii, multi libertini in foro gratiosi navique versantur;* Cic. *De or.* 1.118: *haec turba et barbaria forensis;* Livy 9.46.10, where the *forensis factio* is distinguished from the *integer populus.* Cf. *contionarius populus* (Cic. *Q Fr.* 2.3.4), *contionalis plebecula* (*Att.* 1.16.11).

[31] See Schneider, *RE* iva (1932) 1864–70; Loane 1938: 113–53; Coarelli 1985: 140–55; Morel 1987: 140–45; Andreau 1987; Döbler 1999: 107–17. For *tabernae* in the podium of the temple of Castor, see

access to *contiones*, and we should suppose that they were the most consistent and often the greatest constituent of any contional audience.[32] But – to anticipate a later topic – the nature of the audience will also have varied widely with the circumstances and agenda of the meeting. We must allow, too, for efforts to "pack" the audience with partisans and claqueurs. Those who came to a *contio* were always symbolically constructed as "the Roman People" (except by those who wished to undermine that impression), yet the gap between the symbol and the reality of indistinct, ever-changing crowds opened a conveniently wide field for polemical interpretation of the signs by which they made known their responses to the words directed to them by élite speakers.

PHYSICAL SETTING

It is obvious that the physical setting of any speech contributes to its meaning and its reception by its immediate audience; consequently, it is important mentally to insert the practices of this institution and its rhetoric into the urban topography of Rome. A brief sketch of contional spaces, focusing in particular upon the associations of the monumentalized urban landscape most relevant to the *contio*'s nature as communicative meeting-point between Senate and People, will give a sense, however tantalizing, of the wider symbolic context in which Roman mass oratory resounded.

From distant antiquity, the traditional location for such public meetings was in the Forum, the great central "square" of Rome – actually an irregular, narrow rectangle some two hundred meters long (measuring from northwest to southeast) and seventy meters across – occupying the valley between the Capitol, Quirinal, Esquiline, and Palatine hills (see maps 1 and 2, pp. 43–44). In a slightly elevated area in its northwest corner, just to the south of another, somewhat higher eminence to the north where the Senate-house stood, a hallowed space called the Comitium was demarcated,

---

Nielsen and Poulsen 1992: 56, 109–11. The Forum itself grew gradually more "upscale" and by the late Republic the bankers and moneychangers had pushed most of the more menial *tabernae* into the exit-streets.

[32] Contra Mouritsen, for whom "the Forum belonged to the world of the elite" (2001: 45), and thus that the "natural participants" (p. 78) in the *contio* – Cicero's "people of the *contio*" (*contionarius populus*: Cic. *Q Fr.* 2.3.4) – were "respectable *boni*" (p. 45), representatives of "the propertied classes rather than the working population" and "socially far superior to the mass of urban plebeians" (p. 43). This remarkable conclusion flies in the face of virtually all our characterizations of contional crowds: see chap. 4. It also turns out, on Mouritsen's own account, not to apply straightforwardly to the late Republic, since in a different context he also accepts that from the late second century popular politicians mobilized a base of support among the poorer urban population (pp. 79–89; cf. p. 59 for Clodius' "probably working-class" supporters).

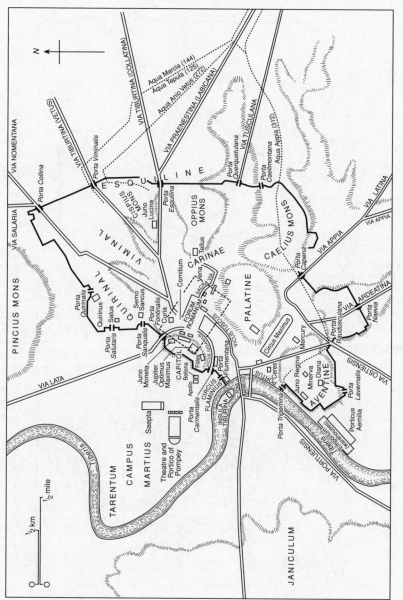

Map 1 Rome in the late Republic.

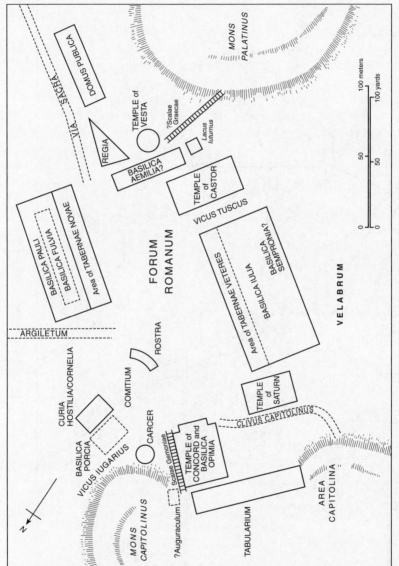

Map 2 The area of the Forum in the late Republic. Some locations and dimensions can only be approximate. For the controversial location of the Basilica Aemilia, see p. 104, n. 16;.

where from earliest times Roman kings and then magistrates had addressed the Roman People, and where the *curiae*, the primordial divisions of the citizenry, had met and voted.[33] Archaeological evidence for a permanent, stone speaker's podium marking off the area of the Comitium from the greater Forum to the south and southeast, perhaps goes back to the early fifth century BC: the so-called "Suggesto C," of which parts of the bottom three steps and several courses of masonry facing the Forum survived for the modern excavator to find beneath later building (figure 1, a).[34] In 338 this platform took on truly monumental form when, we are told, the rams or "beaks" (*rostra*) of the rebellious Latins' warships were torn from their prows and mounted on the podium – which thus became the Rostra – and statues of the victorious consuls, C. Maenius and L. Camillus, were placed upon it.[35]

According to Plutarch, orators originally spoke from the steps of the podium and faced northwest, toward an audience crowded into the Comitial space, consequently numbering only a few thousand at most;[36] there seems to be no good reason to reject this claim, even if (quite understandably) he mistakenly ascribes the subsequent change of direction toward the open Forum to Gaius Gracchus rather than C. Licinius Crassus, tribune in

---

[33] For this and the following assertions, see now the excellent study by Carafa 1998, which includes the first comprehensive examination of the stratigraphy of the Comitium. Despite Carafa's revision of various points, Coarelli 1986: 119–99 and especially 1985: 11–123, remain fundamental. For a résumé, see F. Coarelli, in *LTUR* 1.309–14.

[34] Carafa 1998: 132–43. Photographs of the steps and wall facing the Forum at pp. 138–39, figs. 87, 88. (Further good photographs from the post-war excavations in Nash 1961: 272–75.) For the Rostra specifically, Gjerstad 1941 is still essential, as well as Coarelli's study of the Comitium (above, n. 33), whose rather theoretical discussion, however, takes little account of the actual state of excavation after the last modern campaigns between 1954 and 1961 (which are ill published, to be sure). An up-to-date plan of the successive phases of the Rostra is badly needed: published plans all go back to Gjerstad, but as I discovered on my own examination of the site under the present pavement of the Forum on May 30, 1995, subsequent excavation has revealed more of the platform's eastern wing than is shown there, including the well-preserved northeast edge of the later Rostra ("Suggesto J") and, extending roughly one meter beyond it, the corner of the earlier platform ("C"). An excellent photograph of the whole area during the excavations of 1956–61 is printed by Carafa at p. 74, fig. 65.

[35] Below, nn. 46–48. Carafa 1998: 143–47 notes that there is no archaeological evidence of large-scale alterations to the Rostra or Comitium at this time, *pace* Coarelli 1985: 145–46.

[36] Plut. *C. Gracch.* 5.3. Estimates of the size of audiences *inside* the Comitium (i.e. before the middle of the second century: see n. 40) are particularly unreliable, given the lack of firm evidence for its size: Thommen's figure of no more than 1,000 seems far too low (Thommen 1995: 364), MacMullen's 5–6,000, based on Coarelli's plan, is probably too high (MacMullen 1980: 456); Carafa 1998: 140, n. 52 offers a happy medium of about 3,000 within a smaller space. Mouritsen 2001: 18–20 now calculates 3,800–4,800, depending on whether Carafa's or Coarelli's plan is adopted. In the middle Forum, Thommen 1995: 364 guesses that room existed only for some 6,000; MacMullen's figure is 15–20,000 (1980: 455–56). Mouritsen's maximum of around 10,000 is based on the scenario of a voting assembly (2001: 20–23); *contiones* that were not part of such a proceeding will not have been constrained by the *pontes*.

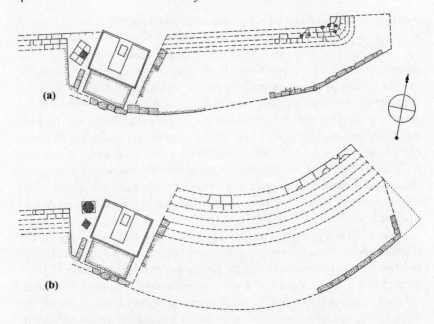

(a)

(b)

Figure 1 Plans of the Republican Rostra. (a) "Suggesto C" (second phase), the
mid-Republican Rostra. (b) "Suggesto J," the late-Republican Rostra. The structure
abutting the west end of the platform is generally identified as the traditional "Tomb of
Romulus" (or Faustulus), with the famous *Lapis Niger*.

145, who is otherwise well attested to have initiated the practice of turning
toward the Forum for conducting legislation, and to have first "led out"
the voting-tribes for that purpose from the Comitium into the large open
square.[37] Strictly speaking, this might suggest two sequential innovations,
the first pertaining to the place where the voting-tribes assembled *only after*
the final *contio* (still held, on this account, in the Comitium), and the presiding officer's order to regroup in the central Forum, and the second, to
the location *only* of *contiones*.[38] But it seems more economical and plausible

---

[37] Cic. *Amic.* 96: *atque is* [sc. *C. Licinius Crassus*] *primus instituit in forum versus agere cum populo*;
Varro, *Rust.* 1.2.9: *C. Licinius, tr. pl. cum esset, post reges exactos annis CCCLXV primus populum ad
leges accipiendas in septem iugera forensia e comitio eduxit.*

[38] Thus Coarelli 1985: 157–66 (but cf. 1986: 158); Mouritsen 2001: 20–25, whose insistence on excluding
any practical motivation for the change(s) seems arbitrary – especially if popular politicians did
indeed seek to mobilize larger sectors of the population (above, n. 32). Taylor 1966: 23–25, on the
other hand, rejected Plutarch entirely as a (misunderstood) "doublet" of the tradition about Crassus,
partly on the assumption that orators must have spoken facing the Forum from the beginning. There
is, however, no evidence for that assumption, which seems implausible at a time when the tribes
voted in the Comitium. Still, it remains most probable that Plutarch's evidence is a "doublet": it

to suppose that magistrates presiding over legislation always (both before Crassus and after) faced the direction where the tribes formed up (thus, before 145, toward the Comitium; from 145, increasingly, toward the open Forum) than to imagine Crassus, and those following him for the next twenty-two years, turning a pirouette on the Rostra between final *contio* and vote. Much greater numbers could be assembled on the Forum side of the Rostra anyway, which well suited the efforts of Crassus (and the Gracchi later) to mobilize a larger mass of supporters.[39] The rebuilding of the speaker's platform in a more graceful arc whose eastern end was now curved back (north) noticeably more than its predecessor ("Suggesto J": figure 1, b), perhaps the better to face the portion of the crowd assembled in the large open space to the east, in front of the Basilica Fulvia (Aemilia?) and Temple of Castor, appears, on the best evidence, to fall suggestively at about the middle of the second century.[40]

According to the widely accepted view of Filippo Coarelli, whose plan is frequently adapted and reprinted, from the early third century down to circa 80 BC (and thus for the earlier part of the period with which I am directly concerned), the Comitium took the form of a circular, stepped, theatral area, of whose arc the Rostra was simply the southeast portion.[41] But this was always merely hypothetical, based ultimately on the existence of arguably comparable Curia-Comitium complexes at the third-century colonies of Cosa, Alba Fucens, and Paestum; and others have recently pointed out the lack of actual evidence on the ground for the reconstruction, which would have produced difficulties in any case.[42] Decisive, however, is the

will have been an easy slip wrongly to attribute to Gracchus a "popular" innovation involving the Rostra that properly belonged to Crassus, given the tradition that made the former the inventor of a populist, histrionic style of speaking (cf. David 1983a: 105).

[39] At *Amic.* 96 Cicero explicitly sets Crassus' innovation in the context of the development of *popularis* politics, as Plutarch also does the supposed one of Gracchus ("transforming, in a way, the constitution from aristocracy to democracy": *C. Gracch.* 5.3). That is, of course, a gross exaggeration, not least because the traditional orientation was not simply toward the Curia but also the tribes gathered in the Comitium (Coarelli 1985: 158).

[40] Carafa's careful examination of the confused stratigraphy of the poorly documented excavations (1998: 75–80, 86–88, 148–51) yields a date around the middle of the second century, which is more persuasive than the rather abstract case offered by Coarelli (1985: 146–51) for the early third century. For the shifting location of the Basilica Aemilia, see chap. 3, n. 165.

[41] Coarelli 1985: 11–20; 1986: 146–57. Cf. Vasaly 1993: 62–66; Ulrich 1994: 75–81; Millar 1998: 40; Mouritsen 2001: 18–20.

[42] Pina Polo 1989: 190–96; Vaahtera 1993: 116; Carafa 1998: 150–51. Already before Coarelli, Krause 1976: 61, 66 had ruled out a circular plan. Among the difficulties are that the Sacra Via seems to have run through the Comitium and thus right through the conjectured stepped, circular area (see F. Coarelli, *LTUR* 1.312; 4.227); that a circular theatral area would naturally call for a speaker in its center, as in the Greek models, not standing atop its steps. Pliny's reference to statues *in cornibus comitii* (*HN* 34.26) does not imply a circular Comitium, *pace* Coarelli 1986: 149–59; 1985: 120–21:

fact that the bottom courses of a wall defining the northeastern side of "Suggesto J" are actually extant, which shows clearly that the stepped arc came to end precisely where it is shown on E. Gjerstad's old plan (see figure 1, b) and did not continue around to describe a circle.[43] Paolo Carafa's study of the stratigraphy of the area, furthermore, strongly suggests that there was no major reconstruction of the area by Sulla, such as would be implied by the destruction of a supposed theatral area with the exception of its southeast arc (to remain as "Suggesto J") – nor indeed before Caesar's well-known, radical intervention, which more or less obliterated the old Comitium.[44] Consequently, the organization of the contional space did not change significantly through our period: "Suggesto J" is to be recognized as the late-Republican Rostra, the platform from which Tiberius Gracchus as well as Cicero spoke to the crowds gathered below and around in the open Forum. Sadly, even less remains of it than of its predecessor, although Gjerstad's often-reprinted drawing (see figure 2)[45] can give a rough conception of its probable appearance – stripped, however, of the famous statues that adorned its surface and will be enumerated presently.

The Rostra, as already noted, received its name from the ships-rams or "beaks" (*rostra*) torn from the captured ships of Antium after the Latin revolt of 340–338 and fixed to the wall of the podium facing the central Forum.[46] There were six, according to the one source that specifies the number.[47] As has been noted above, on the platform itself stood equestrian statues of the victorious consuls in the Latin war, C. Maenius and L. Camillus, perhaps accompanied by one of the great Marcus Camillus, Rome's "Second

---

the Romans were happy to call *cornua* not only the ends of an arc, but also the ends of extended lines (e.g. battle lines) or rectangles, and even the corners of quadrangles: *TLL* IV.970–71 (cf. Livy 25.3.17 [where, despite *TLL* and Coarelli 1985: 121, n. 113, the location is not the Comitium but the voting-platform for a *concilium plebis* in the Area Capitolina]; Tac. *Ann.* 1.75.1 [*in cornu tribunalis*]; Plin. *Ep.* 5.6.23 [*in cornu porticus*]; Flor. *Epit.* 2.21 [*utraque Aegypti cornua*]).

43 My own examination of the remains (above, n. 34) satisfied me that the block shown on Gjerstad's plan as forming the northeastern limit of the bottom step of "J" was indeed at the edge of the platform: later excavation has laid bare a well-dressed exterior wall, clearly defining the northeast flank of "J," running for some four meters roughly southeast from this block toward the southeast corner of the platform. The wall is clearly evident in photographs printed by Carafa 1998: 74, fig. 65 (cf. p. 47, figs. 39–40 for more detail).

44 Carafa 1998: 151–55. On Caesar's ruthless revision of the western Forum, see Coarelli 1985: 233–57; Kolb 1995: 260–67; Favro 1996: 60–78; Carafa, pp. 156–59 (on the Comitium).

45 The photograph printed by Carafa 1998: 74, fig. 65, gives a fair sense of its size and shape.

46 Livy 8.14.12; Plin. *HN* 34.20. See Hölscher 1978: 318–19.

47 Flor. *Epit.* 1.5.10. Strictly speaking, Florus gives only the number of Antiate ships equipped with such "beaks," but this is probably inferred from the number on the Rostra, to which he explicitly refers.

Figure 2 E. Gjerstad's reconstruction of the late-Republican Rostra ("Suggesto J").
Statues are omitted, and there is no archaeological evidence for the number of attached
ships' "beaks" (*rostra*).

Founder" and grandfather of the consul of 338.[48] Perhaps toward the end
of the fourth century began the practice of commemorating with half-size
statues on the Rostra ambassadors who had been outrageously killed on
their missions: the envoys to Fidenae slaughtered in 438, Coruncanius, the
victim of the Illyrian queen Teuta in 230, and Cn. Octavius, assassinated in
Laodicea in 163.[49] The senatorial decree ordering the erection of Octavius'

---

[48] Livy 8.13.9; Eutr. 2.7.3; cf. Plin. *HN* 34.23 and Asc. 29 C, who have sometimes been taken to
refer to a statue of the great Camillus (Münzer, *RE* VII.1 [1910] 347). See Sehlmeyer 1999: 48–52;
Wallace-Hadrill 1990: 171–72 rejects Livy's information as "annalistic fantasy," but his objection is
only relevant to the question whether the statues were contemporary.

[49] Sehlmeyer 1999: 63–66. Plin. *HN* 34.23–24 (who gives a different *praenomen* for Coruncanius than
does Polyb. 2.8.3, and mentions a second ambassador killed by Teuta, one P. Iunius); Livy 4.17.6;

statue describes the Rostra already then as "the focal point" of the city (*quam oculatissimo loco*), particularly suited to the purpose of commemoration; Cicero, a little over a century later, would say that there was no more honorific place for a statue than on the Rostra.[50] When the Rostra was rebuilt around the middle of the second century ("Suggesto J"), most of these decorations presumably were transferred to the new structure.[51] The next remarkable addition was a gilded equestrian statue of Sulla as dictator in 81, which graced, or disgraced, the podium for the whole of the Ciceronian age.[52] Toward the end of our period the Sullan precedent was followed in turn by Pompey, perhaps in 52, Caesar probably in 46 or 45, and finally, in 43 (on the new, Caesarian Rostra), Octavian.[53] To complete the picture, I should mention the statue of the satyr Marsyas, the attendant of the god of freedom, Liber Pater. The figure, we are told by Virgil's commentator Servius, was a symbol of *libertas*.[54]

Unfortunately, the remains of the Republican Rostra do not allow more than a guess as to the original height of the platform over the pavement of the Forum. We do, however, know that the podium of the late-Republican temple of Castor, the second-most-frequent location for *contiones* (below), was very high, standing about 2.5 m to 4.3 m above the gradually sloping level of the Forum at that point; and the Caesarian-Augustan Rostra that

---

Cic. *Phil.* 9.4–5 (who omits the embassy to Teuta altogether: perhaps they had been removed already [cf. Wallace-Hadrill 1990: 171]). For the size of the statues, Plin. *HN* 34.24.

[50] Plin. *HN* 34.24: *eaque est in rostris.* Cic. *Deiot.* 34.

[51] The ambassadors to Fidenae, for example, were removed only in Cicero's lifetime (*Phil.* 9.4). Perhaps Coruncanius disappeared even earlier (n. 49).

[52] App. *B Civ.* 1.97; Vell. Pat. 2.61.3; Cic. *Phil.* 9.13. Almost certainly represented on a coin of 80 BC: *RRC* 381.

[53] Vell. Pat. 2.61.2–3; Cic. *Deiot.* 34; Cass. Dio 42.18.2, 43.49.1–2; Suet. *Iul.* 75.4; Sehlmeyer 1999: 231–34. The date of Pompey's statue is unknown; it could hardly have been extant in 66, when Cicero's speech on the Manilian Law was delivered without any mention of the immediate proximity of such an extraordinary honor, and it is difficult to imagine that the Senate would have approved of it thereafter until the remarkable rapprochement of 52. Dio 44.4.4–5 says that two statues of Caesar were erected on the Rostra in 44, one wearing the *corona civica* (cf. App. *B Civ.* 2.106) and the other with the *corona obsidionalis* (see Weinstock 1971: 148–52, 163–67); whether the equestrian statue was one of these or yet a third is unknown (Sehlmeyer, p. 234), but given that Cicero already mentions a statue on the Rostra in November 45, we probably should assume that there were at least three. Which was the one famously adorned with a diadem in January 44 (Cass. Dio 44.9.2) is also uncertain. For Octavian's statue (see Cic. *ad Brut.* 1.15.7), see also App. *B Civ.* 3.51; Cass. Dio 46.29.2; *RRC* 497/1, 490/1 and 3, 518/2; Sehlmeyer, pp. 249–51.

[54] *Libertatis indicium*: Serv. ad *Aen.* 4.58 (cf. ad 3.20); Mythographus Vaticanus 3.2.1. Note the frequent appearance of Liber Pater on the obverses of Republican coinage (*RRC* 266/3, 341/2, 343/2, 385/3, 386, 449/2–3, 494/36), which appears to confirm the ideological significance of the pair. The statue: Pseud. Acr. and Porphyry ad Hor. *Sat.* 1.6.120–21; *RRC* 363. It also appears on a panel of the Anaglypha Traiani: Torelli 1982: 99–106; Coarelli 1985: 91–119 makes good use of a copy of the statue from the Forum of Paestum. On their attempt to assign a precise date to the statue and tease out its original significance, see p. 99.

replaced its Republican predecessor was some 3.5 m high. The clear inference is that at least the late-Republican Rostra fell into this general range.[55] The ancient terminology, then, whereby one spoke *de loco superiore* to an audience in a *locus inferior*, is not misleading. The different levels essentially demarcated the roles of speaking and listening, so that on the occasion when Caesar, as praetor, denied the senior consular Q. Catulus access to the platform and told him to speak *ex loco inferiore*, this was probably tantamount to telling him to be still.[56] Francisco Pina Polo justly contrasts the typical situation in Greek popular assemblies (for example, the Athenian Pnyx, even after its reversal *c.* 404, or in the theaters that were so commonly used for the purpose), where speakers were elevated only moderately or were even looked down upon by the audience, a relationship that well suits the much less sharply demarcated roles of speaker and listener in the Greek *ekklesia* or *boule*.[57] At Rome, the presiding magistrate and speakers loomed above their audience on a fairly high platform, and it is tempting to share Pina Polo's intuition that the elevation of speakers relative to the audience in Rome reflects, and indeed helps to construct, a political hierarchy emphasizing the élite status of the speaking class and encouraging deference from the common citizen to higher authority.[58]

We can, therefore, begin to gain some conception of what the late-Republican Rostra looked like. More informative, however, is in some ways a representation, whose selectivity and focalization can help to highlight an object's meaning in actual, lived experience. Two images, one pictorial and one verbal, are particularly evocative.

A series of *denarii* minted in 45 BC by one (Lollius) Palicanus (figure 3) shows on the coins' reverse a curved, arcaded structure, topped by a bench,

[55] For the podium of the Temple of Castor, Nielsen and Poulsen 1992: 113; for the Imperial Rostra, Richardson 1992: 336. For the unknown height of the late-Republican Rostra, see Carafa 1998: 88; Taylor 1966: 45, reasonably guesses a height of 12 Roman feet = 3.5 m.

[56] Cic. *Att.* 2.24.3, with Shackleton Bailey ad loc. Hölkeskamp 1995: 34, n. 104 follows Mommsen 1887: 3.383–84, n. 5, and Botsford 1909: 149, in holding that those "produced" (*producti*) spoke from an intermediate level, below the top of the Rostra but above the surrounding pavement. So too Cerutti 1998: 302–3 – acknowledging, however, that "it was only for *contiones* that a stairless front would have better suited its tribunal" (p. 296), which appears to concede the absence from regular (non-legislative) *contiones* of the kind of wooden *locus inferior* he posits. In any case, the texts give no reason to doubt that there were only two levels: the *superior locus* for the presiding magistrate and *producti*, and the *inferior locus* where the audience stood (Livy 8.32.3; 8.33.9; cf. 30.37.8 [probably a projection onto Carthage]; Cic. *Vat.* 24; Fronto, *Ep.* 1.2.7). Rightly, Pina Polo 1989: 89–90, with 182, n. 1.

[57] Pina Polo 1996: 23–25. Note, however, that the evidence for the Pnyx is less than decisive, and Camp 1996: 41–46 now argues that in all phases the Athenian speaker stood at a higher level than the audience.

[58] Pina Polo 1996: 23–25. Also, Corbeill 2002: 199–200.

Figure 3 Denarius of M. Lollius Palicanus, 45 BC (*RRC* 473/1). On obverse: Libertas. On reverse: representation of Rostra showing curve and three ships' "beaks"; atop the platform, tribunician bench (*subsellium*).

with three ships' rams attached to the columns; the head of the goddess "Freedom," carefully labelled *Libertatis*, occupies the obverse.[59] Since the remains of the Republican speaker's platform do indeed show a pronounced curve, the ships' "beaks" make it certain that the image is one of the Rostra;[60] the bench is clearly the *subsellium*, the characteristic seat of tribunes and thus a symbol of the office itself, just as the *sella curulis* on other issues is a symbol of curule office.[61] So ingrained is the habit of reading late-Republican coin-types simply as allusions to family history that in the definitive catalog this is taken to be a reference "primarily to the tribunate [in 71] of the moneyer's father," who had been instrumental in securing Pompey's support for restoring the powers of the tribunate taken away by Sulla.[62] No doubt this may be present, at least as a second-order allusion. But I would say that for those into whose hands Palicanus' coin came in 45, the combination of Rostra, tribunician *subsellium*, and *Libertas* on the

---

[59] *RRC* 473/1 ([Lollius] Palicanus). The date, 45 BC, seems fairly secure (M. H. Crawford 1974: 93).

[60] M. H. Crawford 1974: 482, n. 1. Coarelli 1985: 243–45, insists that the coin must represent the "new," Caesarian structure, which was, however, built in 44 according to our only evidence for it (Cass. Dio 43.49.1). Palicanus may, of course, have known of Caesar's intentions, which may well have inspired the choice of type; but unless Dio's chronology is wrong the coin can hardly have represented specifically and exclusively a monument not yet built instead of one still in existence until 44 (according to Dio) and probably more familiar than virtually any other structure in the city. The image is sufficiently "symbolic" to apply easily to both.

[61] Cf. among Palicanus' own issues the curule chair of *RRC* 473/2. For the frequent appearance of that type as a symbol of curule office, see the coins listed in the Crawford's index (1974: 861).

[62] M. H. Crawford 1974: 483. See especially Ps.-Asc. 189, 220 St. For comments on the allusive iconographic language of late-Republican coins, see below, pp. 82–91.

other side would have evoked above all the powerful ideological significance of the tribunician *contio* for the Roman citizen. Like other constitutional ideas linked closely on late-Republican coins with Freedom (*provocatio* and suffrage, including the ballot laws), this coin emphasizes the close connection between that cherished Roman ideal and the *contio*.[63] When a consul in 122 invidiously raised the specter of his audience being crowded out of their place in the *contio* by newly enfranchised Latins, he gave a fair indication of its value,[64] for it offered the urban citizenry face-to-face communication with the leaders of the *res publica* and thus, as will be seen, their greatest opportunity to exert some influence on politics.

The second "depiction" of the Rostra is the opening of Cicero's first contional speech, delivered during the debate over the Manilian law in 66, in which he seeks to reconcile his persona of acute concern with the People's interest with the fact that only now, as praetor, was he making his début on the Rostra:[65]

Although the sight of you in full assembly has always seemed to me far the most pleasing, and indeed this place, the greatest for action and most splendid for speaking, still, Citizens, I have thus far been held back from this path to public esteem, which has always lain wide open to every patriotic citizen, not by my own wish but by the principles that have guided my life from my coming of age. For since I did not yet dare to intrude upon the dignity of this place, and was resolved not to bring forth here anything that was not the product of mature talent or studious application, I thought that I should devote all my time to defending my friends in the courts. Thus, while this place never lacked those who would champion your cause, my scrupulous and principled efforts serving private citizens in their time of need have won, by your judgment, the highest reward.[66]

---

[63] The existence of further symbolic associations (e.g. the *subsellium* as a reference to *auxilium*) cannot and need not be excluded, though the presence of the Rostra should be given its full significance. Weinstock 1971: 140 makes the coin a partisan Caesarian reference to the dictator's stance as Liberator. Again, while such associations may well have been intended, that is surely to privilege a rather narrow reading of the composition; there is nothing on the coin that makes exclusive and direct reference to Caesar, and as Weinstock himself shows, the ideology of Roman freedom was an old numismatic theme and commanded universal assent.

[64] *ORF* 32.3, p. 144; see p. 158.

[65] Of course, in the natural course of things one might have expected a plebeian to have done this as tribune of the plebs, but Cicero, awkwardly for this context, had declined even to run for that office. (See Mitchell 1979: 150–53.) He had some ground to make up.

[66] Cic. *Leg. Man.* 1–2: *Quamquam mihi semper frequens conspectus vester multo iucundissimus, hic autem locus ad agendum amplissimus, ad dicendum ornatissimus est visus, Quirites, tamen hoc aditu laudis qui semper optimo cuique maxime patuit non mea me voluntas adhuc sed vitae meae rationes ab ineunte aetate susceptae prohibuerunt. Nam cum antea nondum huius auctoritatem loci attingere auderem statueremque nihil huc nisi perfectum ingenio, elaboratum industria adferri oportere, omne meum tempus amicorum temporibus transmittendum putavi. Ita neque hic locus vacuus fuit umquam ab eis qui vestram causam defenderent et meus labor in privatorum periculis caste integreque versatus ex vestro iudicio fructum est amplissimum consecutus.*

This passage is as direct an expression as we have of the popular ideological construction of the Rostra, a place which becomes virtually metonymic for deliberation and decision by the Roman People. The Rostra is a "path to public esteem" (*aditus laudis*) invested with all the "dignity" (*auctoritas*) of the Roman People, so much indeed that this rising star of the courts shrank from setting foot upon it until his talents had sufficiently ripened and he could step forth himself as a worthy defender of the People's cause. By asserting the primacy of the Rostra over other *loci* of speech and action on behalf of the Republic, Cicero assures his audience that (despite his record) he cherishes the principles of popular deliberation and decision higher than mere praise for rhetorical brilliance (for which the courts were the chief venue) or the personal power that might be won in the Senate, out of the gaze of the People.[67] The popular orator loves the very sight of the People and understands that defending the People's interests from this spot is the true path to fame in the *res publica*. He will not shun the Rostra and "the sight of you" – a pledge whose significance is more explicitly brought out by Cicero's later claim, when he reached the consulship, that many consuls do just that, thus acknowledging their debt for the honor of public office not to the People but to the "support of powerful men, the extraordinary influence of the few" in the Senate.[68] The emphasis on face-to-face confrontation of the popular gaze is palpable: the Rostra is made into a kind of touchstone for the true sentiments of members of the senatorial élite.

Cicero's picture of the Rostra as the point of intersection between Senate and People, the two constituents of the classic formula *Senatus Populusque Romanus*, is reinforced by topography. The fronts of two buildings in particular constituted the backdrop for an orator speaking from the Rostra: the Senate-house (*Curia*), perhaps only a few strides to the north from the time of Sulla,[69] and the Temple of Concordia, at the northwest end

---

[67] *Ad agendum*, which I have translated broadly "for action," produces a slight echo of the technical phrase for presenting legislation to the People for their vote (*agere cum populo*). Yet the antithesis with *ad dicendum* suggests that the primary meaning is not to be restricted quite so narrowly.

[68] Cic. *Leg. agr.* 2.6–7. For this nexus of ideas surrounding the notion of "debt," see pp. 258–66.

[69] The pre-Caesarian Curia Hostilia/Cornelia is to be put somewhere on the site of the present church of SS. Luca e Martina, thus just to the northwest of the Curia Iulia (which still stands, in its Diocletianic form), more or less atop a small eminence some ten meters higher than the level of the Comitium: Coarelli 1986: 142, 152–60 (cf. 1985: 120, fig. 21; 241); Carafa 1998: 119, 140, 155 (cf. 91–95 and 96, fig. 76, for a description of the original contours of the terrain). Some sources imply that at least after the Sullan expansion of the Curia *c.* 81 (Plin. *HN* 34.26; cf. Cass. Dio 40.50.2–3; 44.5.2), the building pressed very closely on the Comitium: Pliny, loc. cit. and *HN* 34.21; Asc. 42 C: *prope iuncta curiae* (rightly explained by Coarelli 1985: 241). Carafa, however, rejects the idea that the Curia could have been so close, since the summit of the small hill is further distant (some 20 m from the nearest point of the Comitium and perhaps 50 m from the Rostra) and there is no evidence of terracing in between (p. 155).

of the Forum, perhaps some fifty meters away. The intimate connection between Senate and Rostra will have been made physically evident every time the consul, tribune, or praetor presiding over a meeting of the Senate emerged through its doors and made his way to the speaker's platform to describe the proceedings. Popular space, then, or senatorial space? One has the sense of permeable and shifting boundaries at an ideologically fraught meeting-point between *senatus* and *populus*. The Temple of Concordia, for its part, ostensibly a highly suitable divinity to preside over this locus of confrontation, bears that tension within its very name and contentious, even bloody, history. Concordia had originally, it seems, been associated primarily with the concessions of the patrician order that led to resolution of the prolonged ancient civic crisis called the Struggle of the Orders;[70] but its reconstruction by L. Opimius (cos. 121), the man who had ruthlessly pursued the destruction of Gaius Gracchus, can only be regarded as an audacious attempt to coopt the essentially plebeian associations of the cult in the service of violent reaction. The irony of this project was clearly not lost on contemporaries, many of whom will have noted that the man whose name was now inscribed on the Temple of Concordia had grossly violated perhaps the most basic Roman civil right – protection against execution without popular authorization – newly reinforced by a law of the very man in whose destruction he now gloried. Plutarch tells us that after the work was completed, someone expressed the outrage of the People by painting in, just underneath Opimius' own dedicatory inscription, the line, "An act of madness made the Temple of Concord."[71] Six decades afterwards Cicero chose the temple as the venue for the even more legally questionable senatorial condemnation of the "Catilinarian" conspirators: through its doors the consul had gone forth to fetch the men, and under the awe-struck, or horrified, gaze of the citizenry had led them – including one who had the day before been praetor of the Roman People – to the adjacent *carcer* to execution.[72]

Palpable in these events is the evolution of the popular meaning of the temple into a symbol of a very different vision of "Concord" as the product of (ostensibly) emergency bloodletting; in turn, a new popular symbol to set against this "hijacked" ideal was *Libertas*, "Freedom," to which P. Clodius built a shrine on the site of *Cicero's* demolished house after sending him into exile – under a law that was in essence a reconfirmation of

---

[70] For this part of the tradition, see pp. 101–2. On the temple's place in the political topography of the late Republic, see now the very full discussion by Döbler 1999: 48–62.

[71] Plut. *C. Gracch.* 17.6. See chap. 3, n. 159.

[72] Plut. *Cic.* 22.1–2. For the importance of proximity of the *carcer* in the choice of meeting-place, see Bonnefond-Coudry 1989: 97–102.

the law of Gaius Gracchus.[73] The Temple of Concordia was itself an ideological battleground, whose contours nicely match the bitter debate in public discourse over the real meaning of *concordia* as a political catchword, invoked by some in defense of senatorial domination and rejected by popular politicians as merely a cloak for injustice and savagery.[74] The temple may have suggested to many of those standing in a *contio* a bitterly ironical commentary on the rhetoric of concord often served up from the Rostra.

The victor of the civil wars of the 80s, Lucius Cornelius Sulla, launched a further "monumental struggle" for symbolic mastery of the contional space. Coarelli's hypothesis of a thoroughgoing revision of the whole contional area by Sulla is to be rejected,[75] but we have good evidence for two highly conspicuous interventions here by the dictator, both already mentioned above, namely, the construction of a much-expanded Curia to house his new Senate, which was being doubled in size, and the erection on the Rostra of his gilded equestrian statue.[76] The feeling that the Curia Cornelia aroused as a Sullan monument among both Senate and People may be judged both by its use as a funeral pyre for P. Clodius in 52 and the subsequent anxious deliberations of the *patres*, reported by Cassius Dio, regarding the preservation or obliteration of Sulla's name on the structure.[77] Of course, the Senate-house was always senatorial space; but the expanded building seems to have intruded significantly into the ancient Comitium, nearly to the Rostra itself.[78] In 59, before an audience of senators and the well off, Cicero describes the Curia as "watching and pressing upon the Rostra as the punisher of sedition and regulator of conduct" – a phrase that, incidentally, shows that this kind of "reading" of topography was not foreign to contemporaries.[79] The statue on the Rostra, however, was nothing less than Opimian-style annexation of a popular space, quite

---

73 Sources collected by E. Papi, *LTUR* III.188–89. Note that the Porticus of Catulus was also torn down to build the shrine; it was built on the razed site of C. Gracchus' ally, M. Fulvius Flaccus.

74 For the use of *concordia* as a conservative buzzword, see Sall. *Iug.* 31.23 (Memmius); *Hist.* 1.55.24 (Lepidus), with Burckhardt 1988: 70–85.

75 Above, n. 44.

76 Above, nn. 52 and 69.

77 Cass. Dio 40.50.3 (assignment of the repairs to Faustus Sulla: ὅπως ἐξοικοδομηθὲν τὸ ἐκείνου ὄνομα ἀπολάβῃ); 44.5.2 (building of the Curia Iulia: ὅπως μήτε ἐν ἐκείνῳ τὸ τοῦ Σύλλου ὄνομα σώζοιτο). Note also Caesar's decision not to rebuild on the same spot (above, n. 44). For the burning of the Curia Cornelia in 52, see p. 2 (Asc. 33 C) and the recent discussion of Sumi 1997: 98–99.

78 Above, n. 69. According to Cic. *Fin.* 5.2, the enlarged Curia also shed some of the reverence that historical memory had conferred on its predecessor.

79 Cic. *Flac.* 57: *cum speculatur atque obsidet rostra vindex temeritatis et moderatrix offici curia*; Corbeill 2002: 199.

appropriate for the man who, blaming demagogues for the catastrophic civil war and vouchsafing from this very spot that he would "change" the People for the better, "deprived" the Rostra and Comitium of the tribunes' voice and turned them into "deserted" solitudes.[80] While it is probably true that the togate dress of the figure of Sulla and his extension of one hand in the gesture of address (*adlocutio*) attempt to reinvent a man deeply stained with the blood of citizens as the bringer of peace and constitutional government, the statue clearly stuck in the craw of the urban plebs who hated the man so cordially.[81] After news came of Caesar's victory at Pharsalus the plebs pulled down from the Rostra and smashed not only the statue of Pompey but also that of Sulla.[82]

In sum, even from the inadequate evidence we possess we can discern that the very setting of the *contio* was an ideologically contested space, on which were inscribed highly charged polemics which are likely to have shaped Roman citizens' lived experience of the *contio* in ways which cannot be precisely defined (now or indeed then), but may often be inferred with some degree of confidence.

The Rostra in the northwestern corner of the Forum was not the only location for *contiones* within the city.[83] After the late second century the Capitol was no longer a contional venue, since legislation by the tribes had moved to the Forum.[84] Especially after Sulla, it seems, the podium of the

---

[80] Cic. *Clu.* 110: [sc. Quinctius] *qui quod rostra iam diu vacua locumque illum post adventum L. Sullae a tribunicia voce desertum oppresserat multitudinemque desuefactam iam a contionibus ad veteris consuetudinis similitudinem revocarat*... See also especially Sulla's memorable *contiones* of 88 and 82 (App. *B Civ.* 1.59 and 95, cf. τὸν μὲν δῆμον ἐς χρηστὴν ἄξει μεταβολήν. For the emasculation of the tribunate, see Greenidge–Clay, 212–13; Gruen's judicious assessment (1974: 23–28) misses, however, the citizens' perspective on the *contio*, so well expressed by the coin of Palicanus and Cic. *Leg. Man.* 1–2.

[81] For references, see above, n. 52. On the interpretation of the statue, see especially the persuasive arguments of Sehlmeyer 1999: 204–9, against, for example, Behr 1993: 121–23, and Ramage 1991: 104. There has been a long controversy over whether Sulla was given the title *imperator* or *dictator* in the inscription on its base; Appian's Ἡγεμών is in itself unhelpful (Mason 1974: 146, *dux*?), while the legend on the coins (L SVLL FELI(X) DIC) strongly suggests the latter, and the objection that, according to Appian, Sulla had not been elected dictator at the time the statue was voted is probably indecisive (M. H. Crawford 1974: p. 397; contra, Famerie 1998: 124–25). However, if he was titled *dictator* (so too now Mackay 2000: 182–83), this would tend to support the "peaceful" interpretation of the statue. Cicero and Velleius make clear that the statue was *on* the Rostra, not simply (as in Appian) before it. Sulla's claim to have crushed "tyranny" is attractively connected by Reusser 1993: 113–20 with the dedication on the Capitol of a copy of the Athenian "Tyrannicides" group.

[82] Vasaly 1993: 68, n. 56 apparently thinks the statue of Sulla was removed shortly after 78, but Cass. Dio 42.18.2 is clear. Plebs: Suet. *Iul.* 75.4. Re-erected, by Caesar's order, in 44: Cass. Dio 43.49.1–2; Plut. *Cic.* 40.4; *Caes.* 57.4.

[83] For surveys of sites for *contiones*, see Taylor 1966: 19–33; Pina Polo 1989: 182–98.

[84] The Capitol is last heard of as a contional venue (excepting Brutus' obviously extraordinary *contio Capitolina* after Caesar's assassination in 44) in 121, when the tribune Minucius held a meeting as

Temple of Castor at the southeast corner of the Forum was used frequently, especially by tribunes, for the *contio* that immediately preceded legislation by the tribal assembly, a development whose chronology is probably broadly consistent also with the increasing use of that temple for senatorial meetings in that period.[85] In a reconstruction dating to the first half of the second century, the original front row of columns of the pronaos and presumably a frontal staircase had been removed, while the front of the temple platform was brought forward to form a vertical wall facing the Forum, access to which was provided by stairs on each side. When the temple was again restored in 117 by L. Caecilius Metellus Delmaticus to commemorate his victory over the Dalmatians, the older tribunal, used perhaps originally for the censors' viewing of the "passage of the Knights" (*transvectio equitum*), was greatly expanded, to a width of some 21 m and depth of 7 m, rising as we have seen some 2.5 to 4.3 m above the level of the Forum; this alone would point to expanded use of the podium already at this time, probably at least for legislative votes and the *contio* that would immediately precede them.[86] Presumably also those *contiones* that immediately followed meetings of the Senate in the Temple of Castor in order to convey an account of their proceedings to the People will also have been addressed from this

a prelude to a legislative vote of the tribes to abrogate Gaius Gracchus' laws (Oros. 5.12). Since Capitoline *contiones* seem typically to have been part of the legislative procedure of the tribes, the migration of tribal legislation to the Forum around the middle of the century suggests that even Minucius' assembly was a late exception, perhaps born of a concern to secure the area against the Gracchans (cf. Plut. *C. Gracch.* 13.3; similarly, Thommen 1995: 366). The nature of Tiberius Gracchus' final assembly is too problematic to enter into this debate (Taylor 1963: 51–69; contra, Badian 1972: 720–21). Ulrich 1994: 60–72, tries to work out the confused and confusing topographical details.

85 For senatorial meetings, see Bonnefond-Coudry 1989: 80–90, and Cic. *Verr.* 2.1.129 – whose claim is, however, not corroborated by the record of specific cases (see the tables in Bonnefond-Coudry, pp. 32–47). On the use of the temple for *contiones*, Ulrich 1994: 81–107 offers an excellent synthesis, although reference should be made also to the final publication of the Danish excavations of the temple in Nielsen and Poulsen 1992 (cf. I. Nielsen, *LTUR* 1.242–45); Cerutti 1998: 292–305 deals with the podium, but his interpretation of Cicero's charges that Clodius had actually removed its steps takes rhetorical invective too literally. The attractive emendation of Cic. *Mil.* 91 (see chap. 1, n. 5) would add a further known *contio* before the Temple of Castor in 52, not listed by Pina Polo.

86 The earliest certain evidence for the use of the temple podium for legislation (and thus, its preceding *contio*) appears to date to 62 (Plut. *Cat. Min.* 26–29), but App. *B Civ.* 1.64 probably attests to such use as early as 87 (Pina Polo 1989: p. 284, no. 223) and the most straightforward interpretation of the ambiguous reference to a *templum* in Cic. *De or.* 2.197 would take it back to 103 (cf. Pina Polo, pp. 281–82, no. 208). The *lex latina tabulae Bantinae* of the very late second century lays down that magistrates should swear to uphold its terms [*pro ae*]*de Castoris palam luci in forum vorsus*, presumably on the podium (*Roman Statutes*, no. 7, line 17; not, I should think, on the steps of the temple, as stated there, p. 207; cf. Nielsen and Poulsen 1992: 55); it is tempting to conclude that this location was chosen because the law had originated there (Nielsen and Zahle 1985: 26, n. 59). If so, it would be the earliest evidence for *comitia* at the temple. On the Metellan temple, see Nielsen and Poulsen 1992: 80–117. There is no evidence that the podium was fitted with *rostra* (p. 113; so too Coarelli 1985: 309). *Transvectio equitum*: Mommsen 1887: III.493–95; Scullard 1981: 164–65.

tribunal as a rule; this practice would go back to the middle of the second century.[87] But with these exceptions it seems that the traditional Rostra remained the favored location for most *contiones*; as we have seen, in Cicero's *Pro lege Manilia* of 66 the Rostra is still the focus of popular oratory. Not before 44 do we find fairly clear evidence of a *contio* held at the temple of Castor that was *not* part of the proceedings of a legislative vote nor directly consequent upon a senatorial meeting therein; this, however, was a time when the Comitial space was being radically reconstructed in accordance with the plans of Julius Caesar.[88] Presumably, the Rostra's historical and physical centrality still made it the best place to gather a crowd.

Finally, we must take briefer notice of two specialized venues for *contiones* outside the ancient urban boundary (*pomerium*) (see map 1). The Circus Flaminius, an open space just outside the *pomerium* with strong plebeian associations – the first plebeian assembly had been held there, as were also the Plebeian Games, and the area was monumentalized by that great early "popular" politician C. Flaminius – was employed for the special case of meetings at which the presiding magistrate desired the participation of a proconsul (normally a general heading out to a province, or returning from campaign and perhaps awaiting a triumph), for by remaining outside the urban space a commander would not trigger the lapse of his military power (*imperium*).[89] Among the most notable such meetings were that which was called in 61 to raise the question of the Bona Dea trial with Pompey before his triumph, and that of 58 at which P. Clodius desired to have Caesar speak regarding the execution of the "Catilinarian" conspirators before his

---

[87] The use of the temple for senatorial meetings is attested as early as 159: *CIL* I² 586 = *ILS* 19 = *ILLRP* 512, line 1. This may be the context of the fragment of a speech of Scipio Aemilianus delivered *pro aede Castoris* (*ORF* 21.16, p. 126); as Bonnefond-Coudry 1989: 82 notes, there is no need to assign this to 142, the year of Aemilianus' censorship.

[88] App. *B Civ.* 3.41; cf. above, n. 44. It is unclear whether the occasion mentioned by Cicero at *Phil.* 3.27, 5.21 was actually a *contio* (see n. 23), or if so, whether it was consequent upon a senatorial meeting. In 88 the consuls held a *contio* here which the tribune Sulpicius dispersed by force (Plut. *Sull.* 8.3; cf. *Mar.* 35.2); the purpose of this meeting (missing from Pina Polo's catalog) may have been to announce the *iustitium*, perhaps immediately consequent upon a meeting of the Senate. Note that the obscure *gradus* and *tribunal Aurelii*, new in 74, perhaps to be located near the Temple of Castor (so Coarelli 1985: 190–99; cf. K. Korhonen, *LTUR* v.86–87; contra, Richardson 1992: 182), are never explicitly associated with *contiones*: Cic. *Clu.* 93 refers to a trial surrounded, unusually, by the kind of crowd that frequented Quinctius' *contiones*.

[89] The "plebeian" character of the space is well emphasized by Coarelli 1997: 363–74 (see also Thommen 1995: 367). I leave aside the controversy begun by Wiseman 1974 about whether the "Circus" was indeed an elongated oval used for chariot- or horse-racing. Taylor 1966: 20–21, 31, 45–46 gives an exaggerated impression of the frequency of *contiones* here; in the late Republic, at least, it seems never to have been other than an expedient to confront the peculiar circumstance cited in the text. See also Pina Polo 1989: 185–86. Wiseman rightly rejects Taylor's suggestion that, uniquely, the audience of *contiones* at the Circus Flaminius sat (p. 4).

departure for his provinces.⁹⁰ Probably the precise location of the meetings in the rather large space designated by *in Circo Flaminio* was in fact the area in front of the Temple of Bellona, at its very southern end, just outside the triumphal gate and only a few minutes' walk from the Rostra on the other side of the Capitol.⁹¹ Another spot outside the *pomerium* was also used, much more rarely. The final *contio* immediately before a vote of the centuriate assembly meeting in its legislative capacity – a practice mostly dormant in the late Republic, with the notable exception of the law that restored Cicero from exile in 57 – would, of course, necessarily be held in the Campus Martius, the mandatory meeting-place of that body, probably from a tribunal before the entrance at the north end of the Saepta or voting-enclosure.⁹² There, too, would be held the final *contio* of a tribunician capital trial before the People, an anachronism which was revived for the trial of Rabirius in 63: the Campus was almost certainly the setting of Cicero's speech in defence of Publius Rabirius on a charge of "treason" (*perduellio*).⁹³

CICERO ON CONTIONAL SPEECH

Having examined in some detail the physical and institutional contexts of the *contio*, it is time to turn to its communicative context. As noted in the

⁹⁰ Pompey, 62: *Att.* 1.14.1–2 (cf. the similar *contio* before Pompey's first triumph in 71, certainly here as well [*ad urbem*]: Cic. *Verr.* 1.45). Caesar, 58: Cass. Dio 38.16.5–17.2 (cf. Cic. *Sest.* 33, for example, for the location).

⁹¹ Only one source specifies where in the Circus Flaminius a *contio* was held: Plut. *Cic.* 13.4 (see Coarelli 1997: 391–95, and Wiseman 1974: 15–16). This meeting (an impromptu interruption of a play, perhaps on the site of the later Theater of Marcellus) was certainly an extraordinary one, but there seems to be no good reason why Cicero led the crowd to assemble before the Temple of Bellona, in preference to other sites, unless it was the traditional location. The inference is supported by the fact that the temple also appears to have been the most common location for senatorial meetings *extra pomerium* (Bonnefond-Coudry 1989: 151–60); if this was a "second pole of senatorial activity" (p. 154) outside the city corresponding to that within (at the Curia in the Forum), it is tempting to conjecture a similar juncture of senatorial and popular space here.

⁹² Taylor 1966: 56–57.

⁹³ *Pro Rabirio perduellionis reo;* see Taylor 1966: 103. The conclusion depends largely on the fairly secure premise that the speech was indeed a defense against the tribunician capital charge of *perduellio* (see the references at Cic. *Pis.* 4; cf. *Orat.* 102; Tyrrell 1978: 73) rather than a case involving a mere fine, as has frequently been held against the most straightforward interpretation of the ambiguous evidence (cf. chap. 1, n. 90). But note also Cicero's balancing of the "executioner" in the Forum/*contio* and the "gibbet" to be erected *in campo Martio comitiis centuriatis auspicato in loco* (§§10–11), which seems strongly to imply that the current proceedings were indeed those preliminary to a vote of the Centuriate assembly in the Saepta. If Labienus really had brought a portrait of Saturninus to a *contio* at the Rostra (*Rab. perd.* 25), there is no reason why this should not have been an earlier meeting in the Forum (cf. §§10–11, with Tyrrell, p. 79; *habes* in the present tense at the beginning of the section may mean nothing more than "have [in your possession]," as it evidently does in the reference to Sex. Titius immediately afterwards. For such changes of venue in the course of a trial before the populace, see Santalucia 1998: 85–87.

last chapter, the body of evidence that is particularly valuable here consists of (written versions of) the orations themselves. These will be the focus of attention in the chapters to come. Yet Cicero, in his specifically rhetorical works and elsewhere, has a fair amount to say about the requirements and nature of contional speech; and a brief review of this material will both raise central themes to be revisited later and give an idea of how at least some members of the élite, from whose ranks came the speakers in public meetings, were conditioned to view the *contio* and its characteristic rhetorical features. The composite picture it provides should not be confused with objective reality; its ideological underpinnings will become quite apparent. But that too is of interest.

One might expect to learn much about contional oratory from Cicero's rhetorical works. The great store of ancient rhetorical theory comprehended by them, together with the anonymous *Rhetorica ad Herennium*, offers modern critics of Roman oratory invaluable tools for analysis, much contemporary wisdom on matters of strategy and tactics, as well as the fundamental expectations of the genre and sub-genres. But nowhere is the theoretical tradition drier and less illuminating than when it deals with deliberative oratory; its focus is almost exclusively on the rhetoric of the courtroom (forensic), the most comprehensive of the three broad categories, the most pragmatic for the widest range of students, and always, it seems, the most prestigious. The teaching of the schools in Cicero's day on deliberative oratory seems to have offered a tedious series of variations on or reactions against Aristotle's view that the ultimate aim is "utility" (*utilitas*), fleshed out with the standard division of topics between the "honorable" (*honestum*) and the "expedient" (*utile* or *tutum*) and a series of commonplaces upon them.[94] Perhaps the arguments of expediency needed to be given primacy before a popular audience;[95] perhaps not, since "there is no one, particularly in such an illustrious state, who does not desire to pursue the worthy course above all."[96] At this level of abstraction, these "textbook" discussions and notes from the lecture halls shed little light specifically on popular oratory in Rome and its differences from the other major deliberative sub-genre, that of senatorial speeches.

[94] See *Rhet Her.* 3.2–9; Cic. *Inv. rhet.* 2.155–76, *De or.* 2.333ff. (with Leeman, Pinkster, and Wisse 1981–96: IV.44–57); *Part. or.* 83–97; Quint. *Inst.* 3.8. Josef Martin 1974: 167–76 gives a good overview of the body of classical theory on the genre.

[95] Cic. *Part. or.* 92: *apud indoctos imperitosque,* the latter virtually a synonym for the contional audience (below, chap. 3). Leonhardt 1998/99 seeks to substantiate this principle by comparing the relative weight given to the *honestum* and the *utile* in *Leg. agr.* 1 (fragmentary) and 2. But strong emphasis on the *utile* while discussing an agrarian law before the People hardly surprises.

[96] Cic. *De or.* 2.334, with the note of Leeman, Pinkster, and Wisse 1981–96: IV.51. Perhaps, however, Cicero here means nothing more than Quintilian's "no one is so wicked as to want to seem so" (*Inst.* 3.8.44).

More interesting than such jejeune theoretical rules are the remarks, redolent of actual experience, that Cicero puts in the mouth of the great orator M. Antonius in the second book of the rhetorical dialogue *De oratore* (*On the Orator*) (333–40). Antonius emphasizes first that to give advice on matters of high import demands a *gravissima persona*, a "very weighty self-presentation," in whom powers of mind, personal authority, and eloquence are all combined.[97] The People and the *contio* are characterized by their passions;[98] and Cicero's stated ideal of the contional orator is one who, by the mere power of his words and grandeur of his person, can sway those passions, rousing the People when they are inert, calming them when they are aroused.[99] The ideal itself is a traditional one, going right back to Thucydides' Pericles.[100]

The fundamental conception can be fleshed out by other Ciceronian texts directed at élite audiences. Regarding popular passions, Cicero turns out to be much more concerned to calm them than to stir them up. He frequently applies metaphors of storm and sea to the *contiones* of populist politicians, who are condemned for seeking to fill their sails with the "popular wind" (*popularis aura* or *ventus*), the force of which may even carry them farther than they themselves desire.[101] Their meetings are *turbulentae*, "incited" (*concitatae*) by the presiding magistrate, usually a tribune, seeking to "ignite" popular resentment or indignation (*invidia*).[102] On the other

---

[97] Cic. *De or.* 2.333: *nam et sapientis est consilium explicare suum de maximis rebus et honesti et diserti, ut mente providere, auctoritate probare, oratione persuadere possis.*

[98] Cic. *De or.* 2.337: *maximi motus multitudinis*; 2.339; cf. *populi motus*, 1.31; 2.199.

[99] Cic. *De or.* 1.31: [sc. *Quid enim est*] *aut tam potens tamque magnificum, quam populi* motus, *iudicum religiones, senatus* gravitatem *unius oratione converti?* (Cf. Quint. *Inst.* 12.1.26). *De or.* 2.337: *ad animorum motus non numquam . . . in spem aut in metum aut ad cupiditatem aut ad gloriam concitandos, saepe etiam a temeritate, iracundia, spe, iniuria, invidia, crudelitate revocandos*; cf. 2.35 *languentis populi incitatio et effrenati moderatio.*

[100] Thuc. 2.65.8–10, with Yunis 1996: 67–72.

[101] Storm: see especially Cic. *Mil.* 5: *tempestates et procellas in illis dumtaxat fluctibus contionum*, and *Clu.* 138: *id quod saepe dictum est, ut mare quod sua natura tranquillum sit ventorum vi agitari atque turbari, sic populum Romanum sua sponte esse placatum, hominum seditiosorum vocibus ut violentissimis tempestatibus concitari.* The metaphor of the disturbed sea, of course, is very ancient (Hom. *Il.* 2.144ff.); see Austin 1971: 68. Popular winds: see Cic. *Clu.* 77, 130; *Sest.* 140; *Phil.* 11.17; *Har. resp.* 43: *Sulpicium . . . longius quam voluit popularis aura provexit.* Cf. Hor. *Epist.* 1.19.37: *ventosae plebis.* For Cicero's typology of the popular characteristics, see esp. Favory 1976: 163–233.

[102] Note, for example, Cic. *Sest.* 106: *erant illae contiones perditorum hominum necessario turbulentae* (cf. 110); *Clu.* 95: *conflata praesertim invidia et contionibus seditiose concitatis* (cf. 5, 77–79, 103); *Verr.* 1.2: *cum sint parati qui contionibus et legibus hanc invidiam senatus inflammare conentur.* For *contionem concitare* – not merely to "summon" an assembly (so the *OLD*, s.v. 4) – see *Q Fr.* 1.4.3. *Invidia* can take the form of a storm as well as a flame: *Clu.* 94 *illud* [*tempus*] *omnibus invidiae tempestatibus concitatum.* The connection between *contio* and *invidia* has been well emphasized by David 1980a: 181, 184–85, and Pina Polo 1996: 105–19 (cf. Riggsby 1999: 72–77); see especially Cic. *Clu.* 202: *ut omnes intellegant in contionibus esse invidiae locum, in iudiciis veritati*; *Acad.* 2.144: *in*

hand, some men had the awesome presence necessary to impose silence even on a disruptive crowd: the younger Cato, for example, whose *auctoritas*, we are told in the speech for Milo, quieted a turbulent assembly during the battle fought out in *contiones* over what was to be done with Clodius' killer.[103] One is reminded of Virgil's powerful simile to Neptune's calming of the storm, often thought to be based on the posthumous image of Cato:

> And just as, often, when a crowd of people
> is rocked by a rebellion, and the rabble
> rage in their minds, and firebrands and stones
> fly fast – for fury finds its weapons – if,
> by chance, they see a man remarkable
> for righteousness and service, they are silent
> and stand attentively; and he controls
> their passion by his words and cools their spirits:
> so all the clamor of the sea subsided
> after the Father, gazing on the waters
> and riding under cloudless skies, had guided
> his horses, let his willing chariot run.[104]

Cicero would doubtless have agreed with Quintilian that "authority (*auctoritas*) is the most important factor in deliberations."[105]

The *contio* is the fullest test of the consummate orator, claims Cicero's Antonius in the *De oratore*. Speaking in the Senate demands self-restraint in rhetoric and in style, for one's audience is wise, dubious of showmanship – and impatient for its own time to speak; public meetings, however, call for the power of speech in its entirety, an air of authority, and an ability to employ all styles.[106] The enormous variety of emotions that the public orator must inspire demands an acute perception of the ever-changing disposition of the populace and a corresponding versatility of style;[107] still,

---

invidiam et tamquam in contionem vocas (cf. *Att.* 1.16.1). For the association of *invidia* with the "popular" style, see in addition *Brut.* 164: *invidia concitatur in iudicum et in accusatorum factionem, contra quorum potentiam populariter tum dicendum fuit; Verr.* 2.1.151: *me populariter agere atque invidiam commovere; Clu.* 134: *invidiae populariter excitatae.* See pp. 237–39 and 271.

[103] Cic. *Mil.* 58: *Dixit enim . . . M. Cato, et dixit in turbulenta contione, quae tamen huius auctoritate placata est . . .* Cf. M. Popilius, who *venit in contionem seditionemque cum auctoritate tum oratione sedavit* (Cic. *Brut.* 56; traditional date, 359 BC!).

[104] Virg. *Aen.* 1.148–56 (tr. Mandelbaum). On Cato, cf. Plut. *Cat. Min.* 44 and Austin 1971: 69.

[105] Quint. *Inst.* 3.8.12.

[106] Cic. *De or.* 2.333–4: *Atque haec in senatu minore apparatu agenda sunt; sapiens enim est consilium multisque aliis dicendi relinquendus locus, vitanda etiam ingeni ostentationis suspicio: contio capit omnem vim orationis et gravitatem varietatemque desiderat.*

[107] Cic. *De or.* 2.337, esp. *ad dicendum vero probabiliter* [sc. *caput est*] *nosse mores civitatis, qui quia crebro mutantur, genus quoque orationis est saepe mutandum.* For emphasis on the ability to play on emotions, see the end of the section (*maximaque pars orationis admovenda est ad animorum motus,* etc.).

the greatness of the People, the importance of high politics, and the passionate character of the masses all tend to favor a rather majestic oratorical mode,[108] which in any case the grandeur of the setting and the sheer size of the audience conspire to evoke.[109] Certainly, Cicero's own published *contiones* are often marked by an imposing impressiveness of language, particularly notable at beginnings and ends. The massive periodic sentence with which Cicero opens his speech of thanks to the People upon his return from exile, whose sonorous clauses do not achieve resolution until the main verb arrives at the very end, 126 words later (seventeen lines in the Oxford edition), is an awe-inspiring example. A rather literal translation helps to bring out its elaborate structure:

That for which I prayed to Jupiter, Best and Greatest, and the other immortal gods, Citizens, at that time when I sacrificed myself and my fortunes in return for your safety, tranquillity and concord – that, if I had ever set my own concerns before your well-being, I should willingly accept eternal punishment, but if the things which I had done [i.e., the punishment of the "Catilinarian" conspirators], I had done for the sake of preserving the state, and I had undertaken that wretched journey of mine [exile in 58] for your well-being, then the hatred that evil and reckless men had conceived against the Republic and all good men and so long retained they should fix upon me alone rather than in every good man and the entire state; and if such had been my attitude toward you and your children, that memory of me, pity and longing for me would at last come over you, the Fathers, and all Italy – that this prayer of mine was carried out by the judgment of the immortal gods, the avowal of the Senate, the unanimity of Italy, the admission of my enemies, and your undying, divine favor, greatly do I rejoice.[110]

---

[108] Cic. *De or.* 2.337: *genus quoque dicendi grandius quoddam et inlustrius esse adhibendum videtur.*

[109] Cic. *De or.* 2.338: *Fit autem ut, quia maxima quasi oratoris scaena videatur contionis esse, natura ipsa ad ornatius dicendi genus excitemur; habet enim multitudo vim quandam talem, ut, quem ad modum tibicen sine tibiis canere, sic orator sine multitudine audiente eloquens esse non possit.* The point Cicero is making here is not always correctly understood: he is not here asserting that the *contio* ranked above the law courts and the Senate as the "wichtigster Adressat," "die eigentliche [Arena]" (so Hölkeskamp 1995: 26–27); cf. Leeman, Pinkster, and Wisse 1981–96: IV.55. Naturally, the point Cicero makes in the *De oratore* about the rhetorical power required in the *contio* can later be put to good, self-serving use in his polemic with the "Atticists" (*Brut.* 186; cf. the whole section, §§183–200, with Gotoff 1979: 32–66), but the statement that that orator is greatest who most pleases the people cannot really be taken to be a widely held axiom, or even an accurate reflection of Cicero's own thinking: compare how, in the same work, he rates those orators who were pleasing primarily to "ignorant ears" (*Brut.* 223–25).

[110] *Red. pop.* 1: *Quod precatus a Iove Optimo Maximo ceterisque dis immortalibus sum, Quirites, eo tempore cum me fortunasque meas pro vestra incolumitate otio concordiaque devovi – ut, si meas rationes umquam vestrae saluti anteposuissem, sempiternam poenam sustinerem mea voluntate susceptam, sin et ea quae ante gesseram conservandae civitatis causa gessissem et illam miseram profectionem vestrae salutis gratia suscepissem, ut quod odium scelerati homines et audaces in rem publicam et in omnis bonos conceptum iam diu continerent, id in me uno potius quam in optimo quoque et universa civitate defigerent; hoc si animo in vos liberosque vestros fuissem, ut aliquando vos patresque conscriptos Italiamque*

To be sure, this was an extraordinary occasion, calling for the highest degree of solemnity.

The *contio* was like a stage, and like a stage it was a place that gave the best opportunity for illusion, that is (for Cicero) the deception and flattery practiced by populists upon their audiences. But with oratory of "weight" (*gravitas*) and "grandeur" (*maiestas*) one could lead, rather than follow, the Roman People, who thus could be made to see the error of populist ways.[111] The ideal *contio*, in Cicero's eyes, was that exemplary meeting of 57 at which the leading lights of the Republic urged his restoration from exile before a crowd that remained reverentially still, hanging on the words of the *principes*.[112] In Cicero's ideal model of contional speech, communicative influence goes only one way, from élite speaker to mass. Yet he wishes to eat his cake as well as have it, for he insists that such apparently vacuous receptiveness is at the same time an index of the true Will of the People: silence is not just silence, but manifest evidence of unanimous popular approval.[113] In the discussion of contional rhetoric in *De oratore*, actual audience responses are mentioned only as something to be avoided.[114]

Cicero's stated views on contional speech are not to be taken as a simple reflection of reality. As we shall see, orators, even "conservative" ones like Cicero, operated on sharply different assumptions when they came before the Roman People in a public meeting. We need to keep in mind that the texts from which this composite picture of the *contio* is drawn were all produced for élite consumption – students of rhetoric and philosophy or jurors, of the senatorial or equestrian orders. One readily senses therein

universam memoria mei misericordia desideriumque teneret – eius devotionis me esse convictum iudicio deorum immortalium, testimonio senatus, consensu Italiae, confessione inimicorum, beneficio divino immortalique vestro maxime laetor. Prose rhythm is carefully seen to at nearly every sense-pause in the massive sentence, which ends with Cicero's most distinctive clausula, the cretic-trochee. Cf. Nicholson 1992: 106; cf. 104, n. 14. Sentence-structure is in general no simpler in *contiones* than in senatorial speeches: Thompson 1978: 125–32.

[111] *Amic.* 95–97, esp. 96: *Quanti illi* [sc. *Scipioni*], *di immortales, fuit gravitas, quanta in oratione maiestas! ut facile ducem populi Romani, non comitem diceres;* and 97: *si in scaena, id est in contione, in qua rebus fictis et adumbratis loci plurimum est, tamen verum valet, si modo id patefactum et illustratum est.* One is again reminded of Thuc. 2.65.8–10.

[112] See especially *Sest.* 107–8: *Quo silentio sunt auditi de me ceteri principes civitatis!* Cicero repeatedly reverts to the role of the *principes civitatis* in the *contiones* surrounding his recall: *Red. sen.* 26; *Red. pop.* 17; *Dom.* 90; *Pis.* 34. Cf. *Vat.* 24: *cum L. Vettium . . . in contionem produxeris, indicem in rostris, in illo, inquam, augurato templo ac loco conlocaris, quo auctoritatis exquirendae causa ceteri tribuni plebis principes civitatis producere consuerunt?*

[113] *Sest.* 106–8, esp. 107: *tanto silentio, tanta adprobatione omnium, nihil ut umquam videretur tam populare ad populi Romani auris accidisse.* Cf. *Mil.* 91; *Rab. perd.* 18 (cf. Plut. *Brut.* 18.12); and for a senatorial audience, *Cat.* 1.20–21. When Cicero wants it to be, of course, silence *can* be hostile: *Q Fr.* 2.3.3 (senatorial).

[114] Cic. *De or.* 2.339.

powerful anxieties about the role of the People in the *res publica* and the persistent danger posed by those who would break ranks with their own order and exploit the potentially explosive force of the masses, which always lay temptingly ready to hand. In good society a whiff of illegitimacy always surrounded populist methods, like the disagreeable necessity of courting lower-class voters during an electoral campaign;[115] when speaking and writing among themselves, as here, members of the élite may not have been inclined to own up candidly to their own practice. Not even Sallust, for example, despite his own demagogic past and his trenchant critique of the arrogance of the nobility, was inclined to present an alternative, "popular" picture of the *contio* to the readers of his histories: public speeches are repeatedly shown to be a means by which power-hungry demagogues rouse the People's ire against those who hold sway in the Senate, sometimes with justification, sometimes merely out of party spirit.[116] Even Memmius in the *Jugurtha*, the most prominent of the tribunician characters in Sallust's extant works and one whose indictment of a corrupt nobility is generally validated in Sallust's *propria persona*, gives the impression of being one who, like Cicero's *populares*, uses popular speech as a demagogic weapon, "enflaming" the People, arousing *invidia* against the nobility, and more concerned to inspire fear among Roman senators than in the external enemy, Jugurtha.[117] Cicero, on the other hand, even as a senior senator was perfectly prepared under the right circumstances to exploit in his own public speeches the classic populist weapon of stirring popular indignation (*concitatio invidiae*), complete with the call-and-response technique he elsewhere deplores, despite his theoretical observations on the desirability of calming rather than exciting the citizenry.

Still, there are features of Cicero's model of the *contio* that, as we shall see, have a better claim to some credence. The force potentially generated by popular indignation (*invidia*) in the *contio* gives a strong hint of the check it perennially placed upon senatorial "business as usual" in the late Republic. The overall assumption of oratorical *control* over the audience

---

[115] See Cic. *De or.* 1.112; Morstein-Marx 1998: 266–68; Yakobson 1999: 211–25.

[116] With the passages from Cicero (above, n. 102), cf. especially Sall. *Cat.* 38.1: *homines adulescentes summam potestam nacti, quibus aetas animusque ferox erat, coepere* senatum criminando plebem exagitare, *dein largiundo atque pollicitando magis* incendere: *ita ipsi clari potentesque fieri.* Also, *Iug.* 73.5–6; 84.5; *Cat.* 43.1.

[117] Sall. *Iug.* 27.2–3; 30.3 (esp. *prorsus intentus omni modo plebis animum* accendebat); 31; 32.5–34.2. Despite a certain community of sentiment with Sallust's own narrative voice, Memmius' actions must also be assessed against the background of the views of partisan strife sketched at *Cat.* 38; *Iug.* 41.3–5; and *Hist.* 1.12 (M). See Büchner 1982: 190–96, and for the historical circumstances, Morstein-Marx 2000a.

and communication-situation may well be in part a hegemonic fiction shared by the political élite, but we should be open to the possibility that it corresponds to something real in senators' experience. And the metaphor of drama raises interesting questions about the contional audience's ability to discriminate between those who played "Friend of the People" truly and those who falsely took up the role. These ideas all touch upon the central themes of this book.

I have defined the *contio* and set it in its milieu. Now it is time to embark on an analysis of the communication-situation that prevailed in mass-public meetings, beginning with an attempt to assess the level of political knowledge possessed by their audiences.

CHAPTER 3

Civic knowledge

A bestialized urban mob, whose enslavement to its appetites and desperate circumstances make it incapable of reason, is one of the stock characters of the Roman political drama scripted by ancient writers. The contempt in which the plebs was held even by one of its supposed former defenders, the ex-tribune, now historian Sallust, is illustrative: the plebeian masses, with nothing to lose, but much to gain from revolution and upheaval, are rash and treacherous, an enemy within, ready not just to sell their support to any power-seeker but even to plunder their fellow citizens.[1] Cicero seems – at least in public – to take a less harsh view of the People's character as a political agent, though it is still often characterized by "rashness" (*temeritas*) and "fickleness" (*levitas*), and comparable to irrational forces of nature such as the sea or the winds, whose gusts give the populist politician his direction and power.[2]

It is consistent with these conceptions of the multitude that the audiences of public meetings were frequently derided by Cicero, once out of earshot, as composed of *imperiti*, "ignoramuses," an adjective that adheres to references to the plebs or *multitudo* virtually as a formula.[3] The word *imperitus*,

---

[1] Sall. *Cat.* 37, esp. 37.3: *quibus opes nullae sunt bonis invident, malos extollunt, vetera odere, nova exoptant, odio suarum rerum mutari omnia student.* Cf. 48.1–2; *Iug.* 66.2; 86.3.

[2] See pp. 62–63; for Ciceronian references to popular *temeritas* and *levitas*, see Achard 1981: 132. His tone is harsher in private letters to his friend Atticus: see, for example, *Att.* 1.16.11; 2.16.1. There is a concise reconstruction of Cicero's mature political views in Mitchell 1979: 196–204; even less sympathetically, in Perelli 1990.

[3] See Cic. *Amic.* 95: *contio, quae ex imperitissimis constat*; *Brut.* 223; *Verr.* 2.1.151; *Clu.* 5; *Flac.* 2, 96–97; *Mur.* 61; *Fin.* 2.74. On the plebs as *imperiti/imperita multitudo* as a whole, or its violent and seditious part: *Cat.* 4.17; *Mur.* 38; *Sest.* 77, 139, 140; *Har. resp.* 41; *Dom.* 4, 10, 13, 14, 54; *Mil.* 90; *Phil.* 2.116; *Off.* 1.65; and as *barbari: Tusc.* 5.104. Cicero's slanders in the *Pro Flacco* of the *imperiti* who pass decrees in the cities of Asia Minor (§§16, 19, 57, 58) clearly exploit, in part, élite Roman attitudes toward the Roman *contio* (§17). Speaking before the People, Cicero is naturally more careful: *Rab. perd.* 18 (cf. 24). Cf. Hirtius, *BG* 8.21.4 (Gauls); Val. Max. 3.8.6; Tac. *Dial.* 7.4, 41.4 (with 40.3); *Hist.* 1.35; *Ann.* 2.77 (cf. *volgus stolidum, credulum, pronum ad suspiciones*: *Hist.* 2.61, 72, 21). Reference to members of the élite as *imperiti* in philosophical discussion is a different matter (cf. Cic. *Fin.* 4.74 with *Mur.* 61). See further Achard 1981: 133–34; Horsfall 1996: 46, with nn. 340–42.

to be sure, refers in the first instance to ignorance and inexperience, not necessarily the lack of basic mental capacity; and in any case, Cicero on one occasion explicitly allows that even the *imperitissimi* who make up the audience at the *contio* are capable of distinguishing an ingratiating demagogue from a true friend of the People, and thus, with proper instruction, of apprehending the truth.[4] Yet that passage turns out on closer examination to equate the multitude's discernment with its all-too-infrequent deference to the opponents of "popular" politicians, and in general, it may be observed that for Cicero being *imperitus* is indeed more or less identified with the tendency to be influenced by such so-called "*populares*."[5]

The term, then, proves to be ideologically loaded in a variety of ways, which makes the longevity of the ancient stereotype somewhat surprising. For Dietrich Mack in his 1935 Kiel dissertation, a penetrating study overall which remains the fundamental treatment of contional rhetoric, the implied audience of public meetings was made up of "simple m[e]n of the people," whose scant and thin historical knowledge was limited to a disconnected series of commonplace *exempla*, to whom the *res publica* and its traditions meant little or nothing, and who responded effectively only to appeals to their passions and personal interest.[6] But his approving quotation of Adolf Hitler's *Mein Kampf* on the mental laziness of the masses will send up a red flag for today's reader.[7] Such a dismissive view of the multitude is in general no longer politically acceptable; moreover, landmark studies of the crowd as a historical and sociological agent such as those of George Rudé and Elias Canetti,[8] have taught us to be more circumspect toward the grossly partisan misrepresentations of the Roman crowd that we find in élite sources: we no longer take literally Cicero's more venomous or hysterical characterizations of the social makeup of the political crowds mobilized by his enemies.[9] Elite dismissal of contional audiences as *imperitissimi* should warrant no less skepticism. Yet some not-so-distant cousins of the time-worn "ignorant

---

[4] Cic. *Amic.* 95. Further discussion of the passage on pp. 244–46.   [5] Achard 1981: 133–34.

[6] Mack 1937: quoted at p. 43. See also pp. 73–79, and the scattered observations on knowledge of recent and not-so-recent history at pp. 27 (with n. 62), 31 with n. 74, 62 with n. 121, 72.

[7] Mack 1937: 11 with n. 38.

[8] Esp. Rudé 1964; Canetti 1978. McClelland 1989 offers an excellent diachronic survey of thought on crowds.

[9] For slaves (including fugitives), gladiators, assassins, criminals, escaped prisoners, the desperate poor (*egentes et perditi*) among Clodius' bands, see the references from Cicero's *Post reditum* speeches listed by Brunt 1966: 23, n. 73; and for analysis, Benner 1987: 71–83 (on the question of servile participation specifically, pp. 75–77; see also Vanderbroeck 1987: 90–92; Thommen 1989: 184–86; and Favory 1976: 109–51). Note also Cic. *Att.* 1.16.11: *illa contionalis hirudo aerari, misera ac ieiuna plebecula*; *Flac.* 18: *opifices et tabernarios atque illam omnem faecem civitatum* (the setting is Hellenic Asia, but Cicero is exploiting élite prejudices). The characterization of a contional audience as *exules servos insanos* (*Acad.* 2.144) was perhaps not so rare among the élite – in private. See also pp. 128–31.

mob" construct seem still to lurk about even recent scholarship: for a leading art historian, the late-Republican urban citizenry is a "Großstadtproletariat" reached only through the coarsest forms of psychological manipulation and blind to most of the historical allusions on the monuments that surrounded them;[10] a new study of political participation by the Roman plebs represents the mass of potential voters as fundamentally apathetic, having "no natural part" in the élite game of the *res publica* and, absent extraordinary efforts by demagogic politicians, standing aside from it.[11] It is the chief purpose of this chapter to employ the evidence of contional oratory itself to gain some control over the presumption of mass ignorance (or indifference), which has proven all too easy to maintain without challenge or close scrutiny.

While William Harris's shockingly low estimate of the level of literacy (below 20 percent among males) is probably too pessimistic, it still seems fair to characterize the extent of formal education among the lower orders in the city of Rome as rather crudely utilitarian, rudimentary, and scarce.[12] Yet, as noted in the previous chapter, a regular constituent of the contional audience seems to have been the craftsmen and innkeepers (*opifices et tabernarii*) whose businesses and gathering-places ringed the Forum, and who comprised surely the more-prosperous and better-educated constituents of the urban plebs.[13] In any case, literacy rates and formal education need not have had much relevance for informed civic participation in an oral (and visual) political culture such as that of the Republic: important information was on the whole *heard*, not read, above all in the *contio*. Finally, many experiences of lower-class urban life had non-negligible educative effects: Nicholas Horsfall rightly stresses the theater, wandering poets and entertainers, military service (for some), and public monuments as well as the *contio* itself.[14] Direct observation of the frequent succession of major political trials from the *corona* (ring) that encircled the open-air court in the great central space of the Forum must also have produced a good

---

[10] Hölscher 1980: 355; 1984: 19. See now Holliday 2002: esp. 207–19 – but still too dismissive.

[11] Mouritsen 2001: esp. 91–92, 101; cf. 42: "a politically concerned public – outside the ruling circles – did not emerge until the rise of the bourgeoisie in the early modern period."

[12] Harris 1989: 175–284. For less dark views, see, for example, Nicolet 1980: 361–62, 372–73; Kühnert 1991: 60–61; Vanderbroeck 1987: 110–12; and the papers gathered in Humphrey 1991, especially perhaps Corbier's arguments for "alphabétisation pauvre, largement répandue" (p. 117; cf. Corbier 1987: 58–60).

[13] Brunt 1966: 23–25, with 14–16; on professions and skills of freedmen, see Treggiari 1969: 87–161. Mack himself (1937: 64, n. 126) had recognized that appeals to security of property in *contiones* make little sense unless a significant portion of the audience had some. Cf. Rudé 1964: 195–213, for the "respectable" constituents – artisans and shopkeepers – of French and English popular "mobs" in the eighteenth and early nineteenth centuries, which were similarly characterized by élite observers.

[14] Horsfall 1996.

deal of civic knowledge.[15] It is possible, too, that Roman historical dramas (*fabulae praetextae*) played a significant role in the creation of historical knowledge among the general public.[16] And we might speculate about the broadly educational consequences of lower-class participation in, or direct observation of, great civic rituals such as elections, the census, triumphs, sacrifices, processions, and spectacles. Note, for example, that mere voting in elections, exclusive of the preceding months of campaigning, has been estimated to have occupied a minimum of about fifteen days a year.[17]

It would seem that at least the potential existed for the crowd of the *contio* to gain a considerable level of political knowledge, that is, "the range of factual information about politics that is stored in long-term memory," which is the only basis on which a voting citizen can make informed choices, or for that matter even demand choices, about the matters that concern his individual and collective interests.[18] Deprived of an appropriate measure of political knowledge and information, the citizen who casts his vote in relative ignorance is destined to be the plaything of a manipulative élite which mediates and controls communication.[19] On the other hand, we must be careful not to set our standards of civic knowledge for ancient societies at a level unrealistically high even for modern, functioning "democracies" with independent, pervasive mass media. Opinion surveys showing that less than half of the American public could name their member of Congress, only 1.9 percent could name half of the Supreme Court justices, or that in 1986, halfway through the elder George Bush's second term as Vice President, 24 percent either failed to recognize his name or were uncertain of the

---

[15] On the *corona*, see chap. 6, n. 10. In the decade of the 50s an average of nearly ten criminal trials a year are *documented*: see Alexander 1990: nos. 241–351, minus a handful of cases that were either civil or did not actually come to trial. The *corona* is regularly identified with a popular audience like that of the *contio*: Cic. *Flac.* 66, 69; *Fin.* 2.74; 4.74; cf. the *Clodiana multitudo circumstans* who repeatedly disrupted the trial of Milo (Asc. 40–41 C).

[16] Wiseman 1994: esp. 1–22, and 1998: esp. 1–16, 52–59, 60–63. Unfortunately, since so little is known about the actual content of *praetextae*, and about the frequency of their performance in the late Republic (especially whether *praetextae* were performed on a significant portion of the annual fifty days or so of *ludi scaenici*), speculation along these lines tends to be uncontrolled: see Flower 1995. Perhaps one should distinguish between "classics" set in the distant past, such as Accius' *Brutus*, still being revived in the 40s (Flower, pp. 175–76), and ephemeral plays on contemporary themes, which might indeed be of "little long-term relevance" (p. 190). Horsfall 1996: 48, notes the absence of any clear allusion in *contiones* to knowledge drawn from *praetextae*; nor does the subject matter of known *praetextae* (listed in Wiseman 1998: 2–3) overlap notably with the range of historical allusions in Cicero's *contiones*.

[17] Nicolet 1980: 235. For the intense publicity of Republican politics, see chap. 1, n. 39; on the "politics" of electoral campaigns, see now Morstein-Marx 1998: esp. 263–74, and Yakobson 1999: esp. 148–83 and 211–25.

[18] Quotation from Delli Carpini and Keeter 1989: 10.

[19] Delli Carpini and Keeter 1989: 1ff.; Zaller 1992: esp. 6–16, 268ff.

office he held, make the point that modern standards of political knowledge among the citizen public may not be hard to match. "It is easy to underestimate how little typical Americans know about even the most prominent political events – and also how quickly they forget what for a time they do understand."[20]

INTRIGUING ALLUSIONS IN *DE LEGE AGRARIA* 2

We cannot, alas, ever conduct a public opinion survey of the *plebs urbana* – but as we have noted, that basic tool of social-science research anyway offers no direct access to pre-existing "true beliefs" of a population. Following Horsfall's lead, however, we can seek to use the published *contiones* that are available to us as an index, however imperfect and difficult to interpret, of the ideas, assumptions, symbolic associations, and "considerations" that constituted the political knowledge of their implied audience.[21] As was argued in the Introduction, published *contiones* should suit the rhetorical circumstances (including the implied audience) of their originals, even if they are not to be taken as records of what was actually said on the historical occasion; we may, therefore, assume that they reflect the level, and kind, of knowledge their authors thought it reasonable to presume in the sort of crowd who would assemble under circumstances like those of the original performance. Naturally, caution is required in assessing such allusions. Some are so fully contextualized that they explain themselves; in that case, they cannot tell much about an audience's prior state of knowledge. Setting these aside, it is also quite true that historical allusions in the *contiones* did not need to be fully understood, only to "work" rhetorically, perhaps by impressing the audience with the *speaker's* knowledge, triggering vague associations, or by overwhelming them with masses of obscure detail: for example, the substantially greater specificity and quantity of allusion in Cicero's first *contio* against Rullus' agrarian proposal than in the first senatorial speech does indeed give pause.[22] Nor can we make too much of any single example, which can always be explained away; we are looking for an overall pattern, a cumulative picture. With these provisos, however, the attempt is worth making, since the published *contiones* are, after all is said and done, the best evidence we possess for the intellectual and ideological world of the average Roman citizen. We should thrust aside our presuppositions

---

[20] Zaller 1992: 16–22; quotation at p. 16.   [21] Horsfall 1996: 46–50.

[22] Classen 1985: 311–12, 319, 334, 360–64. Thompson (1978: 85–99, 109) plausibly explains this fact as a consequence of the greater amount of rhetorical "work" to be done to pursuade the plebs to reject an agrarian law.

on this matter, including the "burden of proof" that might be mobilized to defend them, and ask ourselves what *this evidence* implies about the level of civic knowledge that a late-Republican orator presumed in his audience.

In the latter portion of the *Second Oration on the Agrarian Law* (76–97), Cicero trains his fire on the part of the bill that proposed to settle a colony at Capua, conjuring up the notion of an innate Campanian rebelliousness and arrogance with which colonists would inevitably be infected and thereby transformed into a terrible threat to Roman freedom.[23] For obvious reasons, this portion of the speech is relatively rich in historical allusions, and thus offers a particularly fruitful field for investigation of the level of historical knowledge presumed in the contional audience. Of special interest for present purposes is the climax of the attack (89–95), in which Cicero vividly recalls a previous attempt, twenty years earlier, to send a colony to Capua, and links its effects with Roman historical traditions about Campania.

Remarkable, to begin with, is the way in which Cicero introduces and fixes the reference to the previous colonial attempt, probably in 83 BC, which he wants to exploit at length as a dark precedent.[24] It is enough for him simply to name its founder, one Marcus Brutus, followed by the assertion that this man and Rullus now were the only "two men we have so far seen who were of a mind to move this entire commonwealth to Capua."[25] Cicero speaks equally cryptically of the destruction of those associated with the colony, including Brutus' own death (he was executed in the aftermath of the Lepidan rising, 77 BC): "they suffered all the severe punishments due to wicked men" (*omnis acerbissimas impiorum poenas pertulerunt*).[26] It is extraordinary that Cicero can fix the historical background for his powerful vignette of the revival of Capuan arrogance in Brutus' colony (chs. 92–94) with such brief and elliptical allusions, especially since this was an *abortive* attempt to resettle Capua; I suggest therefore that they function as mnemonic cues to summon up key elements of a familiar story.

Perhaps the most extraordinary of the historical allusions that are so dense in this portion of the speech comes in the vivid picture of renewed Campanian arrogance that follows. Cicero claims to have seen with his own

---

[23] Classen 1985: 336–43; Vasaly 1993: 231–43.

[24] For detailed analysis of this obscure and ephemeral project, see Harvey 1981 and 1982.

[25] *Leg. agr.* 2.89. After a prejudicial review of the policy of the *maiores* toward Capua, Cicero repeats the claim that "M. Brutus" and Rullus found fault with that tradition (2.92). Harvey 1982: 145–48 confirms the traditional identification of this Brutus with the Caesaricide's father rather than the homonymous praetor of 88.

[26] *Leg. agr.* 2.92. Thompson 1978: 98 doubts, perhaps unnecessarily, that Cicero can have expected his audience to have any recollection of the event.

eyes how, after Brutus' refoundation of Capua, the new colony's *praetor*, L. Consius, once a rather pathetic creature in Rome, was immediately so puffed up with the proud Campanian spirit that he imagined himself the equal of the Roman consuls. Indeed,

Iam vero vultum Consii[27] videre ferendum vix erat. Quem hominem "vegrandi macie torridum" Romae contemptum, abiectum videbamus, hunc Capuae Campano fastidio ac regio spiritu cum videremus, Blossios mihi videbar illos videre ac Vibellios. (*Leg. agr.* 2.93)

But now it was almost unbearable to look upon the face of Consius. A man "shrivelled up, of diminutive thinness," who was despised and loathed when we used to see him in Rome – when we watched him at Capua with a Campanian air of contempt and the pride of a king I felt as if I was watching the infamous[28] Blossii or Vibellii.

This allusion reaches back to minor characters in the Second Punic War, a century and a half before Cicero's speech, and perhaps beyond. The reference to Blossii must be to the Capuan brothers who in 210 BC had led a short-lived rebellion against the Roman dismemberment of their city which merits (just) one page in the sprawling annals of Livy.[29] The identity of the Vibellius or Vibellii mentioned is less clear to us. The best-remembered Vibellius may have been the formidable and rather colorful Campanian knight of the Second Punic War, Cerrinus Vibellius Taurea, whose single combat against a Roman in 215 and suicide at the consul's feet after the capture of Capua were dramatic episodes that exercised the literary art of historians.[30] Taurea may have been the Vibellius who best suited Cicero's interest in evoking implacable hatred of Rome; but if he wished, as seems likely, to call up Capuan arrogance and treachery as well, the other memorable Vibellius in the annals of Rome may also lie behind the allusion. A Campanian officer serving under Roman command in the war with Pyrrhus, D. Vibellius mutinied, treacherously seized Rhegium,

---

[27] Shackleton Bailey 1991: 18; cf. Harvey 1981, who confirms Shackleton Bailey's correction of the MSS (Clark and Marek both print *Considi*) and shows that the man is likely to have been of Campanian origin, despite *Romae contemptum . . . videbamus.*

[28] *Illos*: see *OLD* s.v. *ille*, 4. The plural *Blossios . . . Vibellios* may be merely rhetorical ("men such as": cf. Cic. *Cael.* 39; *Att.* 4.3.3), but in fact, as will be shown, with both names at least two men may well have readily come to mind.

[29] Contra Klebs, *RE* III (1897) 570. See Livy 27.3.4–5; one Marius Blossius, as *praetor* at Capua in 216, had played a role in encouraging support for Hannibal (23.7.8). Another significant Campanian Blossius was the advisor of Tiberius Gracchus (Dudley 1941); but he was from Cumae, while the context of the allusion best suits a Capuan, and in any case there is no reason to think he was remembered by the plebs as a treacherous or arrogant enemy of Rome (cf. Cicero's praise of Ti. Gracchus in this same speech).

[30] Jonkers 1963: 130; cf. Livy 23.8, 46–47; 24.8; 26.15–16.

a city entrusted to his unit to protect, and was ultimately scourged and beheaded in the very Forum itself to make an example of his punishment.[31] This reaches back more than two centuries from the date of Cicero's speech.

For this particular allusion to "work," we need not suppose, it is true, that most of the audience immediately placed the specific individuals whom I have just reviewed, along with their notorious deeds. But it would have been necessary for these names, belonging after all to only minor characters deep in the past, to be a good deal more readily recognizable to his audience as exemplars of Campanian rebelliousness and arrogance than they are even to professional Roman historians today. This allusion is unlike the lists (for example) of obscure Asian toponyms in the same speech (ch. 50) that were pretty clearly meant to sow suspicions of the law's scope;[32] here the names coincide with and contribute to the climax of a heavily sarcastic sentence, heightening the irony by the very absurdity of the comparison. That climax would simply have failed with an audience that did not otherwise recognize these as the names of great Campanian rebels or traitors to Rome.[33]

But the reference to "Blossii and Vibellii" does not exhaust the number of highly specific allusions to the Second Punic War. Cicero goes on to argue that the very richness of the Campanian soil produces such pride and excess:[34]

Ex hac copia atque omnium rerum adfluentia primum illa nata est adrogantia quae a maioribus nostris alterum Capua consulem postulavit,[35] deinde ea luxuries quae ipsum Hannibalem armis etiam tum invictum voluptate vicit. (2.95)

From this great wealth and abundance of all goods was born, first, that pride which demanded from our ancestors that one consul be from Capua, then, that extravagance which defeated Hannibal by means of pleasure, though he was still undefeated by the sword.

The allusions here are to two traditional stories told about Campania's defection to Hannibal in the aftermath of the battle of Cannae: that the Capuans had sent an embassy to Rome demanding, as a price for their continued assistance after the disaster, that one of the two consuls should

---

[31] Polyb. 1.7 (cf. Livy, *Per.* 12) with Walbank 1957–79: 1.53.

[32] See below, chap. 5, n. 161, with surrounding discussion.

[33] Classicists may test my claim by reading the sentence without historical commentary in a typical Latin class, and judging its impact upon the students. Cicero expected much more from *his* audience.

[34] On the environmental determinism Cicero makes use of here, Vasaly 1993: 233.

[35] I follow Marek's Teubner here rather than Clark's OCT.

be Campanian;[36] and that, after Capua went over to Hannibal, one winter in that luxurious place was enough to enervate his once battle-hardened army – an error that some soldiers claimed cost him the war.[37] It has been well observed that in these chapters Cicero makes use of "a centuries-old stereotype," that he presumes his audience's "familiarity with the commonplaces about Campania";[38] but what needs emphasis here is how these stereotypes and commonplaces appear to have been rooted in highly specific references to a shared historical tradition.[39]

Cicero's comment in his ethical treatise *On Ends* that even "men of the lowest class, with no aspiration to do great deeds, even artisans (*opifices*) delight in history" seems well borne out; and we may observe that his reference to *opifices*, a stereotyped constituent of the contional crowd, strongly suggests that he is alluding in the first instance to the oratorical practice of the *contio*.[40] The complex of allusions just examined to events of the third century BC – not all of them particularly salient – increases the likelihood that the many other references to relatively distant history in Cicero's preserved *contiones* were not lost on his plebeian audiences. In the *Sixth Philippic*, Cicero compares the Senate's order to Mark Antony not to attack Mutina with that to Hannibal not to approach Saguntum (*Phil.* 6.6; cf. §4); in view of what we have seen, it is plausible that he actually does expect his audience, or a significant portion of it, to be familiar with the precipitating event of the Second Punic War. In the speech for conferring the Mithridatic command on Pompey (the *Pro lege Manilia*), Cicero alludes to the destruction of Corinth in 146, the wars fought by *maiores nostri* against Antiochus the Great and the Aetolians (192–188), Philip V (200–197), and the Carthaginians, and the ages of Athenian, Carthaginian, and Rhodian sea mastery.[41] Sallust, for his part, makes a late-Republican consul refer (without citing specific names) to the *devotiones* (self-immolation) of the Decii in the late fourth and early third century,[42] while his tribunes frequently exploit public memory of landmarks in the old tradition of the "Struggle of the Orders," which could function as a sort of "charter myth" for contemporary *popularis* politics:[43] Memmius and especially Macer make

---

[36] Livy 23.6.6–8. Livy is skeptical about the story, which he found *in quibusdam annalibus* but not in his better authorities, in part because of its similarity to one told about the Latins.

[37] Livy 23.18.10–16.   [38] Vasaly 1993: 240, 236.

[39] Probably partly preserved by public display of booty from Capua (Horsfall 1996: 49: Livy 26.34.12), but the rhetorical exploitation of such historical anecdotes was surely of primary importance.

[40] *Fin.* 5.52. Horsfall 1996: 45.

[41] *Leg. Man.* 11–12, 14, 54–55. For the destruction of Corinth and Carthage, contrasted with the dissolution of Capua, see *Leg. agr.* 2.87–90; for further lists of great wars – probably a contional commonplace – cf. *Leg. agr.* 2.90 and Sall. *Hist.* 1.55.4 (Lepidus).

[42] Sall. *Hist.* 2.47.10; cf. Cic. *Red. pop.* 1.

[43] Cf. Cicero's use of the history of the tribunate in *Corn.* 1, frs. 48–54 Cr.

repeated play with the tradition of the two fifth-century Secessions of the Plebs, the first of which was associated with the creation of the tribunes, "protectors of all [plebeian] rights."[44] In one noteworthy passage of Macer's speech the establishment of the tribunate (in 494), the opening of plebeian access to the consulship (in 367), and the independence of popular legislation from senatorial ratification (in 337 and *c.* 287) are all alluded to in a manner far too brief and cryptic for ears unfamiliar with these turning points in a rather remote constitutional history.[45]

SPEECH AND MONUMENT

Cicero indulges in a good deal of historical name-dropping in his orations before the People. He recalls as ancestral *exempla* (models of conduct) the decision of "our ancestors" to commit two great conflicts (the Third Punic and Numantine Wars) and the destruction of two great cities (Carthage in 146 and Numantia in 133) to one man, Scipio Africanus (Aemilianus).[46] Before a popular audience in 43 he can merely mention Scipio's great friendship with C. Laelius to produce an invidious contrast with the close association of Mark Antony and his brother, Lucius Antonius.[47] Other great names from the distant past – (Fabius) Maximus and Marcellus, Rome's shield and sword against Hannibal,[48] as well as those paragons of virtue, (Fabricius) Luscinus, (Atilius) Calatinus, (Manlius) Acidinus, the elder Cato, (Furius) Philus, and Laelius[49] – are invoked so swiftly that they must have been instantly recognizable, if stereotyped figures.[50] One may be tempted to think that "honor rolls" of this kind presume little more knowledge than an acquaintance with the *topos* itself.[51] Possible; but we also

---

[44] Sall. *Iug.* 31.17; *Hist.* 3.48.1, 12, 15, 17: see Ogilvie 1965: 309–12, 489–90.

[45] Sall. *Hist.* 3.48.15: *ne vos ad virilia illa vocem, quo tribunos plebei, modo patricium magistratum, libera ab auctoribus patriciis suffragia maiores vostri paravere.* The length of McGushin's notes in his commentary (1992–94: 2.93–94) is a fair index of the knowledge presumed in the implied audience.

[46] *Leg. Man.* 60; cf. *Leg. agr.* 2.51.

[47] Accepting Shackleton Bailey's conjecture at *Phil.* 6.10: *nam hic inter illos <Laelius, ille> Africanus est.* He correctly infers that the younger Africanus ("Aemilianus") is meant, and thus the younger Laelius ("Sapiens," cos. 140), the chief speaker of the dialogue *De amicitia.*

[48] *Leg. Man.* 47, mentioned together with Scipio (Africanus). "Shield and sword," a Roman saying recorded by Posidonius: Plut. *Fab.* 19.3; *Marc.* 9.4.

[49] *Leg. agr.* 2.64. I use parentheses to clarify the reference; in each case Cicero triggers the allusion with a single name. See Thompson 1978: 92–94. *Perspexeratis* is, of course, rather a stretch, but it surely indicates that the "Philus" here cited is the cos. of 136, L. Furius, and Laelius, the friend of Scipio Aemilianus (see n. 47). For Fabricius, see now Berrendonner 2001 and Vigourt 2001.

[50] On the function of such exemplary figures in Roman collective memory, see below, n. 55.

[51] A list in Berrendonner 2001: 103, n. 38. Gendre and Loutsch 2001: 133 justly remark that "le grand homme romain n'est jamais seul: il est un maillon d'une série plus ou moins longue d'autres grands hommes"; Mencacci 2001: 430 sees this feature as a sign of the "genealogical" character of exemplarity.

should be on our guard against our own assumptions, our own tendency to perpetuate the ancient stereotype of ignorant audiences (*imperitissimi!*). Fabricius (cos. II 278) and Calatinus (cos. II 254) indeed belong to the common fund of rhetorical *exempla virtutis* ("models of excellence"), as their not infrequent use in Cicero's speeches before senatorial and equestrian audiences shows.[52] On the face of it, then, their appearance in the speech on the agrarian law suggests that the contional audience shared in a common civic-historical tradition with the élite. And, as we have already seen, Cicero does not "dumb down" his allusions for his plebeian audiences. He does not refer to Fabricius here by his well-known gentile name, as he does regularly elsewhere, but – presumably for the sake of homoeoteleuton (repetition of word-endings) – solely by his less familiar cognomen; and Acidinus (cos. 179), a much more obscure character from the third or second century BC, he elsewhere cites as an *exemplum* only once, in a personal letter to his equestrian friend, Atticus.[53]

The details of any single passage will not, of course, prove anything. But rather than systematically depreciating the possible significance of such allusions in accordance with an *a priori* "presumption of ignorance," I suggest that we interpret them against the background of recent work on the Roman sense of the past. Cicero's audiences belonged to a civic community, the *populus Romanus*, whose sense of identity was forged and maintained by an extraordinarily rich "collective memory" and a tight connection with the glorious past. Indeed, Roman mnemonic practices – for example the extraordinary monumentalization of Roman culture, the "reincarnation" of great figures of the past in noble funerals, or the ever-present invocation of the *maiores* ("ancestors") in the form of *exempla* within a continuous moral-political tradition – tended, to a noteworthy extent, to erase the boundary between past and present.[54] The *maiores* were the fount and measure of moral (and thus political) legitimacy, and paradigms

---

For Späth 2001: 382–83, on the other hand, it serves as evidence of the progressive abstraction of exemplary figures into an undifferentiated collectivity; but in fact the narratives associated with these names have great specificity and are rarely, if ever, interchangeable. With David 1980b: 72–73, I would suppose instead that a multitude of specific associations were sparked by mere names in such sequences.

52 Cic. *Pis.* 14, 58; *Sest.* 72, 143; *Cael.* 39; *Balb.* 50; *Planc.* 60. Calatinus appears also in the form "Caiatinus" (*MRR* 1.207, n. 1). On Fabricius, see Berrendonner 2001 and Vigourt 2001.

53 Cic. *Att.* 4.3.3, with Shackleton Bailey ad loc. and Oppermann 2000: 65–66. Cf. Münzer, *RE* xiv (1928) 1162.

54 On "collective memory" in the Republic (or "social memory" [Fentress and Wickham] or "cultural memory" [Jan and Aleida Assmann]: the terminological debate can be set aside here), see esp. Hölkeskamp 1996 and 2001; Späth 1998; and Hölscher 2001. On the blending of past and present, see the somewhat divergent perspectives of Hölkeskamp 2001: 125–26; Späth 1998: 42–47, esp. p. 45 on the "dual parallel temporalities" of the recent past and "le passé sublime"; Hölscher 2001:

of excellence (or the reverse) passed down to the present in exemplary narratives.[55] This "cult of the ancestors" may well be seen as a source of aristocratic power, authorizing the special claims of the nobility to leadership of the Republic;[56] but precisely to that extent, the plebeian mass must have embraced it and joined with the élite in a *common* orientation toward the communal past.

I suggest that the contional allusions we have thus far surveyed give a clear hint as to how this participation in a communal past was activated: through continual evocation in public speech, "playing off" the visible and ever-present monuments that filled the central spaces of the city. The audiences of public meetings lived in an environment saturated with history, or better, memory. As David Lowenthal reminds us, the chaos of lived experience is reduced to order by the constant activity of forgetting, selectively staved off by mnemonic cues;[57] the monuments and speech that came together in the Forum and other central public spaces will have functioned as just such cues to recollection, complementing each other in their work of creating, sustaining, and reshaping cultural memory to conform to present, lived experience. Returning for a moment to the "models of excellence" above, for example, Fabricius and Calatinus were certainly both inscribed in the "monumental history" of the center of the city, and some noteworthy commemoration of Acidinus as well, a founder of Aquileia

---

esp. 199–201, with the compelling observation that the effect of Republican monumentalization practices was to make the present a kind of "past for the future"; Stemmler 2001: 237, on "[die] Zeitlosigkeit des Historischen."

[55] On *exempla* and the "great men" who incorporated them, see now, in addition to the works cited in n. 54 above, Hölkeskamp 1995: 45–48; Coudry and Späth 2001 (including Späth's own chapter on Camillus, pp. 341–412); Stemmler 2000, and 2001 (also Haltenhoff 2001). David 1980b draws good connections with collective memory and the "visual culture" of Rome and its monuments. On the *maiores/mos maiorum* in particular, see now Bettini 2000: esp. 321–39; Blösel 2000 (see n. 56 below); and for Cicero specifically, Roloff 1938 (major extracts reprinted in Roloff 1967). On Cicero's use of *exempla* in general, see Schoenberger 1910; Rambaud 1953; in the correspondence, Oppermann 2000; cf. Litchfield 1914.

[56] Unpersuasive, however, is Blösel's insistence that, until Cicero, the *maiores* were an exclusive possession of the nobility (Blösel 2000). To attribute radical novelty to Cicero's use of the concept is inherently dubious, given what a small proportion of earlier Latin prose survives, especially of contional speech; it may be no accident that where our evidence is slightly less exiguous – among the fragmentary history and orations of Cato the elder – Blösel discerns a "failed" effort to broaden the concept of *maiores* so that it would apply not to the nobility alone but to the whole Roman People, as Cicero supposedly later "succeeds" in doing. (Contrast the more compelling conception of the whole *populus* as a quasi-family, for which the great *exempla* were a *common* inheritance from "elective" ancestors: Stemmler 2000: 192, and Mencacci 2001.) In general, Blösel's interesting essay tends to neglect the communicative contexts through which such ideologies will have been propagated throughout Roman society: the *laudatio funebris* (pp. 37–46) was not the only, or most important, site of communicative interaction between the élite and People.

[57] Lowenthal 1985: 204–5.

and a Fulvius by birth who had held the consulship with his brother, seems quite probable.[58] As for some of the other great names "dropped" by Cicero, we may recall that Fabius Maximus had erected on the Capitol a colossal bronze statue of Hercules by Lysippus, part of his rich booty from the sack of Tarentum in 209, with an equestrian statue of himself underneath.[59] Already after his early Ligurian victory, Fabius had built a temple of Honos outside the Porta Capena, which was later, after the capture of Syracuse, integrated into Marcellus' splendid complex of Honos et Virtus; that public monument, with its extraordinary display of plundered Greek art, clearly preserved both the brilliance of Marcellus' name and the traditional pairing with Fabius.[60] Finally, Scipio Aemilianus had dedicated in the Forum Boarium a temple of Hercules, vowed almost certainly in the Carthaginian war, bearing frescoes that are likely to have illustrated events of that conflict.[61] At least two equestrian statues of Aemilianus also stood on the Capitol, though in Cicero's day Metellus Scipio could mistake them for likenesses of P. Scipio Nasica Sarapio.[62] If we allow for a mutually reinforcing effect produced by allusions in mass oratory interacting with the material record, built into the urban landscape, of great men and the events associated with them (and vice versa), then the assumption that the references surveyed in this chapter would actually have been comprehended by their audiences seems far more probable than the reverse.

Explicit references to known monuments in the surviving *contiones* are rather scarce; this is not really surprising, given the relatively small sample of such speeches that are extant.[63] The most overt is Cicero's invidious comparison in the *Sixth Philippic* (delivered January 4, 43) of a new statue of Lucius Antonius, brother of Mark Antony, with the ancient monument

---

[58] Calatinus vowed and dedicated two prominent temples, Fides on the Capitol and Spes in the Forum Holitorium (Pietilä-Castrén 1987: 38–44; Ziolkowski 1992: 28–31, 152–54); his tomb and epitaph at the Porta Capena were also well known (Cic. *Sen.* 61; *Fin.* 2.116; *Tusc.* 1.13). Fabricius was honored by the Thurians with a statue in Rome (Plin. *HN* 34.32), and he would later (early Augustan era?) receive an *elogium* in the Forum, probably in the Basilica Paulli (*IIt* XIII.3.63; cf. now Chioffi, in Panciera 1996: 99–139); this double triumphator is likely to have left other memorials as well. Acidinus was honored with a statue at Aquileia (*ILLRP* 324). For family monuments, cf. the *III Marcelli* (see below, n. 172), the *Fornix Fabianus* (n. 167), and Metellus Scipio's group on the Capitol (n. 168).

[59] Plut. *Fab.* 22.6; Pape 1975: 8; Sehlmeyer 1999: 25–26.

[60] On the temple complex, see Pietilä-Castrén 1987: 48–51, 55–58; Ziolkowski 1992: 58–60. For the art, see Livy 25.40.1–3, Plut. *Marc.* 21; Cic. *Verr.* 2.4.120–21, with Pape 1975: 6–7, and Gruen 1992: 94–101.

[61] Pietilä-Castrén 1987: 134–38. Frescoes: Plin. *HN* 35.19 and below, n. 174. Coarelli 1988: 164–80.

[62] Cic. *Att.* 6.1.17, on Shackleton Bailey's persuasive interpretation (ad loc.).

[63] Horsfall 1996: 48–49.

of Q. Marcius Tremulus, consul of 306 and victor over the Hernici and Samnites in the "Second" Samnite War:[64]

In foro L. Antoni statuam videmus, sicut illam Q. Tremuli, qui Hernicos devicit, ante Castoris. o impudentiam incredibilem! (*Phil.* 6.13)

We look upon a statue of Lucius Antonius in the Forum, like the one before the Temple of Castor of Quintus Tremulus, who crushed the Hernici. How unbelievably shameless!

One might be tempted to dismiss this brief allusion to the distant memory of a triumphator over a people (the Hernici) long buried in the annals of history. Yet the location of Tremulus' statue – one of the oldest equestrian statues in Rome – before the Temple of Castor and Pollux, a common site of public meetings in the late Republic, must have assured wide acquaintance with it among Cicero's audience (see map 2, p. 44).[65] And in fact an image of Tremulus' statue almost certainly graced the denarii minted by a late-Republican member of his *gens*, one L. Marcius Philippus.[66] It would be reasonable to suppose that the Marcii Philippi saw fit to remind the People of this ancient hero of their clan not merely on one or two coin issues, but also in *contiones*[67] and of course in funeral eulogies, also held in the Forum. Polybius says that such eulogies included an enumeration of the great deeds of the dead man's ancestors, starting from the earliest; "whereby, since the reputation for excellence of great men is always being renewed, the renown of those who have achieved something splendid is immortalized, and the glory of those who have served their country well is made known to the general citizenry (γνώριμος δὲ τοῖς πολλοῖς) and passed down to posterity."[68] The variety of allusions on the

---

[64] Livy 9.43, with reference to the monument at §22; Plin. *HN* 34.23; cf. *IIt* XIII.1.71 (*de Anagnineis Herniceisq[ue]*). On the statue, see Sehlmeyer 1999: 182–83, who inclines to identify it on a coin of 56 (below, n. 66).

[65] Hölkeskamp 2001: 115–17 draws the statue, commemorating victory over the Hernici, into a "chain of associations" anchored by the temple of Castor, whose original was a monument of victory over the Latins at Lake Regillus. But note that according to the canonical traditions, as represented here by Livy 2.19–20 and Dion. Hal. 6.2–21, the Hernici did not actually participate in the Latin effort to restore king Tarquin.

[66] The problem is to decide which one: Crawford identifies the statue on *RRC* 293, a denarius of the future consul of 91, dating to *c.* 113 or 112; Sehlmeyer (1999: 57–60), who objects to that identification (above, n. 64), finds the statue on a coin dating to *c.* 56 (*RRC* 425/1; cf. Hersh and Walker 1984: table 2, dating to 57) minted probably by the future consul of 38.

[67] It was traditional, for example, to include praises of one's forebears in the speech of thanks to the People upon entering a magistracy: Cic. *Leg. agr.* 2.1.

[68] Polyb. 6.54.2; see the whole passage, §§53–54. Cf. Flower 1996: 128–58: "Designed as the climax of the whole funeral spectacle, [funeral orations] were *central in shaping the citizens' sense of a common past*" (p. 157, my emphasis). Cf. Flaig 1995b; Hölkeskamp 1996: 320–23; Döbler 1999: 101–6; Blösel 2000: 37–46.

late-Republican coinage to impressive services to the *res publica* performed by ancestors reaching back to the fourth, third, and early second centuries is only comprehensible against such a background of public verbal commemoration, often reinforced and prompted by monuments. If Cicero's allusion to Tremulus' statue is not seen in isolation but inserted into its topographic setting and related to specific and well-known social and political practices, it looks more like an attempt to exploit a variety of civic associations evoked by a familiar monument, including some awareness of a wider narrative to which the man and his statue belonged, than a strained effort to use the unnoticed statue of a forgotten patriot to denigrate a contemporary. A reference such as this suggests that a much wider and deeper stratum of historical and civic knowledge is likely to lie hidden or half-submerged beneath the surface of the oft-cursory explicit allusions in our texts.[69]

If so, then where might we find further clues to the extent of this knowledge? The intersection of rhetoric, monument, and numismatic representation just noted in the case of Tremulus' statue encourages a look at the Republican coinage and the "monumental landscape" of Republican Rome for some corroboration of the impression we have gained thus far from allusions in Ciceronian *contiones*. The coins are the place to start, for in their combination of a remarkably demanding allusiveness in their imagery and legends with a clear orientation of "message" toward the politically engaged citizen, they offer a thought-provoking parallel to the picture of contional rhetoric that I have been developing in this chapter.

The most noteworthy development in the coin-types of the late Republic (strictly speaking, already from 137 BC) is the profusion of allusions, explicit or symbolic, to the *res gestae* (achievements) of ancestors and other relatives. This is often interpreted as a perversion of traditional public-spiritedness into an increasingly personal, individualistic ethos;[70] but the distinction is exposed as illusory when we recognize that such allusions to inherited glory typically refer to signal services *to the res publica*.[71] We might recall Polybius' description of the recitation of the great deeds of ancestors at noble funerals; as the passage quoted above shows, the Megalopolitan observer, at least, saw the practice as an inspiring celebration of men who had *served their*

---

[69] Cf. David 1980b: 72–73.

[70] See, for example, Alföldi 1956; even M. H. Crawford 1974: 712–44 adopts a forced dichotomy between "public types" and "private types." It should be noted as well that supposedly "private" types may in fact not be "private" at all: the tendency to ferret out possible allusions to the moneyer's forebears has clearly at times eclipsed the symbolic meaning of a type (e.g. the coin of Palicanus discussed above, pp. 51–53).

[71] See now Meadows and Williams 2001: esp. 44.

country with distinction.[72] The "monumentalization" of the coinage[73] from 137 through a proliferation of allusions to ancestral deeds may well reflect increased competition for public support and the honors it conferred, and thus may indeed serve as a visible index of one element of the crisis of the late Republic; but the *character* of the allusions does not reflect a dramatic reorientation of political values such as has often been postulated.

Since the *tresviri monetales* (or, for a brief period from 44 BC, *quattuorviri*) who were responsible for striking coins were typically young officials at the beginning of a senatorial career, aspiring to electoral success in the immediate or very near future,[74] it is generally and reasonably acknowledged that references to ancestral exploits must have been intended largely to further their chances by advertizing their claims to *dignitas*. For example, when Faustus Sulla, son of the former dictator, facing in 56 BC a quaestorian election the next year, ordered an issue of *denarii* with a representation of the famous monument on the Capitol, dedicated by King Bocchus of Mauritania, depicting his father's reception of the bound Jugurtha (figure 4) – a deed which at last decided the Numidian War when Sulla was at the very rank (quaestorian) to which Faustus now aspired – there can be little doubt that his purpose was to establish a claim to inherited *virtus* in view of the upcoming election; successfully, we might add, since he was quaestor in 54.[75] C. Memmius in 56, on the other hand, facing a tribunician contest the next year, not only decorates his coins with agreeable references to the plebeian god Ceres and the contribution of the Memmian family to her honor in Rome, but places on the reverses of about half of his *denarii* an image of a trophy and a kneeling captive, helpfully labelled C. MEMMIVS

---

[72] Polyb. 6.54.2: ἡ τῶν εὐεργετησάντων τὴν πατρίδα γίνεται δόξα.

[73] So Meadows and Williams 2001, recasting the question in exactly the right way.

[74] On the mint officials, see M. H. Crawford 1974: 598–604; Burnett 1977: 37–44. The careers of the moneyers (on Crawford's chronology: pp. 708–11) indicate that they typically held this office within a few years of the quaestorship (in the 50s, it seems, usually a year or two *before* that magistracy), thus on average, probably, at not far from thirty years of age. *Monetales* must often have been striking coins immediately before their next election – quaestorian, tribunician (see the cases of C. Memmius and Q. Pompeius Rufus in the 50s: *RRC* 427 and 434), or even aedilician (see the "aedilician" types of some coins: M. H. Crawford 1974: 739, n. 3). This is not to say that other influences besides personal electoral hopes will not have impinged upon the choice of types; note that, according to Burnett's attractive suggestion, the moneyers may have been appointed by the consuls, often relatives themselves.

[75] *RRC* 426/1: see further below. "Famous": according to Plut. *Sull.* 6.1–2 and *Mar.* 32.2–3, its dedication had come near to sparking civil war. The date of the series seems fairly secure (M. H. Crawford 1974: p. 88; Hersh and Walker 1984: cf. table 2) in contrast to that of many other late-Republican issues, whose chronological indeterminacy is somewhat obscured by Crawford's rather forceful presentation in his catalog (cf. his discussion of the individual problems at *RRC*, 47–102, along with the objections of Hersh 1977: 24–27, and Hersh and Walker 1984). In general, I shall cite only Crawford's date unless a chronological divergence is relevant to the argument.

Figure 4 Reverse of denarius of Faustus Cornelius Sulla, 56 BC (*RRC* 426/1). L. Sulla, father of the moneyer, seated above; Mauretanian king Bocchus kneeling on left, with olive-branch; captive Jugurtha, with bound hands, kneeling on right.

IMPERATOR, just as the very man thus honored, the moneyer's homonymous uncle, having returned from a command in Bithynia-Pontus whose rewards so bitterly disappointed Catullus, was preparing his candidacy for the consulship.[76] Evidently, a "double" electoral appeal.

As to the "target audience," the manifestly "popular" nature of many of the types strongly implies that these symbolic appeals were directed above all to the People – the voting populace. Various types promise a spectacular or otherwise generous aedileship (an office that will normally have followed service as *monetalis*, sometimes immediately).[77] Particularly noteworthy are symbols that celebrate such "popular" institutions and ideas as the suffrage or *provocatio*, and the association of both with *Libertas*.[78] When two different late-Republican Cassii place images on their coins that link "Freedom" with the *lex Cassia tabellaria* of 137 – a law which introduced the secret ballot in trials before the *Populus* except for *perduellio*, and, as a Ciceronian reference of 56 claims, was seen as a highly "popular" expression

[76] *RRC* 427/1, with Crawford's comments. Crawford's date for the coin is corroborated by Hersh and Walker 1984: table 2; a Macedonian command for one C. Memmius in the later second century – otherwise an attractive object of reference (cf. *MRR* III.141) – is a mirage: Kallet-Marx 1995: 352. Since Memmius was laying claim to a substantial military victory, Catullus' criticism of his meanness takes on stronger significance.

[77] M. H. Crawford 1974: 739, n. 3. Note, e.g., the coins of the Minucii noted below.

[78] Suffrage: *RRC* 292/1 (113 or 112 BC), the famous voting scene, complete with *pontes*, on *denarii* of P. Nerva. (See B. A. Marshall 1997: 67–68.) *Provocatio*: *RRC* 301/1 (110 or 109 BC) and 270 (125 BC), of the Porcii Laecae, with Crawford's commentary. For references to the *lex Cassia tabellaria*, see below, n. 79. Cf. the celebration of tribunician speech on *RRC* 473/1 (45 BC): above, pp. 51–53. On the significance of *Libertas*, see Weinstock 1971: 133–42, and now Ritter 1998 (see, however, below, n. 79).

(or defense) of the People's freedom but detested by the leading senators as an inducement to mob-rule – we may doubt that they were currying favor with the senatorial élite.[79]

All this, of course, presupposes that citizens were actually thought to notice the Republican images and legends on the coins. But I see no good reason to reject that reasonable assumption, which is in any case obviously suggested by the attention lavished on producing this complex profusion of images from 137: the characterization of the coinage (from that date) as *monuments* is again apposite.[80] The argument against a "propagandistic" function for Roman coinage was developed in an Imperial context; it has little pertinence to the Republic, in which the citizen's vote actually counted and had to be courted by a variety of means, and whose electorate – those who frequented the city with some regularity – will have had a much broader and deeper common fund of knowledge of their political leaders, their common physical environment and political traditions, and thus a rich backdrop of allusion to be drawn upon by those wishing to influence them, than the extremely diverse inhabitants of the Roman Empire.[81] In the present context, "propaganda" is likely to be a misleading concept, suggesting a degree of dissemination, centralized control, and tendentious manipulation of ideas that is quite alien to the Republic; the coin-types are better seen as instruments of "publicity" than "propaganda."[82] But to deny that the common citizenry was capable of working out their sometimes complex iconographic language[83] presumes what for present purposes is the point at issue and conflicts directly with the signs we have noted that

---

[79] *RRC* 266/1 (126 BC, C. Cassi[ius]), described below, p. 86, and *RRC* 428/2 (55 BC, Q. Cassius Longinus) with *Libertas* on the obverse and a judicial voting-tablet on the reverse. Cic. *Sest.* 103. Ritter 1998 vindicates the "popular" character of the allusions to the *lex Cassia tabellaria*, but surprisingly rejects any direct connection between *libertas* and voting rights, opting instead for an indirect reference to the strengthening of *provocatio*; but see Cic. *Corn.* 1, fr. 50 Cr *Cassiam qua lege suffragiorum ius potestasque convaluit*, with Asconius' commentary (78 C). Whether the *lex Cassia* was *originally* unpopular with the nobility is not clear: chap. 8, n. 18.

[80] Meadows and Williams 2001: 42–43; cf. already Belloni 1976.

[81] M. H. Crawford 1983, focused as it is on the Imperial coinage, is presumably not intended to contradict Crawford's own stated views on the *Republican* coinage, e.g. 1974: 728: "Once the possibilities had been seen, the consequences of the Lex Gabinia [i.e. of 139, introducing the secret ballot for elections] provided a consistent inducement to potential contestants for office to use the coinage for self-advertisement." Most responses to Crawford (see especially Wallace-Hadrill 1986, and most recently, Levick 1999) also concentrate on the Imperial coinage and do not distinguish sharply enough the peculiarly Republican context of the Republican coinage; see, however, now the good discussion of Flower 1996: 79–86.

[82] See Belloni 1976; good remarks by Hölscher 2001: 203, and Meadows and Williams 2001: 49.

[83] As does Hölscher 1994: esp. 83–85 and 234, n. 27 (similarly, Holliday 2002: 208–9). This conclusion belongs in the context of Hölscher's broader thesis that in the last century or so of the Republic, the urban plebs was an uncomprehending witness to the historical allusions and ideological references on public monuments, constructed (on this argument) *by* the aristocracy *for* a more or less exclusively

the coinage was an instrument of political self-advertisement with the electorate. After all, to defend that thesis it would not be necessary to show that every numismatic allusion, however récherché, will have been instantly understood by the shopkeeper or soldier who turned the coin over in his palm. Coins, like any monument, will often have had what we might call first-order allusions – an easily understood symbolic reference to broadly held values – and second-order allusions – more obscure or elaborate references demanding more specific knowledge. For example, on the *denarius* of C. Cassius (Longinus, probably), minted around 126, which shows on the obverse a voting-urn beside the traditional head of the goddess Roma and on the reverse a personification of *Libertas* in a chariot, holding the rod and cap of freedom (*vindicta, pileus*), we may perceive a straightforward first-order allusion to the idea that suffrage was intimately linked with Freedom, the special prize of the Roman citizen, and a second-order allusion to the recent *lex Cassia tabellaria* carried by a relative (perhaps even the moneyer's father), L. Cassius Longinus Ravilla.[84] In this case, even the second-order allusion is to a political change so recent, important, and controversial that it may readily have been picked up by a citizen who voted and frequented public meetings.

If, then, we may consider the iconography and legends on Republican coins to be an index of plebeian civic consciousness parallel and complementary to the references in extant public speeches, the hypothesis of a relatively impressive level of civic *memoria* seems again to correspond most straightforwardly with the evidence. We find allusions on the coins to Romulus' Sabine War and King Tatius, Ancus Marcius' foundation of Ostia, and the sacrifice of a heifer to Diana under Servius Tullius that assured Rome's primacy over the Latins.[85] On *denarii* minted by Marcus Brutus the Caesaricide, L. Brutus, first consul and founder of the Republic, is linked with *Libertas* in one issue, on another with C. Servilius Ahala, whose killing of Sp. Maelius in 439 was a frequently invoked *exemplum* of Republican freedom.[86] Great – but chronologically remote – victories are invoked, such as Panormus (250) and the Aegates Islands (241) in the First

---

aristocratic audience (esp. 1984: 12–19). His conception of a development from the "Sachlichkeit" of earlier Roman public art, expressive of common political values, to the "polemical," "demagogic," and increasingly "spectacular" appeals for personal allegiance directed at the late-Republican masses (the turning point coming around 200 BC) is sketched out more fully in Hölscher 1980: 352–55.

[84] *RRC* 266/1, with Crawford's commentary and Ritter's remarks on the identification of the urn (1998: 609–10); cf. Marshall 1997: 63–64. On the link with suffrage, see n. 79 above. Cf. no. 428/2, 55 BC, of Q. Cassius (above, n. 79).

[85] *RRC* 344 (cf. 404/1), 346/3–4; 372/1 (cf. 335/9).

[86] *RRC* 433 (54 BC). Brutus traced his ancestry to both men.

Punic War;[87] Marcellus' *spolia opima* and five consulships, and L. Aemilius Paullus' three imperatorial acclamations, all receive commemoration in the waning years of the Republic.[88] "Badges" such as the encircling torque of the Manlii Torquati or the elephant's-head of the Metelli allude to great events of the fourth and third century whose legendary status among men of the first can hardly be doubted.[89] An ancestor's famous deeds of valor were a particularly popular source of allusion, though they might date back centuries: besides the reference just mentioned to T. Manlius Imperiosus' despoliation of the massive Gaul's neckwear, particularly noteworthy are the probable allusions on coins of the late second century to famed warriors of the Second Punic War, M. Servilius Pulex Geminus (cos. 202), who killed no fewer than twenty-three men in single combat,[90] and Catiline's great-grandfather, M. Sergius Silus (pr. 197), who after losing his right hand and suffering a total of twenty-three wounds in his first two campaigns, continued to take the field for many years thereafter. (Sergius is shown upon a rampant horse, appropriately enough holding both a sword and an enemy's severed head in his single, left hand.[91]) We have already noted the intersection of extant contional rhetoric and the coins in the case of Q. Marcius Tremulus' statue; if public interest in such an ancient figure seems to strain credulity, one might point for comparison to the effort of P. Plautius Hypsaeus, the Pompeian protégé later to be one of Milo's rivals for the consulship of 52, to add an ancient consul to his marginally

---

[87] Panormus: see below, n. 89. Aegates Islands: *RRC* 305 (109 or 108 BC). The victory of C. Lutatius Catulus was particularly memorable, not merely because it brought an end to the First Punic War, but did so in the consulship of the victor's own brother, and the coiner's namesake, Q. Lutatius Cerco. Cf. the reference to T. Flamininus' defeat of Philip V on the *denarius* of T. Q[uinctius] (*RRC* 267/1, 126 BC).

[88] Marcellus: *RRC* 439 (50 BC), of [P. Cornelius Lentulus] Marcellinus; cf. *RRC* 329/2. Paullus: *RRC* 415 (62 BC), of [L. Aemilius] Lepidus Paullus.

[89] Torquatan torques: *RRC* 295 (113 or 112 BC); 337/1–2 (91 BC, coin of D. Silanus, presumably a descendant of D. Iunius Silanus Manlianus, pr. 141); 411 (65 BC). For the story, see especially Livy 7.10.13: [sc. *Torquati cognomen*] *celebratum deinde posteris etiam familiae honori fuit*. For its earlier fame, see Claud. Quad. ap. Gell. *NA* 9.13.4–20 and the numerous Ciceronian references cited in *MRR* 1.119. Metellan elephants: *RRC* 262 (128 BC), 263/1 (127 BC), 269 (125 BC), 369 (82–80 BC), 374 (81 BC), 459 (47–46 BC). For the victory at Panormus in 250 and the capture of 60 to 142 Carthaginian elephants, see Walbank 1957–1979: 1.102–3; for Metellus' temple of Ops on the Capitol, dedicated to commemorate that triumph, see below, n. 168.

[90] Servilius: *RRC* 264/1 (127 BC) of C. Servilius [Vatia]. See Livy 45.39.16; Plut. *Aem.* 31.4.

[91] *RRC* 286 (116 or 115 BC), M. Sergi[us] Silus. See Plin. *HN* 7.104–6 for Sergius' preeminence in *virtus* throughout Roman history. Compare also *RRC* 419/1 (61 [Crawford] or 58 BC [Hersh and Walker]), fairly certainly alluding to a youthful feat of M. Aemilius Lepidus (cos. II 175) presumably in the Second Punic War: at about fifteen years of age, he slew an enemy, saved a citizen, and received the honor of a statue on the Capitol (Val. Max. 3.1.1). *RRC* 429/1, 454/1–2, 513 and 514 are also likely to have commemorated deeds of valor, though the specific points of reference are now lost to us because of the lacunose state of our sources.

noble heritage by making much on the reverses of his coins of 60 and 58 of the capture of Privernum in 329 by C. Plautius Decianus – changing the general's name to "C. Hypsaeus" in order to make the spurious connection clearer.[92]

As in the contional allusions with which I began, some of these references are virtually self-explanatory and thus require little to no prior knowledge to put together: Hypsaeus' advertisement of his false forebear's deed, for example, is helpfully labelled "Gaius Hypsaeus, consul, captured Privernum."[93] One can readily understand why that minor entry in the annals of Rome needed full elucidation. But many other allusions on the late-Republican coinage require considerable background knowledge to be appreciated in the manner that seems likely to have been intended. For example, on coins of two Cassii Longini minted in the late sixties and mid-fifties, heads of Vesta on the obverse and voting-tablets on the reverse clearly recall the stern but "popular" justice meted out in the famous trial of the Vestals in 113 by their relative of a few generations back, L. Cassius Longinus Ravilla – none other, in fact, than the proposer of the *lex Cassia tabellaria* celebrated on other types.[94] There is nothing "generic" about this reference, which attempts to extract from the collective memory an event of remarkable specificity just passing the threshold of personal recollection into oral tradition.[95] Equally challenging allusions are not rare.[96] In general, we must

---

[92] *RRC* 420 (60 [Crawford] or 57 [Hersh and Walker]) and 422 (58 BC). Hypsaeus could only legitimately boast of one consular ancestor, in 125 (Gruen 1974: 107, n. 62), which makes his efforts to advertise ancient nobility here, complete with obverse types that suggest divine descent from Neptune and Leuconoe (*RRC* 420/1–2), all the more . . . understandable.

[93] *RRC* 420 C YPSAE[VS] COS PRIV[ERNUM] CEPIT (or CAPTV[M]: *RRC* 422). Cf. *RRC* 427/2, MEMMIVS AED. CERIALIA PREIMVS FECIT, making a fairly obscure reference to an event of 211 BC.

[94] *RRC* 413 (63 [Crawford] or 60 BC [Hersh and Walker]), 428/1 and 428/2 (55 BC), the last-named with a clearly labelled *Libertas* on the obverse. See Marshall 1997: 64–66. For the Cassian coins alluding to the other most memorable achievement of Ravilla, see above, n. 79. For the "popular" character of Ravilla's judicial severity, see Asc. 45–46 C; Cic. *Brut.* 97; for the trial, Gruen 1968: 127–31.

[95] Besides the usual oral media of commemoration, the memory of this event must also have been cued by the temple to Venus Verticordia constructed near the southeast end of the Circus Maximus to expiate the sacrilege: Iul. Obs. 37; Ovid, *Fasti* 4.157ff.; see Richardson 1992: 411; F. Coarelli, *LTUR* v.119. Despite Crawford ad *RRC* 463/1, it is tempting to conjecture that the Venus, holding scales, shown on the reverses of coins of one MN. CORDIVS, is a punning Verti*cordia*.

[96] Another notable example: an issue, variously dated (*RRC* 401, 71 [Crawford] or 65 BC [Hersh and Walker]), minted by one "Manius Aquilius, son of Manius, grandson of Manius" shows a bust of *Virtus* (so labelled) on the obverse, and on the reverse, a soldier helping a kneeling figure to its feet, apparently from a prostrate position, which bears below the label SICIL[IA]. The moneyer's name, his patronymic unusually extended to the name of his grandfather, appears on the sides of the image. That grandfather, Manius Aquilius, had, as consul and then proconsul, put down the great Sicilian slave revolt in 100, thus restoring the major source of grain to Rome's urban market. The allusion, then, is evident – to anyone who saw or had heard of Aquilius' victory some three

beware of supposing that references that seem remote from our vantage point would in fact have been so in a lively civic culture as dependent on *memoria* as was that of Republican Rome. When M. Aemilius Lepidus, the future Caesarian triumvir, advertises the (legendary) guardianship over the kingdom of Egypt exercised by his famous homonymous ancestor, the censor of 179,[97] this might strike one as a pretty obscure piece of family lore, were it not for the great contemporary controversy over the status of Rome's Egyptian legacy which we can also trace in Cicero's speech against the Rullan agrarian bill (see below, pp. 113–14) and then, from 59, over the legitimacy of Ptolemy Auletes, expelled from his throne in 58.[98]

The coins, too, help to flesh out the suggestion made above about the "cuing" of historical memory by the monuments of the city of Rome, for some coin-types manifestly require a sort of "triangulation" with a well-known monument to effect their allusion. Faustus Sulla's reference to his father's capture of Jugurtha, ending the Numidian War in 105, has already been mentioned (see figure 4, p. 84). What is of particular interest here is that the coin-type is a *representation of a representation*: what is shown on the coin must be the monument on the Capitol depicting the moment of the handover. The only legend on the reverse, FELIX (= Sulla), is quite inadequate to fix the allusion to the event for anyone unfamiliar with the monument, while the composition, on the other hand, is sufficiently unique to suggest the identification at once to anyone who knew the Capitol.[99] Another famous issue makes use of general public acquaintance with the ancient Minucian Column which, according to (no doubt spurious) tradition, the People had paid for by subscription and set up outside the Porta Trigemina (see map 1, p. 43) in honor of L. Minucius Augurinus in 439 BC, after (so went the story) he had informed the Senate about the

---

decades before the minting of the coin, his *ovatio* on the Capitol, or, perhaps, the mutual slaughter of his prisoners that brought a climax of pathos to his celebratory spectacle (Greenidge–Clay, 113). (See now Holliday 2002: 116–17, whose attractive conjecture that the scene refers to a monument harmonizes well with my larger argument.) For one who does not, the composition makes little sense, for it is only scantily labelled, nor does it easily fit into any common, generic patterns of imagery on the Republican coins. Crawford's date would suit the allusion particularly well, since that was the year in which the great Spartacan slave revolt in Italy was finally crushed.

[97] *RRC* 419/1 (61 [Crawford] or 58 BC [Hersh and Walker]). No other evidence for this story before Justin (30.2–3; 31.1) and Valerius Maximus (6.6.1): see Gruen 1984: 680–82. For another reverse in the series celebrating M. Aemilius Lepidus, see n. 91.

[98] A resumé of the events in Wiseman 1985: 54–62.

[99] *RRC* 426/1. Consideration of how the allusion works virtually necessitates identification of the scene on the coin as one of the Bocchus monument itself rather than merely of Sulla's signet ring (Plut. *Mar.* 10.5–6; *Sull.* 3.4; *Mar.* 806d; Val. Max. 8.14.4; Cic. *Cat.* 3.10 hardly demonstrates that the designs on aristocrats' signet rings were familiar to the urban populace); there may, of course, have been no real difference between the two compositions (Hölscher 1980: 358, n. 54).

tyrannical plot of Sp. Maelius and then, after the conspirator was killed, had as *praefectus annonae* distributed Maelius' hoard of grain at a generously subsidized price.[100] In *c.* 135 and 134 two descendants (probably brothers), C. and Ti. Minucius Augurinus, recall the stories surrounding their ancient ancestor by placing the column at the center of their reverses, flanked on each side by sheaves of wheat; on the left of the column, one figure seems to be distributing loaves of bread – which looks like a fairly direct allusion to Augurinus' benefaction – while on the right, another carries an augural staff (*lituus*) – either a reference to the name both of the great ancestor and of current coiners, or to the Minucius who was among the five plebeians first inducted into the augural college in 300 (figure 5).[101] The allusion is certainly there, and it could hardly have been more apposite, at a time when the slave war in Sicily had caused, or was still causing, severe interruptions to the grain supply of Rome (one happens to be recorded in 138);[102] we might well suppose that the coins promise a subsidy or grain distribution from members of a clan famed for such activity, or perhaps at least a generous aedileship.[103] One wonders how far the coins might have prompted in some viewers recollection of the whole story, including Maelius (whose punishment was monumentalized by the Aequimaelium, an open space at the site of Maelius' razed house) and his execution by Ahala (whose portrait, as we have seen, M. Brutus placed on his coins in the mid-fifties).[104] However that may be, the fact remains that the allusion to L. Augurinus' ancient benefaction is "fixed" not by explicit labelling but by the association of the homonymous moneyer's name with images

---

[100] Pliny alone mentions the column explicitly (*HN* 34.21; cf. 18.15); cf. Dion. Hal. 12.4.6 (statue, erected by the Senate), Livy 4.16.2–4 (gilded bull). Comparison of the two Pliny passages makes fairly clear that the statue shown atop the column on the coins (see n. 101) must by his time have commonly been *taken* to be of Minucius, although the monument was probably in fact an ancient tomb or even the shrine of a semi-divine progenitor of the *gens* (see now Wiseman 1998: 90–105).

[101] *RRC* 242/1, 243/1, with Wiseman 1998: 90–105, who rejects Crawford's view that the figure atop the column is a statue of L. Minucius himself, which is the identification he prefers for the figure on the left. (Cf. M. Torelli, *LTUR* 1.305–6 for yet another interpretation.) On the significance of the coins, see now also Meadows and Williams 2001: 43–44. It remains unclear whether the figures flanking the column represent statues in a monumental complex (Richardson 1992: 96), or were added to the composition by the moneyers to create a richer, but more demanding, complex of allusions to the dual traditional characteristics of the Minucian house (Wiseman 1998: 104 and 105 seem ambiguous). The date of the coins is inexact (cf. M. H. Crawford 1974: 55–65, with Hersh 1977: 24–27).

[102] Garnsey and Rathbone 1985: 22.

[103] See Coarelli 1997: 300–301, for "la tradizionale vocazione 'annonaria' della *gens Minucia*."

[104] For the Aequimaelium, see Richardson 1992: 3; G. Pisani Sartorio, *LTUR* 1.20–21. Brutus' coin: *RRC* 433 (54 BC). On the nature of the story, which illustrates the virtues of a paternalistic response to the kind of popular desires that demagogues were wont to exploit, see Momigliano 1969: 331–49.

Figure 5 Reverse of denarius of Ti. Minucius Augurinus, *c.* 134 BC (*RRC* 243/1). Minucian Column, flanked by two illustrious ancestors. (Precise identification of the three figures remains controversial: see nn. 100, 101.)

among which the essential "cue" is a well-known monument, the *columna Minucia.*[105]

My suggestion is, then, that the late-Republican coinage can be viewed as a medium of communication comparable to late-Republican mass oratory in certain ways significant for the present research: above all, its apparent intended "audience," and its frequent use of relatively subtle, yet highly specific allusions to the services to the Republic of great men of the past, which place high demands upon the civic consciousness of their viewers. This would strengthen what I have argued is, in any case, the most straight-forward interpretation of the challenging historical allusions in contional speech, that is, that they appear to presume considerable civic *knowledge* in their listeners, not ignorance. Of course, one is just as free to play down the significance of the numismatic references, treated separately, as that of the oratorical ones. But it becomes harder to do so when the two media are considered together, as distinct and complementary testimony to the same phenomenon. And it becomes harder yet when one contemplates the sheer monumentality of the urban environment: the visible, public *memoria* of the Roman People.

---

[105] Note also *RRC* 425 (Marcian aqueduct, and perhaps the statue of its builder, Q. Marcius Rex [pr. 144] on the Capitol: see Crawford's comments, and, contra, Sehlmeyer 1999: 58–60; the aqueduct was "claimed" as well by the Aemilii Lepidi: see *RRC* 291); *RRC* 363 (statue of Marsyas: see below, n. 144; the column in the background is presumably intended to help the interpreter recognize the allusion to a monument in the Comitium, where more than one conspicuous column stood; which column this is, or whether it is meant to be individuated at all, remains uncertain [Sehlmeyer 1999: 57]).

MONUMENTAL MEMORY

The central spaces of the city, in particular the Forum and the Capitol, were a veritable museum of Roman history. The ubiquitous and persistent cuing of collective memory by means of monuments defining the urban landscape gives further impetus to the idea that the mass of allusions – both visible and "merely" verbal – among which the urban plebs lived their lives was no neutral backdrop but a series of vivid reminders, needing only a subtle prompt to be evoked and set to work in a specific discursive context.[106] This idea tends to be more readily embraced in the study of major monuments than it usually is in connection with coins and speech – though the basis of this discrimination is, I would argue, very doubtful – since of course it is readily agreed that the point of a *monumentum* is to perpetuate *memoria*. It certainly is easier to substantiate the assumption that the audience "heard" and responded to the historical references made in major monuments rather than in the media that have thus far been examined. We might recall, for example, the uproar that divided the city over Sulla's apparent appropriation of the victory over Jugurtha by means of the monument that King Bocchus dedicated on the Capitol: this was no internal squabble among the aristocracy within the walls of the Curia, but an explosive competition for *gloria* among the citizenry.[107] Later, in 65, great crowds came to marvel at Marius' restored trophies on the Capitol, filling the area with their applause and pouring out tears of joy at the sight of the great man's image, arousing grave concern in the Senate for obvious reasons;[108] and in the wake of Caesar's victory at Pharsalus, in 48, a crowd destroyed the gilded statues of Sulla and Pompey on the Rostra.[109] The urban plebs' behavior on such occasions gives force to Tonio Hölscher's observation that monuments are "provocations" demanding undeviating assent or forcing rejection: "Neutrality is impossible."[110] But such responses,

---

[106] For historical commemoration in Republican art generally, see now the important monograph by Peter Holliday (Holliday 2002). On collective memory and the monuments, with a focus on the embedded memory of the Comitial area, see now especially Hölkeskamp 1996: 305–8, and 2001; Hölscher 2001. Cf. more generally Favro 1988. Vasaly 1993: 62–75 also offers a detailed picture of the monumental setting of the Rostra, which, however, needs revision in the light of Sehlmeyer 1999: esp. 103–8. Like Hölkeskamp, Vasaly adopts F. Coarelli's circular Comitium, rejected above (pp. 47–48).

[107] Plut. *Sull.* 6.2: τῆς πόλεως ὅσον οὔπω διακεκαυμένης ὑπ' ἀμφοῖν. Note that, according to Plutarch, Bocchus' "target audience" was the *People* as well as Sulla (τόν τε δῆμον ἅμα θεραπεύων, 6.1).

[108] Plut. *Caes.* 6; Suet. *Iul.* 11; Vell. Pat. 2.43.4.

[109] Chap. 2, n. 82. Compare the destruction of Cn. Piso's statues in AD 20: Tac. *Ann.* 3.14.4, with the *Senatus Consultum de Pisone Patre*, lines 155–58.

[110] Hölscher 2001: 207.

too, imply that crowds brought a pool of communal knowledge to their interpretation of monuments; and since, once again, the "audiences" of the various media that I have been examining seem roughly identical, there is no obvious reason to think that this knowledge differed significantly from that which helped similar crowds construe what they heard at the Rostra (or what they saw on coins).

Thanks in particular to the groundbreaking studies of Filippo Coarelli,[111] the monumental environment of Republican Rome is at last coming into focus, although the thoroughness of the Augustan makeover of the city and subsequent building make its reconstruction and interpretation more a textual than an archaeological exercise. It will be worth our while, in the present connection, once again to cast our mind's eye around what may be called the "contional" area of the Forum, from the Temple of Concord at the west end of the roughly rectangular square to the far side of the Temple of Castor some two hundred meters (*c.* 660 ft.) to the southeast, centering on the Rostra (see map 2, p. 44) – the visual focus of the city (*oculatissimus locus*), as one second-century senatorial decree aptly describes it.[112] In the previous chapter we looked at how the cultural meaning of the Rostra was affected by its physical setting and topographical context; now, necessarily exploiting some of the same material, I wish to bring to the fore how the Comitium itself functioned as a "site of memory." The result of this sketch should be a better sense of the extraordinary richness and density of mnemonic cues that surrounded *contio*-goers where they spent much of their days, and indeed at the very site where they listened, interpreted, and responded to the kind of allusions with which I began this chapter.

Here in the Forum, at the physical juncture of Senate and People, where orators harangued a populace hungry for information – a space filled with the busy activity of the courts and, on festal days, a stage for wild-beast hunts, gladiatorial combat, triumphs, the *transvectio equitum*, and even the running of the wolf-men in the Lupercalia[113] – stood a mass of monuments that both grounded and further stimulated the persistent process of creating the Roman past for the urban citizen. The most ancient legends of the city were recalled by a living monument, a fig-tree that commemorated the original *Ruminalis*, which had protected Romulus and Remus with its shade while they were suckled by the she-wolf;[114] beside it stood

---

[111] Esp. Coarelli: 1985 and 1986, supplemented by his entries in the *LTUR*.
[112] Plin. *HN* 34.24. For contional sites, see above, pp. 42–60.
[113] Sehlmeyer 1999: 173; Carafa 1998: 109–10. For the various courts that spread increasingly across the Forum, see David 1992: 14–18 and 39–41, with a plan at 44–45.
[114] Plin. *HN* 15.77 is clear about the *commemorative* nature of the tree in the Comitium (*pace* F. Coarelli, *LTUR* II.249); the original *Ruminalis* was, as he says, at the Lupercal on the other side of the Palatine,

a bronze representation showing the wondrous event, probably the statue group of the three dedicated by the brothers Ogulnii in 296.[115] This was a numinous spot, where things struck by lightning were buried; and at least as late as the first century AD, the periodic withering and re-efflorescence of the tree, tended by priests, were taken to be omens of the fortune of the Roman People.[116] In close proximity to this ensemble and the adjacent Rostra stood a series of other monuments alluding to Rome's founder and first king. Beside the Rostra – just to the left, from the viewpoint of a late-Republican contional audience – was the area sacred to Vulcan (the Volcanal), a hallowed site especially associated with Romulus, the Sabine king Tatius, and their great war.[117] That battle had ranged across what would become, at the war's conclusion, the Forum; it seems therefore no accident that the conflict was memorialized by monuments which, in combination with the Volcanal, more or less defined the limits of the public center – the temple of Jupiter Stator at the eastern end of the Sacred Way and the edge of the Palatine, where the god halted the Roman rout, and to the south, the Lacus Curtius.[118] From that war, according to legend, emerged

but was apparently dead by Ovid's time (*Fasti* 2.411–12). By Tacitus' day, at least, the tree in the Comitium too had come to be called the *Ruminalis* (although some sources use the name *ficus Navia*, evidently because it was adjacent to the statue of Attus Navius [cf. Dion. Hal. 3.71.5], on whom see further below, n. 124); if on other grounds the best location for the Ogulnian monument is in the Comitium, then this was so at least as early as Livy and probably before. Modern scholarship on the relationship and significance of the two trees is interwoven with the arguments about the location of the Ogulnian monument, on which see below, n. 115.

[115] Livy 10.23.11–12, with Plin. *HN* 15.77 *miraculo ex aere iuxta* [sc. *ficum*] *dicato*, which, if the text is sound, must refer to the scene just described (*pace* Evans 1992: 79, n. 62, and others), as Rackham saw with his Loeb translation. It may be that the Ogulnii added the twins to a pre-existing statue of the wolf. The monument is often thought to have been the model of the didrachm of 269–268 (*RRC* 20; cf. E. Papi, *LTUR* v.290–91); a larger composition, complete with tree and shepherd, appears on a coin of *c.* 137 (*RRC* 235: on that point I am not shaken by Metcalf 1999: 4–7; for the tree, see also the *adlocutio* panel of the *Anaglypha Traiani* [detail at Coarelli 1985: 108]). On the meaning of the monument, see Sehlmeyer 1999: 105, with references to earlier work. For the location of the Ogulnian monument, the arguments of Torelli 1982: 95–118, and Coarelli 1985: 28–38, 87–90, in favor of the Comitium seem more persuasive than the alternative view that the ensemble was located at the Lupercal (Dulière, *Lupa*, 58–62; Evans 1992: 74–83; Richardson 1992: 151; Wiseman 1995: 72–76). However that may be, Pliny's text as transmitted (see below, n. 126) clearly testifies to a bronze depiction of the scene in the Comitium.

[116] Plin. *HN* 15.77; Tac. *Ann.* 13.58; cf. Festus 170 L, as restored by C. O. Müller.

[117] Coarelli 1986: 161–78; Carafa 1998: 102–16, rejects Coarelli's placement of the Volcanal in the Comitium (down to the age of Sulla: Coarelli, p. 197) and locates it on a slight eminence just to the southwest (pp. 103–5). The dispute matters little for present purposes; indeed it seems that the two terms were often used interchangeably. Tatius was the traditional founder of the precinct (Dion. Hal. 2.50.3; Varro, *Ling.* 5.74), and the association of the *area Vulcani* with Concordia (Livy 9.46.6) may suggest that this was the spot where the first great act of concord, the settlement between Romulus and Tatius, took place (Plut. *Rom.* 19.7 says in the Comitium [cf. Livy 1.12.10]; for a place on the Sacred Way, Dion. Hal. 2.46.3 and Serv. ad *Aen.* 8.641, with Sehlmeyer 1999: 81).

[118] Establishment of the Forum: Dion. Hal. 2.50.2. Lacus Curtius: Livy 1.12.9–10, 13.5 *monumentum eius pugnae* (though there were other etiologies: Richardson 1992: 229). Jupiter Stator: Livy

the first true Roman community, a "twinned" city (*geminata urbs*: Livy) made one from the two peoples: Rome became the seat of government, but in return the new, composite people took the Sabine name of *Quirites*, a title that would henceforth always be used for addressing the Roman People in this spot.[119] An ancient bronze quadrigate statue that was said to represent Romulus himself kept the association with the founder alive.[120] The Volcanal, finally, was one of the two places pointed out as the spot where Romulus disappeared; the story associated with this place was that he was torn to shreds by senators who afterwards appeased the unhappy populace with a deceptive claim of apotheosis – not an auspicious beginning for communication between Senate and People in the Forum.[121] Indeed, a tradition recorded by Varro located Romulus' tomb (or, according to another story, that of his foster-father Faustulus, the shepherd who found him and his brother) on, or in the immediate vicinity of, the Rostra (see figure 1, p. 46).[122] One might speculate that in 67, when the consul, C. Piso, fighting tooth and nail the highly popular proposal of Gabinius to give Pompey extraordinary resources to fight the pirates, declared from the Rostra that if Pompey wanted to be another Romulus he would not escape Romulus' fate, the allusion was reinforced by the fact that he was standing beside the founder's very tomb. If so, when the crowd came close to killing him on the spot, it was reenacting, by a neat reversal, the legendary dismembering of Romulus by the senators at that very spot.[123]

1.12.3–7, with Richardson, p. 224; cf. Ziolkowski 1992: 87–90, for the controversy over the temple's location. For a recent study of the interaction of historical imagination and monumentalized space in Livy's account of the battle of the Forum, see Jaeger 1997: 30–56. Surviving panels, probably late-Republican, of a frieze (internal?: A. Bauer, *LTUR* 1.185) found in the site of the building traditionally identified as the Basilica (Fulvia et) Aemilia, and certainly from 54 the Basilica Pauli, include the killing of Tarpeia and rape of the Sabine Women, thus reflecting back to the spectator the foundation story of the Forum itself (Evans 1992: 129–34). For Steinby 1987: 181 (cf. n. 165 below), the frieze originated on the Basilica Aemilia, which she would locate elsewhere.

[119] Livy 1.13.4–5, with Ogilvie 1965: 79. For the Volcanal as the earliest place of assembly, see Dion. Hal. 2.50.2; 6.67.2; 7.17.2; 11.39.1; cf. Plut. *Rom.* 27.5–6 and *Mor.* 276b (Senate).

[120] Dion. Hal. 2.54; Plut. *Rom.* 24.3. We cannot, however, be certain how late the statue was still displayed: see Coarelli 1986: 174–77; Sehlmeyer 1999: 74–76.

[121] Plut. *Rom.* 27.5–6; Fest. 184 L identifies the spot as the famous *Niger lapis in Comitio*. For Romulus as senatorial victim, see Cic. *Rep.* 2.20; Dion. Hal. 2.56.3–4; Livy 1.15.8–16.8; Plut. *Rom.* 27.3–28.3.

[122] Pseud.-Acr. and Porphyry ad Hor. *Epod.* 16.13–14 (both citing Varro; texts quoted by Coarelli 1986: 167, n. 9); Fest. 184 L; Dion. Hal. 1.87.2. Festus and Dionysius (3.1.2) seem to record another tradition, placing here the grave of the Roman champion who fell in the battle in the Forum, Hostus Hostilius (Livy 1.12.2–3, 22.1; *De vir. ill.* 2.7). See Coarelli 1986: 166–78, and 188–99, who connects these texts with the *Lapis Niger* complex (in his view, actually a heroon for Romulus until covered over *c.* 80), and the skeptical discussion of Carafa 1998: 111–14.

[123] Plut. *Pomp.* 25.4.

Other important stories of early Rome were also cued by monuments in or beside the Comitium. A small, ancient statue – its head strikingly covered, in priestly attitude – of Attus Navius, the founder-figure of augury who was said to have made his science central to all matters of state in the reign of Tarquin the Proud, evoked the story of the miraculous demonstration of his powers before the tyrannical last king of Rome.[124] Since that myth focused on a priest's successful veto of the constitutional innovations of a power-hungry *rex*, we should probably consider the monument to have been emblematic not so much of "the victory of religion over politics" but more broadly of fundamental Republican constraints, often taking the form of religious objections, upon the exercise of power in Rome.[125] The placement of this statue in the Comitium, at the spot where augurs "inaugurated" magistrates and priests, was obviously no accident.[126] And a statue of Horatius Cocles in full armor, who in the Republic's infancy had held off Porsenna's army at the Tiber bridge, must have reminded viewers of the more martial demands of *virtus* upon the Roman citizen.[127] As powerful evocations of the portentous origins of the city and Republic destined to rule the world, standing at the nexus of Senate and People, the very heart of political action, and in various ways noted above associated with the activities that characterized the place in the present, all of these monuments will not merely have functioned as shrines to a quasi-mythical past maintaining a diffuse patriotism, but challenged contemporary participants in

---

[124] Sehlmeyer 1999: 83–86, 103. Famous versions of the story in Livy 1.36 and Cic. *Div.* 1.31–33; for Attus as founder of Roman state augury, see also Cic. *Att.* 10.8.6; *Rep.* 2.36. The base of the statue was burnt when Clodius' cremation consumed the Curia in 52 (Plin. *HN* 34.21), but there is little reason to assume that the statue itself did not survive (Sehlmeyer, p. 83, n. 230, *pace* Coarelli 1985: 33, and Vasaly 1993: 67), esp. in view of Plin. *HN* 15.77 (above n. 115), though it will have been moved to a new location with the construction of the Curia Iulia.

[125] For the quoted words and a different view of the myth, see Beard 1989: esp. 50–53. Her view seems to overlook what precipitated the conflict between Tarquin and Navius: cf. Linderski 1986: 2207–8.

[126] Sehlmeyer 1999: 103. The difficult text of Plin. *HN* 15.77 (*tamquam comitium sponte transisset Atto Navio augurante*) has given rise to the fanciful idea that Navius' augural powers were credited with miraculously transplanting the original Ruminalis to the Comitium (see above, nn. 114 and 115: Coarelli 1985: 89; 1986: 226; *LTUR* II.249; Evans 1992: 79; Wiseman 1995: 74). Yet Pliny himself evidently distinguishes the tree in the Comitium from *that other* in the Lupercal (*magisque ob memorium* eius quae . . . prima protexit, *ruminalis appellata*; and cf. perhaps *nata*); and no other source mentions such a "miracle" of Navius. If the reference to Navius is not corrupt, I suspect this is nothing more than Pliny's wry joke, invoking the adjacent statue to explain the mysterious connection between the two locations.

[127] Livy 2.10; Plut. *Publ.* 16.4–7; Plin. *HN* 34.22; Dion. Hal. 5.25; Gell. *NA* 4.5.1–4 (the sources vary as to its location: in the Comitium or Volcanal, or each successively [Gellius]). For Cocles' paradigmatic status, see Polyb. 6.54.6–55.4. Pliny attests to the statue's survival to his own day. Sehlmeyer 1999: 92–96, who is also rightly skeptical of the existence in the Comitium of a series of other monuments of Porsenna's invasion (96–103).

the communal actions of the Republic to maintain a heritage rooted in specific primordial events heralding Rome's destiny.[128]

Displays of spoils and a host of victory monuments in the Forum and on the Capitol charted some of the earliest phases of the expansion of the *imperium populi Romani* and trumpeted the special claim of the Romans to martial *virtus*.[129] It is fitting that the central feature of the Comitium, the Rostra, was itself a historical memorial, celebrating the victory over the Latins which launched the great period of Roman expansion; not coincidentally, the adornment of the podium in 338 opens the first phase of historical monumentalization in Rome.[130] The podium received statues of both consuls of that year, C. Maenius and L. Camillus (perhaps also one of the greater Camillus who had saved Rome from the Gauls), and the adjacent Maenian column completed the assemblage.[131] In an interesting juxtaposition, down to Cicero's lifetime there stood behind the Rostra a bronze pillar inscribed with the text of the ancient Treaty of Cassius with the Latins (traditionally, 493 BC) – a well-known monument of the new Republic's first great victory, but also perhaps, in combination with the Rostra, of the Roman mission to "fight down the proud," since the treaty had established the alliance broken by the Latins' revolt in 341, whose triumphant conclusion was commemorated by the Rostra itself.[132] Perhaps the gilded Samnite shields which had lent magnificence to the triumph of L. Papirius Cursor in 310, and had been affixed to the shops then flanking the Forum, were still hung outside the basilicas of the late

---

[128] Consequently I have reservations about Hölscher's strong demarcation of "two pasts" in Roman memory: a mythical-legendary "Frühzeit," detached from the concrete realities of everyday life and the uncontroversial possession of all, and a more tendentious "aktuelle Vor-Geschichte der Gegenwart" present in historical monuments (Hölscher 2001: 200–201, 202–4).

[129] Cic. *Mur.* 22: *Haec* [sc. *rei militaris virtus*] *nomen populo Romano, haec huic urbi aeternam gloriam peperit, haec orbem terrarum parere huic imperio coegit*, etc.

[130] Hölscher 1978: 315–24. Sources and details on pp. 48–49.

[131] For the column, see especially Plin. *HN* 34.20, perhaps *RRC* 363/1, and Coarelli 1985: 39–53. Pliny makes fairly clear that the column was an honorific memorial of the victory over the Latins built in Maenius' consulship (*eodemque in consulatu*) (*pace*, for example, Sehlmeyer 1999: 53–57, who is tempted by the notion that the column was a purely utilitarian construction of Maenius' censorship of 318; he is convincing, however, against the hypothesis that a statue, especially an equestrian one, stood atop it). The column – neither, it seems, rostrate (so Vasaly 1993: 66), or a commemoration of naval victory (so Richardson 1992: 94) – functioned as a primitive sundial before the First Punic War (Plin. *HN* 7.212, a passage used brilliantly by Coarelli 1985: 138–60 to reconstruct the topography of the Comitium).

[132] Cic. *Balb.* 53: *cum Latinis omnibus foedus esse ictum Sp. Cassio Postumo Cominio consulibus quis ignorat? Quod quidem nuper in columna ahenea meminimus post rostra incisum et perscriptum fuisse* (cf. Livy 2.33.9). Note how the orator appeals to recent memory of the monument to verify the date of the alliance, supposedly known by all. Cf. Cornell 1995: 299. Coarelli 1985: 234 dates the disappearance of the monument to Sulla, without very strong reason.

Republic;[133] certainly, statues of Pythagoras and Alcibiades, "the wisest and bravest of the Greeks," monuments – or booty – of the Samnite wars, stood at each "end" or "flank" of the Comitium until *c.* 81.[134]

The First Punic War was especially conspicuous in the "monumental history" of the Forum. The southwest exterior wall of the Senate-house was graced by a conspicuous mural showing the Roman victory over King Hiero and the Carthaginians at Syracuse in 263, under the leadership of M.' Valerius Messala.[135] After his triumph Messala also set up in the Comitium a sundial he had plundered from Catania, whose time was stubbornly followed in the Forum for nearly a century despite its inaccuracy due to the difference of latitude.[136] And the first triumph celebrated for a naval victory, that of C. Duilius over the Carthaginian fleet at Mylae in 260, was commemorated by a column in the Volcanal decorated with the prows of the defeated ships, crowned by the consul's statue.[137] The surviving portion of the inscription on the base, reinscribed and linguistically updated in the early Principate, gives a brief description of his exploits, the number of ships captured and sunk, a separate accounting of gold and silver seized and handed over to the Roman People at the triumph, and the boast to have led many freeborn Carthaginians before his chariot.[138] This well-placed inscription was sufficiently familiar to be cited by Quintilian for its preservation of archaic Latin forms.[139] That the first naval *triumphator* still maintained his place among the many ancient *exempla* of martial prowess in Cicero's day and beyond, despite his lack of biographical "depth,"

---

[133] Livy 9.40.16 (cf. 10.39.14). The fire of 210 burned only the northern *tabernae argentariae* (Livy 26.27.2); the Cimbric trophy-shields mounted on the Basilica Fulvia after Marius' triumph in 101 (Coarelli 1985: 176–77; cf. 199–209) may suggest that the Samnite precedent remained familiar.

[134] Plin. *HN* 34.26 (see chap. 2, n. 42); Plut. *Num.* 8.10. Wallace 1990: 289 suggests that the statues were actually Samnite booty; cf. Sehlmeyer 1999: 88–90. Coarelli 1985: 119–23 attributes their installation to C. Marcius Censorinus (below, on the Marsyas). Hölscher 2001: 193, n. 26 emphasizes the exemplary over the commemorative character of these statues.

[135] Plin. *HN* 35.22; Cic. *Vat.* 21; *Fam.* 14.2.2. Zinserling 1959/60: no. 4; Coarelli 1985: 53–59. Cicero's references show that the mural somehow remained even after Sulla's expansion of the Curia.

[136] Plin. *HN* 7.214. Since Pliny says (cf. Censorinus, *De die natali liber* 23.7, where, as Broughton, *MRR* II.57, n. 2, saw, Philippus' praenomen is mistaken or corrupt) that Q. Marcius Philippus, cens. 164, set a more accurate device beside it (*iuxta*), presumably Messala's sundial remained as a memorial until the Late Republic.

[137] Plin. *HN* 34.20; *IIt.* XIII.3.13, line 5 (*pr[ope a]ream Vulc[ani]*); and nn. 138, 139 below. Cf. Pietilä-Castrén 1987: 28–32; L. Chioffi, *LTUR* 1.309; Sehlmeyer 1999: 117–19. Duilius also dedicated a temple to Janus at the Forum Holitorium, on the triumphal route outside the Porta Carmentalis (Tac. *Ann.* 2.49; Festus 358 L; Pietilä-Castrén 1992: 61–62) and perhaps a second Rostrate column before the Circus Maximus (Serv. ad *Georg.* 3.29).

[138] To be consulted in Degrassi's version, *IIt.* XIII.3.69 = *ILLRP* 319 = Gordon no. 48. See Gordon for a useful summary of the arguments for regarding the text as a copy, if somewhat inexact, of a third-century original.

[139] Quint. *Inst.* 1.7.12.

seems to be largely due to Duilius' monuments here and on the triumphal route.[140]

The Rostra itself received additional monuments over the course of time which recalled great events of domestic history and the development of the Republican civic tradition. The twelve bronze plaques which contained the ancient law-code (thus "Twelve Tables"), are said to have been mounted on the Rostra, where they will have served not only as texts for consultation at the original seat of the urban praetor but also as a memorial of a landmark in the Struggle of the Orders closely associated with the myths of Appius Claudius, the tyrannical Decemvirate, and the Second Secession of the Plebs which put an end to it.[141] A statue of Hermodorus of Ephesus, who was thought to have assisted in the drafting of the laws or in their subsequent elucidation, stood close by.[142] It has been strongly argued that the statue of Marsyas on the Rostra too was associated with a specific moment in the Struggle of the Orders: erected (so the argument goes) by the censor C. Marcius Rutilus Censorinus in 294, it was intended to commemorate recent measures against usury and *nexum* (a form of debt-slavery) as well as unprecedented accomplishments of the Marcii in the plebeian quest for honors (Censorinus was among the first contingent of plebeian pontifices and augurs, his father the first dictator and censor from the plebs).[143] The hypothesis is attractive, but perhaps over-bold, since it depends ultimately on the fact that one L. Marcius Censorinus, as moneyer in 82, placed an image of the statue on the reverse of his *denarii*, which might be explained simply by its punning effect on Marcius' name.[144] Still, an association between Marsyas and the plebs' freedom from debt-slavery, won in the Struggle of the Orders, seems highly plausible. The satyr was generally associated with *Libertas*; here he was represented wearing broken shackles, and furthermore the

---

[140] Gendre and Loutsch 2001: 136. Cf. above, n. 137. Another rostrate column from the First Punic War (M. Aemilius Paullus, cos. 255) stood in this area until destroyed by lightning in 172 (Livy 42.20.1: Sehlmeyer 1999: 119–20; D. Palombi, *LTUR* 1.307–8).

[141] Twelve Tables: Diodorus' reference to the Rostra (12.26.1) would be a minor anachronism, since the speakers' platform did not, strictly speaking, become "the Rams" until 338, but he may thus indicate where they were known to have stood in living memory. Dion. Hal. 10.57.7 ἐν ἀγορᾷ τὸν ἐπιφανέστατον . . . τόπον and Livy 3.57.10 *in aes incisas in publico posuerunt* are vaguer (but cf. 3.34.2 and Pomponius, *Dig.* 1.2.2.4, on the story of their temporary display, apparently at the speaker's platform). See Ogilvie 1965: 507.

[142] Plin. *HN* 34.21; cf. Cic. *Tusc.* 5.105; Strabo 14.1.25; Pomponius, *Dig.* 1.2.2.4: Sehlmeyer 1999: 86–88.

[143] Pseud.-Acr. and Porphyry ad Hor. *Sat.* 1.6.120. Torelli 1982: 99–106; Coarelli 1985: 91–119. See chap. 2, n. 54.

[144] *RRC* 363; cf. M. H. Crawford 1974: 378, such punning references are common enough (e.g., *RRC* 259/1, 293, 344/1–2, 512). Note that Censorinus' gentile name otherwise appears nowhere on the coin.

statue marked the place where disputes between creditors and debtors were heard.[145]

Eventually, to the statues of the consuls of 338 on the Rostra were added further images of great men of the Republic: Cicero was to say in 45 that there was no more honorific place in Rome for a statue than on the Rostra.[146] Perhaps around the end of the fourth century began the first phase of this most exclusive form of commemoration, which consisted in the erection of statues of ambassadors who had been murdered on their missions and thus sacrificed their lives for the Republic: men such as C. Fulcinius, Cloelius Tullus, Sp. Antius, and L. Roscius, envoys to Fidenae in 438 and slaughtered by the vicious Lars Tolumnius; one Coruncanius, allegedly killed at the order of the Illyrian queen Teuta in 230, precipitating Rome's first crossing of the Adriatic; and Cn. Octavius, murdered on his mission to cripple the Seleucid kingdom.[147] Cicero, cheekily (but successfully) urging the Senate to add a statue of Ser. Sulpicius Rufus, who had succumbed to illness on a senatorial mission to Mark Antony before the war of Mutina in 43, declares that because of this honor his embassy would never be forgotten.[148] That might not prevent eventual confusion about details, as is shown by Pliny's conflation of the deed of Cn. Octavius, hamstringer of Antiochus V's elephants, with the much more famous one of C. Popilius, who drew the line in the sand around King Antiochus IV in 168.[149]

The Rostra and the immediate rostral area received further distinctive "historical" monuments during the late Republic. The podium itself was further embellished in 97 with the spoils – perhaps additional rams? – of M. Antonius' naval campaign five years earlier against the Cilician pirates.[150] An extraordinary statue of Hercules in his final mortal agonies,

---

[145] *Libertas*: see chap. 2, n. 54. By the late Republic, the urban praetor had moved to the east end of the Forum, but the civil procedure *in iudicio* was still located in the Comitium: Hor. *Sat.* 1.6.120–21; David 1992: 15, and 1995. The shackles are shown on the Paestum copy: Coarelli 1985: 97–100.

[146] Cic. *Deiot.* 34: *nullus est ad statuam quidem rostris clarior.* Cf. Plin. *HN* 34.24.

[147] References in chap. 2, n. 49.

[148] *Phil.* 9.10: *nulla eius legationem posteritatis obscurabit oblivio.* Cicero was right: *Dig.* 1.2.2.43. For Cicero to suggest the alternative of a gilt equestrian statue (only to deprecate it as inconsistent with Sulpicius' modesty) is itself a bit of *huius saeculi insolentia* (*Phil.* 9.13), for that kind of honor would have been utterly unprecedented for a legate's memorial; the older legates' statues were only half-size (Plin. *HN* 34.24).

[149] Perhaps after the reconstruction of the Rostra under Caesar and Augustus the statue or its inscription (a senatorial decree which Pliny quotes) could no longer be directly consulted; or the confusion may have been in Pliny's source.

[150] Cic. *De or.* 3.10, with which see Murray and Petsas 1989: 109–10, 118–19. Of course, other types of *manubiae* are conceivable: cf. n. 151. Antonius' triumph, probably in 100: Plut. *Pomp.* 24.6; cf. Cic. *Rab. perd.* 26.

brought back by L. Lucullus from Asia Minor or Armenia, was set up by the great general's son beside the Rostra, bearing an inscription that specifically marked it as a dedication from the triumphal booty.[151] But the most striking late-Republican development was the addition of new equestrian statues to the original ones of Maenius and L. Camillus after the passage of more than two and a half centuries. Sulla was the first to receive this extraordinary honor, followed by Pompey, Caesar, and finally Octavian.[152]

Earlier I touched on the traditions associated with the Temple of Concordia, which was so close to the Rostra.[153] From a plebeian perspective, its very name seems ironic on an almost Orwellian scale, since the traditions surrounding it spoke volumes about the tense relations between the plebs and the Senate over the centuries. Tradition traced the foundation of the cult of Concord overlooking the Comitium back to key moments in the effort of the plebs to broaden their civic rights and gain access to positions of power in the Republic. One story looked back to the struggle over the fourth-century Licinian–Sextian rogations, by which, according to tradition, plebeians won access to the consulship and debt relief: the temple had been vowed by the great Marcus Camillus in order to resolve the civic strife and was dedicated immediately after it was settled in 367.[154] Another described how in 304 the upstart aedile Cn. Flavius – son of a freedman and a mere scribe, but elected in the face of noble indignation by a recently empowered urban plebs – had hopefully vowed a temple to Concord after his publication of the arcane legal procedures and of the calendar, which together permitted plebeians full recourse to the law. The enraged nobility responded with attempts to block construction of the shrine by rejecting public funding and ritual objections. Flavius at last financed his shrine to Concord independently of the Senate, by means of fines extracted from usurers, while the religious challenge was overcome when the Pontifex Maximus was actually forced by popular pressure to dictate the ritual formula over his own objections.[155] That version again brings together central themes of the tradition about the "Struggle of the Orders":

[151] *L. Luculli imperatoris de manubiis* (Plin. *HN* 34.93). The import of the series of inscriptions is capably disentangled by Pape 1975: 47–49.

[152] Chap. 2, nn. 52, 53. Sulla's and Pompey's statues were toppled after Pharsalus: chap. 2, n. 82.

[153] See pp. 55–56.

[154] Plut. *Cam.* 42.3–4; Ovid, *Fasti* 1.640–44, where the association of the vow with a secession of the plebs is heterodox. It does not matter for present purposes that this version is generally discounted as an unhistorical "myth" (Momigliano 1942: 115–17; recently, Ziolkowski 1992: 22–24).

[155] Livy 9.46; Plin. *HN* 33.19. Curti 2000: 80–83 picks up Momigliano's observation (1942: 117–20), that the Greek cult of *Homonoia* must have been Flavius' model and noting that, at least in contemporary Syracuse, this cult may have been associated with the transition from oligarchy to

the jealous guarding of religious authority by patricians, the problem of debt (disputes regarding which were adjudicated, it will be remembered, immediately adjacent, by the Maenian column), as well as the plebeian attempt to break into the ruling circles and (not least) the exploitation of demagogic methods. As we have seen above (pp. 76–77), it will not do to assume that traditions about the "Struggle of the Orders" were unknown to the urban plebs.

More salient in the late Republic, no doubt, will have been the connection of the Temple of Concordia with the suppression of the Gracchi. The temple bore the name of L. Opimius, who in 121, by authority of the Senate, crushed the insurrection of C. Gracchus and M. Fulvius Flaccus on the Aventine[156] and unleashed an inquisition against their supporters, whose harshness and arbitrariness were long remembered. Some three thousand men perished in the fighting and the executions that followed: Sallust's view that the nobility cruelly exploited its victory among the plebs was doubtless widely shared among the urban populace.[157] Opimius then crowned his actions by building the first truly monumental Temple of Concordia on the site, among the most conspicuous monuments of the Forum,[158] transparently seeking to put the outrage to rest and to usurp the positive associations of this spot, where plebeian victories in the struggle for their rights were commemorated. That was to twist the meaning of Concord into a buzzword for the extermination of popular heroes, a fact not lost on the People, according to Plutarch, who were more offended by this exultation over the slaughter of citizens than by Opimius' original acts of cruelty: one night, some brave souls painted or scrawled under the dedicatory inscription a parody of the regular formula: "An act of madness made the Temple of Concordia."[159] The anecdote reminds us again that the plebeian crowd

---

[156] democracy, suggests that this was the symbolism of Flavius' initiative as well. The controversy of 304 seems authentic in broad outline, if perhaps not in details: Orlin 1997: 163–65.

[156] That Gracchus and Fulvius strove to exploit the tradition of plebeian secessions to the Aventine (Stockton 1979: 196) seems highly probable, in view of the resonance of that tradition we have discerned in contional oratory.

[157] Sall. *Iug.* 16.2 (cf. 31.7, Memmius' *contio*); Oros. 5.12; Vell. Pat. 2.7.3; Plut. *C. Gracch.* 17.5. It is true that Opimius was afterwards acquitted, in a trial before the Centuriate Assembly, of having violated the rights of those he had imprisoned (and killed) without trial (Alexander 1990: no. 27; see Drummond 1995: 90–93). But this does not seem to have lessened the widespread popular hatred of the man (*flagrantem invidia*, Cic. *Sest.* 140), as is suggested also by his condemnation in 109 in a trial characterized by anti-noble animus (*Iug.* 40.3; cf. Cic. *Brut.* 128; *Planc.* 69–70; Gruen 1968: 144).

[158] *Cuius* [sc. Opimi] *monumentum celeberrimum in foro*: Cic. *Sest.* 140. On the remains of the Opimian temple and the possible traces of earlier structures, see A. M. Ferroni, *LTUR* 1.316–20.

[159] Plut. *C. Gracch.* 17.6: ἔργον ἀπονοίας ναὸν ὁμονοίας ποιεῖ. The jingle ἀπονοίας – ὁμονοίας suggests a comparable play on *vecordia* and *concordia* in the original; furthermore, ποιεῖ (perhaps to

was not oblivious to the monuments that surrounded its activities in the Forum; indeed (as is also seen in the toppling of statues on the Rostra) some of its constituents might even occasionally use them for their own, non-authorized communicative purposes.[160]

By the end of our period the senatorial usurpation of Concordia seems virtually complete: the frequent use of the temple for meetings of the Senate from at least 63 will doubtless have nurtured identification of the two entities, and its memorable role as the setting for the uncovery and suppression of the "Catilinarian" conspiracy, whose agents were executed in the conveniently adjacent *carcer* (prison), might be seen as perpetuating the Opimian interpretation of Concordia as the product of repressive violence directed by the Senate against treacherous citizens.[161] Cicero, standing before Opimius' Temple of Concordia as he delivers his *Third Catilinarian Oration*, wishes to reassure the People that he will not repeat the bloody excesses of the past: distinguishing between the "slaughter of citizens" (*internicio civium*) seen in the recent civil wars and the "restoration of concord" (*reconciliatio concordiae*) that is his aim, he reassures the Roman People that punishment will fall only on the most guilty few.[162] The Catilinarian meetings, in turn, marked a new stage in the ongoing contest over the meaning of the Temple of Concordia. Nearly a century afterward (October 18, AD 31), after L. Aelius Sejanus had been "unmasked" as a conspirator against the Princeps during the famous senatorial meeting in the Palatine Temple of Apollo, his "trial" was reserved for a second meeting on that same day at the (Tiberian) Temple of Concordia, next to his eventual place of execution in the *carcer* – given the scarcity of known meetings there under the early Principate, surely an appeal to the memory of the Catilinarian repression.[163]

Enough has been said to show, I hope, that the west end of the Forum, the "contional area" *par excellence*, was a highly evocative locus of historical remembrance which cannot have escaped its occupants, indeed on certain

be emended to ἐποίει = *fecit*) seems to parody the traditional dedicatory formula. Perhaps *exemplum vecordiae templum Concordiae fecit?*

[160] Strictly speaking, we cannot know whether these men, presumably not members of the élite, were acting independently, but note that Plutarch's context, at least, is one of popular indignation. Cf. the anti-Caesarian graffiti that appeared on the statues of Brutus the Liberator and of Caesar himself early in 44, which as A. Yakobson points out to me, are listed by Suetonius among manifestations of *popular* resentment (*Iul.* 80.3; contrast Plut. *Brut.* 9.6–8; 10.6; *Caes.* 62.4).

[161] See above, p. 55.

[162] Cic. *Cat.* 3.23–25, and 27: *mihi cum eis vivendum est quos vici ac subegi.* Vasaly 1993: 60–87 neglects the ideological associations of the temple, whence Cicero had just emerged (*Cat.* 3.21; cf. Sall. *Cat.* 46.5), and which stood behind his right shoulder.

[163] Cass. Dio 58.11.4; Talbert 1984: 119.

occasions demonstrably did not. We should keep in mind also that there are likely to have been a good many more notable monuments in this area than happen to be mentioned by our surviving sources, which eschew detailed description of the urban landscape and mention such things fairly casually (with the exception of Pliny, whose discussion is heavily biased toward "firsts" and distant antiquity). Furthermore, of course, the monuments of the rostral area did not nearly exhaust the display of "monumental history" throughout the central spaces of the city. There was, for example, the second major contional area, dominated by the Temple of Castor, rebuilt in 117 with the Dalmatian spoils of a triumphant Metellus,[164] the Basilica Aemilia,[165] celebrating with external portrait-shields and inscriptions the deeds of that illustrous family,[166] and the triumphal arch of Q. Fabius Maximus Allobrogicus (*Fornix Fabianus*), honoring as well the Aemilian and Scipionic victors of Pydna and the Third Punic War.[167] Casting our eye more broadly, we should call to mind the great commemorative complex on the Capitol, with its mass of victory monuments and other memorials of the great figures of the Roman past,[168] and the arches and

---

[164] L. Caecilius Metellus Delmaticus, cos. 119. For the use of the temple's podium as a contional site, see pp. 57–59. The later Metellus who adorned a temple of the Dioscuri with statues and paintings (Plut. *Pomp.* 2.4) was probably Pius, consul of 80, after his Spanish triumph in 71 (*pace* Poulsen, in Nielsen and Poulsen 1992: 56), and the temple probably the less well-known one in the Circus Flaminius (so now Coarelli 1997: 505–7).

[165] Now distinguished by E. M. Steinby from the Basilica Fulvia (later Paulli) on the north side of the Forum and reconstructed as a portico to the east of the Temple of Castor, closing the east side of the square: Steinby 1987: 167–77; *LTUR* I.167–68; cf. Wiseman 1998: 106–20 (with map at p. 109). Steinby attributes the original construction to L. Aemilius Paullus, the victor of Pydna, censor in 164. With the Basilica Aemilia move its *imagines clipeatae* (see n. 166).

[166] Plin. *HN* 35.12 (that the portraits were of the Aemilii, and bore inscriptions, is inferred from the example, previously cited by Pliny, of Ap. Claudius' Temple of Bellona); illustrated on *RRC* 419/3, which suggests that the *clipei* decorated the exterior of the building as well as the interior (Coarelli 1985: 203–9). On these *imagines clipeatae*, see Sehlmeyer 1999: 201–3. See Steinby 1987 for the "Aemilian" character of this edge of the Forum in the middle and late Republic (cf. *Aemilia monimenta*, Tac. *Ann.* 3.72.1), manifested by a monument at the *lacus Iuturnae*, the Fornix Fabianus (with its statues of Aemilius Paullus and his sons), and the Basilicas Aemilia and Paulli. Cf. Wiseman 1998: 106–20; a summary of the complicated argument concerning the location of the Basilica Aemilia in E. M. Steinby, *LTUR* I.167–68. The remarkable gallery of *summi viri* that seems to have graced the Basilica Paulli in an Augustan reconstruction (*IIt.* XIII.3.60–65, with Chioffi, in Panciera 1996: 99–139: now *CIL* VI.8.3, 40912–28) was part of that era's gradual "erasure" of the *monumenta Aemilia*.

[167] The best-known Republican arch, at the eastern entry to the Forum, originally erected by Q. Fabius Maximus after his victory over the Gauls in 121 and restored by his grandson, aedile in 57: Maria 1988: 264–66 no. 54; L. Chioffi, *LTUR* II.264–66; Sehlmeyer 1999: 168–69. Its statues, as shown by the extant inscriptions (*ILS* 43), also honored illustrious blood relatives outside the clan of the Fabii, such as L. Aemilius Paullus, Allobrogicus' grandfather, and Scipio Aemilianus, his uncle.

[168] A selective list of known monuments and objects with strong historical references on the Capitol will give a sense of the scale of the phenomenon: (1) the group of Rome's *kings*, joined by a likeness

temples that increasingly lined the spectacular triumphal route leading up to Jupiter's temple on the height.[169] Hosts of statues virtually littered the Forum and the adjacent thoroughfares of the city.[170] And scores of temples

of *L. Brutus* that emerges in our narratives as an important "site of memory" in 44 BC (Sehlmeyer 1999: 68–74; see above, n. 160); (2) a colossal bronze statue of Jupiter on the Capitol made from the armor of Samnites defeated by *Sp. Carvilius* in 293 (or 272), with a likeness of the consul beside it; the statue could be seen from the Alban Mount some fifteen miles to the southeast (Plin. *HN* 34.43, with Sehlmeyer, pp. 113–16); (3) *A. Atilius Calatinus'* Temple of Fides (above, n. 58); (4) a statue of *L. Caecilius Metellus* (Dion. Hal. 2.66.4), victor at Panormus in 250, probably stood by the Temple of Ops Opifera he had dedicated on the Capitol (see now Coarelli 1997: 228–34; cf. Ziolkowski 1992: 122–25; for the statue, Sehlmeyer, pp. 120–21), to which the elephant-badge on numerous Metellan coins probably alludes (above, n. 89); (5) *Fabius Cunctator's* equestrian statue and colossal statue of Hercules (above, n. 59); (6) a portrait of *Scipio Africanus the elder*, kept in the Temple of Jupiter Optimus Maximus and used in Scipionic funerals (Val. Max. 8.15.1; App. *Hisp.* 23; Cic. *Verr.* 2.4.81, whose relevance is properly noted by Sehlmeyer, p. 47, n. 18 and p. 275); (7) a painting showing *L. Scipio Asiaticus'* victory over Antiochus (Plin. *HN* 35.22; Zinserling 1959/60: no. 9), as well as a statue of him in Greek dress (Cic. *Rab. Post.* 27; Val. Max. 3.6.2; Sehlmeyer, 144); (8) an equestrian statue of one *Aemilius Lepidus* (probably the censor of 179) that celebrated a youthful martial exploit was sufficiently well known to be illustrated on a coin with a highly elliptical legend (Val. Max. 3.1.1 and RCC 419/1, with Crawford's commentary; see now Sehlmeyer, pp. 142–43); (9) at least two equestrian statues of *Scipio Aemilianus* (above, n. 62); (10) *M. Aemilius Scaurus* rebuilt, and decorated with impressive spoils, the temples of Fides and Mens (Cic. *Scaur.* 47; *Nat. D.* 2.61; Plut. *Mor.* 318e; see Reusser 1993: 55–58); (11) *Marius'* Cimbric and perhaps African trophies (below, n. 192); (12) the Bocchus-monument celebrating *Sulla's* capture of Jugurtha (above, n. 75; Sehlmeyer, pp. 194–96, and Behr 1993: 114–21, with references to earlier work); controversial fragments of a triumphal monument found near St. Omobono have been attributed to the monument (see now, contra, Reusser, pp. 121–37); (13) an extraordinary monument of the Peoples and Kings of Asia Minor, dedicated in thanks to the *Fides* of the Roman People (and next to its temple), most likely after *Sulla's* recovery of Asia Minor (Reusser, pp. 138–58; see also Kallet-Marx 1995: 287–89); (14) *Q. Metellus Scipio's* squadron of gilded equestrian statues of his ancestors, reaching back at least to his great-grandfather, *P. Scipio Nasica Sarapio* (Cic. *Att.* 6.1.17), which evidently recalls the *turma Alexandri* of the Porticus Metelli (Reusser, p. 48; *pace* Coarelli 1997: 231, there is no reason to assume that the group belonged to L. Metellus' Ops Opifera complex).

[169] On the monumentalization of the triumphal route, see Favro 1994: 151–64, and now Hölscher 2001: 194–98. On the triumphal arches, Maria 1988: 31–53, 262–66, nos. 49–54 (the six known Republican arches). In addition to the Fornix Fabianus (above, n. 167), note esp. *L. Stertinius' fornices* built in 196, the earliest recorded, see Livy 33.27.3–5; Pietilä-Castrén 1987: 71–74, and the *Fornix Scipionis* on the Capitol, constructed only six years later by *Scipio Africanus* before his departure for Asia (Livy 37.3.7: perhaps a commemoration of the victory over Hannibal: cf. Sehlmeyer, 124).

[170] On honorific statues in the Republic, see Sehlmeyer 1999. Among the more notable, I mention those of *T. Flamininus*, with a Greek inscription, by the Circus Maximus (Plut. *Flam.* 1.1; Sehlmeyer, pp. 143–44 thinks, however, of the Circus Flaminius); that of *Ti. Sempronius Gracchus the elder* (cos. II 163), conqueror of Sardinia (below, n. 174), at one entrance to the Forum (Plut. *C. Gracch.* 14.4–5; Sehlmeyer, pp. 150–51); and esp. that of *C. Hostilius Mancinus*, evidently shown bound and naked (Plin. *HN* 34.18), a striking reference to his *fides* and self-sacrifice for the Republic after the official repudiation of the Numantine treaty of 137 (Sehlmeyer, pp. 166–67; see Rosenstein 1990a: 148–50). The statues of the Forum and Capitol were subject to special, though sporadic, control (note the clearing activities of the censors of 159 [Plin. *HN* 34.30]; for the Capitol, cf. Non. 548 L; Sehlmeyer, pp. 152–61); elsewhere, it seems, self-commemoration was restrained only by custom, which prescribed that those so honored had held a magistracy (Sehlmeyer, pp. 272–78).

and other public structures dedicated by victorious commanders in Rome's wars around the Mediterranean,[171] with their sculpture,[172] triumphal plaques or dedicatory inscriptions,[173] murals,[174] and displays of triumphal

[171] Orlin 1997: Appendix 1 lists over seventy temples founded in the Republican period, the overwhelming majority of them consequent upon a victory. In addition to those cited in the notes that follow, I have already had occasion to mention *Calatinus'* temples of Fides and Spes on the Capitol and in the Forum Holitorium (n. 58) and *Marcellus'* temple to Honos et Virtus (n. 60). Particularly noteworthy as well are *M. Atilius Regulus'* (cos. 294) Temple of Jupiter Stator, recalling turning points both in Romulus' battle with the Sabines in the Forum and in the Third Samnite War (above, n. 118), and *Q. Lutatius Catulus'* Temple of Fortuna Huiusce Diei on the Campus, dedicated on the very anniversary of the battle of Vercellae, which along with his Porticus Catuli on the Palatine (Richardson 1992: 312; E. Papi, *LTUR* IV.119) competed for the glory of the Cimbric victory with Marius' Temple of Honos et Virtus on the upper Sacra Via (Richardson 1992: 190).

[172] A statue group boasting of the total of nine consulships won by three *Marcelli* in three generations (Asc. 12C: *III Marcelli Novies Coss.*; Sehlmeyer 1999: 164–65) was set up by the youngest, cos. III 152, in the Temple of Honos et Virtus built by his grandfather, the great general of the Gallic and Second Punic Wars (above, n. 60); this will have been paid for with his own spoils from the Celtiberian war in Spain, with which he probably also further embellished the complex (B. A. Marshall 1985: 102). A statue of the virtuous maiden *Claudia Quinta* who had received the Magna Mater in Rome graced the entry-way of the goddess's temple (Val. Max. 1.8.11; Sehlmeyer 1999: 126–28); some kind of drama seems to have told the story (Ovid, *Fasti* 4.326, with Wiseman 1998: 3, 23). Cato the Censor's likeness stood in the Temple of Salus (Plut. *Cat. Mai.* 19.3; Sehlmeyer, pp. 146–48). The Theater of *Pompey*, crowned by a temple complex celebrating victory (Venus Victrix and Victoria) and its various constituents (Felicitas and Honos et Virtus: see Coarelli 1997: 567–70), housed a statue group of the fourteen peoples subdued by Pompey in his eastern wars of 67–63 (probably those represented in his triumph, listed at Plut. *Pomp.* 45.2), apparently positioned around a representation of Pompey himself (Plin. *HN* 36.41). On the (perhaps spurious) *Porticus ad nationes*, which is often brought into connection with these, see F. Coarelli, *LTUR* IV.138–39 and 1997: 166–68; P. Liverano, *LTUR* V.286.

[173] Livy 40.52.5–7: a *tabula triumphalis* mounted over the doors of the Temple of Jupiter Optimus Maximus and that of the Lares Permarini celebrating the naval victory at Myonessus of *L. Aemilius Regillus* over Antiochus (190). Livy 41.28.8–10: a great *tabula*, dedicated to Jupiter in the Temple of Mater Matuta set up by *Ti. Sempronius Gracchus the elder* (cos. II 163), in the form of Sardinia and containing depictions of the campaigns (cf. Zinserling 1959/60: no. 11) as well as describing his subjugation of Sardinia and second triumph. *ILS* 20: *L. Mummius'* dedication of the Temple of Hercules Victor commemorating his Achaean victory and destruction of Corinth: Pietilä-Castrén 1987: 140–44. Val. Max. 8.14.2; *Schol. Bob.* 179 St: lines of Accius, who is also known to have written a *praetexta* called *Brutus* about the ancient hero of the clan, inscribed on the Temple of Mars in the Circus Flaminius dedicated by *D. Iunius Brutus Callaicus* (note *prompta laudatione delectatus*; see Coarelli 1997: 492–96). *Pompey's* dedicatory tablets to Minerva and another, unknown goddess (Venus Victrix?), summarizing his eastern campaigns: Plin. *HN* 7.97; Diod. Sic. 40.4. *M. Fulvius Flaccus'* capture of Volsinii in 264 was noted on the base of some of the two thousand statues he had seized and dedicated at the Fortuna–Mater Matuta complex, just inside the Triumphal Gate (Torelli 1968: 71–76; cf. Plin. *HN* 34.34, and the mural showing him as triumphator in his own Temple of Vortumnus: Zinserling 1959/60: no. 3). But Fulvius' monument was short-lived (Wiseman 1994: 44–47).

[174] See Zinserling 1959/60: 403–48. (Cf. now Holliday 2002: esp. 30–33, 104–12.) His numbers 1–3, 5, 7, 9, 11, beginning with the painting in the Temple of Consus on the Aventine of *L. Papirius Cursor* as triumphator in 272 and ending with the *tabula picta* of *Ti. Sempronius Gracchus* (above, n. 173), are explicitly described as housed in temples. See above (nn. 135, 168) for murals showing the victories of *Valerius Maximus* and of *Scipio Asiaticus*; Sid. Apoll. 22.158–68 probably describes

booty,[175] would preserve the splendor of the dedicator's *res gestae*, or even of his family, for all posterity.[176] Their cumulative effect may have been as overwhelming as the last several footnotes; but no one has to remember everything at once. Rather, this enormous mass of *potential* reminiscence may be seen as so much material for *actual*, specific recollection, activated by the appropriate cuing and often directed by an external agent, as we saw in the case of Cicero's reference to the statue of Tremulus.

THE RECENT PAST

It is time to pause and survey the path travelled thus far. I began with what may have seemed at first appearance to be implausible demands upon the historical knowledge of the contional audience. Yet the comparable historical allusiveness of late-Republican coin-types suggests that it is, in fact, the most reasonable hypothesis to suppose that allusions in *contiones* are a rough, but not deceptive, index of listeners' knowledge; and thus that orators, like those who developed the complex iconography on the coins, could presume, and exploit, a fairly impressive level of cultural memory in their "target audience." The above review of the extraordinarily rich "monumental landscape" of the ancient city of Rome – a civic environment that not only perpetuated cultural memory but to a remarkable degree was created with that set purpose – shows that the hypothesis of a relatively acute consciousness of the past is by no means implausible, and affords some hints about the processes through which such "knowledge" of the great men of

a copy of a near-contemporary painting of *Lucullus'* capture of Cyzicus (Hölscher 1980: 353–54). Zinserling reasonably conjectures that the paintings carried in triumphs (e.g. in those of Scipio Africanus, Aemilius Paullus, Pompey and Caesar: nos. 8, 12, 17, 18) were often subsequently set up in temples and other public buildings (pp. 407–8, 417–18). For the "propagandistic purpose" of such paintings, see Zinserling, pp. 413–20, who, however, tends to neglect the longer-term striving for *gloria* (see Plut. *Cat. Mai.* 19.4, for explicit mention of paintings in this connection) and exaggerate their specifically electoral impact.

[175] Most notably, the two great porticos at the Circus Flaminius built after the victories over Macedon in 168 and 146: the Porticus Octavia, built by *Cn. Octavius* (whose fame was redoubled by a statue on the Rostra voted after his murder in 162) after his naval triumph in 167 (Pape 1975: 15; Pietilä-Castrén 1987: 118–23), and rated by Velleius as the most opulent of all such structures (2.1.2); and the *Porticus Metelli*, a virtual museum of Greek art taken in the war against Andriscus of 146, including the group of Alexander and his squadron by Lysippus: Cic. *Verr.* 2.4.126; Vell. Pat. 1.11.4–5; Plin. *HN* 34.64, 36.35; Pape, pp. 15–16; Pietilä-Castrén, pp. 128–34. Booty dedicated by *M. Fulvius Nobilior* after his triumph over the Aetolians adorned his censorial Temple of Hercules and the Muses: *CIL* I² 615 = VI 1307 = *ILLRP* 124, with Pape, pp. 12–14.

[176] Cf. Pape 1975: 53–54. Orlin 1997 places such temple-building in a larger communal context than has often been suggested (a greater proportion of public relative to private financing, senatorial control of religious aspects, including initial approval and the dedication), but does not contest the evident fact that to build a temple was, among other things, to stake a personal claim to lasting *gloria* (e.g. 66–73, 161, 192).

the past and their services to the Republic was produced. Mass oratory, in the main forms of ubiquitous political *contiones* and the less frequent, but more spectacular funeral eulogies of the nobility, was able to exploit a huge array of mnemonic cues embodied in the monuments among which all public life, and much life in public, took place – simultaneously, of course, reviving, and perhaps reshaping, the commemorative meaning of those same monuments. Set in the context of Rome's peculiar dedication to *memoria*, rather than judged in accordance with *a priori* assumptions about the ignorance of an urban proletariat, the challenging historical allusions with which this chapter began start to take on real significance as evidence of the civic awareness of contional audiences.

Although the discussion of comparative material from the coinage or monumental landscape has ranged more widely in order to elucidate various points about the commemorative dynamics of Republican Rome, thus far the allusions in contional speech that have been examined belong to relatively distant history, certainly beyond the direct and personal knowledge of their audiences. I have argued for a fairly high degree of participation by contional audiences in Roman cultural tradition, which would be, if accepted, a significant finding; but of course the kind of knowledge and awareness most directly relevant to the audience's role as political agents will be that of recent history, issues, and practices, references to which will be the subject of the remaining part of this chapter.

A dividing line is certainly discernible in Cicero's *contiones* between the age of "our ancestors" (*maiores nostri*) and that in the direct experience of "you and your fathers"; it falls roughly fifty to sixty years before the present.[177] For example, Cicero's references to the Gracchi, on or just beyond that threshold of popular memory, are perceptibly stereotyped and lacking in precise detail,[178] and it is noteworthy in this context that in 63

[177] See *Leg. Man.* 60 (for a secular shift between 133 and 107), *Red. pop.* 6–11 (where the exiles of Metellus Numidicus in 100 – *c.* 98 and of Marius in 88–87, but not that of P. Popilius in 123–121, are placed in the time of *vos patresque vestri* or *vestra patrumque memoria*), and *Rab. perd.* 2 (where the so-called "final decree of the Senate," first used in 121, is an inheritance from the *maiores*; below, n. 179). The break is considerably more recent than is the division between "cultural memory" and "communicative memory" (80–100 years back) adopted by the leading contemporary theorists of memory, Aleida and Jan Assmann (1988: 29–30); but that is explicitly a maximum, and we should perhaps keep in mind the relative scarcity of living grandfathers in Rome (Saller 1994: 229). Roloff 1938: 128–31 (= 1967: 318–22), implausibly sees the terminus of the age of the *maiores* as a fixed rather than a sliding one, and rather arbitrarily sets it just before the "Gracchan Revolution." (Cf. Stemmler 2000: 185, n. 164.) The honorific aura of *maiores*, of course, produces a natural bias toward antiquity in the use of the word. *Pace* Horsfall 1996: 47, the suppression of Saturninus in 100 was hardly beyond living memory in 63.

[178] *Leg. agr.* 2.10, 31; *Rab. perd.* 14–15. However, *pace* Mack 1937: 30–31 with n. 74, comparison of the references to P. Popilius Laenas and Q. Metellus Numidicus at *Red. pop.* 10–11 and at *Red. sen.* 38

he can call upon his audience to defend the so-called Final Decree of the Senate as "that ultimate defence of (sc. the Republic's) authority and power bequeathed us by *the ancestors*" even though it goes back only to the suppression of C. Gracchus in 121.[179] But toward the end of the second century – roughly from the age of Marius – events come into much sharper focus. Defending C. Rabirius in 63 on the charge of having killed Saturninus in 100, Cicero takes his audience through a detailed argument about the events of thirty-seven years before which at times makes remarkable demands on their historical and procedural knowledge.[180] Indeed, the trial of Rabirius itself and the popular response it elicited sufficiently show that the terrible events of those days, and their contemporary implications, remained very much alive in the minds of the men of the Forum.[181] Our sources, naturally, stress the fears for senatorial authority that the charges against Rabirius raised among the élite.[182] But for the *populus*, which was to serve as the jury in Rabirius' final trial and heard the speeches of Labienus and Cicero in that capacity, the fundamental question would have been the validity of the basic Roman civil right of *provocatio*, understood by common citizens to be the foundation of their liberty.[183] Hence Cicero's attempt to turn the prosecution's weapons against them with his (specious) emphasis, early in his speech, on the customs and laws protecting the person of a Roman citizen, including specific reference to the *lex Porcia* restricting corporal

hardly shows that the People considered the circumstances of their return (especially the destruction of their enemies) roughly identical to those of Marius, or had no recollection of these men's hostility to C. Gracchus and Saturninus. If the real difference is that Marius gets better billing in the speech to the People, that is surely no surprise (see below). See Nicholson 1992: 32–34, with 102–3.

[179] *Rab. perd.* 2; cf. 34, a reference to the consular summons (*evocatio*) consequent on the *SCU* (*senatus consultum ultimum*). (It remains convenient to use the conventional, non-technical name for the decree *ut dent operam magistratus ne quid res publica detrimenti capiat*.) Cf. Sall. *Cat.* 29.3 (*more Romano*), with the comments of Stemmler 2000: 182, n. 150; according to Drummond 1995: 79–95, that reference is a rhetorical misrepresentation in any case. See also pp. 225–28 with n. 108.

[180] *Rab. perd.* 20–31, with Tyrrell 1978: 107–33. Living memory of the crisis is also presumed at *Cat.* 3.15 from the same year: a highly elliptical reference to Marius' failure, or refusal, to prevent the killing of a praetor in office, C. Servilius Glaucia. As for the audience's knowledge of the seemingly obscure duumviral procedure, see Tyrrell, p. 79.

[181] Cass. Dio 37.27.3; note the (popular) *invidia* the case aroused (Cic. *Pis.* 4, quoted in n. 182). Cicero's stated wish that Rabirius *had* killed Saturninus (*Rab. perd.* 18) brings forth a shout; by displaying Saturninus' *imago* (*Rab. perd.* 25), the prosecuting tribune, Labienus, presumably aimed at, and may well have achieved, the kind of effect provoked by Caesar's production of Marius' *imago* six years before. The attitude of the plebs to the events as they unfolded in 100 is difficult to ascertain (see Schneider 1982/83; Badian 1984: 108; Burckhardt 1988: 143, n. 190; Cavaggioni 1998: 153–54, 160–65, 182–84) and anyway was mostly beside the point in 63. On the procedure followed in this trial, see chap. 1, n. 90, and chap. 2, n. 93.

[182] Cicero later characterized the trial as one in which *senatus auctoritatem sustinui contra invidiam atque defendi* (*Pis.* 4; see also chap. 6, n. 100) – essentially also Dio's interpretation (37.26.1–3).

[183] Brunt 1988: 330–34. On *provocatio* and its various problems of interpretation, see Lintott 1972 and 1999: index, s.v.; also now Santalucia 1998: 29–46, 52–55, 70–75.

punishment of a citizen, and the *lex Sempronia* forbidding the execution of a citizen without authorization by the People.[184] The traditional view that the fundamental issue of the case was the validity (or limits) of the so-called "Final Decree of the Senate" is of course not incorrect, so far as it goes, but adopts the élite rather than the popular perspective.[185] The importance of this case, too often reduced to an arcane and anachronistic charade, simply cannot be understood without due recognition of the strong popular interest at stake.

The very fact that there is such a clear distinction between the distant and recent past, the latter marked by appeal to the personal memory of contemporaries and their fathers, is itself significant, implying as it does that the history of the last few decades was something in which his audiences were involved as a politically engaged public. "You yourselves saw" in 88 how credit in Rome was linked to conditions in Asia; "have you forgotten" how many armies were maintained in the Social War solely on the revenues of Campania?; "who among you is unaware" that Egypt was said to have been willed to the Roman People by King "Alexas"?[186] "You have often observed from this very place [sc. the Rostra]" the dignified and fluent manner of Pompey's oratory.[187] "You and your fathers" invested your hopes for the empire in Marius alone by conferring upon him the commands against Jugurtha, the Cimbri, and the Teutones; many scions of the Metelli "supplicated you and your fathers" for the return from exile of Numidicus; "you gave me the role" (he says in 63) of defending Pompey's honor in his absence three years previously; "you" defeated Catiline by "your" zeal and courage.[188] This is partly, of course, a rhetorical construction, founded on the fiction that the audience of every *contio* impersonated the *populus Romanus*. Yet in this very fiction we sense the presumption of persistent and immediate involvement by the audience in the affairs of the *res publica*;[189] and surely it does little good to call upon a rhetorical fiction as witness.

It is possible to sketch out some of the outlines of recent history as they appeared to the implied audience of the published *contiones*. Even as late as Cicero's popular speeches of the 60s and 50s, Marius remains a great figure.[190] "You and your fathers decided to put all hopes for our empire in the hands of a single man, Gaius Marius, to give the same man command of the war with Jugurtha, with the Cimbri, and with the Teutones"; he was

---

[184] *Rab. perd.* 10–17.   [185] Below, pp. 225–26.
[186] Cic. *Leg. Man.* 19; *Leg. agr.* 2.80, 41 (see pp. 113–14).   [187] Cic. *Leg. Man.* 42.
[188] Cic. *Leg. Man.* 60; *Red. pop.* 6; *Leg. agr.* 2.49; *Phil.* 4.15.
[189] Cf. Thompson's observation (1978: 83 and elsewhere) that the use of the second-person pronoun emphasizes the audience's personal stake in the matters under deliberation.
[190] See Mack 1937: 26–30, 44–46, who, however, tends to invoke too easily a presumption of popular ignorance (see below, e.g., chap. 6, n. 107).

"the father of our country, I say, the founder of your freedom and of this very Commonwealth," "the guardian of your state and empire."[191] Such effusions fit well with our knowledge of the popular enthusiasm that met Caesar's display of Marius' *imago* during his aunt's funeral in 69, and his restoration, during his aedileship in 65, of Marius' trophy or (trophies) on the Capitol, formerly destroyed by Sulla.[192] Even as late as 44 the (apparently false) claim of an ambitious oculist to be Marius' grandson met with a warm reception among the urban plebs, as well as in various towns of Italy.[193] The colorful details of Marius' flight from Sulla thirty-five years in the past, including his refuge in the marshes, the pity of the people of Minturnae, and the small boat in which he fled to Africa, can all be brushed in with the swiftest of strokes.[194] Darker episodes in Marius' career, such as the constitutionally and politically troubling lynching of Saturninus and Glaucia in 100, the former a tribune and the latter a praetor in office, despite his pledge of protection, or the massacre he unleashed upon his return from exile in 87, are not forgotten, but justified or at least palliated.[195]

Sulla, on the other hand, remains, with great consistency, an object of popular revulsion and hatred. In *contiones* offered by Sallust in his *Histories*, Sulla is nothing less than the enslaver of the Roman People;[196] but even in Ciceronian popular speeches the cumulative picture of Sulla is very dark.[197] The one ostensibly laudatory mention he receives – purely as a general – is

[191] *Leg. Man.* 60; *Rab. perd.* 27; *Red. pop.* 9; cf. *Cat.* 3.24 *custos*. Carney 1960. Cf. how Sallust's "Lepidus" exploits against Sulla the memory of Marius' Cimbric victory (*Hist.* 1.55.17).

[192] Plut. *Caes.* 5–6; Suet. *Iul.* 11. The "false Marius" (n. 193) returned the compliment in 44, attempting to dedicate an altar at the spot in the Forum where Caesar was cremated. On the victory monuments, see now Sehlmeyer 1999: 192–93, 196–97, 217–18; Mackay 2000: 162–68 (but note that "Dio" = Plutarch: 165, n. 15, 166 with n. 18). Mackay (p. 164, with nn. 10, 13) is probably correct against Sehlmeyer (p. 193 with n. 84) on the interpretation of the distributive numeral *bina* (*tropaea*), used by Val. Max. (6.19.14; cf. Kühner and Stegmann 1974–76: II.1.660). But I see no suggestion that the Jugurthine trophy was not itself on the Capitol, a point on which Mackay seems to be of two minds (cf. p. 163 with 164); reference to Κιμβρικὰ κατορθώματα at Plut. *Caes.* 6.2 may be only a venial simplification. Cf. also Richardson 1992: 402; C. Reusser, *LTUR* v.91.

[193] Esp. App. *B Civ.* 3.2, Val. Max. 9.15.1; other sources and discussion in Denniston 1926: 69–70; Weinstock 1971: 364–67.

[194] *Red. pop.* 20.

[195] *Rab. perd.* 20–21, 27–31 (note how Cicero here uses Marius' *gloria* to cast doubt on the idea that he gave Saturninus a false guarantee that his life would be spared; Tyrrell 1978: 131, seems to miss the rhetorical point), 35; *Cat.* 3.15, 24 (where Marius is distanced from the killings of 87 by means of the ablative of accompaniment [*Cinna cum Mario*] and the passive voice: cf. Carney 1960: 115–16); *Red. pop.* 7, 9–10, 19–21.

[196] 1.55.1–8 (speech of Lepidus); 3.48.1, 9 (Macer).

[197] For Cicero's expressed views on Sulla, see esp. Diehl 1988, who, however, does not attempt to distinguish the utterances before popular audiences from the rest. Mitchell 1979: 65–76, 86–90 produces a different picture of Cicero's sympathies by stressing his actual, if inexplicit, affinity with Sulla's political principles, rather than his overt and relatively frequent condemnation of his moral character.

loaded with irony,[198] while he is blamed for the massacre of citizens and "catastrophe" he inflicted on the state in victory[199] and designated outright a "tyrant," though one imposed on the Republic by (illegitimate) legal form.[200] His utterly unscrupulous (*sine ulla religione*) sale, or gifts, to his loyal supporters of property confiscated from citizens without due process played well before the contional audience;[201] Cicero's attack on Rullus' credibility depends in fact largely on painting him as a covert agent of the *Sullani possessores* who had received that largesse, and indignation is heightened by the allegation that their interests are being served by a tribune, a man holding the very office – emasculated by Sulla! – that should have been a source of terror to them given the source of their gains and the ill-will (*invidia*) that burdens them: Rullus pretends to be a Marian but is really a Sullan worse than Sulla![202] Cicero's playing of the "Sulla card" against Rullus, involving a number of clear and specific historical references, indicates that a vivid awareness of the major episodes of bloodshed and disruption in the eighties persisted in the minds of his plebeian audiences.[203] Noteworthy, too, is the relish with which Cicero associates Catiline with the "spendthrift" Sullan colonists who can only hope to evade their creditors if they raise their benefactor from the grave, or with which he invests

---

[198] *Leg. Man.* 8. Possibly as praetor in 66, with *Sullani* still in a position of great power, Cicero was not prepared publicly to derogate Sulla's memory. Note that at §30 he somewhat surprisingly openly acknowledges (if with the utmost brevity) Pompey's service to Sulla in the "freeing" of Italy.

[199] *Cat.* 3.24: *ne dici quidem opus est quanta deminutio civium et quanta calamitate rei publicae*. This review of the internecine bloodshed of the 80s (the Lepidan insurrection seems to have been tacked on for the sake of completeness), while ostensibly even-handed (note the *crudelitas* of Cinna's victory *cum Mario*: cf. n. 195), in fact assigns chief responsibility to Sulla by placing him at the beginning and end of the cycle of violence. The review begins not with P. Sulpicius' violence, in Marius' interest, but with Sulla's crushing of Sulpicius, expulsion of Marius, the "protector of this city," and the killing or expulsion of "many excellent men," and reaches its climax with the Sullan "catastrophe." Note also *Leg. agr.* 2.56 (*funesta illa auctione*), and *Cat.* 2.20. Cf. Sall. *Hist.* 1.55.14, a cryptic but instantly recognizable allusion to the murder of Marius Gratidianus in 82.

[200] *Leg. agr.* 3.5: *Omnium legum iniquissimam dissimillimamque legis esse arbitror eam quam L. Flaccus interrex de Sulla tulit, ut omnia quaecumque ille fecisset essent rata. Nam cum ceteris in civitatibus tyrannis institutis leges omnes exstinguantur atque tollantur, hic rei publicae tyrannum lege constituit.* The *excusatio temporis* that Cicero appears to concede to the Lex Valeria in the passage immediately following (§§5–6) is doubtless intended only to heighten indignation against Rullus' proposal. On Sulla's "tyranny" in *contiones*, see also Sall. *Hist.* 1.55.1, 7, 22, 24 (Lepidus). Cf. Diehl 1988: 149–52, 182–91.

[201] *Leg. agr.* 2.56, 81; Sall. *Hist.* 1.55.12 (Lepidus).

[202] *Leg. agr.* 2.68–70, 98; 3 *passim*, esp. §§6–7, and §10 *repentinus Sulla nobis exoritur!* Worse than Sulla: note the invidious comparison of provisions of Rullus' bill with Sulla's actions at 2.56, 81; 3.5–13.

[203] *Leg. agr.* 3.6: who could be so dull as not to recall that Sulla was dictator after the joint consulship of C. Marius (sc. the younger) and Cn. Papirius (Carbo) – i.e., in 82? References to the Valerian law conferring the dictatorship on Sulla and the Cornelian laws regarding confiscations and allotments: §§5–8 and 2.78. The "Sullan strategy" is naturally absent from the extant portion of the speech before the Senate: Classen 1985: 313, 359.

P. Lentulus Sura, the conspirator of 63, with the desire to repeat Sulla's (and Cinna's) *regnum*.[204] Three decades and more after Sulla's triumph in civil war, the attitude of the Roman plebs toward the memory of the dictator can be inferred from the burning of the Cornelian Senate-house in 52 and the destruction, after Pharsalus, of the gilded statue of the dictator which stood on the Rostra, at the center of public life.[205] One might have thought that the statue of the dictator of more than three decades past would be too passé to be the target of an angry mob. No doubt memory of Sulla and his civil war was kept green by Caesar's own spectacular identification with the Marian legacy (above, p. 111), and after Pompey's adherence to the senatorial cause it will have been easy, especially in view of the latter's origins as a Sullan partisan, to see the Caesarian civil war as a replay of the former one, with a different ending.[206] According to this version of history, which may have been widely current among the plebs, Caesar's victory in 48 will have taken on the appearance of just revenge upon the tyrant and the last remnants of his régime. This, too, is a product of "collective" or "social" memory.

Even far less momentous events of the last generation or so appear to be sufficiently fresh in the historical memory of Cicero's audiences to serve as material for rhetorical allusion. We have already noted the use that Cicero makes of his listeners' recollection of M. Brutus' colonial foundation at Capua *c.* 83 in the second oration against Rullus' agrarian bill. In the same speech he appeals to his audience's knowledge of Rome's reliance on the Campanian revenues during the war against the Italian allies more than two decades before, and before another crowd he recalls the financial crisis that followed Mithridates' invasion of Asia twenty years thence.[207] It is true that in these two cases he offers some prompting. That can hardly be said, however, of the remarkably elliptical way in which, in 63, Cicero refers to the controversy over the supposed inheritance of Egypt by the Roman People. This is common knowledge for his audience: "Who among you is unaware of the claim that that kingdom was inherited by the Roman People according to the will of King Alexas [i.e. Ptolemy Alexander I or II]?"[208] And Cicero does indeed presume familiarity with the events when

---

[204] *Cat.* 2.20 (cf. Sall. *Hist.* 1.55.23 [Lepidus]); 3.9 – doubtless the source of the story repeated by Sallust (*Cat.* 47.2).

[205] Chap. 2, nn. 77, 82.

[206] Note that Pompey's statue on the Rostra was destroyed simultaneously: chap. 2, n. 82.

[207] *Leg. agr.* 2.80; *Leg. Man.* 19.

[208] *Leg. agr.* 2.41. For a résumé of the known details, see J. W. Crawford 1994: 43–46, accepting Badian 1967 on the identification of the testator as Alexander I (d. 88); Braund 1983: 24–28, prefers the second king of that name (d. 80).

he mentions the time "when, following [Ptolemy Alexander I or II's] death, we sent three envoys to Tyre to recover a debt deposited there by him"; depending on which of the two homonymous kings Cicero means, he is reaching back some sixteen to twenty-three years to that relatively obscure step in the story.[209] Such a presumption of knowledge clearly rests on the fact that the relevant questions received much public ventilation in *contiones* two years previously – a public debate which, a few paragraphs further on, Cicero evidently regards as well known to his audience.[210] The coins again corroborate the impression we gain from the speeches, strongly suggesting by the subtlety of their allusions that their "audience" was both well aware of events of the recent past and able to pick up on the symbolic language employed by the designers of the types.[211]

Contional allusions suggest that popular audiences were not only expected to be aware of recent and current events; they also had to make sense of references to a variety of laws. Cicero cites the Licinian and Aebutian laws which forbade proposers of legislation from receiving powers or administrative responsibilities under their own laws, the Valerian and Cornelian laws on Sulla's dictatorship and his acts as dictator, the *lex Fabia* on illegal detention, the *lex Porcia* protecting the citizen from the magistrate's rods, and Gaius Gracchus' law requiring trial in a court established by the People for capital charges against Roman citizens.[212] The allusions on Republican coins to the same *lex Porcia*, as well as others to various ballot laws, suggest that such references were expected to be understood rather than merely to impress.[213] Cicero relies on easy and immediate

---

[209] *Leg. agr.* 2.41; for the alternative dates, see Badian 1967, and n. 208 above. Note the unelaborated reference to the diplomatic actions of the year 65 (*Leg. agr.* 2.44).

[210] *Leg. agr.* 2.44: *eosdem cursus hoc tempore, quos L. Cotta L. Torquato consulibus cucurrerunt?* On *contiones*, see Suet. *Iul.* 11; for the public dispute between the censors on this question, see Plut. *Crass.* 13.1. Cicero's fragmentary speech of 65 on the controversy (*De rege Alexandrino*) was probably delivered, however, in the Senate (scholia to frs. 4 and 8 Crawford = *Schol. Bob.* 92, 93 St). Cf. how details such as Hiempsal's possession of *ager publicus* in Africa had been brought up *non numquam ex hoc loco* (Cic. *Leg. agr.* 2.58).

[211] Note especially the allusions to the crisis of 88 and to the remarkable achievements, at around the beginning of the century, of the new man C. Coelius Caldus (cos. 94) on *RRC* 434/1–2 (54 BC) and 437/1–4 (51 BC [or 53: Hersh and Walker]). Though the span of time is short, references on the coins of Pompey's officers to their role in quite obscure episodes of his eastern campaigns (*RRC* 422, 58 BC; 431, 55 BC) are also of interest, and should be connected with recent and contemporary public commemoration of those campaigns in great detail, from Pompey's triumph of 61 (Plut. *Pomp.* 45.2–3; App. *Mith.* 117) to his dedicatory plaques (Plin. *HN* 7.97; Diod. Sic. 40.4) and the construction of his theater (above, n. 172). Note also Faustus Sulla's use in 56 (*RRC* 426/4) of an unlabelled composition of wreaths, globe, *aplustre*, and sheaf of grain to refer to Pompey's pacification of the world *terra marique*.

[212] *Leg. agr.* 2.21, 3.5–6; *Rab. perd.* 8, 12–13.

[213] See above, n. 78.

comprehension of his allusions to the so-called Final Decree of the Senate in the speech for Rabirius in 63, although it had not been used for fourteen years.[214]

All of this points, then, to an audience not only well versed in its historical traditions but firmly engaged as participant and observer in the rituals and practices of a very public political sphere. Only this assumption can make reasonable sense of the extraordinary fragment of a *contio* delivered by the tribune T. Munatius Plancus, one of the leaders of the attack on Milo after the murder of Clodius, on March 1, 52, the day following the senatorial debate over the legal procedures to be used against those responsible for the violence in which the killing took place and the explosive aftermath of that event in Rome. The fragment is particularly valuable to us since, unlike Cicero's *contiones*, it was not preserved in "literary" form but was extracted verbatim by Cicero's commentator, Asconius, from the register of daily events (*acta diurna*); consequently, there can be little serious doubt (as has sometimes been entertained about Cicero's *contiones*) that it fairly faithfully reflects the actual circumstances and dynamics of its occasion.[215] Asconius quotes Munatius as follows:

Cum Hortensius dixisse<t> ut extra ordinem quareretur apud quaesitorem – existima<bat> futurum ut, cum pusillum dedisset dulcedinis, largiter acerbitatis devorarent – adversus hominem ingeniosum nostro ingenio usi sumus: invenimus Fufium, qui diceret "Divide"; reliquae parti sententiae ego et Sallustius intercessimus.[216]

When Hortensius had moved that there should be a trial with priority, presided over by a Special Investigator – he supposed that if he offered a sweet morsel they would devour the whole bitter meal – against this clever man I made use of my own wits. I arranged with Fufius to call for a division of the motion; Sallust and I vetoed the other part.

---

[214] *Rab. perd.* 2–4, 20, 34–35. In the *Fourth Philippic* he presumes general recognition of the principle, quite abstract from the audience's personal experience, that "all provinces should be subject to a consul's authority and *imperium*": *Phil.* 4.9. Note also Cicero's rebuttal of the arguments against Gabinius' legateship to Pompey at *Leg. Man.* 57–58.

[215] Asc. 44–45 C: Asconius is clearly quoting from the *acta diurna*, which he has just perused for the detail about the *SC* of *pridie Kal. Mart.* See in general B. A. Marshall 1985: 56–57, 193, and now P. White 1997. On regularly published *contiones*, see pp. 25–30.

[216] Asc. 44–45 C, with B. A. Marshall 1985: 193–95. Following Clark (*pace* Sumner 1965 and Marshall 1985: 193), I take the manuscripts' *dixisse* and *existimare* to be a scribe's clumsy attempt to put the original, direct quotation into *oratio obliqua*, following *haec dixit ad verbum*. The latter half of the sentence is clearly in *oratio recta* and I see no good reason to assume that *in the acta* it began in *oratio obliqua*, particularly after *haec dixit ad verbum*. *Quom* (= *cum*) is easily corrupted by medieval abbreviation to the MSS q, que, and Q.; once this was done, alteration of the following subjunctive to infinitive was inevitable. But *existimare* is likely to represent *existimabat* rather than *existimaret*, which would give, as Marshall complains, "a messy construction."

Munatius was describing to his plebeian audience a clever parliamentary maneuver by which he foiled the growing senatorial consensus in favor of a proposed decree pronouncing that the killing of P. Clodius and the ensuing violence were indeed "harmful to the Republic" (*contra rem publicam*; this, the content of the "sweet morsel," will have preceded the surviving fragment), but that the trials should be conducted under existing laws and be given only special priority. This was no doubt a carefully crafted package deal, with something "sweet" and something "bitter" for everyone. For Munatius and those working for the condemnation of Milo, the former part was desirable since it was highly prejudicial to the case, as Cicero's labored attempt to deny this at the beginning of his published speech clearly shows;[217] the latter half, however, was full of "bitterness" for them, since judicial "business as usual" would no doubt have given Milo's friends a fighting chance to win his acquittal.[218] So Munatius arranged with the praetorian senator Q. Fufius Calenus to call for a division of the two halves of the motion, and after they were each approved separately, he and another tribune, the historian Sallust, exercised their veto against the half pertaining to judicial procedures. The way was thus opened for Pompey's special legislation comprehending these cases *ad hoc*, which proved to have provisions for a jury hand-picked by the new sole consul, special procedures to limit bribery, and distressing constraints upon orators' ability to manipulate the evidence rhetorically.[219]

That Munatius would entrust to the ears of his plebeian audience – *imperitissimi* indeed! – such a detailed reference to a complex parliamentary maneuver in the Curia is itself illuminating, not merely of their presumed level of knowledge but also of their political engagement. The tribune palpably expects his listeners to be *interested* in following an adroit move in the senatorial chess game, which was closed to their direct scrutiny but could have weighty consequences.[220] Just grasping what is going on here requires a fairly detailed prior understanding of the immediate background

---

[217] Cic. *Mil.* 12–14.   [218] See Clark's entertaining paragraph (1895: xxiv–xxv).

[219] The content of the two parts of the division is, unfortunately, described explicitly only by the Bobbensian Scholiast (117 St), who may simply be inferring from Cic. *Mil.* 14, the passage on which he is commenting. Bonnefond-Coudry 1989: 527–31 offers an excellent analysis, rejecting the alternative view, based on the *Schol. Bob.*, most recently championed by Gruen 1974: 234–35. (Cf. also B. A. Marshall 1985: 194; further bibliography in Libero 1992: 35, n. 36.) On the provisions of the *lex Pompeia de vi*, Gruen gives a concise summary (p. 235), but it should be stressed as well that Pompey's law saw to it that testimony was to be heard *first*, contrary to regular practice, and over a period of three days compared to one for the prosecution and defense speeches together (Asc. 39–40 C).

[220] Note the emphasis in the fragment on *ingenium*. On the effects of exclusion from senatorial deliberation, see below, chap. 7.

to the controversy, as well as of a number of technical matters – not merely the meaning of *quaestio extra ordinem* and *quaesitor*, but also of a procedural device peculiar to the Senate (division of a motion) and of its effects.[221] Since his audience could not directly observe senatorial meetings, it is evident that their implicit knowledge of procedure derives from reports like this one. What one might call the "educative" function of the *contio* is thus underscored, and in view of the great frequency of such public meetings we should be careful not to underestimate the depth and extent of this "political education" for the *imperita multitudo*.

One might, with sufficient *a priori* conviction, explain away individually every one of the allusions and references I have cited.[222] Certainly, we cannot be sure in individual cases that the published form of the allusion was indeed wholly suitable to its implied context in a *contio* nor, of course, that it was (or would have been) *successful*. But the overall picture, I submit, stands out clearly: that the audiences of public speeches were expected to be quite aware of the Roman past and present, and were treated as involved and regular participants in political affairs.

Careful comparison of Cicero's pairs of senatorial and popular speeches has well shown that the demands of mass oratory differed from the principles of effective persuasion in the aristocratic council: emotional effects, for example, are indeed heightened for the Rostra, while rational proof and political abstractions play better in the Curia.[223] Here Mack, for instance, found ready, but I think specious, verification of his assumptions about mass ignorance. No one would claim that even the most attentive *contio*-goer could equal the typical senator in his grasp of the affairs of the *res publica*; some aspects of public life, such as the language of the law, must have remained relatively opaque and forbidding to the general populace, who were in addition shut out of a crucial arena of deliberation, the Curia.[224] But before mass audiences are faulted too gravely for some of the deficiencies in rationality apparent in *contiones*, the difference in venue needs also to be considered. Anyone who has spoken to a large free-flowing

---

[221] A little over a century later, in very changed historical circumstances, the scholar Asconius thought it necessary to explain the significance of "dividing the motion" to his young sons (43–44 C).

[222] Many more are listed by Horsfall 1996: 94–95, nn. 353, 355.

[223] I refer to the work of Mack and Classen (above, pp. 39–40); cf. also Thompson 1978: 110–32. One of the more intriguing differences between the senatorial and the contional speeches *De lege agraria* is the *greater* detail of the latter, including copious citation and discussion of the text of the law. As Classen 1985: 362–63 points out, this in itself need have little to do with knowledge or the lack of it; rather, the contional audience's natural prejudice in favor of agrarian distribution arguably forced Cicero to create the image of one "penetrating" a subtle "trap" hidden behind its benign façade.

[224] On these points, see pp. 197–200 and chap. 7.

crowd will readily understand that the open spaces of the Forum before "the orator's greatest stage,"[225] filled with several thousand people, without amplification, and with no compulsion upon most of the audience to remain other than the orator's sheer dynamism, will have demanded something very different than the enclosed Senate-house or temple, packed with no more than several hundred listeners who were perhaps impatient of lengthy speechifying but pretty much obligated to keep to their seats.[226] The emotionalism of *contiones*, their lack of any great legal or constitutional subtlety, and highly manipulative strategies (which I shall consider in detail in due course) are all undeniable; but we should not hasten to ascribe these to a stereotyped mass ignorance that appears to be belied by the empiricial evidence of the allusions in the *contiones* themselves.

The urban plebs, however *imperita* it seemed to Cicero and his friends, was far from ignorant about the history, constitution, laws, practices, and procedures of the *res publica*, the People's possession, as the ancient phrase put it; as participants in and observers of the political dramas of the Forum and Campus, they passed their lives surrounded by multiple verbal and visual sources of civic knowledge. As I shall argue in later chapters, a sharp asymmetry of knowledge between Senate and People, and the favorable position of senators in the flow of political information, clearly did open a wide field for strategic manipulation. But a presumption of generalized plebeian ignorance will no longer do; the acquaintance of the plebs with the traditions and workings of the Republic would probably compare favorably to that of the citizens of many a modern democratic state.

---

[225] *Maxima quasi oratoris scaena*: *De or.* 2.338, on which see chap. 2, n. 109.
[226] *De or.* 2.333–34; *Leg.* 3.40.

CHAPTER 4

The Voice of the People

Fergus Millar has rightly lamented that modern students of Republican politics have been "deaf both to the voice of the orator and to the reactions of the crowd."[1] As everyone knew who climbed the Rostra and confronted the sea of faces across the Forum and around the surrounding temples,[2] the Roman People itself had a voice – a loud and sometimes terrifying one. When a tribune who opposed A. Gabinius' law creating a special command against the pirates for Pompey was unable to speak above the noise of the multitude, and thus tried to indicate with his fingers that two commanders should be chosen instead of one, the crowd let loose a shout that – according to Plutarch and Dio – knocked a crow out of the sky "as if struck by lightning."[3] Falling crows are a topos in such narratives, but we may still conclude that a source common to both writers was trying to say that the roar was stunning. Sallust describes the reaction of a different crowd to an unpopular use of a tribunician veto: "the crowd that was present in the meeting was violently agitated and tried to intimidate him with its shouting, its expression, indeed with frequent rushes at him, and every other sort of action that anger tends to incite."[4] Communication in the *contio*, then, worked both ways, a point that has not hitherto been accorded its due significance.[5] On the face of it, the power of a crowd to react favorably or unfavorably would seem to offer real opportunities for imposing its will upon the élite.[6] A similar mechanism, by which highly expressive audiences

---

[1] Millar 1984: 3.
[2] *Leg. Man.* 44: *referto foro completisque omnibus templis ex quibus hic locus conspici potest.*
[3] Cass. Dio 36.30.3; Plut. *Pomp.* 26.6.
[4] Sall. *Iug.* 34.1. In this instance, the tribune's *inpudentia* prevailed.
[5] Brief discussions in Achard 1991: 88–90; Pina Polo 1996: 21–22; and Döbler 1999: 200–203; many good, but scattered observations are to be found in Laser 1997: 138–82. See however Noè 1988, an excellent treatment of the larger subject of creating an (artificial) consensus by means of the *contio*. Aldrete 1999: 85–164 has now well brought out the political significance of popular acclamations in the late Republic and especially the early Empire; see his pp. 114–18 on interruption of speeches by the audience.
[6] Achard 1991: 89; Laser 1997: 142.

in public deliberation created an "ideological hegemony of the masses," has been proposed by J. Ober for Classical Athens;[7] why not in Rome?

THE WILL OF THE PEOPLE

In the published version of his defence of Sestius in the year 56, Cicero included a long digression on what it meant to be an "optimate" and how the "optimate" was to be distinguished from the *popularis*.[8] Among other things, Cicero wishes to anticipate the potential criticism that the "optimate" ignores or defies the wishes of the People, which would clash intolerably with universally shared Republican principles. So he declares that there are actually three places in which the "will and judgment of the Roman People" is manifested: the *contio*, the elections, and the shows (where it is shown in the form of applause, hissing, and so on).[9] The real purpose of this distinction turns out to be to diminish the significance of the massive demonstrations of popular support that Clodius had enjoyed since 58, by tendentiously downplaying the *contio* as a measure of the Popular Will in comparison to the other two.[10] Cicero's very strategy here reveals that in fact it was the *contio* above all that was watched for expressions (*significationes*) of the "will and judgment of the Roman People," which, once expressed formally in legislation – and barring, of course, the veto of the gods – all had to accept in principle as sovereign.[11]

By a convention that is, however, highly significant for us, orators speak to whatever contional audience has assembled before them as if it were

---

[7] Ober 1989: e.g. 43–44, 104, 332–39. [8] *Sest.* 96–143. On these terms, see further below, chap. 6.

[9] *Sest.* 106: *Etenim tribus locis significari maxime de <re publica> populi Romani iudicium ac voluntas potest, contione, comitiis, ludorum gladiatorumque consessu.*

[10] Cic. *Sest.* 106–12. On the dubiousness of the claim that the *verus populus* gave its views at the spectacles, see now Laser 1997: 96–102, in part a polemic against the exaggerated importance attached to the theater as a political field by Flaig 1995a: 118–24 (on which, see also Perelli 1982: 41; Vanderbroeck 1987: 77–81; Tatum 1990). On the *ludi* as a central locus of "publicity," however, see now Döbler 1999: 67–95, esp. 89ff.

[11] See Brunt 1988: 342–46, acknowledging that even "opponents of the power or liberty of the people" "were bound by respect for constitutional convention, on which the authority of the senate was itself based, to pay lip-service to its sovereignty" (p.345). Millar's seminal articles (1984 and 1986) opened the current debate about Roman "democracy" by making the case – still under adjudication – that the principle of popular sovereignty was no merely rhetorical ideal but firmly embedded in institutions and political practice. On the power of the *populus* in the constitution and constitutional discourse, see (recently) also Laser 1997: 26–31; Lintott 1999: 199–208; Mouritsen 2001: 8–14; the attribution of popular sovereignty to Rome is, however, bound to be complicated by judgments about social and institutional realities (cf. Bleicken 1975: 288–94; 1982: 104–6) or the contradictions that inevitably emerge if it is mistaken for a concrete principle in a system of constitutional law (cf. Meier 1966: 116–18). On "the veto of the gods" exercised through their agents, senatorial priests, or the Senate as a body, see Burckhardt 1988: 178–209; Libero 1992: 53–68; briefly, Lintott 1999: 102–4.

identical to *populus Romanus*,[12] and thus rhetorically transform their continually changing, proportionally negligible, and, as we shall see, self-selected audiences into the citizen body of the Republic.[13] This was no mere courtesy: by means of this rhetorical fiction the response of any contional audience could be construed, by one who wished to do so, as an expression of the Popular Will, and its shouts, murmuring, even silence, thus take on great significance in our sources as the reactions of the *populus Romanus*. When Cicero's recall from exile was being discussed in Rome, his enemy's brother Appius Claudius, then praetor, used to ask his audiences in *contiones* whether they wanted Cicero to return; when they shouted "no" he would declare that this was the verdict of the Roman People. Absurd, sniffs Cicero: these were the "half-dead voices of hirelings."[14] Yet, for Cicero speaking in the Verres case, the *maximus clamor* that greeted Pompey's comment about changing the makeup of the juries in a *contio* of 71 was an unambiguous expression of the Will of the Roman People, and a clear sign that they sought this reform even more eagerly than the restoration of the powers of the tribunes, mention of which had only aroused a modest approving hubbub.[15] In 43, the favorable reception given by audiences to the *contiones* that became the *Fourth* and *Sixth Philippics* was, for Cicero, a clear expression of the zeal of the Roman People for recovering their freedom.[16] Although in his private correspondence Cicero typically treats the *contio* as representative of nothing more than the dregs of the urban plebs,[17] even there, when it suits him, he can construe contional audiences as the Roman People, as when, in a letter to Atticus, Cicero writes that the "approval" a *contio* gave to Pompey's reply to Caesar at the beginning of February 49 showed that it was "pleasing to the People,"[18] or when to Cassius in 43 he is

---

[12] Especially noteworthy is the ubiquitous use of the second-person plural pronoun, or its adjectival form *vester*, as the equivalent of *populus Romanus* (*vestra vectigalia, vestrum imperium, vestra commoda*): e.g. *Leg. Man.*1–6, 26 ("you" recalled Lucullus), 43 ("your" judgment on Pompey), 45 ("you" would have lost Asia if not for Pompey), 63 ("you" gave Pompey command in the Pirate War). Cf. also p. 110.

[13] On audiences, see next section below.

[14] Cic. *Sest.* 126: *At vero ille praetor, qui de me non patris, avi, proavi, maiorum denique suorum omnium, sed Graeculorum instituto contionem interrogare solebat, "Velletne me redire," et, cum erat reclamatum semivivis mercennariorum vocibus, populum Romanum negare dicebat . . .*

[15] Cic. *Verr.* 1.45: *ubi, id quod maxime exspectari videbatur, ostendit se tribuniciam potestatem restituturum, factus est in eo strepitus et grata contionis admurmuratio. Idem . . . cum dixisset . . . iudicia autem turpia ac flagitiosa fieri; ei rei se providere ac consulere velle; tum vero non strepitu sed maximo clamore suam populus Romanus significavit voluntatem.*

[16] Cic. *Phil.* 7.22: *Nam quid ego de universo populo Romano dicam? qui pleno ac referto foro . . . declaravitque maximam libertatis recuperandae cupiditatem.*

[17] See below, n. 49.

[18] Cic. *Att.* 7.18.1: *grata populo et probata contioni.* Cf. 7.19: *contionis voluntatem.*

glad to pass on that "a great and unanimous roar of approbation from the People, the likes of which I have never seen" attended Cicero's *contio* in his behalf.[19] The equation of a contional audience with the Roman People was evidently, then, not a polite fiction ignored in practice, but an argument, a rhetorical move, the staking of a claim to a certain kind of legitimacy, which was more or less plausible depending on circumstances.

Responses of contional audiences gave a measure of a politician's standing – a central concern for a competitive élite. In his correspondence, Cicero will often assess a senator's political position by considering the strength of his support not only among the nobility, Senate, or "right-thinking men" (*boni*), but also among the "masses" (*multitudo*) or the "common horde" (*infima plebs*). So, for example, Cicero writes to Atticus in the summer of 61 that his standing with the *boni* is the same as when his friend had left Rome at the end of the previous year; but "among the dregs and filth of the city I am doing much better than when you left." He goes on to say that the failure of his testimony to prevail in the Bona Dea trial did him no harm under the circumstances, and even "bled off" some of the hostility toward him aroused by the Catilinarian executions. Moreover, he notes, "this wretched starveling rabble that comes to meetings and sucks the treasury dry" believes him to be Pompey's closest ally.[20] This way of taking the measure of a senator's political position by reference to distinct segments of the population *including* the urban plebs, was not unique to Cicero. In 56, Pompey worried to Cicero that he was facing political catastrophe, "since the people – those, at least, that frequent public meetings (*contionario illo populo*) – are nearly against him, the nobility hostile, the Senate unfavorable, and the young men ill-behaved."[21] In view of a recent claim that the audiences of *contiones* were predominantly composed of "men of substance" rather than the "working class,"[22] I must also note here parenthetically that, on this evidence, the composition and expressed sentiments of these crowds are quite consistently popular and plebeian, and obviously distinct from the Senate and other respectable elements, who

[19] Cic. *Fam.* 12.7.1: *tanto clamore consensuque populi ut nihil umquam simile viderim.* Cf. the *contio* as a measure of the attitude of the plebs at *Att.* 1.14.1; 1.16.11; *Q Fr.* 2.3.4 (below, nn. 20, 21).

[20] Cic. *Att.* 1.16.11; the latter quotation in the text is in Shackleton Bailey's translation. Cf. *Att.* 1.14.1: *Prima contio Pompei qualis fuisset, scripsi ad te antea: non iucunda miseris, inanis improbis, beatis non grata, bonis non gravis; itaque frigebat; Q Fr.* 2.5.3: *apud perditissimam illam atque infimam faecem populi propter Milonem suboffendit* [*sc.* Pompeius] *et boni multa ab eo desiderant, multa reprehendunt.*

[21] Cic. *Q Fr.* 2.3.4. For the *iuventus* ("young men") here mentioned, a distinct force in Roman politics, see Hellegouarc'h 1963: 468–70.

[22] Mouritsen 2001: 43–45; cf. chap. 2, n. 32 and n. 62 below.

could hardly be described as a "wretched starveling rabble that comes to meetings and sucks the treasury dry."

The contional crowd, then, was closely watched, and its responses to speakers – applause, shouts, even silence – are regularly noted by our sources and even "written into" published speeches.[23] In letters to Atticus, Cicero is not above noting that his name was applauded by a crowd at a meeting as a senatorial decree passed on his motion was read out,[24] or that a *contio* reacted favorably to his speech lending qualified support for the Flavian agrarian bill in 60.[25] Few moments in Republican history are as clouded by partisan *Tendenz* as the response of the crowd when Julius Caesar was offered the diadem at the Lupercalia of 44, which, while not a *contio* in the normal sense, exemplifies the same crowd dynamics; or the reaction of the inhabitants of the city to the mass meetings that immediately followed the murder of Caesar a month later. To those who recounted these events it was evidently of crucial importance whether Caesar was applauded when he was offered the diadem or when he cast it off; or whether there was any authentic expression of public support or toleration for Caesar's assassins *before* Antony whipped up feelings against them at the funeral.[26] The absence of a significant response might itself be noteworthy: Cicero writes to Atticus that Pompey's first *contio* in 61, upon returning from his eastern campaigns, pleased neither the poor nor the wealthy, neither subversives nor right-thinking men; it fell flat.[27] And Cicero is glad to observe the failure of Caesar's attempt in 59 to incite the crowd at one of his meetings to besiege Bibulus in his house: Caesar and his allies now "perceive that they have no support from any constituency."[28] To avoid such public embarrassments, a magistrate conscious of his unpopularity avoided holding public meetings altogether, as allegedly Caesar did after he had offended the People by trampling the intercession of the tribune L. Metellus in 49.[29]

---

[23] For "scripted" audience responses in published contional speeches see, besides *Rab. perd.* 18 and the several instances in *Phil.* 4 discussed below: *Leg. Man.* 37; *Leg. agr.* 3.2; *Phil.* 6.3, 12. For the preservation of "orality" in published speeches, see Fuhrmann 1990.

[24] Cic. *Att.* 4.1.6: *quo senatus consulto recitato continuo, <cum multitudo> more hoc insulso et novo plausum meo nomine recitando dedisset, habui contionem.* I follow Shackleton Bailey's translation over those of Gelzer 1969: 153, and Millar 1995: 107, n. 57 (who believe that the crowd chanted Cicero's name), although he is actually inclined to emend (note repetition of *recitato / recitando*) to *meo nomine iterando* (Shackleton Bailey 1965–67: II.168).

[25] Cic. *Att.* 1.19.4: *secunda contionis voluntate.* On this, see further below, pp. 210–12.

[26] On popular *significationes* after Caesar's death, see below, pp. 150–58.

[27] Cic. *Att.* 1.14.1: *non iucunda miseris, inanis improbis, beatis non grata, bonis non gravis. itaque frigebat.*

[28] Cic. *Att.* 2.21.5: *sentiunt se nullam ullius partis voluntatem tenere.* See, however, n. 147 below.

[29] Cic. *Att.* 10.4.8 (report of C. Curio, whose father's "desertion" by his audience in 90 was also well remembered: chap. 2, n. 12).

The function of the *contio* as an index of popular support was of particular importance during the run-up to a legislative vote, when heated tribunician activity could produce "daily *contiones*" with popular orators "virtually sleeping on the Rostra,"[30] and the responses of their audiences provided plausible evidence of a bill's reception by the Roman People, helping, or failing, to generate unstoppable "momentum" (in the modern jargon). It is a curiosity of the Republic that proposed legislation was very rarely defeated in the actual balloting: the assemblies rarely, it seems, voted bills down (although our evidence is, no doubt, skewed in favor of success).[31] Some infer therefore that élite control of the legislative process was so complete that voting was a mere "consensus ritual" whose function was to demonstrate public approval of decisions taken by their betters, or, alternatively, that only small groups of people whose "outlook and interests" closely reflected those of the élite actually bothered to vote.[32] But a more attractive hypothesis, suggested by what we have already seen and to be corroborated throughout this chapter and the next, is that by the time a vote actually took place the fate of a bill had almost always already been determined by its reception in prior mass meetings.[33] Wherever we have sufficient evidence to mark the correlation, there is remarkably close consistency between the final result of a legislative campaign and the reception the proposal had received in prior public meetings: in no case known to me was a bill defeated, by veto or vote, after having won sustained approbation in *contiones*.

This view may be supported by a brief consideration of the use of the tribunician veto – manifestly one reason why some bills did not survive long enough to be voted down.[34] A serious complication for any use, or threat, of a tribunician veto against legislation was the simple fact that it took from the People what was otherwise seen as their sovereign power

---

[30] Tac. *Dial.* 36.3: *hinc contiones magistratuum paene pernoctantium in rostris.* See chap. 1, n. 40.

[31] See Flaig's list (1995a: 80, n. 13) of eight instances in which a negative vote seems to be explicitly mentioned, only one of which falls in the traditional bounds of the "late Republic" (defeat of Carbo's bill for iteration of the tribunate in 130). Cf. Laser 1997: 67; Mouritsen 2001: 64–65. Such lists of course exclude cases in which we have no secure knowledge of a vote actually being taken (e.g., it is generally, and probably rightly, assumed that Gaius Gracchus' bill on the extension of citizenship was killed by the threat of Livius Drusus' veto, but Appian is not explicit [*B Civ.* 1.23] and Plutarch [*C. Gracch.* 12.2] suggests that the loss of public support was crucial). But in broad terms, the existence of the phenomenon seems undeniable.

[32] The first view is that of Flaig 1995a: 79–91, and 1998 (cf. the earlier observation of Burckhardt 1990: 91–92); the second, of Mouritsen 2001: 64–67, 78–89.

[33] Nippel 1988: 55–56; Thommen 1995: 365; and especially Laser 1997: 66–69, 138, rebutting Flaig (see n. 32).

[34] Cf. the defeat of the consular bill on the Bona Dea sacrilege, or of the Rullan agrarian law, both considered in chap. 5.

to pass laws – a particularly awkward sort of intervention, given that the tribune existed to serve the plebs.[35] Thus, for example, when, in 188 BC four tribunes interceded, or threatened to intercede, against a bill to confer full Roman citizenship on three towns of southern Latium (including Cicero's *patria* of Arpinum), on the grounds that it had not won prior approval in the Senate, they stood aside after being reminded that the extension of citizenship was a matter for the People, not the Senate, to decide – and the measure was duly passed by the popular vote.[36] Clearly, then, the use of this potentially devastating political weapon needed to be defensible before the very People whose interest it ostensibly served; thus, in practice, it was subject to a host of customary and ideological constraints. For example, we happen to hear explicitly on one occasion (in 167 BC) that custom forbade use of the veto before discussion had been allowed to proceed in *contiones* for and against a proposal. While the relevant text for this episode emphasizes the need for those casting the veto to ensure that *they* were fully informed, the custom probably also derived from a general consensus that the veto was not supposed to prevent the People from receiving the advice necessary to form *their* opinion.[37] Certainly, as in the case of the law extending citizenship in 188, vetoes whose manifest function was to *deprive* the People of their sovereign right of decision over legislation were apt to be seen as illegitimate throughout the late Republic.[38] Thus the highly controversial vetoes cast in 133 and 67 immediately before the balloting, with the manifest intent of frustrating a decisively favorable expression of the People's will, brought forth the unimpeachable doctrine voiced by none other than Cicero himself that in a matter concerning the well-being of the Roman People "the unanimous voice of the citizenry" should prevail over that of a single tribune.[39] When in the latter case, A. Gabinius immediately

---

[35] Polyb. 6.16.5. For the explicit argument, largely sanctioned by subsequent practice, that the tribune's veto was itself contingent on serving the People, see Tiberius Gracchus' apologia in 133: App. *B Civ.* 1.12; Plut. *Ti. Gracch.* 15.2–6.

[36] Livy 38.36.7–9: *huic rogationi quattuor tribuni plebis quia non ex auctoritate senatus ferretur cum intercederent, edocti populi esse, non senatus, ius suffragium quibus velit impertire, destiterunt incepto.*

[37] Livy 45.21.6, with pp. 162–63 below.

[38] Lintott 1999: 124–25, for the principle (although he appears to think this would apply only once "the voters [had] separated into their various units").

[39] Cic. *Corn.* 1, fr. 31 Cr *neque . . . passus est* [sc. *A. Gabinius*] *plus unius collegae sui quam universae civitatis vocem valere et voluntatem.* See also Asc. 72 C; Cass. Dio 36.30.1–2. It is significant that a vote on removing a tribune from office seems not to have been subject to the veto (where was Roscius in 67?: Asc. 72 C). Badian's hypothesis (1988: esp. 212) that, shortly after, and specifically in reaction to Ti. Gracchus' deposition of Octavius, wording was adopted in all Republican laws that made such a maneuver strictly illegal (what he calls the "*exceptio sacro sancti*"), lacks supporting evidence and must be considered doubtful in view of the fact (it seems) that no ancient source makes a connection between the two things, despite the notoriety of that case and its near-repetition in 67. (See further

followed Tiberius Gracchus' precedent and instituted a vote on removing the vetoing tribune from office, L. Trebellius gave up his intercession; not only was Gabinius not brought to account for this action, but Cicero actually brings the case up to bolster his own defence of another tribune, C. Cornelius, charged with a more direct violation of tribunician sacrosanctity.[40] All of this implies that a legislative veto will in practice have been nearly impossible to sustain against strong evidence of the Roman People's overwhelming support for a law; and when we consider where that impression would have been gained (or created), we are led necessarily to the *contio* and the *significationes* of the Popular Will expressed in it.[41] The hypothesis is confirmed by the fact that there is no single instance in the late Republic in which a popular bill likely to be passed by the voting assembly was actually killed prematurely by a veto;[42] the real power of the legislative veto lay in the *threat* of its use to second the effort in the *contio*.[43]

On this view, then (to which I shall return in the next chapter), the *contio* becomes the main locus of legislative decision, and its peculiar significance

---

Ehrhardt 1989 with Badian 1989.) Nor does it seem very likely that, without any surviving evidence of public argument about such a controversial matter, the People/plebs could repeatedly, and with absolute consistency from *c.* 130, have voted into law a formula that at a stroke deprived themselves of the right to abrogate an office that enjoyed sacrosanctity from one who had so signally failed (it was argued) to carry out his responsibilities as tribune of the plebs. Such an innovation would have greatly diminished popular influence over the exercise of the legislative veto, and have made any threat of veto, however unjustified, virtually decisive.

[40] J. W. Crawford 1994: 120–21, thus has it backward, to my mind.

[41] Cic. *Leg.* 3.24 is, then, so much wishful thinking, as often in that tract. Meier 1968: 93–99, rightly stresses the contingency of the power of the tribunician legislative veto upon the apparent degree of popular acquiescence in it: "Gegen wichtige populare Gesetze ist die Intercession nicht mehr [sc. after the Gracchi and Saturninus] eingelegt worden oder jedenfalls nicht mehr wirksam gewesen" (p. 99). Cf. Burckhardt 1988: 159–77; Thommen 1989: 207–32 (with lists of known intercessions); Libero 1992: 29–49.

[42] The pattern is very clear in the cases on which we are best informed: the tribunician veto could not stop Ti. Gracchus' land law, the *lex Gabinia de piratis*, and Julius Caesar's agrarian bill (all discussed in chap. 5), nor, of course, Clodius' legislative onslaught in 58, despite the presence of anti-Clodian tribunes that year (e.g. Ninnius: see Cass. Dio 38.14.1–2, with Tatum 1999: 137, for the closest we come to a serious threat of veto). A separate, more complicated matter is the melees precipitated by the intercessions of P. Servilius Globulus against Cornelius in 67 (Asc. 58 C) or of Cato and Q. Minucius Thermus against Metellus Nepos in 62 (Cass. Dio 37.43.2; Plut. *Cat. Min.* 28), the first of which induced the proposer to retreat from confrontation and to compromise, while the second broke up the voting assembly. A non-legislative veto, such as that at Sall. *Iug.* 34.1 (above, p. 119), will not have been subject to the same degree of popular pressure, since of course this was not an act directly depriving the People of their opportunity to express their will in a vote; still, Sallust underscores the pressure exerted by the crowd, and clearly marks that tribune's *inpudentia* as exceptional.

[43] See pp. 188 and 193 for the role of the veto in the legislative controversies over the Bona Dea sacrilege and the Rullan agrarian bill. But lacking the appearance of strong popular support, the threat could not be effectively realized; note Cic. *Leg. Man.* 58: *neque praeter intercessionem quicquam audiam, de qua, ut ego arbitror, isti ipsi qui minitantur etiam atque etiam* quid liceat *considerabunt.*

for members of the urban plebs becomes readily understandable, since they will generally have predominated in such mass meetings called in the city with little advance warning and lacking any formal power of decision, but their preponderance must have been comparatively diminished at regularly scheduled votes on legislation of broad importance, when a substantial influx from the countryside and other regions of Italy was likely.[44] The mass urban meetings that preceded voting on any bills, however, gave the city plebs a privileged role in the framing of any "popular" legislation, which was apt to fail if it did not kindle strong expressions of support from those impersonating the *populus Romanus* at the preliminary *contiones*. This power will have been especially gratifying to freedmen, a large proportion of the urban plebs on any account and probably often of contional crowds, whose influence on voting day itself was hampered by their restriction to only four of the thirty-five legislative voting units ("tribes").[45] Gaius Fannius, while speaking as consul against Gaius Gracchus' proposal to extend citizenship to those with Latin rights, invidiously asked his audience at a *contio*: "Once you have given citizenship to the Latins, well, do you think that there will be any space for you in the *contio*, or that you will attend the games and festivals? Don't you think they will take over everything?"[46] Notably absent from the consul's list of the more jealously guarded privileges of the urban citizen is that of voting; attendance at the *contio*, however, is listed in first position, for it afforded the opportunity to speak for the Roman People in face-to-face, two-way communication with the leaders of the *res publica*.[47] The right to shout in the *contio* could even be seen as the mark of freedom itself.

---

[44] On summoning *contiones*, see pp. 38–40; on the constituents of audiences, see next section. For an influx from the countryside for a legislative vote, see App. *B Civ.* 1.10, 13, and Diod. Sic 34/35.6.1; Plut. *C. Gracch.* 12.1 (see also 13.2, and C. Gracchus' speeches against Popilius delivered in the towns around Rome: *ORF* 48.34, p. 184, with Stockton 1979: 20, n. 49); cf. also the law restoring Cicero in 57 (below, pp. 148–49). It seems likely enough on general grounds that many urban voters were dispersed among the thirty-one crucial rural voting-tribes (Brunt 1988: 25–26; cf. Lintott 1968a: 86–87), but it is not at all clear that "in the late Republic the tribal assembly was *dominated* by urban dwellers" (Brunt [my emphasis]), even if few country people will have turned up for votes on "corn doles" and other matters of burning interest only to the urban populace. (For a recent discussion of the problem, tending toward Brunt's conclusion, see Mouritsen 2001: 80–82.)

[45] See next section on *tabernarii et opifices*, with n. 59. Cf. also n. 57.

[46] *ORF* 32.3, p. 144: *si Latinis civitatem dederitis, credo, existimatis vos ita, ut nunc constitistis, in contione habituros locum aut ludis et festis diebus interfuturos? nonne illos omnia occupaturos putatis?*

[47] The argument from silence has some force here, in view of Julius Victor's framing commentary (*ORF* ad loc.). This is not to say that Fannius' audience was *indifferent* to their right of *suffragium* (see chap. 3, nn. 78–79; Cic. *Leg. Agr.* 2.70, 103, with chap. 6, n. 82); perhaps the threat of being swamped by new voters seemed more remote than the others. For a sharply different view of the fragment, see Mouritsen 2001: 67 n. 13: the *contio* is mentioned as "one among various other diversions open to the upper echelons of society." I would associate Fannius' "urban benefits" with *commoda plebis Romanae*: see pp. 222ff.; see also Purcell 1994: 681.

When the consul of 56, Cn. Lentulus Marcellinus, denounced Pompey's excessive power in a *contio* the crowd roared its agreement. "Shout!," he continued, "shout, Citizens, while you still can! Soon you will no longer be able to do so with impunity!"[48]

BUT WHICH PEOPLE?

On one interpretation, then, any *contio* will have represented nothing less than the Voice of the Roman People; on another, however, it produced nothing more significant than the noisy squawking of the most questionable elements of the urban mob. Everyone in fact knew that the audiences of mass public meetings were not *actually* identical with, or even properly representative, of the Roman People. Except on a couple of occasions when he is trying to boost his claims to popular support, Cicero in his private letters tends to associate *contiones* with the "filth and shit" of the city.[49] It has already been remarked that the location of contional venues and the procedure of summoning public meetings must have ensured that, barring coincidence with a market- or festival-day, or an imminent legislative vote on a matter that would draw rural and Italian constituencies, in the normal run of events they must have attracted almost exclusively urban dwellers.[50] The urban plebs not only lived in close proximity to the meeting-places but through their neighborhood and trade organizations enjoyed a clear advantage of organization.[51]

Very likely, the small businessmen whose livelihood and habits kept them close to the vicinity of the Forum were an important constituent of most contional crowds. Some scholars, however, go so far as to hypostatize a *plebs contionalis* and identify this closely with the "craftsmen and shopkeepers" (*opifices et tabernarii*), probably overwhelmingly ex-slaves, who, according to a number of texts, comprised the crowds, mobs, and gangs involved in civil disturbances in the late Republic.[52] Yet it may be a mistake to

---

[48] Val. Max. 6.2.6 (*ORF* 128.5, p. 418): "*adclamate,*" inquit, "*Quirites, adclamate, dum licet: iam enim vobis inpune facere non licebit.*" Cf. Brunt 1988: 315–16.

[49] Cic. *Att.* 1.16.11: *apud sordem urbis et faecem,* clearly the *contionalis hirudo aerari, misera ac ieiuna plebecula* mentioned two sentences later. Cf. *Q Fr.* 2.5.3: *apud perditissimam illam atque infimam faecem populi*; *Flac.* 18 (quoted below, n. 52).

[50] See pp. 41–42.   [51] See n. 72 below.

[52] References in Meier 1965: 614, and in Vanderbroeck 1987: 87, n. 74. Add Sall. *Hist.* 1.63: *Quin lenones et vinarii laniique <et> quorum praeterea volgus in dies usum habet pretio compositi.* For discussion see also Brunt 1966: 24–25; Meier 1966: 114–15; Perelli 1982: 207–15; Vanderbroeck, pp. 83–84, 86–93; Pina Polo 1996: 129–33; Tatum 1999: 143; for objections, see below, n. 62. On the "freed" character of this class, see Treggiari 1969: 91–106. Cf. Rudé 1964: 195–213, for the "respectable" elements – artisans and shopkeepers – among the "mobs" of France and England in the eighteenth and early nineteenth centuries. But *tabernarii et opifices* was no honorific title (see Cic. *Flac.* 18: *opifices et tabernarios*

equate too closely the crowds that were mobilized particularly for violence with those who gathered to listen to public speeches, even if some, such as P. Clodius, may arguably have tried to blur the distinction.[53] The "seditious" tribune's tactic of gathering a crowd for collective action by ordering the closure of the shops (*tabernas occludi*) may not tell us very much, since it is only infrequently attested, and indeed it is not reliably brought into connection with any specific known *contio*.[54] As Cicero points out in the *Fourth Catilinarian*, "those who are in the *tabernae*" are, after all, engaged in business and suffer a loss when their shops are closed – which presumably explains both why an edict was necessary to ensure that supportive *contio*-goers did not lose much business to their rivals, and why such drastic action is so rarely attested.[55]

Starting from the assumption that "shopkeepers and artisans" essentially constituted the contional audience, some have been surprised by the appeals of speakers in public meetings to interests supposedly not shared by this segment of society, such as agrarian distribution. This leads to the paradoxical conclusion that "a large part of the 'program' of the popular leaders did not fit the needs and expectations of the *plebs contionalis*," that is to say their own audience.[56] To begin with, the common assumption that the "urban mob" was quite uninterested in promises of land is itself open to question: in the *Second Oration on the Agrarian Law* Cicero asserts that the four urban voting-tribes – in which freedmen will have predominated because of their

---

atque illam omnem faecem civitatum); consequently, to designate a crowd as such may have been a rhetorical move against them rather than an attempt, however generalized, at description.

[53] Characterizations of crowds as *tabernarii et opifices*, or, which presumably amounts to the same thing, as having been gathered by closing the *tabernae*, refer less often to *contiones* than to actual or planned violence or intimidation: Cic. *Cat.* 4.17 (cf. Sall. *Cat.* 50; App. *B Civ.* 2.5); Dom. 13, 54, 89, 90; Asc. 41 C. Cic. *Flac.* 18 is a loose slander set in Greek Asia Minor. Laser 1997: 104, 199–209, may exaggerate the quiescence of the *tabernarii*; see Tatum 1999: 147–48.

[54] Cic. *Acad.* 2.144: *Quid me igitur, Luculle, in invidiam et tamquam in contionem vocas, et quidem, ut seditiosi tribuni solent, occludi tabernas iubes? quo enim spectat illud cum artificia tolli quereris a nobis, nisi ut opifices concitentur?* The order would go out in the form of a tribunician edict (*Dom.* 54: *cum edictis tuis tabernas claudi iubebas*). Despite Cicero's *solent* at *Acad.* 2.144, and his (perhaps unreliable) suggestion that this was a common tactic of Clodius' at *Dom.* 54, 89–90, we know of only one specific occasion on which the shops were closed in this fashion in the late Republic: the culmination of Milo's trial (Asc. 41 C). Before the late Republic, the closing of the shops seems regularly to have been associated with an edict imposing a *iustitium* (suspension of public business) during a public emergency (cf. Livy 3.27.2; 4.31.9; 9.7.8; 23.25.1). Spontaneous closure in the midst of some disturbance (Plut. *Caes.* 67.1; App. *B Civ.* 5.18), or the closing of the *tabernae* of the *argentarii* around the Forum in order to hold a judicial *contio* there (Varro, *Ling.* 6.91; cf. Andreau 1987; Coarelli 1985: 140–49) is of course a different matter. On the tactic, whose employment may be generally overestimated, see Vanderbroeck 1987: 126–27; Pina Polo 1996: 132–33 with n. 22; Tatum 1999: 143 ("often").

[55] *Cat.* 4.17.

[56] Vanderbroeck 1987: 102; cf. 93–103; similarly, Perelli 1982: 175–79, 199–202, 235; Brunt 1988: 245, 250–51.

restriction to these units – were the "target audience" of Rullus' proposal of 63, and he does so in a way that implies that his immediate audience was of the same type.[57] This and other late-Republican agrarian proposals were justified before the Senate on the grounds that they would "drain off" the city's excess population; even if this argument overlooked rural beneficiaries for tactical purposes, it must imply that large numbers among the urban plebs were thought to be interested.[58] This is not to say, however, that these potential beneficiaries were solely or largely drawn from the "craftsmen and shopkeepers" of the city, a category far from coextensive with the urban plebs as a whole.[59] Recent migrants to the metropolis will have been especially interested. And the closer the proximity of a *contio* to the actual legislative vote, the more likely it is that interested parties from nearby regions of central Italy will have constituted significant constituents of the audience as well.[60]

What merits particular stress here is that while most *contiones* will indeed have been dominated by the urban plebs (subject to the important exceptions noted above), the makeup of their audiences must have been highly variable.[61] There is no good reason to think that any one distinct segment of the urban mass consistently preponderated in public meetings.

[57] Cic. *Leg. agr.* 2.79: *ante rusticis detur ager, qui habent, quam urbanis, quibus ista agri spes et iucunditas ostenditur?* The complaint about Rullus' stated intention to begin the voting with the *tribus Romilia* will have been gratuitous, even counterproductive, before an audience that was not overwhelmingly drawn from the urban voting units.

[58] Cic. *Leg. agr.* 2.70; Cass. Dio 38.1.3; cf. Cic. *Att.* 1.19.4. Gruen 1974: 387–404, esp. 387, 393–94, argues that the Rullan and Julian agrarian bills aimed at the *urban* population, in particular recent arrivals from the country. Cf. Flach 1990: 71–81; Meier 1965: 591–92, 608–9; contra, Havas 1976b: 154–55.

[59] Purcell 1994: 661 makes the class of freedmen *tabernarii* more or less identical with the urban plebs as a whole, but his model seems to underestimate the influx of freeborn rural peasants (pp. 650–58), which is repeatedly emphasized in our sources (see Brunt 1971a: 380–81 and elsewhere), and which Appian (from Pollio?) considered a major source of "hirelings" for the *contio* (*B Civ.* 2.120). Brunt conjectured that the number of urban freeborn citizens (*ingenui*) was roughly half that of freed citizens (pp. 102, 387); but his suppositions were confessedly conjectural, and were probably too much influenced by variations in epigraphic commemoration (see Treggiari 1969: 31–36). Lintott 1968a: 87–88, makes it something like an even split between *ingenui* and freedmen, which would also be roughly consistent with the recent conjecture of Virlouvet 1991: 48–55 that Caesar's reduction of the grain rolls from 320,000 to 150,000 was arrived at largely by eliminating freedmen (recruitment of 80,000 transmarine colonists [Suet. *Iul.* 42.1], presumably both freeborn and freed, also has to be factored in).

[60] See above, n. 44. Note too the arrival in Rome of many Italians, who were not even entitled to vote, to press – surely in *contiones* – for Gaius Gracchus' law on extension of the citizenship (Plut. *C. Gracch.* 12.1–2).

[61] See now also Mouritsen 2001: 39–46 (but cf. chap. 2, n. 32). Millar, however, tends to refer to "the crowd" as if it were a reasonably consistent entity, giving little emphasis to the tactics of "creating" favorable contional audiences (on bribery, e.g., see Millar 1998: 38; yet cf. 212, 225), and preferring to speak of contional audiences as more or less *randomly* selected ("the ever-available crowd consisting of whoever was already there [sc. in the Forum], or whoever turned up": Millar 1984: 19) and therefore as at least a plausible, if imperfect, stand-in for the urban plebs as a whole. It is, furthermore,

If their proximity to the Forum made "shopkeepers and artisans" a natural and important constituent of most *contiones*, we must also allow that the actual makeup of any one audience will have depended on highly particular circumstances such as the timing and location of the meeting, the extent and nature of preparations, length of notice, the reputation of the magistrate calling the meeting, and its professed or expected purpose.[62]

It stands to reason that those who attended a magistrate's *contio* were more likely to be his supporters than not. A contional audience was a self-selecting group, and given that the meeting provided a good opportunity for a member of the urban plebs to make his voice count, we may infer that at times of political controversy a major motive for attendance was precisely to shout approval for some people and to shout down their opponents.[63] In particular, we should expect those who could to turn out for *contiones* summoned by those politicians they backed in any controversy, in order to make manifest their support and thus, by noise and numbers, to increase the plausibility of their claim to be representing the "Will of the People." Ciceronian references make clear that the sheer size of a contional audience was an important factor when one sought to define its response as an expression of the Popular Will.[64] After all, an audience would simply drift

a little misleading to suggest that "the crowd" in the *contio* and the Roman People at the *comitia* were more or less interchangeable on the grounds that "the same crowd could . . . be transformed into a sovereign assembly of voters simply (in principle) by being instructed by the presiding magistrate to separate (*discedere*) into its voting *tribus*" (Millar 1998: 47; cf. 35). The distinction is crucial between a *contio* on the day of legislative *comitia*, immediately preceding the vote, and the far more frequent *contiones* that stood alone; it was, in fact, illegal to convert this last type into a voting assembly.

[62] Mouritsen's objections (2001: 41, 56–57) to the idea that there was a *plebs contionalis* with any consistent social composition are salutary, except when they lead him to deny the popular character of contional crowds and to replace the "working-class" *plebs contionalis* with an even more dubious well-off version (pp. 43–45; cf. chap. 2, n. 32). Against the simple equation of *plebs contionalis* with *tabernarii et opifices*, see also the objections of Benner 1987: 78–80, and Thommen 1989: 183–87. But *pace* Benner, it seems unlikely that *tabernarii et opifices* and *mercenarii/conducti* are really so distinct from the élite perspective (Cic. *Cat.* 4.17; *Dom.* 89).

[63] Cf. the contrary view of Mouritsen 2001: 42: "For why would a small section of the *plebs* regularly turn up for political meetings in which it had no voice – *apart from cheering and jeering* – and which took no decisions?" (my emphasis). This is a legacy of the misleading dismissal of *contiones* as merely "informal assemblies" (see chap. 2).

[64] Cic. *Leg. Man.* 69: *deinde, cum tantam multitudinem tanto cum studio adesse videamus quantam iterum nunc in eodem homine praeficiendo videmus; Leg. agr.* 2.103: *qualis vos hodierno die maxima contione mihi pro salute vestra praebuistis; Phil.* 6.18: *multas magnasque habui consul contiones, multis interfui: nullam umquam vidi tantam quanta nunc vestrum est. unum sentitis omnes, unum studetis;* cf. *Pis.* 34; *Phil.* 1.32, 4.1, 7.22, 14.16; *Fam.* 11.6a.2. Contrast *In Clod. et Cur.* fr. 16 Cr: *accesserunt ita pauci, ut eum non ad contionem, sed sponsum diceres advocasse.* Achard 1981: 69. (Actual numbers in the *contio* are not transmitted; estimates of a *maximum* range from 6,000 to 20,000: chap. 2, n. 36). Cf. Cicero's similar rhetorical use of *frequens/frequentissimus senatus* (Merguet 1880: 11.384), which, however, is somewhat complicated by the controversy over whether *frequens* had a technical sense ("quorate": Ryan 1998: 36–41, but cf. contra, Bonnefond-Coudry 1989: 425–35).

away if the speaker failed to move it, and might never return.[65] If so, the audiences of *contiones* must have tended to be broadly favorable to those who summoned them. These inferences seem to be confirmed by a remarkably consistent pattern in our rather copious evidence of *contiones* in the late Republic, consisting not merely of published speeches but also of narrative histories and Cicero's letters, in which hostile interruptions and outbursts by the audience take place as a rule *not* against the presiding magistrate's words but against those of opposing speakers whom he has brought before "his" *contio*. The norm is clearly implied by, for example, Cicero's comment about Clodius on one occasion that "*even his own contio* laughed at the man."[66]

Furthermore, there were well-established ways to make them rather more partisan. One way, clearly, was to pay them; opponents saw this as bribery, though a friendly perspective will have viewed it as proper and needed compensation for missing a day's wages or business.[67] Appian, describing the attempt of the assassins of Caesar to influence public opinion by means of a hired crowd, attests to the presence of a large pool of underemployed people in the city, sufficient to supply a "rent-a-mob"; harsh economic realities in the streets must have set the price of an unskilled set of lungs at an attractively low level.[68] When Cicero, speaking of Clodius' "paid audiences" (*conductae contiones*) of "hirelings" (*mercenarii*),[69] and Appian, distinguishing between the "bribe-takers" who packed the meetings that supported Milo or Caesar's assassins from the "uncorrupted portion of the populace,"[70] both from their divergent political perspectives assume that the practice of hiring audiences was widespread, it would seem naive to insist that this is only a mirage called into existence by partisan cant. But we also need not suppose that whole audiences were thus "compensated";

---

[65] Cic. *Brut.* 305.

[66] Cic. *Har. resp.* 8: *etiam sua contio risit hominem.* On the phenomenon in general, see now also Mouritsen 2001: 50–53. The rare contrary example (Gran. Licinian. 36.33 C) need not be dismissed: the aim here is to establish pragmatic norms, not scientific laws.

[67] An excellent observation made in passing by Tatum 1999: 143; also now Mouritsen 2001: 60. In combination with the (perhaps rare) "stick" of shop-closing, the "carrot" of even modest payment must have been quite an incentive.

[68] App. *B Civ.* 2.120–21. In the next century courtroom claqueurs could be hired for three denarii (Plin. *Ep.* 2.14.6) – not a paltry sum, as Sherwin-White 1966: ad loc points out, but perhaps more was demanded of them than of contional shouters. The link between urban misery and political violence is neatly sketched by Brunt 1966: 24.

[69] See esp. Cic. *Sest.* 106–8, 113, 126–7; *Dom.* 89. Achard 1981: 137–38.

[70] *B Civ.* 2.22: τοὺς παρ᾽ αὐτοῦ δεδωροδοκηκότας / τοῦ δήμου τὸ ἀδιάφθορον; 2.120–23, 131–32: τὸ καθαρὸν τοῦ πλήθους / οἱ μισθωτοί. See further below.

rather, as in Appian's description of the use that the murderers of Caesar made of a bribed crowd in the *contiones* following the Ides of March, the method was rather to use this partisan core in the manner of a claque to overwhelm opponents with its noise, and to prompt the uncommitted portion of an audience to join in its shouts.[71]

An effective organization was another good way to see that the right kind of crowd gathered. Rome, of course, had no political parties. But P. Clodius in the mid-fifties built up and made frequent use of a remarkable political "machine" that seems to have dominated the quarters of Rome (*vici*), especially through their professional and neighborhood associations (*collegia*).[72] It stands to reason that this kind of organization gave him a comparative advantage in gathering a receptive crowd, quite apart from what they did once they got there.[73] The depth, extent, and potency of Clodius' urban organization seem to have been unprecedented, and unparalleled again after his death in 52. Yet he did not invent these techniques of orchestrating political action. Well before Clodius' heyday there are scattered but valuable glimpses in our evidence of low- and medium-level "bosses" available in the Forum, often freedmen, who were able to mobilize paid crowds for action at the behest of a major political actor.[74] Nor is there any reason to think that such a useful practice passed away with Clodius' death in 52.[75] But the denizens of the Forum and the underemployed urban poor were not the only source of political crowds. If even a fraction of the alleged twenty thousand *equites* from all over Italy actually gathered on the Capitol in 58 to demonstrate their support for Cicero in his hour of need, we are given a glimpse of a different kind of organizational resource available for those

---

[71] App. *B Civ.* 2.120; full discussion below.

[72] On Clodius' political organization, Tatum 1999: esp. 142–48, gives an admirably balanced and broad view; see further Perelli 1982: 203–15; Benner 1987: 63–71; Vanderbroeck 1987: 112–16; Nippel 1988: 113–14; Laser 1997: 104–6. Cicero makes much of Clodius' use of gangs of toughs (*operae*) for intimidation, but even in Cicero the actual employment of Clodian *operae* in *contiones* is not very well attested (*Sest.* 34, 127; *Q Fr.* 2.3.2).

[73] Laurence 1994: 68–71.

[74] Plut. *Aem.* 38.4: ἀνθρώπους ἀγεννεῖς καὶ δεδουλευκότας, ἀγοραίους δὲ καὶ δυναμένους ὄχλον συναγαγεῖν καὶ σπουδαρχίᾳ καὶ κραυγῇ πάντα πράγματα βιάσασθαι. Cic. *Corn.* 1 fr. 13 Cr, with Asc. 45, 59, 60 C; Sall. *Cat.* 50.1: *qui pretio rem publicam vexare soliti erant*; Livy 4.13.9. On *duces multitudinum* or *operarum* (not a Clodian invention), see Vanderbroeck 1987: 52–59; on the gangs generally, see Lintott 1968a: 74–88. Q. Cicero's reference to "those who control the *contiones*" (*Comment. pet.* 51: *eorum studia qui contiones tenent adeptus es*; cf. Cic. *Sest.* 34) – not "those who hold them" (*contionem habere*), that is, magistrates or tribunes – is unfortunately extremely elliptical. Cf. the use of low- and mid-level vote-brokers in elections: *Comment. pet.* 29–30, with Morstein-Marx 1998: 274–83.

[75] See, for example, App. *B Civ.* 2.120–21, set in 44.

with a strong base outside the city.[76] There are times when Cicero's famous boast that he had an "army of the rich" might almost be taken literally.[77]

Organized claques are clearly attested in our evidence; certainly, the rather complicated and relatively articulate audience responses that appear on certain occasions will have required a high level of training and coordination from prompters, who may well have been professional claqueurs, perhaps maintained otherwise by work in the theater and the lawcourts.[78] Dio tells us that Clodius had trained his followers to shout "Pompey!" whenever in public meetings he asked an insulting or invidious question of the form "Who did (or said) something-or-other?"[79] A letter of Cicero describes just such an occasion, when Clodius tried to overwhelm the shouts of an opposing crowd by leaping up on the Rostra and starting a call-and-response with his followers: "Who was killing the plebs by famine?" His henchmen shouted back "Pompey!" "Who wanted to go to Alexandria?" "Pompey!" "Whom do you want to go?" "Crassus!" – incidentally revealing that the claqueurs operated somewhat less mechanically than Dio suggests.[80] Plutarch gives another sampling of such questions referring to Pompey's alleged lechery and homosexuality – and his "effeminate" habit of scratching his head with one finger.[81] But Clodius can hardly have been the only one to use such techniques. In the Ciceronian letter just cited, Clodius' call-and-response is itself an attempt to overwhelm a lengthy and noisy demonstration by those whom Cicero calls "our people" (*nostri*): after first disconcerting Clodius with a huge *clamor* when he first rose to speak, they hurled insults and finally shouted *versus obscenissimi* about his supposed incest with his sister.[82] Completely spontaneous *clamor* can hardly be so articulate; and this scene leads us to suspect that if indeed the audience of Cicero's *Fourth Philippic* raised an intelligible cry that he had saved the Republic a second time, or another, later audience, that

---

[76] For the demonstration, Cass. Dio 38.16.2–3; Cic. *Sest.* 25–26; *Planc.* 87; *Red. sen.* 12; for the number, Cic. *Red. pop.* 8; Plut. *Cic.* 31.1. See Tatum 1999: 154; Vanderbroeck 1987: 241, no. 43; see chap. 5, n. 23.

[77] *Att.* 1.19.4: *exercitus . . . locupletium.* Recall the troop of *equites*, led by Cicero's friend Atticus, stationed on the *clivus Capitolinus* during the "Catilinarian" debates (e.g. *Att.* 2.1.7; *Phil.* 2.16; *Sest.* 28) and his personal guard of *adulescentes* from Reate (*Cat.* 3.5), a town in his *clientela* (*Scaur.* 27; *Att.* 4.15).

[78] Plaut. *Amph.* 64–85; Plin. *Ep.* 2.14.6 (above, n. 68); cf. 7.24.7. There is an amusing review of the evidence and history of Roman claques in Cameron 1976: 230–49; see now also Aldrete 1999: 135–38; more bibliography in Vanderbroeck 1987: 114, n. 47.

[79] Cass. Dio 39.19.1.

[80] *Q Fr.* 2.3.2. See also *Sest.* 118: *is qui antea cantorum convicio contiones celebrare suas solebat.*

[81] Plut. *Pomp.* 48.7. On monodactylic head-scratching, see *Mor.* 89e: πορρωτάτω θηλύτητος καὶ ἀκολασίας; on its place in the politico-moral discourse, see Edwards 1993: 85; Corbeill 1996: 164–65.

[82] Cic. *Q Fr.* 2.3.2.

he had always been loyal to the Republic, then this may well have been prompted by claqueurs.[83]

By all these means one sought to "procure" a crowd that would bellow its support for one's own views and shout down those of one's adversaries.[84] Dio points out perceptively that it was in the nature of the thing that when Clodius' men began the cry others would join in.[85] It is indeed a powerful social instinct of the human animal, exploited by claqueurs in all ages, to join in applause once it has begun;[86] this is well understood by anyone who has been coerced into participating in the increasingly common standing ovation. But claqueurs cannot actually *force* an audience to applaud; rather, they are most useful when they can build upon a pre-existing favorable inclination among a significant portion of the audience – as was, I argue, typically the case with contional crowds. Appian, at one point in his description of the attempts of the conspirators to influence popular opinion after Caesar's assassination, interestingly hints that claqueurs also helped others embolden themselves to express their *true* feelings effectively.[87] As we shall see, approving audiences need at least a minimal degree of cuing in order to produce something better than the sort of confused, tepid applause that can be more damning than its absence. Control of space will have been another way for partisans to influence crowd responses. The area immediately around the Rostra must have been particularly valuable to partisans, who, if they arrived early and clustered tightly about the platform, were in the best position to embolden and insulate "their" speaker, directly intimidate any adversaries brought to the Rostra, and provide a sufficiently dense core to make their *plausus* and *clamor* prevail over scattered and isolated voices.[88] An imaginative reconstruction of an early-Republican *contio* seems to describe some such strategy, while one account of the Lupercalia incident of 44 (below) appears to corroborate the suggestion by distinguishing between

---

[83] Phil. 6.2: *cum vos universi una mente atque voce iterum a me conservatum esse rem publicam conclamastis*; 14.16: *una voce cuncta contio declaravit nihil esse a me umquam de re publica nisi optime cogitatum.* Note also the shout that Brutus should descend from the Capitol (Plut. *Brut.* 18.11; App. *B Civ.* 2.142) or its "demand" for Pompey in 67 (Cic. *Leg. Man.* 44). Cf. Cameron 1976: 239–40.

[84] Cic. *Sest.* 104: *conductas habent contiones, neque id agunt ut ea dicant aut ferant quae illi velint audire qui in contione sunt, sed pretio ac mercede perficiunt ut, quicquid dicant, id illi velle audire videantur.* Cf. παρασκευάζειν (ὅμιλον, for example) in Greek authors: Cass. Dio 39.19.1; 45.12.4 (cf. §6: ἔκ τε τῆς ἄλλης παρασκευῆς); Plut. *Brut.* 18.12.

[85] Cass. Dio 39.19.1–2.   [86] Atkinson 1984: 17–21.

[87] App. *B Civ.* 2.120, quoted below, n. 170. See Achard 1981: 78–81, for Cicero's apparently contradictory attitudes toward the practice, and further below.

[88] For threats and even violence that arose from a hostile crowd, which obviously were mostly phenomena of the front ranks (although a *lapidatio* from the rear could second the efforts of those at the front: Asc. 58 C), see pp. 165–66.

a friendly portion of a contional audience in front and a hostile one toward the rear.[89]

CONTIONAL VENTRILOQUISM

Having gathered the sort of crowd one wanted, how did one make the Voice of the Roman People "say" something useful? The most obvious method was of course to ask it a direct question. We have noted Clodius' use of an interrogatory call-and-response with an audience prompted by a claque. Cicero ridicules the similar technique of Clodius' brother and ally, Ap. Claudius: "[he] used to ask his audience at the *contio* whether it wanted me to return [from exile], and when he was answered by the shouts of half-dead hirelings used to say that the Roman People refused."[90] Cicero brands this a Greek invention; this kind of chanting does at least seem to have been a novelty in the mid-fifties, as was the practice of applauding, in the *contio*, the name of the proposer of a popular senatorial decree when it was read out to the People.[91] But there were older, essentially rhetorical techniques of giving a voice to the Roman People.

The burst of applause (or any other such sign of approval) that follows a particularly agreeable statement does more than simply demonstrate an audience's appreciation of the speaker. More interestingly, it is also an act of appropriation by the audience; and if the applause is swift and powerful enough, it further creates the impression that the sentiment just expressed reflects a unanimous consensus throughout the group. Yet, as Max Atkinson's fascinating study of "applause-elicitation" in modern political speeches compellingly shows, spontaneous as such outbursts superficially appear, "favourable audience responses are almost always prompted by the politicians themselves" through certain clearly definable techniques.[92]

More important than any particularly apt or agreeable verbal expression is the need to "cue" an audience to the imminent emergence of what Atkinson calls an "applaudable message" *and* to the appropriate moment at which to deliver applause.

---

[89] Strategy: Dion. Hal. *Ant. Rom.* 10.40.3–4. This was the day of the vote, but the context (note λόγοις μὲν πρῶτον, ἐὰν δὲ μὴ πείθωσι τὸν δῆμον, ἔργοις, and 10.41.1–2) suggests that these preparations were intended not only to block the taking of the vote but also to help during the tumultuous discussion in the preliminary *contio*. Front and rear audiences: Nic. Dam. *FGrH* 90 fr. 130.72 (below, p. 145).

[90] Cic. *Sest.* 126 (quoted at n. 14 above).

[91] Cic. *Att.* 4.1.6: *more hoc insulso et novo.* See above, n. 24. Cf., in the next century, Nero's importation of the Alexandrian arts of applause and acclamation: Suet. *Nero* 20.3; Tac. *Ann.* 14.15.5; Cass. Dio 61.20.4.

[92] Atkinson 1984: 47–85, with quotation from p. 84.

Atkinson writes,

[M]essages have to be packaged in a way which deals with two potential sources of difficulty for those in the audience. In the first place, the speaker must make it quite clear to them that he has launched into the final stage of delivering an applaudable message. Secondly, he has to supply enough advance information for them to be able to anticipate the precise point at which the message will be completed. So long as both these things are done, audiences will be led through the first two stages of the type of sequence exemplified by "Hip, hip – Hooray!" and "On your marks, get set – Go!" And once they have committed themselves to participating in such a process there is little to stop them from coming in on cue.[93]

The consequence of failing to "cue" a response in this way is observed all too often at the conclusion of an unfamiliar piece at a concert, when the applause may be weak or at least awkwardly slow in building because few of its members even know whether the piece has actually ended. Operas, often long and complicated (and once, after all, new), have long raised a similar problem of "cuing" applause at the right moment – a service traditionally performed by the house claque, who, at least in the account of a former member of the claque of the Vienna State Opera, were not parasitic extortionists but helped an inexpert audience give star performers their due.[94]

For a speaker, then, the key is to produce an effective "claptrap," a term which has come to mean "pretentious nonsense" but which originally meant "a device, expression, etc., to elicit applause."[95] An effective claptrap needs to give a series of cues to the audience:

An orator has to communicate with his audience in much the same way as a conductor communicates with an orchestra or choir. A single movement of the hand, arm, head, lips or eyes is unlikely to be enough to get musicians to come in on time. They may not all be equally attentive, and some of them will not have a sufficiently good view of the conductor to be able to notice one isolated signal on its own. But if he waves his baton, nods his head, and mouths the word "Now!", synchronizing them all to occur at the same time, the chances of everyone spotting at least one of them are greatly increased. Because each different move conveys an identical message, none of the musicians should be in any doubt as to what to do and when to do it. In the same way, an effective claptrap must provide audience members with a number of signals which make it quite clear both *that* they should applaud and *when* they should start doing so.[96]

Atkinson finds that *tricolon* (lists of three: Lincoln's "Government of the People, by the People, for the People") and *antithesis* (Martin Luther King's

---

[93] Atkinson 1984: 48.   [94] Wechsberg 1945: 70–100. I owe the reference to Cameron 1976: 239.
[95] *Shorter OED*, s.v.   [96] Atkinson 1984: 48.

"I have a dream that one day my four little children will not be judged by the color of their skin but by the content of their character") are particularly useful cuing devices: both produce a kind of road map toward the point of resolution that assures an impressive response from a friendly audience.

With these observations in mind, I turn now to a notable contional claptrap. A large portion of Cicero's late rhetorical dialogue, the *Orator*, is dedicated to the discussion of prose rhythm. In a review of the various rhythms that were recommended particularly for the close of sense units (*clausulae*), Cicero illustrates the power of the "dichoreic"[97] rhythm with a historical example – a fragment of a speech delivered in a public meeting by C. Papirius Carbo, tribune in 90,[98] with the youthful Cicero himself, then aged sixteen, in the audience. To clarify the structure of the passage I shall break it up into its syntactical units.

> O Marce Druse, patrem appello!
> tu dicere solebas sacram esse rem publicam;
> quicumque eam violavissent, ab omnibus esse ei poenas persolutas.
> patris dictum sapiens temeritas fili comprobavit.

> Marcus Drusus – the Elder I mean [cos. 112] – I call upon you!
> You used to say that the Republic was sacrosanct;
> all who had desecrated it had paid the penalty.
> The principle that the father wisely pronounced, the son [tr. pl. 91]
>   has brazenly proven."[99]

These last words, Cicero claims, provoked an amazing shout from the audience because of their pleasing dichoreic rhythm (*temeritas fili comprobavit*, – ∪ | – ∪); one might therefore marvel at the remarkably refined ear of the Roman plebs.[100] Cicero must be partly right: rhythmic *clausulae* were no doubt one effective means of articulating the structure of a claptrap, and of alerting the audience to the presence of the completion point. But he is certainly stretching a point, clearly in the service of his larger agenda in this work to validate his own rhetorical practice against its "Atticist" detractors; it is no accident, for example, that by thus emphasizing the efficacy of a dichoreic clausula, Cicero defends a rhythm much used by himself which had, however, come under attack as "Asian."[101] There is, after all, much more going on in this sentence than a felicitous use of prose rhythm. It is,

---

97 That is, double-trochaic: – ∪ – ×.   98 *MRR* 2.30, n. 8.
99 Cic. *Orat.* 213–14 = *ORF* 87.4, p. 304.   100 E.g. Horsfall 1996: 45.
101 Cic. *Orat.* 212, 215. See Gotoff 1979: 37–66, an excellent exposure of the polemical nature of the discussion in the *Orator* of prose style, including prose rhythm.

in fact, a perfect Atkinsonian "claptrap," reinforced indeed by prose rhythm but whose irresistable provocation of an audience's response is not limited to *clausulae*.[102]

Immediately arresting is the dramatic and jarring apostrophe to a dead man – at first apparently to the recently murdered, highly controversial tribune of 91, but as *patrem* then makes clear, actually to his father, the rival of Gaius Gracchus in 122. A key element of an effective claptrap, according to Atkinson, is just such a way of marking a new course, demanding closer attention, and communicating to listeners that a "completion point" is imminent.[103] Second, after the apostrophe the claptrap is clearly articulated in three short, yet periodic sentences, each maintaining, with the help of an internal pause, suspension of syntax and sense until its final word, and each rounded off, as Cicero demonstrates, with rhythmic *clausulae*. The careful three-part articulation of the claptrap meets Atkinson's demand that the timing of the approach of the completion point be clearly signalled.[104] "Cuing" is intensified in the final segment by the highly effective antithesis between the two apostrophized men – the wisdom of the father and recklessness of the son, the proposition enunciated by the one and the proof fatefully delivered by the other. Atkinson observes, "Once members of the audience have recognized that a contrast is being delivered, it is easy enough for them to anticipate exactly when the completion point will be reached";[105] all the more so when the antithesis is compressed into six words in evenly balanced isocolon (two groups of three). The final word, *comprobavit*, rounds off sense, syntax, and rhythm with a neat paradox. In sum, Carbo's claptrap perfectly exemplifies Atkinson's findings: it was irresistible because of its masterly combination of the essential techniques of eliciting an audience's response. Consequently, notwithstanding the applause it won, the relationship of the *sentiment* it expressed to the pre-existing opinions among its audience, not to mention the Roman People or even the urban plebs generally, is open to question.

Cicero himself was extremely adept at "working" a crowd, despite the contempt he professes in élite circles for popular applause and the impression he liked to give his peers that one entered the *contio* only to calm the wild impulses of the People.[106] His mastery of *eloquentia popularis*,

---

[102] Sandys 1885: ad loc. long ago observed the power of antithesis in the sentence; see now Hutchinson 1995: 491. Cicero himself observes elsewhere in the essay (*Orat.* 202) that "what is called prose rhythm does not always arise from meter (*numerus*), but sometimes from the symmetry or artful arrangement of words (*concinnitas aut constructio verborum*)."
[103] Atkinson 1984: 49–57.   [104] Atkinson 1984: 57–73.
[105] Atkinson 1984: 74; pp. 73–82 on "contrastive pairs."   [106] See pp. 62–66.

the style of speech appropriate to public meetings, is in general too little noted, presumably because it seems sharply inconsistent with our image, or caricature, of the man as a staunch senatorial conservative. The use of claptraps and rhetorical questions to elicit *clamor* and *plausus* are much on display in the *Fourth Philippic*, a published version of the speech delivered at a *contio* on December 20, 44.

First, however, a little of the immediate background in order properly to assess his strategy.[107] At the end of November, 44 BC, Mark Antony, harassed by mutinies among his soldiery and the suddenly open hostility of Octavian, had left Rome and marched north to take over his province of Cisalpine Gaul. On December 20 a dispatch arrived in Rome from D. Brutus, the governor of that province, saying that he was putting himself at the disposal of the Senate and People and announcing that he would bar Antony from the province. Cicero leapt to the attack, and carried a motion in the Senate that day in praise of Brutus, Octavian, and the mutineers against Antony. The decree made no mention of Antony or of any explicit threat of war – it certainly could not have passed if it had. But it was a step in that direction. As was usual, a *contio* was called immediately after the senatorial meeting to inform the People of the decree and explain its significance. Cicero, invited to speak by the presiding tribune, M. Servilius, then delivered the speech which he later wrote up as the fourth in the series of Philippics.[108] We hear from other, independent sources that at this time Antony's stock was low among the populace in Rome and Octavian's high;[109] Cicero could therefore count on a favorable reception and make use of the opportunity to construct and objectify the People's Will, which then would serve to stiffen a wobbly Senate.[110]

I shall not summarize the speech; the purpose here is only to appreciate Cicero's use of the standard techniques of "applause elicitation." Near the beginning, Cicero announces that the Senate has judged Antony an enemy of the state even if it has not yet openly declared him such: "Antonius, says the Senate, is a public enemy; it has not yet used the word, but so it

---

[107] See most fully and recently, Gotter 1996: 92–146; summaries in English in Syme 1939: 141–48, 162–75; Frisch 1946: 144–64; Mitchell 1991: 303–11.

[108] It is again immaterial to my argument whether the published speech represents what was actually said; what matters is that it be appropriate to the implied occasion and therefore give insight into actual rhetorical techniques. See pp. 27–30. On Servilius, see *Phil.* 4.16; cf. *Fam.* 12.7.1. For the speech, see Pasoli 1957 and Wooten 1983: 68–70.

[109] App. *B Civ.* 3.41, 46; Cass. Dio 45.11.3, 12.4–6, 15.1, 15.3. The execution of Amatius in April had already generated popular hatred of Antony, according to App. *B Civ.* 3.3–4; cf. Cass. Dio 45.6.2.

[110] Pasoli 1957: 26–27.

has judged in deed."[111] Particularly in the original, the sentence exemplifies essential features of the claptrap: a hostile comment against an outsider, it conforms to a regular type of "applaudable message," emphasized by balanced antithesis (*nondum verbo / re iam*) reinforced by internal rhyme (*appellatus / iudicatus*) and the suspension of the subject until the last word, the climactic nomination of the enemy. Cicero "writes in" the audience's response by continuing, "Now indeed I am much heartened, since with such a great shout you have unanimously agreed that he is a public enemy"; we are therefore mentally to insert a roar of approval from the crowd during a pause of several seconds while Cicero allows the response to build.[112] A second claptrap comes just two sentences later when he declares that the Senate has warmly commended Octavian for his zeal on behalf of the Republic and "your freedom"; again Cicero writes the audience into his speech by then praising it for its response to Octavian's name: "Excellent! Excellent, Citizens, I commend your grateful response upon hearing the name of this brilliant young man."[113] Somewhat further on Cicero praises the soldiers of the so-called legion of Mars, for their mutiny against Antony and adherence to Octavian: by its actions it had in effect declared Antony a public enemy. Another claptrap, greeted again by the roar of the crowd: "Most plainly and appropriately, Citizens, has your outcry shown your approval of the brilliant deed of the legion of Mars!"[114] Another few sentences and Cicero invites the crowd again to respond: "the brave, true decision of these legions is ratified by the Senate, is approved by the entire Roman People," then, as if checking himself, but in fact to elicit another roar "that is, unless you, Citizens, judge Antony to be consul rather than a public enemy!" A pause for the audience to respond with disapproving *reclamatio* or *admurmuratio*, and then: "Yes, Citizens, I thought your view was as you now express it."[115] Another question: Could anyone hold Decimus Brutus' manifesto to be of

---

[111] *Phil.* 4.1: *nam est hostis a senatu nondum verbo appellatus, sed re iam iudicatus Antonius.* Unfortunately, the effects referred to in the text are almost entirely lost in translation. On "unfavourable references to 'them,'" see Atkinson 1984: 40–45.

[112] *Phil.* 4.2: *nunc vero multo sum erectior quod vos quoque illum hostem esse tanto consensu tantoque clamore approbavistis.* Atkinson 1984: 21–31, shows that the applause after modern "claptraps" typically takes about one second to reach full intensity and lasts, with remarkable consistency, between seven and nine seconds.

[113] *Phil.* 4.3: *laudo, laudo vos, Quirites, quod gratissimis animis prosequimini nomen clarissimi adulescentis.* Atkinson 1984: 35–37, on "favorable references to persons." Since "favorable references to 'us'" are another fundamental "applaudable message" (pp. 37–39) it is tempting to regard *laudo, laudo vos* as a kind of secondary claptrap, with the intention of extending the audience's response still further.

[114] *Phil.* 4.5: *praeclare et loco, Quirites, reclamatione vestra factum pulcherrimum Martialium comprobavistis.*

[115] *Phil.* 4.6–7.

no account? "No you say, Citizens, and rightly so!"[116] And again he returns to his main theme, inviting the Roman People to demonstrate its hostility to Antony: which of the two is the enemy, Brutus or Antony? Is there any room for hesitation? "Just as you say with one mind and voice that you are in no doubt, so the Senate has now decreed."[117] The audience, in Cicero's construction, is unanimous;[118] "In no other cause have you ever been more united."[119]

The dynamics at work are clear. Repeatedly the speaker invites the audience to give its predictable assent to "applaudable messages" offered to it; repeatedly Cicero then takes up its response with a comment, often praise for its apparent resolution, that suggests that he is only taking his cue from the audience when it is, in fact, just the other way around.[120] The orator effectively creates the politically important illusion that he is merely the articulate mouthpiece of the audience, which for its part amasses enormous power behind his words with its orchestrated blasts of approval. The appearance of totally harmonious two-way communication collapses the distance between speaker and audience and gives a powerful impression of unanimity. The objective, clearly, is to make it seem as though the People "themselves" were declaring Antony a public enemy.[121] And, just as in reporting speeches the modern media habitually select or emphasize those statements that received the most conspicuous applause, it seems likely that those assertions and claims to which the audience had most loudly responded will have stuck in the minds of participants and observers, and been reported to those who were not present.[122] Cicero got what he wanted; he would later recall the great enthusiasm of this audience, which even shouted – surely not without someone's prompting – that he had saved the Republic a second time.[123] Not at all implausible, given Antony's current unpopularity among the urban populace.

In a later *contio* Cicero refers back to this audience's response as nothing less than a manifest verdict (*iudicio tanto tamque praeclaro*) for war with Antony. Cicero thus forges from the chaotic mass of oft-contradictory views and perceptions current in any crowd a concrete popular mandate for war with Antony for him to carry out in the Senate: "Aroused by so weighty and unambiguous a verdict, I entered the Senate on the Kalends of January

---

[116] *Phil.* 4.7.
[117] *Phil.* 4.8: *atque ut vos una mente unaque voce dubitare vos negatis, sic modo decrevit senatus.*
[118] See also *Phil.* 4.10: *tantus consensus omnium.*
[119] *Phil.* 4.12: *numquam maior consensus vester in ulla causa fuit.*		[120] Pasoli 1957: 35.
[121] Cf. the comments of Mack 1937: 55–56, 61–62. Pina Polo 1996: 21–22 seems to miss the mark.
[122] "Quotability": Atkinson 1984: 124–51.		[123] *Phil.* 6.2; cf. 7.22.

mindful of the *role for which you had cast me* and which I was sustaining. Seeing that a wicked war had been launched against the Commonwealth, I considered that no delay should be allowed to hold up the pursuit of Marcus Antonius . . ."[124] And indeed, having won his "popular mandate" Cicero returned to the senatorial debates of January, 43, urging the Senate to "catch up" to the People and not forfeit its proper role of leadership.[125] In fact, Cicero's misrepresentation to his audience of the Senate's will on December 20 had been crucial for prompting their "verdict": while reassuring his audience that the Senate stands shoulder-to-shoulder with them in the fight against Antony, Cicero actually pushes them far out in front.[126]

Cicero's demagogy is embarrassing for conventional views of the man and his attitude toward popular politics.[127] The *Fourth Philippic* shows with unusual clarity how rhetorical techniques of applause elicitation were used to objectify a popular "verdict" on the Rostra, to be exploited in turn to sway the Curia.[128] It would be off the mark to conclude, from the manifestly "staged character" of many *contiones*, that the significance of mass oratory was more or less limited to "the rousing effect it had on the faithful" (as well as providing some "soundbites" to those not present).[129] The purpose of such "staging" was precisely to amplify the oratory outward, to make a persuasive claim before others (uncommitted or opposing voters, and the Senate) that the Roman People spoke with one clear voice.

THE AMBIVALENT POPULACE

In fact, the reality was much messier than the objective, concrete "verdicts" cited by Cicero and others. A curious consequence of the particularity and

---

[124] *Phil.* 6.2: *hoc vestro iudicio tanto tamque praeclaro excitatus ita Kalendis Ianuariis veni in senatum ut meminissem quam personam impositam a vobis sustinerem. itaque bellum nefarium illatum rei publicae cum viderem, nullam moram interponendam insequendi M. Antonium putavi* . . . Trans. Shackleton Bailey (my emphasis). For other popular "mandates" drawn from the *contio*, see *Leg. Man.* 69–71; *Leg. agr.* 2.49, 101–2; below, p. 224.

[125] Cic. *Phil.* 5.2, 25, 31; 7.22. Cf. the similar appeal in *Cat.* 1.14–19. For the proper relationship between the two parties as seen in élite circles, see *Amic.* 96: *quanta in oratione maiestas! ut facile ducem populi Romani, non comitem diceres.* Laser 1997: 40.

[126] *Phil.* 4.8: *atque ut vos una mente unaque voce dubitare vos negatis, sic modo decrevit senatus.* §12: *numquam maior consensus vester in ulla causa fuit; numquam tam vehementer cum senatu consociati fuistis.* Cf. Mack 1937: 53.

[127] Such as those expressed by Pina Polo 1996: 123, 150 ("ein obligatorische Komplement zum Kontakt zum Senat, dem stets der Vorrang eingeräumt wurde"); Mack 1937: 10.

[128] The technique remains familiar: according to the *New York Times* for October 8, 2002, an unnamed "White House official" comments that "The strategy is to use the Congress as leverage, leverage to bring around the public, and leverage to make it clear to the UN that it's not only George Bush who is prepared to draw a line in the sand, it's the whole country."

[129] Mouritsen 2001: 54–56.

partisanship of contional audiences is that at times the People appear to be quite schizophrenic because of the contradictory actions of quite different crowds.[130] Immediately following the murder of Clodius on the Appian Way, the tribunes Plancus, Pompeius, and Sallust whipped up public outrage in their *contiones*, the first of which, on January 19, 52, led to the burning of the Senate-house and a roving riot.[131] Yet in the midst of this campaign, another tribune, M. Caelius, called a *contio* at which the killer himself, Milo, and Cicero were heard sympathetically as they argued a plea of self-defense.[132] For Cicero, this crowd was the *populus Romanus*; but for Appian, it had been bribed by Milo (who had indeed also "bought" Caelius), and it was the other crowd, the one that broke up Caelius' *contio*, that was "the uncorrupted portion of the People."[133] (Even so, two sentences later Appian describes this very group, once it has begun a general rampage, as for the most part composed of armed slaves!)[134] But Cicero's identification of Caelius' crowd as the Roman People *tout court* is no doubt even more tendentious, at least if Asconius, a detached and reasonably well-informed source for these events, has rightly understood the popular mood. And Appian's allegation that Milo hired Caelius' audience may not be far wrong. According to Asconius, only a few days before this *contio* Milo had reopened his consular candidacy and distributed 1,000 *asses* a man among the tribes – something like a quarter of a year's rent or more for most of them, and more than would be left to them under Caesar's will.[135]

It would not be difficult to find other diametrically opposed contional *significationes*. I shall consider at length below Appian's complex narrative about the relationship between two opposing crowds and their expressions of sentiment after the assassination of Julius Caesar. But other cases can be readily discerned outside Appian's pages. After the execution of the "Catilinarian" conspirators, in the midst of the apparently successful effort of the tribunes Q. Metellus Nepos and L. Calpurnius Bestia to arouse popular indignation against Cicero, their colleague M. Cato seems to have been able to elicit an approving shout from a *contio* for his declaration that Cicero was the Father of his Country.[136] During the controversy surrounding

---

[130] Rightly, Laser 1997: 218, n. 174.   [131] Especially Asc. 33, 42, 50–51 C.

[132] App. *B Civ.* 2.22; Asc. 33 C; Cic. *Mil.* 91. Nippel 1988: 132–33.

[133] Cic. *Mil.* 91; App. *B Civ.* 2.22: τοῦ δήμου τὸ ἀδιάφθορον.

[134] App. *B Civ.* 2.22: θεράποντές τε ὄντες οἵ πλείους καὶ ὡπλισμένοι.

[135] Asc. 33 C. Kühnert's interpretation of *tributim* (1991: 39–40) is to be rejected (cf. Yakobson 1992: 33–35). Asconius: 33 C: *Populus . . . corpus P. Clodi in curiam intulit cremavitque . . .* ; 37–38 C: the *maxima pars multitudinis* hostile to Milo and Cicero (cf. *populi a se alienatione*).

[136] App. *B Civ.* 2.7: Κάτωνος δ᾽ αὐτὸν καὶ πατέρα τῆς πατρίδος προσαγορεύσαντος ἐπεβόησεν ὁ δῆμος; cf. Plut. *Cat. Min.* 23.3; Cic. *Fam.* 15.4.11: *tu . . . qui me . . . in contionibus ad caelum extulisti.*

Cicero's return from exile, the crowds that attended *contiones* held by Clodius' brother, Appius Claudius, and by Lentulus Spinther expressed quite contradictory popular sentiments;[137] indeed when Cicero re-entered the city the humblest of the plebeians (*infima plebs*) filled the steps of the temples at the Porta Capena to greet the great man with applause, *Clodiani* notwithstanding, and a similar crowd followed him to the Forum and Capitol.[138] And during the grain shortage that closely followed Cicero's return, Clodius' crowd shouted that Cicero was to blame; but others called upon him to move the proposal for a special grain commission, and applauded him when his name in the *senatus consultum* was read out.[139]

Often, no doubt, opposing partisans were mixed together with neutrals in any one audience, resulting in a response ambiguous enough to be interpreted in contrary ways even by eyewitnesses, not to mention by those reporting the event. Consider the famous Lupercalia incident of 44, when Mark Antony offered Julius Caesar the diadem in what was not technically a *contio* but whose setting (on the Rostra in the Forum, surrounded by "the Roman People"), if not necessarily audience, was identical with one. Our sources for the crowd's reaction are irreconcilably and tendentiously contradictory; but a feature that is found in all accounts but Cicero's is a certain ambivalence. In Plutarch, feeble prearranged applause greets Antony's offer of the diadem; a great ovation, Caesar's refusal. Appian's picture is similar, except that after the first attempt the crowd falls silent until it sees who would prevail. Nicolaus of Damascus, on the other hand, has "the People" cry for the diadem to be placed on Caesar's head, continuing even as he pushes it away. After Antony places it on his head and he throws it to the crowd, those in the back of the crowd (οἱ μὲν τελευταῖοι) applaud, but those in front (οἱ δὲ πλησίον) shout that he should accept the People's gift. "The People" shout their approval again when Antony

---

This report is sometimes rejected as a conflation with the senatorial acclamation on the motion of Catulus mentioned by Cicero at *Pis.* 6. But the senatorial decree would have been announced to the people in a *contio*; why should it not have been Cato who did so? For the attacks of Nepos and Bestia, see especially Cass. Dio 37.38.1–39.1, with a radically different version of the audience's reception of Cicero's oath on leaving office from Cicero's own (*Fam.* 5.2.7; *Rep.* 1.7; cf. Plut. *Cic.* 23.1–2); Cic. *Mur.* 81, *Sest.* 12; *Schol. Bob.* 127 St.

[137] Cic. *Sest.* 126 for Ap. Claudius' *contiones*; *Red. sen.* 26, *Sest.* 107–8; *Pis.* 34, for those of Lentulus. Note that in Dio's view τὸ πλῆθος was favorable to Cicero in direct opposition to Clodius (39.7.2).

[138] Cic. *Att.* 4.1.5; cf. *Dom.* 76: *populus Romanus*, and App. *B Civ.* 2.16: λαμπρῶς δ' αὐτὸν περὶ τὰς πύλας ὑποδεχομένων πάντων.

[139] Cic. *Att.* 4.1.6 (on which see above, n. 24); cf. *Dom.* 6–7, 9, 11–16. Nippel's analysis (1988: 124–26) is excellent; Laurence's insistence (1994: 69–70) that Clodius lay behind every popular demonstration leads to perverse results.

puts the diadem on Caesar's head a second time, but when Caesar refuses it again "the same people as before applauded again," presumably those to the rear. In direct contrast to Nicolaus, Cicero gives the simplest, and doubtless most misleading, picture: "You (Antony) kept placing the diadem on him, while the People groaned; he kept casting it off while they applauded."[140]

As Nicolaus' account suggests, different segments of a crowd might of course react differently than others. A moment's thought upon the behavior of real crowds rather than literary ones will also encourage us to give the inherent diversity and even confusion of spontaneous collective actions their due. This, selectively and tendentiously interpreted, may well lie behind such utterly contradictory characterizations as those given by Cicero and Dio of the *contio* in which the consul of 63 spoke on his last day in office.[141] And the natural variations of responsiveness within a crowd gave further room for rhetorical "redefinition" of its constituents. In the published speech in defense of C. Rabirius for the murder of Saturninus, whose original was delivered in the final *contio* in a trial before the People, Cicero represents himself as *intentionally* eliciting a hostile *clamor* from some of his audience by lamenting that he cannot unfortunately give Rabirius the credit for killing the demagogue; he then exploits the supposed feebleness of the predictable response to "define" the shouters as a negligible minority of imbeciles, and himself as the consul specially chosen by the silent majority to stand up to such disruptions.[142] That his audience was largely, in fact, a fairly hostile one can reasonably be inferred not merely from the nature of the charge but from the evidence of Dio, who reports that the People (ὁ δῆμος) were pressing almost irresistibly for conviction.[143] Whether or not Cicero actually did any such thing in his final speech at Rabirius' trial, I assume that by highlighting the device in the published version he is offering an example of how to handle a crowd of which a large constituent is unfavorable. Since a hostile element has not been "prepared" by him, even those capable of hearing him without difficulty

[140] Plut. *Caes.* 61.5; App. *B Civ.* 2.109; Nic. Dam. *FGrH* 90 fr. 130.72; Cic. *Phil.* 2.85.

[141] Cic. *Fam.* 5.2.7; *Pis.* 6–7; *Rep.* 1.7; *Sull.* 33–34 (Plut. *Cic.* 23.2 follows Cicero); Cass. Dio 37.38.1–39.1.

[142] *Rab. perd.* 18: *Utinam hanc mihi facultatem causa concederet ut possem hoc praedicare, C. Rabiri manu L. Saturninum, hostem populi Romani, interfectum!* [CLAMOR] *Nihil me clamor iste commovet sed consolatur, cum indicat esse quosdam civis imperitos sed non multos. Numquam, mihi credite, populus Romanus hic qui silet consulem me fecisset, si vestro clamore perturbatum iri arbitraretur. Quanto iam levior est acclamatio! Quin continetis vocem indicem stultitiae vestrae, testem paucitatis!* See Vanderbroeck 1987: 230–31 (B-21); Primmer 1985: 17–18. For the controversy over the nature of this trial and its background, see chap. 1, n. 90; cf. chap. 2, n. 93).

[143] Cass. Dio 37.27.3. Suet. *Iul.* 12 does not, strictly, contradict Dio on this point.

would presumably not have been able to react speedily and simultaneously, which permits Cicero, making use of his frequent interpretation of silence as an expression of approval, to characterize all those who, for whatever reason, did not respond immediately as favorable to his provocative statement.[144]

Clearly, then, *significationes* of the "judgment and will of the Roman People" sometimes pointed in sharply contradictory directions. Here we should recall John Zaller's findings about public opinion, which I discussed briefly in the introduction:[145] "public opinion" is not a concrete, independent object that is "out there" to be "found" and "measured" by a neutral observer or "heard" by a politician, but an artefact *created* in the process of being articulated, frequently by someone with a political objective in doing so, out of the chaotic mass of often contradictory actual concerns and interests that exist in a given population. Consideration of the difficulties of interpreting even modern polls, in which apparently subtle variations in phrasing and statistical sampling can be decisive, give some idea of the complexity of the issue: for example, on one occasion, 45 per cent of Americans would not have "allowed" a communist to make a speech in their country – but only 20 per cent would have "forbidden" it.[146] The reactions of different contional crowds, assembled by different magistrates and "asked" different questions, were something like the divergent results obtained in modern times by polls paid for by opponents – though without even their quasi-scientific constraints (especially quantification). There was enormous leeway for any observer of the *contio* to abstract what he wanted (and could rhetorically use) from the often debatable evidence provided in mass meetings and other popular demonstrations. No wonder Cicero himself notoriously misapprehended the popular will at some key moments, mistakes that should now be considered quite understandable in the light of what we have just seen.[147] It was certainly possible, despite the methods of engineering an audience reviewed above, for a *contio* to fall flat.[148] And we should certainly shy away from assertions that underestimate the

---

[144] For the meaning of silence, see chap. 2, n. 113.   [145] See pp. 18ff.

[146] Zaller 1992: 28–29, who notes also the finding that purely linguistic "framing" of the question changed the proportion of support for a "freeze" on nuclear weapons in a poll conducted by the *New York Times* in 1983 from 18 percent to 83 percent.

[147] Nippel 1988: 127. "Unpopularity" of the "triumvirs" in 59: Cic. *Att.* 2.18.1; 2.19.2–3; 2.20.3–4; 2.21.1–5. It may be, however, that Cicero was less deluded about the popular attitude toward the assassins in 44 than is commonly thought (*Att.* 14.2.1; *Phil.* 1.30, 36–38; 2.31; 10.8): see Achard 1981: 80, and below, pp. 155–56.

[148] Millar 1998: 131, perhaps over-interpreting Cic. *Att.* 2.21.5 (see above, n. 147); but see *Att.* 1.14.1; 2.21.5; *Brut.* 305.

variability and volatility of public sentiments, such as "Cicero remained thereafter [i.e. after he was sent into exile] unpopular with the plebs."[149] Even Clodius was not always the undisputed darling of the urban populace.[150] The fact that at times the *populus* seems not really *popularis* is not really a paradox.[151]

Given the uncertainties about the makeup of individual audiences, the lack of controls over access, and the natural ambiguity of many crowd responses, if one was faced with a hostile outcry it was possible and of course advantageous, as we saw in Cicero's speech for Rabirius, rhetorically to revoke the credentials of the shouters to represent the Roman People. A central axiom of Ciceronian political rhetoric is that the "true People" (*verus populus*) is unanimous in its support for the "right-thinking men" (*boni*), who in turn safeguard their interests, while "immoral" politicians (*improbi*) misrepresent the noise of a hired or otherwise unrepresentative crowd (*peculiaris populus*) as an expression of the Will of the Roman People. It follows that the former, men like himself, are the ones who are "truly" (*vere*) Friends of the People (*populares*), while the latter pretend to be so "hypocritically and deceptively" (*ficte et fallaciter*).[152] For Cicero, the *contiones* over which Clodius and his associates presided were "bought" (*conductae*) and consisted of "hirelings" and "gangs" (*mercennarii, operae*), while those that listened in reverential silence to the "chief men of the community" (*principes civitatis*) pleading for Cicero's return were the "true Roman People."[153] *That* audience, Cicero avers, was gathered by closing not the shops but the towns (*municipia*) of Italy[154] – a riposte that incidentally, however, serves to remind us of the different, but apparently comparable, means by which Cicero's own partisans mobilized public opinion through the peninsula. The consular *contio* that opened the final push for Cicero's recall took place during the festival period of early July, when the city was filled with visitors from all Italy; the Senate voted thanks to those who had

---

[149] Brunt 1988: 334. The passages he cites at p. 486, n. 76 hardly demonstrate this; nor do those at p. 487, n. 80, perhaps the correct cross-reference. See also below, chap. 6, n. 30.

[150] See nn. 137–39 above, with Nippel 1988: 124–26.

[151] Jochen Martin 1965: 66, 95–96, 195; Laser 1997: 190–91.

[152] The classic statement is Cic. *Sest.* 103–27 (§125 *peculiaris populus*); on "true" and "false" *populares*, see *Leg. agr.* 2, *passim*, esp. 2.7–10; *Rab. perd.*, esp. 10–17; also *Leg. agr.* 1.23, 25; *Cat.* 4.9; *Dom.* 77, 88; *Har. resp.* 42; *Phil.* 7.4. Hellegouarc'h 1963: 534–41; Meier 1965: 569–70; J. Martin 1965: 50–52; Seager 1972a; Achard 1981: 67–71, 131–40, 193–97; Perelli 1982: 39–41; Pina Polo 1996: 119–21. On the terms *populares* and *optimas*, see further chap. 6.

[153] Cic. *Sest.* 106–8, 126; cf. *Red. sen.* 26, *Pis.* 34. Also *Dom.* 89–91: *An tu populum Romanum esse illum putas qui constat ex iis qui mercede conducuntur . . . quem tu tamen populum nisi tabernis clausis frequentare non poteras.*

[154] Cic. *Dom.* 90.

come from the *municipia* and specifically urged them to return to Rome for the vote, an invitation reinforced by consular letters and the personal advocacy of Pompey.[155] Cicero was later to declare thankfully that Lentulus "brought it about, with Italy standing by as his audience, that no one could hear any hired scoundrel emit a harsh cry hostile to the *boni*."[156] It was certainly possible for the *boni* to raise, or hire, a crowd too.[157] We can guess that Clodius would therefore simply have reversed Cicero's categories; we know that Clodius complained, hypocritically but perhaps with some grounds, that Cicero's return had been effected by means of hired armed gangs.[158]

This kind of rhetorical redefinition of Roman crowds was particularly important in the face of a hostile uproar (*adversa acclamatio*). This was in general much to be feared; one such disturbance ruined Cicero's defense of Milo, a speech which, although an open-air trial and not a public meeting, was attended by a huge crowd of *Clodiani* whose responses were essentially contional.[159] As we have already seen in Cicero's deft handling of the shouts in his defence of Rabirius, a speaker could try to make use of a hostile clamor by defining it as the howling of a few idiots, criminals, or slaves. In the published version of the (spoiled) speech for Milo, Cicero suggests that a similar tactic might have been used (perhaps it had been, unsuccessfully): he identifies those who have raised a fearful tumult as mere slaves and criminals and tries to turn the outcry to his advantage with his immediate audience of mostly equestrian and senatorial jurors by characterizing the defendant as one who had "always ignored that kind of men and the loudest shouts where your security was concerned."[160] But the most famous example of the tactic was the retort that P. Scipio Aemilianus is said to have given when he was brought by a tribune before a hostile *contio* and asked to give his opinion of the killing of Tiberius Gracchus.[161] The audience raised a

---

[155] Cic. *Red. sen.* 26–7; *Pis.* 34, 80; cf. *Sest.* 129. For the chronology, see Gelzer 1969: 148–49; Mitchell 1991: 154–56. But the *contio* on the Campus Martius to which Cicero often alludes must be that which immediately preceded the vote: Pina Polo 1989: 301, no. 308. Nicholson 1992: esp. 51–60, offers a convenient summary of the efforts of Pompey and the consul Lentulus on Cicero's behalf.

[156] Cic. *Red. sen.* 26.   [157] Cic. *Att.* 3.23.5. Cf. above, n. 76.

[158] Cic. *Sest.* 127; cf. *Att.* 3.23.5 and 4.2.7, with Shackleton Bailey's notes.

[159] *Adversa acclamatio*, causes and remedies: Cic. *De or.* 2.339–40. Interruptions in the *Pro Milone*: Asc. 41–42 C (cf. 40); Quint. *Inst.* 4.3.16–17, to be preferred to the exaggerations of Dio and Plutarch (B. A. Marshall 1985: 190–91).

[160] *Mil.* 3: *Quorum clamor si qui forte fuerit, admonere vos debebit ut eum civem retineatis qui semper genus illud hominum clamoresque maximos prae vestra salute neglexit.*

[161] Unclarity about the nature of the setting in which Scipio made his remark leads to misapprehension of its significance in Astin 1971: 233–34.

great roar at his judgment that Gracchus had been justly killed, if he had planned to overthrow the republic,[162] but Scipio famously responded that, never having been frightened by the enemy's war cry, he was unimpressed by the shout of men for whom Italy was only a stepmother,[163] apparently adding for good measure that he had himself brought these men to Rome – as prisoners of war, to be sold as slaves![164] An insult, yes, but more than that: his comments turned the standard representation of the contional audience as the Roman People on its head, for he rhetorically reconstituted the audience as only a mob of foreign-born ex-slaves and recent enemies of Rome, to whose opinion he was obviously not bound to defer. The riposte is a rhetorical move in the discourse we have been examining here, not, as it is sometimes naïvely taken to be, testimony to the size of the freed population in Rome.[165]

THE *CONTIONES* AFTER CAESAR'S ASSASSINATION

I turn, finally, to a momentous episode which, as it is described in some detail and from different points of view, well illustrates some of the central themes of this chapter: above all, the significance attributed to expressions of the Popular Will in the *contio*, not only by contemporary agents but also by those who, often tendentiously, described the events in their histories, biographies, or speeches. For, as will be seen, the efforts of contemporaries to create the impression of a favorable communal consensus were

---

[162] The condition is given only by Vell. Pat. 2.4.4. But such qualification rings true to the rhetorical situation (cf. the responses of Piso, Gabinius, and Caesar to Clodius' questioning in 58: Cic. *Pis.* 14; *Red. sen.* 17; Cass. Dio 38.16.6–17.2) and would easily vanish from the tradition. Livy's epitomator appears to think that the famous comment was part of a set speech by Aemilianus (*Per.* 59), but all other references (Cic. *De or.* 2.106; *Mil.* 8) put beyond doubt that it was originally a response to a question put to him by Carbo in a *contio* called by the latter. The famous oration that carried so much weight against Carbo's proposal and was later published (Cic. *Amic.* 96; Livy, *Per.* 59) evidently belongs in another *contio*; it may, of course, have reiterated and explained the point about Gracchus' death. On the date, see Sumner 1973: 58–9.

[163] So Vell. Pat. 2.4.4: *et cum omnis contio adclamasset, "hostium," inquit, "armatorum totiens clamore non territus, qui possum vestro moveri, quorum noverca est Italia?"* Cf. Plut. *Mor.* 201e–f; *ORF* 21.28–29, pp. 31–32 for full testimonia. Deissmann-Merten 1974 rejects this part of Scipio's response, unpersuasively. In its Roman political context, the retort is not at all about autochthony, thus should not be seen as a dubious transplantation of a Platonic figure (*Menex.* 237b); nor is the absence of this part of the reply from two other Ciceronian contexts troubling (*De or.* 2.106 [discussing *status*-theory!]; *Mil.* 8, where it would have been distracting if not indeed counterproductive).

[164] Val. Max. 6.2.3: *orto deinde murmure, "non efficietis," ait, "ut solutos verear quos adligatos adduxi";* *De vir. ill.* 58.8: *et addidit, "quos ego sub corona vendidi."*

[165] Nor, in fact, the violation of a contional convention, as Hölkeskamp 1995: 38 sees it, but a strategic use of that convention.

seconded, or complicated, by literary/rhetorical interpreters who had their own agendas to pursue. The result, I shall argue, is a profoundly confused picture, whose lack of clear resolution ultimately goes back to the fundamental indeterminacy of the Popular Will in such circumstances – an indeterminacy that was exploited, but also in the aggregate compounded, by the partisan interpretations of the original actors (of the sort that I have been examining). A secondary purpose here will be to show how these accounts highlight, or otherwise illustrate, the methods employed by contemporary agents to create the appearance, and ultimately the reality, of a communal consensus. The methods will by now be familiar, but there is value in seeing them working in their narrative context, integrated into a specific sequence of momentous events. It will be apparent that we cannot take any of these narratives at face value as transparent descriptions of the facts; but we will see how their authors thought Roman "opinion- and will-formation" might work.

A central issue in all ancient accounts of the crisis following the assassination of Julius Caesar on the Ides of March, 44, is the attitude of the urban plebs toward the conspirators, made manifest in at least six *contiones* distinguishable in the evidence over the four tense days following the killing.[166] The scrutiny the ancient authors devote to these meetings is equalled by that of modern scholars, among whom the consensus view is that the plebs was deeply resentful of the assassination and hostile to the conspirators.[167] My observations thus far, however, would suggest that much more caution is required of those inclined to read the significance of public demonstrations, which was regularly open to contestation even among contemporaries.

By far the fullest and most complex picture of the popular reaction to Caesar's assassination is that painted by Appian, on whom I shall therefore focus. In his version, the immediate reaction of the urban population to the assassination was panicked flight. The markets were plundered (perhaps due to fear of impending civil war rather than criminal opportunism or class

---

[166] So Pina Polo 1989: 308–9, nos. 346–51, whose distribution of the texts among these six entries needs some revision. No. 352 is a mirage: Suetonius' *pridie* (*Iul.* 85) is either a slip, Cinna's speech having taken place almost certainly on March 15 (Appian, Plutarch), or a corruption of *pridem*.

[167] The fullest examination of the question is that of Yavetz 1969: 62–69, with Yavetz 1974: esp. 64: "It was only after the murder that the true state of mind [of the plebs] was revealed"; see Jehne 1987: 286–331; Pina Polo 1996: 143, 159–62. Nippel 1988: 145–47, is somewhat more cautious. On the speeches in the accounts of Appian and Dio, see now Gowing 1992: 228–34; on the *contiones* of March 17, see Motzo 1940. A recent examination of these events in Gotter 1996: 21–41; Frisch 1946: 44–62, is still useful.

vengeance) and "all" barricaded themselves inside their houses.[168] When the conspirators emerged and called upon Rome to restore its constitution they were dismayed to find that the *populus* did not rush to their support and as their hopes for assistance from the Senate were outweighed by their suspicion of the populace and fear of the soldiery, Lepidus, and Antony, they fled to the Capitol.[169] Once on the Capitol "they decided to distribute bribes to the mob; for they hoped that if some should begin to praise what had happened, the rest, taking thought for freedom and longing for the Republic, would take up the cry."[170] In an interesting digression, Appian explains that the conspirators mistakenly believed that the People were still true Romans, such as they had been when the ancient Brutus had expelled the kings, and failed to recognize that this was inconsistent with their current mercenary condition; for a long time already "hirelings" had been copiously available because of the corruption of the state.[171] Foreigners, freedmen, slaves (whose dress, according to Appian, made them indistinguishable from citizens), the poor who flock to Rome for the grain dole, and not least the demobilized soldiery waiting to be settled in colonies, were all ready to be bought.

From these groups the conspirators easily gathered a great mass (πλῆθος) in the Forum. Despite having been bribed, the crowd did not dare to praise the conspirators because they feared Caesar's reputation and what "the others" (the rest of the People and perhaps the Caesarian leaders) would do, but in order to save the conspirators they repeatedly shouted in favor of peace, calling upon the magistrates to champion it as being in the interest of all.[172] The praetor L. Cornelius Cinna advanced into their midst, and laying aside his magisterial robe (for Caesar had given him his office), declared Caesar a tyrant and thus that the conspirators were tyrannicides worthy of the *maiores*; he demanded that they be invited down from the Capitol and honored as benefactors. At first the hired crowd observed that the "uncorrupted portion of the People" did not join them and therefore did nothing but continue their cries for peace.[173] But after P. Cornelius Dolabella, assuming what he claimed was his rightful status as consul, came

---

[168] App. *B Civ.* 2.118 ἅπαντες.

[169] App. *B Civ.* 2.119; note τοῦ δήμου δὲ αὐτοῖς οὐ προσθέοντος / τὸν δὲ δῆμον ὑφορώμενοι / μὴ [sc. Antony] ἀντὶ τῆς βουλῆς τῷ δήμῳ μόνῳ χρώμενος ἐργάσαιτό τι δεινὸν αὐτούς.

[170] App. *B Civ.* 2.120: ἔδοξεν ἐπὶ τὰ πλήθη μισθώματα περιπέμπειν· ἤλπιζον γάρ, ἀρξαμένων τινῶν ἐπαινεῖν τὰ γεγενημένα, καὶ τοὺς ἄλλους συνεπιλήψεσθαι λογισμῷ τε τῆς ἐλευθερίας καὶ πόθῳ τῆς πολιτείας.

[171] App. *B Civ.* 2.120. The reference to "true Romans" alludes to Appian's version of Brutus' prior speech, 2.119.

[172] App. *B Civ.* 2.121: ἐπεβόων καὶ θαμινὰ τοὺς ἄρχοντας ὑπὲρ αὐτῆς παρεκάλουν.

[173] App. *B Civ.* 2.121: οἱ δὲ τὸ καθαρὸν τοῦ πλήθους οὐχ ὁρῶντες ἐπιμιγνύμενον αὐτοῖς. Pina Polo 1996: 160, n. 44, wrongly places the attack on Cinna (see below) at this *contio*.

before them and denounced Caesar, the "hirelings" gained confidence and called for the conspirators to come down from the Capitol.[174] Thus Cassius and Brutus descended and defended their policy, calling upon the People to emulate their ancestors who had expelled the kings, who indeed, unlike Caesar, had at least been chosen according to law; further, they should recall Sextus Pompeius and the tribunes recently deposed by Caesar. But unsure of present circumstances, the two leaders of the conspiracy returned to the Capitol after their address.[175]

The distinction Appian has drawn between the "hirelings" (μισθωτοί / μεμισθωμένοι / ἔμμισθοι) and the "pure," or "unbribed," part of the People (τὸ καθαρὸν τοῦ πλήθους / ὁ καθαρώτατος λεώς / ἀδέκαστοι) continues to structure his account of mass response to the crisis. In his view, the uncorrupted portion of the populace begins to rally itself only after the meeting just described, as they learn how few the conspirators are; and "the first open expression of opinion in favor of Caesar" is an attack on the praetor Cinna by "some of the unbribed people and Caesarian veterans" on the morning of the meeting of the Senate in the Temple of Tellus – an act that of course alarms the "hirelings" and conspirators.[176] Then, in a pause during the protracted senatorial negotiations, Antony and Lepidus emerge to speak to the crowd that had gathered outside. Lepidus "asked" the *contio* what they wished him to do about the killing of Caesar; "while many shouted, 'avenge Caesar,' the 'hirelings' shouted against them, 'seek peace for the city.' "[177] The "hirelings" began to praise Lepidus and called upon him to take up the chief pontificate vacated by Caesar's death; pleased with his response, they "insisted still more forcefully on peace" so that the Master of the Horse finally declared that he would do what they wished even if it were impious and illegal.[178]

The decree of amnesty is at last passed by the Senate,[179] after which Brutus and Cassius "began sending messengers to the plebs and inviting them to come up and meet them on the Capitol." Interestingly, at this point the division between the corrupt and uncorrupted populace dissolves. "Many" respond to the conspirators' summons, and "many" even of the

---

[174] App. *B Civ.* 2.122: τότε δὴ καὶ οἱ μεμισθωμένοι ἀνεθάρρουν. The validity of Dolabella's election was, in fact, under dispute: e.g. Cic. *Phil.* 2.79–84, 88.

[175] App. *B Civ.* 2.122–23.

[176] App. *B Civ.* 2.125, 126.   [177] App. *B Civ.* 2.130–31.   [178] App. *B Civ.* 2.132.

[179] It has long been assumed, following Drumann 1.416–17 (cf. Gotter 1996: 25, n. 95), that Cic. *Phil.* 1.31–32 (*quo populus Romanus* [sc. *die laetior*]?) disproves Appian's explicit claim that the *contio* immediately following this meeting was held only on the morning of the next day, March 18 (*B Civ.* 2.142). But Cicero's attention is focused on the senatorial meeting; perhaps the rhetorical cluster of marvellous events in *unum illum diem* should not be pressed so far against Appian's remarkably explicit testimony. Postponement of the corresponding *contio* to the following day would also seem consistent with the protracted length of the senatorial meeting.

Caesarian veterans destined for colonial settlement are present for Brutus to address specifically.[180] The *entire audience* now approves of Brutus' words as being most just, and admired the conspirators as "intrepid men and most particularly as friends of the people." Since Appian says that they thus "changed over to an attitude of goodwill toward them" we must assume that this *contio* included those whom he had previously called the "pure portion" of the plebs and not merely the "hirelings," who make no further appearance.[181] On the next day the consuls summon the People to a *contio* in which the senatorial decrees are read out and Cicero delivers a great encomium on the amnesty.[182] The audience is "delighted" and calls for the conspirators to descend from the Capitol; when Brutus and the others are spied there is applause and a shout, and the audience does not permit the consuls to speak before they have shaken hands and made peace with the conspirators.[183] It is also, in Appian's view, the people in their entirety that subsequently turn violently hostile to the conspirators after they learn the terms of Caesar's will and are roused by Antony's emotional speech at the funeral.[184]

The first, rather obvious, point to note is how much attention is paid, both by the conspirators in this account and by Appian, to the *contio* as the recognized venue for expression of the attitude of the Roman People[185] – so much so, in fact, that according to Appian the assassins attempt to

[180] App. *B Civ.* 2.137 συνδραμόντων δὲ ὀξέως πολλῶν, 140 ἐπισημηναμένων δὲ πολλῶν.
[181] App. *B Civ.* 2.142: τοιαῦτα τοῦ Βρούτου λέγοντος ἀκροώμενοί τε ἔτι πάντες καὶ διαλυόμενοι κατὰ σφᾶς ἐπήνουν ὡς δικαιότατα, καὶ τοὺς ἄνδρας ὡς ἀκαταπλήκτους δὴ καὶ μάλιστα φιλοδήμους ἐν θαύματι ἐποιοῦντο, καὶ ἐς εὔνοιαν πρὸς αὐτοὺς μετετίθεντο . . . This is the speech whose written form Cicero thought so insipid (*Att.* 15.1a.2), though his lack of enthusiasm about the written version does not imply that its delivery fell flat, contra Pina Polo 1996: 161 (see Motzo 1940: 142–43). Appian highlights the importance of Brutus' speech by relating it in *oratio recta* and at remarkable length – it is the longest speech in Book 2 (Gowing 1992: 231–32). Plutarch and Dio evidently agree (below).
[182] App. *B Civ.* 2.142. On the chronological question, see above, n. 179. On the basis of Cic. *Phil.* 1.1, Motzo 1940: 138 rejects Appian's explicit claim and assumes that Cicero spoke only in the Senate, not in the subsequent *contio*. This seems unwarranted: the motion may not have originated with Cicero, but his great senatorial oration on *concordia* surely entitled him to speak to the People (see chap. 6, n. 23). He was doubtless present at the meeting, whether or not Motzo's hypothesis is correct that the laudatory reference to Caesar spoken at a *contio* mentioned at *Att.* 14.11.1 and 15.20.3 is from Antony's speech to the People on this occasion (Motzo 1940: 136–43, not noted by Shackleton Bailey).
[183] App. *B Civ.* 2.142.
[184] App. *B Civ.* 2.143–46. There is a notorious contradiction between Appian and Suetonius (*Iul.* 84.2) regarding Antony's role at the funeral: see Gotter 1996: 267, to mention only the most recent discussion.
[185] Likewise, Plutarch uses Brutus' first *contio* to characterize the attitude of ὁ δῆμος/οἱ πολλοί before the revulsion provoked by the funeral (not entirely consistently, perhaps: *Brut.* 18; *Caes.* 67.4). In Nicolaus of Damascus, this *contio* is summoned precisely "to test the People's attitude, and that of the magistrates" toward themselves and their deed (*FGrH* 90 fr. 130. 99: συγκαλέσαντες

manipulate a satisfactory result to the series of public meetings (and succeed in doing so). Their strategy is to employ a bribed claque to prepare the ground for acquiescence in their deed by the "real" People, ultimately bringing about a real (if transient) change in sentiments which is only ruptured by Caesar's funeral. Appian's narrative gives a fairly sophisticated picture, consistent with the above discussion of how the Will of the People might be studiously prompted and "created" by partisan agents in pursuit of Republican legitimacy – and an instrument with which to apply pressure on the Senate.

Also worthy of comment is Appian's distinction between the "authentic" People and the "hirelings" who try to impersonate them. We are by now familiar with this kind of tendentious "defining" of audiences and, consequently, their responses. Appian's claim that those who called for peace from the beginning were motivated purely by bribery is more likely to be founded on a prior assumption (based on what evidence? perhaps the ultimate outcome) about the authentically pro-Caesarian sentiments of the People than on any positively known facts. It is indeed quite plausible that, as Appian relates in connection with the first meeting in the Forum and that of Lepidus, in the unsettled aftermath of the assassination directly conflicting expressions of the Popular Will were voiced in successive *contiones* that may well have attracted significant and increasing numbers from among the free inhabitants of the city. Yet under the immediate threat of civil war (always a special horror for the plebs) such vicissitudes need not be explained by the exclusive indulgence in bribery by one side. It is, after all, somewhat embarrassing for his interpretation that what Appian strenuously insists is an undivided consensus of the "authentic" People against the assassins reverses itself so suddenly and completely (if temporarily), to become actually identical with what the "hirelings" had been shouting for all along. Certainly, a very different interpretation seems to have been possible from a different partisan viewpoint. Cicero's identification of the "real People" is just the opposite of Appian's: immediately after the assassination the People had been "enflamed with zeal" in favor of Brutus and Cassius, who had lost a splendid opportunity to stir it up more vigorously. This claim he makes in a letter to Atticus (thus without the most obvious motives for partisan misrepresentation), and characterizes as "no news, but

δὲ τὸν δῆμον διάπειραν ἔγνωσαν αὐτοῦ καὶ τῶν ἐν τέλει ποιήσασθαι πῶς ἔχουσι γνώμης πρὸς αὐτοὺς κτλ.); he is then at pains to explain why ὁ δῆμος listened quietly to Brutus' speech (§100). Dio, on the other hand, takes relatively little interest in the popular reaction to Caesar's assassination; his neglect of the conspirators' speeches "deprives the reader of any real appreciation of their demagogic tactics" (Gowing 1992: 230).

what everyone says daily."[186] It was at least possible to interpret the popular mood in this way, since Cicero felt able to make this argument to Brutus' and Cassius' face less than three months after the event. Those inclined to dismiss his assessment as mere self-delusion should ask themselves whether Appian's own tendentious interpretation of a series of contradictory signals sent by different public meetings is really so definitive.

Our other sources offer a less orderly picture of popular opinion following the assassination than that of either Appian or Cicero. For Appian, as we have seen, the turning point appears to be Brutus' great speech on the Capitol, when a crowd that is not merely made up of "hirelings" but includes even Caesarian veterans is filled with admiration at the conspirators' bravery and devotion to the People, and the dichotomy within the People dissolves.[187] Plutarch, on the other hand, lays the rhetorical emphasis on Brutus' earlier speech in the Forum, during the conspirators' brief descent from the Capitol in the midst of the crisis. In the *Life of Brutus*, his fullest account of these events, he says that Brutus spoke from the Rostra to a "motley rabble" that had been prepared to shout him down; yet even they were dumbstruck at his appearance and listened in orderly silence.[188] (It is noteworthy that he thus appears to reverse Appian's characterization of the audience as prompted by the conspirators' agents, since his phrase "prepared to raise a disturbance," παρεσκευασμένοι θορυβεῖν, suggests an organized claque on the other side.[189]) The crowd is quieted by Brutus' words; but that the deed itself did not please all is shown by an angry outburst when Cinna takes the podium and begins to denounce Caesar.[190] A second version of this *contio* in his *Life of Caesar* omits Cinna's intervention and takes the crowd's "deep silence" to have been a sign both of pity toward

---

[186] Cic. *Att.* 15.11.2: *nec vero quicquam novi sed ea quae cottidie omnes . . . senatum vocare, populum ardentem studio vehementius incitare, totam suscipere rem publicam . . .* It is clear from *senatum vocare . . . totam suscipere rem publican* that he is speaking here of the immediate aftermath of the assassination, not the subsequent amnesty decree, for which Cicero (*Phil.* 1.32) and Appian both claim strong popular support.

[187] App. *B Civ.* 2.142, quoted above, n. 181.

[188] Plut. *Brut.* 18.12: πρὸς δὲ τὴν ὄψιν οἱ πολλοί, καίπερ μιγάδες ὄντες καὶ παρεσκευασμένοι θορυβεῖν, διέτρεσαν [*sic* MSS, but clearly wrong, despite LSJ s.v. διατρέω: perhaps διετράπησαν (cf. *Mor.* 196a)] καὶ τὸ μέλλον ἐδέχοντο κόσμῳ καὶ σιωπῇ. For μιγάδες, see Plut. *Mor.* 661c; *Rom.* 14.2; *Ages.* 38.1; *Tim.* 1.3. Note that Plutarch contrives a simpler narrative by transferring the famous *contio Capitolina* to the immediate prelude of this speech in the Forum: cf. *Brut.* 18.9–11 and App. *B Civ.* 2.121–23.

[189] See n. 84.

[190] Plut. *Brut.* 18.12–13: προελθόντος δ' αὐτοῦ πάντες ἡσυχίαν τῷ λόγῳ παρέσχον· ὅτι δ' οὐ πᾶσι πρὸς ἡδονὴν ἐγεγόνει τὸ ἔργον, ἐδήλωσαν ἀρξαμένου λέγειν Κίννα καὶ κατηγορεῖν Καίσαρος ἀναρρηγνύμενοι πρὸς ὀργὴν καὶ κακῶς τὸν Κίνναν λέγοντες . . . Note the contrast drawn at the beginning of the sentence between the calm hearing the crowd gives Brutus' λόγος and its subsequent expression of feelings about the ἔργον.

Caesar and of respect for Brutus. About the event itself, its feelings were unresolved: "the *demos* [was] neither angered at the deed nor yet appearing to praise it."[191] Finally, Nicolaus of Damascus, who has nothing good to say about the men who killed Caesar, acknowledges that the crowd fell silent to hear Brutus, but assures us that this was due to their shocked curiosity about the conspirators' next move of "revolution," along with personal regard for the man and his ancestors.[192] It will be recalled, finally, that Appian has a very different answer for the relatively favorable reception given the conspirators at this point: the crowd was composed merely of "hirelings," a claim inconsistent with Plutarch's and Nicolaus' presentation.

One senses that all of these characterizations of the crowds and their mental states are no more than speculations (if not tendentious fabrications) based largely on one simple, awkward fact: that the reception of the first *contio* held by the assassins after the bloody deed was relatively neutral, or ambiguous.[193] Plutarch and Nicolaus "define" the crowd's feelings in various complicated ways; Appian makes it an audience dominated by "hirelings" making their first attempt to turn public opinion away from taking vengeance for Caesar, a construct that also helps to explain the favorable reception subsequently of Brutus' *contio Capitolina* while still maintaining the core idea that the Roman People were in fact *essentially* Caesarian in sympathies. Alternatively, Cicero was able to take comfort in what seems to have been at least the surface appearance of the audience's reaction to Brutus' two major *contiones*, as well, of course, as the meeting of reconciliation in the Forum that marked the conspirators' final descent from the Capitol.

Ultimately, then, precious little can be learned about the "true" attitude of the Roman People, or even of the urban plebs, from the confused political theater of the days following Caesar's assassination and the fog of controversy that quickly enshrouded the accounts. Perhaps the one incontrovertible fact is that there was no strong and unambiguous show of popular anger toward the conspirators until Caesar's funeral (probably on March 20).[194] That may have been a turning point, or perhaps, indeed, a "defining moment," through which in a spectacular collective action a

---

[191] Plut. *Caes.* 67. 4: ὁ μὲν δῆμος οὔτε δυσχεραίνων οὔτε ὡς ἐπαινῶν τὰ πεπραγμένα . . .

[192] *FGrH* 90 fr. 130.100. Unfortunately, a lacuna interrupts the account of the beginning of the *contio*, and the excerptors relegated Nicolaus' version of Brutus' speech to another collection (Περὶ Δημηγοριῶν), now sadly lost.

[193] Which seems reinforced by Dio's reference to the effect of the *contio*, 44.21.2: τοιαῦτα ἄττα εἰπόντες τοὺς μὲν πολλοὺς κατέστησαν, where οἱ πολλοί presumably means "the majority" (cf. 44.35.1).

[194] Appian *B Civ.* 2.143–48 (see n. 184); Plut. *Brut.* 20; Cass. Dio 44.35.1–4 (cf. 44.50).

variety of inconsistent considerations crystallized into a generalized and concrete Caesarian sentiment. But the idea that the urban plebs, a mass of many thousands, was of a clear, decided opinion regarding the killing of Caesar in the confused days immediately after the event should strain the credulity of all but the most dedicated modern Caesarians.

The importance of the shout of the crowd in the *contio* rested precisely on its potential to be interpreted as a concrete demonstration of the Will of the People in a system in which that concept deeply mattered; so much, indeed, that various devices were employed to make the "Roman People" say what an orator wanted them to say and to give his words the force of a universal consensus. Yet, in good part because of those devices, but also because of the natural variability among and within audiences, the meaning of the crowd's response and the relationship of its responses to the *real* People's *real* will – a "political artefact" anyway, something that must be *created* in order to be used, usually to partisan effect – were generally open to contestation. The *contio* is best seen as political theater, that is, a dramatic staging of political argument, characterized by highly developed methods of audience creation and response solicitation that activated a kind of ventriloquism. While it was no doubt impossible to make the Roman People "say" things in the *contio* that would find *no* echo among some sectors of the urban plebs, the methods of articulating the Voice of the People functioned to filter out a chaotic and ineffable diversity of opinion and were in fact designed to create a false impression of near-total consensus.

It would be naïve to interpret contional responses as relatively straight-forward expressions of the Popular Will. This is not to say that contional audiences, or even the urban plebs generally, were without opinions, "a slate on which the schemers of the Senate wrote whatever they wanted."[195] But the plural "opinions" is used advisedly; what ultimately emerges – say, a "universal consensus" for war with Antony or for concord after Caesar's as-sassination – was something very different in quality from the unqualifiable and unquantifiable mass of "opinions" in the heads of (urban) citizens at the end of 43, or mid-March 44. A more productive way to view the phe-nomenon that is being examined is therefore as a *process* of "opinion- and will-formation" in which the *contio* was not merely the central venue but above all the essential instrument in the hands of members of the élite seek-ing to create and objectify a "verdict of the Roman People." This "artefact"

---

[195] Purcell 1994: 678. Cf. Brunt 1966: 24; Perelli 1982: *passim* (see, e.g., pp. 19–20); North 1990a: 18–21; Pina Polo 1996: 134–40.

or "fiction" might well be (but was not necessarily) quite misleading or even false: we might hypothesize in anticipation of the next chapter that the aim of the actors was precisely to produce concrete manifestations of collective action – size of *contio*, impressive response of the audience, and so on – that were sufficient to rout all visible (and audible) opposition. At that point, what has objectively been no more than a symbol of consensus would take on objective reality itself, as powerful if not as definitive as any vote formally constituting the Will of the People, and further would exert its own, strong secondary effects, such as intimidation and the well-known "bandwagon."

CHAPTER 5

Debate

The quantity and broad scope of political matters decided by the People in the form of legislation are indeed impressive, and give some substance to the argument that the Roman Republic was a form of democracy.[1] But more revealing than any argument over definitions and labels would be an examination of how, in late-Republican Rome, the Popular Will came to be expressed – ultimately in the form of a vote, but as we have seen in the last chapter, originally in mass meetings whose strategic function was, as far as possible, to determine that vote in advance.[2] There I began to work out a model of popular decision-making with, at its center, the conception of the *contio* as an instrument whereby the Popular Will was artificially (if not necessarily falsely) fashioned by political leaders and then given the symbolic weight and apparent legitimacy needed for it to be used in political controversy. The methods of audience creation and rhetorical "ventriloquism" that we have studied raise serious questions about the extent to which even members of the political élite who wished to capitalize on the power of the *populus* were constrained to "listen" to the autonomous opinions of the (urban) citizenry. What we have seen so far certainly favors a "top-down" model of public deliberation.[3]

But this cannot be the whole story. For the *contio* was also a forum for de-liberation and debate before an audience standing in for the Roman People, in which only members of the élite participated directly, but (as we have seen) the audience/*populus* also participated indirectly, as observers, judges, and even vocal interlocutors. The central question, from this perspective, is one about the quality of debate: first of all, at a minimum, the opportunity of every voting citizen to hear the opposing arguments on any issue, coher-ently formulated and presented in reasonably good faith. But, of course,

---

[1] Millar 1984 for the middle Republic, Millar 1995 for the later period.   [2] Above, esp. pp. 123–28.
[3] Cf. now also Mouritsen 2001: esp. 46–56 on the factors militating against open debate.

as we saw in the above discussion of some ideal models of democratic deliberation,[4] much more than these essentially procedural requirements is needed to make ordinary citizens real, rather than illusory, participants in the process, and thus to make it more than marginally responsive to their needs and desires: in essence, a strong version of equality (of education, access to information, culturally privileged forms of expression, and so on). Now, ideal models are fine as heuristic devices – ways of revealing aspects of our problems and evidence that otherwise may not stand out in sharp relief – but they can gravely mislead if they are mistaken for realistic standards of actual social behavior. It is no refutation of the "democratic" thesis on the Roman Republic to show that it fails (as does every known polity) to meet Habermasian standards of unconstrained, open deliberation. But that does not make the ideal model useless to the present analysis; on the contrary, it offers a thought-provoking framework within which to reflect on the practical consequences of the inevitable divergences from the ideal, especially on how seriously these particular conditions will have affected the responsiveness of the Republican political system to needs and desires that emerged "from below." Such divergences admit of degrees, and will accordingly affect the distribution of power in public deliberation more or less seriously.

GUEST SPEAKERS

As was just noted, it is a minimal requirement of democratic deliberation that citizens be fairly exposed to opposing views on a given topic of public interest. Rightly objecting to a common misapprehension about the absence of formal deliberation before a legislative vote, Fergus Millar and Peter Brunt point out that there were opportunities for speech-making beforehand, both for and against any proposal – indeed even immediately before voters were sorted into their units (tribes) on the voting day itself. Thus (according to Millar) "any citizen who wished to do so could hear opposing views on any topic, either at different *contiones* held by different officeholders or, sometimes, at the same *contio*"; and (Brunt) "as any magistrate could summon a *contio*, and not only he who would preside over the *comitia*, rival views on controversial questions would be fully presented."[5] This is a perfectly legitimate statement of what was theoretically possible.

---

[4] Viz., the Habermasian "ideal speech-situation" and the "deliberative-democracy" school: above, pp. 21ff.

[5] Millar 1998: 46–47 (cf. 92); Brunt 1988: 26.

As we saw in chapter 2, any of the numerous magistrates with the power of holding *contiones* could call his own meeting and thus, in principle, create a forum for the presentation of an alternative view.[6] And it was a common practice, to be discussed presently, for the advocate of a proposal to bring one or more opponents before a public meeting and offer them some kind of opportunity to speak; this was, as we shall see, considered more or less obligatory at the last occasion for speeches, the final *contio* before a vote. The question for us, however, is whether the realization of these principles in practice justifies these rather sanguine characterizations of what happened in public meetings leading up to legislation as a more or less pluralistic, comprehensive debate.

The evidence does occasionally reveal a degree of conscious concern about the undesirability of circumventing or suppressing public discussion before the fate of a bill was decided. Livy, describing an incident of 167 BC, when two tribunes sought to veto a declaration of war against Rhodes promulgated by a praetor, asserts that tradition held that a veto was premature before the opportunity had been given for *privati* – that is, senators not currently holding a magistracy – to speak for and against a proposal, clearly in public meetings before the vote.[7] Livy's interpretation of the norm (or that of his source) is that it served to assure that the vetoer did so on the basis of full knowledge of the merits and demerits of the bill, as they emerged from the speeches of non-magistrates on both sides of the issue; but, given the ideological constraints upon the use of the tribunician veto reviewed in the last chapter, we may also suppose that this custom was at least equally founded upon the idea that the People must not be robbed of their right of legislative decision before they had even had the opportunity both to hear the views of leading senators on the issue in *contiones* and (simultaneously) to make their feelings known.[8] Either way, some minimal standard of "open-ness" is implied: one should at least have the chance of hearing both sides of the question.[9] More notable, perhaps, is the expectation that in the last *contio* on a legislative proposal, on the day of the vote itself and immediately preceding the formation of the voting units, opponents of a bill should be allowed to speak as well as supporters; even Clodius was allowed to speak at the *contio* immediately preceding the vote on Cicero's

[6] See above, pp. 38ff.
[7] Livy 45.21, esp. §6; *cum ita traditum esset, ne quis prius intercederet legi quam privatis suadendi dissuadendique legem potestas facta esset.* Rilinger 1989: 492–94, corrects Meier 1968: 86–87.
[8] See above, pp. 125–26.
[9] Note the emphasis on *opportunity*, rather than necessarily the actuality, of bipolar debate: *suadendi dissuadendique legem **potestas*** (Livy 45.21.6).

recall from exile.[10] However, realization of this customary expectation was entirely at the discretion of the presiding magistrate (the proposer), who could pick and choose from among the "opposition" speakers and also impose a time limit.[11] Further, we hear on one occasion of a rule, probably pertaining only to a "final" *contio* such as this one, that *privati* should speak before any magistrate, ostensibly to protect their full freedom of speech.[12] The emphasis on hearing from *privati*, especially just before the final vote, is interesting;[13] it implicitly acknowledges some need to compensate for magistrates' monopoly of the power to control speech in the *contio*, as well, of course, as it does the superior authority of many senior ex-magistrates over those "in office" at any one time.[14] It also appears, on occasion, to have given a magistrate a plausible excuse to prevent his colleagues in opposition from having their say immediately before the vote; and of course it tended to reserve the last word for him.[15]

[10] Cic. *Sest.* 108; *Dom.* 90. See Dion. Hal. 10.40.2. Whether or not it was normal practice for the magistrate presiding over the *contio* just before a vote to make a general invitation to *privati* to speak (as is suggested by the following section of Dionysius' text [10.41.1]; also Livy 45.36.1–2; cf. Millar 1998: 46; but note that this is not mentioned in Dio's detailed account of the debate over the *lex Gabinia*), it seems that one could approach the Rostra and request the opportunity to speak on the spot (Plut. *Cat. Min.* 43.1). The request might not be granted, however (Cass. Dio 36.30.1; this is surely also the meaning of Cic. *Att.* 2.24.3: above, p. 51 with n. 56). In any case, of course, only senators were seriously in question here: the important thing for the People was what those with authority thought (Livy 45.21.7; Cic. *Vat.* 24). *Pace* Mommsen 1887: III.395, n. 6, App. *B Civ.* 1.11–12 does not prove that Tiberius Gracchus prevented Octavius from addressing the final *contio* before the vote on his land bill: if the reading of the law regularly opened proceedings, as I am inclined to think (below, n. 64), Octavius had in effect forfeited that opportunity; alternatively, he may simply have declined to offer a *dissuasio*, in keeping with his apparent practice up to then (see below).

[11] Cass. Dio 39.34.2; Plut. *Cat. Min.* 43.1; cf. Livy 45.36.2–3, with 37.6. The proceedings for the final *contio* of a trial before the People seem to have been identical in this respect: note Labienus' restriction of Cicero's final defense-speech for Rabirius to half an hour (Cic. *Rab. perd.* 6). For "picking and choosing," which is implicit in the whole procedure, see most clearly the exclusion of the opposing tribunes from the debates on the *lex Gabinia* and the *lex Trebonia*: below, pp. 179–86; Cass. Dio 39.35.1 with 34.2.

[12] Cass. Dio 39.35.1–2: ἐν γάρ τοι ταῖς συνόδοις ταῖς τοῦ δήμου, ἐν αἷς γε καὶ ἐβουλεύοντο, πάσαις τοῖς ἰδιώταις πρὸ τῶν τὰς ἀρχὰς ἐχόντων ὁ λόγος ἐδίδοτο, τοῦ μηδένα αὐτῶν, ὡς ἔοικε, τῇ τοῦ κρείττονος γνώμῃ προκαταλαμβανόμενον ὑποστέλλεσθαί τι ὧν φρονοίη, ἀλλ' ἐπὶ πάσης παρρησίας τὰ δοκοῦντα αὐτῷ λέγειν. Although Dio does not appear to restrict the practice to such "final" *contiones*, that is in fact the context and indeed the only one in which *suasores* and *dissuasores* were likely to be allowed opposing *speeches* (as distinct from the question-and-answer technique about to be considered).

[13] Note Cic. *Corn.* 1 fr. 30 Cr. *est uniquoique ius vetandi, cum ea feratur, quamdiu <quibus ius est suffragii* suppl. Buecheler> *ferundi transferuntur; id est <dum recitatur* suppl. Kiessling and Schoell> *lex,* dum privati dicunt, *dum <summovetur populus* suppl. Mommsen>*, dum sitella defertur, dum aequantur sortes, dum sortitio fit, et si qua sunt alia huius generis.* Cf. also Cic. *Leg.* 3.11: *rem populum docento, doceri a magistratibus privatisque patiunto* and above, n. 10.

[14] Cic. *Vat.* 24 (quoted at chap. 2, n. 112). Cf. below, pp. 258ff.

[15] For manipulation of the rule to block speech by opposing magistrates, see the examples of Trebonius and perhaps Gabinius, discussed below (Cass. Dio 39.35.1; 36.30). Last word: not explicit in

On the other hand, it would be naïve to give much emphasis to these abstract principles without attending closely to their operation in practice. The nature of the problem may be well illustrated by a look at the rather common (it seems) practice of "introducing" one's opponents on a given issue before a public meeting called and presided over by oneself.[16]

The magistrate who presided over a *contio* might speak himself (usually *contionem habere*). This is indeed the most common case. But alternatively, he might "bring forth" or "summon to a meeting" (*producere, vocare in contionem*) men of note, either giving them the floor to deliver a speech before the People (*contionem dare*) – something they could not do on their own initiative if they were not currently occupying a magistracy – or demanding from them an answer to a question (*interrogare, vel sim.*). Those "brought forth" (*producti*) might be supporters of the presiding magistrate, in which case the object was evidently to advertise the backing of authoritative senators, or they might be opponents, as in the case of Carbo's questioning of Scipio Africanus about the killing of Tiberius Gracchus (see chapter 4).[17]

This practice is of obvious importance for assessing how far the *contio* permitted, or encouraged, open two-sided debate. On the face of it, a tradition of inviting opponents to a dialogue before the People with the advocate of some political action may seem an impressive manifestation of commitment to open public debate. But recollection of the confrontation between Carbo and Scipio in 130 suggests something rather different. Carbo's question to Scipio was not a gentlemanly invitation to lay out the opposing view to his own proposal for iteration of the tribunate. Rather, as Cicero put it in his speech for Milo, Carbo's intent was nothing less than "seditious" – quite evidently, to put Scipio's feet to the fire of public

---

our evidence, but inferred from the custom just mentioned (Mommsen 1887: 1.201, n. 5; III.395, n. 1). The course of discussion preceding passage of the Gabinian bill – on which we have the most information – offers an apparent contradiction. But this example may be exceptional, for in speaking before Catulus the tribune also does not observe strictly the priority of *privati* before magistrates. Perhaps Gabinius' invitation to Catulus was an *ex tempore* maneuver to block his fellow tribunes from addressing the crowd.

16 Some points in this discussion have now been anticipated by Mouritsen 2001: esp. 53–54, but we differ both in the significance we attribute to these events, which are for him transparent charades, and in our understanding of what was at stake for those "invited" (p. 53: "a 'no-win' situation"). If he is right on the former point it is indeed quite incomprehensible why anyone *did* show his face before an adversary's *contio*.

17 Cic. *Vat.* 24: *in rostris . . . quo auctoritatis exquirendae causa ceteri tribuni plebis principes civitatis producere consuerunt.* Pina Polo 1996: 34–52 notes that fully two-thirds of known *privati* who spoke before *contiones* were consulars (also a high proportion of those holding priesthoods). On *producti in contionem*, see also Pina Polo 1989: 77–80; Thommen 1989: 176–79. On whether opponents could be summoned against their will, see below, p. 171.

outrage.[18] Since, as we have seen, self-selecting contional audiences were most likely to be supportive of the magistrate calling such a meeting and that prudence recommended various means of "packing" the audience, we may suppose that the purpose of the tactic was not in fact to educate the public about the available alternatives but to expose opponents to a (preferably) staged expression of the Will of the People under conditions most unfavorable to them.

The menacing *clamor* of an excited, partisan crowd was a terrifying thing. We have already read Sallust's description of what a tribune casting an unpopular veto might have to face.[19] Valerius Maximus' scene-painting for another occasion gives an equally vivid impression: "you [Sempronia, sister of the Gracchi] were compelled to stand firm in a place where the leaders of the state often lost their composure; the enormous power [of the tribune] pressed upon you, hurling threats with hostile looks, while the roar of the ignorant mob shook the entire Forum. . . ."[20] Again, we must keep in mind the absence of an equivalent of modern police protection under anything but the most extreme circumstances – a fact that, perhaps more than anything else in this system, encouraged a certain circumspection vis-à-vis the masses.[21] And this crowd could certainly get out of hand. Even before the notoriously violent 50s, *lapidationes* (stonings) of speakers were not unheard of, and one consul was pulled from the Rostra and nearly killed as he attempted to defy the popular movement for the appointment of Pompey to deal with the pirates.[22] In 58, during the campaign to drive Cicero into exile, P. Clodius "produced" before a *contio* Q. Hortensius and C. Curio, who had defied Clodius' mobilization of the Popular Will to lead an equestrian delegation to the consuls and Senate to plead for Cicero. He

---

[18] Cic. *Mil.* 8: *cum a C. Carbone tribuno pl.* **seditiose** *in contione interrogaretur* . . . For *concitatio invidiae* as a fundamental strategy of the *contio*, see chap. 2, n. 102, and pp. 237–39 and 271.

[19] Sall. *Iug.* 34.1, quoted p. 119. However, this tribune remained firm and his veto prevailed.

[20] Val. Max. 3.8.6: *coacta es eo loci consistere, ubi principum civitatis perturbari frons solebat, instabat tibi torro vultu minas profundens amplissima potestas, clamor imperitae multitudinis obstrepebat totum forum.* The occasion is the tumultuous *contio* called by an unknown tribune (*a tribuno plebei producta ad populum in maxima confusione*) in 101 to support Equitius' claim to be the son of Tiberius Gracchus.

[21] Nippel 1984, 1988, 1995. Good comments on the importance of "exceptional" plebeian outbursts in Flaig 1998: 66–69.

[22] Plut. *Pomp.* 25.4. This brave or stolid consul, C. Piso, also faced a *lapidatio* in the meeting preceding a different legislative vote (Asc. 58 C) and withstood the menaces of tribunes before "their" *contio* on yet a third occasion (Val. Max. 3.8.3: below). Cf. the manhandling of Vettius in 59: *male mulcatum ac pro rostris in contione paene discerptum,* Suet. *Iul.* 17.2, and the beating allegedly threatened against a consular and pontifex *audiente populo Romano* (thus probably in a *contio*) in 58 (Cic. *Dom.* 110: see n. 23). M. Marcellus' fear of violence from the Clodian crowd surrounding the tribunal at Milo's trial in 52 (Asc. 40 C) belongs technically to a different context, but remains illustrative.

had them physically attacked by his partisans in the audience, who were no doubt "spontaneously" expressing the public outrage at their actions and responses.[23]

Before such crowds a magistrate could force an opponent to face a hard choice: either to back away publicly from his stance of opposition, or face a fearful, even potentially violent, explosion of popular anger, and court the imputation that he despised the Will of the People. The dynamics are well illustrated by the preliminaries to Julius Caesar's first agrarian bill in 59.[24] After the Senate – though ostentatiously given the chance to voice any objections or request revisions – had failed either to support or reject the measure, Caesar presented his bill to a *contio*.[25] He also brought his colleague in the consulship, M. Bibulus, before the meeting and asked him under the direct gaze of "the People" if he had any criticism of the law. Dio explains that Caesar "wished to secure in the *contio* some of the leading men as allies (for he anticipated that they had changed their minds and would have some fear of the multitude)."[26] The mention of "fear" of the People is to be underscored; its use by populist tribunes to intimidate political opponents on the Rostra is easily paralleled.[27] Dio makes very clear that the expectation was not that they would actually speak against his proposal

---

[23] Cass. Dio 38.16.5: καὶ αὐτοὺς ὁ Κλώδιος ἐς τὸ πλῆθος ἐσαγαγὼν πληγαῖς ἐπὶ τῇ πρεσβείᾳ διά τινων προπαρεσκευασμένων συνέκοψε. Both Vanderbroeck (1987: 242, no. 44) and Tatum (1999: 155) think that the men were only verbally abused; but note Dio's πληγαῖς, and Cicero's allusions to the event at *Sest.* 27 (*gladiis et lapidibus*) and *Dom.* 54 (*manibus ferro lapidibus*). Given, however, that at *Sest.* 27 Cicero calls the victims *nobilissimos adulescentis, honestissimos equites Romanos* (cf. *Red. sen.* 12, on the embassy of "knights": *adulescentes nobilissimi cunctique equites Romani*; Plut. *Cic.* 31.1), it seems likeliest that – contrary to the usual view, e.g., Tatum 1999: 154–55 – this Hortensius and this Curio were the noble sons, still technically *equites*, of the senior consulars with the same names (cos. 69 and 76). Dio's reference to them as βουλευταί would therefore be a venial slip. It is uncertain whether Cic. *Dom.* 110 and *Mil.* 37 refer to the same incident, since it seems highly improbable that Cicero would have overlooked the beating administered to a senior senator, or the murder of another senator, in his only secure references to the event (*Sest.* 27 and *Dom.* 54).

[24] Millar 1998: 127, distinguishes this instance from the practice of *productio in contionem*, inasmuch as "the two parties are the consuls of the year, who are evidently sharing the tribunal." This is a technicality. The fact remains that Caesar directs the proceedings, and that just as in the typical instances, Bibulus is questioned invidiously and pressed to answer before a hostile (i.e., pro-Caesarian) audience. It seems inconceivable that Bibulus had issued the summons to the *contio* jointly with Caesar. Perhaps this was normally the function of the consul who held the *fasces*, as Caesar did in January (see Suet. *Iul.* 20.1, and Taylor and Broughton 1949: 4–7).

[25] Cass. Dio 38.1–3.

[26] Cass. Dio 38.4.2: ἐθελήσας δ'οὖν καὶ ὡς ὁμογνώμονας τῶν πρώτων τινὰς ἐν τῇ ἐκκλησίᾳ λαβεῖν (καὶ γὰρ ἤλπιζε μετεγνωκέναι τε αὐτοὺς καί πη καὶ τὸ πλῆθος φοβηθήσεσθαι).

[27] Cf. Diod. 34/35.33.7: after the murder of Ti. Gracchus, the tribunes bring forward each senator onto the Rostra to ask who was responsible; all but P. Scipio Nasica κατεπτηχότες τὴν τῶν ὄχλων ὁρμὴν καὶ βίαν denied responsibility and gave divergent replies. Cf. Cass. Dio 36.24.3–4; 30.3–5 (in connection with the *lex Gabinia*), discussed below: Plut. *Pomp.* 30.4.

but that, if only out of fear of the aroused populace, they would now be forced to acquiesce in it or even to support it.

Dio's subsequent account of Caesar's conduct of that *contio* is consistent with this conjecture. Bibulus, when asked if he had any criticism, avoided all specific discussion and would only say that he would not permit any "innovation/revolution" during his consulship.[28] Caesar began to plead with him and asked the crowd to join in, telling them that they would have the law if only he permitted it. Bibulus roared over the noise of the crowd, "You won't have this law this year even if you all want it!" and departed. Caesar's *contio* demonstrates well that this practice was hardly founded on some principled reverence for free and open debate but was instead a form of political theater designed to stampede opposition to popular measures by forcing opponents to confront the ostensibly manifest Will of the Roman People, or at minimum to elicit an outraged response from the audience that could then be represented as a *significatio* of the people's "judgment and will."[29] If Bibulus showed himself in the *contio* unimpressed by the Will of the People (at least of Caesar's "People"), the same could not be said of his fellow senators, who "enslaved by the enthusiasm of the multitude," refused to annul the law when Bibulus requested this, evidently on the grounds that it had been passed "by means of violence" (*per vim*) or "in defiance of the auspices" (*contra auspicia*).[30]

For a proper understanding of Bibulus' steadiness (as some will have seen it) or exasperating arrogance (as others will have done), we need to recognize that not everyone stood firm. In 56, the keepers of the Sibylline oracles, the "Board of fifteen for sacred actions" (*Quindecimviri sacris faciundis*), were brought before a *contio* by the tribune C. Cato and "forced" to divulge in public, before the traditionally mandatory prior discussion in the Senate, the oracle that blocked the use of military force to restore King Ptolemy to Egypt.[31] Again, in December 66, Cicero, praetor in charge of the extortion court, refused an application by C. Manilius, who had won popular favor with his law transferring the Mithridatic command to Pompey, for

---

[28] Cass. Dio 38.4.3: οὐκ ἂν ἀνάσχοιτο ἐν τῇ ἑαυτοῦ ἀρχῇ νεωτερισθῆναί τι; compare what Cato is supposed to have said in the Senate, 38.3.1. Cf. Latin *res novae* (*OLD* s.v. *novus*, 10).

[29] Note the repeated use of this tactic by tribunes of the early 70s to pressure the consuls to restore the powers of the tribunate, at a time when the political power of the tribunate was virtually limited to their ability to create and express the Popular Will: Gran. Licinianus 36.33 C; Cic. *Brut.* 217, with Sall. *Hist.* 3.48.8 M, [Asc.] 189 St. On the tribunician use of the *contio* in the 70s, see Pina Polo 1989: 127–28; 1996: 113–19; also Millar 1998: 49–72.

[30] Cass. Dio 38.6.4: τῇ γὰρ τοῦ πλήθους σπουδῇ δεδουλωμένοι πάντες ἡσύχαζον.

[31] Cass. Dio 39.15.4: ἔς τε τὸν ὅμιλον τοὺς ἱερέας ἐσήγαγε, κἀνταῦθα, πρὶν ὁτιοῦν τὴν γερουσίαν ἐπ᾽ αὐτοῖς χρηματίσαι, ἐξεβιάσατό σφας ἐκλαλῆσαι τὸ λόγιον· ὅσῳ γάρ τοι μᾶλλον οὐκ ἐδόκει σφίσιν ἐξεῖναι τοῦτο [lacuna] τὸ πλῆθος ἔσχε.

a delay of his trial, citing the rapidly approaching end of his own term of office; he barely accepted an extension until the next day. The populace was outraged, and "the tribunes" compelled him to come before a *contio* in which he was roundly denounced. Cicero, claiming that he had only wanted to spare Manilius from falling into the hands of another praetor, immediately appeased the angry crowd by acceding to its request that he undertake Manilius' defense.[32] Dio, ever hostile to Cicero, sneers that his reputation suffered for this about-face, and says that he was henceforth called a "deserter."[33] It doubtless depended on whom you asked. Someone in that crowd would have represented his action as accepting the "judgment and verdict" of the Roman People, an appropriate return for the *beneficium* of high office it had conferred on him,[34] and indeed Cicero won great credit among the *multitudo* for his promise to defend Manilius, even though it may never have been fulfilled.[35] That is precisely Cicero's claim almost a decade later when, in the midst of a severe grain crisis, he accepted the cries of a crowd – now the "true" Roman People, naturally – that called on him to remedy the situation by making an appropriate motion in the Senate. We have come full circle when we hear that Publius Clodius then complained before the College of Pontiffs that Cicero had betrayed the Fathers and deserted to the People.[36]

Clodius' and Dio's discordant notes of criticism (however hypocritical) reveal that such conduct could be assessed very differently from another perspective. For Cicero it was normally the part of a patriotic citizen to *consistere in contione* – more or less to "stand one's ground" and withstand any tumult,[37] to show *constantia* in the face of tribunician or mob

---

[32] Cass. Dio 36.44.1–2; Plut. *Cic.* 9.4–6; cf. Cic. *Corn.* 1 fr. 6 Cr (= Asc. 65 C). On the event, and whether the speech *pro Manilio* (Nonius p. 700 L) was the published version of Cicero's remarks on this occasion or another one connected with his trial (or trials) in 65, see esp. J. W. Crawford 1984: 64–72, and 1994: 33–41; Ramsey 1980.

[33] Cass. Dio 36.44.2: ἐκ τούτου τά τε ἄλλα κακῶς ἤκουε καὶ αὐτόμολος ὠνομάζετο.

[34] B. Rawson 1971: 26–29, would take the allusion in Cic. *Leg. agr.* 2.49 as referring to this occasion rather than to Cicero's support for the *Lex Manilia*. That would, of course, support my point. But *personam imponere* elsewhere (*Phil.* 6.2) is Cicero's rhetorical representation of the audience's expression of approval of the sentiments expressed by a speaker; in which case the response to the speech for the Manilian Law probably remains the most plausible occasion.

[35] See Q. Cicero (?), *Comment. pet.* 51, with the concise review of the problem by Gruen 1974: 262, n. 7. See Ramsey 1980 against actual participation by Cicero; J. W. Crawford 1994: 33–38, for his involvement in an abortive first trial, but not in the decisive second.

[36] *Dom.* 14–17 (*Ego denique non solum ab operis tuis impulsu tuo nominabar, sed etiam, depulsis ac dissipatis tuis copiis, a populo Romano universo, qui tum in Capitolio convenerat, cum illo die minus valerem, in senatum nominatim vocabar.* §15); cf. §§4, 6, 7, and *Att.* 4.1.6.

[37] For this use of *consistere*: Cic. *Clu.* 108: *nec per multitudinem concitatam consistere cuiquam in dicendo licebat*; *Leg. agr.* 1.25: *pertimescam, credo, ne mihi non liceat contra vos in contione consistere*; *Sest.* 127: *dominos contionum omni odio populi notari, quibus autem consistere in operarum contionibus non*

intimidation,[38] to despise the uproar and tempests of the *contio* in the struggle for what was good and right.[39] We get a vivid picture of what was required when Cicero describes Pompey's fortitude in speaking over the shouts of a pro-Clodian crowd during the trial of Milo in 56: "Pompey spoke – or rather tried to speak, for as soon as he rose, Clodius' gangs raised a shout, and throughout the speech he was harassed not only by their cries but by jeering and insults . . . To be sure, he was resolute; he was not intimidated; he delivered his whole speech and occasionally enjoyed silence when his authority prevailed . . ."[40] But what happened to Clodius on the same occasion may have been more typical: "Our side raised such a shout (they had decided to return the favor) that he lost command of his thoughts, words and facial expression."[41]

As is suggested by Cicero's description of Pompey's *constantia*, such steadiness in the face of a turbulent crowd was an impressive sight and actually might win the speaker some credit, not only among those who had little sympathy with popular politics, if our evidence is not totally skewed by pious mythologizing, but even among the audiences themselves. Members of the élite liked to recollect such stories as P. Scipio Nasica's refusal to be cowed by the angry crowd before which the tribunes had hauled "all the senators" to answer for Ti. Gracchus' murder: when he alone admitted and justified the act, "the crowd, despite its resentment, became calm, awed by the man's *gravitas* and frankness."[42] It was recalled that the same man, when during a serious grain shortage in his consulship a tribune demanded his presence at a *contio* in order to pressure him to make a relevant motion in the Senate, replied to the shout of plebeian outrage that interrupted his speech, "Quiet, please, Citizens! – for I know better than you what is good for the Republic." We are told by Valerius Maximus that "With a reverential silence everyone paid greater respect to his authority than their

---

[38] *liceat, eos omni populi Romani significatione decorari?* Val. Max. 3.8.6 (quoted above, n. 20). There is an important element of "steadiness," "firmness" in such uses that the *OLD* suppresses (s.v. 6a), in part by relegating an example like *Q Fr.* 2.3.2: *ei tantus clamor a nostris . . . ut neque mente nec lingua neque ore consisteret* to another heading (5c).

[38] As Cicero, notoriously, failed to do in the face of the hostile interruptions of the *Clodiani* during his original speech for Milo (Asc. 41–42 C). Note the phrase *constanter agere/dicere* in Cic. *Mil.* 58 and Val. Max. 3.8.3.

[39] Cic. *Mil.* 3: *ut eum civem retineatis qui semper genus illud hominum clamoresque maximos prae vestra salute neglexit*; ibid., 5: *Equidem ceteras tempestates et procellas in illis dumtaxat fluctibus contionum semper putavi Miloni esse subeundas, quia semper pro bonis contra improbos senserat . . .*

[40] Cic. *Q Fr.* 2.3.2. The setting was either one of the three required *contiones* (*anquisitiones*) before the vote in a trial before the People (*iudicium populi*) or a public meeting preceding a trial in the *quaestio de vi*: Alexander 1990: no. 266, with Shackleton Bailey 1980: 174–75.

[41] Cic. *Q Fr.* 2.3.2.

[42] Diod. 34/35.33.7: ἡσύχασεν ἐντραπεὶς τὸ βάρος καὶ τὴν παρρησίαν τἀνδρός.

own sustenance."[43] In the prelude to the trial of Milo, M. Cato had been brought before a *contio* to explain what he thought of Milo's suspicious manumission of slaves that made them unavailable for interrogation under torture. The audience was hostile, but Cato spoke "firmly and bravely" (*constanter et fortiter*), and the disruptive crowd "was pacified by his authority" – so, at least, says Cicero.[44] We do not need to accept these accounts as the literal truth of what took place in each instance; yet both Valerius and Cicero strongly suggest that fortitude and candor in the face of intimidation might indeed raise a senator's public stature, proving in effect his authority and moral strength.[45] Conversely, failure in the ordeal was a public humiliation, involving loss of "face" and, presumably, corresponding political clout.[46] Scipio's insulting response to Carbo's *contio* evidently did not diminish his standing with the People, who promptly rejected Carbo's proposal for iteration of the tribunate at his urging.[47] Perhaps his retort only enhanced his *auctoritas* while simultaneously heading off any criticism that he despised the *real* Roman People. Similarly, in the published version of Cicero's speech for Rabirius, the orator's intentional elicitation of a hostile clamor makes good sense as a device to stress before the citizenry his readiness to face down the shouts of the ignorant, as the *real* Roman People had elected him to do.[48]

Bringing opponents before a meeting, then, held opportunities and dangers for both sides, and could backfire. In 133 Tiberius Gracchus surely assumed, when he "dragged" T. Annius to the Rostra from the Senate-house after the latter had denounced the deposing of Octavius as a violation of tribunician sacrosanctity, that before an angry crowd his own counterattack would gain force and Annius' nerve would fail.[49] But Annius seems to have caught Gracchus off guard by requesting leave to ask his own questions, which then proved so effective, it was said, that Gracchus disbanded the

---

[43] Val. Max. 3.7.3 = *ORF* 38.3, pp. 157–58.

[44] Cic. *Mil.* 58: *Dixit enim hic idem qui semper omnia constanter et fortiter, M. Cato, et dixit in turbulenta contione, quae tamen huius auctoritate placata est . . .*

[45] Above, p. 63.

[46] Cic. *Fam.* 12.3.2: [Antonius] *productus in contionem a Cannutio turpissime ille quidem discessit . . .* See also Cic. *Leg. agr.* 3.1, 16, with n. 133 below.

[47] Cf. Stockton 1979: 92, n. 27. The bill did come to a vote: *itaque lex popularis suffragiis populi repudiata est* (Cic. *Amic.* 96).

[48] *Rab. perd.* 18. See above, pp. 146–47.

[49] Plut. *Ti. Gracch.* 14.4: ἐκπηδήσας . . . τόν τε δῆμον συνεκάλει καὶ τὸν Ἄννιον ἀχθῆναι κελεύσας ἐβούλετο κατηγορεῖν. Note that it is only when Annius is given leave to ask his questions that silence falls (σιωπῆς γενομένης). Livy, *Per.* 58: *T. Annius consularis, qui cum in senatu in Gracchum perorasset, raptus ab eo ad populum delatusque plebi.* Plutarch and Livy both use verbs implying physical compulsion, which probably allude to the tribune's power of *prensatio*: see below, n. 53.

meeting without answering them; as a result "the People" became more alienated from Tiberius, who finally called another *contio* to deliver a full apologia.[50] A generation later, in 90, the tribune Q. Varius was forced to disband a meeting at which he had "produced" the aged *princeps senatus*, M. Aemilius Scaurus to answer to the charge of inciting the Italian War, so completely did Scaurus' famous reply sway the audience.[51] Still, on the whole the advantage lay with the presiding magistrate, above all because he controlled the proceedings and, as we have seen, the political drama could be played out before "his" audience. It is surely significant that opponents have sometimes to be "ordered" or "compelled" to come before a *contio*.[52] Scholars debated even in antiquity whether a tribune actually had the legal authority to order anyone to appear on the Rostra,[53] but in practice it seems to have been virtually impossible to refuse, not least because failure to come was bound to be represented as a sign of lack of conviction and candor, or cowardice.[54]

Recognizing the "pressure to justify himself" under which the *productus in contionem* was placed, Millar nevertheless views this optimistically: "the health of the political system required that they should explain themselves and their views on current issues of policy."[55] There is something in this, of course. No doubt the possibility that a refractory senator might be hauled before a *contio* to account for his words or actions might have been seen positively as one assurance of accountability.[56] Yet in practice, the invidious framing of the question by the presiding officer, the restriction of those questioned to answering such questions rather than presenting an opposing

---

[50] Such is the version of Plut. *Ti. Gracch.* 14.5–16.1, who introduces the comment about Tiberius' adjourning the meeting with λέγεται. Livy's epitomator (*Per.* 58) may reflect another tradition, according to which the two gave successive speeches, first Tiberius, then Annius (*delatusque plebi, rursus in eum* [Gracchum] *pro rostris contionatus est*); but it is rarely clear how closely the Livian *Periochae* reflect their original. A speech purporting to be that of Annius against Gracchus was known to the grammarian Festus (*ORF* 17.5, p. 106), but it would seem to be a natural subject for a late rhetorical exercise, and (as Andrew Dyck points out to me) its absence from Cicero's *Brutus* probably tells against authenticity.

[51] Asc. 22 C = *ORF* 43.11, p. 167; below, pp. 258–60.

[52] Language of command or even physical compulsion is not uncommon in references to the *productio* of opponents: see, e.g., Cic. *Sest.* 27 and *Dom.* 54 (*iussisti*); Asc. 22 C (*iuberet*); Livy, *Per.* 58 (*raptus ab eo*); Val. Max. 3.8.3; Plut. *Ti. Gracch.* 14.4 (ἀχθῆναι κελεύσας); Dio 36.44.2 (ἀναγκασθείς). The tribune's *viator* seems to have conveyed the demand: Cic. *Font.* 39; Asc. 22 C; Gell. *NA* 13.12.4.

[53] Varro and Antistius Labeo pedantically denied that tribunes had the formal right of *vocatio* (i.e., to issue a compulsory summons) in addition to *prensio* (i.e., to lead by the hand), and Labeo claims even to have refused a tribune's order on these grounds (Gell. *NA* 13.12.4–9) – a unique example in the evidence. See Mommsen 1887: II.313, n. 2; Botsford 1909: 148; Pina Polo 1996: 48.

[54] See above, n. 46.   [55] Millar 1998: 60, 134.

[56] So perhaps Cic. *Leg. agr.* 2.99 ad fin., if *ad populum Romanum . . . producere* is here equivalent to *in contionem producere*.

argument, and the intense social pressure brought to bear on them, do not suit very well the idea that these men were really being asked to "explain themselves and their views" to a public that desired exposure to credible alternatives. Whatever the theory, in actual practice the "production" of political opponents before a mass meeting was directed not at the audience at all but at those political leaders who had taken an unpopular stand; its purpose was not to help voters make an informed choice but to force adversaries to drop their opposition; and despite the fact that the tactic sometimes backfired, it was not intended to foster real debate but to cut it off.

ROUTING THE OPPOSITION

We have seen, then, that a central feature of contional "debate" corresponds little, if at all, with the minimal criterion of public deliberation, that is, that the citizenry be fairly exposed to opposing viewpoints on a given issue. Indeed, the tactic that I have been analyzing at some length offers a good example of how a feature that at first appearance would seem to suit one model of the function of the *contio* (a venue for open debate) in fact, on closer examination, proves more consistent with the alternative model (an instrument with which to create a symbolic manifestation of the Popular Will and to exert the pressure of an ostensible communal consensus). This should warn us against too readily assuming that this institution worked in a manner consistent with the principles of modern liberal democracies. With this example in mind, I now turn to the hypothesis that the equal right of a plurality of magistrates to summon public meetings will have ensured that alternative views on any question of major public import were fully aired. A review of the best-known and best-documented cases of public "debate" on major controversial legislative proposals of the late Republic will offer the best chance to assess this proposition.

The struggle over Tiberius Gracchus' agrarian law in 133 is a good place to start, for it well illustrates both the power of contional rhetoric and the tendency of public meetings, even over such a momentous matter, to stifle rather than to nourish authentic debate.[57] Appian tells us that Gracchus was known to everyone because he was noble, ambitious – and a fine speaker. At the beginning of their accounts of Gracchus' tribunate, both Appian and Plutarch stress the effectiveness of his rhetoric as he laid

---

[57] Cf. the recent, extended analysis of the public controversies of 133 by Döbler 1999: 221–56.

out and justified his proposal in *contiones*.[58] But what about the opposing view? The public "debate" that ensues in Appian appears to be a plausible compilation of discussion and complaints: there is no mention, however, of a formal counterargument from the Rostra.[59] This might mean little in itself, except that Plutarch is quite explicit that after some rather vague attempt by "the rich landowners" to turn the People against the law by alleging revolutionary motives, Gracchus' adversaries beat a hasty retreat from the rhetorical contest and set their hopes on interposing a veto on voting day. "None of his opponents could stand their ground against these arguments, which, arising from great conviction and sincere sympathy, filled the people with corresponding transports of enthusiasm; so forfeiting the verbal argument they turned to Marcus Octavius, one of the tribunes [that is, to veto the law]."[60]

Now it is true that Plutarch goes on to mention nearly daily "contests" (ἀγῶνες) between the two tribunes before the vote, in which (supposedly) neither said a bad word about the other.[61] Were these debates, then, offering Octavius, at least, the opportunity now to make the case that Plutarch has already said was forfeited? The specific example he supplies, however, fits more convincingly the tactic just studied of "producing" opponents rather than an airing of opposing policy alternatives. Gracchus is said to have pleaded with Octavius to yield his opposition to the law, adding an offer to compensate Octavius out of his own funds for any damage to the value of Octavius' land caused by the law – "although his means were not great!"[62] The only plausible context for such an appeal is a *contio* called by Gracchus before which Octavius was "produced" in the same way that, much later, Bibulus was "produced" by Caesar; and when we observe that the invidious implication of Gracchus' reported offer – before the *populus Romanus* as audience – was that the other tribune was opposing the law merely to protect his own financial interest, it becomes clearer what kind of "contest" this was. Ἀγῶνες, after all, need not imply speeches, and Plutarch never mentions one delivered by Octavius. Gracchus was evidently using the power and symbolism of the *contio* to try to force Octavius to drop his threat of a

---

[58] Plut. *Ti. Gracch.* 9.4–10.1; App. *B Civ.* 1.9.

[59] App. *B Civ.* 1.10. The impression that this is meant to be a representation simply of the "talk" of the city is bolstered when a great influx from the citizen and Latin colonies joins in the argument.

[60] Plut. *Ti. Gracch.* 10.1: τούτους ἀπὸ φρονήματος μεγάλου καὶ πάθους ἀληθινοῦ τοὺς λόγους κατιόντας εἰς τὸν δῆμον ἐνθουσιῶντα καὶ συνεξανιστάμενον οὐδεὶς ὑφίστατο τῶν ἐναντίων. ἐάσαντες οὖν τὸ ἀντιλέγειν ἐπὶ Μάρκον Ὀκτάβιον τρέπονται τῶν δημάρχων ἕνα. Cf. 9.3–4. Whether or not Gracchus now retaliated, as Plutarch says, by introducing a tougher version of the law is not material to the present argument: see Stockton 1979: 57–58.

[61] Plut. *Ti. Gracch.* 10.4. [62] Plut. *Ti. Gracch.* 10.5.

Mass Oratory and Political Power

veto; but Octavius bravely, or shamelessly, stood his ground. Gracchus ratcheted up the pressure by proclaiming a legal suspension of business (*iustitium*) until the vote, to which the opposition replied by changing into the dress of mourning.[63] On voting day, Octavius' intercession finally came during the reading of the text of the law in what would have been the final *contio* before the formation of voting units; he does not seem to have taken the opportunity to present any final arguments against the law.[64] After the tribune was himself removed from office by a vote of the majority of the voting-tribes, the bill passed into law; no further public discussion of the bill, by *privati* or others, is mentioned.

Since this is our first encounter with a pattern of contional "debate" that will prove paradigmatic, it will be useful to linger over it for a moment. What must be stressed first of all is that the ostensible right of the opposition to present its views, either in public meetings presided over by sympathetic magistrates or in those held by a bill's proponent, was not actually realizable in practice when the proposer had succeeded in tapping some strong vein of popular sentiment and used it in his *contiones* to sweep the opposition aside. Once effectively banished from the Rostra, the opposition naturally evaded public argument on the merits of the law and instead resorted to constitutional obstruction (in the form of Octavius' veto) and symbolic resistance (such as the change into mourning). Gracchus had successfully routed the opposition from the sphere of verbal discourse and driven it into other avenues: symbolic modes of resistance would ultimately have greater effect on citizens' hearts and minds than the explicit and open confrontation of arguments. Indeed, a popular reaction began to set in against Gracchus as soon as he was driven by Octavius' obstruction to the extremity of having

---

[63] Plut. *Ti. Gracch.* 10.6-7. The symbolic rhetoric of changing into mourning in such crises warrants full examination elsewhere.

[64] Burckhardt 1988: 161–62, following Meier 1968: 90–91 (a confused treatment, for the *potestas suadendi dissuadendique* had indeed already existed from the date of promulgation to the day of the vote: see above, n. 7), believes that Octavius vetoed the first reading of the bill before a *contio*, that is, its promulgation; this hardly suits the narratives of Appian (1.11–12) and Plutarch (*Ti. Gracch.* 12–13). Appian is explicit (Plutarch's picture is somewhat blurry on this point) that the veto was imposed during the *final* reading of the law, immediately before the vote, which Libero 1992: 37–41 demonstrates was the usual moment throughout the late Republic for the actual casting of the veto (as distinct from merely threatening to do so). Rilinger 1989: 492–95 argues that this was also the last possible moment for a veto; but this appears to be contradicted by Cic. *Corn.* 1 fr. 30 Cr *dum sitella defertur*, etc. (text above, n. 13; cf. Mommsen 1887: III.397, n. 1; cf. 1.285, n. 1). The sequence of the *loca intercessionis* given in that text suggests that the reading of the law opened the proceedings of the *contio* that took place immediately before balloting, and that final speeches on a proposal followed the reading. (B. A. Marshall 1985: 249 asserts that "there is no particular order observed" at Cic. *Corn.* 1 fr. 30 Cr, but the objection seems to overlook the fact that the sequence begins only at *id est.*) Vetoing the recitation of the law would thus have had the advantage of impeding proceedings at the very outset, before the speeches and above all before actual voting arrangements had commenced.

him deposed; thus the political and ideological groundwork was laid for the senatorial reaction against the tribune that culminated in his murder.[65]

The quality of debate here is not high: one might actually speak more aptly of a "non-debate." Of course, the forfeiting of the case by the opposition might just be seen as an indication of the debilitating weakness of their argument: perhaps there was simply no legitimate case to be made against Tiberius Gracchus' plan for agrarian redistribution. But that does not seem to do justice to Appian's report of the complaints against the bill both before it was passed and after – or indeed to modern criticisms.[66] Cicero's attack on the agrarian bill of 63 (see below) gives an idea, further, of the sort of thing a little ingenuity might have produced under more favorable circumstances. Rather, what we see here is that once one side had prevailed in what we saw in the last chapter was a symbolic battle, fought in the *contio*, to impersonate the Popular Will, then debate – even such as it was up to this point – was over. Whatever the objective merits or de-merits of Tiberius Gracchus' land bill, the actual political dynamics of the Republic in 133 BC were such that success in passing it into law depended not on argument and public deliberation but on swift mobilization of over-whelming, mass support. Recalling the techniques reviewed in the previous chapter for creating manifestations of the "will and verdict of the Roman People," we are entitled to doubt that mounting this kind of mass demon-stration demanded, in turn, much in the way of *persuasion*. The other side of this coin is that of course a politician seeking to make use of the potentially explosive power of "the People" needed to formulate his proposal in such a way that it would not *need* much in the way of persuasion; persistent and quite real economic hardships and social injustices would always provide ready material for those brave, ambitious, or vengeful enough to take this path.

The prelude to voting on Julius Caesar's agrarian bill of 59, which I touched upon earlier, bears important similarities to the events of 133 just reviewed and therefore deserves a second look.[67] The story begins rather differently, for we are told that Caesar scrupulously brought his proposal before the Senate for any objections to be considered before its submission to the People; but no one could find anything wrong with the specific provisions, even though many disapproved of the law because of the power

---

[65] Plut. *Ti. Gracch.* 15.1. Cf. App. *B Civ.* 1.14; Cic. *Leg.* 3.24, *Brut.* 95: *iniuria accepta, fregit Ti. Gracchum patientia civis in rebus optimis constantissimus M. Octavius,* with Linderski 1982 (= Linderski 1995: 291–94). See also below, n. 74.

[66] App. *B Civ.* 1.10, 18–19. See Stockton 1979: 51–52; Flach 1990: 38–48.

[67] Cf. now Döbler 1999: 316–33.

it would bring to Caesar, and so all kept silent.[68] Cato, it is true, while avoiding direct criticism of the bill, declared that the present arrangement should not be changed – and came close to being dragged off to prison by Caesar, presumably for the length of his filibuster.[69] At last, despairing of obtaining a sponsoring decree from the Senate, Caesar brought the matter directly before the People in a *contio*. Yet even now the opposition remains virtually a silent one. As we have seen, considerable pressure was brought against M. Bibulus in Caesar's *contio* to bow to popular pressure and lend his support to the law; Bibulus, however, conceded no ground and declared that he would prevent the law's passage during his consulship regardless of the audience's wishes.[70] No *contio* held by the opposition appears in the evidence, which in view of prevailing popular pressure would anyhow have been doomed. In the end, it seems, only M. Cato was prepared to face the crowd on voting day and speak against the law, proclaiming that the people were establishing a tyrant in the citadel by means of their votes; but he was dragged from the Rostra, from which it seems likely that he had not had Caesar's leave to speak, and if we are to take our sources at their word it appears that Caesar gave no one else (certainly, no opponent) the opportunity to speak against the law immediately before the vote.[71] Once again, the opposition had been silenced by a powerful combination of sharp political practice and public indignation. From that point there was no recourse for opposition but obstructionism. Bibulus' effort to secure the annulment of the law from the Senate failed completely.[72] By shutting himself in his house for the rest of the year, however, and advertising thereby and in published edicts Caesar's contempt for constitutional traditions, Bibulus attempted to deflect popular indignation from himself against the man who was acting as if he were sole consul,[73] just as M. Octavius had tried, perhaps with more success, to erode Tiberius Gracchus' popularity by forcing him to take extreme measures. As in 133, obstructionism laid the

---

[68] Cass. Dio 38.2. Here this version differs sharply from Appian's (*B Civ.* 2.10), which has it that ἐνισταμένων δὲ τῇ γνώμῃ πολλῶν in the Senate. But Dio is on the whole much better informed about the events of 59 than is Appian.

[69] Cass. Dio 38.3: cf. 38.2.3: διατριβαὶ καὶ ἀναβολαὶ τὴν ἄλλως ἐγίγνοντο. On filibusters, see Libero 1992: 15–22.

[70] Cass. Dio 38.4.2–3.

[71] Plut. *Cat. Min.* 33; App. *B Civ.* 2.11. The quotation preserved by Plutarch probably indicates that Cato was not merely filibustering, which would get him dragged off the Rostra in 55 (Cass. Dio 39.34.3–4; Plut. *Cat. Min.* 43.1–2). Note that in Dio's version Bibulus too had tried to speak – apparently interrupting Caesar's speech – but was prevented from doing so: 38.6.2–3.

[72] Cass. Dio 38.6.4: above, n. 30.

[73] "Sole consul:" Suet. *Iul.* 20.2. Cf. Cic. *Att.* 2.21.3, 5; cf. 2.19.2–3, 20.4: *populare nunc nihil tam est quam odium popularium.*

groundwork for a counterattack against the populist politician: the status of Caesar's laws of 59 was under attack from the moment Caesar stepped down from the consulship.[74] Republican obstructionism should itself be understood not as the abdication of ideological struggle but as a form of symbolic rhetoric whose purpose was to shift the contest decisively onto what we might call a "constitutional" plane. This was an interesting kind of ideological guerilla warfare that tells much about the importance of public opinion in Republican Rome; but such tactics fundamentally diverted attention from the specific content of proposed legislation and attempted instead to manipulate the power of broad, more or less universally held civic values in order to lay the basis for a decisive counterstroke (like the assassination of Tiberius Gracchus).

The strategy of arousing indignation among the populace and exploiting popular anger to silence all opposition is again and perhaps most strikingly demonstrated by Clodius' attack against Cicero early in 58.[75] Clodius pressed his attack in what Cicero calls "daily" *contiones*; "but no one said a word in my defence, or the Republic's."[76] Dio, it is true, says that the tribune Ninnius urged the People – presumably then in a *contio* – to change to the dress of mourning to show support for Cicero. This may only be a confused reference to Ninnius' motion in the Senate to that effect, which was decreed but then vetoed; or, alternatively, Ninnius attempted to fight or undermine the veto by carrying the argument before a *contio*.[77] But clearly he achieved nothing of note. The large demonstration in support of Cicero held by *equites* on the Capitol, joined by Q. Hortensius and C. Curio, does not seem to have been accompanied by a *contio*; again no magistrate came forward to speak for Cicero. As already noted, Clodius subsequently seems to have hauled Hortensius and Curio before a well-primed *contio* and then had them "thrashed" in what was presumably intended to be a strong show of public indignation.[78] The decisive moment seems to have been one particularly noteworthy meeting, summoned at the Circus Flaminius

---

[74] The peculiar power of obstructionism in the ideological battle for legitimacy is properly noted by Libero 1992: esp. 72–76, 79–80, and 99–101 on Bibulus' efforts against Caesar. See also Burckhardt 1988: 196–202.

[75] Detailed recent discussions are in Nippel 1988: 114–20; Tatum 1999: 151–66; Döbler 1999: 334–46.

[76] *Sest.* 42: [*cum viderem . . .*] *contiones haberi cotidie contra me; vocem pro me ac pro re publica neminem mittere . . .* See also *cotidianis contionibus* (*Sest.* 39); other references (mostly from the *Pro Sestio*) in Pina Polo 1989: no. 298.

[77] See esp. Cass. Dio 38.16.3; Cic. *Sest.* 26, *Dom.* 99.

[78] On the equestrian demonstration, and the participation of Hortensius and Curio (the younger?), see chap. 4, n. 76, and above, n. 23. Cic. *Fam.* 15.21.2 might, if it refers to this year, indicate that C. Trebonius supported Cicero *in contionibus* as quaestor. But the reference is vague, and might refer to 60 (so Broughton) or indeed 57.

outside the walls to accommodate the presence of Caesar, now proconsul and preparing to depart for his provinces, to which the consuls, L. Piso and A. Gabinius, were also brought forward to state their views on the proposed law.[79] Piso, asked about Cicero's consulship, replied cagily that he did not approve of cruelty; Caesar disapproved of retroactive penalties, a key feature of Clodius' law, but did not beat around the bush in condemning the execution of the "Catilinarians"; Gabinius not only failed to praise Cicero but criticized the behavior of the *equites* and Senate.[80] We may rest assured that Clodius' intent in bringing the consuls and Caesar before a *contio* was not to create an opportunity for an instructive exchange of views before an undecided populace, but to exploit the urban crowd and a series of *civitatis principes* to create a powerful impression of political and social consensus against Cicero's actions. After this meeting gave Cicero the clearest possible signal of his isolation he soon turned to flight, and the law was passed with no significant public debate, all opposition having melted away.

These three great legislative controversies (over Tiberius Gracchus' agrarian law, Caesar's agrarian law, and Clodius' law directed at Cicero) clearly demonstrate the use of the *contio* by those proposing "popular" legislation to generate unstoppable "momentum" for their projects, and cast serious doubt on the notion that in actual practice such meetings afforded a space for authentic public debate about serious alternatives of policy. The insignificance or even absence from our record of *contiones* called by the opponents of these three contentious laws strikes a blow against the rather theoretical assumption that opposing views would be fully heard in *contiones* before a vote. Instead, these cases tend to confirm my hypothesis about the actual functioning of the *contio*, and indeed suggest a further elaboration of it: the proposer of a bill aiming at popular support against potential resistance from the Senate sought to arouse in his own *contiones* such a strong and persistent show of public enthusiasm (or indignation) that his opponents would be forced to yield the Rostra. Thus unable to mount any effective (verbal) counterargument before the People, they would have publicly forfeited their case – with consequences for the relative "turnout" of voters

---

79 The main sources are Cass. Dio 38.16.6–17.2; Cic. *Sest.* 33; *Pis.* 14; *Red. Sen.* 17; Plut. *Cic.* 30.4; see Pino Polo 1989: no. 296.

80 Piso, surely, gave his answer to a question about Cicero's consulship (Cic. *Pis.* 14), not about the proposed Clodian law (so, somewhat vaguely, Cass. Dio 38.16.6). Gabinius' failure to praise Cicero (Dio, ibid.) makes best sense too if he was responding to a query about Cicero's actions in 63. Dio 38.17.1–2 gives a more complete version of Caesar's careful response than does Plut. *Cic.* 30.4. (Mitchell 1991: 136, n. 113, however, prefers Plutarch; contra, Tatum 1999: 299, n. 19.) When Cicero speaks of *maximo cum gemitu vestro* at this *contio* (*Sest.* 33) he is explicitly limiting his characterization – possibly an imaginative one – to his present audience, men of the senatorial and equestrian orders.

on balloting day that are easy to conjecture. In a legislative campaign the *contio* was an offensive weapon, never neutral ground. It was used, above all, to win and maintain control of public discourse by *excluding* the serious consideration of alternatives that is essential to debate.[81]

ELEVENTH-HOUR DEBATES

The picture so far is consistent: despite the frequency and salience of *contiones* in the evidence for political action in the late Republic and the considerable emphasis they typically receive in that evidence, the great contests over legislation that give shape to late-Republican history hardly merit the word "debate," even in a minimal sense: the reasonably full and fair discussion of alternative courses of action that alone would give a listening and voting public an authentic power of choice over matters concerning their own interests. Still, as we have seen, it was apparently customary at least *on the day of the vote* for the magistrate presenting a bill to the People to offer his opponents an opportunity to speak against it. An instance that is relatively well documented is the discussion which in 67 immediately preceded the passage of the *lex Gabinia*, conferring an extraordinary command against the pirates on Pompey, a case that has been invoked as a paradigmatic example of serious and fundamental public debate about the constitution and the empire.[82]

When the tribune A. Gabinius announced in a *contio* his proposal to give a specially constituted command with extraordinary resources to an ex-consul for the eradication of piracy, it was immediately met with a chorus of popular approbation: immediately "everyone outside the Senate turned to Pompey."[83] But Gabinius was very roughly handled by the Senate, which

---

[81] Compare Cicero's presentation in the *Pro Cluentio* of Quinctius' campaign *in contionibus* against the verdict on Oppianicus in 74: Pina Polo 1996: 113–19.

[82] A "genuine debate on matters of principle" (Millar 1998: 84; cf. 80–82); "a fundamental argument about the nature of the constitution on one hand, and the needs of imperial security on the other . . . conducted in public through the medium of speeches" (Millar 1995: 101–2).

[83] Cass. Dio 36.23.4–24.1; Plutarch's claim that among the senators only the young Julius Caesar supported the proposal (*Pomp.* 25.4) cannot but be a gross simplification (Watkins 1987). I take Cic. *Leg. Man.* 44 to refer to the *contio* mentioned by Dio and its audience's response: *cum universus populus Romanus referto foro completisque omnibus templis ex quibus hic locus conspici potest unum sibi ad commune omnium gentium bellum Cn. Pompeium imperatorem depoposcit.* This is regularly taken to refer to the actual vote, but this is not a necessary interpretation of *deposcere* (the crowd will have shouted for Pompey) and ill fits the phrase *referto foro completisque omnibus templis ex quibus hic locus* [the Rostra] *conspici potest*, which emphasizes observation, not the activity of voting (cf. *Phil.* 7.22). Nor was the Rostra any longer the likely venue for legislative voting (chap. 2). Plutarch seems to refer to the same *contio* at *Pomp.* 25.3 (ἀναγνωσθέντων δὲ τούτων [the terms of the proposal] ὁ μὲν δῆμος ὑπερφυῶς ἐδέξατο), but proceeds to confuse the precise sequence of

resisted putting so much power in the hands of one man; indeed Dio implies that the tribune was actually threatened with physical violence. Gabinius fled the meeting, and when the multitude learned the mind of the Senate – presumably at a *contio* called immediately by the tribune – it rioted and set out to attack the House; if the senators had not anticipated the crowd and fled they would have been massacred (so says Dio). The mob did manage to catch the consul C. Piso, but Gabinius saved his life.[84] "After this," Dio goes on, "the leading senators kept quiet, content to be left alive, but persuaded the other nine tribunes to oppose Gabinius." But in fact, with the exception of L. Trebellius and L. Roscius, Gabinius' colleagues were too fearful of the multitude to speak in opposition to the law.[85] Yet, when the day of voting arrived and the *contio* that regularly immediately preceded a legislative vote was being held, Gabinius prevented even these two from speaking after Pompey and he had done so. Trebellius now made an attempt to stop the proceedings by means of a veto, but Gabinius immediately instituted a vote to depose him from office, and Trebellius ultimately yielded only when the eighteenth voting unit was about to decide the issue by adding its vote to the unanimous consensus of the seventeen previous "tribes."[86] "Seeing this, Roscius did not dare to utter a word," and had to be satisfied with making gestures with his hand to indicate that two men should be chosen rather than one. But the crowd raised such a deafening roar that Roscius was induced to "keep quiet not only with his tongue but with his hand."[87]

So far the progress of Gabinius' rogation fits closely the pattern we have observed, in which the combination of the power of the presiding

subsequent events, bringing forward Catulus' speech against the law and Roscius' finger-gestures to some vague occasion before the final voting of the law (25.5–26.1). *Pace* Libero 1992: 40–41, Dio's account has no technical flaw, since the final *contio* immediately before forming the "tribes" for balloting was the normal setting for a confrontation of opposing *speeches* on a law, and its clarity, together with Plutarch's known indifference to details of chronology irrelevant to his purpose, make it clearly preferable to the biographer's account. Note that Dio's information about the timing of Trebellius' veto – our only information, in fact – raises one exception to Libero's thesis that the *locus intercessionis* was as a rule during the final reading of the law (p. 40 at n. 67). But since Dio explicitly notes that the tribune changed his plan after being denied permission to speak in the *contio* (36.30.1), this instance is clearly marked as aberrant. If the order of proceedings suggested by Cic. *Corn.* 1 fr. 30 Cr be followed (above, n. 64), Trebellius had allowed the normal time for interposing a veto to pass, in the expectation of addressing the voters; once that opportunity was denied him, he had no further reason to delay.

84 Cass. Dio 36.24.1–2. See Plut. *Pomp.* 25.4, and on the possible allusion to Romulus, above, p. 95. Perhaps Piso was seized while futilely attempting to hold an opposing *contio*.

85 Cass. Dio 36.24.3–4: αὐτῶν οἱ μὲν ἄλλοι φοβηθέντες τὸ πλῆθος οὐδὲν ἀντεῖπον.

86 Cass. Dio 36.30.1–2; Asc. 72 C; see p. 158. The tribes voted in sequence, and since voting stopped as soon as a majority was reached, the consensus of the first eighteen of the thirty-five tribes produced (formally) a unanimous decision.

87 Cass. Dio 36.30.3–4 (§3: ὁ ὅμιλος μέγα καὶ ἀπειλητικὸν ἀνέκραγεν); cf. Plut. *Pomp.* 25.6.

magistrate with that of a thoroughly aroused populace produced a comprehensive "silencing effect" upon real and potential opposition. Indeed, on this occasion the presiding magistrate's power to authorize speech is demonstrated with particular forcefulness: Gabinius explicitly quashes opposing speech by his fellow *tribunes*, magistrates whose right to advise the People from the speaker's platform, one would suppose, would have been hard to contest. But as we have seen, custom sanctioned the expectation that at some point the opportunity would be given to present a contrary view to the People; further, tradition gave special emphasis to the rights of *privati* to speak before the vote.[88] Thus Gabinius compensated for the silencing of the tribunes by unexpectedly giving the podium last to the leading consular, Q. Catulus, and perhaps Q. Hortensius as well; these two can fairly be assumed to have been the moral leaders of the opposition.[89] On the surface, therefore, Gabinius would appear to have yielded the floor to the most eloquent voices on the other side, which would have helped considerably to justify, after the event, his silencing of the tribunes. But Dio's interpretation is interesting: "Catulus would have remained silent [the context is the "silencing" of Trebellius and Roscius], but Gabinius urged him to say something both because he was preeminent among the senators and he thought that because of him the others as well would come over to his view; for he expected that after seeing what had happened to the tribunes he would add his voice in favor of the law."[90] In other words, according to Dio (or his source), Gabinius' action was purely strategic, intended in effect to import into this final legislative *contio* the dynamics characteristic of those other meetings at which opponents were "produced" before a strongly partisan audience in order not to encourage open discussion, but to suppress it through intimidation.

The fact that Gabinius seems to have misjudged his man does not weaken the force of Dio's interpretation. In the event, Catulus maintained his *constantia* against the tactics of intimidation and spoke against the proposal, among other things apparently giving voice to Roscius' objection that if

---

[88] See pp. 162–63, and n. 13.

[89] Catulus: Cass. Dio 36.30.4–36a; Plut. *Pomp.* 25.5; Catulus' question, and the crowd's response to it, are often reported: Cic. *Leg. Man.* 59; Vell. Pat. 2.32.1; Sall. *Hist.* 5.24; Val. Max. 8.15.9. Hortensius is said by Cicero to have said *permulta* against Gabinius' proposal from the Rostra, presumably on this same occasion (*Leg. Man.* 52), but his speech is not noted by any other source. Unfortunately a lacuna in Dio's text leaves the immediate sequel to Catulus' speech in obscurity.

[90] Cass. Dio 36.30.4–5. In favor of Dio's view that the decision appeared to be spontaneous, and that Catulus had not expected to speak, is the fact that, according to the customary order, a *privatus* should not have spoken after Gabinius (above, n. 15).

such a special command were created two men should be chosen.[91] But what was remembered about this speech was how the audience had punctured one part of his argument: when he asked the crowd rhetorically in whom would they entrust their hopes if something happened to Pompey after they had put everything in the hands of this single man, it is said to have roared back, "You!"[92] Nothing is known of Hortensius' speech, though it may reasonably be guessed that he took the same line.[93] Catulus and Hortensius, then, had – under highly disadvantageous conditions, apparently without prior notice and in any case only at the last moment – been given an opening to press for an alternative; but the forcefulness with which Catulus had made use of that opportunity was a result of Gabinius' miscalculation (according to Dio), and in any case, under the circumstances, it mattered little. A last-minute *dissuasio* before a crowd that, given the prior reception of the bill in public meetings, was doubtless present largely in order to vote in its favor, was bound to be a futile exercise; in this case, certainly, it is perfectly clear that minds were by then made up. Indeed, as the Gabinian case shows, the playing field could be tilted even further on voting day, since the very proposer of the bill decided who would be permitted to speak against it – if anyone – in that final *contio*, and could exercise that discretion in a manner designed to weaken the force of the opposition.[94]

Two other known cases confirm the emptiness of such eleventh-hour "debates." The Manilian proposal of the next year to transfer the command in the Mithridatic War to Pompey from the consul of 67, M'. Acilius Glabrio, was rather less controversial, since it enjoyed considerable support from leading senators, and the preparation for the decision was correspondingly less contentious.[95] But it was indeed highly "popular,"[96] and again the "silencing" effect is clear. We know from Cicero's speech in favor of the

---

[91] Dio's lengthy version of the speech cannot be taken as authentic; he evidently wishes to present opposing speeches at this turning point in his work. Nevertheless, he included, of course, the famous question: 36.36a. While Catulus' arguments may have been much the same as those he later brought against the Manilian law (Cic. *Leg. Man.* 60: *at enim ne quid novi fiat contra exempla atque instituta maiorum*), the wording of the memorable question (below) seems to suggest that he took the same line as Roscius.

[92] Cic. *Leg. Man.* 59. One suspects a hostile claque here, given that such an effective interruption could hardly have been carried off without preparation.

[93] See above, n. 89. Against the *lex Manilia*, at least, Hortensius argued *si uni omnia tribuenda sint, dignissimum esse Pompeium, sed ad unum tamen omnia deferri non oportere* (Cic. *Leg. Man.* 52).

[94] See above, n. 15.

[95] Cf. Kallet-Marx 1995: 320–21. Cic. *Leg. Man.* 68 gives a list of consulars who favored the law. Still, Cicero may have been the highest-ranking senator actually to speak in a *contio* in favor of the law (Cass. Dio 36.43.2 mentions also the merely quaestorian Julius Caesar).

[96] Note that, according to Dio, Manilius resorted to his proposal in order to recover popular support, which he had forfeited with his abortive effort to distribute the freedmen among the tribes (36.42).

proposal that before voting day Catulus and Hortensius had both spoken against the law, the former rejecting constitutional innovation and the latter arguing again that everything should not be put in the hands of one man.[97] We do not know in what precise context the two leaders of the opposition had made their remarks, but their apparent brevity would be consistent with their being "produced" before a *contio* by Manilius in the familiar manner. In Plutarch's narrative, the opposing case seems to be presented only on the day of the vote: "the senators" urged each other to resist the law and "not forfeit their freedom; but when the time [for the vote] came, all but Catulus gave up for fear of the people and held their tongue."[98] Catulus inveighed against the law and Manilius, but when he saw that his speech had no effect on the People he sought to make an impression with a paradoxical appeal, nominally to the senators present, to flee to some mountain in order to preserve freedom.[99] The allusion was evidently to the so-called Second Secession of the Plebs to the Aventine or the Sacred Mount, which according to tradition brought an end to the tyranny of the Decemvirs nearly four centuries before. When we consider that reference to this event was a standard form of populist exhortation to the plebs to take up its hereditary defense of freedom, the force of Catulus' allusion becomes clear: ostensibly directed to senators but in fact to the plebeian multitude, this was a highly emotive plea to consider the consequences of their present actions for "freedom," whose preservation had by tradition been among their most hallowed duties.[100] Yet, although Catulus enjoyed great authority among the plebs, the appeal was in vain – after all, the bill enjoyed wide approval even among leading senators – and the vote of the tribes was unanimous.[101]

The Trebonian rogation of 55, which would confer special provinces on the consuls, Pompey and Crassus, is a further notable instance of the expression of dissenting views before a vote. Here again, despite gestures

---

[97] Cic. *Leg. Man.* 52, 60. Cicero himself evidently delivered his speech in a *contio* "given" him by Manilius (cf. the address to him at §69; Pina Polo 1989: 93, n. 4) which does not, however, appear to have been the *contio* immediately preceding the vote (to which the pledges and requests of §§69–71 appear unsuited).

[98] Plut. *Pomp.* 30.4: ἐνστάντος δὲ τοῦ καιροῦ, τὸν δῆμον φοβηθέντες ἐξέλιπον καὶ κατεσιώπησαν οἱ λοιποί.

[99] Plut. *Pomp.* 30.4. Millar 1998: 86 notes the paradox.

[100] It is intriguing, incidentally, that the only recorded Manilius in the early Republic was one of the two military tribunes elected, according to Livy (3.51.11), by the secessionist army on the Aventine before its move to the Sacred Mount. Cf. Sall. *Iug.* 31.17 and pp. 76–77 for the vitality of the tradition of the Secessions. For the "preservation of freedom" theme, see pp. 217–22.

[101] Catulus: Cass. Dio 36.30.5; Plut. *Pomp.* 25.5; Cic. *Leg. Man.* 51, 59. Support: Cic. *Man.* 68, with Kallet-Marx 1995: 321.

that satisfied the minimal customary requirements of open discussion, the practical realities of the case invite skeptical reflection. Once again we hear that opponents, "happy just to survive," were deterred by fear from expressing any objection to the law with the exception of M. Cato and M. Favonius, supported by two tribunes, C. Ateius Capito and P. Aquilius Gallus.[102] However, as in 67, the fact that they had two tribunes in their camp, with the right to hold *contiones* of their own, seems not to have given the opposition a practical opportunity to present contrary arguments to the People, for we again hear of verbal resistance to the law only on the day of voting itself. At the final *contio* immediately preceding the vote, the sponsor of the law, the tribune C. Trebonius, granted Favonius an hour to make his case, Cato no less than two – and the tribunes, consequently, nothing.[103] Three hours for the opposition appears remarkably generous, but the suspicion obtrudes that at this point no amount of verbal persuasion would have a significant effect. And that is precisely the assumption that Dio represents Favonius and Cato as adopting. The former used up all his time protesting against being given so little (*sic*); while Cato, "since he knew well that not even if he used up the whole day would he be able to persuade them to vote anything that he wanted," simply decried the general situation, hoping, as actually happened, that he could force Trebonius to cut him off and thus add this grievance as well.[104] Cato was right: it was clearly much too late for verbal persuasion about the merits of the law. The only chance he and Favonius had was to leave the law aside and to focus attention instead on Trebonius' arguably high-handed procedure, ostensibly so inimical to *libertas*. Cato managed to drive Trebonius to the extremity of having him pulled down from the Rostra to interrupt his filibuster, thus instigating an act of political theater loaded with invidious symbolism that gave a powerful visual demonstration of his complaint. When Trebonius made the mistake of having Cato expelled from the Forum and led off to prison, a sympathetic crowd gathered and began at last to listen to his remonstrances; Trebonius "took fright" (δείσαντα) and released him.[105] As with Gracchus' and Caesar's agrarian laws, when the circumstances were so unfavorable to verbal dissuasion the opposition's hopes of turning the wave of popular support rested on symbolic acts

---

[102] Cass. Dio 39.33.4: τῶν ἄλλων τὸ μὲν πολὺ δουλωθὲν ὑπὸ τοῦ φόβου ἡσυχίαν ἤγαγον, ἀγαπῶντες εἰ καὶ ὡς περισωθεῖεν. Cf. Plut. *Cat. Min*: 43.1 οἱ μὲν ἄλλοι τὴν ἀντίπραξιν καὶ κώλυσιν ἀπεγνωκότες ἐξέλιπον καὶ τὸ ἀντειπεῖν. For the persistence of Cato, Favonius, and the tribunes, see 39.34.1 with 39.32.3.

[103] Cass. Dio 39.34.2–35.1. Trebonius' apparent attempt to prevent his colleagues in opposition from addressing the People recalls Gabinius in 67.

[104] Cass. Dio 39.34.2–3. [105] Cass. Dio 39.34.4; Plut. *Cat. Min*. 43.2–3.

of obstruction that would push their adversaries into repressive measures apparently contrary to Republican traditions.

The prelude to passage of the Gabinian, Manilian, and Trebonian laws shows that, however much opponents' ability to speak against a bill was circumscribed in practice during the weeks leading up to the voting, they were at least likely to be given the formal opportunity to express their view just before the vote. This much was demanded by custom, and, I suppose, by the notion that the *populus Romanus* should be given the advice necessary for it to make a sovereign decision. But the evidence also shows that such protection of dissenting views existed only at the *contio* immediately preceding the vote. Up to that point, *contiones* were used to whip up public enthusiasm and indignation, and opposing speakers, if they were introduced at all by presiding magistrates, were as a rule brought on in order to force them to yield to the "manifest" Will of the People, as expressed by a particular contional audience. Consequently, as we have just seen, if a bill managed to be carried by such signs of popular enthusiasm all the way to voting day (in the face of the possible veto threat), clearing the Rostra of its opponents, then any last words of resistance on the final day were typically bound to be useless: it was "all over but the counting." For if the proposer of the bill had done his work well in the *contiones*, opponents now faced an overwhelmingly hostile crowd, and moreover they were subject to the power of the proposer of the bill to manipulate his wide discretion to authorize and deny speech on that day – a power, we have seen, that was apt to be exploited strategically. The ineffectuality of final speeches of opposition (as a rule) after the "battle for the Rostra" had been won, along with the fact that legislation that actually came to a vote seems almost never to have failed, thus further confirms the hypothesis that the *contio* was the main locus of legislative decision.[106] This, in turn, throws doubt upon the claim that, for all their self-selecting and frequently partisan composition, contional audiences were so arbitrarily constituted that they had no discernible relationship with the *populus* that came together on the final day to vote.[107] On the contrary, the decisiveness of the contional contest would appear to suggest that a central objective therein was to bring it about – by demoralizing potential voters on the other side, invigorating partisans, by impressing potential sympathizers with the power of apparent social consensus, and by exerting the "bandwagon effect" on the rest – that it was a decidedly favorable *populus* that assembled on voting day.[108] This would

[106] See pp. 124–28.   [107] Mouritsen 2001: esp. 50, 65–66.

[108] I here make use of Mouritsen's own powerful, and I think central, insight that Republican political action should be viewed above all as a matter of *mobilizing followers* among various constituencies

make good sense of the fact that, even on those rare and transient occasions in some eighty years of sharp and divisive political struggles where we do find something befitting the word "debate," such as before the voting on the Gabinian, Manilian, and Trebonian laws, it is such an inconsequential thing.

LEGISLATIVE FAILURE IN THE *CONTIO*

So far this discussion has focused on *successful* use of the *contio* by proposers of legislation to silence opposition and generate a powerful impetus that would carry a bill to success right through voting day. Of course, it did not always work that way: on more than one well-documented occasion, the "contional campaign" appears to have produced the *defeat* of a proposal. This, then, leaves open a final possibility that authentic debate before the People played a significant role in Republican politics, since it seems at first appearance quite plausible that here, at last, a full and open airing of competing arguments took place and indeed decided the issue. Reporting in our sources is biased in favor of success, so we cannot expect the same richness of testimony to this phenomenon as there is to its reverse, but a few glimpses in the evidence, as well as one well-attested contional debate, will help to sketch out a coherent picture.

Cicero gives a tantalizingly elliptical account, narrated over the course of three separate letters to his friend Atticus, of the vigorous campaign in the first months of 61 to pass a law instituting a special trial for P. Clodius' alleged desecration of the Bona Dea ceremony the previous December.[109] We hear of a senatorial decree specifying the nature of the court and ordering the consuls to bring the proposal before the People to vote into law; then of the attempts of one of the consuls, M. Pupius Piso, to undermine the proposal, among other things by inducing a tribune, Q. Fufius Calenus, to hold a *contio* in which he attempted (in vain) to prod the popular hero Pompey, just back from his victorious campaigns in the East and awaiting his imminent triumph outside the pomerium, to express dissent from the senatorial plan.[110] Cicero does not mention further *contiones* until the day

whose active participation, in the face of various disincentives, could not simply be presumed without further ado. This, of course, need not have been combined with a general depreciation of the political importance of the *contio*, nor is it necessarily inconsistent with the "democratic" interpretation of the Republic that is his main target.

[109] See the detailed accounts of the legislative maneuvers over the Bona Dea trial in Moreau 1982: 81–129, and now Tatum 1999: 71–80.

[110] Cic. *Att.* 1.13.3; 14.1–2. Fufius' motives are clear from *Pisonis consulis impulsu* (14.1), the invidious form of the question (*placeretne ei iudices a praetore legi, quo consilio idem praetor uteretur*), and

of the vote itself, when a fiasco ensued because of M. Piso's failure to carry out his charge from the Senate: after C. Curio and other friends of Clodius had spoken against the law, Piso too spoke – but in a way that was interpreted as opposing it. The *contio* actually seems already to have been dismissed in preparation for voting when Cato, Hortensius, Favonius, and other "good men" forced their way onto the Rostra and roundly attacked Piso, who finally postponed the assembly.[111] A senatorial decree ordering the consuls to urge the People to accept the law was then probably vetoed by Fufius;[112] in any case, the scene now shifts to public meetings, and we next hear of "plaintive speeches" (*contiones miseras*) held by Clodius against numerous leading senators, including Cicero, which apparently made great headway in the court of public opinion.[113] Cicero, at least, launched his own counterattack, but his vague account of the matter suggests that he did so before the Senate rather than facing a (hostile) People from the Rostra.[114] It

Pompey's current standing (*Att.* 1.16.11), as well as the pattern of contional tactics already described. An obvious precedent, which Fufius may well have had in mind, was Pompey's first *contio* upon his return from Spain in 71 (Cic. *Verr.* 1.45).

[111] Cic. *Att.* 1.14.5: probably not to be taken as evidence that the voting was to be conducted on the Rostra rather than the tribunal of the temple of Castor and Pollux, contrary to what seems to be the regular practice at this date. It was, likely enough, only because the voting was focused at the other end of the Forum that Cato and others were able to climb onto the Rostra, which, however, still served as an excellent platform for harangues. Their action was, of course, strictly illegal (Moreau 1982: 112–14).

[112] Cic. *Att.* 1.14.5: Shackleton Bailey's attractive emendation *Fufius intercessit* for the MSS *tertium concessit* (1965–67: 1.311), which would be the only explicit reference to Fufius' veto, has come in for repeated criticism (Moreau 1982: 117–19; Tatum 1986; Libero 1992: 32, n. 18.) Yet the emendation makes excellent sense, explaining above all why, in Cicero's narrative, the effort to bring the law immediately before the People again grinds to a sudden halt and the Senate is obliged to proceed to a new pressure tactic: *decernebat ut ante quam rogatio lata esset ne quid ageretur*. And the objections brought against it are weak: contra Moreau, Fufius had every reason to relieve the pressure on Pupius Piso and avoid a comitial veto if possible; contra Tatum, Cicero emphasizes the senatorial isolation of Fufius and need not have considered a veto of this decree decisive; contra Libero, the *senatus consultum* at *Att.* 1.16.2 is that which authorized the rogation itself, not this effort to put pressure on Pupius. Furthermore, it is hard to find any more suitable context for Asconius' comment *illud vos meminisse non dubito per Q. Fufium illo quoque tempore quo de incesto P. Clodi actum est factum ne a senatu asperius decerneretur* (45 C: *pace* Moreau 1982: 119–20, Asconius says nothing about a *divisio* in 61), inasmuch as there is no good evidence that Fufius' own tribunician rogation was sanctioned *ex senatus consulto* – rather the reverse is suggested at *Att.* 1.16.2, where the consular law is distinguished from Fufius' *legem de religione* by the phrasing *ei legi . . . quae ex senatus consulto ferebatur*.

[113] Cic. *Att.* 1.14.5 (cf. 1.16.1); for "headway," see Plut. *Caes.* 10.5 (*pace* Cicero's invective at *In Clod. et Cur.* fr. 16 Cr).

[114] Cic. *Att.* 1.16.1, a remarkably vague passage, perhaps designedly so, its purpose being to impress Atticus. Moreau 1982: 124 (preceded and followed by most others, notably Balsdon 1966: 71; J. W. Crawford 1984: 106–7; Pina Polo 1989: 295, n. 90; Millar 1998: 119) argues strongly that the *contio* was one of the venues for Cicero's counterattack as well as the *Curia*. Yet *clamor concursusque maxima* may refer only to the kind of welcome he received in public, perhaps particularly among senators and equites. (Cf., e.g., the *frequentia* of §5; and for *clamor* in the Senate, see §10

certainly looks as though the leadership of the Senate now largely forfeited the public contest of words, ultimately shelving the consular bill in the face of Fufius' continued threat of a legislative veto and yielding the tribune's point on the vital issue of how the jury was to be constituted.[115]

There is much that is remarkable here. It seems that the role of advocating the senatorial bill fell mechanically upon a consul who happened to be a friend of Clodius and strove throughout to undermine the bill, in preference to his zealous colleague, the "excellent" M. Valerius Messalla, probably simply because Piso was the consul who held the *fasces* in January; the expectation of the senatorial leadership seems to have been that on a matter in the religious domain, where the Senate enjoyed a monopoly of authority, the senatorial decree, with the exhortation of the consul, would inevitably yield the proper result on voting day.[116] (The patrician Clodius was of course not yet the darling of the urban plebs that he would later become.) It was Piso's shocking rejection of the role scripted for him that threw everything into disorder, exposing senatorial disunity at the highest level and leading to the extraordinary spectacle of Hortensius' and Cato's impromptu demonstration on voting day – nothing less than "a spectacular dressing down" of the consul, who would in the normal course of events have been thought to represent the senatorial consensus.[117] This blew the matter wide open; significantly, it is only now that we begin to hear of a determined counterattack against the bill, mounted in public meetings by Fufius and P. Clodius himself: apparently only after the fiasco of the original voting day brought the controversy fully into the public sphere could these partisans

---

of this letter; also *Q Fr.* 2.1.2; 2.6.1.) Note in any case that these happened *before* Clodius "fled" to his *contiones* (§1: *cum enim ille ad contiones confugisset*), presumably the moment described at §5; it seems hardly plausible that Cicero resorted to the People first. The nature of his counterattack (*quas ego pugnas et quantas strages edidi!*) is then described without any indication of setting, and in terms that suggest senatorial cut-and-thrust (cf. §8–10). Note too that the known *In P. Clodium et Curionem* (apparently to be identified with the speech described at Cic. *Att.* 1.16.9–10: J. W. Crawford 1994: 227–63) and the *Contra contionem Q. Metelli* (1994: 215–26) were both responses delivered in the *Senate* to hostile *contiones*.

[115] Cic. *Att.* 1.16.2; Moreau 1982: 125–29. Not, it is true, a complete victory for Clodius: Tatum 1999: 80.

[116] This may indeed have been standard practice for consular bills: cf. Cic. *Leg. agr.* 2.6: *non eadem mihi qua superioribus consulibus lege et condicione utendum esse decrevi, qui aditum huius loci conspectumque vestrum partim magnopere fugerunt, partim non vehementer secuti sunt.* The law on Cicero's return from exile may be exceptional, in this as in other ways. On Messalla, see Cic. *Att.* 1.14.6. On Piso, see Moreau 1982: 100–102; for the alternation of the *fasces* at this date, see Taylor and Broughton 1949: 4–7.

[117] The quoted phrase is Shackleton Bailey's translation of *commulcium Pisoni consuli mirificum*, Cic. *Att.* 1.14.5. The outrage of Cato and Hortensius at the consul's failure to advocate acceptance of the bill is echoed by the decree the Senate then tried to pass *ut consules populum cohortarentur ad rogationem accipiendam.*

effectively exploit the invidious potential of the *contio* to stir up ill will against several leading consulars, including Cicero.[118] Only in concert with this campaign emerged Fufius' ultimately decisive threat of a tribunician veto, whose use before the Popular Will was sufficiently mobilized might well have been counterproductive.[119]

The neglect of the *contio* by the senatorial leadership during the presentation of the consular bill on the Bona Dea sacrilege reminds us that many matters on which the Senate possessed recognized special expertise and authority – religion, of course, and perhaps also relatively minor details of "foreign relations" typified by the *lex Antonia de Termessibus* of perhaps 68 or the *lex Gabinia Calpurnia de Delo* of 58[120] – may have been approved by the People as a matter of routine, perhaps in the kind of assembly Cicero mentions in which some tribes were represented by five or six voters drafted in from other units.[121] But for matters that might touch upon any popular interest, this was a highly unstable equilibrium, vulnerable to any tribune prepared to resort to the *contio*. Like the battle over the trial of Milo with which this book began, the struggle over the law on the Bona Dea sacrilege shows how the *contio* lay ready to hand, for those ready and able to use it, as a tool by which political matters that might otherwise have been handled according to a kind of senatorial routine could be torn from the hands of the Fathers and thrust into the public gaze, cast, of course, in a highly invidious light.[122] The circumvention of the consular bill well exemplifies, again, the power that could be mobilized, through the *contio*, on the popular side of the ancient pair, *Senatus Populusque Romanus*. But it does not alter the picture thus far developed of a rather pale version of public deliberation and "debate"; it would be hard to sustain the proposition that alternative views on this legislation were offered to the citizenry in anything like the manner that would permit an informed choice. As in the regular pattern that has been discerned, the *contiones* that feature so centrally in the story of the failure of the senatorial bill on the Bona Dea sacrilege are used by one side only, and, as we have repeatedly seen, they are used as an instrument not so much of persuasion, but of mobilization.

---

[118] Cic. *Att.* 1.14.5, 1.16.1; *Schol. Bob.* 85 St: *cum illo anno potestate quaestoria fungeretur, apud populum creberrimis eum contionibus lacessebat.* Fufius' earlier *productio* of Pompey had failed to arouse a significant response: *Att.* 1.14.1. For Clodius' "flight" to *contiones*, see above, n. 114.

[119] First mention of Fufius's veto threat: Cic. *Att.* 1.16.2. Note that there is no word in *Att.* 1.14 of such a threat – not even when the consular law is first brought before the People.

[120] *Roman Statutes*, nos. 19 and 22. [121] Cic. *Sest.* 109.

[122] Cf. Memmius' use of the *contio* after Jugurtha's capture of Cirta in 112: Sall. *Iug.* 26–27, with Morstein-Marx 2000a.

Over the ninety-odd years comprehended by the term "the late Republic" it is indeed remarkably difficult to find an instance in which it can plausibly be held that "debate," in the sense of a open exchange of opposing views before the mass public, appears to have been decisive in bringing about the defeat of major legislation. Two cases spring to mind;[123] yet too little is known about one to exclude other, at least equally probable causal reconstructions, while the other looks more like the exception that proves the rule than a seriously countervailing example.

The first is the defeat of the Papirian rogation of 130 for reiteration of the tribunate – the occasion of Scipio Aemilianus' famous counterthrust to C. Papirius Carbo's invidious question.[124] Not only was Carbo's proposal defeated, but Cicero and Livy both make it clear that public argument between the principal figures on each side determined the final vote: we hear that Scipio's weighty and authoritative speech won the day over the arguments of Carbo himself and of Gaius Gracchus, brother of the recently martyred tribune. "Thus," writes Cicero, "a 'popular' law was rejected by the People's votes."[125] Excellent; but we must immediately acknowledge that our information about this event is too scarce for us to force it into any pattern, much less make it paradigmatic. For all we know, Scipio's impressive performance in Carbo's *contio* decisively checked the popular momentum of the bill, leaving it susceptible, as others often were not, to the objections of an extraordinarily authoritative opponent on the day of the vote. But speculation on this case is almost uncontrolled, and it should be left aside.

A second example in which legislation appears to have been defeated chiefly by means of a rhetorical confrontation in *contiones* is much better known: Cicero's campaign, as consul in 63, against the agrarian bill proposed by the tribune, P. Servilius Rullus. With the help of Cicero's three extant orations and references in the late narratives of Plutarch and Dio, the nature

---

[123] The defeat of Gaius Gracchus' proposal in 122 to extend the franchise might at first look promising, given the admiration felt in Cicero's day for the consul Fannius' published speech against it (Cic. *Brut.* 99–100). But our sources in fact have nothing to say about "debate" *in contionibus* – they do not even mention any speech by the bill's advocates – and focus instead on the consular edict banishing Italians from the city and M. Livius Drusus' threat of a veto (App. *B Civ.* 1.23; cf. Plut. *C. Gracch.* 12.1–2). The suspicion must be strong that the proposal was, for obvious reasons, unpopular among Roman voters and that the campaign for the law lost all its force after the removal of non-Romans. As for Fannius, the doubts entertained in Cicero's day about his ability as an orator, and thus even about the genuineness of the published speech, do not encourage belief that the delivered version had been decisive in 122.

[124] Above, pp. 149–50.

[125] Cic. *Amic.* 96: *Itaque lex popularis suffragiis populi repudiata est.* Cf. Livy, *Per.* 59: *rogationem eius P. Africanus gravissima oratione dissuasit . . . <C.> Gracchus contra suasit rogationem, sed Scipio tenuit.*

of the debate on this occasion can be reconstructed more fully than for any other bill. And a fascinating debate it is, too, from which one scholar has recently concluded that "there was serious public argument about law in Rome," for Cicero reviews the Rullan bill "very methodically," "deals with concrete issues of constitutional substance and legal draftsmanship, and . . . delivers precise details to back up his criticism."[126] On this view, the speech is evidence for the high level of contional debate. Moreover, here, for once, we know that the two sides did make their cases in public meetings before the People, and we have reason to believe that the rhetorical confrontation was, in fact, decisive. The argument over the Servilian land bill of 63 thus has special significance for the thesis that "serious debate" characterized the Republican *contio*.

First, a brief review of the immediate background. Shortly after the tribunes for 63 took office on December 10, 64, one of their number, P. Servilius Rullus, held a *contio* in which he promulgated a long-anticipated and far-reaching plan for agrarian purchase and distribution.[127] Cicero's fellow consul, C. Antonius, and a number of senators were thought to favor the measure; but when it was discussed in the Senate with the new consuls on the first day of the new year, Cicero delivered a stinging counterattack, later published as the first of his collection of speeches *On the Agrarian Law*, which appears to have routed Rullus' senatorial supporters while an exchange of provinces with Antonius brought the other consul back into the fold.[128] If the published *First Oration* reflects the original in this respect, Cicero aggressively challenged Rullus to debate the measure in the *contio* – evidently, from what we have seen thus far, an altogether novel procedure for a consul confronted by "popular" legislation. He would even

---

[126] Williamson 1990, quotations at pp. 275, 269. Millar 1998: 105 claims less, but still in a positive vein: "The debate over the *lex agraria* . . . illustrates the complexity of the arguments that . . . could be put before the people, as well as the need to generate such arguments on both sides."

[127] Cic. *Leg. agr.* 2.11, 13. Against Madvig's emendation, which would yield a date for this *contio*, see above, chap. 2, n. 18. A text of the law was certainly published before the end of the year (§13: *me designato*). The recoverable details of the plan are not material to the present discussion: for references, see below, n. 148.

[128] Plut. *Cic.* 12.3–4; Antonius' support for the law, though not that of other senators, is noted as well by Cass. Dio 37.25.3–4. The date of the exchange of provinces with Antonius (Cic. *Pis.* 5, cf. *Leg. agr.* 1.26 and 2.103; Sall. *Cat.* 26.4; Cass. Dio 37.33.4; Plut. *Cic.* 12.4), to be distinguished from Cicero's later resignation of Cisalpine Gaul (add Cic. *Att.* 2.1.3; *Fam.* 5.2.3), is an old chestnut, but on the whole the context of the agrarian controversy, which is the only narrative into which it is explicitly integrated (by Plutarch or his source), seems preferable to that of the harrying of Catiline, which may be inferred weakly from Cass. Dio 37.33.4; cf. Cic. *Mur.* 49 and Cass. Dio 37.30.3. See Vretska 1976: 361, and McGushin 1977: 167. For the date of the *Leg. agr.* 1, see *Att.* 2.1.3, as well as fr. 1 and §26 of the speech itself.

call his own *contio* and force Rullus to defend himself![129] And so he did almost immediately thereafter, turning the traditional consular speech of thanks to the People for election into a long diatribe against Rullus and his land bill.[130] Since we may fairly suppose that the members of the urban populace who came to the Rostra for Cicero's first, celebratory *contio* were disproportionately friendly, it appears that he chose his audience well for a shocking series of revelations of what the new year would bring and a blistering counterattack upon the (perhaps unsuspecting) tribune.[131] This was just not the way in which consuls were expected to behave.[132]

Cicero announced to the People that this bill, taking cover behind the fair name of agrarian legislation, was nothing less than an attempt to impose a tyranny over the Republic and to empty the patrimony of the Roman People into the pockets of Rullus and his friends, including the hated "Sullan occupiers" (*Sullani possessores*) who owed their possession of other men's property to the fiat of the dictator. There followed at least one *contio* called by Rullus and the other tribunes supporting his proposal, to which, however, Cicero claims not to have been invited; despite the disadvantages that I have reviewed for one who was thus "produced," Cicero subsequently represents this refusal to attack him to his face as a violation of custom and fairness as well as a sign of cowardice.[133] Nevertheless, even Cicero had to acknowledge that in this *contio* the tribunes made headway by means of a

---

[129] *Leg. agr.* 1.23–25: *Lacesso vos, in contionem voco, populo Romano disceptatore uti volo . . .* (§24) [*C*]*um populo Romano vox et auctoritas consulis repente in tantis tenebris inluxerit . . . verendum, credo, nobis erit ne vestra ista praeclara lex agraria magis popularis esse videatur.* (§25) *Cum vero scelera consiliorum vestrorum fraudemque legis et insidias . . . ostendero, pertimescam, credo, ne mihi non liceat contra vos in contione consistere.*

[130] Speech of thanks: *Leg. agr.* 2.1. Plutarch describes only one speech before the People, which was decisive (ἐκεῖνον ἐξέβαλε τὸν νόμον, *Cic.* 12.6). Yet we know that Cicero published two short *quasi* ἀποσπάσματα *legis agrariae* in addition to the major speeches before the Senate and before the People (*Att.* 2.1.3), so at the minimum Plutarch is foreshortening the progress of the debate. In fact it seems probable that he has conflated *Leg. agr.* 2 with another, later *contio*, for the setting he sketches is a *contio* called by the tribunes to which the consuls were invited, while *Leg. agr.* 3.1 indicates that no such occasion had yet arisen. If so, it is attractive to apply Plutarch's description of the circumstances of the speech to the lost, fourth agrarian speech, which indeed was conclusive, as Plutarch says.

[131] An acute observation of Mouritsen 2001: 55.

[132] *Leg. agr.* 2.6: *non eadem mihi qua superioribus consulibus lege et condicione utendum esse decrevi, qui aditum huius loci conspectumque vestrum partim magno opere fugerunt, partim non vehementer secuti sunt.*

[133] *Leg. agr.* 3.1: *Commodius fecissent tribuni plebis, Quirites, si, quae apud vos de me deferunt, ea coram potius me praesente dixissent; nam et aequitatem vestrae disceptationis et consuetudinem superiorum et ius suae potestatis retinuissent. Sed quoniam adhuc praesens certamen contentionemque fugerunt, nunc, si videtur eis, in meam contionem prodeant et, quo provocati a me venire noluerunt, revocati saltem revertantur.* At the end of the speech (§16), Cicero reverts to the theme: the tribunes should have the courage to come forward and face him (*veniant et coram . . . disserant*). Since, as §1 makes clear, he is referring now to his own *contio*, the manuscripts' *convocaverunt* should be emended not to

vigorous attack on his credibility, above all by claiming that he, not they, was the one actually seeking to protect the *Sullani possessores* and to curtail the People's benefits.[134] Cicero's response was a *contio* of his own to which – so he claimed – the tribunes, though invited, refused to come, and a speech (the *Third Oration*) throwing their allegation back in their teeth.[135] The tribunes apparently at last took up the challenge to confront Cicero face to face, ordering him and Antonius to be present at their *contio*; but Cicero's short speech on this occasion, unfortunately now lost, was conclusive.[136] A tribune, L. Caecilius Rufus, had announced (presumably also in a *contio*) his intention to veto the measure, a threat that was likely (as we have seen) to be decisive only when the voting-tribes appeared ready to accept the result.[137] Almost certainly, the bill was withdrawn without coming to a vote, a result for which Cicero's oratory must have been largely responsible.[138] Cicero was deeply interested in appropriating the "popular" weapon of aggressive, invidious contional speech to buttress, rather than harass, senatorial power; with the speeches *On the Agrarian Law* he produced his own triumph in the genre, worthy of a place beside Lucius Crassus' *suasio* of the Servilian judiciary law which had been "like a teacher" to him in his youthful study of rhetoric.[139]

Here, then, we have the sort of discursive give-and-take from opposing perspectives that meets at least the basic requirements of debate. This, for once, was a real, and somewhat protracted, rhetorical confrontation over legislation that was apparently not simply pre-empted by overpowering

evocaverunt (Madvig, followed by Clark and Marek) but to *non vocaverunt*: despite the Roman People's demands, the tribunes had not summoned Cicero to their own meeting.

[134] *Leg. agr.* 3.2–3.

[135] For the alleged invitation, *Leg. agr.* 3.1, quoted above, n. 133. The *proxima mea contione* of which Cicero speaks at 3.2 is presumably that at which the *Second Oration* was delivered.

[136] See n. 130 above, with J. W. Crawford 1984: 79–81. Note that according to Plutarch Cicero requested the senators to attend.

[137] Cic. *Sull.* 65. See above, pp. 124–26.

[138] Plutarch and Pliny attribute the defeat of the bill entirely to Cicero's oratory (*Cic.* 12.6; *HN* 7.117); Dio writes vaguely of timely action by Cicero and his confederates (37.25.4). Pliny alone seems to think the bill came to a vote (*te dicente* [*Marce Tulli*] *legem agrariam, hoc est alimenta sua, abdicarunt*) but his comment is potentially ambiguous and too brief to bear much weight. Cf. Cic. *Rab. perd.* 32; *Fam.* 13.4.1–2, with Hardy 1924: 89.

[139] Cic. *Brut.* 164; *Clu.* 140; see above, pp. 27–28, and Brunt 1988: 50, n. 84. For Cicero's abiding interest in this strategy, note his praise for the eloquence of a tribune, M. Octavius Cn. f., who induced the People to replace C. Gracchus' grain-distribution law with a more moderate one (*Brut.* 222; *Off.* 2.72; probably between 99 and 87: *MRR* II.471, III.151); for M. Livius Drusus' counter-demagogy against C. Gracchus in 122 (*Brut.* 109; *Fin.* 4.66; see Plut. *C. Gracch.* 9.3–10.2, Suet. *Tib.* 3.2); and for Sp. Thorius' successful "populist" rhetoric that evidently concluded the Gracchan project of land distribution (Cic. *Brut.* 136: chap. 6, n. 160). See also Cic. *Amic.* 96 on C. Laelius in 145 and Scipio Aemilianus in 130.

displays of the Popular Will. Cicero's counterarguments are indeed impressively detailed and (seemingly) comprehensive. But there are at least two serious problems for anyone who would use this case to argue for a generally high level of debate in the late-Republican *contio*. The first difficulty is that, as the other examples suggest, this kind of rhetorical confrontation of populist legislation appears to be quite exceptional – as Cicero's own emphasis on the paradoxical nature of his reaction shows.[140] It was, it seems, simply Rullus' bad luck to be challenging a consul who also happened to be a master orator eager to use the power of his extraordinary gift. The debate over the land bill of 63, then, cannot be taken as typical. The second difficulty is that Cicero's extraordinarily manipulative rhetorical tactics on this occasion (as he himself represents them),[141] and, above all, their success, suggest that such debate as was to be found in the late-Republican *contio* was so unequal in the distribution of power between speaker and audience that the latter was, to an extraordinary degree, at the mercy of speakers and their representations.

AN UNEQUAL ARGUMENT

I start with Cicero's central strategy in the second speech against Rullus – that is, his exploitation of the old trick of pretending to agree with ends that in fact one wishes to subvert but are unassailable in the audience's mind,[142] while diverting attention instead to the infinitely malleable (because ultimately inscrutable) realm of motive: the inevitably vicious and self-interested plans of one's opponents. Disarming public suspicions of a consul who came forward to oppose an agrarian law, Cicero proclaims, brazenly, that he is predisposed to favor "popular" measures like agrarian laws – especially those that made the *possessores* nervous! – praises the "objectives, wisdom, and laws" of the Gracchi, and adopts for himself

---

[140] Above, pp. 191–92 with nn. 129, 132.

[141] Again, strictly speaking, *Leg. agr.* 2–3 do not necessarily exactly reflect what Cicero actually said on the original occasions, although there are good reasons to believe that there was little difference between the delivered and published arguments (above, pp. 26–30). I do assume, however, that in memorializing this triumph in the genre of populist speech for anti-"popular" ends (above, n. 139) Cicero put on display the *kinds of arguments* that were effective before audiences like those that heard the originals.

[142] Thus violating the one of Habermas's four "validity claims" pertaining to "sincerity" or "truthfulness" ("Wahrhaftigkeit": see pp. 21–22; McCarthy 1982: 282–91, with Habermas 1973: 256), whose fundamental importance for communicative rationality is precisely that it certifies that the true reasons for action are not being studiously hidden from public scrutiny, and consequently that any agreement that results is not a "sham" one based on false pretences.

the paradoxical title *consul popularis*, that is, "the People's consul."[143] (It is important for the proper appreciation of these claims to know that else-where – in writings or speeches directed to the élite – Cicero attacks agrarian redistribution as subversion of the most fundamental bond of society, the sanctity of property rights; considers the Gracchi to have been justly killed for their assaults on the Republic; and classifies those who claimed to be *populares* as a singularly depraved class of demagogues).[144] Having ostensi-bly established his credentials, Cicero now lays aside what by any objective measure was the real political question at hand – the merits of agrarian distribution and of this example of the policy – but would leave him with an impossible case to make before a popular audience. Instead, he defines the argument quite differently, by asserting that he will demonstrate to the people that Rullus' bill is not really a proper agrarian law at all but a vast, deadly confidence scheme aimed at stealing away the freedom and patrimony of the Roman People and, not coincidentally, robbing the Peo-ple's hero, Pompey, of his rights.[145] Dark forces, unnamed and thus all the more insidious, lurk behind the scam, which was cooked up by a tribune of the plebs, of all people: one who is supposed to be a "protector and guardian of freedom" (*praeses libertatis custosque*) was establishing "tyrants in the community" (*reges in civitate*)![146]

Declaring with pretended deference that once he lays out the basis of his personal views he will follow whatever the People decide about their validity,[147] he proceeds to bury his audience in an avalanche of misrep-resentations and distortions of various clauses of the proposal, with the covert aim of building up a specious structure with which to support his

[143] Cic. *Leg. agr.* 2.6–10 (quotation at §10); on the Gracchi see also §§31, 81, with Robinson 1994. (For the remainder of this chapter citations from the *De lege agraria* 2 will be given by section numbers only.) For the contional construction of the *popularis*, see chap. 6. For anti-*possessor* sentiment, see §68, where it is treated as suspect that this law satisfies their claims; regarding the *Sullani possessores*, whose legal claim Cicero otherwise upheld (cf. *Att.* 1.19.4; cf. Quint. *Inst.* 11.1.85), see esp. §70.

[144] On agrarian redistribution, *Off.* 2.73, and 78–83 are particularly illuminating; see Dyck 1996: 471–77; Mitchell 1979: 200–204; Wood 1988: 202–4; Perelli 1990: 86–87. On the Gracchi, see especially *Cat.* 1.3–4, 29; *Sest.* 103 (senatorial orations); *Fin.* 4.65–66; *Off.* 2.43, 80; *Rep.* 1.31–32 (essays); Béranger 1972; see also chap. 6, at n. 12.

[145] The plot: §§10–15, 98–99, and *passim*; Pompey: §§23–25, 49–55, 99. Sumner 1966 powerfully demonstrates the unverifiability, as well as the rhetorical usefulness, of Cicero's claim that the law was designed in part as an attack on Pompey. On Cicero's strategy, see especially Classen 1985: 304–67; Thompson 1978: 28–46. See also below, pp. 198–99.

[146] §15; cf. §20 *regia potestas*. For "dark forces," see §23 *Viderunt ei qui haec machinabantur* and esp. §§63, 98. The old argument over the identification of the men to whom Cicero is alluding here is probably a red herring: Cicero *needs* an anonymous menace and thus creates one.

[147] §16. This should be taken in the same spirit as Cicero's slightly earlier request for the guidance of the People's *sapientia* in understanding the term *popularis*: §7.

devastating allegations about the intention behind the law, while giving the impression of undertaking a painstaking and detailed refutation of its provisions.[148] Admiration for the technicality and detail displayed in the *Second Oration* would seem therefore to be misplaced.[149] On the contrary, the opacity of arcane legal language – a province of specialists then as now – is Cicero's strongest card here, his hand strengthened by the layman's natural deference in such matters to the senatorial expert, whose privileged access to information and familiarity with the law lend his presentation extraordinary authority.[150] This is surely why the *First Oration*, delivered before the Senate, contains much less detailed argumentation about the text of the law than the *Second Oration* before the People and almost no direct citation of its clauses.[151] Jean-Louis Ferrary has demonstrated that despite the impression the contional speech gives of examining the bill comprehensively, the three extant orations together in fact quote only nine bits of its text, all but one of which are mere fragments of sentences.[152] Carl Joachim Classen shows that the misleading citation and quotation of such disconnected fragments furthers the impression Cicero wishes to give of systematically unpacking a vicious plot from the "impenetrable, mysterious text."[153] Such bewildering complexity strongly reinforces Cicero's message that the bill is nothing but a speciously attractive trap – but the real trap was, almost certainly, the one laid by Cicero himself. His techniques have been so effective that only in this century was it recognized, or perhaps rather rediscovered, that "the vagueness and ambiguity which hangs

---

[148] Ferrary 1988 gives the best edition of the fragments, with commentary and bibliography; this serves as the basis for *Roman Statutes*, no. 52. On the content of the proposal, see Gruen 1974: 389–96; Flach 1990: 71–76; a different view in Havas 1976b. Hardy 1924: 68–98 is still useful, if too dependent on the unverifiable assumption that Caesar lay behind the measure; Sumner 1966 is a healthy corrective on that point and on the bill's alleged anti-Pompeianism (though he still brings Caesar in by the back door, as it were: p. 579); Mitchell 1979: 184–96 remains too susceptible to Cicero's hostile rhetoric. On the speech, see especially Classen 1985: 304–67, and Vasaly 1993: 217–43; Jonkers 1963 is particularly good on Cicero's disingenuous distortions.

[149] Cf. Williamson 1990: 270.

[150] For an astringent taste of Roman legal language in epigraphically attested products of popular legislation, see nos. 1–2 in *Roman Statutes*. Popular awareness of the difficulty of seeing the true import of a law behind its language is illustrated by an anecdote Cicero tells on another occasion about the "popular" politician C. Servilius Glaucia (the ally of Saturninus in 100): he used to warn the Roman People (i.e., in his *contiones*) that whenever a law was read out to them they should pay particularly close attention to the first clause: if it ran "Whoever after the passing of this law" instead of listing regular magistrates they should suspect that they were about to be subjected to a novel criminal court (*Rab. Post.* 14).

[151] See Classen 1985: 334, 362–63.

[152] Ferrary 1988: 164. The quotations are conveniently assembled in *Roman Statutes*, pp. 758–59.

[153] Classen 1985: 315 for the quotation; see esp. 326, 365.

over the law are due," in fact, "to Cicero's method of presenting it to his audiences."[154]

The welter of detail in the *Second Oration*, in which nothing is quite what it seems, provides a hospitable environment in which to produce a number of truly remarkable distortions that presumably would never have survived concentrated scrutiny. Some examples will serve to make the point. After putting as sinister a construction as possible on the clause calling for election of the ten land commissioners (*decemviri*) by half of the Roman voting-tribes selected by lot – the procedure introduced in 104 for the election of the pontifex maximus and in this year extended to all priesthoods – Cicero persistently declares that they would be chosen without an election.[155] He then boldly claims that the provision in the law for a *lex curiata* to sanction the *imperium* of the men chosen is only a device for giving legal authority to Rullus' henchmen without a vote.[156] Cicero tries to shock his audience with the idea that there will be no checks on the *imperium* of the commissioners; he even envisions them acting as generals![157] Yet it emerges at one point that their *imperium* would in fact be only praetorian,[158] and obviously if the usual protections of *provocatio* or intercession were formally suspended as he says, Cicero would have lost no time in quoting the relevant passages of the law on that point. G. V. Sumner judiciously concludes that "in reality, the *imperium* of the Decemviri appears to be related strictly to their judicial authority and the power of taking auspices." "A land commission," he drily observes, "was not really a suitable instrument for ruling the Roman Empire."[159]

Cicero cries that the territory placed by the law under the commissioners' unaccountable adjudication covers the entire empire: they could sell off at will all Asia, Bithynia, and even Egypt, arbitrarily settling the question of the Ptolemaic inheritance that had been hanging fire since the 80s.[160]

---

[154] Hardy 1924: 72, strongly seconded by Ferrary 1988: 164, after his minute study of the preserved fragments.

[155] §26: *Iam hoc inauditum et plane novum, uti curiata lege magistratus detur qui nullis comitiis ante sit datus*; cf. §§27, 29, 31.

[156] §28: *Vidit et perspexit sine curiata lege Xviros potestatem habere non posse, quoniam per VIIII tribus essent constituti.* See Hardy 1924: 84; Ferrary 1988: 148: "Cicéron abuse son auditoire." Mitchell 1979: 190–92 accepts Cicero's sinister portrayal of the proposed election.

[157] For some of the extraordinary references to their powers, see §§15, 33–34, 99. Generals: *Leg. agr.* 3.16. At 2.32, Cicero further implies that they would have a bodyguard (*ministros et satellites potestatis*) numbering in the hundreds, even if Mommsen's emendation of 2.32 (*vicenos*, defended by Dilke 1978) produces a wildly exaggerated number.

[158] §32: *Dat praeterea potestatem verbo praetoriam, re vera regiam.*

[159] Both quotations at Sumner 1966: 576.   [160] §§38–44.

In fact, the relevant clause of the law pertains only to "public land" (*ager publicus*) outside Italy that had become the property of the Roman People after 88 BC; it almost certainly did not name Asia, Bithynia, and Egypt, nor, probably, the impressive roster of cities of Asia supposedly to be put on the block.[161] In fact, the extent of Roman public land in Asia Minor cannot now have been great; Cicero's argument on this point actually appears to rest on getting his audience to confuse Roman public land with reconquered territory, combined with the invidious, but extremely dubious, suggestion that the commissioners would have totally unrestricted discretion to declare territory "public land" at will.[162] Likewise Egypt was "smuggled in" by the orator under the pretense that the commissioners might arbitrarily decide that it was covered under the clause authorizing the sale of Roman public land abroad appropriated since 88.[163] It is fairly clear, despite Cicero's clouding of the issue, that the powers of the commissioners could hardly have been such as to allow them to determine, at their own discretion, the highly controversial question of the status of the Ptolemaic kingdom.[164]

While requiring commanders and former commanders to hand over to the commissioners for sale any plunder belonging to the Roman People that still remained under their control (*manubiae*), the law

---

[161] §38: *extra Italiam, quod publicum populi Romani factum sit L. Sulla Q. Pompeio consulibus aut postea*; Hardy 1924: 75; Ferrary 1988: 154. On the list of cities (§§39–40), see Jonkers 1963: 81–82; Vasaly 1993: 219–21 well points out that the series of impressive foreign names here and at §§50–51 would have "left the listener with the sense that the scope of the power granted by the bill would be limitless" (p. 225). In like vein, it is possible indeed that Capua was not explicitly named in the law as the destination for a colony, despite §76 and *Leg. agr.* 1.18, with fr. 2 (Vasaly, pp. 221–22; cf. 227–38): the opportunity to create a vision of the revival of Capua as a hostile *altera Roma* was in any case not to be missed (§§76–97).

[162] The tactic is clear at §39: *Primum hoc quaero, ecqui tandem locus usquam sit quem non possint xviri dicere publicum populi Romani esse factum . . . Commodum erit Pergamum, Smyrnam, Trallis, Ephesum, Miletum, Cyzicum, totam denique Asiam quae post L. Sullam Q. Pompeium consules recuperata sit populi Romani factam esse dicere . . .* Ferrary 1988: 154 suggests that a considerable amount of land in Asia may still have been of questionable status following the Mithridatic Wars; cf. Kallet-Marx 1995: 264–73. That may be so; but there is no real evidence that the commission had the authority to intervene radically, to the point of altering the status of whole cities and overturning decisions by Roman commanders since 88 (Sulla above all), some of them ratified by the Senate, and all of them now sanctioned by the passage of roughly two decades. "There is no reason to suppose that their judicial powers would have enabled them to declare public or private at will any territories in the empire": Hardy 1924: 94.

[163] Gabba 1966: 769–75.

[164] As is claimed by Hardy 1924: 74–77, whose treatment of this aspect of the law is otherwise admirable. Sumner was surely correct to argue that a separate law of the people or *senatus consultum* authorizing annexation of Egypt would have been required before the prospective *decemviri* could proceed; in which case if, as seems likely, the phrasing of the law left open the possibility of activity in Egypt (cf. Sumner 1966: 577; Ferrary 1988: 154–55), this was by no means sinister. Again Mitchell 1979: 195–96 is too generous to Cicero.

explicitly exempted the great haul of booty that Pompey was about to bring home from his victorious campaigns that spanned the *imperium*.[165] This would seem to undercut the argument that Pompey was the chief intended victim of this law; so instead Cicero waxes indignant over the projected use by the commissioners of the rich revenues expected from Pompey's conquests, suggesting that this was a covert way of getting at the great man's winnings after all. The claim that this was an affront to Pompey's dignity thus depends on inducing the audience to associate conceptually future revenues, which were not, of course, in his custodial control, with *manubiae*, which were.[166]

Cicero's discussion of Rullus' plans for the purchase of land in Italy stands out as a particularly brazen misrepresentation. An article of the law called for the commissioners to purchase cultivable land from willing sellers in Italy.[167] Cicero, quoting only perhaps five words of the clause, proceeds to discuss it as if it concerned only, or chiefly, the grants of Sulla (*Sullani agri*): the circumstances of these grants made them a liability, but Rullus had engineered a massive public buyout that would rid their owners of great ill will and danger and fill their pockets through collusion over the price with the commissioners.[168] Cicero "reveals" that article 40 of the law would give full legal title to the recipients of these grants, the *Sullani possessores* – a concession to civic harmony made by the drafters of the law – and pretends that the chronological terminus mentioned in the law – "after C. Marius and Cn. Papirius were consuls" (82 BC) – is used to conceal Rullus' aim to benefit "Sulla's men" under unimpeachable, anti-Sullan names, although it is hard to see how a provision that had the realistic aim of accepting the results of Sulla's victory could have been phrased otherwise.[169] The nadir is perhaps reached when Cicero tries to tell his audience that the standard phrase Rullus used to confer full legal ownership on the recipients of public grants in fact would give it better legal status than hereditary ownership and would by sleight of hand free it of all servitudes, encumbrances, or

---

[165] §§59–60; cf. *Leg. agr.* 1.13. I follow Churchill 1999 against Shatzman's view (1972) that *manubiae* were considered a general's personal property. The provision in the Rullan bill clearly supports Churchill (cf. Gnoli 1980); and if *manubiae* were indeed property of the Roman People, Cicero's subtle conflation of the category with *vectigalia* has a certain specious logic.

[166] §62: *ita remissis manubiis vectigalibus eius virtute partis se frui putat oportere.* See Sumner 1966: 580 citing the same provision in the Flavian and Julian land bills, both supported by Pompey. Ferrary 1988: 156–57, no. 12; contra, Mitchell 1979: 193.

[167] §§66–67, 71; cf. 1.14 (Ferrary 1988: 157, no. 13).   [168] §§68–70.

[169] *Leg. agr.* 3.6–7, 11, with Ferrary 1988: 158–59, no. 14. Hardy 1924: 88: "But the next year was that of Sulla's dictatorship, and *post Sullae dictaturam* would have cut out the very lands intended by the clause." In any case, it may also have been intended to disallow claims based on possession during the anarchic period of intermittent civil war immediately preceding Sulla's victory.

taxes placed upon it.[170] It is striking how often Cicero bases his attacks on this bill on arbitrary and disingenuous misinterpretation of standard legal language.[171] No doubt, it is precisely in this arcane realm, presided over by senatorial and equestrian experts, where the plebeian audience was likely to feel least capable of challenging a forceful presentation by an impressive authority with undoubtedly superior competence in such matters.

None of this implies that Cicero's audience was sunk in abysmal ignorance. I have indeed already made use of the *Second Oration* to support a relatively favorable assessment of civic knowledge among Cicero's audience, too easily dismissed as an ignorant and disaffected proletariat (chapter 3); certainly, the level of detail at which Cicero works in this speech implies that on matters close to its interests contional crowds would be attentive to the terms of a given proposal and sufficiently engaged to listen to highly specific arguments about it, including citation of its actual wording.[172] It is rather a matter of a large imbalance between the élite speaker and his mass audience in *relative* knowledge, most acutely in knowledge of a certain, somewhat esoteric kind: of the law, its language, and its technicalities. In combination with the accumulated authority conferred by Cicero's consular position, this produces a skewed communication-situation that offers listeners virtually no handle with which to exert some control over his misrepresentations.[173]

Rullus' speeches are unfortunately not extant; probably some of these misconstructions would have been answered therein. We do know from Cicero that Rullus responded in kind, claiming that the consul was simply protecting *Sullani possessores* like a certain Septimius and Turranius, to which his opponent replied that Rullus had written the law to accommodate the financial interest of his shadowy father-in-law, Valgius.[174] I suppose that their respective audiences knew as little about these men as we do, which was of course precisely the point: a murky scheme calls for obscure machinators. In any case, in the absence of independent evidence to decide the matter, Rullus' responses depended equally on a perception of personal

---

[170] *Leg. agr.* 3.7–9. The phrase in the law: *ea omnia eo iure sint ut quae optimo iure privata sunt.* Jonkers 1963: 143; Ferrary 1988: 159, citing A. W. Zumpt.

[171] Classen 1985: 315, 319.

[172] M. H. Crawford, *Roman Statutes*, 12, is unduly skeptical that delivered *contiones* can have been as complex as the published version of *De lege agraria* 2; but nothing at Cic. *Brut.* 91–92 suggests that an orator preserving a speech in writing would have made it unworkable in its implied rhetorical context. Cf. above, n. 141.

[173] Compare the familiar quandary faced by well-informed modern citizens when "classified" intelligence reports are cited by authoritative government officials to justify extraordinary military or legal measures.

[174] *Leg. agr.* 3.3, 8, 13.

credibility to be believed; and it is sobering to reflect that it was, after all, Rullus who lost this confrontation of rhetorical personae. The relevant point for present purposes, however, is that, somehow, the circumstances of late-Republican public deliberation gave Cicero the opportunity, which he masterfully exploited, *to avoid the policy issue entirely* (agrarian redistribution, in this law specifically and in general) and, behind a breathtakingly hypocritical façade, to convert it into an argument about credibility and motives: the tribune is not what he pretends to be, a real Friend of the People, but an aspiring tyrant, and the bill, Cicero seeks to show, is only a well-baited and deadly trap with which to secure his domination. It is to *that* end that all the ostensibly "factual" details marshalled by Cicero are subordinated; thereby it is "shown" that it would be naïve fantasy for anyone in the audience to entertain the hope of receiving in the end something better than blood-stained Sullan prizes with doubtful title unloaded by their nervous possessors, or "desolate and plague-ridden" "sand and marshes" – if anything at all![175]

A reader may reasonably object that such stratagems of political rhetoric, including the pretence of agreement with the intent behind a law while attacking the motives and sincerity of its authors, are by no means foreign to modern democratic states, and are not infrequently successful. Of course; indeed, the persistence and force of the tactic derive from the quite real issues of trust and credibility that are always present in polities that demand accountability of those who possess institutional power. But there are discernible degrees of disingenuousness and manipulation, which have real consequences for the distribution of power in public deliberation. My claim is not that late-Republican Rome was unique in this way, but that various concrete facts that structured the communication-situation of the *contio* made this an extraordinarily powerful and hence pervasive rhetorical move in the late Republic. Cicero's ability to prevail in this debate while baldly lying about his position on the basic policy issue is important, for it suggests that in Republican Rome, for reasons yet to be fully examined, the voting audience had a very limited capacity to force those who advised it to live up to their ingratiating rhetoric.[176] This in turn implies that no speaker had reason to depart from pious nostrums in addressing the People

---

[175] §§65–85 (*harenam aliquam aut paludes*, 71; *desertos ac pestilentes*, 98).

[176] One might suppose that hopes for further electoral success would impose some real consistency of action upon those posing as Friends of the People. That presumes the existence of some effective way of "unmasking" imposters (which I would deny: see Cicero's own record) and of course has little to no relevance for consuls (precisely the ones to whom this strategy was best suited), who in the normal course of events could have had no real expectation of running for another office.

("I have always been *popularis*"), since objections to "populist" measures could always be made, disingenuously, on grounds of trust and credibility without directly confronting them as policies – a hopeless proposition. Under these circumstances of minimal "transparency," the senators whose tongues formulated the Popular Will were under very little constraint to take their legislative cues from their perceptions of citizens' real needs, or to "educate" them by offering viable policy alternatives that could face public scrutiny, for the system neither forced opponents of legislation to formulate and advocate plausible alternatives, nor subjected those who sought to mobilize a popular backing by means of legislative proposals to the discipline of competition with well-articulated solutions from a contrary point of view.

Speech in the *contio* does bear marks of a traditional notion of the value of open public deliberation before the citizenry. Bills were aired extensively before a vote, in public speeches delivered in mass gatherings in a central urban space; constitutional custom demanded that the views of opponents of a bill, and of authoritative senators not currently holding public office, be heard before the moment of decision; the Roman People could be expected to follow a highly detailed, technical discussion as speakers grounded their views in the very text of a bill. Yet a close look at actual practice, represented by major legislative controversies and discussions before the People, corroborates the finding of the last chapter that *contiones* before legislative votes normally functioned not as the venue for debate but as a tool in the hands of the proposer of legislation for mobilizing public support, stampeding the opposition, and generally dominating public discourse about a measure. The rare emergence of a sustained and detailed two-sided debate (for which the only clear example is that over the Rullan agrarian proposal) is a mark of the proposer's failure, not success, in making full and effective use of the *contio*.

The practice of inviting opposing speakers to a *contio* to justify their positions was an act of political theater that in reality had little to do with ensuring that rival views were presented but aimed instead at intimidating and isolating the opposition. Powerful manifestations of the Popular Will would make it all but impossible to respond directly or candidly to a popular proposal in the *contiones* that marked a legislative campaign, while the customary opportunity at the last moment to dissuade voters, whose very appearance at the assembly was a sign of commitment, was almost always doomed. A clear indication (and consequence) of the "silencing effect" of *contiones* upon opponents is their early abandonment of the verbal realm on some notable occasions in favor of a strategy of obstruction, often dramatized by symbolic action which descended at times to farce but held out the hope at least of inspiring an eventual reaction. The manipulative disingenuousness of Cicero in the debate over Rullus' land bill, and specifically his evasion of all substantive discussion, is another product of this "silencing effect."

The other side of the "silencing effect" is, of course, that public discourse in the late Republic was, on the face of it, overwhelmingly *popularis* in character (if often hypocritically so). If the élite speakers who, as we have seen, held such power over this discourse justified their proposals and recommendations with reference to an overwhelmingly *popularis* consensus, we must assume that they had no other choice: to this extent at least late-Republican contional audiences imposed their preferences upon those who had the sole right to articulate their will authoritatively. But the paradox might be viewed from the other perspective as well. If, despite the extent of control they enjoyed over the generation of this discourse, senators of every stripe – including those who opposed ostensibly *popularis* projects – were prepared to accommodate themselves at least publicly and verbally to a *popularis* consensus, this must be because it was somehow not incompatible with their own interests, individual and collective. One way in which *popularis* discourse could be brought safely into line with anti-*popularis* actions is shown by Cicero's deceptive strategy against the Rullan land bill. But closer study of the ideology of the *contio* will show that it would be superficial to take the "popular" consensus of contional discourse as evidence of an almost "democratic" responsiveness of the Roman public sphere to the views and concerns of the common citizen.

CHAPTER 6

Contional ideology: the invisible "optimate"

Our chief contemporary witnesses to the political life of the late Republic, Cicero and Sallust, are fond of analyzing the political struggles of the period in terms of a distinction between *optimates* and *populares*, often appearing with slight variations in terminology, such as Senate, nobility, or *boni* versus People or plebs.[1] But what precisely is denoted and connoted by this polarity? Clear enough, one who is designated in these sources as *popularis* was at least at that moment acting as "the People's man," that is, a politician – for all practical purposes, a senator[2] – advocating the rights and privileges of the People, implicitly in opposition to the leadership of the Senate; an "optimate" (*optimas*), by contrast, was one upholding the special custodial and leadership role of the Senate, implicitly against the efforts of some *popularis* or other.[3] The polarity obviously corresponds with the dual sources of institutional power in the Republic – Senate and People – and was realized in practice through contrasting political methods (i.e., striving to keep real decision-making power within the Senate, or, alternatively, using popular organs such as the *contio* and *comitia* to shake, or overrule, a senatorial consensus) and distinctive types of rhetorico-ideological appeals suited to

---

[1] On *optimates* and *populares* the bibliography is immense. Some notable, recent treatments are: Perelli 1982: esp. 5–61, and 1990: 53–91; Achard 1981: 3–8, and 1982; Vanderbroeck 1987: 26–52, 104–12, 174–86; Burckhardt 1988; Brunt 1988: 32–45; Mackie 1992; Laser 1997: 188–93; Ferrary 1997; Tatum 1999: 1–7. Still fundamental are Strasburger 1939: 773–98; Wirszubski 1960: 31–65; Hellegouarc'h 1963: 500–505, 518–25; Jochen Martin 1965; Meier 1965: 549–615.

[2] Even tribunes will normally have enjoyed senatorial status (that is, at least have counted among those *in senatu* until the next censorial *lectio*) on the basis of a prior quaestorship; and the most straightforward reading of Gell. *NA* 14.8.2 is surely that after the *lex Atinia*, dated probably late in the second century, tenure of the tribunate entitled one to sit in the Senate as a *tribunicius* (for which term see Cic. *Phil.* 13.27) and gave a presumptive right to inclusion in the next censorial *lectio*. See Mommsen 1887: III.862–63; Lintott 1999: 69; Thommen 1989: 33–35, with references to newer literature; on junior members of the Senate, Bonnefond-Coudry 1989: 655–82 and Ryan 1998: 52–95.

[3] The most illuminating texts are Sall. *Cat.* 38.3 *alii sicuti populi iura defenderent, pars quo senatus auctoritas maxuma foret*, and Cicero's highly tendentious digression in the *Pro Sestio*, 96–143. Meier 1965: 598–612 usefully articulates a "complex" of proposals and aims pursued at one time or another by those actually identified in texts as *populares*.

tapping those alternative sources of power (i.e., the "optimate" construction of the populist "demagogue," on one side, or the "popular" politician's
concitatio invidiae on the other).[4] It is important to recognize that references to *populares* in the plural do not imply a co-ordinated "party" with
a distinctive ideological character, a kind of political grouping for which
there is no evidence in Rome, but simply allude to a recognizable, if statis-
tically quite rare, *type* of senator whose activities are scattered sporadically
across late-Republican history. Further, these labels do not in themselves
carry any suggestion that the tactics and ostensible goals implied by them
were durably linked to an individual throughout his career. Indeed the
norm was otherwise, the tendency being for younger men at the outset of
their careers to flirt transiently with *popularis* politics in order to make their
name and gain a jump on their peers in the increasingly competitive rush
toward higher office.[5] The "life-long" *popularis* – and, one must add, one
who actually lived long enough to make this a meaningful phrase – was a
new and worrying phenomenon at the time of Julius Caesar's consulship
of 59: an underlying reason why the man inspired such profound fears.[6]

During the long domination of the patron–client model and the associated "prosopographical school" of Republican history, analysis in terms of
"ops-and-pops" was highly unfashionable, and apt to be dismissed as the
residue of a nineteenth-century supposition that the ancient Republic functioned rather like a modern parliamentary system.[7] Now that the narrow
focus on private, interpersonal relationships has been found by many to be
insufficient to explain the communal, civic manifestations of Republican
political life (e.g. elections, legislation, *contiones*), the importance of the
ideological realm is no longer so easily denied, and the *optimates/populares*
distinction lies ready to hand as a way to delineate the ideological content
of the political struggles of the late Republic. The natural result is to see
Republican politics largely as a competition before the citizenry between
representatives (even if only temporarily so) of two distinct political ideologies, one (broadly speaking) subordinating the authority of the Senate to
the rights and privileges of the People, the other, the reverse.[8]

This sounds plausible. But the examination in chapter 5 of the best-
documented late-Republican debates raises a serious problem with this

[4] See above, pp. 62ff., and below.
[5] Sallust points to the phenomenon at *Cat.* 38.1. See now Tatum 1999: 5.
[6] See Cic. *Phil.* 5.49.
[7] Ferrary 1997 offers an illuminating historiographical review. On the changing paradigms of the
discipline, see chap. 1 above.
[8] Fundamental are Perelli 1982: esp. 25–69; Ferrary 1982: esp. 726–66; Brunt 1988: 32–56. Ferrary 1997:
227–29 defends the construct of a "*popularis* ideology."

hypothesis that has never, to my knowledge, been accorded its due weight – specifically, that none of these legislative confrontations unfolded before the populace as a competition between two explicitly opposing political ideologies (which we might define for this purpose as distinctive and somewhat coherent complexes of means and ends corresponding to distinguishable views of the public good). Rullus may have called himself a *popularis*; Cicero's answer was that *he* was himself the true *popularis*, Rullus not at all. (In the trial of Rabirius, the strategy against Labienus was in essence the same.) At least from the Rostra – which is most of what the Roman People saw – neither the opponents of Tiberius Gracchus, nor Catulus against Gabinius, nor Bibulus against Caesar, nor Cato against Trebonius even so much as suggested that their advice to the *populus* was predicated on an "optimate" policy based on a different arrangement of political ends and means from those of the "popular" advocates of a bill. Rather, the strategy was always to invoke against one's *popularis* opponent the equally *popularis* (or rather, universally Republican) ideal of freedom – freedom from the sort of tyrannical domination (*regnum*) that supposedly lurked behind the fair face of "false" *populares*. Usurping the honorable title of "People's Man," either explicitly (as does Cicero in the agrarian speeches) or implicitly, they sought to appropriate to themselves the great ideological power of the *true* Friend of the People. This is obviously consistent, too, with the "silencing effect" noted in the last chapter and the overwhelmingly *popularis* character of contional debates. There was, it seems, virtually no place on the Rostra for ideological bifurcation. To the extent that one resorted willingly to the *contio* in the late Republic, one did so as a *popularis*;[9] and if unwillingly, then one still did not openly espouse any alternative to being *popularis*.

There is ideology in play here, and there is certainly also competition; but that does not necessarily produce ideological competition. On the contrary, an alternative thesis suggests itself, as follows. In the fully public sphere – that is, the *contio*, where members of the élite confronted the mass, not in less open or even closed sites of élite discourse such as literature, philosophy, private correspondence, senatorial or forensic speeches[10] – there was, in fact, no *overt*, fundamental clash of political ideology but rather a contest

---

[9] "A speech to the people was therefore almost by definition 'popular'" (Mouritsen 2001: 14, with a good discussion at pp. 8–14).

[10] For the exclusion of the public from direct observation of meetings of the Senate, see pp. 246ff. below. Forensic speeches are of course a special, "blended" category, since unlike senatorial orations they were delivered in the open air in the Forum, and a *corona* of ordinary (?) citizens surrounding the tribunal and the primary audience of jurors constituted a secondary audience which might have some influence upon a speaker's performance (most notably at the trial of Milo in 52: chap. 4,

between individuals' claims to embody paternalistic ideals of solicitude for the People and their interests on which all *ostensibly* agreed. Seen from the perspective of the People, gathered around the Rostra, the question before them was not, "Do I agree with this *popularis* in favor of agrarian distribution (or grain subsidies, etc.), or that 'optimate' against it?," but "Is the proposer of this agrarian (or frumentary, etc.) law really championing our interests, as he avows, or is he rather pursuing some private benefit for himself or someone else behind the scenes?" The competition – at least the one the People were invited to judge – was one between rhetorico-political personae that constituted credibility and authority rather than one between ideas to which all, at least in public, made obeisance. Hence the emphasis in contional rhetoric on themes of deception and privileged knowledge, of obligation, gratitude, and self-sacrifice, which, in the absence of any acknowledged ideological dichotomy, produced the crucial "evidence" with which to distinguish between the opposing claims to credibility.

CICERO *POPULARIS*: A "PLEBS'-EYE VIEW"

Cicero's characterization of himself near the beginning of the second speech against Rullus as a *consul popularis*, an enthusiastic standard-bearer for any agrarian bill that advanced the People's interests, evokes puzzlement and consternation in the modern reader who is aware of his real views on such matters as they are expressed in his less public writings and speeches.[11] In those works, written for a different audience, the *popularis* or rather the "so-called *popularis*" (for he will not concede to him any real dedication to the People's good), is uncompromisingly denounced as a demagogue, seeking power for himself and dividing the Republic against itself by dangling largesse plundered from the treasury before a duped citizenry; he is not simply pursuing alternative political goals, he is morally diseased

---

n. 159) and thus perhaps even on what he said or how he said it (cf. Cic. *Flac.* 66: *sic submissa voce agam tantum ut iudices audiant*). While the forensic speaker might seek to "play to the crowd" for the pressure it could exert on jurors (as Cicero accuses D. Laelius of doing against Flaccus: *Flac.* 69: *a iudicibus oratio avertitur, vox in coronam turbamque effunditur*; the Milo case is again illustrative: see Munatius' exhortation to the populace, Asc. 40 C), and his opponent might try to stiffen the jurors by characterizing any hostile element among the *corona* as a mob of foreigners and slaves (as does Cicero in the defense of both Flaccus and Milo [for the latter, *Mil.* 3]), still both knew that what ultimately counted was their effect upon the equestrian and senatorial jurors. Hence, things were said in the courts that could never be said in a *contio* (much of the *pro Milone*, for instance, or the defense of the "optimate" way of life in *Sest.* 96–143, which was, be it noted, forced on him by the invidious question put by the prosecution [§96]; note also the conceptual opposition between *contio* and *iudicium* that underlies much of the *pro Cluentio*: e.g. §§2–5, with Riggsby 1999: 72–77).

[11] For appropriation of the title *popularis* in *De lege agraria* 2, see §§6–16, and further above, pp. 194–95.

(*improbus, perditus*), driven by madness (*furor*) and brazen criminality (*audacia*).[12] Scholars often deplore the orator's insincerity, cynicism, inverted demagogy in the *contiones* against Rullus – but fail to come fully to grips with the problem of how and why such an extraordinarily disingenuous strategy could have worked. There is a tendency to depreciate its significance, perhaps on the assumption that its insincerity or artificiality would have been easily detected. On the contrary: if Cicero chose this framework for his published models of popular persuasion we must proceed on the assumption that he thought it effective rhetoric – indeed, the sort of rhetoric that conduced to his actual success.[13] How such a claim could actually be made before the People and what the implications are of such successful ideological appropriation are the questions to ask here.

Let us therefore perform a kind of thought-experiment. Stripping away the evidence that is regularly mined by those reconstructing Cicero's "real" political views but was (practically speaking) inaccessible to the ordinary citizen, and focusing our attention on his fully public words, his *contiones*, let us try to sketch a "plebs'-eye view" of Cicero.[14] It will be seen that the meeting-going citizen's picture of Cicero's political views will have differed significantly from that which prevails among modern scholars, and that the difference is due, essentially, to the availability to us, but not to the contional audience, of information from various sources (letters, essays, senatorial speeches) that will not have been well known, or known at all, outside élite circles. The misleadingly partial view of himself that Cicero presented to the *populus Romanus* at the Rostra corresponds exactly to the misleadingly partial view of senatorial political principles revealed in the "debates" that were scrutinized in the last chapter, corroborating the hypothesis that the most salient and pressing issue for listeners, that is potential voters, in public meetings was not one of ideas but of men: specifically, their *true* moral character and fidelity to the "popular" principles to which all who sought to play the game of the *contio* expressed undying devotion.

I start with a brief review of Cicero's public persona in the late 60s, around the time of the speeches *On the Agrarian Law*, as it might have

---

[12] The central texts are *Off.* 2.72–85 (with Dyck 1996, ad loc.) and *Sest.* 96–143. Especially illuminating is Achard 1981: esp. 186–355, a comprehensive delineation of the structure of Cicero's political thought as it is expressed in his "optimate" speeches (thus, generally excluding or subordinating the *contiones*). Among the many modern discussions of Cicero's objections to *popularis* politics, I have also found particularly useful: Mitchell 1979: 196–205, and 1991: 9–62; Perelli 1982: 25–45, and 1990: 53–91; Seager 1972a; Wood 1988: 193–99.

[13] Chap. 5, n. 141.

[14] See above, n. 10. For the care taken by Cicero to make his published orations reflect the differing implied audiences, see pp. 27ff.

appeared to those who frequented the Rostra. During his campaign in 64 for the consulship, Cicero had the urban plebs "and those who control the *contiones*" behind him because of his support for Pompey's *dignitas* (doubtless by speaking for the Manilian law of 66), his promise to undertake the defense of the tribune C. Manilius in response to popular pressure (whatever his eventual, actual role in the trial), and his advocacy for the ex-tribune C. Cornelius.[15] Cicero had been "*popularis* at least in speeches in *contiones* or the courts," which, in the view of the author of the *Handbook on Electioneering* (probably Cicero's brother Quintus), encouraged the urban masses to believe that he would be friendly to its interests.[16] His subsequent election as a "new man" in the consulship created a presumption in favor of the idea that he was the People's candidate against the jealous exclusivity of the nobility and therefore bound to defend their interests and to justify their choice: he could hardly *but* be *popularis*, Cicero asserts, not only as consul but for the rest of his life.[17]

What about after Cicero took his stand in 63 against that year's agrarian and debt agitation, along with the "Catilinarian" conspiracy? A common view is that Cicero laid aside the mask, "frankly declared his optimate principles," became a "champion of senatorial authority," and ended his insincere flirtation with the *popularis* line, after which point he was discredited in the eyes of the urban plebs.[18] One scholar even suggests that the *plebecula* ceased to come to Cicero's public speeches after he had proved himself far from *popularis* in 63, so that his *contiones* become more "optimate" thereafter as his audience, by self-selection, underwent a corresponding change.[19] The

---

[15] Q. Cicero (?), *Comment. pet.* 51. On *qui contiones tenent* see above, chap. 4, n. 74. On Cicero's public profession of support for Manilius in 66, see pp. 167–68. For cultivating public favor in the *Comment. pet.*, see Morstein-Marx 1998.

[16] Q. Cicero (?), *Comment. pop.* 53: *multitudo* [*existimet*] *ex eo quod dumtaxat oratione in contionibus ac iudicio popularis fuisti te a suis commodis non alienum futurum.* On the authenticity of the work see Nardo 1970; see now Morstein-Marx 1998: 260–61.

[17] Cic. *Leg. agr.* 2.1–7, esp. 7: *Neque enim ullo modo facere possum ut, cum me intellegam non hominum potentium studio, non excellentibus gratiis paucorum, sed universi populi Romani iudicio consulem ita factum ut nobilissimis hominibus longe praeponerer, non et in hoc magistratu et in omni vita essem popularis.* Clark's emendation in the OCT of *essem* to *esse* <*videar*>, in order to avoid a slightly irregular use of secondary sequence, introduces precisely the wrong tone here of potential dissimulation. As Andrew Dyck points out to me, the attraction into secondary sequence is in fact defensible (cf. Kühner and Stegmann 1974–76: II.2.195): so Marek's Teubner, who prints the text given above, following C. F. W. Müller.

[18] Brunt 1988: 334, 377, 478. Mitchell 1979: 107–76 minimizes Cicero's exploitation of *popularis* associations before 63; but for present purposes what matters is not whether the oligarchy thought him dangerous but whether the plebs saw him as a plausible "friend."

[19] Achard 1981: 28–29. I reject Achard's view (29–30) that the published versions of Cicero's *contiones* were also more "optimate" than what was delivered, on the grounds that the reading public was "optimate." He is immediately obliged to make special allowance for *Leg. agr.* 2–3

fact is, however, that no such drastic change in Cicero's standing with the populace is apparent from the evidence. Indeed, according to Sallust, once Cicero revealed the Catilinarians' plans to the plebs "they exalted him to the skies" as one who had rescued them from slavery; we should note that the very acceptance by the urban populace of his version of the conspirators' objectives depended on his credibility with themselves.[20] There were popular demonstrations in favor of Cicero as well as against him during the invidious campaign unleashed by the tribunes Metellus Nepos and Calpurnius Bestia at the end of 63: one audience, prompted by Cato, pronounced him "Father of his Country."[21] In 61, Cicero was convinced that he continued to be much favored by the urban plebs because of Pompey's special esteem for him.[22]

But perhaps most noteworthy, given the point of departure here – Cicero's demarche against the agrarian bill of 63 – is his public attitude toward a major land proposal three years later, and the People's response to him in turn. In 60 Pompey, looking to reward the veterans of his eastern campaigns, prompted the tribune L. Flavius to revive the cause of agrarian distribution.[23] If Cicero had clearly compromised himself in 63 with regard to *popularis* principles in general and agrarian legislation in particular, we should expect both that he would be treated as a patent opponent of the Flavian bill and that the public reaction to him would be overwhelmingly hostile. Both expectations, however, are defied by a close reading of the portion of a letter to Atticus that relates to the matter. It is necessary to quote the relevant section in full.[24]

This is the state of affairs in Rome: with Pompey's backing, Flavius, the tribune of the plebs, has been strongly pushing a land bill that had nothing "popular" except its backer.[25] With the approval of a public meeting [*contio*] I proposed that everything be struck from the bill that was to the disadvantage of private property-holders.

("très démagogique"); but if he wanted to leave those speeches as models of effective demagogy (see chap. 5, n. 141), why would he have shied away from this project when publishing his other *contiones*?

[20] Sall. *Cat.* 48.1: *coniuratione patefacta* [doubtless, as commentators have noted, by means of the *contio* published as the *Third Catilinarian*: McGushin 1977 ad loc.] . . . *mutata mente Catilinae consilia execrari, Ciceronem ad caelum tollere: veluti ex servitute erepta gaudium atque laetitiam agitabat.*

[21] Chap. 4, n. 136.   [22] Cic. *Att.* 1.16.11.

[23] On the bill in its context, see Gruen 1974: 396–97; Flach 1990: 76–78.   [24] Cic. *Att.* 1.19.4.

[25] *Agraria lex a Flavio tribuno pl. vehementer agitabatur auctore Pompeio, quae nihil populare habebat praeter auctorem.* Despite Shackleton Bailey 1965–67: 1.336, the transmitted *auctorem* ["backer"], referring back to the just-mentioned popular hero, Pompey, does not call for emendation to *actorem* ["mover"], referring to Flavius. *Auctorem* hardly "ruins" the point, as one may judge by replacing the word in question with *Pompeium.* Nor is this quite tantamount to calling Pompey "a" *popularis*; rather, his backing is a *popularis* feature of the *law.* See Badian 1977; Shackleton Bailey has himself gone back and forth on this (cf. the 1987 Teubner and 1999 Loeb). *Pace* Shackleton Bailey

I was for exempting the land that had been public in the consulship of P. Mucius and L. Calpurnius [133 BC], confirming the holdings of the Sullan grantees, and keeping the people of Volaterrae and Arretium, whose land Sulla had confiscated but not distributed, in possession. The one provision I did not reject was that land be bought with the windfall that is to be collected over the next five years from the new revenues. The Senate was opposed to this entire agrarian plan, suspecting that some novel position of power was being sought for Pompey; certainly he had set his mind to pushing the law through. But with the warm thanks of the landholders I strove for confirmation of all private property. For that is my army: the wealthy, as you well know.[26] At any rate, by means of my support for purchase I met the People and Pompey halfway (for I also wanted to do this). I felt that if this was carefully carried out, both the dregs of Rome could be drained off and the desolate parts of Italy could be peopled.

Cicero's strenuous, yet rhetorically subtle, attempt to reassure his opulent friend, very much a member of his "army of the well-to-do," about his flirtation with an agrarian proposal against the will of the Senate, has given the wrong impression.[27] He refers to his own provisos that anything that tampers with private-property rights should be removed from the bill, that the land that was public in 133 BC (in the first instance therefore the Campanian *ager publicus*) be exempted, and that the rights of possession that go back to Sulla be confirmed. Yet what he lets drop as the "one provision I did not reject" is in fact the foundation of the plan: to purchase lands, using the expected new revenues from Pompey's conquests, for distribution to the poor, "the dregs of Rome." He makes clear that despite his quibbles approval of this point was tantamount to approval of the plan, for thereby he satisfied both Pompey and the People ("for I also wanted to do this"); we should note that even his requests for minor alterations met a *favorable*

1965–67: 1.337, *refrixerat*, though itself an epistolary tense, suggests by its meaning that the preceding imperfects are not.

[26] *Ego autem magna cum agrariorum gratia confirmabam omnium privatorum possessiones; is enim est noster exercitus, hominum, ut tute scis, locupletium.* Here the context strongly suggests that *agrarii* must be those who already possess land, as often (*OLD*, s.v. 1), not, as Shackleton Bailey insists, "prospective colonists," which leads to the paradox and ellipsis discussed in his commentary. The objection that *"agrariorum* could not point to the same group as *privatorum"* seems to me invalid, since the two terms have different meanings and *privatorum possessiones* is in any case a phrase for "private property" (cf. Cic. *Leg. agr.* 3.3; cf. also 2.15: *privatorum pecunias augeri, publicas exhauriri*).

[27] Note how Cicero protests at the outset that there was "nothing 'popular' about it except its backer." The assertion about the lack of popular support is highly paradoxical in view of Dio 37.50.1, as Shackleton Bailey points out; I would explain this as due to Cicero's desire to assuage the qualms of his addressee rather than as mere "wishful thinking." Consider also the tone of reassurance in *ego autem magna cum agrariorum gratia confirmabam omnium privatorum possessiones; is enim est noster exercitus, hominum, ut tute scis, locupletium.* It looks as though Cicero's protestations did not completely mollify his friend: Cic. *Att.* 2.1.6–7.

response from the audience at the *contio* where he delivered them. He also has to acknowledge that the Senate was set against it. In sum, at this *contio* (if not before) he had emerged publicly as a *supporter* of an agrarian proposal that was attractive to the People, and strongly disapproved of by the Senate, even in the form he advocated (i.e., modified, or interpreted, so as not to interfere with property rights). It does not matter for present purposes that Cicero was at this time cultivating Pompey;[28] what the People saw, they liked. It becomes rather less surprising that later in the year Cicero learned that Caesar actually expected him to lend his support to the agrarian bill being planned for 59.[29] I could continue with further signs of Cicero's "popularity" after 60,[30] but enough has been said to establish the present point: that despite what *we* happen to know about Cicero's real views on the measures typically pursued by *populares* (for agrarian distribution, for example),[31] he was surprisingly able for the most part to maintain before the urban populace the image of one who was friendly to these goals, and thus consistent with his declarations, so blatantly hypocritical to *us*, in the second and third orations against Rullus.

What Cicero said to the People in his appearances on the Rostra is worth particularly close attention. Here we may broaden the chronological purview somewhat in order to make full use of the evidence, that is, the published versions of nine orations delivered by Cicero to the People in public meetings between 66 and 43 BC.[32] A brief review of some of the ways in which Cicero rhetorically establishes his *popularis* credentials will show how strong a "family resemblance" the sentiments and ideas he expresses in his *contiones* exhibit with what are frequently taken to be the mainstays of a "*popularis* ideology."[33] The *popularis*/"optimate" dichotomy is persistently occluded or deconstructed by Cicero in his speeches to the mass public, thus raising the question whether it has any real meaning in this context – and correspondingly highlighting, by contrast, the real choice with which audiences of contional debates were confronted: whom to trust as their authentic, rather than feigned, standard-bearer.

---

[28] Alliance with Pompey: Cic. *Att.* 1.16.11, 17.10, 18.6; 2.1.6–7. Note Atticus' disapproval. Much to Cicero's relief, presumably, the bill lost its momentum during a war scare in Gaul (*sed haec tota res interpellata bello refrixerat*) and in the face of Metellus Celer's determined opposition, Pompey dropped the matter (Cass. Dio 37.50.5).

[29] Cic. *Att.* 2.3.3.

[30] See above, p. 145 on Cicero's reception after his return in 57. The popular reaction against him at the beginning of 58 stands out as exceptional, and might be attributed to Clodius' successful exploitation of the sort of tactics studied in chap. 4. The plebs' hostility to Cicero in 52 was provoked by a specific offense of that year – his defense of Milo (Asc. 37 C) – and may be balanced against his effective demogogic leadership in 44–43 (*Phil.* 4, 6; *Fam.* 12.4.1).

[31] See chap. 5, n. 144.   [32] Above, pp. 24–25.   [33] See above, nn. 1 and 8.

The word *optimas* does not even cross Cicero's lips in a *contio*. It appears to have had a divisive and invidious ring to it even among the élite, for Cicero generally avoids using it before senatorial and equestrian audiences: the famous excursus on "optimate" politics in the *Defense of Sestius* (a judicial speech, not a *contio*) was forced on Cicero by the opposing counsel, M. Albinovanus, who had posed an invidious question about the identity of "the tribe of optimates."[34] But there is a more fundamental reason why no politician regarded by scholars as "optimate" is known to have so much as acknowledged the fact in a speech before the People: if the term *optimas* implied anything, it implied subordination of popular to senatorial decision-making – a view not likely to win applause around the Rostra! On the other hand, despite his many bitter attacks on actual *populares* in his political essays and speeches before élite audiences, Cicero regularly appropriates that title to himself whenever he publicly opposes an apparent or self-proclaimed *popularis*, whether speaking *in contione*, in the courts, or even in the Senate.[35] It was impossible for a senator in any public forum to concede that one was not guided by the "real" interests of the "true" People, however misguided (or worse) the motley mobs might be that were gathered by the "false," self-proclaimed *populares*.

Drawing a distinction between the "true" *popularis*, who serves the People's interests, and the "supposed" *popularis*, who masks his lust for domination under populist proposals, rhetoric, and symbols, Cicero relentlessly carves out a place for himself in the former category and thrusts his opponent into the latter. In the speeches against Rullus, he stakes his own claim in various ways: his election in the face of a resentful nobility;[36] his (supposed) approval of any law, including a plan for agrarian redistribution, that would increase the benefits and privileges (*commoda*) of the People;[37] his pious invocation of the Gracchi;[38] his (fictive) stance as a defender of the current popular champion, Pompey, against insidious attack;[39]

---

[34] *Natio optimatium*: *Sest.* 96. See Hellegouarc'h 1963: 503–4; Achard 1981: 61–62, 372. In *Har. resp.* Cicero is obliged by the haruspices' use of the word (§40) to discuss it. Note that here he treats it as equivalent to *principes* (§§45, 53, 55).

[35] See p. 148 with n. 152, and below, n. 163. On the commonplace of dissimulation by alleged *populares*, see below.

[36] Above, n. 17.

[37] Cic. *Leg. agr.* 2.10–12. *Commoda*: §§7, 17, 71, 77, 78 (cf. 12 [*utilis plebi Romanae*], 22 [*populi utilitatem et fructum*]); *Leg. agr.* 3.3. On the *commoda populi Romani*, see further below.

[38] Gracchi: see below, n. 50. Note also his respectful reference to Cn. Domitius Ahenobarbus (tr. pl. 104), responsible for the *popularis* innovation of popular election for priests (*Leg. agr.* 2.18–19).

[39] See esp. *Leg. agr.* 2.23–25 (§25: *non eos in primis id acturos ut ex omni custodia vestrae libertatis, ex omni potestate, curatione, patrocinio vestrorum commodorum Cn. Pompeius depelleretur?*), 49–50. On the emptiness of the Pompey theme, see above, chap. 5, n. 145.

his (professed) hostility to the memory of Sulla and the *Sullani possessores*;[40] his unwavering defense of the *libertas* of the Roman People against a faction seeking to overthrow it;[41] and, not least, his avowals of deference to the People's "wisdom" and "authority."[42] In a similarly difficult case later in the year, the trial of C. Rabirius – which probed at its sensitive core the fundamental civil right of *provocatio* – Cicero again was called upon to resist a highly "popular" cause pressed by an ostentatiously *popularis* tribune, T. Labienus.[43] Cicero again fashions himself as the true heir of the *popularis* tradition, this time (a nice paradox) by standing firm for the protection of the citizen from tyrannical cruelty and arbitrary magisterial punishment, an essential part of the freedom of the Roman People founded on "popular" laws – above all that of C. Gracchus, whom Cicero invokes at length as his own moral exemplar, and whose honorable legacy, he claims, Labienus had betrayed.[44] An indignant outburst in defense of the memory of Marius, the enemy of Sulla – "truly the father of our country, I say, the founder of your freedom and of this very Commonwealth,"[45] reverential words for the People's power and wisdom,[46] and the representation of his own purpose in the case as the preservation of "freedom," "security," and resistance to the "assault against your majesty" and the Republic itself[47] all serve further to ground Cicero's credibility among the populace. Quite striking is the way in which Cicero reverses the roles of consul and tribune in this speech, donning a tribunician persona by associating himself both subtly and explicitly with civic freedom, clemency, and the rule of law in

---

[40] *Leg. agr.* 2.68–72, 81, 98; 3.3–14. See above, p. 112.

[41] See below, pp. 217–22. For the implicit identification of the "faction," see below, pp. 215–16 and pp. 218–19.

[42] *Leg. agr.* 2.7: *Sed mihi ad huius verbi* [sc. *"popularis"*] *vim et interpretationem vehementer opus est vestra sapientia*; 16: *si falsa vobis videbuntur esse, sequar auctoritatem vestram, mutabo meam sententiam.* For the People's wisdom and authority, see below, nn. 91, 92.

[43] Cicero himself looks back on the speech as one in which he defended *senatus auctoritatem . . . contra invidiam* (*Pis.* 4).

[44] *Rab. perd.* 10–13, esp. §10: *Quam ob rem uter nostrum tandem, Labiene, popularis est, tune qui civibus Romanis in contione ipsa carnificem . . . qui in campo Martio comitiis centuriatis auspicato in loco crucem ad civium supplicium defigi et constitui iubes, an ego qui funestari contionem contagione carnificis veto, qui expiandum forum populi Romani ab illis nefarii sceleris vestigiis esse dico, qui castam contionem, sanctum campum, inviolatum corpus omnium civium Romanorum, integrum ius libertatis defendo servari oportere?* Cf. §§15–17. On Gracchus, see §§12–15, and below, n. 50. It misses the point to declare that Cicero's self-presentation as *popularis* is "ironical" (so Tyrrell 1978: 75–76).

[45] *Rab. perd.* 27. See below, n. 52.

[46] *Rab. perd.* 5: *vos, Quirites, quorum potestas proxime ad deorum immortalium numen accedit, oro atque obsecro . . . adhibeatis in hominis fortunis misericordiam, in rei publicae salute sapientiam quam soletis.*

[47] *Rab. perd.* 34; 35: *quoniam . . . accusatio perniciosa, iudicium acerbum, res tota a tribuno pl. suscepta contra rem publicam, non vos ad arma vocandos esse, verum ad suffragia cohortandos* contra oppugnationem vestrae maiestatis *putavi. Populi Romani maiestas*: cf. §20: perhaps Cicero's own ingratiating modification of the wording of the "Final Decree."

opposition to the ostensible arbitrariness, cruelty, and lust for domination shown by the prosecuting tribune-tyrant.[48]

With such references and phrases, Cicero signalled to a contional audience that he deserved credence as a devoted custodian of their interests. The attitude Cicero takes toward heroes of the plebs must have been a particularly clear token of this kind. In his début speech on the Rostra, in 66, Cicero immediately constructs himself before the People as the successor to those who had been "defending your cause" on the orator's platform: implicitly, at this moment, the *popularis* tribunes A. Gabinius and C. Cornelius. His ostensibly gratuitous defence of the rights and honor of the author of the *Lex Gabinia* reinforces the point.[49] Later, in the two speeches in which he most labors to counteract the *popularis* appeal of his adversaries, his pious references to the Gracchi brothers and his invidious contrasts between their actions and those of his own "pseudo-popular" opponents, indicate clearly how such name-dropping defined the rhetorical *ethos* of the speaker for the popular audience. "I am not the common run of consul, who thinks it an abomination to praise the Gracchi," those men "who dearly loved the Roman plebs" (*amantissimi plebis Romanae*). Cicero commends the "plans, wisdom, and laws" of the Gracchi, explicitly including their distribution of public land to the plebs; he cites the "generosity" of both brothers and their commitment to the interests of the Roman People; he stresses Tiberius' "fairness and restraint," and recalls how deeply he is mourned among the Roman People; he sets Gaius up as a model of justice, possessing in addition a series of other virtues such as "familial devotion," "wisdom," and "authority" beyond all other men.[50] Such partisan comments – against a kind of consular taboo, Cicero claims – serve to "show" that his attacks against an ostensibly *popularis* agrarian proposal or a highly "popular" tribunician prosecution (and in that context in effect against the memory of a popular hero of the past, Saturninus) are not founded on anti-*popularis* sentiment. On the contrary, these are expressions of allegiance to the People's cause, and attempt to assure the audience that despite superficial appearances no ideological gap in fact separates them from the speaker. Such is the function, too, of Cicero's pose in the anti-Rullan *contiones* as the defender of Pompey's dignity against the attack of Rullus and a shadowy group of *Sullani*, a notion that "had its origin solely in Cicero's fertile and inventive

---

[48] An excellent observation of Tyrrell 1973: 295–97.
[49] Cic. *Leg. Man.* 2: *neque hic locus vacuus fuit umquam ab eis qui vestram causam defenderent.* Gabinius: below, n. 97.
[50] Cic. *Leg. agr.* 2.10 (emending, with Baiter, the MSS *plebi* to *plebis*, as Ciceronian usage seems to require), 31, 81; *Rab. perd.* 14–15. See Robinson 1994; Béranger 1972, a nuanced survey of Cicero's comments on the Gracchi in all contexts, well shows how disingenuous he is being here.

brain" but had some plausibility after his public advocacy of the Manilian Law over the objections of the pillars of the Sullan oligarchy, Catulus and Hortensius.[51] His various tributes to the memory of C. Marius, the third founder of Rome and enemy of the hated Sulla, work in a similar way.[52]

No less surprising than Cicero's praise of the Gracchi to one familiar with his real views on *popularis* heroes is the remarkable moderation with which he speaks of his personal enemy Clodius in the speech to the People delivered upon his return from exile in 57 – an injury inflicted on him by precisely that man. An aggressive attack on his popular enemy would have risked angry outbursts, would certainly have interfered with his primary message of loyalty to the People (who had, after all, also passed the legislation that sent Cicero into exile), and no doubt have raised suspicions that he was going to use their benefaction in restoring him to pursue a private, élite vendetta. So the few words Cicero directs at his chief enemy are remarkably mild. Clodius is portrayed as having "lent his voice to the common enemies of all for my destruction," these being a rear guard of the "Catilinarians" who hated Cicero for having saved the Republic in 63.[53] The real source of the attack, then, is elsewhere, and Clodius' error – for he is never branded a "criminal," an "enemy within" driven by violence and madness, as he is in the corresponding senatorial speech – is one of complicity rather than direct agency; perhaps it is suggested that he had allowed merely personal hostility toward Cicero to go too far, aligning himself with the enemies of the Republic as a whole because of his own private enmity.[54] Cicero, on the other hand, rejects the precedent of his great predecessor, Marius, in this one way: he will not settle his scores in blood, but only with words

---

[51] The quotation is from Sumner 1966: 578, in reference to "the ingenious 'anti-Pompey' theory." On the *Sullani*, see below. Plausibility: Q. Cicero (?), *Comment. pet.* 51; cf. *Leg. agr.* 2.49; *Leg. Man.* 59–68; cf. below, p. 218.

[52] Marius: *Rab. perd.* 27–30; *Red. pop.* 7, 9–10, 19–20. "Third Founder": Plut. *Mar.* 27.5; cf. Cic. *Rab. perd.* 27. For Marius' stature as a popular hero in the mid-sixties, note especially Plut. *Caes.* 6 and above, pp. 110ff. The difference between the *Red. pop.* and the *Red. sen.* (cf. §38) in the treatment of Marius is a clear indication of the esteem in which the victor over the Germans was still held among the citizenry: Mack 1937: 26–27, 30–31.

[53] *Red. pop.* 10: *ad meam perniciem vocem suam communibus hostibus praebuisset*, 13, 21. Cf. the phrase *domestici hostes* at §13, used repeatedly of the conspirators in the *Third Catilinarian* (14, 22, 28). Clodius is never explicitly named in either speech (and the consuls Gabinius and Piso, only once, in the Senate), but this is not in the first instance evidence of tact or circumspection (Nicholson 1992: 95–96): in general one sought to deny one's enemy the status, dignity, and even power accorded by a name (cf. Vittinghoff 1936: 19–20, 23–24).

[54] For contrast, note *Red. sen.* 19: *sceleratum civem aut domesticum potius hostem*, marked by *vis, audacia, furor, temeritas*, and *manus* (cf. §3 *scelere*); direct mention of Clodius' agency at 4 and 19, with characterization of the law as intended to raise the "Catilinarian" conspirators from the dead. Similarly, the crimes of the consuls Gabinius and Piso are characterized as essentially "active" in the senatorial speech, "passive" in the popular one (Mack 1937: 34).

and patriotic policy.[55] The absence of personal invective in the popular speech, sharply contrasting with Cicero's acrid salvoes before the Senate against the consuls of 57, reinforces the point.[56] Cicero's ostentatious self-restraint in the matter of vengeance "proves" his neglect of his own interest in favor of that of the Roman People, among whom aristocratic feuding will have seemed at best a distraction irrelevant to the public interest, at worst a troubling harbinger of bloodshed for a populace that well remembered Sulla and Marius.[57] All of this serves to consolidate the guiding theme of this speech: Cicero's complete personal subordination to the People, to whom he owes everything in exchange for his rebirth from civic extinction.[58] On Cicero's day of triumph and vindication over his *popularis* opponent, there is nothing here that marks the "optimate" or indeed exposes any ideological division at all in the fully public sphere of the *contio*.

Turning to a review of some of the political ideas that Cicero expresses in his *contiones*, we should be struck by how plausibly he mouths the central "popular" slogans and catchwords. "The Freedom of the Roman People," *libertas populi Romani*, is frequently seen as the central *popularis* slogan, repeatedly invoked, as for example by Sallust's tribunes, C. Memmius and C. Licinius Macer, against the domination of an oligarchy and in defense of the rights and powers of the People.[59] But so does Cicero: *libertas* is the keynote of the second speech against Rullus, where the word appears twenty-two times.[60] Crying out his warning that Rullus and his co-conspirators are dangling land grants before the People while snatching away their freedom and establishing tyrants in their midst, Cicero reminds

---

[55] *Red. pop.* 20–21.

[56] *Red. sen.* 10–18. Mack 1937: 32–34; Nicholson 1992: 152, n. 168, with 90–97.

[57] See above, pp. 110ff; cf. Nicholson 1992: 44–45, 108. For peace as a popular "good," contrary to Sallust's nasty characterization of the sentiments of the plebs (chap. 3, n. 1), see also Cic. *Leg. agr.* 2.9, 102 (*pacem, tranquillitatem, otium*); *Cat.* 2.28; 3.1–2; 3.23–29; for a tribune's denunciation of the *potentium inimicitiae*, see Sall. *Hist.* 3.48.27 (cf. §11).

[58] *Red. pop.* 21–24, sealed with a majestic oath; cf. 1–8.

[59] Sall. *Iug.* 31, esp. 4–5, 16–17; *Hist.* 3.48, esp. 1–4. On *libertas* as a key element in popular ideology, see especially Brunt 1988: 330–50; see also Wirszubski 1960: 40–96; Hellegouarc'h 1963: 551–58; Meier 1965: 594–98; Bleicken 1972: esp. 34–48; Perelli 1982: 48–49; Ferrary 1982: 755–66; Vanderbroeck 1987: 105–8; Laser 1997: 153–58; Mouritsen 2001: 8–13. While some (e.g. Wirszubski) give equal emphasis to the "optimate"/senatorial uses of the same catchword, there is a tendency among others to define it as essentially *popularis*, and thus only cynically manipulated by *optimates* (see, for example, Seager 1972a: 333–38; Brunt, pp. 56, 331, 345; Perelli 1990: 75–76). For the specifically Ciceronian doctrine of *libertas* in essays and non-contional speeches, partly oriented against the alleged threat to *libertas* posed by *populares*, see especially Hellegouarc'h, pp. 560–63; Achard 1981: 316–23, 455–60; Perelli 1990: 69–91.

[60] In addition to the passages quoted below, see *Leg. agr.* 2.9, 15–17, 20, 24–25, 29, 71, 75, 102; 3.16. It is illuminating to note how much more the theme is emphasized in the *Second Oration* than in the extant portion of the *First Oration*, delivered before the Senate: Classen 1985: 331.Cf. Thompson 1978: 28–46.

one of the Sallustian tribune Macer's warning that a recent revival of grain distributions was only a "trap" to divert the People from their proper aim of restoring the power of the tribunate.[61] The consul further assimilates himself to the rhetorical tradition of tribunician denunciation by his use of the invidious word *pauci*, essentially "oligarchs." Sallust's *popularis* tribunes never tire of warning the People about the "slavery" imposed upon them by a narrow, exclusive clique among the nobility seeking domination of the State. There, the enemies of freedom are the *factio* ("clique," almost "conspiracy") of the *pauci* and *potentes* ("powerful") – terms which function as cues of a highly pejorative concept of illegitimate power resting on personal resources and conspiracy rather than on legal rights and public approval.[62] In Cicero's *contiones* on the Rullan land bill, he uses *pauci* to designate the powerful men who lurk behind the tribune, preparing to seize the patrimony of the Roman People and make themselves tyrants.[63] Indeed, his insinuations strongly hint that these men are precisely the sort of men whom Sallust's *popularis* orators denounce: the leaders of the Sullan oligarchy.[64] They are Sullan partisans, the sort of men "for whom political office, powers, and riches are habitually won by violence and discord between citizens," possessors of large tracts of land seized in the proscriptions and handed out by that tyrant; indeed, they are the very people who make a habit of complaining bitterly that the lands and seas have been handed over to Pompey – an allusion to the controversies over the *lex Gabinia* and *lex Manilia* that must immediately have brought to mind Catulus and Hortensius, the leaders of the opposition to both laws.[65] The whole purpose of the

---

[61] Cic. *Leg. agr.* 2.15: *ostentari populo Romano agros, eripi etiam libertatem . . . denique, quod est indignissimum, per tribunum plebis, quem maiores praesidem libertatis custodemque esse voluerunt, reges in civitate constitui.* Sall. *Hist.* 3.48.21: *Qua tamen quinis modiis libertatem omnium aestumavere, qui profecto non amplius possunt alimentis carceris . . . Cavendus dolus est; namque alio modo neque valent in univorsos neque conabuntur.* On Macer's warning, see below, pp. 253–54.

[62] *Servitus/dominatio/tyrannis*: Sall. *Iug.* 31.11, 16, 20, 22 (Memmius); *Hist.* 3.48.1, 3, 6, 9, 10, 11, 13, 19, 20, 23, 26, 28 (Macer); cf. *Hist.* 1.55.1–2, 6, 7–13, 22, 25–27 (Lepidus). *Pauci/potentes/factio*: *Iug.* 31.1–4, 19–20 (Memmius); *Hist.* 3.48.3, 6, 8, 27–28 (Macer); cf. *Hist.* 1.55.23 (Lepidus). Paul 1984: 33, 88. On the term *factio*, cf. Hellegouarc'h 1963: 100–109; Seager 1972b; Brunt 1988: 447, n. 5. *Pauci*: Hellegouarc'h, pp. 443–46.

[63] *Leg. agr.* 2.25 (*pauci homines*), 78, 82; 3.12, 13. *Certi homines* is functionally equivalent: 2.6, 15, 25, 63, 70; cf. 2.12, *privatos quosdam* in a sketch of the tribunes' "conspiratorial" activity. Cf. 2.7: *me . . . non hominum potentium studio, non excellentibus gratiis paucorum, sed universi populi Romani iudicio consulem . . . factum.* Hellegouarc'h 1963: 446, with n. 4, rightly sees that Cicero's words point invidiously toward leaders of the oligarchy; *pace* Achard 1981: 18, Cicero conspicuously does *not* suggest that the mysterious backers of the land bill are "populaires."

[64] For Sulla as the destroyer of the People's freedom: Sall. *Hist.* 1.55.1–2 (Lepidus); 3.48.1, 9 (Macer).

[65] Cic. *Leg. agr.* 2.102: *Etenim illis honores, potestates, divitiae ex tumultu atque ex dissensionibus civium comparari solent. Sullani possessores*: above, n. 40. §46 Catulus and Hortensius (see above, pp. 181ff.):

law, he declares, is to establish "the tyranny of the few" (*ad paucorum domi-nationem*).[66] When in his Catilinarian *contiones* Cicero represents Catiline's following as a chiefly aristocratic cabal seeking personal enrichment and domination in civil war,[67] or on the other occasions when he hints at the dark machinations of powerful individuals off the public stage against the People's will and interests or against their advocates like himself,[68] he is composing simple variations on the familiar invidious theme of narrowly oligarchic power detached from, and hostile to, popular control.

No less than any "real" *popularis*, Cicero too offers himself as the People's aggressive champion in the great fight for freedom. "If you find these charges false once I have presented my case, Citizens, I shall follow your lead and change my opinion; but if you come to see that under the guise of a handout a plot is being hatched against your freedom, do not hang back but defend, with the help of your consul and no effort for yourselves, that freedom won by the sweat and blood of your ancestors and handed down to you!"[69] The passage recalls the stirring exhortation with which Sallust's tribune Macer opens his great speech: "Citizens! If you were not well aware of how great the difference is between the rights you inherited from your ancestors and this slavery imposed by Sulla, I would have to give a lengthy speech and recount

---

Atque idem qui haec appetunt queri non numquam solent omnis terras Cn. Pompeio atque omnia maria esse permissa. A similar hint in their direction at §23, where "those who are orchestrating this matter" have decided not to allow all tribes to vote on the decemviri for fear that "you will entrust the job without hesitation to Cn. Pompey in the first place." Cicero's ostensible hesitation to name names, on the grounds that that would be *contumelia* (63), as well as the notion that the backers aim to make themselves decemviri under the law, insinuates that the anonymous schemers are powerful senators and are not limited to men such as Rullus' father-in-law, Valgius (69; 3.3, 8, 13–14). The old argument whether Cicero is hinting at the complicity of Crassus and Caesar is off the mark: they were not good material for kindling popular indignation.

[66] Cic. *Leg. agr.* 3.13.

[67] *Coniuratio contra rem publicam* (*Cat.* 2.6; cf. 3.3, 14, 17, 21), aiming at exclusive domination (esp. *Cat.* 2.19, 3.9). Cicero's emphasis in the *Second Catilinarian* on Catiline's supporters among the élite is a further noteworthy link with the tradition: the first two categories that Cicero enumerates encompass *locupletes* who have squandered their huge patrimonies (§18) and aristocrats prevented by their crushing debts from seeking *honores* except in civil war (§19), while his final category consists of high-living young men (§22–23; cf 5); *luxuria* has led them to crime (§§10–11); gladiators are more patriotic than some patricians (§26; cf. 3.22: *spem . . . a patriciis hominibus oblatam*). The audience must have appreciated Cicero's application to Catiline's fancy followers of an insulting phrase that the urban plebs rightly suspected was often used of them (*sentina urbis*: *Cat.* 2.7; cf. *Att.* 1.19.4; *Leg. agr.* 2.70).

[68] *Leg. Man.* 58, 70–71; *Leg. agr.* 2.5–6, 7: *me . . . non hominum potentium studio . . . consulem ita factum*; *Cat.* 3.27–29; *Red. pop.* 24 (cf. the theme of senatorial *invidia* at §§13, 21).

[69] Cic. *Leg. agr.* 2.16: *Quae cum, Quirites, exposuero, si falsa vobis videbuntur esse, sequar auctoritatem vestram, mutabo meam sententiam; sin insidias fieri libertati vestrae simulatione largitionis intellegetis, nolitote dubitare plurimo sudore et sanguine maiorum vestrorum partam vobisque traditam libertatem nullo vestro labore consule adiutore defendere.* Cf. also n. 44, for the Rabirius case.

to you how often, and for what injuries, the plebs under arms abandoned the Senate, and how they created the tribunes of the plebs as champions of all their rights; but it remains now only to call upon you and to make the first step on the road by which I think freedom is to be won!"[70] Cicero, then, appears in 63 to be capably exploiting a topic of *popularis* exhortation. But this is no once-off stab at a persona rendered increasingly implausible by the consul's actions through the rest of the year and beyond. Nineteen years later, on December 20, 44, Cicero steps forward as the protector of "your freedom," long silent of necessity but now ready to resume leadership in the People's struggle, and begins his first Philippic *contio* against Antony by defining the issue as essentially one of freedom versus servitude.[71] In the *Sixth Philippic*, delivered on January 4, 43, Cicero reminds the People of his record of service in their interest and declares that he will attend day and night to their freedom.[72] His *contio* concludes with a great encomium of *libertas*: "The Immortal Gods willed that the Roman People rule over all nations; it is against their law that the Roman People should be slaves. The ultimate crisis is upon us. The stake is freedom. Either you must be victorious, Men of Rome, as you surely will be in virtue of your patriotism and united will, or – anything but slavery! Other races can endure servitude, but the birthright of the Roman People is freedom."[73] The speech closes resoundingly on the word *libertas* – a device used elsewhere in Sallust's speeches of M. Lepidus and of Macer in the *History*.[74]

The useful versatility of the slogans of freedom in Republican Rome, which commended it equally to "popular" politicians and *optimates* in their efforts to brand their opponents as aspiring tyrants (*reges*), is well known.[75] One might even distinguish a negative, "optimate" idea of

---

[70] Sall. *Hist.* 3.48.1–2: *Si, Quirites, parum existumaretis quid inter ius a maioribus relictum vobis et hoc a Sulla paratum servitium interesset, multis mihi disserundum fuit docendique <vos> quas ob iniurias et quotiens a patribus armata plebes secessisset utique vindices paravisset omnis iuris sui tribunos plebis: nunc hortari modo relicuom est et ire primum via qua capessundam arbitror libertatem.*

[71] *Phil.* 4.1: *Frequentia vestrum incredibilis, Quirites, contioque tanta quantam meminisse non videor et alacritatem mihi summam defendendae rei publicae adfert et spem <libertatis> recuperandae. quamquam animus mihi quidem numquam defuit: tempora defuerunt, quae simul ac primum aliquid lucis ostendere visa sunt, princeps vestrae libertatis defendendae fui.* Cf. §11 and esp. §16: *me auctore et principe ad spem libertatis exarsimus.*

[72] *Phil.* 6.17: *An ego non provideam meis civibus, non dies noctesque de vestra libertate, de rei publicae salute cogitem?*

[73] *Phil.* 6.19 (trans. Shackleton Bailey): *Populum Romanum servire fas non est, quem di immortales omnibus gentibus imperare voluerunt. res in extremum est adducta discrimen; de libertate decernitur. aut vincatis oportet, Quirites, quod profecto et pietate vestra et tanta concordia consequemini, aut quidvis potius quam serviatis. aliae nationes servitutem pati possunt, populi Romani est propria libertas.*

[74] Sall. *Hist.* 1.55.27; 3.48.28. Achard 1981: 455 considers this a typical *popularis* touch.

[75] See above, n. 59. For the prominence of "freedom" in the anti-tribunician rhetoric of the (Sullan) senatorial leadership, see Sall. *Hist.* 3.48.22 (Macer): *vindices uti se ferunt libertatis.*

freedom, emphasizing prevention of any individual's personal domination of the Republic, from a more positive, *popularis* focus on fundamental civic rights (*provocatio* above all) and material benefits exploited by those who sought to enlist popular support as a counterweight against the authority of the Senate.[76] Such a distinction makes sense of the ways in which the same political idea could be invoked to support diametrically contrary actions. But it obscures the fact that in *contional speech* any hint of such a distinction appears to have been studiously suppressed. On the contrary, the figure of the *rex*, properly emphasized, tightly reunified any divided strands of the concept of freedom, since this stereotype was fundamentally as inconsistent with the citizen's Republican civil rights as it was with an aristocrat's honor. The clearest proof that Rullus and his fellow would-be tyrants offer of their hatred of freedom is their assault on the People's right of suffrage, upon which Cicero elaborates first and at great length; next there is the matter of their "tyrannical" legal powers, not least the (supposed) suspension of *provocatio*.[77] Similarly, when Q. Catulus evoked the Secessions of the Plebs in his speech against Manilius' law conferring the Mithridatic command on Pompey, crying out ostensibly to the senators (but in fact before the People) that they should flee to a mountain like their ancestors, or to some other place where freedom could be preserved, he was quite forcefully asserting the unity of the Republican *libertas*-tradition among plebs and *patres*, for he thereby implicitly identified the current "struggle for freedom" fought by himself and (ostensibly) some senators with that pursued by the plebeians when they had won their fundamental rights.[78] The anti-*regnum* appeal often used before the People against "popular" politicians does not, therefore, involve a redefinition of the common ideal of freedom in such a way that it was left empty of positive content for the ordinary citizen; and for their part *popularis* leaders made equal use of the argument when, as often, they denounced the domination of the "few," or the "tyranny" of

---

[76] This kind of distinction, echoing Isaiah Berlin, seems to underly most important treatments: see especially the magisterial essay by Brunt 1988: 281–350, esp. 327–34 (for popular hostility to *regnum*, however, see also his pp. 51–52); also Ferrary 1982: 761–67; Perelli 1990: 69–85; Vanderbroeck 1987: 105–106.

[77] Cic. *Leg. agr.* 2.17: *Hic quaero quam ob causam initium rerum ac legum suarum hinc duxerit ut populus Romanus suffragio privaretur*; see on this theme 2.16–22, 26–31. The *regia potestas* of the "tyrants" comes next (31–35); note *orbis terrarum gentiumque omnium datur cognitio sine consilio, poena sine provocatione, animadversio sine auxilio* (33). I part company from Thompson 1978: 31 *et passim* chiefly in her claim that Cicero is promoting a specifically senatorial/"optimate" idea of *libertas* in the *Leg. agr.* 2.

[78] Plut. *Pomp.* 30.4; above, p. 183. Interesting also is Cn. Lentulus Marcellinus' equation of contional shouting with freedom: Val. Max. 6.2.6 = *ORF* 128.5, p. 418 (chap. 4, n. 48). The occasion is apparently that mentioned at Cass. Dio 39.28.5 (Pina Polo 1989: 302–3, no. 317).

their opponents – such as Cicero.[79] To judge from its exploitation by all sides in the tumult of the late Republic as a "catchword" to arouse popular indignation or suspicion, *libertas* even in the specific sense of rejection of *regnum* (*dominatio, tyrannis, potentia*) was broadly embraced not merely by senators but by the general populace as well.[80]

Nor will Cicero yield to anyone in his concern for the *commoda populi Romani* (or *plebis Romanae*), the "advantages" or "benefits" of the Roman People – a vague but rhetorically powerful catch phrase generally thought to be the special preserve of *populares*.[81] These "benefits" formed a broad collection of goods, running from fundamental legal protections and voting rights to state largess (such as land grants or subsidized grain), public festivals, and enjoyment of the self-promoting generosity or vote-catching deference of ambitious senators.[82] The protection or augmentation of the *commoda populi Romani* was indeed something associated in the public mind with popular heroes, in particular the Gracchi.[83] That made it all the more important for Cicero loudly to espouse the same goal, most strikingly

---

[79] Sall. *Iug.* 31 (Memmius), esp. §§11–17 and 26: *Nam inpune quae lubet facere, id est regem esse*; *Hist.* 3.48, esp. §§1–7 (Macer); *Hist.* 1.55 (Lepidus). See also above, n. 62. Cicero: Plut. *Cic.* 23.2; Cic. *Att.* 4.2.3 (on Clodius' shrine of *Libertas* on the site of Cicero's demolished house, see *Dom.* 108, 110–12; Cass. Dio 38.17.6), *Sest.* 109; *Dom.* 75, 94; *Mil.* 12 (so too in non-contional contexts: Cic. *Att.* 1.16.10; *Sull.* 21–25; Ps.-Sall. *In Cic.* 5). Cato: Plut. *Cat. Min.* 29.1. Achard 1981: 318–19; Hellegouarc'h 1963: 560, 562–63.

[80] Brunt 1988: 51–52. Brunt explains away the wide appeal of this idea by labelling it "aristocratic ideology" uncritically accepted by the masses because they were not "capable of political or historical reflection" (p. 51).

[81] See Hellegouarc'h 1963: 556–57; Ferrary 1982: 750–55; Brunt 1988: 346–49; Vanderbroeck 1987: 106; Purcell 1994: 687.

[82] Most comprehensive is Cic. *Leg. agr.* 2.71: *Vos vero, Quirites, . . . retinete istam possessionem gratiae, libertatis, suffragiorum, dignitatis, urbis, fori, ludorum, festorum dierum, ceterorum omnium commodorum . . .* This particular list naturally emphasizes the *commoda* to be enjoyed in the city that would be diminished by emigration: *gratia, dignitas*, and *forum* must allude to the special power the voters in Rome enjoyed to demand "supplication" before elections (see Yakobson 1992 and 1999: esp. 211–25; Morstein-Marx 1998: 265–69) and the gestures of deference to its will in the *contio*, while *ludi* and *festi dies* doubtless refer in good part to enjoyment of the forward-looking beneficence of the aspiring politicians in charge of public festivals. For the link between *gratia* and *suffragia*, see Cic. *Leg.agr.* 2.17: *unus quisque studio et suffragio suo viam sibi ad beneficium impetrandum munire possit*; 102 *vos, quorum gratia in suffragiis consistit* (cf. also pp. 260ff. below). For legal protections as *commoda*, see also *Verr.* 2.5.172; voting rights, *Sest.* 103 (Cassius' *lex tabellaria*); agrarian and frumentary laws, *Sest.* 103; *Leg. agr.* 2.10–15. Note the similarity between the list of *commoda* in *Leg. agr.* 2.71 and C. Fannius' famous rhetorical question from his *dissuasio* against Gaius Gracchus' citizenship-law (*ORF* 32.3, p. 144, quoted at chap. 4, n. 46).

[83] Cic. *Leg. agr.* 2.81: *duo Gracchi qui de plebis Romanae commodis plurimum cogitaverunt*; *Sest.* 103–5 (the Gracchi and L. Cassius, tr. pl. 137, who carried the second of the secret-ballot laws); *Leg. agr.* 2.25 (Pompey). The phrase suitably appears in a fragment of C. Gracchus, *ORF* 48.44, p. 188 = Gell. *NA* 11.10.1: *ut vectigalia vestra augeatis, quo facilius vestra commoda et rem publicam administrare possitis* (cf. fr. 30: *rei publicae commoda*). *Leg. agr.* 2.7 shows that avowed *populares* claimed to be defending the *populi commoda*, while 3.3 shows that a *popularis* tribune was expected to be *vestrorum commodorum patronus*.

in his speech of thanks in 57 for the popular vote to restore him from exile: Cicero concludes with a long and solemn vow of eternal loyalty to the Roman People, ending with a promise that the "good will of my grateful heart will not fail you in increasing your benefits (*commoda*)."[84] In the speeches *On the Agrarian Law* Cicero had also repeatedly linked himself to the same tradition, not only indirectly through his praise of the Gracchi and other popular heroes but also by explicitly declaring his desire to further the *commoda populi Romani*.[85] Despite Cicero's sharp personal animosity toward *popularis* projects, this claim probably caused him no embarrassment. Even before an audience of senatorial and equestrian jurors he was prepared to declare it nothing less than the Senate's duty "to maintain and increase the freedom and benefits of the plebs"; and in his essay *On the Commonwealth* (*De re publica*) he makes clear that it was crucial to the proper functioning of the Republican system that the People should not *think* that their *commoda* were neglected by their leaders.[86] This paternalistic notion of the Senate's custodial responsibility was nothing less than standard Republican "theory," not the property of any political sect but shared (ostensibly) by senators and People alike.[87] While speaking before the People, Cicero had only to omit those key provisos that the *commodum populi* might sometimes be contrary to the utility of the Republic, or that the People's good was not necessarily the same as their wishes.[88]

Strong advocacy of popular sovereignty is often categorized as another distinctly *popularis* theme.[89] If so, then Cicero, when he spoke from the Rostra, will have made a respectable *popularis*. He speaks freely of the Roman People's "honor" (*dignitas*) and "greatness" (*maiestas*).[90] He announces his deference to their wisdom; he will even change his own mind and yield to their contrary view if they find his arguments weak.[91] The

---

[84] *Red. pop.* 24: *nec in vestris commodis augendis grati animi benivolentiam defuturam.*

[85] *Leg. agr.* 2.15: *itaque hoc animo legem sumpsi in manus ut eam cuperem esse aptam vestris commodis;* cf. 71, 76, 77, 78 (cf. *utilis plebi Romanae:* §§12, 14).

[86] *Sest.* 137: *plebis libertatem et commoda tueri atque augere. Rep.* 1.52.5: *neque committendum ut sua commoda populus neglegi a principibus putet.* Important also for election: cf. Q. Cicero (?), *Comment. pet.* 53 (quoted above, n. 16).

[87] Laser 1997: 31–43, and compare his conception of the "bilateral resonance" that bound the People to their leaders: pp. 231–41.

[88] Cic. *Sest.* 103; *Sull.* 25. Contrast C. Gracchus, *ORF* 48.30, p. 183: *si nanciam populi desiderium, conprobabo rei publicae commoda.*

[89] See especially Wirszubski 1960: 47–50; Meier 1965: 603–5; Brunt 1988: 330–50 (who, however, goes much too far in speaking of "that ultimate control by the people which the *populares* championed" [341]). On the general acceptance of the People's sovereignty in principle, see chap. 4, n. 11.

[90] *Leg. agr.* 2.65, 71, 76, 79; cf. *Rab. perd.* 20, 35 (quoted above, n. 47); *Red. pop.* 4. Cf. Achard 1981: 389, nn. 95–99.

[91] *Leg. agr.* 2.7, 16 (quoted above, n. 42); *Leg. Man.* 17–18; *Rab. perd.* 5 (quoted above, n. 46).

People, too, not merely the Senate, have *auctoritas*, which the leaders of the Republic should follow.[92] As for himself, the People's gift of the honor of public office imposes on him the duty of following their will and consensus regardless of personal interest;[93] accordingly, he takes his cues from them: in speeches two decades apart (63 and 43) Cicero characterizes audience responses to his *contiones* as "casting him in a role" that he is bound to carry out, like an actor in a play produced by the *populus Romanus*.[94] In sum, he reveres the Roman People as pious men do the gods; nay more, they *are* like gods to him.[95] If deference to the People's Will was an important mark of the "People's Friend," then Cicero made sure that here too his persona was rhetorically plausible.

One would suppose that the polar nature of the "optimate"/*popularis* opposition would cause real difficulties for the champion of senatorial leadership of the Republic who emerges from élite texts such as *On the Commonwealth*, *On the Laws*, or the *Defense of Sestius*. Not so, above all because Cicero undermines the polarity systematically, though with great subtlety, sometimes indeed by significant silences; and never speaks in such a way as to cast doubt on his primary bond with the People. Cicero's subtlety is at its most notable when he is confronting manifestly "popular" initiatives against which institutional opposition was most firmly located within the Senate. In his two extant *contiones* against the Rullan agrarian bill, the Senate hardly features at all – except as a place where one is hardly permitted to use the word *popularis*, or where Rullus, now out of the public

---

[92] *Leg. Man.* 63; *Leg. agr.* 2.16 (quoted above, n. 42); *Phil.* 6.18. In these passages, *auctoritas* means "decision" in the first instance, but in these contexts precisely the authoritative nature of the decision is stressed.

[93] *Leg. Man.* 71: *ego me hoc honore praeditum, tantis vestris beneficiis adfectum statui, Quirites,* vestram voluntatem *et rei publicae dignitatem et salutem provinciarum atque sociorum* meis omnibus commodis et rationibus praeferre *oportere*. *Phil.* 6.18: *quis est civis,* praesertim hoc gradu quo me vos esse voluistis, tam oblitus benefici vestri, *tam immemor patriae, tam inimicus dignitati suae quem non excitet, non inflammet tantus vester iste consensus?* For the bond of obligation alluded to here, see further below, pp. 260ff.

[94] *Leg. agr.* 2.49: *Vos mihi praetori biennio ante, Quirites, hoc eodem in loco* personam hanc imposuistis *ut, quibuscumque rebus possum, illius absentis dignitatem vobiscum una tuerer; Phil.* 6.2: *hoc vestro iudicio tanto tamque praeclaro excitatus ita Kalendis Ianuariis veni in senatum ut meminissem quam personam impositam a vobis sustinerem.* The Roman People as *auctor/auctores: Leg. Man.* 69; *Leg. agr.* 2.101. Contrast chap. 4, n. 125.

[95] *Red. pop.* 18: *qua sanctissimi homines pietate erga deos immortalis esse soleant, eadem me erga populum Romanum semper fore, numenque vestrum aeque mihi grave et sanctum ac deorum immortalium in omni vita futurum*; 25: *vobis, qui apud me deorum immortalium vim et numen tenetis.* It is amusing to find that these passages were adduced by critics in the eighteenth and nineteenth centuries against the authenticity of the speech (Nicholson 1992: 156, n. 16; cf. 104–5). The metaphor does not merely grow out of the peculiar circumstances of 57: cf. *Rab. perd.* 5 (quoted above, n. 46).

view, was supposedly given license to speak insultingly of the "excessive" power of the urban plebs.[96] We should note the mildly invidious nature of these references, which, like the paradoxical title *consul popularis*, help to locate Cicero in an independent position outside the "hard core" of the Senate, unlike that common run of consul who shuns the Rostra, who hates agrarian laws, who thinks it sacrilege to praise the Gracchi.[97] This stance is undergirded by his self-representation, methodically built up in the proemium of the speech, as a consul who owes loyalty exclusively to the People, for they had elected him in preference to members of the nobility, who, it is suggested, are still enviously scheming to seize upon some stumble and fault the People's choice.[98] Thus in his person he resolves and super-sedes traditional oppositions: rising above the "war" long waged between the offices of consul and tribune with the assertion that their struggles derive not from some institutional logic (i.e. Senate and People, though neither is expressed) but from the moral failings of their holders, he implicitly justifies "tribunician aggressiveness" (*vis tribunicia*!) against the arrogance of some consuls along with the frequent battles of other, patriotic consuls against "seditious" tribunes.[99]

Eight years after his defence of the senator Gaius Rabirius on the charge of having murdered the tribune Saturninus during the tumult of 100, Cicero represented this speech as a vindication of the "authority of the Senate" against (popular) indignation: a perfect "optimate" intervention, so it would seem.[100] Since Saturninus had been killed after he was in custody, and

---

[96] *Leg. agr.* 2.6: *Ego autem non solum hoc in loco dicam ubi est id dictu facillumum, sed in ipso senatu in quo esse locus huic voci non videbatur popularem me futurum esse consulem prima illa mea oratione Kalendis Ianuariis dixi.* Rullus: §70 (quoted at chap. 7, n. 42).

[97] *Leg. agr.* 2.6, 10. Compare how in the speech for the Manilian Law Cicero represents himself as perhaps the sole champion in the Senate of Gabinius' claim under the law to a legateship (*Leg. Man.* 57–58), hints vaguely at the underhanded attacks likely to be launched against himself for his dedication to the People's will (§§70–71), and aligns himself with the *populi Romani auctoritas* against even the *principes* Catulus and Hortensius (§§63–64).

[98] *Leg. agr.* 2.1–7. On the nobility, see esp. §6: *sed mihi videntur certi homines, si qua in re me non modo consilio verum etiam casu lapsum esse arbitrabuntur, vos universos, qui me antetuleritis nobilitati, vituperaturi* – a theme with which Cicero also chooses to close the speech (§103). The *certi homines* are not explicitly *nobiles*, though this is surely implied (note the close of the immediately preceding sentence: *non dubitanti fidele consilium* [*nobilitatis*], etc.); for the "oligarchic" ring of *certi homines*, see above, n. 63. For other slightly invidious references to the nobility, see §§3, 7.

[99] *Leg. agr.* 2.14. Cf. Sall. *Hist.* 3.48.12 (Macer): *vis tribunicia, telum a maioribus libertati paratum.*

[100] *Pis.* 4: *Ego in C. Rabirio perduellionis reo XL annis ante me consulem interpositam senatus auctoritatem sustinui contra invidiam atque defendi.* Contra Primmer 1985: 28–29, *auctoritas* here is not used in the narrow sense of "decree" (i.e. the "*SCU*" of 100) but of senatorial "authority" whose consolidation in his consulship Cicero saw as his greatest achievement (*Att.* 1.16.6–8, 18.3; *Fam.* 1.9.12; Mitchell 1991: 9–14). For the phrase *auctoritatem . . . interponere*, see *OLD interpono*, 6a; cf. *Rab. perd.* 2,

therefore after the emergency that justified any suspension of the citizen's right of protection against magisterial coercion (*provocatio*) had passed, the case evidently struck directly at the view that the so-called "Final Decree of the Senate" placed virtually no limits upon those who chose to carry out severe punitive measures – or political murders – under its broad umbrella. But that was what one might fairly call the "optimate" view, espoused by Cicero before élite audiences, and its controversial nature is seen not only here but in the polemic over Opimius' first execution of the decree in 121.[101] Hence, though the case against Rabirius might look to us like a relatively narrow challenge to peripheral aspects of the "Final Decree," to Cicero and all others for whom the "authority of the Senate" was paramount its import was much greater.[102] If thirty-seven years after the fact, one who had taken up arms in answer to the Senate's decree and consuls' summons could now be called to account and perhaps exiled for the actions he had undertaken in consequence of those authoritative appeals, then there is little wonder that, whatever the possible technicalities, in fact the Senate's whole power to authorize suppression of violent insurrection was felt to be on the line.[103]

That being so, it is indeed remarkable how diminished a role Cicero allots in this speech to the Senate as an institution. Having established his "popular" credentials at length, as we saw, with the pious appeals to the memory of Gaius Gracchus and cries of outrage at the prosecuting tribune's un-civic "cruelty", Cicero frees his hands to paint Saturninus in uncompromisingly dark colors: driven by "depravity," "madness," and "criminality," he had slaughtered citizens, broken open the prison, seized the Capitol, and made himself the enemy not so much of the Senate but of the whole citizenry.[104] As later in the defense of Milo, the emotional, if not the rational, force of the defense would have dissolved had the victim of

as well as the comparable phrasing of *Brut.* 164 and Dio's understanding of the tribunes' motive (37.26.2–3). The passage remains good evidence that the speech Cicero published was indeed a defense against a charge of *perduellio*, which Primmer is only the most recent to deny (see chap. 1, n. 90).

[101] Cf. *Cat.* 1.3–5; *Mil.* 70; cf. *Phil.* 5.34: *consulibus totam rem publicam commendandam.* Opimius: Sall. *Iug.* 31.7; 42.4; Livy, *Per.* 61; Oros. 5.12.10; Vell. Pat. 2.7.3. For Labienus' argument, see Tyrrell 1973: 293–95, and 1978: 129–30; Primmer 1985: 10–11. On the contingency of the "*SCU*" upon what was politically practicable rather than upon clearly delineated principles of law, see Drummond 1995: 79–95; Lintott 1999: 89–93.

[102] Cicero: see n. 100; Cass. Dio 37.26.3.

[103] See Tyrrell 1973: 294–95, and Primmer 1985: 11, whose emphasis on the broad importance of the case is preferable to the somewhat minimalist views of Gruen 1974: 278; Ungern-Sternberg 1970: 83–85; Drummond 1995: 84–86; and esp. the narrow perspective adopted by Phillips 1974: 97–101. Havas 1976a speculates about the covert movers behind the prosecution.

[104] *Rab. perd.* 22 (*improbitas et furor*), 24 (*furoris et sceleris*), 35 (*caedem civium fecisset ut L. Saturninus, si carcerem refregisset, si Capitolium cum armatis occupavisset,* with Niebuhr's restorations). On the prison break, which may have been gratuitously attributed by Cicero to Saturninus, see Tyrrell

the defendant's violence not been seen as fully deserving of his fate, even if it was impossible to admit the defendant's direct agency[105] – particularly as Rabirius had doubtless himself come in for bitter vituperation at the hands of Labienus: the story that he had passed around Saturninus' head at his dinner parties must have been recounted with gusto.[106] Opposing him, in the interest of "the safety of the fatherland and freedom," stood the consuls, among them the popular hero, Marius; all the chief men of that age, along with the entire senatorial and equestrian orders; leaders of the present, then in their youth, such as P. Servilius Vatia (cos. 79), Q. Catulus (cos. 78), and C. Scribonius Curio (cos. 76); indeed, the whole Roman People.[107] In this unanimous confrontation of all patriotic citizens with those in the grip of violent insanity, Cicero is careful to draw attention away from the institutional role of the Senate in the conflict by emphasizing the force of the consular order to take arms against Saturninus over the legal status of the senatorial decree which lay behind it; thus he draws the populist sting from the prosecution's attack by refocusing responsibility sharply upon the *popularis* hero, Marius, who executed the decree.[108] Furthermore, by concentrating attention almost exclusively upon the moment of the consular summons, Cicero is also able to avoid entirely the central issue of the limitations upon the extent of repressive action, while the prestige of Marius can answer for what followed.[109] Finally, having aligned Senate and People on the same side, mediated through the figure of Marius, Cicero is able in the peroration to offer an explicit, "popular" defense of repressive action under the so-called Final Decree, which now emerges as a highly

---

1978: 133, with Val. Max. 9.7.1. For the events, see Badian 1984; Burckhardt 1988: 141–51; Cavaggioni 1998: 137–71.

[105] Cicero's ostensibly counterfactual wish that Rabirius *had* killed Saturninus, *hostem populi Romani* (*Rab. perd.* 18–19; above, pp. 146–47) might be compared with the so-called *pars extra causam* of the Miloniana (*Mil.* 72–91).

[106] *De vir. ill.* 73: the story may indeed have entered the historical tradition via Labienus' speech. The portrait-bust of Saturninus which Labienus brought before the *contio* (Cic. *Rab. perd.* 25) would have been a useful prop.

[107] *Rab. perd.* 22: *patriae salutem ac libertatem*; cf. 20, 27: *salus rei publicae*; 27: *pro communi libertate*. Marius: esp. §§27–30. It is quite unnecessary to assume that Marius' opposition to Saturninus had dropped out of the collective memory: so Mack 1937: 27 at n. 62. Social consensus: §§20–21, 26–27, 31. Roman People: §20: *Parent omnes; ex aede Sancus armamentariisque publicis arma populo Romano C. Mario consule distribuente dantur.* On *salus rei publicae*, see Burckhardt 1988: 120, with n. 114.

[108] The senatorial decree is indeed described at §20, and mentioned secondary to the consular command at §21, but thereafter the focus is sharply on the consular order (§§22, 27, esp. 34: *vocem illam consulis, "qui rem publicam salvam esse vellent"*). This subtle shift, I believe, misleads Loutsch 1982, who insists that §2 refers narrowly to the consular *evocatio* rather than to the "*SCU*" that authorized it: that is to impose specious precision while overlooking a central element of Cicero's strategy. Cf. Primmer 1985: 57, n. 119.

[109] Primmer 1985: 17–19.

salutary device for protecting the People against their enemies, their very guarantee of "freedom, security, and greatness."[110]

What is noteworthy here is not so much the subtlety and ingenuity of the rhetoric but the much more important point that, despite the fact that this case seems virtually designed to expose the ideological fault lines between "optimate" and *popularis* (since the most controversial and vulnerable aspect of the "Final Decree" lay at its heart), Cicero was not forced to come out in the open and articulate any distinctly "optimate" political principle in his justification of the killing of Saturninus. The very real ideological differences that were indeed in conflict in Rabirius' case were hidden from public view rather than thematized, just as they had been in the sham debate over the Rullan agrarian bill.

The rhetorical self-image that Cicero constructs by means of the various claims, interpretations, and "buzzwords" that I have reviewed bears little resemblance to the traditional picture of the orator's political views, drawn for the most part from different source material intended for élite audiences. This fact alone sets the special character of contional speech in sharp relief, and demonstrates its unique value for constructing a distinct "plebs'-eye view" of Republican civic ideology. But the divergence between Cicero's contional persona and the views he expresses in other venues and genres further raises important questions about the nature of Republican debate. Cicero never permits "optimate" political principles to be clearly recognized by his contional audience for what they are, even – or least of all – when they do arguably determine his actions (as in the rebuttal of Rullus' land bill, or the defense of Rabirius). Instead, he is able to evade ideological confrontation altogether by donning the mask of the *popularis* – and to succeed in doing so.

The full significance of Cicero's contional makeover as a *popularis* needs to be appreciated. No doubt it may be seen as merely an ancient version of the familiar modern political strategy, recently perfected by left-leaning parties in the United States and the United Kingdom, of coopting the "best" ideas of the opposing party in an effort to win the center; we may be reminded of the broad consensus on central ideas like the free market or "big government" that appears to have settled over western political discourse since the crumbling of the Iron Curtain. Comparable forces were indeed at work in Republican Rome: a Cicero could not hope to prevail over a Rullus before a popular audience by attacking the principle of land distribution,

---

[110] *Rab. perd.* 33–35 (§34: *spem libertatis, spem salutis, spem maiestatis*). Cf. the brevity and vagueness of the reference at §2.

nor could he hope to defend Rabirius successfully in a trial judged by the
People if he sweepingly subordinated *provocatio* to magisterial discretion
and a broadly phrased authorization by the Senate to see to it that "the
State suffered no harm." A voting audience does indeed impose certain
fundamental constraints upon the speaker. But the differences between the
scenarios are as important as the similarities. In the modern context, a party
structure tends to ensure that, even as broad consensus forms on certain
ideas, the oppositional dynamic itself will force the emergence of sufficient
differentiations to form alternatives recognizable to voters. Something very
different is evidently going on here, for Cicero's practice makes clear – and
the review of major "debates" in chapter 5 is fully consistent on this point –
that in the late Republic any discernably distinct "optimate" ideology
tended to be carefully kept out of the *contio*, that is, out of the public's
gaze.

It was apparently not always this way: in the midst of a grain crisis in
138, the consul P. Scipio Nasica, eventual leader of the lynch mob that
killed Tiberius Gracchus, is said to have told an angry, hungry crowd that
it should be quiet, since he knew better than they what was good for the
Republic.[111] But Nasica ended up a hated figure who had to be discreetly
removed, and after his departure to Asia in 132 it looks as though this kind of
plain speaking, or aristocratic arrogance, rather quickly became an anachronism.[112] Thereafter, at least, as the "plebs'-eye view" of Cicero and my
earlier review of the content of several important late-Republican "debates"
make sufficiently clear, no "optimate" alternative to the broadly "popular"
consensus of contional discourse appears to have been openly introduced
to the fully public sphere of the *contio*. What is of special interest here is
not that in the late Republic no one dared any longer to assert from the
Rostra the primacy of senatorial authority over the popular will – although
that too needs emphasis.[113] More important, both those seen as *populares
and their opponents* reinforced an "ideological monotony" by competing
to be seen as the true representatives of the same "popular" ideology. And
a most effective element in that strategy for one, like Cicero, who was
equal to the role was the effort to assimilate one's persona explicitly to
that consensus, as a "true" *popularis* – a strategy that was greatly facilitated

---

[111] Val. Max. 3.7.3 = *ORF* 38.3, pp. 157–58: "*tacete, quaeso, Quirites,*" inquit: "*plus ego enim quam vos
quid rei publicae expediat intellego.*" See Diod. 34/35.33.7 for another instance of Nasica's lack of his
colleagues' "fear" of the People.

[112] Plut. *Ti. Gracch.* 21.2–3; Val. Max. 5.3.2e; Cic. *Rep.* 1.6.

[113] Against, e.g., Hölkeskamp 1995: 40 (cf. 2000: 214–15, 222), or Döbler 1999: 204, n. 756, who treat
Nasica's reply as paradigmatic.

by the exclusion of the public from direct observation of meetings of the Senate, which created two, relatively distinct spheres of action in which a senator might play two, remarkably different roles.[114] As cynical as one may justifiably be about modern democratic politics, it is difficult to imagine a Democratic (or Labour) candidate seeking to win an election not just by taking up some of the most successful sloganeering of the other side but by suppressing any overt distinction at the level of ideas even to the extent of proclaiming that it is she, in fact, not her opponent, who is the "true" Republican (or Tory).

IDEOLOGICAL MONOTONY

This kind of rhetorical assimilation returns us to the question first adumbrated while noting Cicero's disingenuous pose as *popularis* during his attack on the Rullan land bill: whether there was, in fact, any ideological competition in public political discourse – whether the voting populace was actually presented with a choice of alternative solutions (and indeed problems) or only of men who, with greater or less plausibility, claimed to be the authentic representatives of ideas that no one could openly challenge.

At this point one might well object that, even with Cicero's emphasis on the primacy of his bond to the People, even with his rhetorical creation of an independent position for himself within the Senate and the subtle notes of criticism of that body that occasionally obtrude, he never adopts in his *contiones* the oppositional, even hostile, stance toward the Senate that may be felt to be the distinctive mark of the "real" *popularis*. But this formulation, plausible as it appears, overlooks precisely the complications that made the "strategy of impersonation" so effective, and make it so interesting from the point of view of this investigation. Cicero does indeed frequently speak as a defender of "the authority of the Senate" – and seems to expect his audience to respect this as a good.[115] Defending Rabirius and the "Final Decree" against Labienus, Cicero does not shy away from construing his opponent's aim as an attack on the "authority of the Senate" (*auctoritas senatus*) – and appears to think this will count against him.[116] And why not? Even Sallust's tribune, Memmius, deplores the betrayal of the

---

[114] See below, pp. 246ff.

[115] *Red. pop.* 16: [*Pompeius*] *hortatusque est ut auctoritatem senatus, statum civitatis, fortunas civis bene meriti defenderetis* (cf. 18). Cf. §§10, 14: *Ego autem in qua civitate nihil valeret senatus . . . rem publicam esse nullam putavi.* Note that *senatus auctoritas* and *vestra libertas/voluntas vel sim.* are repeatedly paired on the side against Antony: *Phil.* 4.5, 8, 15; 6.3, 5, (cf. 19). Cf. 4.12: *numquam tam vehementer cum senatu consociati fuistis*; 4.15: *vestra cum senatu concordia.*

[116] *Rab. perd.* 2 (see n. 100 above); cf. 3, 17.

"authority of the Senate" by the "powerful few."[117] For the *popularis* critique was not based on contrasting political *ideals* but on contrary claims about the political *facts* of the present.

None of those who laid strongest claim to the title *popularis* appears ever to have represented conflict between Senate and People as fundamentally an institutional one. No *popularis* is known to have publicly called for an alteration of the constitution in order to remove the Senate from its position of leadership in the Republic or to make it simply an instrument of the Popular Will: what was, broadly speaking, lifetime tenure in the Senate was never challenged, nor was it ever proposed seriously to circumscribe the Senate's formal powers.[118] The *contiones* in Sallust, which are our best guide to the nature of *popularis* rhetoric (namely, the speeches of the tribunes Memmius and Macer, as well as those of the consul-elect Marius and the anti-Sullan consul Lepidus), contain no word against the Senate as an institution; indeed, as we have just seen, Memmius is actually made to deplore the betrayal – by the Senate itself – of the *auctoritas senatus*. Rather, they diagnose a moral collapse among the élite whose symptoms were a breach of the trust given to senators by citizens' votes and the formation of a conspiratorial clique that had seized domination of the Senate and begun a covert war against the People.[119] Those who took up an oppositional stance against "the Senate" did not, as a rule, decry the hallowed institution as such but its present corrupt leadership.[120] Labienus, Cicero's avowed *popularis* opponent in the Rabirius trial, did not decline to praise the

---

[117] Sall. *Iug.* 31.25: *hosti acerrumo prodita senatus auctoritas, proditum imperium vostrum est*; cf. 18–19. Paul 1984: ad loc.

[118] Meier 1965: 549–68, 593–99, 610–12; Jochen Martin 1965: 23, 223; Laser 1997: 158, 165–69, 188–93. Perelli 1982: 16–19 polemicizes against the "old Prussian school" of Gelzer and Meier on this point, but has to acknowledge that *populares* were no more than reformists. Syme 1939: 153: "If the political literature of the period had been more abundantly preserved, it might be discovered that respect for law, tradition and the constitution possessed a singular unanimity of advocates."

[119] Cf. Meier 1965: 594–95. Macer attacks the *nobilitas, factio,* or *pauci* (Sall. *Hist.* 3.48.3, 6, 8) but never mentions the Senate as such. Memmius inveighs against the *nobiles*, the *factio*, and *pauci potentes* (Sall. *Iug.* 31.1–2, 4, 9, 19–20); the sole reference to the Senate is to deplore its loss of *auctoritas* through the actions of these men (§25). The *contio* of Lepidus (Sall. *Hist.* 1.55) is directed against Sulla and his *satellites*, that of Marius, in part, against the *nobilitas* (*Iug.* 85); neither has a word against the Senate as such. Recall Caesar's portrayal, at the beginning of the *Civil War*, of a Senate cowed by a truculent *factio* in 49. "Sallust is intent to demonstrate that the heirs of a great tradition had betrayed their trust" (Syme 1964: 126; cf. Earl 1961: 28–59), a strand in his thinking that the ex-demagogue evidently drew from the tradition of "oppositional" rhetoric.

[120] I set no store by loose characterizations such as Diod. 34/35.25.1: ὁ Γράκχος δημηγορήσας περὶ τοῦ καταλῦσαι ἀριστοκρατίαν, δημοκρατίαν δὲ συστῆσαι, or Plutarch's comments about the significance of the orators' reversal of direction on the Rostra (see pp. 45–47). Jochen Martin 1965: 198: "Für den Popularen war der Gegensatz zur Senatsmehrheit konstitutiv." Meier 1965: 593–94.

Senate of the previous generation even while attacking that of the present.[121] The emphasis is strongly on the moral quality of the persons who had "seized" power in the Senate, which usefully makes the situation remediable: Sallust's tribunes imply that if the People would only throw off their fear and inertia and use their *suffragia* to choose men of *virtus* for public office, as they once had, everything would once again be well.[122] (Naturally: even *popularis* tribunes looked forward to continuing their political career and, in due course, wielding power in the Senate themselves.) That is, there would then again be a proper aristocracy of virtue rather than its specious semblance, the rule of the powerful and well-born under the name of *optimates*.[123] Therefore, what looks at first like an ideological dichotomy – "pro-" and "anti-Senate" – actually resolves itself, upon closer examination, to a divergence of claims about the moral worthiness of the current senatorial leadership: "pro-" and "anti-*principes*" or, less precisely, "nobility." The issue turns on men, not ideology.

Taking hold of the problem at another end, we may observe also that it was not self-evidently true that to be a true Friend of the People entailed hostility to the Senate – or vice versa – and that there is no reason to think that the efforts of Cicero and others to deconstruct that simple equation fell on deaf ears; quite the contrary, as the defeat of the Rullan rogation (to take a particularly striking example) makes manifest. After the shock of Tiberius Gracchus' tribunate in 133, it did not take the champions of the Senate long to "prove" their devotion to the People's welfare in concrete form: against Gaius Gracchus' "popular" program in 122, M. Livius Drusus offered land in a great series of colonial settlements, insisting in his *contiones* that the Senate was the source of his proposals and was thus motivated by concern

---

[121] Cic. *Rab. perd.* 20: *cunctus senatus, atque ille senatus quem etiam vos ipsi, qui hos patres conscriptos qui nunc sunt in invidiam vocatis, quo facilius de hoc senatu detrahere possitis, <laudare consuevistis>* . . .

[122] Sall. *Iug.* 31.12 (Memmius): *At qui sunt ii qui rem publicam occupavere? Homines sceleratissumi, cruentis manibus, immani avaritia, nocentissumi et idem superbissumi, quibus fides decus pietas, postremo honesta atque inhonesta omnia quaestui sunt.* (§16) *Quod si tam vos libertatis curam haberetis quam illi ad dominationem adcensi sunt, profecto neque res publica sicuti nunc vastaretur et beneficia vostra penes optumos, non audacissumos forent. Hist.* 3.48.5–6 (Macer): *omnes alii, creati pro iure vestro, vim cunctam et imperia sua gratia aut spe aut praemiis in vos convortere meliusque habent mercede delinquere quam gratis recte facere. Itaque omnes concessere iam in paucorum dominationem . . . quom interim more pecorum vos multitudo singulis habendos fruendosque praebetis, exuti omnibus quae maiores reliquere, nisi quia vobismet ipsi per suffragia, ut praesides olim, nunc dominos destinatis.* Cf. *Rhet. Her.* 4.48: *inimicos eorum* [sc. *defensorum vestrorum*] **vestris suffragiis** *in amplissimum locum pervenisse.* Livy puts this reproach into the mouths of a number of plebeian leaders delivering *contiones* during the Struggle of the Orders (see esp. 4.35.5–11 [note: *contiones seditiosae*]; other references in Yakobson 1999: 192–93) – which probably indicates how characteristic it was.

[123] See Cic. *Rep.* 1.51: the "optimate" does not reject the principle employed in the *popularis* critique (n. 122) but differs in his assessment of the *virtus* of those who actually held positions of power. Again, the moral quality of men, not ideas, is at issue.

for the multitude.[124] In the same year the consul M. Fannius defended the privileged nature of the Roman citizenship against Gracchus' proposal for its extension to the Latins.[125] The Sullan *factio* and even Cato himself – in his tribunate – carried laws to subsidize the purchase of grain – a cause that Asconius calls *summa popularis*.[126]

It is also clear that the popular audience was fully alert to the possibility that those laying claim to the title of *popularis* might in fact be furthering interests other than theirs.[127] We are told that "the greatest proof of [M. Livius] Drusus' [the tribune of 122, rival to Gaius Gracchus] goodwill to the People and of his honesty was that he appeared to be proposing nothing for his own personal benefit or in his interest": for he made sure that others were named to lead out his colonies, and kept himself clear of the distribution of funds, in pointed contrast to the way in which Gaius Gracchus carried out his projects.[128] This is also one of Cicero's best weapons against Rullus, who seems to have made the mistake of naming himself as the magistrate charged with conducting the election of the agrarian Board of Ten: "If indeed you are taking thought for the People, clear yourself of the suspicion of any personal benefit, give a guarantee that you are seeking nothing but what is useful and beneficial to the People, let power go to others while gratitude for your service goes to you!" But Rullus will obviously appoint himself in a rigged election, along with his colleagues co-sponsoring the legislation; there will be quite enough booty to go around.[129] In 59 Caesar was more careful, explicitly excluding himself from consideration for the Board of Twenty to be selected under his law, "so that he should not be thought to have drafted

---

[124] Plut. *C. Gracch.* 9.3: καὶ μέντοι καὶ αὐτὸς ὁ Λίβιος ἀεὶ δημηγορῶν ἔλεγεν, ὡς γράφοι ταῦτα τῇ βουλῇ δοκοῦντα κηδομένη τῶν πολλῶν. On the elder Drusus, see Burckhardt 1988: 54–70.

[125] Cic. *Brut.* 99, *ORF* 32.2–5, p. 144 (above, chap. 4, nn. 46–47).

[126] Cic. *Verr.* 2.3.163; 2.5.52; Sall. *Hist.* 3.48.19; Plut. *Caes.* 8.4; *Cat. Min.* 26.1. Cf. also the grain law of M. Octavius, perhaps to be dated between 99 and 87: Cic. *Off.* 2.72, with *Brut.* 222; *MRR* III.151. Burckhardt 1988: 240–56, on "optimate" grain policy. Cato's dramatic move as quaestor against those who had accepted rewards for killings under the Sullan proscriptions might also be noted: Plut. *Cat. Min.* 17.4–5; Cass. Dio 47.6.4; Fehrle 1983: 79–81. (I owe the reference to A. Yakobson.)

[127] See Cic. *Rab. perd.* 15 for the phrase *alienus a commodis vestris*.

[128] Plut. *C. Gracch.* 10.1: Μεγίστη δὲ τῷ Δρούσῳ πίστις εὐνοίας πρὸς τὸν δῆμον ἐγίνετο καὶ δικαιοσύνης τὸ μηδὲν αὐτῷ μηδ' ὑπὲρ ἑαυτοῦ φαίνεσθαι γράφοντα. Gracchus and M. Fulvius Flaccus were explicitly named as leaders of the "Gracchan" colony of Junonia: App. *B Civ.* 1.24. Naturally, direct involvement could be seen in a positive light, as is suggested by Plut. *C. Gracch.* 6.3–4; it may be that Drusus was the first to make an issue of it. Legislation attempting to restrict this kind of conflict of interest (the obscure *leges Licinia et Aebutia*: Cic. *Leg. agr.* 2.21; *Dom.* 51; Mommsen 1887: 1.501, n. 2) is likely to be a post-Gracchan response to the perceived problem.

[129] Cic. *Leg. agr.* 2.22, esp. *etenim si populo consulis, remove te a suspicione alicuius tui commodi, fac fidem te nihil nisi populi utilitatem et fructum quaerere, sine ad alios potestatem, ad te gratiam beneficii tui pervenire.* For Rullus' counter-insinuation, see 3.3.

anything in his own interest."[130] The hapless Rullus had sought to reassure voters with a similar provision excluding Pompey from consideration in 63 – thus anticipating the criticism that he was only acting as the general's agent – which Cicero, however, pounces on as a telling sign of his ill will toward the People's champion.[131] We might compare the oath Cicero himself took at the end of his speech advocating the transfer of command in the Mithridatic War to Pompey, by the gods "who preside over this holy spot [and] see right into the minds of those who take up the business of the Commonwealth," that he was not supporting the law at anyone's prompting, that he was certainly not moved by the expectation of any favor from Pompey, and that he was not seeking from some powerful personage (Pompey again) any protection from danger or advancement in honor.[132] This whole discourse attests to the fact that the People were perfectly well aware of what might otherwise be supposed to have been a Sallustian revelation: that young mavericks suddenly invested with the extraordinary potential power of the tribunate might well be seeking their own advancement rather than the public good with their wild denunciations of the current leaders of the Republic and promises of handouts to the People.[133]

Fundamentally, after all, a broad social consensus – not just "optimate" fantasy – affirmed that the Senate was not the adversary but the natural ally of the People. This simple truth tends to be overlooked, as we are generally more interested in points of conflict and tension than in the "centripetal" forces of social cohesion, but it would be hard to explain otherwise how the Republic could have survived as long as it did, especially given the high degree of face-to-face interaction that has been traced in this study alone.[134] Pro-senatorial contional rhetoric that presumes a cooperative relationship

---

[130] Cass. Dio 38.1.7: ὅπως μὴ δι' ἑαυτόν τι γράφειν νομισθείη. Cf. §2.

[131] Cic. *Leg. agr.* 2.23–25.

[132] Cic. *Leg. Man.* 70: *me hoc neque rogatu facere cuiusquam, neque quo Cn. Pompei gratiam mihi per hanc causam conciliari putem, neque quo mihi ex cuiusquam amplitudine aut praesidia periculis aut adiumenta honoribus quaeram* ... Note also in this speech Cicero's impassioned defense of Pompey's right under the Manilian law to name A. Gabinius, author of the *lex Gabinia* of the previous year, as one of his legates (§§57–58); the objection, surely, was to the appearance of a "quid pro quo," not simply to the fact that Gabinius was just out of the tribunate.

[133] Sall. *Cat.* 38.1: *homines adulescentes summam potestatem nacti, quibus aetas animusque ferox erat, coepere senatum criminando plebem exagitare, dein largiundo atque pollicitando magis incendere: ita ipsi clari potentesque fieri.*

[134] Meier 1966: 53: "Adel und Volk in Rom bildeten eine im Grunde monistische Gesellschaft." Much recent work has helped to elucidate the bonds that joined mass and élite in the late Republic, with some scholars emphasizing the ways in which the élite won popular acquiescence in their hegemony (notably Flaig 1993, 1995b, and 1998; Hölkeskamp 1995 and 2000; Jehne 2000a), others stressing reciprocal interdependence (Laser 1997: esp. 231–40: "bilaterale Resonanz"; Yakobson 1999: esp. 228–33).

between Senate and People suggests that this kind of thinking was by no means alien to popular audiences. For example, in the *contio* on his return from exile, Cicero is able to use the Senate rhetorically as a self-evident marker of legitimacy.[135] It represents the conscience of the Republic and the locus of initiative on his case; but Cicero also emphasizes its powerlessness to effect its will without assuming the submissive position of pleading with the People to vote for his restoration: it is, ultimately, to the Roman People that Cicero owes his "rebirth."[136] Thus the Senate leads – and the People decide: a contional example of the great Ciceronian project of harmonizing senatorial *auctoritas* with popular *libertas*. In the two *Catilinarian* and the first of the *Philippic contiones*, Senate and People stand shoulder to shoulder to confront the common enemies of freedom; if the Senate later became slightly remiss in the confrontation with Antony, this merely makes it more incumbent on the People to give it its cue.[137] The primary bond of the contional orator is always with the People, but so is – on a favorable view – that of the Senate as a whole.

Implicit in all this is a notion that the Senate was subordinate to and dependent on the People – an idea most forcefully expressed in a famous section of a public oration delivered in 106 by L. Licinius Crassus, tribune in the previous year, a speech that may well have exerted great influence on the development of a "popular" response to *populares*.[138] Speaking in support of a bill that would readmit senators to criminal juries after these had been staffed exclusively by *equites* for almost two decades, Crassus upheld "the authority of the Senate" in what at first appears to be a highly paradoxical way. The most famous line of the speech contained a striking phrase, well remembered two generations later, concerning the relationship between Senate and People: "Do not permit us [i.e. senators] to be subject to anyone but all of you together, as we can and should be!"[139] Crassus' rhetorical point was that control by the *equites* of the courts that judged senators was tantamount to subjugation of the Senate to exclusive equestrian domination, to the detriment, obviously, of the interests of the

---

[135] *Red. pop.* 8, 10–14, 16, 18.

[136] *Red. pop.* 15–16; cf. 7–8. "Rebirth:" §§1–5. Nicholson 1992 is surprisingly uninterested in how Cicero constructs his relationship to the People (see, e.g., pp. 104, 106: "pandering"); it is indicative of the "senatorial" perspective of this useful book that a review of those to whom Cicero needed "to repay his debt of *gratia*" (p. 45) omits the *populus Romanus*.

[137] *Cat.* 2.27, 3.13–14; *Phil.* 4.1–2. Cf. *Phil.* 6.1, 3, 7, 18: *itaque senatum bene sua sponte firmum firmiorem vestra auctoritate fecistis.*

[138] Cic. *Brut.* 164, quoted below, n. 142; see also chap. 5 at n. 139.

[139] Cic. *De or.* 1.225: *Nolite sinere nos cuiquam servire, nisi vobis universis, quibus et possumus et debemus.* Note the preceding: *eripite nos ex miseriis, eripite ex faucibus eorum, quorum crudelitas nostro sanguine non potest expleri.* Cf. *ORF* no. 66, fr. 22–26, pp. 243–45.

rest of the citizens, who were after all the Senate's rightful masters. Like some of Cicero's contional remarks (on the People's authority, say), this sounds more *populare* than any known *popularis*, and clearly it did ruffle feathers among the élite.[140] Its dramatic force should not be overlooked in a society in which the senatorial order commanded no small degree of awe and deference. In Cicero's rhetorical dialogue, *On the Orator*, M. Antonius, Crassus' oratorical rival, cites this very quotation as an example of highly effective rhetoric that lacks a strict relation to the truth: no philosopher, no matter how lax, would approve of the statement that the Senate is in servitude to the People, when in fact the People have handed over to the Senate the power of restraining and controlling themselves, like a rider controls a horse.[141] Yet, as Cicero explains, the appeal did work paradoxically in *favor* of the Senate's authority: "He was arousing indignation (*invidia*) against the collusion of judges and prosecutors [of the equestrian order], against whose power he had to speak in the 'popular' style (*populariter*)."[142] Crassus made a populist gesture of élite deference to the primacy of the Roman People in order to stir up resentment against the equestrian order by suggesting that the *equites* had, through their control of the courts that tried the offenses of senators, set themselves up as the People's rival. I shall consider below the standard ideological construction of senators' personal subjugation to the People as a "debt" originating in popular election, a connection that helps to make full sense of this short fragment: *equites*, of course, were free of this bond, hence unaccountable and potentially suspect to the People in any political role. But for the present it is enough to note how this appeal, which must have been effective given Antonius' high praise (the Servilian law passed), establishes a rhetorical basis for popular trust in the Senate: namely, senators are in some plausible sense "subject" to the People.

L. Crassus' "popular" advocacy of the Servilian judiciary law highlights another way in which the *popularis/*"optimate" distinction was dissolved

---

[140] *Divinitus . . . dicta* in the view of M. Antonius, the orator, but *turpiter et flagitiose dicta* according to the Stoic P. Rutilius Rufus (Cic. *De or.* 1.227) – another anachronistic figure of senatorial rigidity (on whom see Kallet-Marx 1990). Cf. Cic. *Parad.* 5.41: *copiosa magis quam sapiens oratio* (another Stoic judgment). The phrase must also have been among those selected by the prosecutor, M. Iunius Brutus, to juxtapose invidiously with contrary sentiments in Crassus' earlier speech on the colony at Narbo in a trial around the turn of the century: Cic. *De or.* 2.223; *Clu.* 140; Quint. *Inst.* 6.3.44 (cf. Alexander 1990: no. 98).

[141] Cic. *De or.* 1.226: *cui* [sc. senatui] *populus ipse moderandi et regendi sui potestatem quasi quasdam habenas tradidisset?*

[142] Cic. *Brut.* 164: *in qua* [oratione] *et auctoritas ornatur senatus, quo pro ordine illa dicuntur, et invidia concitatur in iudicum et in accusatorum factionem, contra quorum potentiam populariter tum dicendum fuit.* Cf. also *Clu.* 140: *in suasione legis Serviliae summis ornat senatum laudibus, et multa in equites Romanos . . . asperius dicta.*

before the People. Crassus is described as speaking *populariter* ("in the 'popular' style"/"like a *popularis*") and this is immediately linked with the arousal of popular resentment, outrage, or indignation (*concitatio invidiae*).[143] The prevalence of the tactic is easy to understand: the power of contional speech as a political instrument rested essentially on its ability to mobilize collective action or a demonstration of the Popular Will by an audience that could drift away if its attention were not seized and held; while popular suspicion – often well earned – of the real intentions of powerful individuals and groups among the élite made *invidia* a natural and potent emotional "hook." In the courts, the rhetorical handbooks advised forensic speakers to create *invidia* toward their opponents by calling attention to their power, wealth, nobility, factiousness, and aristocratic connections;[144] if this tactic worked well among juries of the well-to-do, how much more effective must it have been when a tribune used it before a popular audience![145]

Sallust's representation of a *contio* of Gaius Memmius in 111 conveys the flavor (and puts today's "negative campaigning" to shame). Memmius' plan was to push through the popular assembly, over senatorial objections and delays, a law designed to gain information on senators' and commanders' alleged recent complicity with the enemy.[146] Bitter denunciation of the "power of the junta"[147] and the "arrogance of the oligarchs"[148] vastly outweighs any discussion of the terms of the proposal: they are bloody-handed criminals and greedy cheats,[149] who plunder public funds, extort personal tribute from allies, betray the Senate's authority and "your" empire and sell off the very Commonwealth itself,[150] who ostentatiously flaunt their offices and public honors as so much spoils before the People,[151] while protecting their tyrannical dominance by savage and lawless retribution against any

---

[143] Cic. *Brut.* 164 (above, n. 142); cf. the assessment of Crassus as a master of the *popularis dictio* (§165, quoted at chap. 7, n. 124). For *concitatio invidiae* see also chap. 2, n. 102 and pp. 271–72.

[144] *Rhet. Her.* 1.8: *In invidiam trahemus si vim, si potentiam, si factionem, divitias, incontinentiam, nobilitatem, clientelas, hospitium, sodalitatem, adfinitates adversariorum proferemus, et his adiumentis magis quam veritati eos confidere aperiemus.*

[145] P. M. Martin 2000: 30–34, for further good examples of some of the *topoi* of populist rhetoric against the powerful.

[146] Note that Memmius exploits the pre-existing *apud plebem gravis invidia* (Sall. *Iug.* 30.1) by "pointing out the many arrogant and cruel deeds of the nobility" (§3). On the speech, see Paul 1984: ad loc.; La Penna 1968: 190–93; Büchner 1982: 190–96. This is the second time in the text that Memmius exploits popular *invidia* to force the hand of the Senate: see 27.2–3, with Morstein-Marx 2000a: 474–76. For the law, which would bring King Jugurtha to Rome to give information about funds extorted or received by Roman commanders and envoys in betrayal of the Republic, see Sall. *Iug.* 32.1, 5, and Gruen 1968: 141.

[147] *Iug.* 31.1, 4: *opes factionis, factionis potentia.*

[148] *Iug.* 31.2: *superbia paucorum*; cf. §20: *divina et humana omnia penes paucos.*

[149] *Iug.* 31.12, 14.   [150] *Iug.* 31.9, 25.   [151] *Iug.* 31.10.

popular champions who emerge;[152] in sum, they have reduced the Roman People, born to rule, to abject slavery.[153] This is strong stuff indeed, largely echoed in Sallust's other tribunician *contio*.[154] More generally, whether or not the word *invidia* appears, we repeatedly observe the conjunction of *popularis* politicians with the stirring (exploiting) of popular outrage (*concitatio invidiae*) in public meetings, from Tiberius Gracchus' attacks in *contiones* of 133 on the selfishness of "the rich" opposing him – including the vetoing tribune, M. Octavius – and the "lies" of Roman military commanders,[155] or Gaius Gracchus' violent denunciations of his brother's killers and his own enemies, and his harangues on the debased morality that currently prevailed in the Senate,[156] right down to the tribunician agitation for the destruction of Milo after the murder of Publius Clodius, with which this book opened.[157] The inflammatory assertion of L. Marcius Philippus, while urging his own agrarian bill as tribune, that "there are not two thousand citizens who hold property" is another notable example: this comment, delivered while acting in the *popularis* manner (*cum in agendo multa populariter*), Cicero brands as "vicious" (*male*) and "destructive" (*perniciose*) precisely because of the danger such populist charges posed, mediated through the popular vote, to what he sees as the central principle of government: the protection of private property.[158]

What is particularly worth noting in the case of Crassus, however, is that Cicero tells us explicitly that this sort of "arousal of indignation" was directed against judges and prosecutors among the *equites* and used in *support* of the "authority of the senate"; and despite its evident pro-senatorial character, Cicero treats this as an example of speaking *populariter*, that is, "in a 'popular' manner/like a *popularis*."[159] For Cicero, then, the crucial determinant of "speaking *populariter*" (or, as often, the "'popular' style of speaking:" *populare genus dicendi, popularis dictio, eloquentia popularis*) was

---

[152] *Iug.* 31.2, 7–8, 13, 21.　　[153] *Iug.* 31.11, 16, 20, 22, 26.

[154] Sall. *Hist.* 3.48, with McGushin 1992–94: II.86–98; La Penna 1968: 280–84; Büchner 1982: 221–29. Marius' oration in the *Iugurtha* (85) plays the *invidia*-theme much more softly, as befits one who, now consul, no longer needs the People's outrage but their confidence.

[155] App. *B Civ.* 1.11; Plut. *Ti. Gracch.* 9.5, 10.5. See pp. 173ff.

[156] Plut. *C. Gracch.* 3.3–4.4; App. *B Civ.* 1.22; *ORF* 48.32–34 (p. 184) 44 (pp. 187–88) 48 (pp. 191–92) 55 (p. 194) 58 (p. 195) 61 (p. 196). For the famously histrionic style that Gaius Gracchus introduced, see below, pp. 270–72.

[157] Pp. 1ff. Asc. 33: *Ibi pro contione Plancus et Pompeius . . . invidiam Miloni fecerunt.* Cf. 37: *invidiosas [contiones] etiam de Cicerone [habebant], quod Milonem tanto studio defenderet. Eratque maxima pars multitudinis infensa non solum Miloni sed etiam propter invisum patrocinium Ciceroni.*

[158] Cic. *Off.* 2.73, with Dyck 1996: 464. The date is *c.* 104: *MRR* 1.560.

[159] Cic. *Brut.* 164 (quoted above, n. 142): note especially *contra quorum* [sc. *iudicum et accusatorum*] *potentiam populariter tum dicendum fuit.*

not the choice of target or political ideology,[160] but the rhetorical style and strategy properly suited to a particular audience, the *populus* in the *contio*, marked by increased vehemence of delivery and corresponding exploitation of outrage or indignation (*invidia*).[161] Similarly, I submit, in the context of the fully public sphere of the *contio*, we should think of "*popularis* ideology" not as a complex of political ideas espoused by *populares* in explicit or implied opposition to "optimate" ones, but as the broad popular consensus that formed the background of all effective contional speech, by those we might consider "optimates" in a larger perspective as well as those taking up an oppositional stance. Ideology and rhetorical style/strategy cannot after all really be separated: the "popular" nature of Crassus' appeal for public trust in the senatorial order derives not just, or even chiefly, from its manifest aggressiveness in argument and delivery but from its effective exploitation of certain "popular" ideas, such as the "subordination" of senators specifically to the People and the People alone (founded, as we shall see later, on the concept of popular election as a *beneficium* that imposed a debt), that were certainly specific to the popular sphere (recall the élite criticism of Crassus' appeal).

"*Popularis* ideology," then, becomes "popular" or "contional ideology." That there was a broad consensus on central Republican ideas is of course not news. But because the restricted evidence of contional oratory has not normally been separated out from other communicative genres, and the separation of the "popular" from the "senatorial" spheres of action little emphasized, it has not been sufficiently appreciated that the "optimate"/*popularis* dichotomy, which has its uses in other contexts, breaks down, or rather, disappears in the context of public meetings; to impose the opposition here would suggest an ideological distinction, an alternative, that was not in fact presented to the People. A nakedly "optimate" stance was in straightforward contradiction with the *contio* as a rhetorical setting.[162] If applied to speech, the traditional polarity may, in fact, best be seen as essentially a distinction of "discourses" or discursive genres, turning ultimately upon audience and venue. The complex of concepts, ideas, and (expressed) goals that we tend to associate with *populares* filled the toolbox of any orator who desired to effect anything through the *contio* (at least

---

[160] Cf. also Cic. *Brut.* 136: *Sp. Thorius satis valuit in populari genere dicendi, is qui agrum publicum vitiosa et inutili lege vectigali levavit.* The *vitiosa et inutilis lex* (Badian 1958: 235–42) that Thorius effectively repealed by means of his populist rhetoric must have been none other than Tiberius Gracchus' law of 133: App. *B Civ.* 1.27; Flach 1990: 54–56.

[161] David 1980a: 171–211, esp. 176–77. For the phrase *eloquentia popularis* (*vel sim.*), see Cic. *De or.* 1.81; *Orat.* 13, 151; *Brut.* 136, 165, 191, 247.

[162] Cf. Mouritsen 2001: 8–14; Vasaly 1993: 74.

after 133). In the Senate, for the most part, something quite different was called for, which one might call an "optimate" rhetorico-ideological discourse: never of course going so far as to subordinate overtly the *good* of the People but in general assuming the Senate's superior ability to discern that good, even if necessary against the Popular Will.[163] A Crassus, or a Cicero, was able to move back and forth without difficulty between these discursive genres and the different roles each demanded; most other senators were more at home in one or the other, depending on talent or training, stage of career and personal ambition, and of course political preferences.

But for the citizen standing before the Rostra – men like, say, the freedman grain-merchant Sextus Aemilius Baro whose death in 52 BC is commemorated on a tombstone found in Rome, or Licinius, the modest neighborhood priest who specialized in purifying slaves and was caught up in the Milonian controversy of the same year[164] – the "ideological monotony" of contional discourse posed a difficult problem of discernment. If Cicero and Rullus each pledged their allegiance to the same principles and goals and denounced the other as an imposter, then the problem from the "plebs'-eye view" was constituted as one of deciding which of the two it was. And yet how to unmask him, when the *contio* itself was the exclusive authoritative source of political information? On what grounds to make a judgment, and confer one's trust?

---

[163] Hence, with this crucial and heavy proviso, it was possible even to claim to be the "real" *popularis* in the Senate: Cic. *Leg. agr.* 1.23. See above, p. 223. Achard 1981 elegantly and comprehensively delineates the fundamental structures of this "optimate" rhetoric.

[164] *ILLRP* 786a; Asc. 51 C.

CHAPTER 7

Contional ideology: the political drama

Disillusioned by the failure of a flurry of progressive legislation in the United States to live up to its promise, the American political theorist Murray Edelman formulated a "symbolist" model of democratic politics, which he laid out in three thought-provoking, now classic works published between 1964 and 1977.[1] Edelman sought to construct a model of modern democratic politics that would explain how formally democratic political regimes can survive, even flourish, despite the continual failure of their policies to produce real and lasting benefits for their voters. He took the perspective that functionally, if not in theory, modern "democratic" politics was best seen as a kind of symbolic manipulation whereby ruling élites engineer the acquiescence of the mass and thus perpetuate their power. They do so, in Edelman's view, not by actually *solving problems* but by *staging dramas of problem-solving*, to which the public responds with anxiety at the dangers confronted and acquiescence in the efforts of their leaders to assuage that anxiety. At the core of theory is the idea that

Political "events" . . . are largely creations of the language used to describe them. For the mass of political spectators, developments occur in a remote area where there can be no direct observation or feedback. The bewildering political universe needs to be ordered and given meaning. People who are anxious and confused are eager to be supplied with an organized political order – including simple explanations of the threats they fear – and with reassurance that the threats are being countered.[2]

Elites respond with what Edelman would eventually call "dramaturgies of coping":

In contrast to the complicated network of competing influences in the empirical world, the world of the myths [i.e. self-serving élite representations] is simple: It revolves around hostile plotters and benevolent leaders, and both factions carefully plan the future and can shape it in accordance with their plans. The language

---

[1] Edelman 1964, 1971, 1977. A later development of the theory may be found in Edelman 1988.
[2] Edelman 1971: 65.

of political discussion, analysis, and debate frequently evokes these themes by personifying observed, feared, or desired trends into plotters and heroes.[3]

Among such "themes" or "myths" is the "evocation of an outgroup, defined as 'different' and as plotting to commit harmful acts"; then, in order "to reassure those who are frightened" by this menace, "the view that the political leader is benevolent and effective in saving the people from danger"; and finally the "corollary," "that a group . . . can achieve victory over its enemies if it will only work, sacrifice, and obey its leaders."[4] Thus

> The willingness of mass publics to follow, to sacrifice, to accept their roles is the basic necessity for every political regime. Without a following there are no leaders. For government and for aspirants to leadership it is therefore important both that people become anxious about their security and that their anxiety be assuaged, though never completely so.[5]

There must, therefore, always be designated "enemies" of the People, for without their help there can hardly be plausible and authoritative "friends" to lead and govern them.

Whatever its value for the analysis of modern democratic politics, Edelman's "symbolist" theory has suggestive points of contact with the discourse of the Republican *contio*. We have observed that contional rhetoric avoided an overt confrontation between larger political ideas and instead focused attention on competition between persons, essentially revolving around the question who was the true and who the false Friend of the People. This recalls Edelman's central idea that élite leadership of "mass publics" is founded upon the exploitation of popular anxiety to produce acquiescence, especially by scripting a political "drama" turning upon the plots of "enemies" and the "heroic" and ultimately successful efforts of leaders to overcome them with popular support. As we shall see shortly, the illusionistic world of drama happens to be the metaphor that Cicero himself adopts to characterize the *contio* and the central problem faced by its popular audience of distinguishing truth-telling from manipulative deception. This problem is not merely a rhetorical or ideological creation, since (as we shall see) the ordinary citizen, in fact, had only a partial view of his leaders, and depended for the rest on mediated information controlled by senators, whose goals were not necessarily those of the People. But the invidious "drama" scripted and performed on the public stage by members

---

[3] Edelman 1971: 77. "Dramaturgy of coping": Edelman 1977: 147.
[4] Edelman 1971: 78.   [5] Edelman 1977: 5.

of the élite may be seen as Edelman-style "symbolic politics," bypassing possible arguments about divergent visions of the public good – a less exciting script, and one potentially threatening to the privileged position of the élite – and instead stimulating and assuaging by turns a (not-unjustified) pre-existing public anxiety about the real intentions and trustworthiness of their leaders. Above all, the model suggests how this "dramaturgy of coping" can have served to perpetuate popular acquiescence in paternalistic rule by a powerful élite. For "heroes" from the ranks of that élite would always be called upon to defend the People against those "plotters" in their midst whom they had "unmasked." If Cicero was a vigilant *popularis*, Rullus was a tyrant in tribune's clothing; if the nobles were corrupt abusers of the public trust, then the tribune who alerted the public to this condition was a brave, lonely champion of the People's interests. Gaius Gracchus, speaking for the Aufeian bill about 124, declares somewhat alarmingly that everyone who comes before the People is trying to "make off with" something; others are seeking bribes from the rival parties – the Bithynian King, the Pontic King, or both – but he, Gracchus, seeks from the People "not money, but a good reputation and public distinction."[6] So long as the foundations of this discourse remained sound, withdrawal of public trust from certain members of the élite (anxiety) can only have reinforced it in others (acquiescence); thus there would always be provident and loyal "heroes" to look to for guidance.

DRAMATIC ILLUSION

Recall the point in the argument we had reached by the end of the last chapter. We saw that there was no clearly marked (or even acknowledged) ideological dichotomy in political argument before the People; all senators who sought any influence in the *contio* publicly espoused the shared principles, assumptions, and pieties of "popular ideology," whatever their real views or personal inclinations. The most striking illustration of this fact is Cicero's attempt – successful, it appears – to pass himself off as a card-carrying

---

[6] Gell. *NA* 11.10 = *ORF* 48.44, pp. 187–88: *Nam vos, Quirites, . . . neminem nostrum invenietis sine pretio huc prodire. omnes nos, qui verba facimus, aliquid petimus, neque ullius rei causa quisquam ad vos prodit, nisi ut aliquid auferat. ego ipse . . . non gratis prodeo; verum peto a vobis non pecuniam, sed bonam existimationem atque honorem. qui prodeunt dissuasuri ne hanc legem accipiatis, petunt non honorem a vobis, verum a Nicomede pecuniam; qui suadent ut accipiatis, hi quoque petunt non a vobis bonam existimationem, verum a Mithridate rei familiari suae pretium et praemium; qui autem ex eodem loco atque ordine tacent, hi vel acerrimi sunt; nam ab omnibus pretium accipiunt et omnis fallunt.* On the *rogatio Aufeia*, see Kallet-Marx 1995: 110–11.

popularis in the public speeches against Rullus and the defense of Rabirius. Rather than dismissing Cicero's "strategy of impersonation" as if it were perfectly evident that it could not work in the public forum (clearly a most dubious assumption, given Cicero's gifts and the pattern of rhetorical assimilation that I have traced), a far more fruitful course will be to take seriously what this strategy implies: that in the absence of a clearly marked (or even simply acknowledged) ideological bifurcation, the central problem that faced the mass audience of the *contio* was how to distinguish the "true" *popularis* from the "false" one. With this background, I now consider how this problem was "dramatized" in contional discourse, as well as the reasons why this "drama" could have been so convincing.

In his dialogue *On Friendship*, Cicero makes his central speaker, C. Laelius, historically the close friend and ally of the great Scipio Aemilianus, take up the important question of how to distinguish between the flatterer and the true friend. Laelius insists that it is possible to do so, and as befits a senator, he uses the *contio* as an analogy. In the *contio*, "which is made up of the most ignorant men" and is like the dramatic stage in that "there is the most room for falsehood and illusion," the audience "is accustomed to distinguish the difference between the *popularis*, that is, a flatterer and a weathervane, and the steady, stern and statesmanlike citizen"; even there, truth prevails "if only it is revealed and explained." It must therefore be possible for wise and virtuous men, with some care, to detect a true friend.[7] To illustrate his point, Laelius then cites two cases that were in recent history at the implied date of the dialogue (129 BC), in which highly attractive *popularis* bills were voted down by the People after successful contional speeches against them – that of Scipio Aemilianus, full of authority and grandeur (*gravitas* and *maiestas*) against C. Papirius Carbo's bill on iteration of the tribunate in 130; and Laelius' own speech in 145 as praetor – which he modestly claims depended more on the arguments than on authority – against C. Licinius Crassus' bill to institute election for the priesthoods.[8] These are encouraging examples, Laelius hopefully claims, of how the People can be made to see the error of "popular" legislation.[9]

The passage is sorely in need of some simple deconstruction. It revolves around the fundamental assumption that the *popularis* simply "flatters" the

---

[7] Cic. *Amic.* 95–97. Note esp. §95: *Contio, quae ex imperitissimis constat, tamen iudicare solet, quid intersit inter popularem, id est assentatorem et levem civem, et inter constantem et verum et gravem;* 97: *Quod si in scaena, id est in contione, in qua rebus fictis et adumbratis loci plurimum est, tamen verum valet, si modo id patefactum et inlustratum est . . .*

[8] Perhaps the very occasion when the orator's position on the Rostra was reversed: p. 46 with n. 37.

[9] Cic. *Amic.* 96: *Itaque lex popularis suffragiis populi repudiata est.*

People with enticing but specious and self-serving proposals, while the opponent of such seduction is the People's true "friend," can perceive the People's true interests, and can, with enough "weight" and "grandeur" (*gravitas* and *maiestas*), *make the People see* the "truth" through the illusionist manipulation of the "flatterer." Obviously, inherent in this whole complex structure is the questionable notion that Scipio, and Cicero, and other opponents of *populares*, were more honest and accurate diagnosticians of what was good for the People than were the Papirii, the Rulli, or the Clodii of the late Republic. We, at least, are entitled to doubt whether, when the People were persuaded to reject reiteration of the tribunate in 130 or agrarian distribution in 63, or for that matter when they restored senators to the juries in 106 or emended C. Gracchus' grain law in the early first century, they had really been induced, by sober consideration of the merits of the law, to see "the truth."[10] The real interest of the passage for the present study, however, lies among the assumptions about the nature of contional communication that lurk just beneath its surface. The citizenry are at a disadvantage in their access to knowledge and thus the *contio* is a place of illusion, like the dramatic stage; the person behind the mask and the character he is playing before the People are not – or rather, even more insidiously, not necessarily – one and the same.[11] The challenge for the audience is to determine – without being able to strip off the mask – which speaker actually is the "true friend" of the People behind the "cajolery" (*blanditiae*) of one and the authoritative bearing (*gravitas, maiestas*) of the other that bespeaks a "leader of the People rather than a follower."[12] The emphasis on an intuitive interpretation of external signs of trustworthiness rather than on assessment of rational argument is interesting.[13] But although here Cicero/Laelius seems piously to assume that ultimately sincerity is palpable, at least in direct comparison with "flattery," in actual speeches it turns out to require the keen insight of a Cicero to penetrate the deceptive appearance of men like the tribune Rullus or the unspeakable Piso – whose noble eyebrows had tricked the Roman People into electing him consul – and equally powerful

---

[10] See above, p. 193 with n. 139.

[11] Compare how Cicero's imagery of the dramatic "role" assigned to him by the People functions in just the opposite way: *Phil.* 6.2 and *Leg. agr.* 2.49, quoted at chap. 6, n. 94. For the stage metaphor put to a different use, see *De or.* 2.338.

[12] Cic. *Amic.* 96: *Quibus blanditiis C. Papirius nuper influebat in auris contionis . . . Quanta illi* [sc. Scipioni], *di immortales, fuit gravitas, quanta in oratione maiestas! ut facile ducem populi Romani, non comitem diceres.*

[13] Cf. Cic. *Off.* 1.145–46 (*videndum est in vita ne forte quid discrepet*), with Dyck 1996: 326: "The discrepancy would presumably be . . . between the given action and the social rôle one was assuming."

oratory to expose their underlying character.[14] External signs, it seems, may not then be so straightforward for an audience to "read."

The difficulty faced by the contional audience was enormously magnified by the separation, in Republican political life, between the two spheres of action and sources of power – Senate and popular assembly – and the rigid exclusion of the People from direct observation of the former, even as a hierarchical practice of mediated communication emphasized its primacy. This can only have invested goings-on inside the Curia with an awesome mystery, at the same time dramatizing the "masquerade," since one had no idea – other than what a rival senator might say, whether truthfully or not one could not easily say – how this Friend of the People really behaved in that mysterious locus of power when free of the citizenry's monitoring gaze.

All non-senators, with negligible exceptions, were sent forth from the House before any question was formally referred to it, and the presence of a member of the general public was held to invalidate any decree.[15] Although the doors of the meeting-place seem actually to have been closed only in extraordinary circumstances, the area immediately outside the doors (sometimes called the "forecourt of the Curia"), from which it was possible to follow the proceedings to some degree, seems normally to have been kept clear of the general public and reserved for a privileged group: the sons of senators and, when foreign business was transacted, ambassadors.[16] Naturally, then, on momentous occasions great crowds assembled outside wherever the Senate was meeting, sometimes, as we have seen, hoping to influence the deliberations inside by means of their noise and numbers, but

[14] On Piso, see now Corbeill 1996: 169–72; cf. "if one can judge a person's moral character simply by visual scrutiny – and give proof of that character to others – then all bodes well for the state" (p. 169); cf. also Corbeill 2002: 192–93. At *Pis.* 14 – a reference to Piso's performance in the Clodian *contio* discussed elsewhere (chap. 5, n. 80) – Cicero underscores the consul's deceit by configuring his expression as a comic mask, that of the *senex iratus*: Hughes 1992 (following Grimal).

[15] Cass. Dio 39.28.3 (an episode of 56). See Mommsen 1887: III.978 (cf. 932), adducing also Cass. Dio 80.1.2; Livy 22.60.2; cf. Livy 27.51.5.

[16] Mommsen 1887: III.931, with n. 5; Willems 1883–85: 2.163–64; Talbert 1984: 154–55, 195–200. Cf. Harris 1979: 255; Bonnefond-Coudry 1989: 54, n. 21. Presumably the practice was identical when the Senate met elsewhere than in the Curia. An open-door policy is implied by Cicero's complaints at *Phil.* 2.112, 5.18, as well as by the fact that those clustered about the doors could to some extent see and listen to the proceedings (see esp. Cic. *Q Fr.* 2.7.1: *Id. Mai. senatus frequens divinus fuit in supplicatione Gabinio deneganda. adiurat Procilius hoc nemini accidisse. foris valde plauditur;* cf. *Cat.* 4.3 *in conspectu meo;* Livy 22.59.16 *intueri;* Val. Max. 2.2.7; Zonar. 7.15; Plin. *Ep.* 8.14.5; Talbert 1984: 198). Livy 27.50.9 suggests that in extraordinary times a crowd of excited citizens might actually press upon the threshold (those in 2.48.10, 22.59.16 do not appear to be the common citizenry), but the passage itself indicates how unusual that must have been: the entrance was blocked. On the whole, the requirement of a *contio* to inform the public of what had taken place in the Senate suggests that for all practical purposes meetings were closed to the general public.

doubtless always hungrily awaiting the release of authoritative information in the *contio* that traditionally followed the Senate's adjournment. The great throngs that flocked about the Senate's meeting-place to learn of its investigation of the "Catilinarians" on December 3, 63, and of its deliberations on their punishment two days later are two of the best-known examples.[17] A crowd of citizens gathered in front of the Temple of Tellus during the discussion of amnesty after Caesar's assassination and went so far as to interrupt the meeting, demanding that Antony and Lepidus address them even in the midst of senatorial deliberations.[18] Nothing better expresses the agonizing dependence of the citizenry on senatorial control of authoritative information than Livy's dramatic reconstructions of the arrival of the news of the devastating defeat at Trasimene or the splendid victory at the Metaurus – reconstructions which, I suggest, illuminate contemporary practices and assumptions even if they cannot be assumed to be accurate descriptions of the actual events of 217 and 207. Anxiety, rumor and expectation drew the citizenry to the Forum while senators met in the Curia; the anguished pleas for some word by relatives of the soldiery were put off until the Senate heard the information and its meeting was concluded. Then, at last, came the announcement in a *contio* – reportedly, in the case of the disaster at Trasimene, amounting to nothing more than M. Pomponius' famous "we have lost a great battle," after keeping the hysterical mob waiting until close to sundown.[19]

Decrees of the Senate were normally read out to the People in a *contio* immediately after the meeting had adjourned.[20] The *contio* was formally convened by the magistrate who had presided over the meeting of the Senate; he might now also deliver a speech.[21] The most familiar example

---

[17] Plut. *Cic.* 19.3; Cic. *Cat.* 4.14. Cicero represents these as demonstrating their support of strong measures; we may recall the guard of overzealous equites at the entrance (Sall. *Cat.* 49.4 [cf. Cic. *Cat.* 1.21], with McGushin 1977: 234) and Cicero's emergency enlistment order (Cass. Dio 37.35.4), but these alone will not have crammed the entire Forum and the adjacent temples and streets.

[18] App. *B Civ.* 2.130–32: ἐκ πολλοῦ συνδραμόντες ἐκάλουν (130). The crowd obliged Lepidus to descend from the temple, on the Carinae, to the Rostra so that all could hear (131); presumably the space in front of the temple was too restricted for all. One wonders whether that was the intention.

[19] Livy 22.7.6–8 (Trasimene); 27.50.4–11, 51.5 (Metaurus). Cf. Pina Polo 1989: 141–42; Achard 1991: 207.

[20] See, e.g., Cic. *Att.* 2.24.3; 4.1.6. Pina Polo 1989: 139–40. App. *B Civ.* 2.142 seems to show (chap. 4, n. 179) that the *contio* might be delayed by failing daylight until the morning after a late-running senatorial meeting. Alternatively, the presiding magistrate might only have the decree read out on the day of the senatorial meeting, leaving the speeches for the next day: so, apparently, during the Vettius scandal of 59 (Cic. *Att.* 2.24.3).

[21] Pina Polo supposes that the *contio* immediately following a senatorial meeting would be held by the highest official in the city; but on his own showing, the presiding magistrate was sometimes

of such a speech is Cicero's *Third Catilinarian*, the original of which he
delivered toward dusk, at the end of a long meeting of the Senate, without
even waiting for the decree to be written up and read: he recounts it from
memory.[22] The magistrate, at his discretion, might also offer others the
opportunity to address the People: the mover of the decree, or one who
had delivered a particularly important opinion (*sententia*) on the matter.[23]
This might be called the "official" *contio*; magistrates other than the presiding official in the Senate could hold *contiones* of their own, in which,
for example, the mover of an important minority *sententia* might be given
the opportunity to offer the People a different (and probably tendentious)
version of what had taken place outside their view: hence, for example,
Cicero's *Sixth Philippic*.[24] Even when there was no decree to be publicly
communicated, meetings of the Senate on matters of general interest were
perhaps often followed by corresponding *contiones* that brought the discussion before the People: immediately after Cicero's speech of thanks to the
Senate for his recall from exile, the consuls P. Lentulus Spinther and Q.
Metellus Nepos brought him into a public meeting to thank the other half
of the Republican dyad.[25]

Not surprisingly, contional speakers often betray an acute consciousness
of popular exclusion from the senatorial sphere and define their own role

a tribune. Surely the magistrate who had presided over the meeting of the Senate would normally
hold the following *contio* as well, as did, for example, the tribune M. Servilius on December 20, 44,
when Cicero delivered the Fourth Philippic (Cic. *Phil.* 4.16); he might be joined by other magistrates
as well (Cic. *Att.* 4.1.6: *omnes magistratus praesentes praeter unum praetorem et duos tribunos*; both
consuls at App. *B Civ.* 2.142).

[22] Dusk: Cic. *Cat.* 3.29. Decree: §§13–15.

[23] Cic. *Att.* 4.1.6; *Phil.* 4 with 3.37–39; App. *B Civ.* 2.142, with Cass. Dio 44.22.3. At *Cat.* 4.11 Cicero
implies that the mover of the decree would be his "companion" in the *contio* to follow: *sive hoc
statueritis, dederitis mihi comitem ad contionem populo carum atque iucundum* (sc. *Caesarem*). Cicero
probably spoke at the *contio* after the meeting at the Temple of Tellus on March 17, 44: chap. 4,
n. 182.

[24] After the senatorial debate regarding Antony that closed on January 4, 43, the tribune P. Apuleius
held a *contio*, at which he apparently asked Cicero, whose motion had been defeated, to give his
opinion of the decree (*Phil.* 6.1; Cicero later claimed that the crowd had summoned him: *Phil.* 7.21).
Note that the audience had already received an account of the proceedings (below, n. 27), presumably
in an "official" *contio* held by the consul, Pansa, and probably also from Apuleius himself. Another
tribune, M. Servilius, did much the same thing in March: *Fam.* 12.7.1, with *Phil.* 11; this *contio* is
lost. In principle, Cicero's procedure was not so very different from that of Clodius in 57, who had
communicated to the People in a *contio* held by his brother, Appius Claudius, a praetor, a highly
misleading (though not strictly false) version of the Pontiffs' decree in regard to the restoration of
Cicero's domestic site (Cic. *Att.* 4.2.3, with Tatum 1993). The parallel is not exact, since that did not
follow upon a meeting of the Senate as a whole.

[25] Cass. Dio 39.9.1 (which, with *Schol. Bob.* 110 St, surely shows, *pace* Pina Polo 1989: 133, 139–40, that
Cicero's speech of thanks to the People is not identical with his speech in favor of Pompey's grain
commission; Cicero simply omitted it from its proper place at *Att.* 4.1.5); cf. Cass. Dio 43.18.6 and,
further, Nicholson 1992: 127.

partly as one of mediators of crucial knowledge of that world. Near the beginning of his *Third Catilinarian Oration*, Cicero begins a long and minute exposition of the momentous senatorial meeting that had occupied nearly the whole day, and the events that led to it, with the words, "I shall briefly lay out for you what has been scrutinized, revealed, and discovered in the Senate through my efforts, so that you, who have no knowledge of this and are awaiting information, may know their extent, how patent they are, and by what method they have been investigated and detected."[26] Cicero's following narration covers thirteen paragraphs of the speech, not much less than half of the whole. Here, of course, as consul and presiding official, Cicero will have had a special responsibility to relate the events in detail. On the occasion of the *Sixth Philippic*, however, on January 4, 43, his invitation by a tribune to give the People his opinion of the Senate's decree came after they had already heard "what was done in the Senate, and the various opinions expressed." But Cicero will answer the tribune's question "in such a way that you may know about what you did not witness": a very short, tendentious narrative follows, which must be to some extent an alternative version from that already offered to the People.[27] Doubtless that was also the nature of the remarkable fragment of a *contio* that I have already had occasion to quote, in which T. Munatius Plancus described to the People in some detail the procedural maneuvers by which he managed to outwit the cunning Hortensius and to maneuver the Senate into formally condemning the killing of Clodius.[28]

We need not share W. V. Harris's extreme pessimism about the extent of literacy in Rome to doubt that the average citizen drew much benefit from written sources of information about what went on in the Curia – if for practical purposes such sources really existed.[29] As a rule, decrees of the Senate were copied onto wooden tablets and filed away in the *aerarium*, probably the basement level of the Temple of Saturn in the Forum; there appears to have been no regular provision for posting them up for public scrutiny after they were recited in the *contio*.[30] True, Suetonius makes two vague comments about a novelty of Julius Caesar's first consulship (in 59)

---

[26] Cic. *Cat.* 3.3: *Quae quoniam in senatu inlustrata, patefacta, comperta sunt per me, vobis iam exponam breviter ut et quanta et quam manifesta et qua ratione investigata et comprehensa sint vos qui et ignoratis et exspectatis scire possitis.*

[27] Cic. *Phil.* 6.1: *ita respondebo ut ea quibus non interfuistis nosse possitis.* Cf. *audita vobis esse arbitror, Quirites, quae sint acta in senatu, quae fuerit cuiusque sententia.* See above, n. 24.

[28] Asc. 44–45 C: *in contione exposuisse populo quae pridie acta erant in senatu: in qua contione haec dixit ad verbum;* the full text is quoted above, p. 115.

[29] Harris 1989: 175–284; cf. above, Chap. 3, n. 12.

[30] But see below, on White's hypothesis of Caesar's "publication" of senatorial *acta*. On the filing of decrees in the state archive (against anachronistic modern assumptions about its function, see

involving the "publication" in some manner of a senatorial record (*acta senatus*), but we do not really know just how accessible this was for the common citizen: was it posted on notice-boards, on the analogy of magisterial edicts and promulgated bills, or simply made available for consultation by resourceful individuals in archives?[31] In any case, since we hear nothing else about this practice in the otherwise remarkably detailed and copious evidence we have for this period – historical narratives and biographies, contemporary letters, and Cicero's speeches, including several *contiones* – we should take care not to exaggerate its practical significance for a society in which oral communication remained the primary medium for the transmission of news and information to the citizenry in Rome.[32] Augustus' edict on the Secular Games of 17 BC makes sufficiently clear that the display of a written text was a form of "publication" secondary to oral announcement and recitation: "Following ancestral tradition we have publicly announced the edict in a *contio* and have likewise posted it on a whitened board so that anyone who was absent from the *contio* or did not fully understand it might be informed."[33] Written publication was neither the essential act of

---

Culham 1989; Bonnefond-Coudry 1989: 570–73), see von Schwind 1940: 53–63; Sherk 1969: 4–13. The so-called Tabularium on the slope of the Capitol facing the Forum is commonly taken to be an appendage to the *aerarium*, but its identification is now in dispute: in favor of the traditional identification, see now A. Mura Sommella, *LTUR* v.17–20. Livy 3.55.13 attests to a practice of filing *senatus consulta* in the Temple of Diana on the Aventine as well. The elaborate procedure of publication described in the *SC de Bacchanalibus* (*CIL* 1² 581 = *ILS* 18 = *ILLRP* 511, lines 22–23, 25–27: repeated oral and simultaneous written publication on bronze) is clearly highly exceptional, as von Schwind emphasizes (pp. 59–61). Cic. *Att.* 4.3.3 <*Milo*> *proposita Marcellini sententia* might be thought to reveal a tribune posting up in public an opinion delivered in the Senate (so translated by Shackleton Bailey). But with *sententia*, *proposita* surely means "stated, put forward" (cf. Cic. *Lig.* 26: *de suscepta causa propositaque sententia nulla contumelia, nulla vis, nullum periculum posset depellere*); thus, wherever we add Milo's name (I prefer Klotz's placement, at the beginning of the main clause, rather than here, with Tunstall), he cannot be the agent of *proposita Marcellini sententia*. Cicero is simply saying that, after Marcellinus delivered his opinion in the Senate that a trial regarding the attacks on Cicero and his property should take precedence over the elections, Milo posted up his edict to the same end, declaring his intention to postpone any election on religious grounds.

31 Suet. *Iul.* 20.1: *primo omnium instituit, ut tam senatus quam populi diurna acta confierent et publicarentur* (cf. *Aug.* 36). For the former interpretation of *publicarentur*, see P. White 1997: 78–84, who powerfully rebuts the "gazette" hypothesis of Riepl 1913: 387–94, 405–10. Talbert 1984: 308–23 interprets the much more copious information about the *acta senatus* from the Imperial period; "next to nothing is known of these [senatorial] *acta* before the beginning of the Principate" (p. 310). White's skeptical treatment of a host of fundamental questions surrounding both *acta senatus* and *populi* (see also Baldwin 1979; B. A. Marshall 1985: 56) should dampen any temptation to attribute much political significance to this transitory innovation.

32 See Harris 1989: 29, 164–66, 206–18; of course, this suggests that literacy is somewhat beside the point for the effects of communication on the distribution of power. The great attention apparently attracted by the posted texts of Bibulus' "Archilochian" edicts in 59 (*Att.* 2.20.4, 21.4) will have been extraordinary, a consequence of his remarkable withdrawal from the public stage.

33 *CIL* vi 32323, lines 26–27: *more exsemploque maiorum in contione p[alam ediximus . . . item in albo proposui]mus, uti, si qui a contione afuissent aut non sat[is intellexissent, cognoscerent . . .]*.

publicizing information, nor a substitute for oral presentation in the *contio*, but a recourse for those unable to attend or to hear it.

The *contio*, then, offered the citizenry their only authoritative insight into that shadowy world where their leaders deliberated amongst themselves. Those who spoke in *contiones* – essentially, tribunes and consuls and those designated by them – "revealed" that information and in so doing created it for the public, a position that cannot but have conferred substantial power upon them, individually and collectively. This communicative power, derived from magistrates' and other important senators' privileged place in what might be called an economy of knowledge, can be readily perceived when, as often, orators before the People assume the persona of a "revealer of hidden truth," disclosing – in fact, of course, constructing – what had transpired in the corridors of power outside the popular gaze. The role is marked by what we might call a "revelatory" rhetorical mode, recognizable even at the level of diction, in which speakers teach and warn the People (*docere*, *monere*), demonstrate and explain to them (*ostendere*, *exponere*), make them see and understand – verbs and phrases rarely used of speakers in the Senate.[34] The best-known example is Cicero's self-representation in the Catilinarian *contiones* (*In Catilinam* 2 and 3). He never sleeps; always wakeful, always anticipating hidden plots against the People's safety, he spends his days and nights monitoring the activities of their enemies while they are themselves left in peace.[35] His foresight is amazing: he knows in advance every scheme that Catiline and his friends adopt and reveals them at the proper time first to the Senate, then to the People in turn.[36] The verb *providere*, in the sense "to take appropriate steps in anticipation" of something, but never losing the idea of vision contained

---

[34] *Exponere*: Cic. *Cat.* 2.17; 3.3; 3.13, *Leg. agr.* 2.16. *Docere*: Sall. *Hist.* 3.48.1; Cic. *Leg. agr.* 3.3, 4, 15; *Red. pop.* 16; cf. *Leg.* 3.11: *rem populum docento, doceri a magistratibus privatisque patiunto*. *Ostendere*: Cic. *Leg. agr.* 2.21, 71; 3.3, 15. *Monere*: Sall. *Iug.* 31.25; *Hist.* 3.48.13; Cic. *Rab. Post.* 14. Cf. also descriptive passages in Sallust: *Iug.* 30.3; 33.4; 42.1. Cic. *Cat.* 2.6: *adsecutus ut vos . . . videretis*; *Cat.* 3.3: *in eo omnis dies noctesque consumpsi ut . . . rem ita comprehenderem ut tum demum . . . maleficium ipsum videretis*.

[35] *Cat.* 3.3: *semper vigilavi et providi, Quirites, quem ad modum in tantis et tam absconditis insidiis salvi esse possemus*; §4: *in eo omnis dies noctesque consumpsi ut quid agerent, quid molirentur sentirem ac viderem*; §27: *Mentes enim hominum audacissimorum sceleratae ac nefariae ne vobis nocere possent ego providi. Cat.* 2.19: *me ipsum vigilare, adesse providere rei publicae*; §26: *mihi ut urbi sine vestro metu ac sine ullo tumultu satis esset praesidi consultum atque provisum est*. For the sleeplessness of the People's guardian, see also *Leg. agr.* 2.5, 77; *Phil.* 6.17–18.

[36] *Cat.* 2.6: *omnia superioris noctis consilia ad me perlata esse sentiunt; patefeci in senatu hesterno die*; §12–13: *rem omnem ad patres conscriptos detuli . . . Cum ille homo audacissimus conscientia convictus primo reticuisset, patefeci cetera: quid ea nocte egisset, ubi fuisset . . . Cum haesitaret . . . quaesivi quid dubitaret proficisci eo quo iam pridem pararet . . . Cat.* 3.3 (quoted above, n. 35), and the whole narrative of §§3–15.

in its verbal root, is particularly prominent, and indeed closes the *Third Catilinarian*: *providebo, Quirites*, "I shall see to it, Citizens."[37] Cicero's keen vision, and prevision, have been lent him in some sense as the human agent of Jupiter, whose new, greater statue – erected, it happens, on the Capitol that very day – looking out over the Forum, Curia, and of course the very audience of this speech, penetrated, through the consul, the plots against the Republic and laid them bare to the Senate and People of Rome.[38] Like Jupiter's statue, Cicero not only sees but also makes others see: he produces stunning revelations in the Senate, and shows the People what has been hitherto obscured to their vision.[39] Power of metaphorical vision is perhaps what most fundamentally distinguishes the contional speaker from his audience – an idea itself visually expressed by the great physical elevation of the speaker on the Rostra.[40]

Orators frequently display to the People their special powers of insight into the dark corners of their adversaries' minds – a claim made most plausible by their direct access to the Senate, unlike the mystified populace. And their revelations about this privileged sphere could not be refuted on any independent, unmediated evidence not flowing from a senatorial source, while any rival version offered by another speaker in another meeting was in principle open to the same kinds of questions of credibility as any other. We have seen in previous chapters how, arguing against Rullus' proposal for land distribution, Cicero lays bare, underneath the fair façade of tribunician agrarian distribution, a covert assault on the freedom of the Roman People by a murky clique of Sullan color. He pays lip service to the idea that the audience might reject his revelations;[41] but on what independent basis can they take issue with the penetrating insight of the

---

[37] *Cat.* 3.29. See examples quoted above, n. 35; also 3.14 *providentia mea*, 3.16 *hoc providebam animo*, 3.18 (quoted n. 38). Cf. *Leg. agr.* 2.102, 103; *Phil.* 6.17.

[38] *Cat.* 3.18–22, especially the response of the *haruspices* (§20): *si illud signum quod videtis solis ortum et forum curiamque conspiceret, fore ut ea consilia quae clam essent inita contra salutem urbis atque imperi inlustrarentur ut a senatu populoque Romano perspici possent.* Divine direction: *Cat.* 3.18: *Quamquam haec omnia, Quirites, ita sunt a me administrata ut deorum immortalium nutu atque consilio et gesta et provisa esse videantur;* §22: *Dis ego immortalibus ducibus hanc mentem voluntatemque suscepi atque ad haec tanta indicia perveni;* 2.29: *neque mea prudentia neque humanis consiliis fretus polliceor vobis, Quirites, sed multis et non dubiis deorum immortalium significationibus, quibus ego ducibus in hanc spem sententiamque sum ingressus.* My thinking on this point was partly stimulated by an unpublished paper delivered by Paul Langford at the 1993 meeting of the American Philological Association.

[39] Revelations in the Senate: see above, n. 36. The People's vision: *Cat.* 2.6: *Quod exspectavi, iam sum adsecutus ut vos omnes factam esse aperte coniurationem contra rem publicam* videretis. 3.4: *ut . . . rem ita comprehenderem ut tum demum animis saluti vestrae provideretis cum oculis maleficium ipsum* videretis. Cf. §3: *ut . . . vos qui et ignoratis et exspectatis* scire possitis.

[40] See above, pp. 50ff. Cf. Hölkeskamp 1995: 36–41.   [41] Cic. *Leg. agr.* 2.15–16.

consul who, as his revelations persistently remind them, has direct access to a world outside their ken? In the Senate, out of their earshot, Cicero avers, this fine *popularis* tribune had even complained about the power of the urban plebs and said they should be "drained off" like so much sewage![42] Rullus responded with revelations of his own, exposing Cicero as the agent of the Sullan *possessores*.[43] Whom was the *contio*-goer to believe, and on what basis?

We should not expect this kind of "Trojan-horse" tactic to be exclusively Ciceronian, and as it happens the next-best example in our evidence of contional speech is the warning of Sallust's tribune Memmius in III that the Senate's soft treatment of the enemy Jugurtha is in reality nothing less than another step in a vast oligarchical conspiracy against the People's freedom.[44] An implausible allegation, viewed dispassionately from the historian's desk. But Memmius' law was passed. In Sallust's other great tribunician harangue, C. Licinius Macer cries, "Beware of the trap!": a recent grain law sponsored by the *Sullani* – *ostensibly* a good thing – is really only an insidious attempt to preserve the servitude of the plebs by easing pressure to restore the full powers of the tribunate.[45] Concessions by the oligarchy, he asserts, are driven solely by fear in a strategy that aims to hold off the People's just claims until Pompey can be enlisted as an ally against them; but he adds that he has firm knowledge that on his return from Spain the general will prefer to lead the People instead of joining the oligarchs: they can count on his support for the revival of the tribunate.[46] That Macer's characterization of the situation may not have been far off the mark is not to the point here.[47] What is interesting for us is his implicit claim to what amounts, before this audience, to specialist knowledge of the true minds of their leaders, and the power of his revelatory use of this knowledge. His implied audience, who relied on what they heard in the *contio* not only for authoritative news but for a deeper understanding of complicated political maneuvers, were in no position to refute him, as they could not refute Cicero or Memmius; and the

---

[42] Cic. *Leg. agr.* 2.70: *Et nimirum id est quod ab hoc tribuno plebis dictum est in senatu, urbanam plebem nimium in re publica posse; exhauriendam esse; hoc enim verbo est usus, quasi de aliqua sentina ac non de optimorum civium genere loqueretur.* Of course, in private Cicero uses *sentina* (and worse) to refer to the urban plebs: *Att.* 1.19.4 (translated above, pp. 210–11); chap. 4, n. 49.

[43] See p. 200 with n. 174.   [44] Sall. *Iug.* 31.25–26. Above, pp. 237–38.

[45] Sall. *Hist.* 3.48.19–23; §21: *Cavendus dolus est!* For the *lex Terentia Cassia frumentaria* of 73, cf. Greenidge–Clay, 257; Gruen 1974: 385.

[46] Sall. *Hist.* 3.48.21–23; cf. §8. Note the visual metaphor of §23: *mihi quidem satis spectatum est.*

[47] On the other hand, if Gruen's controversial interpretation (1974: 23–28) of the attitude of the Sullan oligarchy toward restoration of the tribunate be accepted, Macer's assertions would largely be reduced to so much disingenuous populism.

success of a denial by Macer's opponents will have depended, in turn, not on knowledge in the audience's independent possession but on the plausibility of *their* alternative characterization when they came (*if* they came) before the *contio*.[48]

The "revelatory" posture depends for most of its effectiveness on the audience's acceptance of the proposition that things are not always – indeed, hardly ever – what they seem on the surface. So naturally, hand in hand with the orator's claim of privileged perception goes the orator's representation of the relationship between appearance and reality as deceptive and often highly counterintuitive. "Great confusion prevails because of the treacherous shamming of some men who, while they attack and hinder not only the benefits of the People but even their security, seek by means of their speeches to make themselves appear to be *populares*."[49] Offers of state largesse may after all only be demagogic bait, and the true Friend of the People is surely not one who is secretly attempting to further dark schemes that are directly contrary to the hopes he is inspiring in the Roman People.[50] Cicero's opponent Rullus turns out to be just this type of sneaky operator. The moment he had been elected he affected a changed demeanor, tone of voice, and manner of walking; he was unkempt, wore old clothes, grew his hair longer, and shaved less frequently, "so that with his glaring frowns he appeared to threaten tribunician force against everyone and to menace the Republic"; and once he entered into office he gave himself a more aggressive bearing than all the other tribunes.[51] His first *contio* on the

---

[48] It is sometimes claimed that Macer's speech failed (Gruen 1974: 25; McGushin 1992–94: II.98). That presumes that his objective was to restore the full powers of the tribunate immediately – an unrealistic one, since, for all practical purposes, a tribune no longer had the power to initiate legislation. There is no very concrete prescription at Sall. *Hist.* 3.48.14–18; at most, a call for non-cooperation with recruitment (Brunt 1971a: table XIV, shows an increase of *c.* 60 percent in the number of active legions between 75 and 72). The speech makes quite clear that all hopes for the restoration of the tribunate rest on Pompey (§§ 23–24). In the meantime, however, the important right of holding *contiones* still remained to tribunes, and thus, for those willing to risk the consequences (§§3–4, 8–11), an opportunity, if somewhat diminished, to develop the valuable reputation of being "the People's Friend."

[49] Cic. *Leg. agr.* 2.7: *Versatur enim magnus error propter insidiosas non nullorum simulationes qui, cum populi non solum commoda verum etiam salutem oppugnant et impediunt, oratione adsequi volunt ut populares esse videantur.* See the whole discussion, §§7–10, and Cicero's own attempt to use speech to appear *popularis* (above, pp. 207–30.). The theme of *popularis* dissimulation, so congenial to Cicero especially after 58 (cf. *Sest.* 106–39; *Dom.* 77–92; *Har. resp.*, esp. 40–44; also, *Amic.* 95–97, discussed above), is therefore not reserved exclusively for élite audiences. On Cicero's general practice of attributing dissimulation to his political opponents, see Achard 1981: 260–68.

[50] Cic. *Leg. agr.* 2.10: *Neque enim, Quirites, illud vobis iucundum aut populare debet videri, largitio aliqua promulgata, quae verbis ostentari potest, re vera fieri nisi exhausto aerario nullo pacto potest . . . ; nec, si qui agros populo Romano pollicentur, si aliud quiddam obscure moliuntur, aliud spe ac specie simulationis ostentant, populares existimandi sunt.* Cf. *Sest.* 139; *Har. resp.* 42.

[51] Cic. *Leg. agr.* 2.13, quoted below, n. 118. On *vis tribunicia*, see §14 and Chap. 6, n. 99.

agrarian bill was incomprehensible, perhaps a deceptive ploy in itself – or did he just like obscure oratory?[52] This emphasis on dissimulation, again, is not merely a Ciceronian, or pro-senatorial, topos. It is employed also by Sallust's *popularis* tribunes, who seek to "expose" before the People the arrogance, greed, and arbitrary power of the men to whom they have themselves entrusted the honor of high office by means of their votes. To be sure, Memmius to some extent, and Macer explicitly, speak of the sins of the nobility as if they were patent to all – a rhetorical device belied by their very complaints about their audiences' apathy or passivity, and their cry to the People to stop enslaving themselves by means of their own votes.[53]

When we call to mind again the inability of the general populace to verify the words and deeds of their leaders inside the Curia, we may fairly conjecture that the topos of deceptive appearances was no arbitrary invention of senatorial orators but played on a real (and often justified) anxiety among the populace about whether their "friends" were really still so disposed once they stepped over that threshold. In some suggestive passages, the dichotomy between deceptive appearance and underlying reality is coordinated with the public-contional/closed-senatorial distinction in such a way that one easily senses this doubt lurking just beneath the surface. Cicero declares that he is not the sort of consul who will say that he is *popularis on the Rostra* without doing the same thing in the Senate, "where it seemed that there was no place for that word"; likewise, as we saw, he reports to the plebs the nasty, contemptuous way in which Rullus (who boasted of his nobility, after all) spoke of them while among senators.[54] In his speech of thanks on returning from exile, Cicero pledges to the People that he will maintain good faith with them by, among other things, *stating his opinions forthrightly in the Senate*.[55] An earlier pledge, at the conclusion of the speech for the Manilian Law, that Cicero is not speaking at the

---

[52] Cic. *Leg. agr.* 2.13: *utrum insidiarum causa fecerit, an hoc genere eloquentiae delectetur nescio.* Cicero has his little joke with the second alternative, but that does not undermine the insinuation. For a comparable "unmasking" of Labienus, the self-proclaimed *popularis* tribune prosecuting Rabirius, see *Rab. perd.* 11–17: the supposed guardian and defender of the plebs' rights and freedom, stands betrayed by his cruelty, his contempt for a citizen's right to due process and therefore for the freedom and majesty of the Roman People (cf. §35: *oppugnationem vestrae maiestatis*).

[53] Unmasking the oligarchy: Sall. *Iug.* 31.12–15 (Memmius): *At qui sunt ii qui rem publicam occupavere?* (§12); Macer's opening *praeteritio* (*Hist.* 3.48.1) is not to be taken at face value in view of what follows (esp. §§5–6). Passivity: Sall. *Iug.* 31.1–3, 9–11, 20; *Hist.* 3.48.6, 8, 14–16, 25–26. Paradoxical voting: chap. 6, n. 122.

[54] Cic. *Leg. agr.* 2.6: *in ipso senatu in quo esse locus huic voci non videbatur* (fuller quotation at chap. 6, n. 96), §70 (quoted above, n. 42). Nobility: §19.

[55] Cic. *Red. pop.* 24: *In referenda autem gratia hoc vobis repromitto semperque praestabo . . . neque in sententia simpliciter ferenda fidem . . . defuturam.*

bidding of any powerful figure, not even to please Pompey – sworn, be it noted, by the patron gods of the Rostra, who can penetrate the minds of all who take part in politics – responds to the same concern about the consistency of orators' actions and behavior when out of the public eye and back among the circles of the powerful.[56] Finally, we may recall the powerful metaphor, which Cicero twice employs in the extant *contiones*, of himself as an actor assigned by the People a role to play when he returns to the Senate.[57] With this image, Cicero implicitly acknowledges the problem raised by the two spheres in which the senator transacts the business of the *res publica* – on the Rostra, before the People's eyes, and inside the Senate, out of their observation – and the popular anxiety that a senator might play very different roles to different audiences; and he seeks to overcome the tension by inventing a dramatic part in which he has been cast by the Master Impresario, the Roman People, and must play, whatever his personal interests and inclination.

Audiences of public meetings, then, had a partial, obstructed view of their leaders; for what went on outside their gaze and hearing, they were dependent on mediators of information who were, as a rule, themselves the leading participants and thus had the greatest stake in presenting that information in an interested way; and they were constantly reminded of these facts. No wonder that the *contio* was, as Cicero's "Laelius" says, a place of illusion, a "stage," where senators competed in performing the role of "People's Friend" while the audience sought to judge the persuasiveness of the performance.[58] The consequences for the nature of the communication-situation are enormous. Senators could get away with – indeed, were effectively encouraged by the differing audiences and institutions to adopt – the kind of bifurcated persona that I have perceived in Cicero, so long as the public role was not directly and blatantly contradicted by action (not hard to avoid, as we saw in Cicero's case); as a matter of course, rival senators could seek to "puncture" the role by "informing" the People of contradictory "facts," but the informer's credibility was no more independently established than that

---

[56] Cic. *Leg. Man.* 69–70: *defero testorque omnis deos, et eos maxime qui huic loco temploque praesident, qui omnium mentis eorum qui ad rem publicam adeunt maxime perspiciunt, me hoc neque rogatu facere cuiusquam, neque quo Cn. Pompei gratiam mihi per hanc causam conciliari putem . . .*

[57] Cic. *Phil.* 6.2 and *Leg. agr.* 2.49, quoted at chap. 6, n. 94.

[58] Cic. *Amic.* 95: *contio . . . tamen iudicare solet, quid intersit inter popularem . . . et inter constantem et verum et gravem* [*civem*]. For "Laelius," of course, only *populares* are actors; yet since the *contio* as a whole is a *scaena*, what is a *civis constans et verus et gravis* doing there if not playing a role as well (Cic. *Amic.* 95, 97)? The passage obviously connects with the strained effort of rhetoricians to draw a firm line between orators and actors, a distinction which "[has] implications for the speaker's relation to truth," as Corbeill 2002: 189 comments with fine understatement. Cf. also Aldrete 1999: 67–73.

of his target. The ideological sterility of contional oratory becomes readily understandable, since the complications of the communicative context made most salient the problem of personal credibility and personal authority rather than the validity of contestable political principles and goals: thus the competitive dynamic so characteristic of the Republican political élite could play out quite sufficiently on the level of persons rather than ideas – and far less dangerously, collectively, for the élite, who were the ones who had the exclusive right to articulate this discourse.[59]

Finally, it is important to note how the senator-orator's powerful place in the economy of information establishes both in reality and in ideology a steep epistemic hierarchy of speaker over audience in this communication-situation.[60] This is a result not so much of the mere fact of mediated communication – a phenomenon if anything far more pronounced in today's "tele-democracies" than in Rome. It is rather due to the fact that the Republic's "media" of authoritative political knowledge were the very senators who were taking the leading role in political action, and their "informing" the populace was indissolubly bound up with their efforts in the *contio* to mobilize supporters, persuade the uncommitted, and elicit impressive popular demonstrations of their support: they were, as it were, party leaders, television stations, and pollsters rolled into one. In the absence of independent, authoritative media, even strong competition between such comprehensive political-communications complexes is not sufficient to yield substantial autonomy in the consumer of information.[61]

Thus, to the extent that a popular audience accepted an orator's (plausible, even partly justified) self-representation as one possessed of privileged insight, capable of penetrating the mists of political deception that cover the vicious traps into which the ordinary citizen is all too apt to wander, the speaker correspondingly gained authority over his audience. For authority is founded on a community's acceptance, warranted or not, that a person has information, knowledge, and wisdom superior to their own; and the purveyors of hidden truths possess in principle particularly great authority, since hidden truths are especially hard to refute.[62] And on what rational

---

[59] See above, pp. 15–18, and Chap. 4.

[60] For the importance of equality in democratic discourse, see above, pp. 22–23.

[61] On the conditions necessary for mediated communication still to result in a (relatively) autonomous consumer, see chap. 1, n. 79.

[62] On the hierarchy of knowledge in the *contio*, which I believe Burckhardt (1990: 96) was the first to stress in this context, cf. especially Hölkeskamp 1995: 36–41, who also well demonstrates the importance of the *contio* as a stage for aristocratic performance and legitimation. On *auctoritas* in general, see Heinze 1960: 43–58, a classic essay: "das System der republikanischen Verfassung wird getragen durch das Prinzip der *auctoritas*, durch das im Volke lebende Gefühl, innerlich

grounds would the audience, conscious of its exclusion from the senatorial sphere and the superior knowledge and experience of those who are familiar with it, not accept this characterization? Ideology works, in large part, by excluding alternatives, and no alternative was offered to this kind of heavy dependence on the "senatorial expert" – not even by those who laid claim most forcefully to the title of *popularis*.

CREDIBILITY AND AUTHORITY

In the absence of independent knowledge, there was little basis for investing trust in one speaker over another apart from a persuasive appearance of credibility and authority. Hence the crucial importance in the *contio* of an orator's agreeable, trustworthy, and persuasive self-representation, the product, in rhetorical terms, of *ethos* or "ethical argument," one of the three traditional "proofs" (πίστεις) or sources of persuasion alongside *logos* (ratiocination) and *pathos* (arousal of emotion).[63] As I shall try to show in what remains of this chapter, the "ethical" construction of credibility and authority depends on a rich and complex "popular ideology" (in the sense established in the last chapter) of exchange between the élite (recipients of communal gifts of honor) and the mass (who demand in return provident watchfulness in their interest and defence).

An anecdote reported by Asconius, Cicero's scholarly commentator, nicely illustrates the underlying basis of the great authority possessed by senior senators. When in 90 M. Aemilius Scaurus, Chief of the Senate (*princeps senatus*), was summoned to a *contio* by the tribune Q. Varius to defend himself against the charge of having incited Italy to revolt, he famously replied: "Quintus Varius, the Spaniard, says that Marcus Scaurus, Chief of the Senate, incited the allies to rebel. Marcus Scaurus, Chief of the Senate, denies it; there is no witness. Whom, Citizens, should you believe?" This had such an impact on the audience, says Asconius, that the tribune simply sent him home.[64] This anecdote, regarding a *contio* that was also in effect, perhaps even technically, part of a trial, expresses a pronounced

---

gebunden zu sein an den Rat der verhältnismäßig wenigen, denen man politische Einsicht und Verantwortungsgefühl zutraut" (p. 51; see also Hellegouarc'h 1963: 302–5). The present study helps to show, I hope, that this "feeling" was founded on some hard institutional facts and strongly reinforced by ideology.

[63] May 1988, with a good summary of the importance of "ethical argument" in Rome at 1–12; for the theoretical teaching on *ethos* in general, see Wisse 1989.

[64] Asc. 22 C = *ORF* 43.11, p. 167.

feature of Roman forensic oratory:[65] that since evidence for what we think of as "the facts" was in extremely short supply in Rome (with no forensic science to speak of, and testimony usually of quite limited value) most of what functioned as "evidence" in a Roman criminal trial was actually little more than a persuasive construction of character in interaction with the given circumstances.[66] From this perspective, Scaurus' "evidence" of loyalty to the Republic – encapsulated by his status as *princeps senatus* – is far more compelling than any claim made by some "Spaniard."[67] To emphasize his point, Scaurus could have waved toward the Capitol, where two temples bearing his name, those of Fides and Mens, served as warrants of his services to the Republic.[68]

Since whatever the technical status of this meeting, Varius did indeed take the trouble to haul Scaurus before a popular or equestrian court to answer a charge of treason, we must assume that he had *some* kind of case that might appear plausible to his listeners, even in the absence of direct testimony;[69] consequently it is worthy of our notice that Scaurus was thought to have prevailed here by resolving the question into an issue of sheer trustworthiness that is expected to be adjudicated by the criterion of personal status in the *res publica*.[70] This sounds like mere bluster, but there is more here than at first meets the ear. Valerius Maximus, in his version of

---

[65] Gruen 1965: 62–63 (cf. B. A. Marshall 1985: 137–38) argues that the exchange took place in a regular *contio* before the actual trial in a *quaestio*; Alexander 1990: no. 100 (cf. David 1992: 622, n. 88) considers it more probable that this belongs to one of the preliminary *contiones* (*anquisitiones*) of a trial before the People. Either way, the audience is contional; and even if Gruen is correct about the precise nature of this meeting, the issue under discussion, subsequently pursued in the trial itself, is a forensic one (note the reference to testimony).

[66] Quint. *Inst.* 5.7 is illuminating on the Roman attitude to witnesses; Cic. *Cael.* 22 is an excellent example of the commonplace against witness testimony, *quae facillime fingi, nullo negotio flecti ac detorqueri potest*, and of how plausibly an orator could therefore insist upon the primacy of circumstantial inference (the "artificial proofs" of *argumenta, coniectura, signa*: cf. §66). Milo's trial may offer a rare example of an inversion of the traditional hierarchy of orator over witnesses (on the verdict, cf. Asc. 53 C with 40 C), but this cannot be treated as the norm, since the remarkable changes to normal trial procedure imposed by the *lex Pompeia* gave extraordinary emphasis to testimony over speeches (Asc. 36 C; cf. Clark 1895: xxv). On the primacy of "character," see May 1988; however, this does not imply that Roman juries did not see their job as one of judging specific criminal acts (see Riggsby 1997, and 1999: 5–11, with the concept of "instrumental ethical argument" [59, 153 and elsewhere]; note also Asconius' interpretation of the jury's verdict on Milo, cited above).

[67] In the versions given by Val. Max. 3.7.8 (cf. 8.6.4); Quint. *Inst.* 5.12.10; *De vir. ill.* 72.11, Scaurus calls Varius *Sucronensis*: a native of Sucro on Spain's Mediterranean coast, thus obscure as well as outlandish.

[68] Chap. 3, n. 168 (no. 10).

[69] On the trial, see Alexander 1990: no. 100. The standard of evidence need not have been very high: the prosecutions under the Mamilian Commission of 109 come to mind (*quaestio exercita aspere violenterque ex rumore et lubidine plebis*, Sall. *Iug.* 40.5).

[70] Cf. the similar analysis by Jehne 2000b: 167–70.

the challenge, hints at as much when he attributes to Scaurus the following words just before the famous quotation: "It is unfair, Citizens, to defend my actions before men who are not those among whom I have lived my life; but nevertheless I shall make bold to ask you, although most of you [because of disparity in age] could not have been present among my deeds and my magistracies . . ."[71] The implied point is clear: Scaurus has been subject to the persistent scrutiny of the Roman People, and has consistently passed their test of worthiness by repeated election to office (*honores*); contrast Varius, a nobody from nowhere who as tribune has hardly entered into the public eye. Election, and especially continual re-election, proves worth and credibility, producing authority.

The tight (ideological) connection between election and public trust is more fully intimated in some other contional texts, which situate the claim to trust within fundamental Republican values, in particular the nexus of reciprocal obligation between élite individual and the People. This relationship of reciprocity is neatly expressed in the lapidary phrase *bene de re publica meritus*, "one who has earned the gratitude of the Republic," in which both notions, those of prior service and of consequent obligation, so neatly cohere; but this phrase puts the emphasis on the public debt to the élite individual, which is on the whole the perspective preferred in élite discourse.[72] The emphasis is reversed before a popular audience: since election to public office is a "gift" or "award" (*beneficium*) conferred not by powerful individuals but by the People through their votes, the obligation of reciprocity in the exchange requires the recipient to be mindful of the debt (*gratus*) and thus to serve the good of the People exclusively, without regard for personal benefit or disadvantage.[73] When a speaker acknowledges this debt to the People, it certifies that what he counsels derives from his single-minded devotion to the People rather than from consideration of private gain or vested interests. A passage in Cicero's *Sixth Philippic* expresses at some length an idea that normally did not require spelling out at length:

---

[71] Val. Max. 3.7.8: *est enim iniquum, Quirites, cum inter alios vixerim, apud alios me rationem vitae reddere, sed tamen audebo vos, quorum maior pars honoribus et actis meis interesse non potuit, interrogare* . . . Malcovati does not include this as part of the fragment – without good reason, it seems to me.

[72] *Populi grati est praemiis adficere bene meritos de re publica civis* (Cic. *Mil.* 82). The phrase *bene de re publica/de patria* (*in rem publicam*) *meritus/mereri*, common in Cicero's forensic and senatorial speeches (cf. Merguet 1880: 1.409–10), seems to appear only thrice in his popular speeches (*Red. pop.* 16, 23; *Phil.* 4.8).

[73] Cf. above, pp. 233–34.

Should I not look ahead for my fellow countrymen? *Should* I not be thinking day and night about your freedom and the safety of the Commonwealth? What ought I not to do for you, Men of Rome? You preferred me to all offices, a man whose family starts with himself, before the noblest in the land. Am I ungrateful? None less so. When I had won my honors, I went on working in the Forum just as when I was seeking them. Am I a novice in public affairs? Who has more experience? For twenty years I have been waging war against traitors. Therefore, Men of Rome, I shall keep watch and ward for you. I shall advise to the best of my power, and labor almost beyond my power. After all, is any citizen, especially of the rank to which you have been pleased to call me, so forgetful of your favor, so unmindful of his country, so inimical to his own standing, as not to be aroused and fired by your amazing unanimity?[74]

It happens that we have three Ciceronian *contiones* that immediately follow a major public *beneficium*, and in each case Cicero founds his credibility as a loyal servant of the People on this "benefaction" from the People. When he first comes before a *contio* as praetor in 66 he constructs his support for the Manilian Law solely as a return for the People's *beneficium*, and therefore based wholly on his perception of their interest; it never crossed his mind to do Pompey or anyone else a favor that might further his own advancement, for he knows well that public office (*honor*) comes only from the People.[75] At the outset of his consulship he declares before the *contio*, "Since I am conscious that I, far outpacing men of the highest nobility, was made consul not through the support of powerful men or the overwhelming influence of a faction but by the verdict of the entire Roman People, it is impossible for me to act otherwise than to be *popularis* in my tenure of

---

[74] Cic. *Phil.* 6.17: *An ego non provideam meis civibus, non dies noctesque de vestra libertate, de rei publicae salute cogitem? quid enim non debeo vobis, Quirites, quem vos a se ortum hominibus nobilissimis omnibus honoribus praetulistis? an ingratus sum? quis minus? qui partis honoribus eosdem in foro gessi labores quos petendis. rudis in re publica? quis exercitatior? qui viginti iam annos bellum geram cum impiis civibus. quam ob rem, Quirites, consilio quantum potero, labore plus paene quam potero, excubabo, vigilaboque pro vobis. etenim quis civis, praesertim hoc gradu quo me vos esse voluistis, tam oblitus benefici vestri, tam immemor patriae, tam inimicus dignitati suae quem non excitet, non inflammet tantus vester iste consensus?* (trans. Shackleton Bailey).

[75] Cic. *Leg. Man.* 2: *cum et auctoritatis in me tantum sit quantum vos honoribus mandandis esse voluistis . . . si quid auctoritatis in me est, apud eos utar qui eam mihi dederunt;* 69: *quicquid hoc beneficio populi Romani atque hac potestate praetoria . . . possum, id omne ad hanc rem conficiendam;* 70: *me hoc neque rogatu facere cuiusquam, neque quo Cn. Pompei gratiam mihi per hanc causam conciliari putem, neque quo mihi ex cuiusquam amplitudine aut praesidia periculis aut adiumenta honoribus quaeram, propterea quod . . . honorem autem neque ab uno neque ex hoc loco sed eadem illa nostra laboriosissima ratione vitae, si vestra voluntas feret, consequemur.* Interesting is the comment that public office is not won solely "from this place" (the Rostra), that is, as a reward for public support for popular measures, but rather as a result of the People's judgment of a candidate's whole mode of life. The *beneficium* of popular election is not an amoral exchange of favors but involves judgment by the citizenry of the candidate's overall worthiness. Cf. Morstein-Marx 1998.

this magistracy and in my whole life."[76] The force of the oath of undying loyalty that concludes his speech of thanks to the People in 57 is likewise founded on the idea of reciprocity for the *beneficium* of the vote to restore him from exile.[77]

This implicit argument for public trust was no doubt extremely familiar, even conventional, so that it did not require many words to summon up its force. When Cicero wishes to imply that the *principes civitatis* who pleaded with the People for his restoration from exile did so with the public good truly at heart, he characterizes them as "all those on whom you have bestowed your greatest rewards and offices."[78] L. Crassus' representation of the whole Senate as properly in exclusive servitude to the People is surely a claim for popular trust founded on this same complex of ideas, according to which senators, owing their position to the *beneficium* of election, were obliged to reciprocate (as *equites* were not) by devoting themselves selflessly to the interests of the Roman People.[79] Consider, too, how in a Sallustian *contio* put in the mouth of a consul of 75, C. Aurelius Cotta declares in an impressive rhetorical re-creation of the legendary ceremony of self-immolation (*devotio*) that "in return for [your] highest awards" (*pro maxumis beneficiis*), he is ready to lay down life itself for the People's well-being. The populace was panicked over a grain shortage; this man, whom Sallust's tribune Macer elsewhere dismisses as being "at the center of the oligarchy," offers his very life in a mock sacrifice if this would remove any part of the plebs' *incommodum* – broadly, "distress," but a word that picks up the slogan *commoda populi Romani*.[80] For current magistrates, visual symbols will also have given strong reinforcement to the argument: the "curule seat" (*sella curulis*), the bundles of rods (*fasces*) – twelve for consuls – held by as many lictors, but respectfully lowered before the Roman People when the

---

[76] Cic. *Leg. agr.* 2.7, text at chap. 6, n. 42.

[77] Cic. *Red. pop.* 24: *Quapropter memoriam vestri benefici colam benivolentia sempiterna . . . In referenda autem gratia hoc vobis repromitto semperque praestabo . . .* Cf. the very similar appeal of another former exile, C. Aurelius Cotta, in his Sallustian *contio* (Sall. *Hist.* 2.47.4–5; see below) – though this man in fact owed his restoration to Sulla, hardly the People. Cicero too, like Cotta, exploits the idea of *devotio* to develop the bond of popular trust: Nicholson 1992: 37–39; 104, n. 14.

[78] Cic. *Red. pop.* 16 (text below, n. 86). This is of course an appeal to authority; what is of interest here is the foundation of that authority upon the People's *beneficium*. Note, similarly, *vestris beneficiis amplissimis adfectus / summis ornamentis honoris praeditus* in *Leg. Man.* 51 (below, n. 91) – not mere compliments but tokens of credibility.

[79] Cic. *De or.* 1.225 = *ORF* no. 66, fr. 24, p. 244. See above, pp. 235–36.

[80] Sall. *Hist.* 2.47.9–12, esp. §9: *Atque ego, quoius aetati mors propior est, non deprecor, si quid ea vobis incommodi demitur; neque mox ingenio corporis honestius quam* pro vostra salute *finem vitae fecerim,* and §12: [sc. *me*] *volentem* pro maxumis beneficiis *animam dono dedisse.* Cf. Perl 1965 and 1967; Vanderbroeck 1987: 131–32; McGushin 1992–94: 1.208–17; Laser 1997: 226–27. For the grain shortage, Sall. *Hist.* 2.45, with Gruen 1974: 35–36, and Perl 1967: 138–40.

consul mounted the Rostra to speak.[81] Indirectly, the host of monuments clustered around the rostral area that commemorated the signal services performed for the Roman People by many of the revered *maiores*, working seamlessly in an apparent continuum right up to the "great men" of recent memory such as Sulla, Lucullus, and Pompey, may be seen as a kind of physical warrant – albeit contestable – for the claim of the present recipients of the People's highest *beneficia* to a corresponding cumulation of public trust and authority.[82]

As the anecdote involving Scaurus shows, the claim to popular trust founded upon a proven relationship of reciprocity in *beneficia* was heavily biased in favor of those who had received from the People a series of such "favors" culminating in the greatest of all, the consulship and (like Scaurus) a leading position among consulars (ex-consuls). Hence the manifest weight in public deliberation attributed to the *auctoritates* ("opinions," but never losing the sense of "authority") of the Leaders of the State, the *principes civitatis*.[83] Cicero once characterizes the Rostra as "that consecrated space" where "tribunes of the plebs are accustomed to bring forward the *principes civitatis* in order to ascertain their opinion (*auctoritatis exquirendae causa*)."[84] Nothing Cicero says is ever incidental to his rhetorical purpose, which here is to contrast invidiously the odious Vatinius' presentation of a lowly informer on the speaker's platform; nevertheless, the assertion that a central function of the *contio* was to give the citizens an opportunity to learn the views of the leading men of the Republic is obviously quite correct. (Hence the special place allotted by custom for *privati*, which the *principes* almost always were, to speak before a legislative vote.[85]) From Cicero's point of view, the system worked precisely as it should when the consul of 57, Cn. Lentulus Spinther, made sure that the vote on the law to restore him from exile was preceded by *contiones* in which were brought forth the recipients of "your greatest rewards and offices" – veritable parades of the *principes civitatis*, among whom Cicero in his speech of thanks to the People singles

---

[81] See Bell 1997: 10–13. "Curule seat": Wanscher 1980. For the lowering of *fasces*, see Livy 2.7.7: *gratum id multitudini spectaculum fuit, submissa sibi esse imperii insignia confessionemque factam populi quam consulis maiestatem vimque maiorem esse*; Plut. *Publ.* 10.7: μέγα ποιῶν τὸ πρόσχημα τῆς δημοκρατίας, Cic. *Rep.* 2.53; Val. Max. 4.1.1. For the semiotics of the *fasces* and lictors in interaction between magistrates and the People, see A. J. Marshall 1984, and now Goltz 2000.

[82] For the monuments, see pp. 97–101.

[83] A group roughly identical in Ciceronian usage, it seems, to that of consulars (see Hellegouarc'h 1963: 332–33). The most notable exception known to me is its use in *De or.* 1.225 to refer to L. Crassus, apparently at the time of his defense of the Servilian judiciary law in 106, when he was as yet only an ex-tribune. But since the dialogue is set in 91 this use is probably merely anticipatory. See Cic. *Fam.* 3.11.3 on M. Brutus in 50.

[84] Cic. *Vat.* 24. (Latin text at chap. 2, n. 112.)   [85] See above, p. 163.

out for special mention Pompey and the senior consulars P. Servilius Vatia (cos. 79) and L. Gellius (cos. 72).[86]

So important, indeed, were these *auctoritates* that even the sponsors of highly "popular" measures, whose merits one might suppose would have "spoken for themselves" to the average citizen, were well advised to present a good array of accumulated authority on their side, and to counteract that ranged against them.[87] Clodius, mobilizing support for his law that would impose exile on those who put citizens to death without the People's authorization, that is, implicitly on Cicero, took care to advertise in *contiones* that both consuls, L. Piso and A. Gabinius, and Caesar, Pompey, and Crassus as well, were all supporters of his bill; the first three of these he brought before a great *contio* in the Circus Flaminius to deliver their *auctoritas* personally.[88] The strategy is more explicit in the case of the agrarian law in 59, which may be enlisted once again to serve a point. Despite its huge popularity, Caesar did not let the proposal stand on its own merits but thought it best to bring leading members of the Senate before *contiones* to voice their support. His first step was to present his obstructive colleague Bibulus before a meeting, in the expectation that out of fear of the plebs he would back down and support the plan.[89] Bibulus resisted the pressure, so Caesar in another *contio* brought forward Pompey and Crassus to give their opinion of the bill, in order, Dio says, to do them honor, to frighten opponents by thus publicizing the open support of the most powerful men in Rome, and "at the same time to gratify the multitude by demonstrating that they were not reaching for anything outrageous or unjust but for the kind of thing which even these men would approve and encourage."[90]

Somewhat surprisingly, then, "gratifying the multitude" entails displaying support among the *principes*: again, an opposition between the People and those who, in other contexts, might be dismissed as "oligarchs" (*pauci*) is by no means natural. So when one faced the resistance of powerful authorities (as did Caesar here, or Cicero pleading for the "popular" Manilian law), the case was not really made until a good show of authority was lined

---

[86] See esp. Cic. *Red. pop.* 16: *omnes qui vestris maximis beneficiis honoribusque sunt ornati, producti ad vos*; *Sest.* 108: *Quo silentio sunt auditi de me ceteri principes civitatis!* Cf. chap. 2, n. 112.

[87] Cf. Cic. *Sest.* 105: *ac tamen, si quae res erat maior, idem ille populus horum* [sc. opponents of *populares*] *auctoritate maxime commovebatur.*

[88] Sources at chap. 5, n. 79. For Clodius' claims about the support of Pompey, Crassus, and Caesar, see Cic. *Sest.* 39–40; *Har. resp.* 47.

[89] Cass. Dio 38.4.2 (pp. 166–67 and 175–76.)

[90] Cass. Dio 38.4.5–6, esp. §6: τῷ τε πλήθει καὶ κατ' αὐτὸ τοῦτο χαρίσαιτο, τεκμηριῶν ὅτι μήτ' ἀτόπου μήτ' ἀδίκου τινὸς ὀρέγοιντο, ἀλλ' ὧν καὶ ἐκεῖνοι καὶ δοκιμασταὶ καὶ ἐπαινέται γίγνοιντο. For the questions put to Pompey and Crassus, see also App. *B Civ.* 2.10; Plut. *Pomp.* 47.4–5.

up also in favor of a proposal. In the speech for the Manilian law, Cicero must make no small effort to assuage his audience's concern about the objections of the *principes* Q. Hortensius and Q. Catulus. "Q. Catulus, a brilliant man devoted to the Republic who has received your highest marks of favor, and likewise Q. Hortensius, distinguished by the greatest gifts of public esteem, wealth, excellence, and intellectual capacity, disagree with this argument."[91] The enormous respect enjoyed among the People about this time by Catulus, the recognized leader of the Senate, is corroborated by other sources.[92] Cicero uses seventeen paragraphs of the speech, roughly one quarter of the whole, to undercut this authority: "I acknowledge that the authority (*auctoritatem*) of these men has often prevailed with you, and so it ought; but in this matter, although you see that patriotic and distinguished men hold opposing opinions (*auctoritates*), nevertheless we can leave authoritative opinions aside (*omissis auctoritatibus*) and seek out the truth from the facts and logic themselves . . ."[93] However, it turns out that the rebuttal is after all sealed by countervailing *auctoritas*. "If, Citizens, you think that the argument should be confirmed by appeals to authority" it turns out that Cicero has double the number, citing as supporters of the bill four senior consulars, among them two *triumphatores* and one former censor: "so you see that with the authoritative opinions of these men we can respond to the objections of those who oppose the bill."[94]

This emphasis on authority is fully consistent with the deeply hierarchical communication-situation that has emerged in this chapter, and further supports the thesis that the most salient issue in late-Republican public deliberation was one of personal credibility rather than ideological preferences. This is a competition for trust in which the decisive "evidence" for determining the merits of proposals was an evaluation of the persons involved, an evaluation based on externals such as accumulated authority (based, admittedly, on perceptions of prior service) rather than on the obscure and confusing details of legislation, where so many traps could be laid.

---

[91] Cic. *Leg. Man.* 51: *At enim vir clarissimus, amantissimus rei publicae, vestris beneficiis amplissimis adfectus, Q. Catulus, itemque summis ornamentis honoris, fortunae, virtutis, ingeni praeditus, Q. Hortensius, ab hac ratione dissentiunt.*

[92] Cass. Dio 36.30.4–5: τά τε πρῶτα τῆς βουλῆς ἦν . . . ᾐδοῦντο πάντες αὐτὸν καὶ ἐτίμων ὡς τὰ συμφέροντά σφισι καὶ λέγοντα ἀεὶ καὶ πράττοντα; Plut. *Pomp.* 25.5: πολλὴν μὲν αἰδούμενος.

[93] Cic. *Leg. Man.* 51: *Quorum ego auctoritatem apud vos multis locis plurimum valuisse et valere oportere confiteor; sed in hac causa, tametsi cognostis auctoritates contrarias virorum fortissimorum et clarissimorum, tamen omissis auctoritatibus ipsa re ac ratione exquirere possumus veritatem . . .*

[94] Cic. *Leg. Man.* 68: *Quod si auctoritatibus hanc causam, Quirites, confirmandam putatis* . . . [the *auctores* are P. Servilius Isauricus (cos. 79), C. Scribonius Curio (cos. 76), Cn. Lentulus Clodianus (cos. 72), and C. Cassius Longinus (cos. 73)]. *Qua re videte ut horum auctoritatibus illorum orationi qui dissentiunt respondere posse videamur.*

However, it would be quite wrong to claim that this "top-heavy" criterion of credibility based on repeated election was the only one available, or was invulnerable to subversion. On the contrary, the argument that ascent to the top rungs of the ladder of public office was a warrant of trustworthiness had a basic flaw, for after the consulship no further office beckoned (except the rare honor of the censorship or a further consulship). What was to keep the consular from "cheating" on his "debt" for the greatest of all *beneficia* in the People's gift, the consulship itself? This is exactly the fear that was exploited by Sallust's tribune, C. Licinius Macer. The People are repeatedly swindled by those to whom they have given their *beneficia*, he alleges; once in power they turn it against the very People whom, if they had a due consideration for their debt (were *grati*), they would serve. The consequence of such "ingratitude," combined with the People's passivity, is that with their vote – the only remnant of the ancestral patrimony of freedom left them – they no longer select protectors, as once, but masters for their own enslavement.[95] Thus freedom itself depends on respect for, and nurturing of, this crucial relationship of reciprocity. Sallust's Marius, on the other hand, alludes to the same idea when he stresses in his *contio* the persistence of *his* sense of obligation: unlike others, the corrupt nobility, he was the same man after receiving the People's honors and *imperium* as he had been while seeking them.[96] This is the background against which should be understood Cicero's assertion, in his first *contio* upon taking up the consulship, that in consequence of his election in preference to members of the nobility he cannot but be *popularis* for the rest of his life; likewise this context helps us to understand why it is desirable, even necessary, for Cicero to fortify his sense of indebtedness to the People for his restoration from exile by swearing a great oath to repay their benefaction by subordinating himself totally and permanently to their interests.[97]

At the other end of a Roman political career from the *principes civitatis* were the tribunes, the usual proponents of *popularis* challenges to the leadership of the Senate (although with ten tribunes elected every year, and only a handful of notable *populares* among the several hundred who held the office over the course of the late Republic, this should not be seen as

---

[95] Sall. *Hist.* 3.48.5–6, quoted at chap. 6, n. 122. Note *itaque omnes concessere iam in paucorum dominationem*. Note also Cato's cry that by their own votes the People were establishing a tyrant in the citadel (Plut. *Cat. Min.* 33.3).

[96] Sall. *Iug.* 85.3; 85.8: *quae ante vostra beneficia gratuito faciebam, ea uti accepta mercede deseram non est consilium, Quirites*. For the metaphor of *merces*, cf. *Hist.* 3.48.5: *mercede delinquere*. Cf. *Rhet. Her.* 4.49: *Existimatis unum quemque eniti ut perficiat quae vobis pollicitus erit. Erratis et falsa spe frustra iam diu detinemini stultitia vestra*, etc.

[97] Chap. 6, n. 17; above, n. 77.

the usual activity of a tribune). Tribunes stood close to the beginning of their public career (usually, in the late Republic, in their second major of-fice) and belonged to a far less select group than consulars; thus the claim to authority just analyzed was less compelling coming from their mouths. One recourse was to invert it, and to construct the "warrant" of public service not around *past* benefactions but the desire for *future* ones. That is Gaius Gracchus' explicit promise in his speech for the Aufeian bill, prob-ably delivered while quaestor in the year in which he was elected to his first tribunate.[98] Yet it seems unlikely that this rather hypothetical sort of appeal would have held much water unless, like the noble Gracchus, one had the kind of lineage – a "brand name" – that would serve as a credible guarantee of future performance.[99] A more powerful "ethical" source of credibility for tribunes was therefore likely to be the nature and symbolism of the office itself, whose recognized function was to pursue and defend the interests of the plebs.[100] There were physical symbols of the tribunate, too, whose power might be compared and opposed to those of the consuls: especially the tribunician bench, or *subsellium*, so emphatically linked with the Rostra on the coin of Palicanus (see figure 3, p. 52).[101] The mere fact of holding the tribunate created a presumption in favor of the idea that one was a "protector and guardian" of freedom, civil rights, and the People's "benefits" (*commoda*).[102] Yet, since a tribune's opponents could be expected to counterattack in turn by seeking to "expose" him as merely manipulating a specious persona for his own aggrandizement (Cicero's strategy against Rullus), he needed to corroborate this presumption in his favor by setting it within a wider rhetorical context.

Most important, to judge from Sallust's tribunes, was to place oneself in a tradition of popular "martyrs" such as the Gracchi and to emphasize

---

[98] Gell. *NA* 11.10 = *ORF* 48.44, pp. 187–88, quoted above n. 6, especially: *ego ipse . . . non gratis prodeo; verum peto a vobis non pecuniam, sed bonam existimationem atque honorem.*

[99] On the People's electoral bias toward nobility, see Yakobson 1999: 184–227, and Morstein-Marx 1998: 273–74.

[100] Polyb. 6.16.5. It does not seriously affect the present point that the populist zeal of tribunes was in practice curbed by other pressures, including ambition and fear, and that the office may be viewed in Cicero's terms as a pragmatic way of bringing popular *libertas* into harmony with senatorial *auctoritas* (Cic. *Leg.* 3.23–26). See Bleicken 1955 and 1981; Meier 1966: 53, 116–51; Thommen 1989; Lintott 1999: 206–8.

[101] Above, pp. 51ff.

[102] Cic. *Leg. agr.* 2.15: *per tribunum plebis, quem maiores praesidem libertatis custodemque voluerunt*; *Rab. perd.* 12: *Popularis vero tribunus pl. custos defensorque iuris et libertatis!* Sall. *Hist.* 3.48.1 (Macer): *plebes . . . vindices paravisset omnis iuris sui tribunos plebis*; §12 (quoted at chap. 6, n. 99). The presumptive link between tribunes and *commoda populi Romani* is not so explicitly attested, but clearly implied by the entire *Leg. agr.* 2 (esp. §§11–15) and the association of the defense of popular *commoda* with great tribunes of the past, especially the Gracchi (Cic. *Leg. agr.* 2.81; *Sest.* 103–5; Gell. *NA* 11.10.1 = *ORF* 48.44, p. 188).

that not personal benefits but dire risks were the lot of one who embraced the People's cause.[103] Both Memmius and Macer begin their speeches by representing themselves as putting themselves in mortal danger by urging their audiences to assert their rights against the oligarchy.

Many reasons deter me from taking up your cause, Citizens – but patriotism overcomes them all: the power of the oligarchy, your apathy, the absence of justice, and especially because rectitude brings more danger than respect. For it pains me to mention how over the last fifteen years you have been the plaything of an arrogant cabal, how miserably your protectors have fallen unavenged, how your minds have been infected by cowardice and sloth. Even now you do not rise up against your enemies, whom you have in your grip; indeed you still fear men in whom you should strike terror. But this being so, nevertheless my will compels me to confront the domination of the oligarchy. I, at least, will make trial of the freedom my father passed down to me; but whether I do so in vain or to good purpose lies in your hands, Citizens.[104]

Nor am I unaware how great are the resources of the nobility which I – alone, powerless, with the mere empty shell of a magistracy – am now trying to dislodge from dominance, and how much more secure is a clique of malefactors than innocent men acting individually. But in addition to the hope I have in you, which has overcome my fears, I have decided that for a man of resolution defeat in the struggle for freedom is better than failing to struggle at all.[105]

Both, too, are eager to remind listeners of the fate of previous tribunes who championed the rights of the People; Macer explicitly (and Memmius implicitly) appends himself to the list: "What great troubles are being stirred up against me!"[106] The Temple of Concordia behind and to the left of the

---

[103] See now P. M. Martin 2000: 27–41.

[104] Sall. *Iug.* 31.1–5: *Multa me dehortantur a vobis, Quirites, ni studium rei publicae omnia superet: opes factionis, vostra patientia, ius nullum, ac maxume quod innocentiae plus periculi quam honoris est. Nam illa quidem piget dicere, his annis quindecim quam ludibrio fueritis superbiae paucorum, quam foede quamque inulti perierint vostri defensores, ut vobis animus ab ignavia atque socordia corruptus sit, qui ne nunc quidem obnoxiis inimicis exsurgitis atque etiam nunc timetis eos quibus decet terrori esse. Sed quamquam haec talia sunt, tamen obviam ire factionis potentiae animus subigit. Certe ego libertatem quae mihi a parente meo tradita est experiar; verum id frustra an ob rem faciam, in vostra manu situm est, Quirites.*

[105] Sall. *Hist.* 3.48.3–4: *Neque me praeterit quantas opes nobilitatis solus, inpotens, inani specie magistratus pellere dominatione incipiam, quantoque tutius factio noxiorum agat quam soli innocentes. Sed praeter spem bonam ex vobis, quae metum vicit, statui certaminis adversa pro libertate potiora esse forti viro quam omnino non certavisse.*

[106] Sall. *Hist.* 3.48.8–11 (Macer); *Iug.* 31.7–8, 13 (Memmius). It might be noted, however, that Memmius' subsequent career, even if his old enemy M. Aemilius Scaurus testified against him in an extortion trial, shows little sign of serious victimization at the hands of the *principes* (see Gruen 1968: 158, 174–76, 183); Macer, for his part, was not prevented from reaching the praetorship, and there would be no textual support for the assumption that his subsequent condemnation for extortion and suicide was simply belated punishment for his tribunician stance (see Gruen 1974: 273).

orators, that conspicuous monument to the crushing of Gaius Gracchus and perhaps some three thousand of his supporters, will have offered strong visual support for this kind of "ethical" self-representation.[107] As it happens, these *topoi* of indignation can in fact be traced right back to the Gracchi brothers. Tiberius had gone so far as to change into the clothes of mourning and, announcing that he despaired of his own life, brought his children and wife before an assembly and commended them to the care of the People.[108] Gaius had powerfully evoked the slaughter of his brother, a tribune, under a hail of blows "while *you* looked on," his corpse being dragged "through the very middle of the city" to the Tiber – although it was customary even for those who had failed to answer a summons on capital charges to receive a second warning, and despite the fact that the ancestors made war on Falerii for an insult to a certain tribune named Genucius, and condemned one Gaius Veturius to death for failing to step aside for another holder of that office.[109] Clearly Gaius (and others thereafter who made use of the *topos*) was evoking the basis of tribunician sacrosanctity: the ancient oath of the plebeians to forfeit to Jupiter the life of anyone who harmed one of their tribunes.[110]

To "define" oneself thus within the now sacred tradition of the Gracchi was to "prove" that what one counseled was indeed in the People's interest. How else could it be so dangerous to urge the People to reclaim its rights? With equal logic, of course, this rhetorical representation made a direct claim upon the People to be vigilant in supporting their protectors: if they allow their champion to be crushed, they would soon find no one willing to take up this role.[111] Above all, by such an invidious appeal the ostensibly *popularis* tribune hoped to mobilize the People, to forge them into a usable weapon by shaking them out of their (supposed) acquiescence in their own domination – a definition of the situation that implied, once accepted, a program of action.[112] The day before Tiberius Gracchus' death, he announced in what must have been a *contio* in the Forum that he feared that his enemies would break into his house that night to kill him; moved by his appeal, "an enormous number" stood sentry for him through the

---

[107] See pp. 55–56 and 102ff. Note that Memmius goes on to cite explicitly the killings of the Gracchi and of Gaius' ally, M. Fulvius Flaccus: Sall. *Iug.* 31.7.

[108] Plut. *Ti. Gracch.* 13.5; cf. Asellio, fr. 6 Peter (= Gell. *NA* 2.13.5), and Cass. Dio fr. 83.8 (speaking of Tiberius' *mother* – perhaps a misunderstanding). Plutarch places this *contio* well before the similar appeal made on the penultimate day of his life: 16.3, with App. *B Civ.* 1.14–15.

[109] Plut. *C. Gracch.* 3.3–4. These stories are, it seems, unattested elsewhere. On Genucius and Falerii, see *MRR* I.220, n. 2 (tentatively dated to 241). The passage is a further interesting example of the use of historical allusion before the People (chap. 3).

[110] Livy 3.55.7, with Ogilvie's commentary ad loc.; cf. Mommsen 1887: II.286–88.

[111] For explicit expression of the *topos*, see Livy 4.35.7–8, and *Rhet. Her.* 4.48. P. M. Martin 2000: 34–37.

[112] For chastisement of popular *patientia, ignavia*, or "torpor," see n. 53 above.

night.[113] In 67, after Gabinius was physically threatened or even attacked in the Senate-house while presenting his proposal for the piracy command, he slipped out and informed the crowd in the Forum, who then made a rush upon the Curia and (it is said) would have massacred the senators had they not immediately fled.[114] This kind of response was not strictly limited to tribunes but might be accorded to other popular heroes, such as the ex-tribune Clodius, or indeed Julius Caesar. In 56, we are told, a crowd threatened to burn the Senate-house if Clodius, then plebeian aedile (thus also under the plebs' special protection), were harmed; and the Curia actually *was* burnt down after his murder.[115] When Caesar was being accused of complicity in the "Catilinarian" conspiracy a crowd surrounded the Curia threateningly and demanded his safe release.[116] And all know of the violent popular emotions unleashed by his funeral.

Naturally, a rhetorical *ethos* was expressed not only verbally but physically as well: delivery, bodily disposition, gesture, even dress.[117] The physicality of the *ethos* of the tribune well emerges from Cicero's amusing (but highly invidious) description of how Rullus tried to win plausibility for his "act" by assuming an aggressive, accusatory air that extended to facial expression and bodily carriage, complemented by an unkempt appearance, neglected facial hair, and shabby dress.[118] This is ridicule; but it also rests on a general understanding that a harsh, angry comportment was part of the standard "popular" tribunician repertoire. Similarly, Valerius Maximus describes tribunes' physically menacing official behavior, fierce looks, and stalking along the Rostra.[119] Violent body-movement was also, since Gaius Gracchus' tribunates, a mark of the populist *ethos*. Gracchus, the first truly

---

[113] Plut. *Ti. Gracch.* 16.3: παμπόλλους τινάς.　　[114] Cass. Dio 36.24.2.

[115] Cass. Dio 39.29.2–3; Asc. 33 C and above, pp. 1–2. Plebeian aediles were covered by the plebeian *lex sacrata*: Livy 3.55.7, with Mommsen 1887: ii.472–73.

[116] Plut. *Caes.* 8.3.

[117] David 1980a: esp. 181–86, and Corbeill 2002, a fascinating paper to which I am much indebted for what follows. Readers will descry some differences between Corbeill's interpretation of contional "body language" and mine: above all, I suppose that gesture depended not on differences of political/social class (where Bourdieu's *habitus* is most at home) or "political ideology" (seen by Corbeill in terms of *optimates* v. *populares*), but the nature of the case being made – in particular, whether *invidia* was being "enflamed" or dampened/deflected. If Cicero was restrained while delivering *Leg. agr.* 2 or *Phil.* 4 he was open to the objection mentioned below, n. 127; and be it noted that the patricians Caesar and Clodius, or the noble Gracchi, were far more "aristocratic" than Cicero.

[118] Cic. *Leg. agr.* 2.13: *iam designatus alio vultu, alio vocis sono, alio incessu esse meditabatur, vestitu obsoletiore, corpore inculto et horrido, capillatior quam ante barbaque maiore, ut oculis et aspectu denuntiare omnibus vim tribuniciam et minitari rei publicae videretur.*

[119] Val. Max. 3.8.3: *tantum non* manibus *tribunorum pro rostris Piso collocatus, cum* hinc atque illinc eum ambissent [sc. *tribuni*] *ac Palicanum num suffragiis populi consulem creatum renuntiaturus esset interrogaretur . . .* ; 3.8.6: *Instabat tibi* [sc. Sempronia, sister of the Gracchi] torvo vultu *minas profundens amplissima potestas* [sc. *tribuni plebis*].

great *popularis* orator, was remembered both for the vehemence of his speech and his complementary innovations in delivery: he was the first to pull his toga aside to free his left arm for gesture, the first to pace along the Rostra, and even supposedly employed a flautist to help him moderate his tone of voice.[120] According to Cicero, the next great populist figure, Saturninus, compensated for his indifferent talent with an impressive appearance and "movement" (*motus*), while his tribunician colleague and the heir to his policy, Sex. Titius, minced about so daintily that his name was given mockingly to a dance.[121]

J.-M. David has shown how Cicero's stylistic comments in the *Brutus* and elsewhere hint at the emergence late in the second century of an aggressive, emotional style of delivery aimed at the arousal of public indignation (*concitatio invidiae*), and consequently marked by a vehemence in delivery and gesture described by terms such as "sharp/bitter" (*acer*; also *acerbus, asper*) or "violent" (*vehemens*). This was the character of "the popular style of oratory" (*eloquentia popularis, populare genus dicendi*, and the like) – as we have seen, not precisely the style of oratory that served *popularis* political aims (though highly appropriate to, and typically associated with it), but rather that which was suited to a large popular audience, that is, the *contio*.[122] David is particularly interested in the adoption of this style by the increasing numbers of "new" Italian orators from around the end of the second century, attracted by the rewards of successful prosecution in the expanding criminal courts, but its origins lie elsewhere: we need only recall its apparent inventor, the noble Gaius Gracchus.[123] The Roman noble L. Licinius Crassus, who anticipated the full "arrival" of the Italians and indeed shut down the Latin schools of oratory which played such an important role in the expansion of the rhetorical profession, was a master

---

[120] David 1983a, with full citation of sources. On the flute, or rather shepherd's-pipe, see also Wille 1967: 453–54. On keeping the hand inside the toga – in Cicero's day the practice only of novices – see Cic. *Cael.* 11, with Austin 1960: ad loc.

[121] Saturninus: Cic. *Brut.* 224: *seditiosorum omnium post Gracchos L. Appuleius Saturninus eloquentissimus visus est; magis* specie *tamen et* motu *atque* ipso amictu *capiebat homines quam aut dicendi copia aut mediocritate prudentiae.* Titius: Cic. *Brut.* 225, with Corbeill 1996: 167–68. His *mollitia* gave rise to jokes alleging passive homosexuality (Cic. *De or.* 2.265; on the political and rhetorical significance of *mollitia*, see Edwards 1993: 63–97; Gleason 1995: 55–81; Corbeill 1996: 128–73 and 2002: esp. 204–8) – but the plebeian view is likely to have been different; even Hortensius attracted such stock invective for his "excessive" gesturing (Gell. *NA* 1.5.2–3). For Titius' annulled land bill of 99, see *MRR* 11.2, and for his condemnation in the next year, perhaps for *maiestas*, see Alexander 1990: no. 80. Titius allegedly kept a portrait-bust of Saturninus which Cicero, probably tendentiously, claims determined the verdict (Cic. *Rab. perd.* 24–25; cf. Val. Max. 8.1 damn. 3).

[122] David 1980a: 171–211. See above, pp. 238–39 with n. 161.

[123] David 1979, 1980a: esp. 187–91, 1983b; see also 1992: 547–56. Gracchus complicates the effort to interpret the style in terms of *habitus* (above, n. 117).

in the genre of mass oratory, and as we have already seen, famously wielded its characteristic weapon, the arousal of indignation, in his speech for the Servilian judiciary law in 106.[124] The Roman noble was no stranger to the methods of *concitatio invidiae*.[125] Evidently the new oratorical vehemence is most closely linked instead with the emergence of truly mass oratory in Rome after the reversal of the orators' orientation on the Rostra opened up for *contiones* the whole central Forum, where room might be found for a crowd of several thousand, and, not much later, the appearance of the first great populist politicians.[126] In any case the accusatory nature of such forceful body language will have served, as Cicero's "penetration" of Rullus' "disguise" shows, as a visible token of the oppositional stance and the right-eous public spirit of the People's guardian. This must have been a necessary concomitant of the *concitatio invidiae*, since it was a maxim of Roman oratory that if passionate language of accusation were not attended by the repertoire of gestures that expressed matching emotion – stamping the foot, striking the forehead, slapping the thigh, violent movement, pacing, and fluctuation of vocal pitch – it was likely to be found insincere.[127]

A. Corbeill has persuasively argued that in the "late Roman Republic, the external characteristics of an individual carried great representational meaning"; moral character was supposed to lie open to visual scrutiny, unless it was insidiously hidden, as was Rullus', under a false exterior.[128] The tantalizing glimpses we are given of various other visible "marks" of popular heroes therefore take on considerable significance, though they are difficult to interpret. Cicero notes that the populace had loved not

---

[124] Cic. *Brut.* 165: *Et vero fuit in hoc etiam popularis dictio excellens.* For Crassus' *concitatio invidiae*, see §164, quoted at chap. 6, n. 142. Although Crassus did not overdo his "body-language" (below, n. 127) his style of speaking was *vehemens et interdum irata et plena iusti doloris* (Cic. *Brut.* 158; see also *De or.* 2.188). A somewhat different view in Corbeill 2002: 190.

[125] Cf. Cn. Lentulus Marcellinus' *invidiae querela* against Pompey in 56 – as consul (Val. Max. 6.2.6)! – or Catulus, *princeps civitatis* (below, p. 274), or L. Marcius Philippus (p. 238).

[126] Cf. Corbeill 2002: 198–99, 202–3: "To reach the people gathered in such open spaces, exaggerated movement, expansive gesticulation, and open, shouting, mouths were essential." Aldrete 1999: 73–82 interestingly remarks on the ability of gesture to extend listening range in an age without vocal amplification (also Corbeill, pp. 203, 208).

[127] See Cicero's famous comment on Calidius' lackluster performance at *Brut.* 278 (Corbeill 2002: 190). For the importance of delivery generally, see the oft-repeated anecdote about Demosthenes (e.g. *Brut.* 142; *De or.* 3.213). A series of the kinds of gestures we are concerned with is given at Cic. *Brut.* 158. For *supplosio pedis, femur ferire,* and *frons percussa,* see also Cic. *De or.* 3.220; Quint. *Inst.* 11.3.123, 128. For pacing (*incessus* or *inambulatio*) see also Cic. *Orat.* 59; Quint. *Inst.* 11.3.124–27 ("how many miles have you talked?"); below, n. 129. For *iactatio corporis* cf. *excursio* (*Orat.* 59; Quint. *Inst.* 1.11.3), *procursio* (Quint. *Inst.* 11.3.125). Of course, the equal risk at the other extreme was to lose credibility and *auctoritas* by appearing to be a mere actor (see Quint. *Inst.* 11.3.184, and above, n. 58). Hence, sometimes less was more (cf. Cic. *De or.* 2.188, on Crassus' sparing use of his body).

[128] See above, n. 14.

only the "name" and "speech" of the Gracchi and Saturninus, but also their "expression" and "stride."[129] Saturninus – who was, concedes Cicero, the best speaker among the post-Gracchan "demagogues" – added to the tradition of vigorous movement on the Rostra a striking style of dress.[130] But demagogic fashion reached a new low with the outrageously long tunic flapping at the heels of the tribune of 74, L. Quinctius.[131] Only the populist associations of such remarkable divergences from the highly uniform élite dress code make sense of anecdotes about the fears inspired in Sulla by Julius Caesar's long-sleeved, loosely girded tunic: the dictator was moved to thoughts of murder (according to one author) clearly for something worse than an offense to good taste.[132] Perhaps such flamboyant touches, rather like the adoption of vigorous bodily movement instead of the "manly" physical steadiness and restraint in gesture and demeanor that Cicero recommends in general, suggested a "breaking of ranks," taking up a position just a bit, but significantly, askew of the "suits" of the senatorial order.[133]

I have sketched out the two basic forms of ethical appeal for public trust, one naturally serving the "chief men of the state," founded largely on the nexus of mutual obligation between senator and People, the other well suited to the populist opposition figure, an indignant, aggressive posture resting frequently on the premise that those mutual obligations had been broken by the senatorial leadership. These two "postures" also have their proper "signs," for example the calm *auctoritas* of the consular or the aggressive histrionics and eye-catching dress and demeanor of the tribune.

---

[129] Cic. *Sest.* 105: *horum homines nomen, orationem, vultum, incessum amabant.* On the cultural significance of a politician's *incessus*, see Corbeill 1996: 165–67, and especially 2002: 192–96. Gaius Gracchus was of course remembered for his pacing on the Rostra (above); but Cicero *may* not be saying anything specifically about these men's rhetorical performance, if this is actually an allusion to urban crowds' reaction upon hearing their names, listening to their speeches, spotting their faces, and watching them make their way about the public spaces.

[130] Cic. *Brut.* 224 (*amictu*), quoted above, n. 121.

[131] Cic. *Clu.* 111: *Facite enim ut non solum mores et adrogantiam eius sed etiam voltum atque amictum atque etiam illam usque ad talos demissam purpuram recordemini.* The *tunica talaris* would seem to be Greek-style banqueting-dress in *Verr.* 2.5.31, 86; *Cat.* 2.22 (*talaribus tunicis, velis amictos, non togis*), also perhaps associated with entertainers (*Att.* 1.16.3; *Off.* 1.150; Quint. *Inst.* 11.3.58). Corbeill 1996: 160–63 focuses on the charge of effeminacy, but see n. 133 below.

[132] Suet. *Iul.* 45.3; Cass. Dio 43.43.4; Macrob. *Sat.* 2.3.9.

[133] Edwards 1993: 90; Corbeill 1996: 194–95, and 2002: 204–8. Both of these scholars show special interest in the link with effeminacy made by Cicero in a famous wisecrack (Macrob. *Sat.* 2.3.9; Cass. Dio 43.43.5) – but this may be to adopt the hostile perspective: the plebs may not have seen it that way, nor was it necessarily they who mocked Titius' "dance." At its extreme, such as Caesar's later flaunting of triumphal garb and red, regal boots (Cass. Dio 43.43.1–2), one might guess that such gorgeous dress hinted at charisma and a special link with a mass population. Steadiness: see Cic. *Orat.* 59–60; *De or.* 3.213–27.

Being expressions of opposing rhetorical positions rather than competing political ideologies, they are to some extent interchangeable. Senior politicians could, if they were skillful, counterattack against populist tribunes by deploying the indignant "defender-of-the-People" ethos that was the frequent role of their opponents. Crassus' exploitation of this posture in favor of the Servilian judiciary bill well shows that there was no *essential* reason why *eloquentia popularis* could not be turned effectively against targets other than the Senate. And in his attack on Rullus, the consular Cicero alternates between the two roles most effectively, beginning with a carefully constructed portrait of himself as dedicated solely to the People's welfare because of the special nature of their *beneficium* in entrusting the consulship to a "new man," then proceeding to what will have been a frequent tribunician motif of sounding the alarm against insidious tyranny and posing as the standard-bearer for the People's freedom. Indeed, the *topos* of warning against nascent tyranny, the standard rhetorical defense employed by the leaders of the Senate against the more ambitious "popular" proposals, can itself be seen as simply a redirected, and equally invidious, form of the more characteristically tribunician warning against the subversion of popular freedom by the "oligarchs" (*pauci*). When the elder consular Catulus dramatically alluded to the Secessions of the Plebs while "warning" of the attack on the freedom of the Roman People cloaked by the Manilian Law, he was "arousing indignation" (*invidiam concitare*) in a manner borrowed straight from the tribunes' book.[134] One can also hear a "popular" echo in Cicero's plea to the People not to allow him to come to grief for his loyal service to them in his speech of December 3, 63 – a section of the *Third Catilinarian* that is too readily chalked up to late publication and retrospective editing.[135]

None of this is to say that such personae, though they be rhetorically constructed, could simply be donned and doffed like a hat. They had to be credible, which required not merely internal consistency within the presentation but consistency with other public behavior, including recent political facts. When the author of the *Handbook on Electioneering*, probably Cicero's brother Quintus, notes, in 64, that the masses should *think* that he is not indifferent to their interests (*commoda*) from the fact that he has been *popularis* "at least" (*dumtaxat*) in his speeches in *contiones* and the courts, he acknowledges the limitations of public knowledge (exclusion from the Senate, and emphasis on the highly public stage on the Rostra and in

---

[134] Plut. *Pomp.* 30.4, with pp. 183 and 221, above.
[135] Cic. *Cat.* 3.26–28. See McDermott 1972, and cf. the conclusion of the *Leg. Man.* (esp. §71), where the same idea is touched on more briefly and implicitly, as befits its lesser import.

the Forum) but at the same time implies the need to maintain a consistent public ethos over an interval of some duration. We have seen that the Roman plebs did not lack memory, that politically active elements in it were alert and engaged in the affairs of the Republic (chapter 3); Quintus adds that his brother can count on the support of the masses because Cicero had supported Pompey's advancement, defended the tribune Cornelius and, in response to a direct popular appeal, undertaken to defend Manilius.[136] The "esteem" or "reputation" (*existimatio*) of a politician was something laboriously built up by a senator in the course of a career, above all in a series of elections, each one more competitive than the last, that turned essentially on the question of the candidate's moral worthiness.[137] This reputation was of great weight (as we have seen) when thrown into the balance; but the orator on the Rostra was not a Proteus, absolutely free to recreate himself in any image he thought might serve his case.

Recent work has helped to bring to light the manifold ways in which the Republican politician made constant use of a symbolic, visual rhetoric to lay claim to "worthiness" (*dignitas*) before the *populus*.[138] The rituals of election to high public office (significantly called *honores*) are best known, in particular the impressive "walkabouts" conducted by candidates in the central public space of the city, the Forum, attended by diverse crowds that would physically testify to their moral stature, marked by frequent handshakes and polite comments all around, even for the lowest peasant. Roman elections were overwhelmingly "personal," in the sense that overt exploitation of current political issues, though not necessarily strictly avoided (as was urged upon Cicero by his brother), was certainly subordinated to what was, from a certain perspective, the more profound and relevant question of the moral worth and general excellence of the candidate in whom the People were about to entrust power – awesome power, in the case of the consuls.[139] This chapter suggests that the contests of public deliberation should be seen in much the same light. Like an election, if less explicitly, a contional "debate" was fundamentally a competition for public trust in

---

[136] Q. Cicero (?), *Comment. pet.* 51, 53. See above, p. 209.
[137] On *existimatio*, see Yavetz 1974. On elections, see below. For the connection between these circumstances and the great importance of rhetorical *ethos* in Rome, see May 1988: 6–12; in the body of the book May well demonstrates both the importance of Cicero's *ethos* as a source of rhetorical persuasion throughout his career, and the necessity of developing a credible *ethos*, cultivating it, and carefully husbanding it.
[138] Bell 1997; Morstein-Marx 1998.
[139] Yakobson 1999: 148–83 shows that the old view according to which "policy" issues were absent from Roman elections cannot be sustained in an extreme form. But he too acknowledges that elections were expected to be about voters' assessment of candidates' "personal worth" (177).

an image of moral worth and personal excellence, fought out by means of verbal and physical symbols evoking key elements of Republican ideology on which there was, at least in the public sphere, universal consensus. The *ethos* of the candidate and that of the contional orator are not to be distinguished sharply but seen as varying manifestations, appropriate to different contexts, of the Roman ideal of political leadership – an élitist and paternalist ideal, it almost goes without saying, that sets great store by the superior capacity of certain men of recognized and recognizable excellence to discern the genuine interest of all (as ordinary men could not) and to pursue it honorably.

Far from assuring the victory of all "popular" proposals for extending the rights or benefits of the People, the "ideological monotony" of public deliberation refocused the competitive struggle for popular support upon questions of personality rather than ideology: who was the true embodiment of the "popular" ideals that all avowed, rather than which was the more compelling vision of the public good. This relocation of the nub of the argument offered quite favorable terrain for resistance to populist initiatives, since in the competition for public trust on the popular stage the accumulated and cumulative authority of the leaders of the Senate might at least be a match for the the *popularis* tribune's righteous indignation. The division between senatorial and popular planes of political action, and the exclusion of the citizenry from direct observation of the former, both facilitated disingenuous manipulation by the orator (Cicero against Rullus – but perhaps also Memmius or Macer) on this deceptive "stage" and simultaneously made such questions of credibility and consistency of the utmost saliency for the voting audience, whose knowledge of this hidden world was mediated by the very senators who sought, by means of this knowledge, to influence and control them.

Cause is also consequence, for the emphasis upon *ad hominem* and "ethical" argument for public trust over debate about alternative versions of the public good perpetuated, as well as was produced by, the "ideological monotony" discerned above. Cicero did not *have* to articulate an argument against agrarian distribution that might persuade the People, for success was more readily available by other methods. (As we saw in chapter 5, for those without Cicero's, or L. Crassus', rhetorical gifts, sheer obstructionism offered some hope of prevailing on the symbolic plane even while forfeiting verbal argument.) Elite speakers thus competed for mass support by offering not alternative ideas, which might ultimately have threatened the ideological basis of the entire political structure, but alternative rhetorical personae. Competition in mass persuasion, paradoxically, presented no threat to a "closed" ideological system which, regardless of the fate of individuals in their struggle for status and power, helped to immunize the Republican system from serious potential alternatives (such as increasing "democratization" following a Greek model) and consolidated the collective power of the Republican élite.[140] Simultaneously, control of the economy of information by members of the élite produced a steeply hierarchical communication-situation, whose effects include an ideological construction of the élite orator as one possessed of privileged knowledge and penetrating insight into the real forces at work that, hidden from ordinary vision, governed the life of the Republic. "Naturalized" in ideology, this conception of the senator-orator will have been no small source of power for the élite as a whole (even though that élite was often divided against itself), in a manner comparable to the way in which senators as a whole, acting as magistrates, priests, and members of "the prime organ of religious control," drew collective power from another mediating role (frequently used against peers): that between gods and men.[141]

The dependence of the voting citizenry upon the élite for all authoritative political information, the anxiety and confusion this produces, and the preference in élite representation for evocation and designation of "plotters" and "heroes" in place of relatively mundane and complex argument about divergent views of means and ends, all encourage an analysis of the late-Republican *contio* in the "symbolist" terms of Murray Edelman. The hard facts on which the political "drama" was continually improvised were the exclusion of the Senate from the People's gaze and the disinguousness and manipulative methods that this exclusion encouraged.[142] This produced an acute problem of public trust, since knowledge of a senator's activity while out of the People's sight and control was dependent on what he (or other senators, whose motives were equally open to challenge) told them; and the problem of trust conferred authority on those élite speakers who were able to perform most convincingly the role of the People's guardian, with their penetrating insight from their elevated position on the Rostra into the plots of tribunes or oligarchical cabals lurking below the dangerously deceptive surface. The withdrawal of trust in one senatorial champion of

---

[140] Cf. Hölkeskamp 1995: 41–49, on how contional rhetoric reinforced the political "Grundkonsens" upholding the traditional order.

[141] For which see Beard 1990: esp. 30–34 and 43.

[142] It is unnecessary, incidentally, to ascribe wholly cynical motives to the authors of this drama, who will, like Cicero, naturally have identified their enemies with those of the Republic. In any case, a mass public will arguably often not give their attention unless it is seized, and their commitment maintained, through a "symbolic drama" of "heroes" and "enemies."

the public interest (like the tribune Rullus) was the result of conferral of trust in another (the consul, Cicero): anxiety produces acquiescence. Such events in the political spectacle did not threaten the covert, ideological assumption that such a mediating authority would always be necessary, embedded, as we have just seen, in core Republican values. Indeed, it was thereby only reinforced.

CHAPTER 8

Conclusion

Roiled by waves of unrest in the last century of its life, the Roman Republic continually fell into bloody spasms of political violence. Economic distress, prolonged military service, controversies over land redistribution, exclusion from full civic participation, and the savage dispossessions of civil war made the Italian countryside a persistent breeding ground for discontent. The city of Rome, now housing in cramped, unsanitary conditions perhaps a million souls – an enormous population under pre-modern conditions – depended on the agricultural surplus of far-flung lands; its population hung perilously close to the brink of starvation and was apt to panic when poor harvests or disruption of the grain routes caused periodic interruptions in the food supply. Violence and persistent political disruption in the absence of effective institutions for maintaining order made the city ungovernable for extended periods in the 50s; three years in that decade opened without consuls because it had proven impossible to hold elections. The long-suffering soldiery saw its hopes for compensation upon demobilization persistently dashed by a recalcitrant Senate, and looked to its victorious generals to realize them by whatever methods would serve. It seems extraordinary not that the Roman Republic fell (if that is the right word) when it did, but that it survived so long.[1]

Yet the traditional political system maintained the allegiance of its citizens right down at least to the Caesarian civil war, and arguably much further.[2] True, it has been maintained that the Republic (defined somewhat tendentiously as the senatorial *dominance* of the state) "fell" precisely because it had failed to meet the demands of important constituencies, especially the Italians, the plebs, and the army.[3] But this somehow comforting thesis takes for granted a relatively straightforward connection between

---

[1] Meier 1966 (1980 reprint): xv; and see Gruen, n. 16 below.
[2] On this point at least the fundamental studies by Meier (1966: esp. 45–63, 64–161) and Gruen (1974: esp. 498–507) agree, despite their widely differing analyses of the crisis itself.
[3] Brunt 1988: esp. 68–82, a thesis sketched in brief much earlier (Brunt 1971b).

disappointment, even distress, and profound disillusionment with a political system that, on one hand, possessed enormous accumulated prestige and, on the other, faced no plausible rival.[4] Julius Caesar's soldiers, when they crossed the Rubicon, would not have said that they were marching to sweep away the Republic but to protect it – specifically, to defend that precious Republican institution, the tribunate, and the just claims of their victorious general against the aggression of an oligarchical cabal that had illegitimately seized control of the Senate.[5] In fact, no one seems ever to have raised the banner of revolt against the Republican régime as such, which seems incomprehensible if there was a large and powerful reservoir of allies to be won by doing so. Even Caesar needed his Senate.[6]

The power of the Republican political tradition thus would seem highly paradoxical, in view of the litany of crises with which I began this chapter. But an examination of public political discourse, the central linguistic medium of interaction between mass and élite through which fundamental Republican ideas were elaborated and put into wide circulation, helps to resolve the apparent paradox. Mass oratory in the *contio* breathed life into, and constantly renewed, the communal bonds between élite speakers and (potentially) voting listeners, weaving the common citizen into the fabric of the *res publica* as much as did the electoral or legislative ballot. We have seen how the contional audiences were engaged and informed participants in Roman public life and political traditions. Contional rhetoric sustained and revived the wide consensus on fundamental Republican political ideals even while members of the élite competed against one another's claims truly to embody those ideals. The "publicity" of the Republic, and the power of the idea of the "will and judgment" of the sovereign Roman People, become most conspicuous when we observe how élite orators strove to create objective signs of overwhelming popular support for their aims – the cries of approval, applause, and ultimately, the effective silencing of the opposition when it became impossible to mount a counter-demonstration or to sustain a veto.

At the same time, these same methods, manipulative as they were, also reveal the other side of the picture: an élite hegemony over what was consequently a highly paternalistic public discourse that served, notwithstanding

---

[4] Note Meier's reply in the new prologue to the 1980 reprint of Meier 1966 (p. xix) to Brunt's somewhat dismissive review of the original (Brunt 1968).

[5] Caes. *B Civ.* 1.7.

[6] Beyond this anodyne formulation I leave aside as peripheral to my present purpose the controversy whether Caesar himself was able to look beyond the Republic (denied by Meier 1982 but broadly affirmed by Jehne 1987).

its agonistic aspects, to reinforce deference to that élite as a whole rather than to challenge it. If the shouts in the *contio* and subsequent votes in the *comitia* gave the People their "Voice," members of the élite, as orators, gave them their words. While such words, if they are to have persuasive or motivating force, will always involve complex negotiation between perspectives of speaker and of audience, the negotiating power of these two parties to the exchange depends on numerous variables (access to knowledge and information, social prestige, institutional biases such as the direct control of participation by the presiding official in the *contio*), and we have seen that a number of factors tilted the balance of power in these crucial acts of communication toward the élite orator instead of the shouting, or silent, audience whom he sought to impel. These were not audiences of "ignoramuses," and the idea that they could simply be browbeaten or overawed by their social superiors seems to be drawn more from élite fantasy or nostalgic projection than observation of reality. But many factors that have been isolated and examined made the communicative exchange between speaker and audience a distinctly unequal one.

Although certain practices and norms make clear that the Roman People were expected to be informed in public meetings about a bill before they exerted their sovereign right of making it law, it is also clear that a "debate" model of the *contio*'s function does not well fit the facts. Rather, public meetings were, in practice, the means by which members of the élite sought to generate the impression of overwhelming popular consensus behind their projects that would rout their opponents from the Forum or force acquiescence within the Senate, or both. The relatively equal presentation of alternative views that is fundamental to the idea of "debate" – and crucial to an audience for making an informed decision about its own interests – was only minimally respected, on the day of the vote itself, when there was little hope or expectation of changing minds among those who had been successfully mobilized to vote. Up to that point, the power of the presiding magistrate to set the agenda, to determine who would speak, to influence the very composition of his audience, and to shape perceptions of its response by means of various manipulative techniques was apt to be exploited to the full in order to silence any opposing view, either by exposing it invidiously to a hostile crowd (or threatening to do so) or by mobilizing sufficiently wide sectors of the urban population that it could no longer effectively be heard.

The *contio*, then, is best seen in "instrumental" rather than "deliberative" terms. And this instrument was largely in the hands of the élite orators who, after all, summoned it into existence. True, its very instrumentality obliged orators, particularly after 133, to articulate a highly ingratiating rhetoric of popular power which, in isolation, seems almost democratic. Yet, by silencing all contrary argument by means of the power of the crowd, this instrumentality also precluded authentic debate both about specific proposals and broader visions of the public good, which in turn furthered the dependency of the voting audience upon the orator, since without substantial competition between serious alternatives the listener was given no independent leverage over agenda or presentation. The strict separation of senatorial and popular spheres of action, together with the removal of the former from the People's direct surveillance, increased this dependency, since élite orators were the sources of most essential information even as they used it to mobilize the public. Furthermore, the separation of spheres raised a very real problem of public accountability, to which orators responded with a "drama" of treacherous "plotters" and "friends" of the Roman People that effectively supplanted any real argument over policy alternatives that might ultimately even have challenged the bases of élite hegemony. Instead, the competition for public trust in alternative élite mediators of privileged knowledge coincided naturally with an ideological construction of authority for the élite possessors of that knowledge. The result was a steeply hierarchical speech situation that reflected or reproduced other similar socio-political hierarchies very familiar to the Roman citizen, in particular his dependence on senators for mediation of religious knowledge (and its proper use in the community's interest), probably also even more diffuse social hierarchies such as the dependence of client or freedman upon patron.[7]

How effective, then, was the late-Republican *contio* as a means for the Roman People to bring its interests to bear upon élite political actors? John North's well-known formulation that "the popular will of the Roman people found expression in the context, and only in the context, of divisions within the oligarchy" is apt to be quoted in this context, particularly by those unsympathetic to a "democratic" interpretation of Republican politics; yet it turns out, on closer examination, to be fundamentally ambiguous.[8] At first glance it would seem to suggest that there was only a narrow opening for popular involvement in decision-making, specifically only when the senatorial leadership found itself divided.[9] Yet divisions among the élite can

---

[7] Cf. Hölkeskamp 1995: 33–35; Burckhardt 1990: 95: "It is difficult to imagine a society in which so important a part of the social make up and the values lying behind it would not be reflected in some way in political life."

[8] North 1990a: 18 (= 1990b: 285) for the quotation. Cf. Harris 1990: 292.

[9] So Bleicken 1975: 272.

themselves be as readily seen as a *consequence* of the availability of a "popular" avenue for political action as a *cause* for venturing down it.[10] When, after 133, was the Roman élite *not* divided?[11] And what precipitated that division if not the newly explored opportunity, for those prepared to part company with their senatorial leaders, to tap the enormous force of popular power on certain issues? There is a kind of chicken-and-egg problem here that appears to reduce North's formulation almost to a tautology: whenever the "popular will of the Roman people found expression" there were of course "divisions within the oligarchy," since these were two aspects of the same phenomenon, both indeed apt to be played out at the same venue (the *contio*).

Rather than separating out these two interdependent causal factors, we might instead attend to the question, who – speakers or listeners? – exerted the strongest influence over the production of contional discourse. I would like to suggest that while "public opinion" is always a construct, the "Popular Will of the Roman People" was a much more artificial construct than it might at first appear. It was expressed in collective actions that were prompted and to a large extent created by élite orators; indeed, in a basic sense it did not exist unless and until a magistrate summoned a *contio* and articulated it (for the odd *lapidatio* or bread-riot was hardly an unambiguous and explicit *significatio* of the "judgment and will of the Roman People"). Since this meeting would typically also be, not coincidentally, the opening salvo of that politician's campaign to realize some already-determined plan (carry a bill, or influence senatorial deliberations), there can be little question of the Popular Will imposing itself upon those who set its agenda and called it forth. Of course magistrates who sought to tap the power inherent in the Will of the Roman People needed to try to anticipate what kind of proposal, furthered by skillful use of a core of supporters and deft handling of the crowd, would generate the kind of momentum that could withstand not only vocal resistance but the threat of a veto. At times of severe distress and clearly focused discontent (as in 133, I presume, or 67) the sources of that perturbation had to be addressed, more or less adequately, but that bespeaks only a minimal level of responsiveness in the system. As a system of communicative exchange, public political discourse was of course not wholly insulated from the authentic concerns of the (urban) citizenry – whatever they might have been, and however they might have been independently established – but the balance of power between the parties in

---

[10] See North's comments on Perelli that immediately follow (1990a: 18–19).

[11] Cic. *Rep.* 1.31.3–4. *Duo senatus* and the opposing senators listed by "Laelius" show that the division of *populus unus* that he describes runs right through the élite as well.

that exchange was tilted heavily toward the senators who chose the agenda, timing, and even, to some extent, their "crowd," and who, finally, also did the speaking.

If, then, the élite enjoyed a strong hegemony over contional discourse, it makes sense to consider the functions of that discourse as determined more by élite interests than plebeian ones. While contional speech indeed did much to integrate the (urban) plebs into the Republican system, it also tended to coopt the theoretically sovereign power of the Roman People in the service of ideas and proposals formulated by the élite for their consumption, subject to very little constraint on the part of the public. It also did much to yoke the People to an élite vision of what the Republic was and should be: in brief, a system in which those with privileged knowledge and correspondingly high authority repaid the honor granted them by the People by offering loyal advice and guidance in a dangerous world. Whether one put one's trust in an isolated member of that élite – the "popular" tribune – or in the collective body of the Senate, this was, either way, a paternalistic ideological construction of the functioning of the political community that served to reduce the audience's decision-making to a choice between champions in whom to invest their trust. While among the élite there would be individual winners and losers in the competition for public trust, so long as the broad framework was accepted by the People – and no challenge to it seems to appear in our evidence of public discourse – the loss of public trust and credibility for one member of the élite was balanced by its conferral on another. In this way, the ideological function of contional discourse reflected and also continually justified the political hegemony of the Roman élite, and correspondingly legitimized the Republican system as a whole.

Christian Meier, in his seminal book of 1966, *Res Publica Amissa* – a brilliant and even profound work that somehow has never received due recognition in the English-speaking world – built his analysis of the crisis of the late Republic upon the apparently paradoxical fact that the grave troubles of the age failed to give birth to any conception of an acceptable and realizable alternative to the traditional system.[12] Those elements of the social order that had a significant political role maintained an unchallenged allegiance to the ideal of the old order, despite the antagonisms

---

[12] Girardet 1996: 248 objects that the crisis of the Republic was characterized not by the *lack* of an "alternative" but its looming presence – in the form of personal *regnum*. But that is to misunderstand, and trivialize, Meier's point. Setting aside old controversies over Caesar's plans and the expectations of his public, during the period of the Republic a personal domination wholly lacked legitimacy and thus could not represent an "alternative" in Meier's sense.

and discontents that their immediate circumstances often aroused. While the severity of contemporary difficulties was recognized, in the absence of any comprehensible alternative to the old Republic and its institutions, norms, and practices, remedies could only take the form of returning to an increasingly unworkable past, which led inevitably to the perpetuation and worsening of the crisis ("Krise ohne Alternative").[13] For Erich Gruen in 1974, on the other hand, the Senate and its governing élite were by no means crippled by indifference, unresponsiveness, and general ineffectiveness in the "last generation of the Republic"; the system did not collapse because of its own inherent weaknesses but was dealt a fatal blow by a specific, explosive event, the Caesarian civil war.[14] Despite their sharp divergences regarding the nature of the crisis (or even the very existence of a long-standing "crisis"), both are in agreement that "a reconstitution of the social and political structure was unthinkable for *nobiles* and *plebs* alike."[15] It is clear why this would be so for the Republican élite, whose power, stability and resilience, however, continue to demand explanation, especially if we are no longer to have recourse to an exaggerated notion of the political importance of patronage.[16] But Millar's provocative challenge to a narrowly "oligarchical" model of Republican politics has brought to the foreground the fruitful question of how the Roman People were so successfully integrated *as citizens* into this régime that was once thought to be "semi-feudal," and indeed how they came not merely to acquiesce in, but actively to perpetuate, élite power.[17]

This book, I hope, offers an explanation. Like Republican elections, the *contio* served better as a communal arena in which the hierarchies both within the political élite and in the Commonwealth as a whole could be

---

[13] Meier 1966: esp. 201–5, 301–6; see also the retrospective comments in the new introduction to the 1980 reprint, and Meier 1978: 34–42. General, brief summaries of the theory are in Meier 1980: 39–49, and in English in Meier 1982: 349–63. Jehne 1987: 3–13 gives a concise and well-annotated critical sketch of the theory; for criticism, see also Brunt 1968; Rilinger 1982; Heuß 1983: 87–88; Girardet 1996. Also Badian 1990b.

[14] Gruen 1974. See now also, partly in reaction to Meier's *Caesar*, Girardet 1996 and Welwei 1996.

[15] Gruen 1974: 506; the opening of Gruen's new introduction to the 1995 edition (p. vii) is illuminating. Meier's formulation is typically paradoxical: "Das besonders Eigenartige dieses Vorgangs besteht darin, daß von den treibenden Kräften – mit der möglichen (!) Ausnahme Caesars – keine den Untergang der überkommenen Form des Gemeinwesens wollte, den sie allesamt bewirkten" (Meier 1978: 34).

[16] "What should demand more attention . . . is not what splintered the system at the end of the Republic, but what held it together for so long, what enabled the *nobiles* to surmount faction and feud and maintain a nearly unbroken dominance for four centuries" (Gruen 1996: 216; cf. 1991: 251–55). On patronage, see pp. 4–6.

[17] In addition to the articles by Gruen just mentioned (above, n. 16), see the work of Flaig, Hölkeskamp, Jehne, Laser, and Yakobson cited above, chap. 6, n. 134; also, Rosenstein 1990a, 1990b.

established, perpetuated, and validated than as a democratic forum for bringing to light, clarifying, and pursuing the real interests of the voting citizen. That conclusion accords well with the rather obvious fact – somewhat embarrassing for a "democratic" interpretation of the political system – that the late Republic produced relatively few benefits to the Roman plebs in the form either of material assistance or of reforms to the political system itself making it more responsive to pressure "from below." Those material benefits that were won – in particular, progressive improvement of the food supply in the city, and two major, if inadequate, efforts to distribute public land to the poor – tended to address only the most basic (if also most pressing) concerns of existence, were overall relatively limited in scope, and even so by no means swiftly or easily conceded by the Senate. Most notable is the general lack of democratic reform of the system itself, even after the incremental concessions of the secret ballot for elections, most popular trials, and legislation, in the course of the 130s, at the very beginning of our period – concessions that themselves may have been driven as much or more by noble efforts to close off an influx of "new men" from outside the aristocracy than any popular movement to increase the citizenry's influence over the political process.[18] From a large perspective, it appears that the personal advantages available to some senators prepared to face the risks of breaking ranks with their peers by tapping the alternative source of power in the Republic greatly exceeded the benefits that they actually offered and won for the Roman People.

The suppression of debatable alternatives from contional discourse to produce a relatively "closed" ideological system offers a notable example of ideology's ability to naturalize the existing order by covertly excluding alternatives. An important element of Meier's attractive thesis – the Romans' inability to see a way "out" rather than simply a doomed way "back" – becomes rationally comprehensible rather than apparently paradoxical and fatalistic. Popular oratory, perhaps remarkably, did not pry open new possibilities for radically new solutions to the Republic's problems (such as

---

[18] Gruen 1991: 257–61; cf. Jehne 1993. For a "democratizing" interpretation of the ballot laws, however, see Yakobson 1995 and 1999: 126–33; cf. B. A. Marshall 1997. (Harris 1989: 168–70 [cf. 1990: 293], and Hall 1990, take a position in between.) There is early numismatic evidence of the "popular" appeal of at least the *lex Cassia* of 137 (*RRC* 266/1 of *c.* 126 BC: see Marshall, pp. 63–64; Ritter 1998, with chap. 3 above, n. 79) – but as Gruen notes, that does not preclude noble initiative; and the fact that the legislative secret ballot (as well as the first two ballot laws) could be voted into existence without the very protection it afforded seems to qualify the "democratizing" interpretation heavily. (See also Morstein-Marx 2000b: 230–31.) Meier 1966: 131–35 strongly emphasizes the (failed) reformist potential of Gaius Gracchus' legislation, especially his judicial law; but as that potential remained unrealized, it does not affect this point.

an incremental democratization of the system that might conceivably have broadened its base of legitimacy), but revolved perennially around the same unchallengeable premises while continally re-staging an Edelman-esque "drama" of competing personalities. If an important reason for the stubborn survival of the Republican régime was the curious inability of both élite and mass, in the face of repeated trials and traumas, to conceive seriously of an "alternative" to the ancestral Republic, with its paternalist traditions of élite hegemony and popular deference so long as popular interests were seen to be protected, this surprising intellectual impasse was a product precisely of the great success with which contional discourse bound the citizenry to their senatorial leaders.

References

Abbreviations of journal titles correspond to those used in *L'Année Philologique*.

Achard, G. 1981, *Pratique rhétorique et idéologie politique dans les discours "optimates" de Cicéron* (*Mnemosyne* Suppl. 68), Leiden.
    1982, "Langage et société: à propos des *optimates* et des *populares*," *Latomus* 41: 794–800.
    1991, *La communication à Rome*, Paris.
    2000, "L'influence des jeunes lecteurs sur la rédaction des discours cicéroniens," in Achard and Ledentu 2000, pp. 75–90.
Achard, G. and M. Ledentu (eds.) 2000, *Orateur, auditeurs, lecteurs: à propos de l'éloquence romaine à la fin de la République et au début du Principat*, Lyon.
Aldrete, G. S. 1999, *Acclamations in Ancient Rome*, Baltimore.
Alexander, M. C. 1990, *Trials in the Late Roman Republic, 149 BC to 50 BC*, Toronto.
    2003, *The Case for the Prosecution in the Ciceronian Era*, Ann Arbor.
Alföldi, A. 1956, "The Main Aspects of Political Propaganda on the Coinage of the Roman Republic," in *Essays in Roman Coinage Presented to Harold Mattingly*, ed. R. A. G. Carson and C. H. V. Sutherland, Oxford, pp. 63–95.
Althusser, L. 1971, *Lenin and Philosophy and Other Essays*, tr. B. Brewster, London.
Andreau, J. 1987, "L'espace de la vie financière à Rome," in *L'urbs: espace urbain et histoire (Ier siècle av. J.-C.–IIIe siècle ap. J.-C.)*, Rome, pp. 157–74.
Assmann, A. and J. Assmann 1988, "Schrift, Tradition und Kultur," in *Zwischen Festtag und Alltag. Zehn Beiträge zum Thema "Mündlichkeit und Schriftlichkeit,"* ed. W. Raible, Tübingen, pp. 25–49.
Astin, A. E. 1971, *Scipio Aemilianus*, Oxford.
Atkinson, M. 1984, *Our Masters' Voices: the Language and Body Language of Politics*, London and New York.
Austin, R. G. 1960, *Cicero: Pro M. Caelio Oratio*, 3rd edn., Oxford.
    1971, *P. Vergili Maronis Aeneidos Liber Primus*, Oxford.
Badian, E. 1958, *Studies in Greek and Roman History*, Oxford.
    1967, "The Testament of Ptolemy Alexander," *RhM* 110: 178–92.
    1972, "Tiberius Gracchus and the Beginning of the Roman Revolution," *ANRW* 1.1: 668–731.
    1977, "The Auctor of the Lex Flavia," *Athenaeum* 55 n.s.: 233–38.

1984, "The Death of Saturninus: Studies in Chronology and Prosopography," *Chiron* 14: 101–47.

1988, "E.H.L.N.R.," *MH* 45: 203–18.

1989, "The Case of the Cowardly Tribune. C.T.H.R.E. on E.H.L.N.R.," *AHB* 3: 78–84.

1990a, "The Consuls, 179–49 BC," *Chiron* 20: 371–413.

1990b, Review of Meier, *Caesar*, *Gnomon* 62: 22–39.

Baldwin, B. 1979, "The *acta diurna*," *Chiron* 9: 189–203.

Balsdon, J. P. V. D. 1966, "Fabula Clodiana," *Historia* 15: 65–73.

Beard, M. 1989, "Acca Larentia Gains a Son," in *Images of Authority: Papers Presented to Joyce Reynolds* (*PCPhS* Suppl. 16), ed. M. M. Mackenzie and C. Roueché, Cambridge, pp. 41–61.

1990, "Priesthood in the Roman Republic," in *Pagan Priests. Religion and Power in the Ancient World*, ed. M. Beard and J. North, Ithaca, pp. 17–48.

Behr, H. 1993, *Die Selbstdarstellung Sullas: ein aristokratischer Politiker zwischen persönlichem Führungsanspruch und Standessolidarität*, Frankfurt.

Bell, A. J. E. 1997, "Cicero and the Spectacle of Power," *JRS* 87: 1–22.

Belloni, G. G. 1976, "Monete romane e propaganda," in *I canali della propaganda nel mondo antico*, ed. M. Sordi, Milan, pp. 131–59.

Benner, H. 1987, *Die Politik des P. Clodius Pulcher* (*Historia* Einzelschrift 50), Stuttgart.

Béranger, J. 1972, "Les jugements de Cicéron sur les Gracques," *ANRW* 1.1: 732–63.

Berrendonner, C. 2001, "La formation de la tradition sur M'. Curius Dentatus et C. Fabricius Luscinus: un homme nouveau peut-il être un grand homme?," in Coudry and Späth 2001, pp. 97–116.

Berry, D. H. 1996, *Cicero*, Pro P. Sulla Oratio, Cambridge.

Bettini, M. 2000, "*Mos, mores* und *mos maiorum*: die Erfindung der 'Sittlichkeit' in der römischen Kultur," in Braun, Haltenhoff, and Mutschler 2000, pp. 303–52.

Bleicken, J. 1955, *Das Volkstribunat der klassischen Republik*, Göttingen.

1972, *Staatliche Ordnung und Freiheit in der römischen Republik*, Kallmünz.

1975, *Lex Publica. Gesetz und Recht in der römischen Republik*, Berlin.

1981, "Das römische Volkstribunat. Versuch einer Analyse seiner politischen Funktion in republikanischer Zeit," *Chiron* 11: 87–108.

1982, *Die Verfassung der römischen Republik*, 3rd edn., Paderborn.

Blösel, W. 2000, "Die Geschichte des Begriffes *mos maiorum* von den Anfängen bis zu Cicero," in Linke and Stemmler 2000, pp. 25–97.

Bohman, J. 1997, "Deliberative Democracy and Effective Social Freedom: Capabilities, Resources, and Opportunities," in Bohman and Rehg 1997, pp. 321–48.

Bohman, J. and W. Rehg (eds.) 1997, *Deliberative Democracy. Essays on Reason and Politics*, Cambridge, MA.

Bonnefond-Coudry, M. 1989, *Le sénat de la république romaine de la guerre d'Hannibal à Auguste*, Rome.

Botsford, G. W. 1909, *The Roman Assemblies*, New York.

Braun, M., A. Haltenhoff, and F.-H. Mutschler (eds.) 2000, *Moribus antiquis res stat Romana: römische Werte und römische Literatur im 3. und 2. Jh. v. Chr.*, Leipzig.

Braund, D. 1983, "Royal Wills and Rome," *PBSR* 51: 16–57.

Brunt, P. A. 1966, "The Roman Mob," *P&P* 35: 3–27.

1968, Review of C. Meier, *Res publica amissa, JRS* 58: 229–32.

1971a, *Italian Manpower, 225 BC–AD 14*, Oxford.

1971b, *Social Conflicts in the Roman Republic*, New York.

1988, *The Fall of the Roman Republic and Related Essays*, Oxford.

Büchner, K. 1982, *Sallust*, 2nd edn., Heidelberg.

Burckhardt, L. A. 1988, *Politische Strategien der Optimaten in der späten römischen Republik* (*Historia* Einzelschrift 57), Stuttgart.

1990, "The Political Elite of the Roman Republic: Comments on Recent Discussion of the Concepts *Nobilitas* and *Homo Novus*," *Historia* 39: 77–99.

Burnett, A. M. 1977, "The Authority to Coin in the Late Republic and Early Empire," *NC* 17 (ser. 7): 37–63.

Cameron, A. 1976, *Circus Factions*, Oxford.

Camp, J. McK., II 1996, "The Form of Pnyx III," in *The Pnyx in the History of Athens*, ed. B. Forsén and G. Stanton, Helsinki, pp. 41–46.

Canetti, E. 1978, *Crowds and Power*, New York.

Carafa, P. 1998, *Il comizio di Roma dalle origini all'età di Augusto* (Bull. della Comm. Arch. Com. di Roma Suppl. 5), Rome.

Carandini, A. 1988, *Schiavi in Italia. Gli strumenti pensanti dei Romani fra tarda Repubblica e medio Impero*, Rome.

Carney, W. 1960, "Cicero's Picture of Marius," *WS* 73: 83–122.

Cavaggioni, F. 1998, *L. Apuleio Saturnino*. Tribunus plebis seditiosus (Istituto Veneto di Scienze, Lettere ed Arti: Memorie, Classe di Scienze Morali, Lettere ed Arti 79), Venice.

Cerutti, S. M. 1998, "P. Clodius and the Stairs of the Temple of Castor," *Latomus* 57: 292–305.

Churchill, J. B. 1999, "*Ex qua quod vellent facerent*: Roman Magistrates' Authority over *Praeda* and *Manubiae*," *TAPhA* 129: 85–116.

Clark, A. C. 1895, *M. Tulli Ciceronis pro T. Annio Milone ad iudices oratio*, Oxford.

Classen, C. J. 1985, *Recht-Rhetorik-Politik*, Darmstadt.

Coarelli, F. 1985, *Il foro romano (II): periodo repubblicano e augusteo*, Rome.

1986, *Il foro romano (I): periodo arcaico*, 2nd edn., Rome.

1988, *Il foro boario dalle origini alla fine della repubblica*, Rome.

1997, *Il Campo Marzio*, Rome.

Converse, P. E. 1964, "The Nature of Belief Systems in Mass Publics," in *Ideology and Discontent*, ed. D. E. Apter, New York, pp. 206–61.

Corbeill, A. 1996, *Controlling Laughter*, Princeton.

2002, "Political Movement: Walking and Ideology in Republican Rome," in *The Roman Gaze*, ed. D. Fredrick, Baltimore, pp. 182–215.

Corbier, M. 1987, "L'écriture dans l'espace public romain," in *L'urbs: espace urbain et histoire (Ier siècle av. J.-C.–IIIe siècle ap. J.-C.)*, Rome, pp. 27–60.

1991, "L'écriture en quête de lecteurs," in *Literacy in the Roman World* (*JRA* Suppl. 3), ed. J. H. Humphrey, Ann Arbor.

Cornell, T. J. 1995, *The Beginnings of Rome: Italy and Rome from the Bronze Age to the Punic Wars (c. 1000–264 BC)*, London and New York.

Coudry, M. and T. Späth (eds.) 2001, *L'invention des grands hommes de la Rome antique / Die Konstruktion der großen Männer Altroms*, Paris.

Crawford, J. W. 1984, *M. Tullius Cicero: the Lost and Unpublished Orations*, Göttingen.

1994, *M. Tullius Cicero: the Fragmentary Speeches*, 2nd edn., Atlanta.

Crawford, M. H. 1974, *Roman Republican Coinage*, 2 vols., Cambridge.

1983, "Roman Imperial Coin Types and the Formation of Public Opinion," in *Studies in Numismatic Method Presented to Philip Grierson*, ed. C. N. L. Brooke, B. H. I. H. Stewart, J. G. Pollard, and T. R. Volk, Cambridge, pp. 47–64.

1988, "The Laws of the Romans: Knowledge and Diffusion," in *Estudios sobre la* Tabula Siarensis, ed. J. Gonzalez and J. Arce, Madrid, pp. 127–40.

(ed.) 1996, *Roman Statutes* (*BICS* Suppl. 64), 2 vols., London.

Culham, P. 1989, "Archives and Alternatives in Republican Rome," *CPh* 84: 100–15.

Curti, E. 2000, "From Concordia to the Quirinal: Notes on Religion and Politics in Mid-Republican/Hellenistic Rome," in *Religion in Archaic and Republican Rome and Italy: Evidence and Experience*, ed. E. Bispham and C. Smith, London, pp. 77–91.

Damon, C. 1992, "Sex. Cloelius, Scriba," *HSPh* 94: 227–50.

David, J.-M. 1979, "Promotion civique et droit à la parole. L. Licinius Crassus, les accusateurs et les rhéteurs latins," *MEFRA* 91: 135–81.

1980a, "'Eloquentia popularis' et conduites symboliques des orateurs de la fin de la République: problèmes d'efficacité," *QS* 6.12: 171–211.

1980b, "*Maiorum exempla sequi*: l'*exemplum* historique dans les discours judiciaires de Cicéron," *MEFRM* 92: 67–86.

1983a, "L'action oratoire de C. Gracchus: l'image d'un modèle," in *Demokratia et Aristokratia. A propos de Caius Gracchus: mots grecs et réalités romaines*, ed. C. Nicolet, Paris, pp. 103–16.

1983b, "Les orateurs des municipes à Rome: intégration, réticences et snobismes," in *Les "bourgeoisies" municipales italiennes aux IIe et Ier siècles av. J.-C.*, Paris and Naples, pp. 309–23.

1992, *Le patronat judiciaire au dernier siècle de la République Romaine*, Rome.

1995, "Le tribunal du préteur: contraintes symboliques et politiques sous la République et le début de l'Empire," *Klio* 77: 371–85.

Deissmann-Merten, M. 1974, "Zu einem Ausspruch des Scipio Aemilianus," *Chiron* 4: 177–81.

Delli Carpini, M. X. and S. Keeter 1989, *What Americans Know about Politics and Why It Matters*, New Haven and London.

Denniston, J. D. 1926, *M. Tulli Ciceronis In M. Antonium Orationes Philippicae Prima et Secunda*, Oxford.

Diehl, H. 1988, *Sulla und seine Zeit im Urteil Ciceros*, Hildesheim.

Dilke, O. A. W. 1978, "Cicero's Attitude to the Allocation of Land in the *De lege agraria*," *Ciceroniana* 3 n.s.: 183–87.

Döbler, C. 1999, *Politische Agitation und Öffentlichkeit in der späten Republik*, Frankfurt.

Drumann, W. 1899–1929, *Geschichte Roms in seinem Übergang von der republikanischen zur monarchischen Verfassung*, 2nd edn., ed. P. Groebe, 6 vols., Berlin.

Drummond, A. 1995, *Law, Politics, and Power. Sallust and the Execution of the Catilinarian Conspirators* (*Historia* Einzelschrift 93), Stuttgart.

Dudley, D. R. 1941, "Blossius of Cumae," *JRS* 31: 94–99.

Dulière, C. 1979, *Lupa Romana. Recherches d'iconographie et essai d'interprétation*, Rome.

Dyck, A. R. 1996, *A Commentary on Cicero, De Officiis*, Ann Arbor.

Eagleton, T. 1991, *Ideology: an Introduction*, London.

Earl, D. C. 1961, *The Political Thought of Sallust*, Cambridge.

Edelman, M. 1964, *The Symbolic Uses of Politics*, Urbana.

  1971, *Politics as Symbolic Action*, Chicago.

  1977, *Political Language: Words that Succeed and Policies that Fail*, New York.

  1988, *Constructing the Political Spectacle*, Chicago and London.

Edwards, C. 1993, *The Politics of Immorality*, Cambridge.

Ehrhardt, C. T. H. R. 1989, " 'E.H.L.N.R.' Again," *AHB* 3: 45–46.

Elster, J. 1997, "The Market and the Forum: Three Varieties of Political Theory," in Bohman and Rehg 1997, pp. 3–33.

Evans, J. D. 1992, *The Art of Persuasion: Political Propaganda from Aeneas to Brutus*, Ann Arbor.

Famerie, E. 1998, *Le latin et le grec d'Appien: contribution à l'étude du lexique d'un historien grec de Rome*, Geneva.

Fantham, E. 1997, "The Contexts and Occasions of Roman Public Rhetoric," in *Roman Eloquence: Rhetoric in Society and Literature*, ed. W. J. Dominik, London, pp. 111–28.

Favory, F. 1976, "Classes dangereuses et crise de l'État dans le discours cicéronien (d'après les écrits de Cicéron de 57 à 52)," in *Texte, politique, idéologie: Cicéron*, Paris, pp. 109–233.

Favro, D. 1988, "The Roman Forum and Roman Memory," *Places* 5: 17–24.

  1994, "The Street Triumphant: the Urban Impact of Roman Triumphal Parades," in *Streets. Critical Perspectives on Public Space*, ed. Z. Çelik, D. Favro, and R. Ingersoll, Berkeley, pp. 151–64.

  1996, *The Urban Image of Augustan Rome*, Cambridge.

Fehrle, R. 1983, *Cato Uticensis*, Darmstadt.

Ferrary, J.-L. 1982, "L'idee politiche a Roma nell'epoca repubblicana," in *Storia delle idee politiche economiche e sociali*, ed. L. Firpo, vol. 1, Torino, pp. 723–804.

  1988, "Rogatio Servilia Agraria," *Athenaeum* 66: 141–64.

  1997, "*Optimates* et *populares*. Le problème du rôle de l'idéologie dans la politique," in *Die späte römische Republik / La fin de la république romaine. Un débat franco-allemand d'histoire et d'historiographie*, ed. H. Bruhns, J.-M. David, and W. Nippel, Rome, pp. 221–35.

Flach, D. 1990, *Römische Agrargeschichte*, Munich.

Flaig, E. 1993, "Politisierte Lebensführung und ästhetische Kultur. Eine semiotische Untersuchung am römischen Adel," *Historische Anthropologie* 1: 193–217.

1995a, "Entscheidung und Konsens. Zu den Feldern der politischen Kommunikation zwischen Aristokratie und Plebs," in Jehne 1995a, pp. 77–127.

1995b, "Die *pompa funebris*. Adlige Konkurrenz und annalistische Erinnerung in der römischen Republik," in *Memoria als Kultur*, ed. O. G. Oexle, Göttingen, pp. 115–48.

1998, "War die römische Volksversammlung ein Entscheidungsorgan? Institution und soziale Praxis," in *Institutionen und Ereignis. Über historische Praktiken und Vorstellungen gesellschaftlichen Ordnens*, ed. R. Blänkner and B. Jussen, Göttingen, pp. 49–73.

Flower, H. 1995, "*Fabulae Praetextae* in Context: When Were Plays on Contemporary Subjects Performed in Rome?" *CQ* 45: 170–90.

1996, *Ancestor Masks and Aristocratic Power in Roman Culture*, Oxford.

Foucault, M. 1980, *Power/Knowledge: Selected Interviews and Other Writings, 1972–77*, ed. C. Gordon, New York.

Frisch, H. 1946, *Cicero's Fight for the Republic*, Copenhagen.

Fuhrmann, M. 1990, "Mündlichkeit und fiktive Mündlichkeit in den von Cicero veröffentlichten Reden," in *Strukturen der Mündlichkeit in der römischen Literatur*, ed. G. Vogt-Spira, Tübingen, pp. 53–62.

Gabba, E. 1966, "Nota sulla *Rogatio Agraria* di P. Servilio Rullo," in *Mélanges d'archéologie et d'histoire offerts à André Piganiol*, vol. II, ed. R. Chevallier, Paris, pp. 769–75.

1994, "Rome and Italy: the Social War," in *Cambridge Ancient History*, vol. IX: *The Last Age of the Roman Republic 146–43 BC*, ed. J. A. Crook, A. Lintott, and E. Rawson, 2nd edn., Cambridge, pp. 104–28.

Garnsey, P. and D. Rathbone 1985, "The Background to the Grain Law of Gaius Gracchus," *JRS* 75: 20–25.

Gelzer, M. 1969, *Cicero. Ein biographischer Versuch*, Wiesbaden.

Gendre, M. and C. Loutsch 2001, "C. Duilius et M. Atilius Regulus," in Coudry and Späth 2001, pp. 131–72.

Girardet, K. M. 1996, "Politische Verantwortung im Ernstfall: Cicero, die Diktatur und der Diktator Caesar," in Ληναϊκά. *Festschrift für Carl Werner Müller*, ed. C. Mueller-Goldingen and K. Sier, Stuttgart and Leipzig, pp. 217–51.

Gjerstad, E. 1941, "Il comizio romano dell'età repubblicana," *Opuscula archaeologica* 2: 97–158.

Gleason, M. W. 1995, *Making Men: Sophists and Self-Representation in Ancient Rome*, Princeton.

Gnoli, F. 1980, "La 'rogatio Servilia agraria' del 63 a.C. e la responsabilità penale del generale vittorioso per la preda bellica," in *Atti del II Seminario Romanistico Gardesano*, Milan, pp. 293–309.

Goltz, A. 2000, "*Maiestas sine viribus* – Die Bedeutung der Lictoren für die Konfliktbewältigungsstrategien römischer Magistrate," in Linke and Stemmler 2000, pp. 237–67.

Gotoff, H. 1979, *Cicero's Elegant Style: an Analysis of the* Pro Archia, Urbana.

Gotter, U. 1996, *Der Diktator ist Tot! Politik in Rom zwischen den Iden des März und der Begründung des zweiten Triumvirats* (*Historia* Einzelschrift 110), Stuttgart.

Gowing, A. 1992, *The Triumviral Narratives of Appian and Cassius Dio*, Ann Arbor.

Gruen, E. S. 1965, "The *Lex Varia*," *JRS* 55: 59–73.

1968, *Roman Politics and the Criminal Courts 149–78 BC*, Cambridge, MA.

1974, *The Last Generation of the Roman Republic*, Berkeley. Reprinted with new introduction, 1995.

1984, *The Hellenistic World and the Coming of Rome*, Berkeley.

1991, "The Exercise of Power in the Roman Republic," in *City-States in Classical Antiquity and Medieval Italy*, ed. A. Molho, K. Raaflaub, and J. Emlen, Stuttgart, pp. 251–67.

1992, *Culture and National Identity in Republican Rome*, Ithaca.

1996, "The Roman Oligarchy: Image and Perception," in Imperium Sine Fine: *T. Robert S. Broughton and the Roman Republic* (*Historia* Einzelschrift 105), ed. J. Linderski, Stuttgart, pp. 215–34.

Habermas, J. 1973, "Wahrheitstheorien," in *Wirklichkeit und Reflexion: Walter Schulz zum 60. Geburtstag*, ed. H. Fahrenbach, Pfullingen, pp. 211–65.

1984–87, *The Theory of Communicative Action*, trans. T. McCarthy, 2 vols., Boston.

1996, *Between Facts and Norms. Contributions to a Discourse Theory of Law and Democracy*, trans. W. Rehg. Cambridge, MA.

2001, *On the Pragmatics of Social Interaction: Preliminary Studies in the Theory of Communicative Action*, trans. B. Fultner, Cambridge, MA.

Hall, U. 1990, "Greeks and Romans and the Secret Ballot," in *"Owls to Athens." Essays on Classical Subjects Presented to Sir Kenneth Dover*, edited by E. M. Craik, Oxford, pp. 191–99.

Haltenhoff, A. 2001, "Institutionalisierte Geschichten. Wesen und Wirken des literarischen *exemplum* im alten Rom," in Melville 2001, pp. 213–17.

Hardy, E. G. 1924, *Some Problems in Roman History*, Oxford.

Harris, W. V. 1979, *War and Imperialism in Republican Rome, 327–70 BC*, Oxford.

1989, *Ancient Literacy*, Cambridge, MA and London.

1990, "On Defining the Political Culture of the Roman Republic: Some Comments on Rosenstein, Williamson, and North," *CPh* 85: 288–94.

Harvey, P. 1981, "Cicero, Consius, and Capua, I," *Athenaeum* 59: 299–316.

1982, "Cicero, Consius, and Capua, II," *Athenaeum* 60: 145–71.

Havas, L. 1976a, "L'arrière-plan politique du procès de *perduellio* contre Rabirius," *ACD* 12 (1976) 19–27.

1976b, "La Rogatio Servilia (Contribution à l'étude de la propriété terrienne à l'époque du déclin de la République Romaine)," *Oikumene* 1: 131–56.

Heath, J. 2001, *Communicative Action and Rational Choice*, Cambridge, MA.

Heinze, R. 1960, *Vom Geist des Römertums. Ausgewählte Aufsätze*, ed. E. Burck, 3rd edn., Darmstadt.

Hellegouarc'h, J. 1963, *Le vocabulaire latin des relations et des partis politiques sous la République*, Paris.

Hersh, C. A. 1977, "Notes on the Chronology and Interpretation of the Roman Republican Coinage. Some Comments on Crawford's *Roman Republican Coinage*," *NC* 17 (ser. 7): 19–36.

Hersh, C. and A. Walker 1984, "The Mesagne Hoard," *ANSMusN* 29: 103–34.

Heuß, A. 1983, "Grenzen und Möglichkeiten einer politischen Biographie," *HZ* 237: 85–98.

Hölkeskamp, K.-J. 1995, "*Oratoris maxima scaena*: Reden vor dem Volk in der politischen Kultur der Republik," in Jehne 1995a, pp. 11–49.

1996, "*Exempla* und *mos maiorum*. Überlegungen zum kollektiven Gedächtnis der Nobilität," in *Vergangenheit und Lebenswelt. Soziale Kommunikation, Traditionsbildung und historisches Bewußtsein*, ed. H.-J. Gehrke and A. Möller, Tübingen, pp. 301–38.

2000, "The Roman Republic: Government of the People, by the People, for the People?," review of F. Millar, *The Crowd in Rome in the Late Republic*, *SCI* 19: 203–33.

2001, "Capitol, Comitium und Forum. Öffentliche Räume, sakrale Topographie und Erinnerungslandschaften der römischen Republik," in *Studien zu antiken Identitäten*, ed. S. Faller, Würzburg, pp. 97–132.

Hölscher, T. 1978, "Die Anfänge römischer Repräsentationskunst," *MDAI(R)* 85: 315–57.

1980, "Römische Siegesdenkmäler der späten Republik," in *Tainia. Festschrift R. Hampe*, ed. H. A. Cahn and E. Simon, Mainz, pp. 351–71.

1984, *Staatsdenkmal und Publikum vom Untergang der Republik bis zum Festigung des Kaisertums in Rom*, Constance.

1994, *Monumenti statali e pubblico*, Rome.

2001, "Die Alten vor Augen. Politische Denkmäler und öffentliches Gedächtnis im republikanischen Rom," in Melville 2001, pp. 183–211.

Holliday, P. J. 2002, *The Origins of Roman Historical Commemoration in the Visual Arts*, Cambridge.

Hopkins, K. 1983, *Death and Renewal*, Cambridge.

Horsfall, N. 1996, *La cultura della* Plebs Romana, Barcelona.

Howarth, D. and Y. Stavrakis 2000, "Introducing Discourse Theory and Political Analysis," in *Discourse Theory and Political Analysis*, ed. D. Howarth, A. J. Norval, and Y. Stavrakis, Manchester, pp. 1–23.

Hughes, J. J. 1992, "Piso's Eyebrows," *Mnemosyne* 45: 234–36.

Humphrey, J. H. (ed.) 1991, *Literacy in the Roman World* (*JRA* Suppl. 3), Ann Arbor.

Hutchinson, G. O. 1995, "Rhythm, Style, and Meaning in Cicero's Prose," *CQ* 45: 485–99.

Jaeger, M. 1997, *Livy's Written Rome*, Ann Arbor.

Jehne, M. 1987, *Der Staat des Dictators Caesar*, Cologne.

1993, "Geheime Abstimmung und Bindungswesen in der römischen Republik," *HZ* 257: 593–613.

(ed.) 1995a, *Demokratie in Rom? Die Rolle des Volkes in der Politik der römischen Republik* (*Historia* Einzelschrift 96), Stuttgart.

1995b, "Einführung: zur Debatte um die Rolle des Volkes in der römischen Politik," in Jehne 1995a: 1–9.

2000a, "Jovialität und Freiheit. Zur Institutionalität der Beziehungen zwischen Ober- und Unterschichten in der römischen Republik," in Linke and Stemmler 2000, pp. 207–35.

2000b, "Rednertätigkeit und Statusdissonanzen in der späten römischen Republik," in *Rede und Redner. Bewertung und Darstellung in den antiken Kulturen*, ed. C. Neumeister and W. Raeck, Möhnesee, pp. 167–89.

Jonkers, E. J. 1963, *Social and Economic Commentary on Cicero's* De Lege Agraria Orationes Tres, Leiden.

Joslyn, R. A. 1986, "Keeping Politics in the Study of Political Discourse," in *Form, Genre, and the Study of Political Discourse*, ed. H. W. Simons and A. A. Aghazarian, Columbia, SC, pp. 301–38.

Kallet-Marx [Morstein-Marx], R. M. 1990, "The Trial of Rutilius Rufus," *Phoenix* 44: 122–39.

1995, *Hegemony to Empire: the Development of the Roman* Imperium *in the East from 148 to 62 BC*, Berkeley.

Key, V. O. 1966, *The Responsible Electorate: Rationality in Presidential Voting, 1936– 1960*, Cambridge, MA.

Knight, J. and J. Johnson 1997, "What Sort of Equality Does Deliberative Democracy Require?," in Bohman and Rehg 1997, pp. 297–319.

Kolb, F. 1995, *Rom. Die Geschichte der Stadt in der Antike*, Munich.

Krause, C. 1976, "Zur bauliche Gestalt des republikanischen Comitiums," *MDAI(R)* 83: 31–69.

Kühner, R. and C. Stegmann 1974–76, *Ausführliche Grammatik der lateinischen Sprache*, 5th edn., 2 vols., Hanover.

Kühnert, B. 1991, *Die Plebs Urbana der späten römischen Republik. Ihre ökonomische Situation und soziale Struktur*, Berlin.

La Penna, A. 1968, *Sallustio e la "rivoluzione" romana*, Milan.

Laser, G. 1997, Populo et scaenae serviendum est. *Die Bedeutung der städtischen Masse in der Späten Römischen Republik*, Trier.

Laurence, R. 1994, "Rumour and Communication in Roman Politics," *G&R* 41: 62–74.

Lears, T. J. J. 1985, "The Concept of Cultural Hegemony," *AHR* 90: 567–93.

Ledentu, M. 2000, "L'orateur, la parole et le texte," in Achard and Ledentu 2000, pp. 57–74.

Leeman, A. D., H. Pinkster, and J. Wisse 1981–96, *M. Tullius Cicero*, De Oratore Libri III, 4 vols., Heidelberg.

Leonhardt, J. 1998/99, "Senat und Volk in Ciceros Reden *De lege agraria*," *ACD* 34/35: 279–92.

Leovant-Cirefice, V. 2000, "Le rôle de l'apostrophe aux *Quirites* dans les discours de Cicéron adressés au peuple," in Achard and Ledentu 2000, pp. 43–56.

Levick, B. 1999, "Messages on the Roman Coinage: Types and Inscriptions," in Paul and Ierardi 1999, pp. 41–60.

Libero, L. de 1992, *Obstruktion. Politische Praktiken im Senat und in der Volksversammlung der ausgehenden römischen Republik (70–49 v. Chr.) (Hermes* Einzelschrift 59), Stuttgart.

Linderski, J. 1982, "*Patientia fregit*: M. Octavius and Ti. Gracchus (Cic. Brut. 95)," *Athenaeum* 60: 244–47.

1986, "The Augural Law," *ANRW* 11.16.3: 2146–312.

1995, *Roman Questions: Selected Papers*, Stuttgart.

Linke, B. and M. Stemmler (eds.) 2000, Mos Maiorum. *Untersuchungen zu den Formen der Identitätsstiftung und Stabilisierung in der römischen Republik* (*Historia* Einzelschrift 141), Stuttgart.

Lintott, A. W. 1965, "Trinundinum," *CQ* 59: 281–85.

1968a, *Violence in Republican Rome*, Oxford.

1968b, "Nundinae and the Chronology of the Late Roman Republic," *CQ* 62: 189–94.

1972, "Provocatio. From the Struggle of the Orders to the Principate," *ANRW* 1.2: 226–67.

1999, *The Constitution of the Roman Republic*, Oxford.

Liou-Gille, B. 1994, "La *perduellio*: les procès d'Horace et de Rabirius," *Latomus* 53: 3–38.

Litchfield, H. W. 1914, "National *Exempla virtutis* in Roman Literature," *HSPh* 25: 1–71.

Loane, H. J. 1938, *Industry and Commerce of the City of Rome (50 BC–200 AD)*, Baltimore.

Lo Cascio, E. 1994a, "La dinamica della popolazione in Italia da Augusto al III secolo," in *L'Italie d'Auguste à Dioclétien*, Rome, pp. 91–125.

1994b, "The Size of the Roman Population: Beloch and the Meaning of the Augustan Census Figures," *JRS* 84: 23–40.

1997, "Le procedure di *recensus* dalla tarda Repubblica al tardo antico e il calcolo della popolazione di Roma," in *La Rome impériale: démographie et logistique* (Actes de la table ronde Rome, 25 mars 1994), Rome, pp. 3–76.

2001, "Recruitment and the Size of the Roman Population from the Third to the First Century BCE," in *Debating Roman Demography*, ed. W. Scheidel, Leiden, pp. 111–37.

Loutsch, C. 1982, "Cicéron et l'affaire Rabirius (63 av. J.-C.)," *MH* 39: 305–15.

Lowenthal, D. 1985, *The Past Is a Foreign Country*, Cambridge.

McCarthy, T. A. 1982, *The Critical Theory of Jürgen Habermas*, Cambridge, MA.

McClelland, J. S. 1989, *The Crowd and the Mob from Plato to Canetti*, London.

McDermott, W. C. 1972, "Cicero's Publication of his Consular Speeches," *Philologus* 116: 277–84.

McGushin, P. 1977, *C. Sallustius Crispus*: Bellum Catilinae. *A Commentary* (*Mnemosyne* Supp. 45), Leiden.

1992–94, *Sallust: the* Histories, 2 vols., Oxford.

Mack, D. 1937, *Senatsreden und Volksreden bei Cicero*, Würzburg.

Mackay, C. 2000, "Sulla and the Monuments: Studies in His Public Persona," *Historia* 49: 161–210.

Mackie, N. 1992, "*Popularis* Ideology and Popular Politics at Rome in the First Century BC," *RhM* 135: 49–73.

MacMullen, R. 1980, "How Many Romans Voted?," *Athenaeum* 58: 454–57.

Madvig, J. N. 1873, *Adversaria critica ad scriptores graecos et latinos*, vol. II: *Emendationes latinae*, Copenhagen.

Maria, S. de 1988, *Gli archi onorari di Roma e dell'Italia Romana*, Rome.

Marshall, A. J. 1984, "Symbols and Showmanship in Roman Public Life: the Fasces," *Phoenix* 38: 120–41.

Marshall, B. A. 1985, *A Historical Commentary on Asconius*, Columbia.

1997, "*Libertas Populi*: the Introduction of Secret Ballot at Rome and Its Depiction on Coinage," *Antichthon* 31: 54–73.

Martin, Jochen 1965, "Die Popularen in der Geschichte der späten Republik," diss. Freiburg.

Martin, Josef. 1974, *Antike Rhetorik: Technik und Methode*, Munich.

Martin, P. M. "Sur quelques thèmes de l'éloquence *popularis*, notamment l'invective contre la passivité du peuple," in Achard and Ledentu 2000, pp. 27–41.

Maslowski, T. 1976, "Domus Milonis oppugnata," *Eos* 64: 23–30.

Mason, H. J. 1974, *Greek Terms for Roman Institutions: a Lexicon and Analysis*, Toronto.

May, J. M. 1988, *Trials of Character: the Eloquence of Ciceronian Ethos*, Chapel Hill.

Meadows, A. and J. Williams 2001, "Moneta and the Monuments: Coinage and Politics in Republican Rome," *JRS* 91: 27–49.

Meier, C. 1965, "Populares," *RE* Suppl. 10: 549–615.

1966, *Res Publica Amissa. Eine Studie zu Verfassung und Geschichte der späten römischen Republik*, Wiesbaden. Reprinted with new introduction, Frankfurt 1980.

1968, "Die *loca intercessionis* bei Rogationen," *MH* 25: 86–100.

1978, "Fragen und Thesen zu einer Theorie historischer Prozesse," in *Historische Prozesse*, ed. K.-G. Faber and C. Meier, Munich, pp. 11–66.

1980, *Die Ohnmacht des allmächtigen Dictators Caesar: drei biographische Skizzen*, Frankfurt.

1982, *Caesar: a Biography*, trans. D. McLintock, New York.

Melville, G. (ed.) 2001, *Institutionalität und Symbolisierung*, Cologne, Weimar, and Vienna.

Mencacci, F. 2001, "Genealogia metaforica e *maiores* collettivi (prospettive antropologiche sulla costruzione dei *viri illustres*," in Coudry and Späth 2001, pp. 413–37.

Merguet, H. 1880, *Lexikon zu den Reden des Cicero*, 4 vols., Jena.

Metaxaki-Mitrou, F. 1984, "Violence in the *Contio* during the Ciceronian Age," *AC* 54: 180–87.

Metcalf, W. E. 1999, "Coins as Primary Evidence," in Paul and Ierardi 1999, pp. 1–17.

Michels, A. K. 1967, *The Calendar of the Roman Republic*, Princeton.

Millar, F. 1984, "The Political Character of the Classical Roman Republic, 200–151 BC," *JRS* 74: 1–19.

1986, "Politics, Persuasion and the People before the Social War (150–90 BC)," *JRS* 76: 1–11.

1989, "Political Power in Mid-Republican Rome: Curia or Comitium?," *JRS* 79: 138–50.

1995, "Popular Politics at Rome in the Late Republic," in *Leaders and Masses in the Roman World: Studies in Honor of Zvi Yavetz*, ed. I. Malkin and Z. W. Rubinsohn, Leiden, New York, and Cologne, pp. 91–113.

1998, *The Crowd in Rome in the Late Republic*, Ann Arbor.

2002, *Roman Republic in Political Thought*, Hanover, NH and London.

Mitchell, T. N. 1979, *Cicero: the Ascending Years*, New Haven.

1991, *Cicero: the Senior Statesman*, New Haven.

Momigliano, A. 1942, "Camillus and Concord," *CQ* 36: 111–20.

1969, *Quarto contributo alla storia degli studi classici e del mondo antico*, Rome.

Mommsen, T. 1887, *Römisches Staatsrecht*, Leipzig.

Moreau, P. 1982, Clodiana religio: *un procès politique en 61 av. J.-C.*, Paris.

Morel, J.-P. 1987, "La topographie de l'artisanat et du commerce dans la Rome antique," in *L'urbs: espace urbain et histoire (Ier siècle av. J.-C.–IIIe siècle ap. J.-C.)*, Rome, pp. 127–55.

Morley, N. 1996, *Metropolis and Hinterland. The City of Rome and the Italian Economy, 200 BC–AD 200*, Cambridge.

2001, "The Transformation of Italy, 225–28 BC," *JRS* 101: 50–62.

Morstein-Marx, R. 1998, "Publicity, Popularity and Patronage in the *Commentariolum Petitionis*," *CA* 17: 259–88.

2000a, "The Alleged 'Massacre' at Cirta and Its Consequences (Sallust *Bellum Iugurthinum* 26–27)," *CPh* 95: 468–76.

2000b, "*Res Publica Res Populi*," review of A. Yakobson, *Elections and Electioneering in Rome*, *SCI* 19: 224–33.

Motzo, R. B. 1940, "Le contiones di M. Antonio e di M. Bruto dopo la morte di Cesare," in *Studi di antichità classica offerti da colleghi e discepoli a E. Ciaceri*, Geneva, Rome, and Naples, pp. 136–43.

Mouritsen, H. 2001, *Plebs and Politics in the Late Roman Republic*, Cambridge.

Murray, W. M. and P. M. Petsas 1989, *Octavian's Campsite Memorial for the Actian War* (Trans. American Philos. Soc. 79.4), Philadelphia.

Nardo, D. 1970, *Il "Commentariolum Petitionis": la propaganda elettorale nella "ars" di Quinto Cicerone*, Padua.

Nash, E. 1961, *Pictorial Dictionary of Ancient Rome*, 2nd edn., New York.

Neuman, W. R., M. R. Just, and A. N. Crigler 1992, *Common Knowledge: News and the Construction of Political Meaning*, Chicago and London.

Nicholson, J. 1992, *Cicero's Return from Exile. The Orations Post Reditum*, New York.

Nicolet, C. 1980, *The World of the Citizen in Republican Rome*, trans. P. S. Falla, Berkeley and Los Angeles.

Nielsen, I. and B. Poulsen (eds.) 1992, *The Temple of Castor and Pollux*, Rome.

Nielsen, I. and J. Zahle 1985, "The Temple of Castor and Pollux on the Forum Romanum. Preliminary Report on the Scandinavian Excavations 1983–1985 (1)," *AArch* 56: 1–29.

Nippel, W. 1984, "Policing Rome," *JRS* 74: 20–29.

1988, *Aufruhr und "Polizei" in der römischen Republik*, Stuttgart.

1995, *Public Order in Ancient Rome*, Cambridge.

Noè, E. 1988, "Per la formazione del consenso nella Roma del I sec. a.C." in *Studi di storia e storiografia antiche: per Emilio Gabba*, Pavia, pp. 49–72.

North, J. 1990a, "Democratic Politics in Republican Rome," *P&P* 126: 3–21.

1990b, "Politics and Aristocracy in the Roman Republic," *CPh* 85: 277–87.

Ober, J. 1989, *Mass and Elite in Democratic Athens: Rhetoric, Ideology, and the Power of the People*, Princeton.

Ogilvie, R. M. 1965, *A Commentary on Livy, Books 1–5*, Oxford.

Oppermann, I. 2000, *Zur Funktion historischer Beispiele in Ciceros Briefen*, Leipzig.

Orlin, E. M. 1997, *Temples, Religion and Politics in the Roman Republic* (*Mnemosyne* Suppl. 164), Leiden.

Page, B. I. 1996, *Who Deliberates? Mass Media in Modern Democracy*, Chicago.

Page, B. I. and R. Y. Shapiro 1992, *The Rational Public: Fifty Years of Trends in Americans' Policy Preferences*, Chicago.

Panciera, S. 1996, *Iscrizioni greche e latine del Foro romano e del Palatino. Inventario generale, inediti, revisioni*, Rome.

Pani, M. 1997, *La politica in Roma antica*, Rome.

Pape, M. 1975, "Griechische Kunstwerke aus Kriegsbeute und ihre öffentliche Aufstellung in Rom von der Eroberung von Syrakus bis in augusteische Zeit," diss. Hamburg.

Pasoli, E. 1957, *Cicero, Filippica IV*, Brescia.

Paul, G. 1984, *A Historical Commentary on Sallust's* Bellum Jugurthinum, Liverpool.

Paul, G. M. and M. Ierardi (eds.) 1999, *Roman Coins and Public Life under the Empire: E. Togo Salmon Papers II*, Ann Arbor.

Perelli, L. 1982, *Il movimento popolare nell' ultimo secolo della Repubblica*, Torino.

1990, *Il pensiero politico di Cicerone. Tra filosofia greca e ideologia aristocratica romana*, Florence.

Perl, G. 1965, "Die Rede Cottas in Sallusts Historien," *Philologus* 109: 75–82.

1967, "Die Rede Cottas in Sallusts Historien (Fortsetzung)," *Philologus* 111: 137–41.

Phillips, E. J. 1970, "Cicero and the Prosecution of C. Manilius," *Latomus* 29: 595–607.

1974, "The Prosecution of C. Rabirius in 63 BC," *Klio* 56: 87–101.

Pietilä-Castrén, L. 1987, *Magnificentia publica: the Victory Monuments of the Roman Generals in the Era of the Punic Wars*, Helsinki.

Pina Polo, F. 1989, "Las contiones civiles y militares en Roma," diss. Saragossa.

1995, "Procedures and Functions of Civil and Military *contiones* in Rome," *Klio* 77: 203–16.

1996, *Contra arma verbis. Der Redner vor dem Volk in der späten römischen Republik*, Stuttgart.

Primmer, A. 1985, *Die Überredungsstrategie in Ciceros Rede pro C. Rabirio*, Vienna.

Purcell, N. 1994, "The City of Rome and the *plebs urbana* in the Late Republic," in *Cambridge Ancient History*, vol. IX: *The Last Age of the Roman Republic 146–43 BC*, ed. J. A. Crook, A. Lintott, and E. Rawson, 2nd edn., Cambridge, pp. 644–88.

Ramage, E. S. 1991, "Sulla's Propaganda," *Klio* 73: 93–121.

Rambaud, M. 1953, *Cicéron et l'histoire romaine*, Paris.

Ramsey, J. T. 1980, "The Prosecution of C. Manilius in 66 BC and Cicero's *Pro Manilio*," *Phoenix* 34: 323–36.

Rawson, B. 1971, "*De lege agraria* 2.49," *CPh* 66 (1971) 26–29.

Reusser, C. 1993, *Der Fidestempel auf dem Kapitol in Rom und seine Ausstattung: ein Beitrag zu den Ausgrabungen an der Via del Mare und um das Kapitol 1926–1943*, Rome.

Richardson, L., Jr. 1992, *A New Topographical Dictionary of Ancient Rome*, Baltimore.

Riepl, W. 1913, *Das Nachrichtenwesen des Altertums*, Leipzig.

Riggsby, A. M. 1997, "Did the Romans Believe in Their Verdicts," *Rhetorica* 15: 235–51.

1999, *Crime and Community in Ciceronian Rome*, Austin.

Rilinger, R. 1982, "Die Interpretation des Niedergangs der römischen Republik durch 'Revolution' und 'Krise ohne Alternative,'" *AKG* 64: 279–306.

1989, "'Loca intercessionis' und Legalismus in der späten Republik," *Chiron* 19: 481–98.

Ritter, H.-W. 1998, "Zu libertas und den Tabellargesetzen in der republikanischen Münzprägung," in *Imperium Romanum. Studien zu Geschichte und Rezeption (Festschrift für Karl Christ)*, ed. P. Kneissl and V. Losemann, Stuttgart, pp. 608–14.

Robinson, A. 1994, "Cicero's Use of the Gracchi in Two Speeches before the People," *A&R* 39: 71–76.

Roloff, H. 1938, "Maiores bei Cicero," diss. Göttingen.

1967, "Maiores bei Cicero," in *Römische Wertbegriffe*, ed. H. Oppermann, Darmstadt, pp. 274–322.

Rosenstein, N. 1990a, Imperatores Victi. *Military Defeat and Aristocratic Competition in the Middle and Late Republic*, Berkeley.

1990b, "War, Failure, and Aristocratic Competition," *CPh* 85: 255–65.

Rudé, G. 1964, *The Crowd in History. A Study of Popular Disturbances in France and England 1730–1848*, New York, London, Sydney.

Ruebel, J. S. 1979, "The Trial of Milo in 52 BC: a Chronological Study," *TAPhA* 109: 231–49.

Ryan, F. X. 1998, *Rank and Participation in the Republican Senate*, Stuttgart.

Saller, R. P. 1994, *Patriarchy, Property and Death in the Roman Family*, Cambridge.

Sandys, J. E. 1885, *M. Tulli Ciceronis ad M. Brutum Orator*, Cambridge.

Santalucia, B. 1998, *Diritto e processo penale nell'antica Roma*, 2nd edn., Milan.

Schneider, H. 1982/83, "Die politische Rolle der *plebs urbana* während der Tribunate des L. Appuleius Saturninus," *AncSoc* 13/14: 193–221.

Schoenberger, H. 1910, "Beispiele aus der Geschichte," diss. Erlangen.

Schwind, F. von 1940, *Zur Frage der Publikation im römischen Recht mit Ausblicken in das altgriechische und ptolemäische Rechtsgebiet*, Munich.

Scullard, H. H. 1981, *Festivals and Ceremonies of the Roman Republic*, London.

Seager, R. 1972a, "Cicero and the Word *Popularis*," *CQ* 22: 328–38.

1972b, "*Factio*: Some Observations," *JRS* 62: 53–58.

Sehlmeyer, M. 1999, *Stadtrömische Ehrenstatuen der republikanischen Zeit* (*Historia* Einzelschrift 130), Stuttgart.

Shackleton Bailey, D. R. 1965–67, *Cicero's Letters to Atticus*, 6 vols., Cambridge.

1980, *Cicero*: Epistulae ad Quintum Fratrem et M. Brutum, Cambridge.

1991, *Two Studies in Roman Nomenclature*, Atlanta.

Shatzman, I. 1972, "The Roman General's Authority over Booty," *Historia* 21 (1972) 177–205.

Sherk, R. K. 1969, *Roman Documents from the Greek East*, Baltimore.

Sherwin-White, A. N. 1966, *The Letters of Pliny: a Historical and Social Commentary*, Oxford.

Sklenář, R. J. 1992, "Rullus' Colonies: Cicero, *De lege agraria* 1.16–17 and 2.73–75," *Eos* 80: 81–82.

Späth, T. 1998, "Faits de mots et d'images: les grands hommes de la Rome ancienne," *Traverse* 1: 35–56.

2001, "Erzählt, erfunden: Camillus. Literarische Konstruktion und soziale Normen," in Coudry and Späth 2001, pp. 341–412.

Steinby, E. M. 1987, "Il lato orientale del Foro Romano. Proposte di lettura," *Arctos* 21: 139–84.

Stemmler, M. 2000, "*Auctoritas exempli*. Zur Wechselwirkung von kanonisierten Vergangenheitsbildern und gesellschaftlicher Gegenwart in der spätrepublikanischen Rhetorik," in Linke and Stemmler 2000, pp. 141–205.

2001, "Institutionalisierte Geschichte. Zur Stabilisierungsleistung und Symbolizität historischer Beispiele in der Redekultur der römischen Republik," in Melville 2001, pp. 219–40.

Stockton, D. 1979, *The Gracchi*, Oxford.

Strasburger, H. 1939, "Optimates," *RE* 18: 773–98.

Stroh, W. 1975, *Taxis und Taktik. Die advokatische Dispositionskunst in Ciceros Gerichtsreden*, Stuttgart.

Sumi, G. S. 1997, "Power and Ritual: the Crowd at Clodius' Funeral," *Historia* 46: 80–102.

Sumner, G. V. 1965, "Asconius and the Acta," *Hermes* 93: 134–36.

1966, "Cicero, Pompeius, and Rullus," *TAPhA* 97: 569–82.

1973, *The Orators in Cicero's Brutus. Prosopography and Chronology*, Toronto.

Syme, R. 1939, *The Roman Revolution*, Oxford.

1964, *Sallust*, Berkeley, Los Angeles, and London.

Talbert, R. J. A. 1984, *The Senate of Imperial Rome*, Princeton.

Tatum, W. J. 1986, "Cicero, *ad Att.* 1.14.5," *CQ* 36: 539–41.

1990, "Another Look at the Spectators at the Roman Games," *AHB* 4: 104–7.

1993, "The *Lex Papiria de dedicationibus,*" *CPh* 88: 319–28.

1999, *The Patrician Tribune: Publius Clodius Pulcher,* Chapel Hill.

Taylor, L. R. 1963, "Was Tiberius Gracchus' Last Assembly Electoral or Legislative?," *Athenaeum* 41: 51–69.

1966, *Roman Voting Assemblies,* Ann Arbor.

Taylor, L. R. and T. R. S. Broughton 1949, "The Order of the Two Consuls' Names in the Yearly Lists," *MAAR* 19: 2–14.

Thommen, L. 1989, *Das Volkstribunat der späten Römischen Republik (Historia Einzelschrift* 59), Stuttgart.

1995, "Les lieux de la plèbe et de ses tribuns dans la Rome républicaine," *Klio* 77: 358–70.

Thompson, C. 1978, "To the Senate and to the People: Adaptation to the Senatorial and Popular Audiences in the Parallel Speeches of Cicero," diss. Ohio State University.

Torelli, M. 1968, "Il donario di M. Fulvio Flacco nell' area di S. Omobono," *Quaderni dell' Istituto di topografia antica dell' Università di Roma* 5: 71–76.

1982, *Typology and Structure of Roman Historical Reliefs,* Ann Arbor.

Treggiari, S. 1969, *Roman Freedmen,* Oxford.

Tyrrell, W. B. 1973, "The Trial of C. Rabirius in 63 BC," *Latomus* 32: 285–300.

1978, *A Legal and Historical Commentary to Cicero's* Oratio pro C. Rabirio Perduellionis Reo, Amsterdam.

Ulrich, R. B. 1994, *The Roman Orator and the Sacred Stage: the Roman* Templum Rostratum (*Latomus* Suppl. 222), Brussels.

Ungern-Sternberg, Jürgen von 1970, *Untersuchungen zum spätrepublikanischen Notstandsrecht.* Senatusconsultum ultimum *und* hostis-*Erklärung,* Munich.

Vaahtera, J. 1993, "On the Religious Nature of the Place of Assembly," in *Senatus Populusque Romanus: Studies in Roman Republican Legislation,* ed. U. Paananen, K. Heikkulä, K. Sandberg, L. Savunen, and J. Vaahtera, Helsinki, pp. 97–116.

Van Dijk, Teun 1998, *Ideology: a Multidisciplinary Approach,* London.

Vanderbroeck, P. J. J. 1987, *Popular Leadership and Collective Behavior in the Late Roman Republic (ca. 80–50 BC),* Amsterdam.

Vasaly, A. 1993, *Representations. Images of the World in Ciceronian Oratory,* Berkeley.

Vigourt, A. 2001, "M'. Curius Dentatus et C. Fabricius Luscinus: les grands hommes ne sont pas exceptionnels," in Coudry and Späth 2001, pp. 117–29.

Virlouvet, C. 1991, "La plèbe frumentaire à l'époque d' Auguste: une tentative de définition," in *Nourrir la plèbe. Actes du colloque en hommage à Denis van Berchem,* ed. A. Giovannini, Basel, pp. 43–65.

Vittinghoff, F. 1936, *Der Staatsfeind in der römischen Kaiserzeit. Untersuchungen zur "damnatio memoriae,"* Berlin.

Vretska, K. 1976, *Sallust*: De Catilinae coniuratione, 2 vols., Heidelberg.

Walbank, F. W. 1957–79, *A Historical Commentary on Polybius,* 3 vols.

Wallace, R. W. 1990, "Hellenization and Roman Society in the Late Fourth Century BC," in *Staat und Staatlichkeit in der frühen Römischen Republik*, ed. W. Eder, Stuttgart, pp. 278–92.

Wallace-Hadrill, A. 1986, "Image and Authority in the Coinage of Augustus," *JRS* 76: 66–87.

1990, "Roman Arches and Greek Honours: the Language of Power at Rome," *PCPhS* 216: 143–81.

Wanscher, O. 1980, Sella curulis. *The Folding Stool: an Ancient Symbol of Dignity*, Copenhagen.

Watkins, O. D. 1987, "Caesar solus? Senatorial Support for the *Lex Gabinia*," *Historia* 36: 120–21.

Wechsberg, J. 1945, *Looking for a Bluebird*, Boston.

Weinstock, S. 1971, *Divus Julius*, Oxford.

Wellesley, K. 1971, "Real and Unreal Problems in the *Pro Milone*," *ACD* 7: 27–31.

Welwei, K.-W. 1996, "Caesars Diktatur, der Prinzipat des Augustus und die Fiktion der historischen Notwendigkeit," *Gymnasium* 103: 477–97.

White, P. 1997, "Julius Caesar and the Publication of Acta in Late Republican Rome," *Chiron* 27: 73–84.

White, S. K. (ed.) 1995, *The Cambridge Companion to Habermas*, Cambridge.

Wille, G. 1967, *Musica Romana*, Amsterdam.

Willems, P. 1883–85, *Le Sénat de la République Romaine*, 2 vols., Louvain.

Williamson, C. 1990, "The Roman Aristocracy and Positive Law," *CPh* 85: 266–76.

Wirszubski, C. 1960, *Libertas as a Political Idea at Rome during the Late Republic and Early Principate*, Cambridge.

Wiseman, T. P. 1974, "The Circus Flaminius," *PBSR* 42: 3–26.

1985, *Catullus and His World: a Reappraisal*, Cambridge.

1994, *Historiography and Imagination. Eight Essays on Roman Culture*, Exeter.

1995, *Remus. A Roman Myth*, Cambridge.

1998, *Roman Drama and Roman History*, Exeter.

Wisse, J. 1989, *Ethos and Pathos from Aristotle to Cicero*, Amsterdam.

Wodak R., R. de Cillia, M. Reisigl, and K. Liebhart 1999, *The Discursive Construction of National Identity*, Edinburgh.

Wood, N. 1988, *Cicero's Social and Political Thought*, Berkeley.

Wooten, C. W. 1983, *Cicero's Philippics and Their Demosthenic Model: the Rhetoric of Crisis*, Chapel Hill.

Yakobson, A. 1992, "*Petitio et largitio*: Popular Participation in the Centuriate Assembly of the Late Republic," *JRS* 82: 32–52.

1995, "Secret Ballot and Its Effects in the Late Roman Republic," *Hermes* 123: 426–42.

1999, *Elections and Electioneering in Rome. A Study in the Political System of the Late Republic* (*Historia* Einzelschrift 128), Stuttgart.

Yavetz, Z. 1969, Plebs *and* Princeps, Oxford.

1974, "*Existimatio, Fama*, and the Ides of March," *HSPh* 78: 35–65.

Yunis, H. 1996, *Taming Democracy: Models of Political Rhetoric in Classical Athens*, Ithaca and London.

Zaller, J. R. 1992, *The Nature and Origins of Mass Opinion*, Cambridge.

Zetzel, J. 1993, Review of C. P. Craig, *Form as Argument in Cicero's Speeches*, *BMCRev* 4: 446–51.

Zinserling, G. 1959/60, "Studien zu den Historiendarstellungen der römischen Republik," *WZJena* 9: 403–48.

Ziolkowski, A. 1992, *The Temples of Mid-Republican Rome and Their Historical and Topographical Context*, Rome.

Index